Introduction to
Comparative Politics
Political Challenges and Changing Agendas

AP® Edition

SEVENTH EDITION

Mark Kesselman
Columbia University

Joel Krieger
Wellesley College

William A. Joseph
Wellesley College

Contributors

Ervand Abrahamian
Baruch College

Joan DeBardeleben
Carleton University

Louis De Sipio
University of California, Irvine

Halbert Jones
Saint Anthony's College,
University of Oxford

Darren Kew
University of Massachusetts,
Boston

Peter Lewis
Johns Hopkins University

George Ross
Université de Montréal

CENGAGE
Learning·

Australia • Brazil • Mexico • Singapore • United Kingdom • United States

CENGAGE
Learning®

Introduction to Comparative Politics:
Political Challenges and Changing
***Agendas*, AP® Edition, Seventh Edition**
Mark Kesselman, Joel Krieger,
William A. Joseph

Product Director: Suzanne Jeans

Product Team Manager: Carolyn Merrill

Associate Product Manager: Scott Greenan

Managing Developer: Joanne Dauksewicz

Content Developer: Kate Scheinman

Associate Content Developer: Amy Bither

Product Assistant: Abigail Hess

Media Developer: Laura Hildebrand

Marketing Manager: Valerie Hartman

Content Project Manager: Cathy Brooks

Art Director: Linda May

Manufacturing Planner: Fola Orekoya

IP Analyst: Alexandra Ricciardi

IP Project Manager: Amber Hosea

VP, Director, Advanced and Elective
    Products Program: Alison Zetterquist

Content Developer, Advanced and Elective
    Products Program: Ashley Bargende

Senior Media Developer, Advanced and
    Elective Products Program: Philip Lanza

Production Service and Compositor:
    Integra Software Services Pvt. Ltd.

Text and Cover Designer: Rokusek Design

Cover Image:
    © Ints Vikmanis/Shutterstock.com

ISBN: 978-1-285-86535-5

Cengage Learning
20 Channel Center Street
Boston, MA 02210
USA

Cengage Learning is a leading provider of customized learning solutions
with office locations around the globe, including Singapore, the United
Kingdom, Australia, Mexico, Brazil, and Japan. Locate your local office at
www.cengage.com/global.

Cengage Learning products are represented in Canada by Nelson
Education, Ltd.

To learn more about Cengage Learning Solutions, visit **www.cengage.com**.

To find online supplements and other instructional support, please visit
www.cengagebrain.com

AP® and Advanced Placement Program® are trademarks registered
and/or owned by the College Board, which was not involved in the
production of, and does not endorse, this product.

Printed in the United States of America
Print Number: 03   Print Year: 2017

Brief Contents

PART I   INTRODUCTION

    CHAPTER 1: Introducing Comparative Politics   1

PART II   CONSOLIDATED DEMOCRACIES

    CHAPTER 2: Britain   36
    CHAPTER 3: The United States   80
    CHAPTER 4: European Union   125

PART III   MIXED SYSTEMS

    CHAPTER 5: Mexico   168
    CHAPTER 6: Nigeria   213
    CHAPTER 7: The Russian Federation   262

PART IV   AUTHORITARIAN REGIMES

    CHAPTER 8: Iran   313
    CHAPTER 9: China   359

Contents

Preface   *xv*

PART I   INTRODUCTION

Chapter 1   Introducing Comparative Politics   1
Mark Kesselman, Joel Krieger, and William A. Joseph

SECTION 1: The Global Challenge of Comparative Politics   2
Making Sense of Turbulent Times   4

SECTION 2: What—and How—Comparative Politics Compares   5
Level of Analysis   7
Causal Theories   9

SECTION 3: Themes for Comparative Analysis   11
Theme 1: A Globalizing World of States   11
Theme 2: Governing the Economy   13
Theme 3: The Democratic Idea   16
Theme 4: The Politics of Collective Identities   19

SECTION 4: Classifying Political Systems   21

SECTION 5: Organization of the Text   23
1: The Making of the Modern State   23
2: Political Economy and Development   24
3: Governance and Policy-Making   24
4: Representation and Participation   25
5: Politics in Transition   25

Contents

PART II   CONSOLIDATED DEMOCRACIES

Chapter 2   Britain   **36**

Joel Krieger

SECTION 1: The Making of the Modern British State   37

Politics in Action   37

Geographic Setting   38

Critical Junctures   40

*The Consolidation of the British State 40   The Seventeenth-Century Settlement 41
The Industrial Revolution and the British Empire 42   The British Empire 42
Industrial Change and the Struggle for Voting Rights 42   World Wars, Industrial Strife,
and the Depression (1914–1945) 43   Collectivist Consensus (1945–1979) 43
New Labour's Third Way 43   The Conservative–Liberal Coalition 44*

The Four Themes and Britain   45

Britain in a Globalized World of States 45

Themes and Comparisons   47

SECTION 2: Political Economy and Development   48

State and Economy   48

Social Policy 50

Society and Economy   51

Inequality and Ethnic Minorities 52   Inequality and Women 52

Environmental Issues   53

Britain in the Global Economy   54

SECTION 3: Governance and Policy-Making   55

Organization of the State   55

The Executive   56

*Cabinet Government 56   Bureaucracy and Civil Service 58   Public and Semipublic
Institutions 60*

Other State Institutions   60

The Military and the Police 60   The Judiciary 61   Subnational Government 61

The Policy-Making Process   63

SECTION 4: Representation and Participation   63

The Legislature   64

*The House of Commons 64   The Legislative Process 64   The House of Lords 65
Reforms in Behavior 65   Structural Changes: Parliamentary Committees 65*

Political Parties and the Party System   66

The Labour Party 66   The Conservative Party 66   Liberal Democrats 67

Elections   68

*The Electoral System and the 2010 Election 68   Gender, Ethnicity, and
Representation 69   Trends in Electoral Behavior 70*

Contents

Political Culture, Citizenship, and Identity 70
Social Class 71   National Identity 71
Interest Groups, Social Movements, and Protest 72
The Political Impact of Technology 72

SECTION 5: British Politics in Transition 73
Political Challenges and Changing Agendas 73
Constitutional Reform 74   Identities in Flux 75
Youth Politics and the Generational Divide 75
British Politics in Comparative Perspective 77
Chapter Summary **78**

Chapter 3   The United States **80**
Louis DeSipio

SECTION 1: The Making of the Modern American State 81
Politics in Action 81
Geographic Setting 82
Critical Junctures 84
*The Revolutionary Era (1773–1789) 84   The Civil War and Reconstruction
(1861–1876) 86   The New Deal Era (1933–1940) 86   Divided Government,
Frequently Shifting Partisan Dominance, and Political Contestation of the Scope
of Government (1968 to the Present) 87   September 11, 2001, and Its Aftermath 88*
The Four Themes and the United States 89
*The United States in a Globalized World of States 89   Governing the Economy 89
The Democratic Idea 89   The Politics of Collective Identity 90*
Themes and Comparisons 90

SECTION 2: Political Economy and Development 91
State and Economy 91
Society and Economy 93
Environmental Issues 97
The United States in the Global Economy 97

SECTION 3: Governance and Policy-Making 99
Organization of the State 99
The Executive 101
The Presidency 101
The Cabinet and the Bureaucracy 103
Other State Institutions 104
*The Military 104   National Security Agencies 104   The Judiciary 105
Subnational Government 106*
The Policy-Making Process 107

Contents

SECTION 4: Representation and Participation ... 108
The Legislature ... 108
Political Parties and the Party System ... 110
Elections ... 112
Political Culture, Citizenship, and Identity ... 114
Interest Groups, Social Movements, and Protest ... 116
The Political Impact of Technology ... 117

SECTION 5: United States Politics in Transition ... 118
Political Challenges and Changing Agendas ... 118
Youth Politics and the Generational Divide ... 121
United States Politics in Comparative Perspective ... 122
Chapter Summary ... **123**

Chapter 4   European Union ... **125**
George Ross

SECTION 1: The Making of the European Union ... 126
Politics in Action ... 126
Critical Junctures ... 127
Themes and Comparisons ... 129

SECTION 2: Politics and Economics in the Development of the
European Union ... 131
State and Economy: EU Economic Governance ... 131
Starting in the Cold War 131   Crisis and Renewal: 1970–1993 134
Globalization and the EU ... 135
The Great Recession and the Euro zone Crisis 137

SECTION 3: EU Governance ... 140
The Maze of EU Institutions ... 140
The European Commission 141   The Council of Ministers 142   The European Council 143
The European Parliament 143   The European Court of Justice 147   Other Institutions 149

SECTION 4: The EU and Its Policies ... 149
Building a European Market ... 149
Competition Policy ... 151
Agriculture ... 152
Regional Development ... 153
The Euro and EMU ... 154
Shared Policies ... 155
Globalization and Competitiveness 155   Social Policy 157   Environmental Policy 157
Intergovernmental Europe ... 158
Justice and Home Affairs 159   Foreign and Security Policy 160

SECTION 5: Euro-Politics in Transition ... 164

Contents

PART III   MIXED SYSTEMS

Chapter 5   Mexico   168
Halbert Jones

SECTION 1: The Making of the Modern Mexican State   169
Politics in Action   169
Geographic Setting   170
Critical Junctures   172

*Independence, Instability, and Dictatorship (1810–1910) 172   The Revolution of 1910
and the Sonoran Dynasty (1910–1934) 174   Lázaro Cárdenas, Agrarian Reform, and the
Workers (1934–1940) 175   The Politics of Rapid Development (1940–1982) 176
Crisis and Reform (1982–2000) 177   Since 2000: Mexico as a Multiparty Democracy 177*

The Four Themes and Mexico   179

*Mexico in a Globalized World of States 179   Governing the Economy 179
The Democratic Idea 180   The Politics of Collective Identity 180*

Themes and Comparisons   181

SECTION 2: Political Economy and Development   182
State and Economy   182

*Import Substitution and Its Consequences 182   Sowing the Oil and Reaping
a Crisis 184   New Strategies: Structural Reforms and NAFTA 185
The Mexican Economy Today 185*

Society and Economy   187
Environmental Issues   187
Mexico in the Global Economy   188

SECTION 3: Governance and Policy-Making   189
Organization of the State   189
The Executive   190

The President and the Cabinet 190   The Bureaucracy 192   The Parastatal Sector 193

Other State Institutions   193

The Military 193   The Judiciary 194   Subnational Government 195

The Policy-Making Process   195

SECTION 4: Representation and Participation   196
The Legislature   197
Political Parties and the Party System   198

The PRI 199   The PAN 200   The PRD 201   Other Parties 202

Elections   202
Political Culture, Citizenship, and Identity   202
Interest Groups, Social Movements, and Protest   203
The Political Impact of Technology   205

Contents

SECTION 5: Mexican Politics in Transition   206

Political Challenges and Changing Agendas   207

Youth Politics and the Generational Divide   209

Mexican Politics in Comparative Perspective   210

Chapter Summary   **210**

Chapter 6   Nigeria   **213**

Darren Kew and Peter Lewis

SECTION 1: The Making of the Modern Nigerian State   216

Politics in Action   216

Geographic Setting   217

Critical Junctures   219

The Precolonial Period (800–1900) 219   Colonial Rule and Its Impact (1860–1945) 221
Divisive Identities: Ethnic Politics under Colonialism (1945–1960) 221
The First Republic (1960–1966) 222   Civil War and Military Rule (1966–1979) 223
The Second and Third Republics, and Predatory Military Rule (1979–1999) 223
The Fourth Republic (1999 to the Present) 224

The Four Themes and Nigeria   225

Nigeria in a Globalized World of States 225

Themes and Comparisons   227

SECTION 2: Political Economy and Development   227

State and Economy   228

Origins of Economic Decline 228   From 1985 to the Present: Deepening Economic Crisis
and the Search for Solutions 228

Society and Economy   231

Ethnic and Religious Cleavages 231   Gender Differences 232

Environmental Issues   232

Nigeria in the Global Economy   233

Nigeria and the Regional Political Economy 233   Nigeria and the Political Economy of
the West 234

SECTION 3: Governance and Policy-Making   235

Organization of the State   235

The National Question and Constitutional Governance 235   Federalism and State
Structure 235

The Executive   237

The Executive under Military Rule 237   The Fourth Republic: The Obasanjo,
Yar'Adua, and Jonathan Administrations 237   The Bureaucracy 238
Semipublic Institutions 238   Prebendalism 239

Other State Institutions   239

The Judiciary 239   State and Local Government 240

The Policy-Making Process   241

Contents

SECTION 4: Representation and Participation 242

The Legislature 242

Political Parties and the Party System 243

Elections 243

Old Roots and New Alignments: The PDP and the Other Parties of the Fourth Republic 246

Political Culture, Citizenship, and Identity 248

Modernity versus Traditionalism 248   Religion 249   The Press 249

Interest Groups, Social Movements, and Protest 250

Labor 250   The Business Community 251   Other Social Groups 251

The Political Impact of Technology 251

SECTION 5: Nigerian Politics in Transition 253

Political Challenges and Changing Agendas 253

Youth Politics and the Generational Divide 257

Nigerian Politics in Comparative Perspective 257

*A Globalizing World of States 257   Governing the Economy 258
The Democratic Idea 259   Collective Identities 259*

Chapter Summary 260

Chapter 7 The Russian Federation 262

Joan DeBardeleben

SECTION 1: The Making of the Modern Russian State 263

Politics in Action 263

Geographic Setting 264

Critical Junctures 266

*The Decline of the Russian Tsarist State and the Founding of the Soviet Union 266
The Bolshevik Revolution and the Establishment of Soviet Power (1917–1929) 266
The Stalin Revolution (1929–1953) 267   Attempts at De-stalinization (1953–1985) 268
Perestroika and Glasnost (1985–1991) 270   Collapse of the USSR and the Emergence of
the Russian Federation (1991 to the Present) 270*

Themes and Comparisons 272

SECTION 2: Political Economy and Development 274

State and Economy 274

Society and Economy 277

Environmental Issues 279

Russia in the Global Economy 280

SECTION 3: Governance and Policy-Making 282

Organization of the State 282

The Executive 284

The National Bureaucracy 285   Public and Semipublic Institutions 287

Contents

Other State Institutions   288

*The Judiciary 288   Subnational Governments 288   The Military and Security
Organs 290*

The Policy-Making Process   292

SECTION 4: Representation and Participation   292

The Legislature   293

Political Parties and the Party System   294

*The Dominant Party: United Russia 296   Other Parties Represented in the State Duma
(2007–2011) 296   The Liberal Democratic Parties: Marginalized 297*

Elections   298

Political Culture, Citizenship, and Identity   300

Interest Groups, Social Movements, and Protest   301

The Political Impact of Technology   303

SECTION 5: Russian Politics in Transition   **304**

Political Challenges and Changing Agendas   305

Youth Politics and the Generational Divide   309

Russian Politics in Comparative Perspective   310

Chapter Summary   **311**

PART IV   AUTHORITARIAN REGIMES

Chapter 8   Iran   **313**

Ervand Abrahamian

SECTION 1: The Making of the Modern Iranian State   314

Politics in Action   314

Geographic Setting   315

Critical Junctures   318

*The Safavids (1501–1722) 318   The Qajars (1794–1925) 319   The Pahlavis
(1925–1979) 319   The Islamic Revolution (1979) 321   The Islamic Republic
(1979 to the Present) 323   Iran after 9/11 324*

The Four Themes and Iran   325

*Iran in a Globalized World of States 325   Governing the Economy 326
The Democratic Idea 326   The Politics of Collective Identity 327*

Themes and Comparisons   327

SECTION 2: Political Economy and Development   328

State and Economy   328

Iran's Economy under the Islamic Republic 329

Society and Economy   330

Contents

Environmental Issues   333
Iran in the Global Economy   333

SECTION 3: Governance and Policy-Making   335
Organization of the State   335
The Executive   336
*The Leader and Major Organizations of Clerical Power 336   The Government
Executive 338   The Bureaucracy 339*
Other State Institutions   340
*The Judiciary 340   The Military 341   Subnational Government 342
Semipublic Institutions 342*
The Policy-Making Process   343

SECTION 4: Representation and Participation   345
The Legislature   346
Political Parties and the Party System   346
*The Liberation Movement 347   The National Front 347   The Mojahedin 347
The Fedayin 347   The Tudeh (Party of the Masses) 348*
Elections   348
Political Culture, Citizenship, and Identity   349
Interest Groups, Social Movements, and Protest   350
The Political Impact of Technology   352

SECTION 5: Iranian Politics in Transition   352
Political Challenges and Changing Agendas   353
Youth Politics and the Generational Divide   356
Iranian Politics in Comparative Perspective   356
Chapter Summary   **357**

Chapter 9   China   **359**
William A. Joseph

SECTION 1: The Making of the Modern Chinese State   360
Politics in Action   360
Geographic Setting   363
Critical Junctures   364
*Warlords, Nationalists, and Communists (1912–1949) 364   Mao Zedong in
Power (1949–1976) 365   Deng Xiaoping and the Transformation of Chinese
Communism (1977–1997) 367   From Revolutionaries to Technocrats (1997 to
the Present) 367*
The Four Themes and China   369
China in a Globalized World of States 369   Governing the Economy 369

Contents

The Democratic Idea 370   The Politics of Collective Identity   370

Theme and Comparisons 371

SECTION 2: Political Economy and Development 371

State and Economy 371

China Goes to Market 372   Remaking the Chinese Countryside   373

Society and Economy 374

Environmental Issues 376

China in the Global Economy 377

SECTION 3: Governance and Policy-Making 379

Organization of the State 379

The Executive 379

CCP Organization 379   PRC Organization   382

Other State Institutions 384

The Judiciary 384   Subnational Government 385   The Military, Police, and Internal Security 385

The Policy-Making Process 386

SECTION 4: Representation and Participation 387

The Legislature 387

Political Parties and the Party System 388

The Chinese Communist Party 388   China's Non-communist "Democratic Parties" 389

Elections 390

Political Culture, Citizenship, and Identity 390

From Communism to Consumerism 390   China's Non-Chinese Citizens 392

Interest Groups, Social Movements, and Protest 393

Protest and the Party–State 394

The Political Impact of Technology 395

SECTION 5: Chinese Politics in Transition 396

Political Challenges and Changing Agendas 396

China and the Democratic Idea 397

Youth Politics and the Generational Divide 399

Chinese Politics in Comparative Perspective 399

China as a Communist Party–State 399   China as a Developing Country 400

Chapter Summary **402**

Endnotes   405

Glossary   411

About the Editors and Contributors   419

Index   421

Preface

The prefaces to several previous editions of *Introduction to Comparative Politics* (ICP) used Bob Dylan's words to observe that "the times, they are a-changin'." We reflect on how we began previous editions:

- "Politics throughout the world seems more troubled today than even a few years ago, when celebrations around the globe ushered in the new millennium."
  —*Introduction to Comparative Politics*, 3rd edition. © 2004.
- In recent years the "world of politics was as turbulent as at any time in recent memory, with clear-cut trends more elusive than ever."
  —*Introduction to Comparative Politics*, 4th edition. © 2007.
- "[We] have witnessed as much—or more—turmoil and uncertainty as the preceding years."
  —*Introduction to Comparative Politics*, 5th edition. © 2010.
- "The sixth edition of ICP... has been published soon after prodemocracy movements overthrew decades-old dictatorships in Tunisia and Egypt, and repressive regimes unleashed deadly force against similar movements in Algeria, Bahrain, Iran, Libya, Syria, and Yemen."
  —*Introduction to Comparative Politics*, 6th edition. © 2013

When it comes to the degree of uncertainty, and the range and depth of challenges faced by ordinary citizens who yearn for stability, less strife, and a widening circle of opportunities, the present edition is no different than its predecessors. We write these lines just days after a highly controversial referendum was held in Crimea on the question of seceding from Ukraine. Less than 24 hours later, the Crimean parliament voted for Crimea's annexation by Russia, and Moscow moved quickly to make that a fact. Russian forces had taken control of Crimea just a couple of weeks before following a pro-European revolution in Ukraine had ousted an unpopular pro-Russian president. Russia's intervention in Ukraine raises fears in other parts of the former Soviet Union, particularly in the other states in the Black Sea region—Armenia, Azerbaijan, and Georgia—that their hard-won independence is at risk.

The seventh edition of *Introduction to Comparative Politics* does not try to emulate the coverage of fast-breaking daily events by CNN, Fox News, and Twitter. Its mission is to provide students with a clear and comprehensive guide to these unsettled political times through comparative analysis.

Country-by-Country Approach and Thematic Framework

The methods of comparative analysis come alive as students examine similarities and differences among countries and within and between political systems. Our thematic approach facilitates disciplined analysis of political challenges and changing agendas within each country. Like previous editions of *Introduction to Comparative Politics*, this edition (ICP7) employs a country-by-country approach structured around four core themes:

1. **A Globalizing World of States** focuses on the importance of state formation, the internal organization of the state, and the impact of the interstate system on political development. We emphasize the interaction of globalization and state power.

2. **Governing the Economy** analyzes state strategies for promoting economic development and competitiveness, emphasizes the crucial role of economic performance in determining a state's political legitimacy, and stresses the interactive effects of economic globalization on domestic politics.
3. **The Democratic Idea** explores the challenges posed to the state by citizens' demands for greater participation and influence in democracies, mixed systems, and authoritarian regimes, and discusses the inevitable gap between the promise of democracy and its imperfect fulfillment.
4. **The Politics of Collective Identities** considers the political consequences of the complex interplay among class, race, ethnicity, gender, religion, and nationality.

Our approach to comparative politics stresses the analysis of each country's politics by applying these four themes within a context shaped by globalization. This approach strikes a balance between a fine-grained analysis of the richness of each country's distinctive pattern of political development and explicit cross-country comparative analysis. In so doing, our text teaches students that the study of comparative politics is defined by a method that investigates similarities and differences in cases and, at the same time, poses and attempts to answer searching questions that really matter in the lives of students as active citizens. These are questions embedded in the thematic scaffolding of ICP.

Five Critical Junctures in Politics

Chapter 1 helps students navigate through the text by introducing the book's thematic framework, which is combined with a thorough analysis of the political institutions and processes of each country in the chapters that follow. It sets the stage and previews the thematic focus by noting:

1. 1989, which symbolizes the end of the Cold War, and the eruption of capitalist democracies that transcend East versus West divisions in Europe and much of the world;
2. 9/11/01, which reframes globalization, shifting attention away from the development gap and to terrorism, security, and the use of force;
3. 2008, a year of intense financial and economic crisis around the world;
4. 2011, when prodemocracy movements confronted repressive regimes in North Africa and the Middle East, and Japan was rocked by a severe earthquake, tsunami, and nuclear disaster;
5. 2014, when Vladimir Putin's invasion of Ukraine threatened to destabilize the post-Soviet global order and created the very real possibility of a "back to the future" scenario of a new Cold War between Russia and the United States and its European allies.

Chapter 1 also describes the comparative method; presents in some detail our four-theme framework; discusses how we classify the political systems of the countries covered in this book; and provides an overview of the organization of the country chapters.

Consolidated Democracies, Mixed Systems, and Authoritarian Regimes

We classify the seven countries in this edition of ICP in three categories:

- *Consolidated democracies* (Britain, United States, and the European Union—a unique set of democracies)
- *Mixed systems* (Mexico, Nigeria, and Russia)
- *Authoritarian regimes* (Iran and China)

In the Introduction, we define the three regime types and explain the rationale for the typology. In particular, we warn against assuming that there is a linear movement from authoritarian regimes to mixed systems to consolidated democracies. Democratization is often a protracted process with ambiguous results or reversals, rather than a clearly delineated path toward completion. Thus, we stress that the countries we classify as mixed systems are not riding a historical escalator mechanically leading to their transformation into stable or consolidated democracies. We call attention to "hybrid" regimes, in which some elements of democracy co-exist with authoritarian practices.

We also emphasize that the boundaries dividing the three groups are not airtight. For one thing, politics is a moving target. Russia is a good example of a country on the cusp between a mixed system and an authoritarian regime. Furthermore, scholars disagree about the appropriate criteria for classifying regime types as well as about how to classify particular cases. Indeed, instructors may find it fruitful to encourage class discussion of alternative conceptual schemes for classifying groups of countries and how to best characterize the political system of given countries.

NEW! Seventh Edition Content

The content of this edition of ICP has been shaped by our survey of what teachers found appealing about previous editions of the book and their recommended changes. Based on this feedback, we have made the following improvements:

- **NEW!** Shortened country chapters compared to the previous edition. The result is a more streamlined text that strikes a balance between introducing comparative politics to students with little or no background in political science while maintaining coverage of the complexity of institutions, issues, processes, and events.
- **NEW! Focus questions** at the beginning of each major section heading in the country chapters introduce students to the section that follows.
- **NEW! Making Connections** questions at the end of each feature box encourage students to link the topic of the box to the content of the chapter.
- **NEW! Where Do You Stand?** questions at the end of each section in all chapters encourage students to develop and defend original arguments on controversial issues.
- **NEW! Subsections on Environmental Issues, The Political Impact of Technology, and Youth Politics and the Generation Gap** highlight the particular importance of these issues.
- **NEW! The thoroughly updated introduction and country chapters** provide analysis of major recent political developments throughout the world. For example, the chapters on Iran, Mexico, and the United States extensively analyze the implications of recent elections in these countries. The chapter on Russia discusses the crisis in Ukraine and the annexation of Crimea. The China chapter analyzes the rise to power of Xi Jinping, who was installed as head of the Chinese Communist Party in November 2012 and as president of the People's Republic of China in March 2013.

Consistent Country Chapter Organization

At the beginning of each chapter, students will find a map, data on ethnicity, religion, and language specific to that country to aid in comparing countries, and some basic information about the country's political system.

Each country chapter consists of five sections:

1. **The Making of the Modern State**, which begins with an opening vignette that illustrates an important feature of the country's contemporary politics. This is followed by a description of the country's geographic setting, a discussion of the critical junctures in the historical development of the state, and an overview of how the book's four central themes relate to the country. This section concludes by noting the significance of the country for the study of comparative politics.

2. **Political Economy and Development** analyzes the relationship between the state, the impact of economic development on society, current environmental issues, and the country's position in the global economy,

3. **Governance and Policy-making** looks at the general organization of the state, the executive branch, and other state institutions, including the judiciary, subnational levels of government, and the military, police, internal security and other agencies of coercion. This section concludes with a description of the policy-making process.

4. **Representation and Participation** covers the country's legislature, party system, elections, political culture, citizenship, national identity, interest groups, social movements, and protest. The final subsection is a new one on the political impact of technology.

5. **Politics in Transition** begins by highlighting a recent important event that is influencing the country's politics and then proceeds to an analysis of the major political challenges facing the country. This is followed by the new subsection on youth politics and the generational divide. The chapter ends with some concluding thoughts about politics of the country in comparative perspective.

Special Features That Teach

Maps, tables, charts, photographs, and political cartoons enliven the text and present key information in clear and graphic ways. We have provided a more visually interesting presentation of data in a way that is intended to enhance cross-country comparative analysis. At the end of Chapter 1, various data is presented in a way that facilitates comparisons among the countries covered in this book.

Sidebar boxes in each country chapter highlight three interesting and provocative aspects of politics:

1. The **Profile** feature highlights biographies of important political leaders.
2. The **Global Connection** feature provides links between domestic and international politics.
3. The **U.S. Connection** feature compares an important feature of political institutions with its American counterpart or explores a crucial aspect of the country's relationship with the United States.

Key terms are set in boldface and defined in the margin of the page where the term is first introduced and in the complete glossary at the end of the book. The glossary defines many key concepts that are used broadly in comparative politics.

Student Research and Exploration In Chapter 1, students are enabled to do further research using a sidebar box that discusses the use of the Internet in the study of comparative politics. It notes a variety of websites where students can find more information about the countries covered in the book. Each chapter concludes with a list of suggested readings and websites.

An end-of-chapter **Summary** highlights the major themes and facts in the chapter.

Supplemental Teaching and Learning Aids and Database Editions

Teacher's Resource Guide

A complete teaching resource developed by and for AP® teachers. This Resource Guide includes suggestions on how to pace the course, how to review for the exam, and how to assess students' preparedness. Part I of the Guide provides introductory and background material about specific concerns of AP® teachers: overview of the course, teaching the course, your students and the AP® Exam (including scoring), section on specific types of exam questions (multiple-choice, free response), and information on test-taking strategies. Part II provides comprehensive teacher support material for textbook based on the college instructor's edition, with a special "AP Focus" in each chapter that shows how to tailor instruction to the specific requirements and expectations of the AP® course.

Fast Track to a 5

This test-preparation book for students, written by Rebecca Small of Oakton High School, offers comprehensive AP® test-prep practice keyed to *Introduction to Comparative Politics*, 7th Edition—including a diagnostic pre-test, test-taking strategies, review material with study questions, instruction on and practice for interpreting charts, graphs, and cartoons, and full-length practice exams in AP® format. Available for purchase either with the text or separately.

Instructor Companion Website

This Instructor Companion Website is an all-in-one multimedia online resource for class preparation, presentation, and testing. Accessible through www.cengage.com/login with your faculty account, you will find the following available for download: book-specific Microsoft® PowerPoint® presentations; a Test Bank compatible with multiple learning management systems; a Teacher's Resource Guide; Microsoft® PowerPoint® Image Slides; and a JPEG Image Library.

The Test Bank, offered in Blackboard, Moodle, Desire2Learn, Canvas, and Angel formats, contains Learning Objective–specific multiple-choice and essay questions for each chapter. Import the test bank into your LMS to edit and manage questions, and to create tests.

The Microsoft® PowerPoint® presentations are ready-to-use, visual outlines of each chapter. These presentations are easily customized for your lectures and offered along with chapter-specific Microsoft® PowerPoint® Image Slides and JPEG Image Libraries.

Instant Access Code for Cognero

Cengage Learning Testing Powered by Cognero is a flexible online system that allows you to author, edit, and manage test bank content from multiple Cengage Learning solutions, create multiple test versions in an instant, and deliver tests from your LMS, your classroom, or wherever you want. The test bank for *Introduction to Comparative Politics*, 7th Edition, contains Learning Objective–specific multiple-choice and essay questions for each chapter.

Student Companion Website

This free companion website for *Introduction to Comparative Politics* is accessible through cengagebrain.com and allows students access to chapter-specific interactive learning tools including flashcards, glossaries, and more.

CourseReader 0-30: Comparative Politics

CourseReader for Comparative Politics allows you to create your reader, your way, in just minutes. This affordable, fully customizable online reader provides access to thousands of permissions-cleared readings, articles, primary sources, and audio and video selections from the regularly updated Gale research library database. This easy-to-use solution allows you to search for and select just the material you want for your courses. Each selection opens with a descriptive introduction to provide context and concludes with critical-thinking and multiple-choice questions to reinforce key points.

CourseReader is loaded with convenient tools like highlighting, printing, note-taking, and downloadable PDFs and MP3 audio files for each reading. CourseReader is the perfect complement to any Political Science course. It can be bundled with your current textbook, sold alone, or integrated into your learning management system. CourseReader 0-30 allows access to up to 30 selections in the reader. Please contact your Cengage sales representative for details.

As our discussion of the critical junctures of 1989, 9/11/01, 2008, 2011, and 2014 suggest political change is a constant feature of our contemporary world. Not much is certain about what the future will hold—except that the political world will be endlessly fascinating and comparative analysis will continue to be an important tool for trying to make sense of it. Welcome aboard!

Acknowledgments

We are grateful to colleagues who have reviewed and critiqued past and current editions of ICP:

Joseph Ellis, *Wingate University*
Katharina Felts, *Loudoun Valley High School*
Gunther Hega, *Western Michigan University*
Kira Hoilman, *Potomac Falls High School*
Debra Holzhauer, *Southeast Missouri State University*
Anika Leithner, *California Polytechnic State University*

In addition, we thank the talented and professional staff who helped edit and publish ICP7: Scott Greenan, Associate Product Manager; Kate Scheinman, Senior Content Developer; Carolyn Merrill, Product Team Manager; Laura Hildebrand, Senior Media Developer; Amy Bither, Associate Content Developer; and Abigail Hess, Product Assistant.

M. K.
J. K.
W. A. J.

AP® Course Topic	Correlation to Introduction to Comparative Politics, 7th Edition
I. Introduction to Comparative Politics	
A. Purpose and methods of comparison and classification	
1. Ways to organize government	Pages: 6–11, 16, 21–23, 41
2. Normative and empirical questions	Pages: 5–8
B. Concepts (state, nation, regime, government)	Pages: 7–11, 21–26
C. Process and policy (what is politics; purpose of government; what are political science and comparative politics; common policy challenges)	Pages: 5–11, 13–16, 21–26
II. Sovereignty, Authority, and Power	
A. Political culture, communication, and socialization	Pages: Britain 40–41, 50–53, 55–58, United States 114–116, EU 131–135, Mexico 202–203, Nigeria 248–249, Russia 300–301, Iran 349–350, China 390–393
B. Nations and states	Pages: Britain 55–56, United States 99–101, EU 120–131, 145, Mexico 189–190, Nigeria 235–236, Russia 282–284, Iran 335–336, China 379
C. Supranational governance (e.g., European Union)	Pages: Britain 45–47, 54, 76, United States 89, 97–99, EU 131–137, 155–157, Mexico 174, 179, 188–189, Nigeria 225–229, 257–258, Russia 280–282, Iran 325–326, 333–335, China 366, 369, 377–378
D. Sources of power	Pages: Britain 58, 64–66, United States 85, 101–105, 108–110, EU 140–147, Mexico 197–198, Nigeria 237, 242–243, Russia 293–294, Iran 346, China 362, 379–384
E. Constitutions (forms, purposes, application)	Pages: Britain 41, 55–56, United States 99–101, Mexico 189–190, Nigeria 235, Russia 282–284, Iran 346, China 386–387
F. Regime types	Pages: Britain 41, United States 85, Mexico 172, Nigeria 218, Russia 265, 292, Iran 317, China 362
G. Types of economic systems	Pages: Britain 48–51, United States 91–93, EU 149–152, Mexico 182–186, Nigeria 227–231, Russia 274–277, Iran 328–330, China 371–374
H. State building, legitimacy, and stability	Pages: Britain 48–53, 55–56, 70–72, United States 91–93, 99–101, 114–116, EU 129–131, Mexico 182–183, 189–190, 202–203, Nigeria 235–236, 240–241, Russia 274–277, Iran 328–330, 343–345, China 371–374, 379–382, 390–393
I. Belief systems as sources of legitimacy	
1. Religion	Pages: Britain 28, 39, United States 83, Mexico 171, Nigeria 217, Russia 263, Iran 317, China 362
2. Ideology (liberalism, communism, socialism, conservatism, fascism)	Pages: Britain 66–68, United States 110–112, Mexico 172, 198–202, Nigeria 243, Russia 294–298, Iran 344, 346–348, China 362, 379
J. Governance and accountability	Pages: Britain 68–69, United States 112–114, EU 131–135, Mexico 202, Nigeria 243–246, Russia 299–300, Iran 348, China 379–384

(continued)

Correlation Chart

AP* Course Topic	Correlation to Introduction to Comparative Politics, 7th Edition
III. Political Institutions	
A. Levels of government 1. National/regional/local	Pages: Britain 55–56, United States 99–101, Mexico 189–190, Nigeria 235–236, 240–241, Russia 282–284, Iran 335–336, China 379–384
2. Unitary/federal	Pages: Britain 55-56, United States 99–101, EU 129–131, Mexico 189–190, Nigeria 235–236, 240–241, Russia 282–284, Iran 335–336, China 362
3. Centralization/decentralization	Pages: Britain 55–56, United States 99–101, EU 129–131, Mexico 189–190, Nigeria 235–236, 240–241, Russia 282–284, Iran 317, 320, China 379–384
B. Executives (head of state, head of government, cabinets) 1. Single or dual	Pages: Britain 41, 55–58, United States 85, 99–101, Mexico 85, 189–190, Nigeria 218, 237–238, Russia 265, Iran 335–339, China 362, 379–384
2. President	Pages: United States 101–103, Mexico 190–192, Nigeria 237, Russia 284, Iran 336–338, China 379–384
3. Prime Minister	Pages: Britain 41, 55–56
C. Legislatures 1. Unicameral/bicameral (symmetric/asymmetric)	Pages: Britain 64–66, United States 108–110, EU 140–147, Mexico 85, Nigeria 242–243, Russia 265, 293–294, Iran 317, 346, China 362
2. Organization	Pages: Britain 55–58, United States 99–101, EU 140–147, Mexico 197–198, Nigeria 242–243, Russia 293–294, Iran 346, China 379–384, 387–388
3. Membership (representation)	Pages: Britain 66–68, United States 110–112, EU 140–147, Mexico 198–202, Nigeria 243, Russia 292–294, Iran 346–348, China 388–390
D. Parliamentary and presidential systems 1. Institutional relations	Pages: Britain 64–65, United States 108–110, EU 140–147, Mexico 198–202, Nigeria 242–243, Russia 293–294, Iran 346, China 387–388
E. Elections 1. Presidential	Pages: United States 112–114, Mexico 202–203, Nigeria 243–246, Russia 298–300
2. Parliamentary	Pages: Britain 68–70, Iran 348
3. Referendums/Initiatives	Pages: Britain 62, 69, 74
4. Noncompetitive	Pages: Russia 298–300, China 390
F. Electoral Systems 1. Proportional representation	Pages: Russia 298–300, China 390
2. Single member district (plurality, majority runoff)	Pages: Britain 68–70, United States 112–114, Mexico 202–203, Nigeria 243–246, Iran 348
G. Political parties (organization, membership, institutionalization, ideological	Pages: Britain 66–68, United States 110–112, Mexico 198–202, Nigeria 243, Russia 294–298, Iran 346–348, China 388–389
H. Party systems	Pages: Britain 66–68, United States 110–112, Mexico 198–202, Nigeria 243, Russia 294–298, Iran 346–348, China 388–389
I. Leadership and elite recruitment	Pages: Britain 41, 56–58, United States 85, 101–103, Mexico 190–192, Nigeria 237–238, Russia 284–285, Iran 336–339, China 379–384, 387–388
J. Interest groups and interest group systems	Pages: Britain 72, United States 88, 116, Mexico 202–205, Nigeria 250–251, Iran 350–352, Russia 301–302, China 393–395

K. Bureaucracies — Pages: Britain 58–60, United States 103–104, Mexico 192–193, Nigeria 238–239, Russia 285–287, Iran 339, China 371–372

L. Military and other coercive institutions — Pages: Britain 60–61, United States 104, Mexico 193–194, Nigeria 223–225, Russia 290–291, Iran 341–342, China 385–386

M. Judiciaries
   1. Degrees of autonomy — Pages: Britain 61, United States 105–106, EU 147–148, Mexico 194–195, Nigeria 239–240, Russia 288, Iran 340–341, China 384–385

   2. Judicial Review (including European Union in relation to states, citizens) — Pages: Britain 61, United States 105–106, EU 147–149, Mexico 194–195, Nigeria 239–240, Russia 288, Iran 340–341, China 384–385
   3. Types of law — Pages: Britain 61, United States 105–106, EU 147–149, Mexico 194–195, Nigeria 239–240, Russia 288, Iran 340–341, China 384–385

IV. Citizens, Society, and the State

A. Cleavages and politics (ethnic, racial, class, gender, religious, regional) — Pages: Britain 70–72, United States 83, Mexico 171, Nigeria 217, 231, Russia 263, Iran 317, China 361
B. Civil society and social capital — Pages: Britain 70–72, 75, 77, United States 114–116, Mexico 202–203, Nigeria 248, Russia 300–301, Iran 394–350, China 390–393

C. Media Roles — Pages: Britain 58, 72–73, United States 117, Mexico 205–206, Nigeria 249–252, Russia 287–288, 303–304, Iran 352, China 395

D. Political participation (forms/modes/trends) including political violence — Pages: Britain 63–70, United States 108–110, Mexico 196–198, Nigeria 242–243, Russia 292–294, Iran 345–348, China 387–390
E. Social movements — Pages: Britain 72–73, United States 116–117, Mexico 203–205, Nigeria 250–251, Russia 301–303, Iran 350–351, China 393–395

F. Citizenship and representation — Pages: Britain 68–71, United States 112–116, Mexico 202–203, Nigeria 248, Russia 303–301, Iran 349–350, China 390–393

V. Political and Economic Change

A. Revolution, coups, and war — Pages: Britain 38, United States 82–83, 84–89, EU 126–127, Mexico 170–171, Nigeria 214–215, 223–225, Russia 264–271, Iran 314–315, 318–323, China 360–361, 364–369

B. Trends and types of political change (including democratization)
   1. Components — Pages: Britain 38, 40–45, United States 82–90, EU 131–135, Mexico 172–180, Nigeria 219–225, Russia 266–271, Iran 318–326, China 364–370, 397–399

   2. Promoting or inhibiting factors — Pages: Britain 40–45, 48–50, United States 82–83, 91–93, EU 131–135, Mexico 172–179, Nigeria 219–225, Russia 266–271, Iran 318–327, China 364–369

   3. Consequences — Pages: Britain 73–75, United States 118–121, EU 164–166, Mexico 206–207, Nigeria 253–256, Russia 304–309, Iran 352–356, China 396–399

C. Trends and types of economic change (including privatization)
   1. Components — Pages: Britain 48–50, United States 91–93, EU 131–139, 149–153, Mexico 182–186, Nigeria 227–231, Russia 274–277, Iran 328–330, China 371–374

   2. Promoting or inhibiting factors — Pages: Britain 40–45, United States 84–89, EU 155–156, Mexico 171, 177, Nigeria 219–225, Russia 266–272, Iran 318–325, China 371–374

   3. Consequences — Pages: Britain 51–54, United States 93–96, EU 155–156, Mexico 185–187, Nigeria 231–232, Russia 277–279, Iran 330–333, China 374–376

(*continued*)

Correlation Chart

AP* Course Topic	Correlation to Introduction to Comparative Politics, 7th Edition
D. Relationship between political and economic change	Pages: Britain 48–50, United States 91–93, EU 131–135, Mexico 182–186, Nigeria 227–231, Russia 274–277, Iran 328–330, China 371–374
E. Globalization and fragmentation: interlinked economies, global culture, reactions against globalization, regionalism	Pages: Britain 45–47, 54, 76, United States 89, 97–99, EU 135–137, 155–157, Mexico 174, 179, 188–189, Nigeria 225–229, 257–258, Russia 280–282, Iran 325–326, 333–335, China 366, 369, 377–378
F. Approaches to development	Pages: Britain 48–50, United States 91–93, EU 149–153, Mexico 182–186, Nigeria 227–231, Russia 274–277, Iran 328–330, China 371–374
VI. Public Policy	
A. Common policy issues	
1. Economic performance	Pages: Britain 51–53, United States 93–96, Mexico 187, Nigeria 231–232, Russia 277–279, Iran 330–332, China 374–376
2. Social welfare (e.g., education, health, poverty)	Pages: Britain 50–53, United States 93–96, EU 153, Mexico 201, 204, 209, Nigeria 230–231, Russia 287–288, Iran 330, 343, 349, 352, China 366, 371, 374
3. Civil liberties, rights, and freedoms	Pages: Britain 42–43, United States 86, 105, EU 157, 159, Mexico 173, 181, 208, Nigeria 224, Russia 283, 297, 300, Iran 319–320, 327, 349, China 362, 370, 391, 401
4. Environment	Pages: Britain 53–54, United States 97, EU 157–158, Mexico 187–188, Nigeria 232, Russia 279–280, Iran 333, China 376–377
5. Population and migration	Pages: Britain 36, 39, United States 83, EU 125, Mexico 169, 186, Nigeria 213, Russia 263, Iran 313, China 359
6. Economic development	Pages: Britain 45–53, United States 89, 91–93, EU 153, Mexico 179–181, Nigeria 225–227, Russia 274–279, Iran 328–330, China 371–374
B. Factors influencing public policymaking and implementation	
1. Domestic	Pages: Britain 72, 75, 77, United States 116–117, 121–122, Mexico 203–205, 209–210, Nigeria 250–251, 257, Russia 301–302, 309–310, Iran 350–352, China 393–395, 399
2. International	Pages: Britain 54, 76, United States 97–99, EU 158–160, Mexico 180–181, Nigeria 229, 225, 257–258, Russia 280–282, Iran 325–326, 333–335, China 369, 377–378

Preparing for the AP® Exam

Advanced Placement Comparative Government and Politics can be exhilarating. Whether you are taking an AP course at your school or working on AP independently, the stage is set for a great intellectual experience. As the school year progresses and you delve deeper and deeper into the course work, you will begin to make connections between the ideas and concepts that form the basis of comparative government and politics. Understanding these concepts with growing sophistication is exciting, but comparing domestic political systems can provide quite a challenge. More exciting still is recognizing examples of these concepts in the media. Globalization will have a significant impact on today's students, perhaps more than any generation in the past, and AP Comparative Government and Politics will better prepare you to live in a globalized world.

Sometime after New Year's Day, however, when the examination begins to loom on a very real horizon, Advanced Placement can seem downright intimidating—in fact, when offered the opportunity to take the examination for a lark, even adults long out of high school refuse. If you dread taking the test, you are in good company.

The best way to deal with any AP examination is to master it rather than letting it master you. If you can think of these examinations as a way to show off how your mind works, you have a leg up: attitude *does* help. If this isn't your style, you can build confidence and sideline your anxiety by using the strategies we describe in this book to prepare you for the test. This book is designed to put you on a fast track for success on the exam. Focused review and practice time will help you master the material and the art of test taking so that you can walk in with confidence and earn a 5.

Before The Examination

By February, long before the exam, you need to make sure that you are registered to take the test. Many schools take care of the paperwork and handle the fees for their AP students, but check with your teacher or the AP coordinator to make sure that you are on the list. This is especially important if you have a documented disability and need special arrangements for the test. If paying for the test presents a financial hardship for your family, don't be shy. Contact your school's AP coordinator. The College Entrance Examination Board offers reduced fees for those who qualify. If you are studying AP independently, call AP Services at the College Entrance Examination Board for the name of your local AP coordinator, who will help you through the registration process.

The evening before the exam is not a great time for partying nor is it a great time for cramming. If you like, look over class notes or drift through your textbook, concentrating on the broad outlines, not the small details.

The evening before the exam *is* a great time to get your things ready for the next day. Sharpen a fistful of No. 2 pencils with good erasers for the multiple-choice section; set out several black or darkblue ballpoint pens for the free-response questions; get a piece of fruit or a power bar and a bottle of water for the break; and make sure you have your Social Security number and whatever photo identification and admission ticket are required. Make sure you have removed your cell phone from your backpack or purse. Cell phones are not allowed during the exam, so you will need to get a watch to keep track of the time you spend on the free-response questions.

On the day of the examination, it is wise not to skip meals; studies show that students who eat a reasonable meal before testing tend to get higher grades. Be careful not to drink a lot of liquids, as this could make a trip to the restroom necessary during the test and cost you valuable time in the process. It is advisable to bring a snack in case you get hungry during testing—there will be a short break between Sections I and II of the exam, and you should be able to eat something quickly at this time if you need it. You will spend some time waiting while everyone is seated in the right room for the right test. That's before the test has even begun. With a short break between Sections I and II, the AP Comparative Government and Politics Exam lasts for over two and a half hours. So be prepared for a long afternoon. You do not want to be distracted by a growling stomach or hunger pangs.

Be sure to wear comfortable clothes, take along a sweater in case the heating or air-conditioning is erratic. Be sure, too, to wear clothes you like—people always perform better when they think they look better—and by all means wear your lucky socks.

You have been on the fast track. Now go earn a 5!

Taking the AP® Comparative Government and Politics Exam

The AP Comparative Government and Politics course introduces students to the basic concepts used by political scientists to assess and examine the political processes and outcomes of politics in the six core countries: China, Great Britain, Iran, Mexico, Nigeria, and Russia. Students completing this course should achieve several goals, including knowing important facts related to the governments and politics of the six core countries; understanding major comparative political themes, topics, and concepts; understanding patterns of political processes and behavior; being able to compare and contrast political institutions and processes across countries and making generalizations; and being able to analyze and interpret data relating to comparative politics. The AP Exam will test student knowledge of six content area topics relevant to understanding comparative politics and the core countries. These content area topics include introduction to comparative politics; sovereignty, authority, and power; political institutions; citizens, society, and the state; political and economic change; and public policy.

The AP Comparative Government and Politics Examination consists of two sections: Section I has 55 multiple-choice questions; Section II has eight short-answer and free-response questions. You will have 45 minutes for Section I. The questions will be collected, and you will be given a short break. You will then have 100 minutes for Section II. There are eight total questions for the free-response section of the exam, which include five definition and description short-answer questions, one conceptual analysis question, and two country context questions. You must write a response for each of the eight questions—some AP examinations allow you to choose among the free-response questions, but this is not one of them. Each section of the written portion has a suggested amount of time to write your answers. Keep an eye on your watch, and devote the appropriate amount of time to each free-response question. Watch alarms are not allowed.

Strategies For the Multiple-Choice Section

Here are some rules of thumb to help you work your way through the multiple-choice questions:

- **No guessing penalty** There are five possible answers for each question. Each correct answer is awarded one point and no points are deducted for incorrect answers. Test takers should therefore not leave an answer blank.
- **Read the question carefully** Pressured for time, many students make the mistake of reading the questions too quickly or merely skimming them. By reading a question carefully, you may already have some idea about the correct answer. You can then look for it in the responses. Careful reading is especially important in EXCEPT questions and in questions with Roman numeral choices.
- **Eliminate any answer you know is wrong** You may write on the multiple-choice questions in the test book. As you read through the answer choices, draw a line through any answer you know is wrong.
- **Read all of the possible answers, then choose the best answer choice** AP Exams are written to test your precise knowledge of a subject. Sometimes there are a few probable answers, but one of them is more specific or, when weighing the choices, a better response. For example, the Chinese political system allows for the existence of multiple parties, but only the Chinese Communist Party holds

political offices. An answer that referred to China as a one-party state would be more correct than an answer that referred to China as a multiparty state.

- **Avoid absolute responses when choosing between two or more answer choices** These answers often include the words *always* or *never*; for example, the statement "In single-member district elections, regional parties never win seats." This statement is incorrect, because regional parties, such as the Scottish National Party, sometimes win seats in single-member district elections.
- **Mark and skip tough questions** If you are hung up on a question, mark it in the margin of the question book. Questions involving graphs and data analysis can be particularly time consuming. If you notice that it is a lengthy question or you do not immediately know the answer, then skip the question. You can come back to skipped questions later if you have time. Make sure you skip these questions on your answer sheet, too. You do not want to miss the opportunity to answer questions that you possibly know because you spend too much time on a particularly difficult question.

Types of Multiple-Choice Questions

There are various kinds of multiple-choice questions. Here are some suggestions for how to approach each kind:

Classic/Best Answer Questions

This is the most common type of multiple-choice question. It simply requires you to select the most correct answer. For example:

1. After the collapse of the Soviet Union, most Russian citizens wanted the Russian government to be
   (A) communist
   (B) socialist
   (C) a free-market democracy
   (D) czarist
   (E) totalitarian

1. (B) Most Russian citizens preferred a version of socialism that limited corruption and improved living standards. Most Russians were skeptical of democracy due to their limited experience with it. Words such as *most*, *usually*, *typically*, *preferably*, etc., are very important in this type of question. This is a standard question that has one correct answer.

Except Questions

In the EXCEPT question, all of the answers are correct but one. The best way to approach these questions is to use a true/false strategy. Mark a T or an F in the margin next to each possible answer. There should be only one false answer, and that is the one you should select. For example:

1. All of the following countries have experienced a major political revolution in the last century EXCEPT
   (A) Mexico
   (B) Great Britain
   (C) Russia
   (D) Iran
   (E) China

1. (B) Great Britain has not experienced any major political upheaval or conflict in several hundred years, so that is a false answer. You should have put an F next to it. All of the other answers are true.

List and Group Questions

In this type of question, there is a list of possible answers, and you must select the answer that contains the correct group of responses. These questions look hard, but you can simplify them by crossing out items from the list and then eliminating them in the answers below. For example:

1. In which of the following countries is oil a major export commodity?
   I. Great Britain
   II. Nigeria
   III. China
   IV. Russia
   (A) I and II
   (B) II and III
   (C) I, II, and III
   (D) I and IV
   (E) II and IV

To approach the question, draw a line through choice I, because Great Britain does not export oil in any significant amount. Then cross out any response that contains choice I. At this point, you have eliminated responses (A), (C), and (D). Continue to cross out items that are wrong and the responses that contain them. Although China is a top 10 producer of oil, because it is the world's second-largest consumer of oil, it also ranks as one of the top five major importers of oil in the world. Therefore, it exports very little oil. Draw a line through III and answer (B), which contains choice III. Now you have narrowed down the possible responses.

1. (E) Both Nigeria and Russia ranked among the top 10 oil-exporting countries over the past five years. It is no coincidence that both are also among the top 10 in oil exports to the United States, the world's largest oil consumer. This answer choice correctly identifies both countries without including any incorrect answer possibilities.

Paired Questions

In these types of questions, there are two sets of information that are grouped together; you must choose the terms or responses that are correctly paired together.

1. Mexico's current economic and political systems can best be described as which of the following?

Economic System	Political System
(A) *laissez-faire*	authoritarian
(B) socialist	parliamentary
(C) neoliberal	unitary
(D) free-market capitalism	presidential
(E) command	federal

After reading the question and all of the possible answer pairs, you could eliminate choices (B) and (E) since Mexico does not operate under either a socialist or command economy, although its political system does have a federal structure. Understanding that Mexico operates under a federal system would also allow you to eliminate choice (C), because a unitary political structure is the opposite of federalism. Choice (A) is incorrect, as very few countries operate under a *laissez-faire* economic system today; even liberal economic systems have some government involvement. Mexico has also maintained a democratic structure since the authoritarian regime of the Institutional Revolutionary Party (PRI) was voted out of power in the **2000** election.

1. (D) Mexico functions under a free-market capitalist system and openly participates in global trade despite some state-controlled enterprises. Mexico's political system is a strong presidential system in which the executive office oversees and is responsible for most of the key aspects of government.

Chart/Graph Questions

These questions require you to examine the data on a chart or graph. While these questions are not difficult, spending too much time interpreting a chart or graph may slow you down. To avoid this, first read the question and all of the possible answers so that you know what the question is asking. In some cases, before you look at the chart, you may be able to eliminate some obviously incorrect responses. For example:

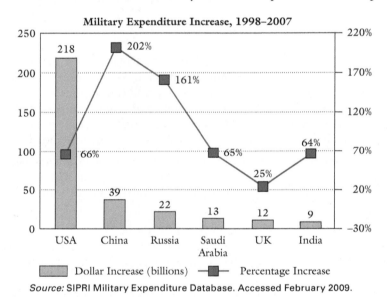

Military Expenditure Increase, 1998–2007

Dollar Increase (billions) ▬ Percentage Increase

Source: SIPRI Military Expenditure Database. Accessed February 2009.

1. The chart above best supports which of the following statements?
   (A) Saudi Arabia decreased its military spending by **34** percent in the last **10** years.
   (B) Military spending in the UK is increasing at a greater rate than India.
   (C) The enlistment of women in the military is increasing at a faster rate than the number of male enlistments.
   (D) China and Russia increased their military spending at a greater rate than the United States.
   (E) China spent more money on the military than any other country in the last **10** years.

After reading the question and the responses, you could eliminate answer (A) just by recognizing that all of the statistics displayed on the chart signify an increase in the military expenditures of the listed countries. You can also eliminate (B) because even though the UK spends a greater overall dollar amount on the military than India, India's military expenditures have increased at more than double the rate of the UK. It is generally known that men make up an overwhelming percentage of military personnel around the world, but more important for test-taking purposes, you can recognize that answer (C) does not relate to the chart in any way, which eliminates it as a possible answer. Answer (E) is wrong because, while military expenditures increased by over **200** percent in China, the United States spent nearly six times as much as China in actual dollars.

1. (D) As the table shows, between **1998** and **2007**, China and Russia increased military expenditures at a percentage rate nearly three times higher than the next-highest country on the chart, the United States.

Political Cartoon Questions

These questions require you to interpret a political cartoon. Every political cartoon contains symbolism and a point of view. Examine the cartoon before you read the question and possible answer choices to determine what each part of the drawing represents and to identify the artist's viewpoint. For example:

Tribune Media Services, Inc. All Rights Reserved. Reprinted with permission.

1. What is the viewpoint expressed in the cartoon about Chinese politics?
   (A) Deng Xiaoping is committed to political freedom.
   (B) China is marching towards democracy.
   (C) The Chinese people prefer free markets to political freedom.
   (D) Deng Xiaoping implemented free market policies without liberalizing the political system.
   (E) The government of China is debating whether or not to free the market or free the people.

1. The answer is (D). The cartoonist is pointing out an irony. Under the leadership of Deng Xiaoping in China, the government liberalized the market, but continued to suppress political freedoms.

Free-Response Questions

There are eight mandatory short-answer and free-response questions on the AP Comparative Government and Politics Examination. The structure of the questions is the following: five short-answer questions and three free-response questions. One free-response question is purely conceptual, meaning that no country-specific information will be required in the response. The other two free-response questions are country context questions and will require country-specific information in the response. These questions may ask the student to respond about one of the core countries or to compare two of the core countries. At least one of the questions usually requires interpretation of a chart, graph, or cartoon. Free-response questions can be written in any order. Whether you write the responses in or out of order, make sure that you put the number of the question in the corner of each page of your responses booklet. In addition, questions are broken into parts, such as (a) and (b). Label each part of your response.

These are not traditional essay questions. The short-answer questions can often be answered in a few sentences and should be completed in a precise and straightforward fashion. Free-response questions frequently do not require an introduction or conclusion (but it depends on what the question asks). Although this may sound easier than writing a traditional essay, it is important that you know the material very well because these are targeted questions. Examination readers want specifics. They are looking for accurate information presented in clear, concise prose. You cannot mask vague information with an elegant style.

You will have a 100-minute block of time for this section, so watch your time. Allow 25 minutes for the five short-answer questions and 25 minutes for each of the free-response questions. Spend approximately five minutes reading each free-response question and jotting down a few words on each point you want to cover in your answer. Then spend 15 minutes writing your response. Save the last five minutes to read over your response to make sure that you have covered each point with enough detail. If 25 minutes have passed and you are not finished with a question, leave some space and start a new question on the next page. You can come back later if you have time.

Vocabulary

In answering the free-response questions, carefully read the question and do exactly what it asks. It is important to note the word choices used in the questions:

- Define means to state the meaning of a word or phrase. For instance, if a question asks you to define *political culture*, the response is "common attitudes, beliefs, and symbols that influence political behavior." Definitions are usually just one sentence, however, it is important to address the core idea of the concept. For example, when defining political culture do not simply provide a list of examples, but *explain* that political culture encompasses commonly held beliefs within a society.
- Identify means to select a factor, person, or idea and give it a name. For instance, if a question asks you to identify one of the reform policies initiated by Mikhail Gorbachev, one possible response is "One of the policy reforms enacted during Gorbachev's regime was *glasnost*."
- Explain why/explain how means to describe how a feature of government or politics operates and give a cause or reason. Excellent student responses to explanations often include the word *because* in the response. For instance, if a question asks you to explain how legislative seats are distributed in a proportional representation system, your response should reason, "Legislative seats in a proportional representation system are distributed in proportion to the percentage of votes each party receives in an election; because of this qualification, voters generally cast their votes for a specific party as opposed to an individual candidate in proportional representation systems."

Scoring for Free-Response Questions

These questions are scored using a rubric that assigns points for each part of the answer. For example, if Part (a) requires you to identify and explain two factors, that part of the response will usually be worth four points (one point for each identification and one point for each explanation). If Part (b) requires you to identify and explain one factor, that part of the response will usually be worth two points (one point for the identification and one point for the explanation), for a total of six points possible on the question. In the AP Comparative Government and Politics Examination, short-answer and free-response questions can range in rubric value anywhere from one to eight points.

For the following free-response question, you will find three sample responses—one excellent, one mediocre, and one poor—and an explanation of how the responses were scored.

QUESTION. The executive office consists of a head of state and a head of government.
  a. Describe the key purpose of the head of state and the head of government.
  b. Identify the office that comprises the head of state in Great Britain AND the office that comprises the head of state in Iran.
  c. Compare the responsibilities of the head of state in Iran with those of the head of state in Great Britain.

Sample Free-Response 1

Part (a): The head of state is the key public representative of the state. The head of state is the person who serves as the official representative of the state and oversees the ceremonial duties of the country. The head of government is responsible for the day-to-day operations of the country's government as well as the functions of government.

Part (b): The head of state in Great Britain is the queen or monarch. The head of state in Iran is the supreme leader, currently Ayatollah Khamenei.

Part (c): The head of state in Great Britain, the queen, is only a ceremonial figurehead who presides over the opening of Parliament and serves as a symbol of British culture and political pride both in Great Britain and abroad. In Iran, the head of state, the supreme leader, is not only a ceremonial figurehead but is also the ultimate voice of authority within the country. The supreme leader is the highest-ranking Islamic cleric and is the ultimate authority in interpreting shar'ia. The supreme leader is also responsible for commanding the armed forces, declaring war, and dismissing the president from office if needed.

SCORING 6/6. The student is awarded all six possible points. In Part (a), the response correctly describes the role of the head of state as the person who serves as the official representative of the country as well as the ceremonial figurehead of a country. The response also describes the role of the head of government as the office and individual responsible for carrying out the operations and functions of government (one point for each description).

In Part (b), the student identifies the monarch, currently the queen, as the head of state for Great Britain and the supreme leader as the head of state for Iran (one point for each identification).

In Part (c), the response accurately explains the responsibilities and differences of the head of state in both Great Britain and Iran. The response demonstrates that the head of state in Great Britain is more symbolic and ceremonial than the supreme leader, the head of state in Iran (one point for the explanation of each head of state).

Sample Free-Response 2

Part (a): The head of state is a ceremonial and symbolic figure that may represent the state in certain political situations. The head of government is responsible for carrying out the functions and actions of a country's government.

Part (b): The head of state in Great Britain is the queen. The head of state in Iran is the president.

Part (c): The queen is responsible for meeting with political leaders and determining things such as trade and international agreements. The president of Iran is the one who heads all government actions and serves as a symbol and central figure of the country.

SCORING 3/6. In Part (a), the student is awarded two points. The response accurately describes the duties of a head of state and the duties of a head of government (one point for each description).

In Part (b), the student correctly identifies the queen as the head of state of Great Britain (one point for identification), but the identification of the president as the head of state of Iran is incorrect; the head of state in Iran is the supreme leader.

In Part (c), the student does not receive any points. Although the queen of Great Britain may meet with other political leaders as a symbolic gesture, she does not make political decisions regarding trade or other political agreements. The president is not the head of state in Iran, although as the head of government, the president does oversee the general functions of government.

Sample Free-Response 3

Part (a): The head of state is responsible for running the government of a nation and guiding its operations. The head of government is a symbolic figure that represents the country in political affairs.

Part (b): The head of state for Great Britain is the prime minister. The head of state for Iran is the supreme leader.

Part (c): The prime minister of Great Britain is responsible for overseeing Parliament and taking care of all aspects of British government. The supreme leader has the ultimate decision-making authority in Iran, and all government actions are run through the supreme leader. The supreme leader supervises all the processes of government in Iran.

SCORING 1/6. The student does not accurately describe the duties and responsibilities of the head of state and the head of government. The student makes a very common mistake of confusing the descriptions for each of the political roles. The student does not earn any points for Part (a).

In Part (b), the student incorrectly identifies the prime minister as the head of state of Great Britain. The head of state for Great Britain is the queen. The student earns one point for identifying the supreme leader as the head of state for Iran (one point for identification).

In Part (c), the student explains the role of the British prime minister, who is the head of government. The head of state is not described in the free-response answer. The student correctly identifies part of the supreme leader's duties in Iran, but inaccurately states that the supreme leader supervises all actions of government. The president, who is the head of government in Iran, would do this. The student earns no points for Part (c).

1

Introducing Comparative Politics

Mark Kesselman, Joel Krieger, and William A. Joseph

THE GLOBAL CHALLENGE OF COMPARATIVE POLITICS

▽ Focus Questions

- What are two examples of how comparison can bring to light features that might otherwise not be observed?

- Describe a discussion in which you used the comparative method to make a point.

It has been said that the personality of students and scholars tends to resemble the characteristics of what they study. We might stretch this observation to speculate that what fascinated you as a child might have attracted you to comparative politics. As a child did you love to observe the shape-shifting images through the lens of a kaleidoscope? If you did, then you are a natural for comparative politics—for you are sure to be fascinated by the endlessly shifting developments of the contemporary world of politics, and the range and depth of challenges faced by political elites and ordinary citizens around the world.

As a subject for study within political science comparative politics is the only subfield within political science that defines a method in its name. Comparative politics is both a subject matter and a method of analysis. As a subject matter it studies the politics of your own and other countries and peoples by analyzing patterns of similarity and difference, primarily at the national (country) level.

The drumbeat of politics goes on and on but as the French say, the more things change, the more they stay the same.

The current era of politics remains a combustible and volatile mix in which uncertainty alternates with stability, and movements for peace and justice confront demonic forces that often divide societies along every axis of collective identities and divisions.

- Young people desperate for jobs and educational opportunity sometimes sinking together with—and sometimes pitted against—middle-aged job-holders and pensioners are burdened by what feels like perpetual austerity, gross inequality, and a loss of faith that things will improve.
- Ordinary citizens in every corner of the globe, from occupy wall Street activists in the United States to people in authoritarian regimes throughout the world, demanding democratic governments and the chance to enjoy the fruits of liberty.
- Ethnic, racial, and national tensions enflamed by hard times and a tightly integrated globalized global order, strain national unity—a precious and increasingly rare commodity.

Like the Internet technology that speeds up and transforms our lives, creates vast far-flung social networks, and makes possible the cell phone images and messages that flash instantly around the globe—and partly as a result of this technology—the political world is changing rapidly too.

Cold War

The hostile relations that prevailed between the United States and the Soviet Union from the late 1940s until the demise of the USSR in 1991.

In a quarter century, we have witnessed the collapse of the Berlin Wall in 1989, which ushered in the end of the **Cold War** era; the attack on the World Trade Center towers in 2001, ushering in a new era of global insecurity in the face of mounting terrorism; and the Great Recession of 2008, which threw the global economy into a tailspin, heightened political conflict, and widespread anxiety about the future. More recently, we have witnessed bellicose rhetoric from Russian president Vladimir Putin, backed by military takeover of the Crimea, which prompted Western countries to expel Russia from the Group of 8 (G-8)—an exclusive club of the eight most industrialized nations in the world: Canada, France, Germany, Italy, Japan, Russia, the United Kingdom, and the United States. Despite overheated rhetoric, we are not on the precipice of a new Cold War—a nuclear confrontation akin to the Cuban missile crisis is unthinkable; and the financial integration of a globalizing world mitigates the likelihood of increasing hostility between Russia and the West.

Russian president, Vladimir Putin (seated second on right), along with Crimean officials, signs the treaty of annexation in Moscow on March 18, 2014. The agreement made the former Ukrainian territory part of the Russian Federation.

Anadolu Agency/Getty Images

While the changes that have occurred in the past quarter century are momentous, they were not unique in magnitude. They were preceded by other—even more momentous—changes, notably the two world wars of the twentieth century. And they will doubtless be followed by other momentous changes in the not too distant future. How can we make sense of the bewildering march of world history? Our aim in *Introduction to Comparative Politics* is to provide the tools to help bring order out of the apparent chaos of kaleidoscopic political change.

Introduction to Comparative Politics studies how different countries both shape and are shaped by the world order created by watershed events such as those that occurred in 1989, 2001, 2008, 2011, and 2014. Each of these dates describes a particularly important moment—what we call a **critical juncture**—that helps define key transitional moments.

Chapter 1 helps students navigate through the text by introducing the book's thematic framework, which is combined with a thorough analysis of the political institutions and processes of each country. It sets the stage and previews the thematic focus by noting five important critical junctures in recent history.

1. 1989, which symbolizes the end of the Cold War, and a wave of capitalist democracies that replaced the former East versus West divisions in Europe and much of the world;
2. September 11, 2001, which reframes globalization, shifting attention away from the development gap to terrorism, security, and the use of force;
3. 2008, a year that ushered in intense financial and economic crisis around the world;
4. 2011, when pro-democracy movements toppled repressive regimes in North Africa and the Middle East, and Japan was rocked by a severe earthquake, tsunami, and nuclear disaster;
5. 2014, when a resurgent Russia under the increasingly authoritarian leadership of Vladimir Putin, annexed the Crimea and violated the sovereignty of Ukraine.

critical juncture

An important historical moment when political actors make critical choices, which shape institutions and future outcomes.

Making Sense of Turbulent Times

The flash of newspaper headlines, television sound bites, and endless tweets can make politics look overwhelming and chaotic. Through the study of comparative politics, we can better understand a rapidly changing world. Political analysis involves more than blogging, talking head debates, or Monday-morning quarterbacking. It requires both a longer historical context and a framework for understanding unfolding developments.

This book describes and analyzes government institutions, policy-making processes, and other key aspects of politics in a wide range of countries. By using a framework that facilitates analyzing and comparing similarities and differences in a representative sample of countries, we can understand longer-term causes of political changes and continuities within nations. Each chapter explores a country's political development by reference to four themes that are central for understanding politics in today's world:

- *The Globalizing World of States:* the historical formation, internal organization, and interaction of states within the international order
- *Governing the Economy:* the role of the state in economic management
- *The Democratic Idea:* the spread of democracy and the challenges of democratization
- *The Politics of Collective Identities:* the sources and political impact of diverse collective identities, including class, gender, ethnicity, nationality, and religion

collective identities

The groups with which people identify, including gender, class, race, region, and religion, and which are the "building blocks" for social and political action.

These themes, discussed below, help us make political sense of both stable and tumultuous times.

The contemporary period presents an extraordinary challenge to those who study comparative politics, but the study of comparative politics also provides a unique opportunity for understanding this uncertain era. In order to appreciate the complexity of politics in countries around the world, we must look beyond any single national perspective. Today, business and trade, information technology, mass communications and culture, immigration and travel, as well as politics, forge deep connections—as well as deep divisions—among people worldwide. We urgently need a global and comparative perspective as we explore the politics of different countries and their interaction and interdependence with one another.

There is an added benefit of studying comparative politics: by comparing political institutions, values, and processes in countries around the world, the student of comparative politics acquires analytical skills that can also be used at home. After you study comparative politics, you begin to think comparatively. As comparison becomes second nature, we hope that you will look at the politics of your own country differently, with a wider and deeper, more analytical, focus that will inspire new reflections, interpretations, and insights. The contemporary world provides a fascinating laboratory for the study of comparative politics. We hope that you share our sense of excitement in the challenging effort to understand the complex and ever-shifting terrain of contemporary politics throughout the world.

Where Do You Stand?

There are more than 200 countries in the world: is it time for other countries to take on more of the burdens of global leadership that America has shouldered since the end of World War II ?

How do you think the study of comparative politics will change the way you understand America—or whatever country you call home?

WHAT—AND HOW—COMPARATIVE POLITICS COMPARES

To "compare and contrast" is one of the most common human mental exercises, whether in the classroom study of literature, politics, or animal behavior—or in selecting dorm rooms or arguing with friends about your favorite movie. In the observation of politics, the use of comparisons is very old, dating in the Western world from the ancient Greek philosopher, Aristotle, who analyzed and compared the city-states of Greece in the fourth century BCE according to whether they were ruled by a single individual, a few people, or all citizens. The modern study of comparative politics refines and systematizes this age-old practice of evaluating some features of country X's politics by comparing it to the same features of country Y's politics.

Comparative politics is a subfield within the academic discipline of political science as well as a method or approach to the study of politics.[1] The subject matter of comparative politics is the domestic politics of countries. Within the discipline of political science, comparative politics is one of four areas of specialization. In addition to comparative politics, most political science (or government) departments in U.S. colleges and universities include courses in political theory, international relations, and American politics.

Because it is widely believed that students living in the United States should study the politics of their own country in depth, American politics is usually treated as a separate subfield of political science. The pattern of separating the study of politics at home and abroad is also common elsewhere, so students in Canada study Canadian politics as a distinct specialty, and Japanese students master Japanese politics.

However, there is no logical reason why study of the United States should not be included within the field of comparative politics—and good reason to do so. Comparative study can make it easier to recognize what is distinctive about the United States and what features it shares with some other countries. This is why we have included a chapter on the United States in this book.

Special mention should be made of the distinction between comparative politics and international relations. Comparative politics involves comparing domestic political institutions, processes, policies, conflicts, and attitudes in different countries; international relations involves studying the foreign policies of and interactions among countries, the role of international organizations such as the United Nations, and the growing influence of global actors, from multinational corporations to international human rights advocates to terrorist networks. In a globalized world, however, domestic and international politics routinely spill over into one another, so the distinction between the two fields is somewhat blurry. Courses in international relations nowadays often integrate a concern with how internal political processes affect states' behavior toward other states, while courses in comparative politics highlight the importance of transnational forces for understanding what goes on within a country's borders. One of the four themes that we use to analyze comparative politics, the " globalizing world of states," emphasizes the interaction of domestic and international forces in the politics of all nations.

It still makes sense to maintain the distinction between comparative politics and international relations. Much of the world's political activity continues to occur within national borders, and comparisons of domestic politics, institutions, and

Focus Questions ▽

- What do we mean by globalization?

- How does increased cross-border contact among countries and peoples affect political, social, and cultural life?

comparative politics

The field within political science that focuses on domestic politics and analyzes patterns of similarity and difference among countries.

globalization

The intensification of worldwide interconnectedness associated with the increased speed and magnitude of cross-border flows of trade, investment and finance, and processes of migration, cultural diffusion, and communication.

processes enable us to understand critical features that distinguish one country's politics from another's. Furthermore, we believe that, despite increased international economic competition and integration (a key aspect of globalization), countries are still the fundamental building blocks in structuring most political activity. Therefore *Introduction to Comparative Politics* is built on in-depth case studies of a sample of important countries around the world.

The comparative approach principally analyzes similarities and differences among countries by focusing on selected political institutions and processes. As students of comparative politics (we call ourselves comparativists), we believe that we cannot

THE INTERNET AND THE STUDY OF COMPARATIVE POLITICS

The Internet can be a rich source of information about the politics of countries around the world. Following are some of the types of information you can find on the Web. We haven't included URLs since they change so often. But you should be able to find the websites easily through a key word search on Google or another search engine.

- **Current events.** Most of the world's major news organizations have excellent websites. Among those we recommend for students of comparative politics are the British Broadcasting Corporation (BBC), Cable News Network (CNN), the *New York Times*, and the *Washington Post*.
- **Elections.** Results of recent (and often past) elections, data on voter turnout, and descriptions of different types of electoral systems can be found at the International Election Guide (IFES), Elections by Country/Wikipedia, and the International Institute for Democracy and Electoral Assistance.
- **Statistics.** You can find data helpful both for understanding the political, economic, and social situations in individual countries and for comparing countries. Excellent sources of statistics are the Central Intelligence Agency (CIA), United Nations Development Program (UNDP), and World Bank*.

There are many websites that bring together data from other sources. These enable you not only to access the statistics, but also to chart or map them in a variety of ways. See, for example, nationmaster.com and gapminder.com.

- **Rankings and ratings.** Many organizations provide rankings or ratings of countries along some dimension based on comparative statistical analysis. We provide the following examples of these in the data that appear at the end of this chapter: the UNDP Human Development Index (HDI), the Global Gender Gap, the Environmental Performance Index, the Corruption Perceptions Index, and the Freedom in the World rating. Others you might consult are the UNDP's Gender-Related Development Index (GDI) and Gender Empowerment Measure (GEM),

the World Bank's Worldwide Governance Indicators Project, the Index of Economic Freedom, and the Press Freedom Index. *A note of caution: Some of these sites may have a political perspective that influences the way they collect and analyze data. As with any Web source, be sure to check out who sponsors the site and what type of organization it is.*

- **Official information and documents.** Most governments maintain websites in English. The first place to look the website of the country's embassy in Washington, D.C., Ottawa, or London. The United Nations delegations of many countries also have websites. Governments often have English-language versions of their official home pages, including governments with which the United States does not have official relations, such as Cuba and North Korea.
- **The United States Department of State.** The State Department's website has background notes on most countries. American embassies around the world provide information on selected topics about the country in which they are based.
- **Maps.** The Perry-Castañeda Library Map Collection at the University of Texas is probably the best currently available online source of worldwide maps at an educational institution.
- **General comparative politics.** Several American and British universities host excellent websites that provide links to a multitude of Internet resources on comparative politics (often coupled with international relations), such as Columbia University, Emory University, Keele University (UK), Princeton University, and Vanderbilt University. Do a search for "comparative politics resources" with the university name to get to these websites.

MAKING CONNECTIONS How has easy access to the Internet changed the way you do research? Is there a down side?

*Definitions of key terms in this boxed feature appear in the Glossary, which begins on p. 411.

make reliable statements about most political situations by looking at only one case. We often hear statements such as: "The United States has the best health care system in the world." Comparativists immediately wonder what kinds of health care systems exist in other countries, what they cost and how they are financed, how it is decided who can receive medical care, and so on. As we know from the ongoing controversies over the Affordable Care Act there is little agreement about what "the Best" means when it comes to health care systems. Is it the one that provides the widest access? The one that is the most technologically advanced? The one that is the most cost effective? The one that produces the healthiest population?

None of us would declare the winner for best picture at the Academy Awards, without seeing more than one—and even better, all—of the nominated movies! Shouldn't we be as critically minded and engaged when we are comparing and evaluating critical public policy issues decisions?

Some comparativists focus on comparing government institutions, such as the legislature, executive, political parties, or court systems, in different countries.[2] Others compare specific political processes, such as voting or policies on a particular issue, for example, education or the environment.[3] Some comparative political studies take a thematic approach and analyze broad topics, such as the causes and consequences of nationalist movements or revolutions in different countries.[4] Comparative studies may also involve comparisons of an institution, policy, or process through time, in one or several countries. For example, some studies have analyzed a shift in the orientation of economic policy that occurred in many advanced capitalist countries in the 1980s from **Keynesianism**, an approach that gives priority to government regulation of the economy, to **neoliberalism**, which emphasizes the importance of market-friendly policies.[5] And many comparativists study politics within a single country, often within a framework that draws on similarities and differences with other countries.[6]

Level of Analysis

Comparisons can be useful for political analysis at several different levels of a country, such as cities, regions, provinces, or states. A good way to begin the study of comparative politics is with **countries**. Countries are distinct, politically defined territories that encompass governments, composed of political institutions, as well as cultures, economies, and collective identities. Although countries are often highly divided by internal conflicts, people within their borders may have close ties to those in other countries, and business firms based in one country may have operations in many others, countries have historically been among the most important sources of a people's collective political identity. They are the major arena for organized political action in the modern world.

Within a given country, the **state** is almost always the most powerful cluster of institutions. But just what is the state? The way the term is used in comparative politics is probably unfamiliar to many students. In the United States, it usually refers to the states in the federal system—California, Illinois, New York, Texas, and so on. But in comparative politics, the state refers to the key political institutions responsible for making, implementing, and adjudicating important policies in a country. Thus, we refer to the "German state" and the "Mexican state." The state is synonymous with what is often called the "government," or, in the United States, the "administration." The state also implies a more durable entity. Governments may come and go, but the institutions that comprise the state generally endure (unless overthrown from within or conquered by other states in war).

comparativist

A political scientist who studies the similarities and differences in the domestic politics of various countries.

Keynesianism

Named after the British economist John Maynard Keynes, an approach to economic policy in which state economic policies are used to regulate the economy in an attempt to achieve stable economic growth.

During a recession, state budget deficits are used to expand demand in an effort to boost both consumption and investment, and to create employment. During periods of high growth when inflation threatens, cuts in government spending and a tightening of credit are used to reduce demand.

neoliberalism

A term used to describe government policies aiming to promote free competition among business firms within the market, including reduced governmental regulation and social spending.

country

A territorial unit controlled by a single state.

state

The most powerful political institutions in a country, including the executive, legislative, and judicial branches of government, the police, and armed forces.

executive

The agencies of government that implement or execute policy.

cabinet

The body of officials (e.g., ministers, secretaries) who direct executive departments presided over by the chief executive (e.g., prime minister, president).

bureaucracy

An organization structured hierarchically, in which lower-level officials are charged with administering regulations codified in rules that specify impersonal, objective guidelines for making decisions.

legislature

One of the primary political institutions in a country, in which elected or appointed members are charged with responsibility for making laws and usually providing for the financial resources for the state to carry out its functions.

judiciary

One of the primary political institutions in a country; responsible for the administration of justice and in some countries for determining the constitutionality of state decisions.

legitimacy

A belief by powerful groups and the broad citizenry that a state exercises rightful authority.

The most important state institutions are the executive—usually, the president and/or prime minister and the cabinet. Other key state institutions include the military, police, and bureaucracy. In some countries, the executive includes the communist party leadership (such as in China), the head of a military government (as in Nigeria until 1999), or the supreme religious leader (as in the Islamic Republic of Iran). Alongside the executive, the legislature and the judiciary comprise the institutional apex of state power, although the inter-relationships and functions of these institutions vary from country to country.

States claim, usually, but not always, with considerable success, the right to make rules—notably, laws, administrative regulations, and court decisions—that are binding for people within the country. Even democratic states—in which top officials are chosen by procedures that authorize all citizens to participate—can survive only if they can preserve dominance internally and protect their independence with regard to other states and external groups that may threaten them. A number of countries have highly repressive states whose political survival depends largely on military and police powers. Even in such states, however, long-term stability requires that the ruling regime have some measure of political legitimacy; that is, the support of a significant segment of the citizenry (in particular, more influential citizens and groups) who believe that the state is entitled to demand compliance. Political legitimacy is greatly affected by the state's ability to "deliver the goods" to its people through satisfactory economic performance and at least a minimum distribution of economic resources. Moreover, as the upheavals in the Arab world in 2011 dramatized, legitimacy is much more secure when there is some measure of democracy.

Thus, *Introduction to Comparative Politics* looks closely at both the state's role in governing the economy and the pressures exerted on states to develop and extend democratic participation.

You will see from the country chapters in this book that the organization of state institutions varies widely, and that these differences have a powerful impact on political, economic, and social life. Therefore, we devote considerable attention to institutional variations, along with their political implications. Each country study begins with an analysis of how the state has evolved historically; that is, state formation. One critical difference among states involves the extent to which citizens in a country share a common sense of nationhood; that is, a belief that the state's geographic boundaries coincide with the political identity of the people who live within those boundaries, what can be described as a sense of solidarity and shared values based on being citizens of the same country. When state boundaries and national identity coincide, the resulting formation is called a nation-state. A major source of political instability can occur when state boundaries and national identity do not coincide. In many countries around the world, nationalist movements within a state's borders challenge existing boundaries and seek to secede to form their own state, sometimes in alliance with movements from neighboring countries with whom they claim to share a common heritage. Such is the case with the Kurds, an ethnic group whose members live in Turkey, Syria, and Iraq. Many groups of Kurds have fought to establish an independent nation-state of Kurdistan. When a nationalist movement has distinctive ethnic, religious, and/or linguistic ties opposed to those of other groups in the country, conflicts are likely to be especially intense. India and Nigeria, for example, have experienced particularly violent episodes of what has been termed ethnonationalist conflict. Tibet is an example of ethnic conflict within a country, China, whose population otherwise has a strong sense of national identity.

Young people were at the forefront of the democracy movements that shook the Middle East and North Africa in 2011.

Yahya arhab/epa/Landov

Causal Theories

Because countries are the basic building blocks in politics and because states are the most significant political organizations within countries, these are two critical units for comparative analysis. The comparativist seeks to measure and explain similarities and differences among countries or states. One widely used approach in doing such comparative analysis involves developing causal theories—hypotheses that can be expressed formally in a causal mode: "If X happens, then Y will be the result." Such theories include factors (the independent variables, symbolized by X) that are believed to influence some outcome (the dependent variable, symbolized by Y) that the analyst wants to explain.

For example, it is commonly argued that if a country's economic pie shrinks, conflict among groups will intensify. This hypothesis claims what is called an inverse correlation between variables: as X varies in one direction (the economic pie shrinks), Y varies in the opposite direction (political and economic conflict over the economic pie increases). This relationship might be tested by statistical analysis of a large number of cases (Large N Analysis) or by analyzing one or several country cases in depth to determine how relevant relationships have varied historically (Small N Analysis). Even when the explanation does not involve the explicit testing of hypotheses (and often it does not), comparativists try to identify significant patterns that help explain political similarities and differences among countries.

It is important to recognize the limits on just how "scientific" political science—and thus comparative politics—can be. Two important differences exist between the

state formation

The historical development of a state, often marked by major stages, key events, or turning points (critical junctures) that influence the contemporary character of the state.

nation-state

Distinct, politically defined territory in which the state and national identity coincide.

causal theories

An influential approach in comparative politics that involves trying to explain why "if X happens, then Y is the result."

independent variable

The variable symbolized by X in the statement that "If X happens, then Y will be the result"; in other words, the independent variable is a cause of Y (the dependent variable).

dependent variable

The variable symbolized by Y in the statement that "If X happens, then Y will be the result"; in other words, the dependent variable is the outcome of X (the independent variable).

"hard" (or natural) sciences like physics and chemistry and the social sciences. First, social scientists study people who exercise their political will and may act in an unpredictable way as the events of 2011 in the Middle East and North Africa powerfully demonstrate. This does not mean that people choose in a totally arbitrary fashion. We choose within the context of material constraint, institutional dictates, and cultural preferences. But there will always be a gulf between the natural and social sciences because of their different objects of study.

In the natural sciences, experimental techniques can be applied to isolate the contribution of distinct factors on a particular outcome. It is possible to change the value or magnitude of a factor—for example, the force applied to an object— and measure how the outcome has consequently changed. There is a lively debate about whether the social sciences should seek scientific explanations comparable to what prevails in the natural sciences, such as physics. An approach largely borrowed from economics, called **rational choice theory**, has become influential—and highly controversial—in political science, including comparative politics, in recent years.[7] Rational choice theory focuses on how individuals act strategically (that is, rationally) in an attempt to achieve goals that maximize their interests. Such actions involve varied activities like voting for a particular candidate or rebelling against the government. Proponents of rational choice generally use deductive and quantitative methods to construct models of political behavior that they believe can be applied across all types of political systems and cultures. The appeal of rational choice theory lies in its capacity to provide theoretical and practical insights about comparative politics through formal models based on the assumption that individual actors pursue goals efficiently. But this approach has been criticized for claiming to explain large-scale and complex social phenomena by reference to individual choices. It has also been criticized for dismissing the importance of variations in historical experience, political culture, identities, institutions, and other key aspects of the political world.

The study of comparative politics offers many challenges, including the complexity of the subject matter, the fast pace of change in the contemporary world, and the impossibility of manipulating variables or replicating conditions. As a result, most comparativists probably agree on a middle course that avoids either focusing exclusively on one country or blending all countries indiscriminately. If we study only individual countries without any comparative framework, comparative politics would become merely the study of a series of isolated cases. It would be impossible to recognize what is most significant in the collage of political characteristics that we find in the world's many countries. As a result, the understanding of patterns of similarity and difference among countries would be lost, along with an important tool for evaluating what is and what is not unique about a country's political life.

If we go to the other extreme and try to make universal claims, we would tend to ignore significant national differences and patterns of variation. The political world is incredibly complex, shaped by an extraordinary array of factors and an almost endless interplay of variables. Indeed, after a brief period in the 1950s and 1960s when many comparativists tried—and failed—to develop a grand theory that would apply to all countries, most comparativists now agree on the value of **middle-level theory**, that is, theories focusing on specific features of the political world, such as institutions, policies, or classes of similar events, such as revolutions or elections.

Consider an example of middle-level theory that would help us understand the developments of 2011—theories of transitions from authoritarian to more

---

rational choice theory

An approach to analyzing political decision making and behavior that assumes that individual actors rationally pursue their aims in an effort to achieve the most positive net result. Rational choice is often associated with the pursuit of selfish goals, but the theory permits a wide range of motivations, including altruism.

---

middle-level theory

Seeks to explain phenomena in a limited range of cases, in particular, a specific set of countries with particular characteristics, such as parliamentary regimes, or a particular type of political institution (such as political parties) or activity (such as protest).

democratic forms of government. Comparativists have long analyzed the processes through which many countries with authoritarian forms of government, such as military **dictatorships** and one-party regimes, have developed more participatory and democratic regimes. In studying this process, termed **democratic transitions**, comparativists do not either treat each national case as unique or try to construct a universal pattern that ignores all differences.[8] Applying middle-level theory, we identify the influence on the new regime's political stability of specific variables such as institutional legacies, political culture, levels of economic development, the nature of the regime before the transition, and the degree of ethnic conflict or homogeneity.

We believe that students will be in a better position to consider these questions—and provide the most powerful answers—after gaining a solid grasp of political continuities and contrasts in diverse countries around the world. It is this goal that we put front and center in *Introduction to Comparative Politics*.

dictatorships

A form of government in which power and political control are concentrated in one or a few rulers who have concentrated and nearly absolute power.

democratic transition

The process of a state moving from an authoritarian to a democratic political system.

Where Do You Stand?

Is declining economic performance or political instability a greater threat to a regime?

Ten years from now will Edward Snowden be viewed as patriot defending civil liberties and conscious or a traitor who has damaged American security?

THEMES FOR COMPARATIVE ANALYSIS

SECTION 3

Our framework in *Introduction to Comparative Politics*, comprised of these core themes, provides a guide to understanding many features of contemporary comparative politics. But we urge students (and rely on instructors!) to challenge and amplify our interpretations. Further, we want to note that a textbook builds from existing theory but does not construct or test new hypotheses. That task is the goal of original scholarly studies.

Focus Questions ▼

- Which one of the themes presented for comparative analysis seems the most important? Why? The least important? Why?

- Give an example of how, in one particular country, features of one theme can affect the features of another theme.

Theme 1: A Globalizing World of States

Our first theme, *a globalizing world of states*, focuses on the central importance of states in the understanding of comparative politics. International organizations, such as the United Nations, private actors like transnational corporations, such as Microsoft, and non-governmental organizations (NGOs), such as Amnesty International, play a crucial role in politics. But states provide security to their citizens, make and enforce laws, and to varying degrees provide citizens with social protection in times and circumstances of need.

Our globalizing world of states theme highlights that states are still the basic building blocks in world politics. The theme also analyzes the importance of variations among the way that states are organized, in other words, the mix of

institutional design

The institutional arrangements that define the relationships between executive, legislative, and judicial branches of government and between the national government and subnational units such as states in the United States.

World Trade Organization (WTO)

A global international organization that oversees the "rules of trade" among its member states. The main functions of the WTO are to serve as a forum for its members to negotiate new agreements and resolve trade disputes. Its fundamental purpose is to lower or remove barriers to free trade.

International Monetary Fund (IMF)

The International Monetary Fund is the global institution with a mandate to "foster global monetary cooperation, secure financial stability, facilitate international trade, promote high employment and sustainable economic growth, and reduce poverty." It has been particularly active in helping countries that are experiencing serious financial problems. In exchange for IMF financial or technical assistance, a country must agree to a certain set of conditions that promote economic liberalization.

political institutions that distinguishes, for example, democratic from authoritarian regimes. Country chapters emphasize the importance of understanding similarities and differences in state formation and **institutional design**. We identify critical junctures of state formation: key events like colonial conquest, defeat in war, economic crises, or revolutions that impact and shape states. We also study variations in states' economic management strategies and capacities, diverse patterns of political institutions, such as the contrast between presidential and parliamentary forms in democratic states, the relationship of the state with social groups, and unresolved challenges that the state faces from within and outside its borders.

The globalized world of states theme also emphasizes the interaction between the national and the international levels in shaping the politics of all countries. Here, the theme points in two directions: One focuses on a state's influence in affecting other states and the international economic and political arena; the other focuses on the impact of international forces on the state's activities within the country's borders.

Regarding the first direction, states still dwarf other political institutions in the exercise of power that matters, whether with regard to war, peace, and national security, or when it comes to providing educational opportunities, health care, and pensions (social security).

The second dimension of the globalizing world-of-states theme underlines the multiple global forces that have significant impacts on the domestic politics of virtually all countries.[9] A wide array of international organizations and treaties, including the United Nations, the European Union, the **World Trade Organization (WTO)**, the World Bank, the **International Monetary Fund (IMF)**, and the **North American Free Trade Agreement (NAFTA)**, challenge the sovereign control of national governments within their own territories. Transnational corporations, international banks, and currency traders in New York, London, Frankfurt, Hong Kong, and Tokyo affect countries and people throughout the world. A country's political borders do not protect its citizens from global warming, environmental pollution, or infectious diseases that come from abroad.

Thanks to the global diffusion of radio, television, twitter and the Internet, and social media of all kinds, people nearly everywhere can become remarkably well informed about international developments. This knowledge may fuel popular demands that governments intervene to stop atrocities in, for example, faraway Kosovo, Rwanda, or Libya, and Syria or provide aid to the victims of natural disasters as happened after a devastating earthquake in China in 2008 and a multiple disaster in Japan in 2011, each killed many thousands of people. And heightened global awareness may encourage citizens to hold their own government to internationally recognized standards of human rights and democracy. Such awareness played a significant role in motivating people to join the prodemocracy movements in North Africa and the Middle East in 2011.

A puzzle: To what extent can even the most powerful states (especially the United States) preserve their autonomy and impose their will on others in a globalized world? And in what ways are the poorer and less powerful countries particularly vulnerable to the pressures of globalization and disgruntled citizens?

Increasingly, the politics and policies of states are shaped by diverse international factors often lumped together under the category of globalization. At the same time, many states face increasingly restive constituencies within their country who challenge the power and legitimacy of central governments. In reading the

The cartoon claims that globalization is flattening the world of states.
© George Riemann

country case studies in this book, try to assess how pressures from both above and below—outside and inside—influence a state's policies and its ability to retain citizen support.

Theme 2: Governing the Economy

The success of states in maintaining sovereign authority and control over their people is greatly affected by their ability to ensure that enough goods are produced and services delivered to satisfy the needs and demands of their populations. Citizen discontent with communist states' inadequate economic performance was an important reason for the rejection of communism and the disintegration of the Soviet Union and its allies in Eastern Europe in 1989. In contrast, China's stunning success in promoting economic development has generated powerful support for the communist regime in that country.

Effective economic performance is near the top of every state's political agenda, and "governing the economy"[10]—how a state organizes production and the extent and nature of its intervention in the economy—is a key element in its overall pattern of governance. The core of governing the economy involves the strategies that states

North American Free Trade Agreement (NAFTA)

A treaty among the United States, Mexico, and Canada implemented on January 1, 1994, that largely eliminates trade barriers among the three nations. NAFTA serves as a model for an eventual Free Trade Area of the Americas zone that could include most nations in the Western Hemisphere.

choose in an attempt to improve economic performance, deal with economic crises, and compete in international markets. A key contrast between various strategies is the relative importance of private market forces versus government direction of the economy.

The term political economy refers to the interaction between politics and economics, that is, to how government actions affect economic performance and how economic performance in turn affects a country's political processes. We place great importance on political economy in *Introduction to Comparative Politics* because we believe that politics in all countries is deeply influenced by the interaction between a country's government and the economy in both its domestic and international dimensions.

Is there a particular formula for state economic governance that produces maximum success in promoting national prosperity? In particular, is there an optimum balance between state direction of the economy and free markets, that is, the ability of private business firms to operate without government supervision and regulation? On the one hand, both economic winners and losers among the world's countries display a pattern of extensive state intervention in the economy. And, similarly, both winners and losers include cases of relatively little state intervention. Thus, it is not the *degree* of state intervention that distinguishes the economic success stories from those that have fared less well. It appears, from comparing the economic performance of many countries, that the winners do not share a single formula that enabled them to excel. For example, a study of the world's affluent capitalist economies identifies two quite different patterns of political economy, both of which have been associated with strong economic performance.[11] Studies seeking to explain the Asian "economic miracles"—Japan, Taiwan, South Korea, and more recently China—as well as the variable economic performance of other countries, highlight the diversity of approaches that have been pursued.[12]

Comparative analysis of how well different states govern their economies becomes even more complex when one considers the appropriate yardstick to measure economic success. Should economic performance be measured solely by how rapidly a country's economy grows? By how equitably it distributes the fruits of economic growth? By the quality of life of its citizenry, as measured by such criteria as life expectancy, level of education, and unemployment rate? What about the environmental impact of economic growth? These are very different measures. Although many of the dimensions are positively correlated, there is far from a complete correspondence. Recently, there has been much greater attention to the issue of sustainable development, which promotes ecologically sound ways to modernize the economy and raise the standard of living. (See "How Is Development Measured?") We invite you to consider these questions as you study the political economies of the countries analyzed in this book.

A puzzle: What is the relationship between democracy and successful national economic performance? This is a question that students of political economy have long pondered—and to which there are no fully satisfactory answers. Although all economies, even the most powerful, experience ups and downs, all durable democracies (with the exception of India) have been notable economic success stories. On the other hand, several East Asian countries with nondemocratic regimes—notably South Korea, Taiwan, and Singapore in the 1960s and 1970s, and Malaysia and Thailand in the 1980s and 1990s—achieved remarkable records of development. China, an authoritarian communist party–state that has enjoyed the highest growth rate among major economies in the

---

political economy

The study of the interaction between the state and the economy, that is, how the state and political processes affect the economy and how the organization of the economy and strategic choices made by the government and state actors affect political processes.

sustainable development

An approach to promoting economic growth that seeks to minimize environmental degradation and depletion of natural resources.

communist party–state

A type of nation-state in which the communist party attempts to exercise a complete monopoly on political power and controls all important state institutions.

GLOBAL CONNECTION

How Is Development Measured?

As we have noted, we put particular importance on understanding the relationship between the political system and the economy in the study of the politics of any country and in our overall approach to comparative politics. Each of the country case studies describes and analyzes the role of the government in making economic policy. They also take special note of the impact of the global economy on national politics. This book makes frequent reference to two commonly used measures of the overall size or power of a country's economy:

- **gross domestic product (GDP)***: The value of the total goods and services produced by the country during a given year.
- **gross national product (GNP)**: GDP plus income earned abroad by the country's residents.

A country's GDP and GNP are different, but not hugely so. In this book, we usually use GDP, calculated according to an increasingly popular method called **purchasing power parity (PPP)**. PPP takes into account the real cost of living in a particular country by calculating how much it would cost in the local currency to buy the same "basket of goods" in different countries. For example, how many dollars in the United States, pesos in Mexico, or rubles in Russia does it take to buy a certain amount of food or to pay for housing? Many scholars think that PPP provides a relatively reliable (and revealing) tool for comparing the size of an economy among countries. In terms of annual total output according to PPP, the world's ten largest economies, in descending order, are the United States, China, India, Japan, Germany, Russia, Brazil, Britain, France, and Mexico.

Total GDP is a useful measure. It helps to understand a country's overall weight in the world economy. But because this measure does not take into account the size of the population, it does not reveal anything about the average standard of living of the country's citizens. China and India are economic powerhouses according to their total GDP, but their citizens' average income ranks far below that of the majority of countries in the world. A better way to measure and compare the level of economic development and citizens' standard of living in different countries is to look at annual GDP *per capita* (per person), in other words, to divide a country's total economic output by its population. Although China

has the world's second-largest economy as measured by total output, it falls to 120th out of 227 economies in terms of its annual GDP *per capita* ($9,800); India, the world's third largest economy ($4,000) ranks 168th. The United States—by far the world's biggest economy—has the thirteenth highest GDP per capita ($52,800). Qatar ($102,100) and Liechtenstein ($89,400), with their tiny populations rank first and second in GDP per capita. Using GDP *per capita* provides a much better idea of which countries in the world are rich (developed) or poor (developing).

The comparative data charts at the end of this chapter provide total GDP and GDP *per capita* as well as other economic, geographic, demographic, and social information for our country case studies. The Comparative Rankings table also provides several ways of evaluating countries' economic, political, or public policy performance.

In 2014, an international team of scholars launched an important new comparative index that ranks countries according to what they call "social progress," which is defined as "the capacity of a society to meet the basic human needs of its citizens, establish the building blocks that allow citizens and communities to enhance and sustain the quality of their lives, and create the conditions for all individuals to reach their full potential." **The Social Progress Index (SPI)** is derived from twelve measures such as shelter, health and wellness, ecosystem sustainability, personal freedom and choice, and tolerance and inclusion. Out of 133 countries, the three with the highest SPI were New Zealand, Switzerland, and Iceland, while the three with the lowest were Chad, the Central African Republic, and Burundi. The countries covered in this book had the following SPI rankings: Britain (13), China (90), Iran (94), Mexico (54), Nigeria (123), Russia (80), and the United States (16).

MAKING CONNECTIONS As you look at the SPI rankings what two country rankings make you want to dig deeper because something about the ranking seemed so surprising?

*Definitions of key terms in this boxed feature appear in the Glossary, which begins on p. 411.

world since the early 1990s, provides a vivid case of development without democracy. An influential study by political scientist Adam Przeworski and colleagues concludes, after an exhaustive comparison of the economic performance of democratic and authoritarian states, that there is no clear-cut answer to the question of which regime is better able to achieve superior economic performance.[13] Similarly, Nobel Prize–winning economist Amartya Sen has argued, "There is no clear relation between economic growth and democracy in *either* direction."[14] As you read the country studies, try to identify why some states have been more successful than others in "governing the economy," that is, fostering successful economic performance.

Theme 3: The Democratic Idea

democracy

From the Greek *demos* (the people) and *kratos* (rule). A political system featuring: selection to public offices through free and fair elections; the right of all adults to vote; political parties that are free to compete in elections; government that operates by fair and relatively open procedures; political rights and civil liberties; an independent judiciary (court system); and civilian control of the military.

One of the most important and astonishing political developments in recent years has been the rapid spread of **democracy** throughout much of the world. There is powerful evidence of the strong appeal of democracy, that is, a regime in which citizens exercise substantial control over choice of political leaders and the decisions made by their governments.

According to statistical analysis of numerous measures of political freedom and civil liberties, the think tank Freedom House has calculated that in 1973, there were 43 countries that could be considered "free" (or democratic), 38 that were "partly free," and 69 that should be classified as "not free."[15] In 2014, the count was 88 free, 59 partly free, and 48 not free. In terms of population, 35 percent of the world's people lived in free countries in 1973, 18 percent in partly free, and 47 percent were citizens of countries ranked as not free. In 2014, the percentages were 40 percent free, 25 percent partly free, and 35 percent not free. (See Table 1.1.) Economist Amartya

Table 1.1	The Spread of Democracy[a]		
Year	**Free Countries**	**Partly Free Countries**	**Not Free Countries**
1973	43 (35%)	38 (18%)	69 (47%)
1983	54 (36%)	47 (20%)	64 (44%)
1993[b]	75 (25%)	73 (44%)	38 (31%)
2014	88 (40%)	59 (25%)	48 (35%)[c]

[a] The number of countries in each category is followed by the percentage of the world population.

[b] In 1993, the large increase in the number of free and partly free countries was mostly due to the collapse of communist regimes in the Soviet Union and elsewhere. The main reason that there was a significant drop in the percentage of world population living in free countries in 1993 was that India was classified as partly free from 1991 through 1997. It has been ranked as free since 1998.

[c] The increase in the number of countries and percentage of people rated as not free countries in 2010 compared to 1993 reflects the fact that several countries, most notably Russia, were shifted from partly free to not free. Half of the world's "not free" population lives in China.

Source: Freedom House (www.freedomhouse.org)

Sen has observed, "While democracy is not yet uniformly practiced, nor indeed uniformly accepted, in the general climate of world opinion, democratic governance has now achieved the status of being taken to be generally right."[16] As authoritarian rulers in countries from Albania to Zaire (now called the Democratic Republic of the Congo) have learned in recent decades, once persistent and widespread pressures for democratic participation develop, they are hard to resist. However, as brutal suppression of protesters in China (in 1989) and Libya and Bahrain (in 2011) demonstrated, dictators do not easily give up their power.

What determines the growth, stagnation, or decline of democracy in a country? Comparativists have devoted enormous energy to studying this question. One scholar notes, "For the past two decades, the main topic of research in comparative politics has been democratization."[17] Yet, for all the attention it has received, there is no scholarly consensus on how and why democratization develops and becomes consolidated, remains incomplete, or is reversed. Just as there is no single route to economic prosperity, we have also learned that there is no one path to democracy, and that democratic transitions can be slow, uncertain, and reversible. Many of the country studies in *Introduction to Comparative Politics* analyze the diverse causes and sources of support for democracy; and some expose the fragility of democratic transitions.

In certain historical settings, democracy may result from a standoff or compromise among political contenders for power in which no one group can gain sufficient strength to control outcomes by itself. The result is that they "settle" for a democratic compromise in which power is shared. In some (but not all) cases, rival groups may conclude that democracy is preferable to civil war. Or, it may take a bloody civil war that produces stalemate to persuade competing groups to accept democracy as a second-best solution. Democracy may appeal to citizens in authoritarian nations because democratic regimes often rank among the world's most stable, affluent, free, and cohesive countries. In some cases, a regional demonstration effect occurs, in which a democratic transition in one country provokes democratic change in neighboring countries. This occurred in southern Europe in the 1970s, Latin America and parts of East Asia in the 1980s, Eastern and Central Europe in the 1990s, and in North Africa and the Middle East in 2011. Another important pressure for democracy is born of the human desire for dignity and equality. Even when dictatorial regimes appear to benefit their countries—for example, by promoting economic development or nationalist goals—citizens may demand democracy.

Is it possible to identify conditions that are necessary or sufficient for the democratic idea to take root and flourish? Comparativists have proposed, among such factors, secure national boundaries, a stable state, at least a minimum level of economic development, the widespread acceptance of democratic values, and agreement on the rules of democratic politics among those contending for power. Institutional design also matters when it comes to producing stable democracies. Do certain kinds of political institutions facilitate compromise as opposed to polarization and hence greater stability? The balance of scholarly opinion suggests, for example, that parliamentary systems that tie the fates of the legislators to that of the prime minister tend to produce more consensual outcomes than do presidential systems, where the legislature and executive are independent from each other and often compete in setting national political agendas. As you read the country studies, note the patterns of similarity and difference you observe in the degree of conflict or polarization in presidential systems (such as the United States and Mexico) and compare those cases to parliamentary systems (such as Britain).

Although certain economic, cultural, and institutional features enhance the prospects of democratic transitions and consolidations, democracy has flourished in unlikely settings. India, for example, is a long-established democracy that ranks in the bottom quarter of the world's countries in terms of per capita income. Hundreds of millions of Indians live in dire poverty. Yet, despite some important instances of undemocratic practices, India has had a vibrantly functioning democratic system since it became independent in 1947.

Democracy has also failed where it might be expected to flourish, most notably and with tragic consequences in highly educated and relatively wealthy Germany in the 1930s. Democracies vary widely in terms of how they have come into existence and in their concrete historical, institutional, economic, and cultural dimensions.

Displacing authoritarian regimes and holding elections does not guarantee the survival or durability of a fledgling democracy. A wide gulf exists between what comparativists have termed a *transition* to democracy and the *consolidation* of democracy. A transition involves toppling an authoritarian regime and adopting the basic institutions and procedures of democracy; consolidation requires fuller adherence to democratic principles and making democratic government more sturdy and durable. Below we further explore the important question of how to distinguish what we term *mixed systems* from *consolidated democracies*. We consider the distinction of such great importance that it forms one basis for our scheme for classifying countries throughout the world.

The theme of the democratic idea requires us to examine the incompleteness of democratic agendas, even in countries with the longest experiences of representative democracy. Citizens may invoke the democratic idea to demand that their government be more responsive and accountable, as in the Civil Rights Movement in the United States. Social movements in some democratic countries have targeted the state because of its actions or inactions in such varied spheres as environmental regulation, reproductive rights, and race or ethnic relations. Comparative studies confirm that the democratic idea fuels political conflicts in even the most durable democracies because a large gap usually separates democratic ideals and the actual functioning of democratic political institutions. Moreover, social movements often organize because citizens perceive political parties—presumably, an important vehicle for representing citizen demands in democracies—as rigid and out of touch with the people.

A puzzle: Is there a relationship between democracy and political stability? Comparativists have debated whether democratic institutions contribute to political stability or, on the contrary, to political disorder.[18] On the one hand, democracy by its very nature permits political opposition. One of its defining characteristics is competition among those who aspire to gain political office. Political life in democracies is often turbulent and unpredictable. On the other hand, and perhaps paradoxically, the very fact that political opposition and competition are legitimate in democracies can deepen support for the state, even among opponents of a particular government. The democratic rules of the game may promote political stability by encouraging today's losers to reject the use of violence to press their claim to power. They may do so because they calculate that they have a good chance to win peacefully in future competition. Although deep flaws often mar democratic governance in countries that have toppled authoritarian regimes, a careful study finds that, once a country adopts a democratic regime, the odds are that it will endure.[19] As you learn about different countries, look for the stabilizing and destabilizing consequences

social movements

Large-scale grassroots action that demands reforms of existing social practices and government policies.

of democratic transitions, the pressures (or lack of pressure) for democratization in authoritarian states, and the persistence of undemocratic elements even in established democracies.

Theme 4: The Politics of Collective Identities

How do individuals understand who they are in relation to the state and other citizens? How and why do they join in groups to advance shared political or other goals within a country? In other words, what are the sources of collective political identities? At one time, social scientists thought they knew. Scholars once argued that age-old loyalties of ethnicity, religious affiliation, race, and locality were being dissolved and displaced as a result of economic, political, and cultural modernization. Comparativists thought that **social class**—solidarities based on the shared experience of work or, more broadly, economic position in society—had become the most important—indeed, nearly only—source of collective identity. They believed that in the typical political situation, groups formed on the basis of economic interest would pragmatically and peacefully pursue their interests. We now know that the formation of group attachments and the interplay of politically relevant collective identities are far more complex and uncertain.

 In many long-established democracies, the political importance of identities based on class membership has declined. Economically based sources of collective identity do remain significant in influencing citizens' party affiliation and preferences about economic policy and how the economic pie is divided and distributed. Especially in this era of austerity, the struggle over who gets what—and who decides who gets what—can be fierce. Indeed, these days class politics is making a comeback. But contrary to earlier predictions, in many countries nonclass identities have assumed growing, not diminishing, significance. Such identities are based on a sense of belonging to particular groups sharing a common language, region, religion, ethnicity, race, nationality, or gender.

 The politics of collective political identity involves efforts to mobilize identity groups to influence political outcomes, ranging from the state's distribution of benefits, to economic and educational policy or the basis for political representation, and even territorial claims. Identity-based conflicts appear in most societies. Politics in democratic regimes (and, often in a more concealed way, in authoritarian regimes as well) involves a tug of war among groups over relative power and influence, both symbolic and substantive. Issues of inclusion, political recognition, representation, resource allocation, and the capacity to shape public policies, such as immigration, education, and the status of minority languages, remain pivotal in many countries.

 Questions of representation are especially hard to resolve: Which groups should be considered legitimate participants in the political game? Who is included in a racial or ethnic community? Who speaks for the community or negotiates with a governmental authority on its behalf? Conflict about these issues can be intense because political leaders often seek to mobilize support by exploiting ethnic, religious, racial, or regional rivalries and by manipulating issues of identity and representation.

 An especially important source of identity-based conflict involves ethnicity. And given the pace of migration and the tangled web of postcolonial histories that link colonizer to colonized, what country is not multiethnic? As political scientist Alfred

social class

A group whose members share common worldviews and aspirations determined largely by occupation, income, and wealth.

Stepan points out, "... there are very few states in the entire world that are relatively homogeneous nation-states...."[20] In Britain, France, Germany, and the United States, issues of nationality, citizenship, and immigration—often linked to ethnic or racial factors—have often been hot-button political issues. Ethnic conflicts have been particularly frequent and intense in postcolonial countries, for example, in Nigeria, where colonial powers forced ethnic groups together when defining the country's boundaries and where borders were drawn with little regard to preexisting collective identities. The process of state formation has often sowed seeds for future conflict in many postcolonial nations.

Religion is another source of collective identity, as well as of severe political conflict, both within and among religious communities. Violent conflict among religious groups has recently occurred in India, Sri Lanka, and Nigeria. Such conflicts may spill over national boundaries and involve an especially ugly form of globalization. For example, leaders of Al Qaeda targeted non-Muslim Western military forces stationed in what they regarded as the sacred soil of Saudi Arabia as a principal reason for the 9/11 attacks. At the same time, the political orientation of a particular religious community is not predetermined. The political posture associated with what it means to be Christian, Jewish, Muslim, or Hindu cannot simply be determined from holy texts. Witness the intense conflict *within* most religious communities today that pits liberal, secular elements against those who defend what they claim is a more orthodox, traditional interpretation.

distributional politics

The use of power, particularly by the state, to allocate some kind of valued resource among competing groups.

A puzzle: How do collective identities affect a country's **distributional politics**, that is, the process of deciding how resources are distributed, concretely, who gets what? when? how? Once identity demands are placed on the national agenda, can a government resolve them by distributing political, economic, and other resources in ways that redress the grievances of the minority or politically weaker identity groups?

Collective identities operate at the level of symbols, attitudes, values, and beliefs as well as at the level of material resources. The contrast between material- and non-material-based identities and demands should not be exaggerated. In practice, most groups are animated both by feelings of attachment and solidarity and by the desire to obtain material benefits and political influence for their members. Nonetheless, the analytical distinction between material and nonmaterial demands remains useful. Furthermore, nonmaterial aspects of collective identities may make political disputes over ethnicity or religion or language or nationality especially divisive and difficult to resolve because in such cases it is harder to purchase peace through distributing material benefits.

These four themes provide our analytic scaffold. With an understanding of the method of comparative politics and the four themes in mind, we can now discuss how we have grouped the country studies in *Introduction to Comparative Politics* and how the text is organized to help students master the basics of comparative analysis.

Where Do You Stand?

It has been said that the ruling ideas of an age are the ideas of the ruling class—in other words that those with power and wealth shape the values in a society. Do you agree—or do you think we are shaped more by the values we learn at home around the dinner table?

Are collective identities or individual identities more important to the understanding of comparative politics?

CLASSIFYING POLITICAL SYSTEMS

SECTION 4

There are more than 200 states in the world today. Although each state is unique, to avoid being overwhelmed by the sheer number, it makes sense to highlight categories of states that share some important features. It is useful to identify what distinguishes one category of relatively similar states from other categories, and to study how a state moves from one category to another as circumstances evolve. When comparativists classify a large number of cases into a smaller number of categories, or types, they introduce a **typology**. A typology is an analytic construct that helps us engage in comparisons that yield useful knowledge. In ICP we will employ a typology that distinguishes among consolidated democracies, mixed systems, and authoritarian regimes.

Typologies are also useful for making comparisons within the same political category. For example, Britain and the United States are consolidated democracies. But Britain has a parliamentary form of government and the United States has a presidential one. How these very different mixes of democratic institutions work in practice is the kind of important and intriguing question that lies at the heart of comparative politics.

As with many other important concepts, the meaning of democracy is a contentious subject among political scientists and citizens. Should democracy be defined solely on the basis of the procedures used to select top governmental officeholders? For a political system to be democratic, occupants of high office be selected on the basis of free and fair elections. There must be respect for civil liberties, due process, the rule of law, freedom of expression and assembly, and the unfettered right to petition and criticize government. Democracy requires the rights of privacy—hot button issues these days in the era of routine mass surveillance and intercepts of communications by government. Democracy requires an independent judiciary. It requires freedom of religion and, we contend, a high degree of gender equality. While there is disagreement, many would agree that true democracy also requires some leveling of the economic playing field.

We believe that these benchmarks establish the base line of any democratic political system. We invite you to keep them in mind as you read the case studies, noting how each of the **consolidated democracies**, which include Britain, France, Germany, Japan, India, and the United States. There is also a chapter on the European Union, which consists of consolidated democracies, including Britain, France, and Germany and the other countries of Western Europe, as well as democratic states that were established more recently, for example, in former communist party–states such as Poland and Bulgaria.

Even in such long-established democratic states, there remains a gap—often a substantial one—between the aspirations and ideals of democracy and the practice and results of the actually existing democracy. When you read the country studies, use this seven-point checklist to assess where the country ranks with respect to each one.

We do not mean that consolidated democracies fully adhere to democratic norms—they don't, and they sometimes violate them in shocking ways. For example, police abuse and unequal legal treatment of citizens who are poor or from a racial or ethnic minority are all too common in countries generally considered high in the democratic rankings.

Focus Questions ▽

• What are the advantages of using a typology based on levels of adherence to democratic practices? What are the disadvantages?

• What alternative would you propose?

typology

A method of classifying by using criteria that divide a group of cases into smaller cases with common characteristics.

consolidated democracies

Democratic political systems that have been solidly and stably established for an ample period of time and in which there is relatively consistent adherence to the core democratic principles.

mixed systems

Countries whose political systems exhibit some democratic and some authoritarian elements.

authoritarian regimes

A system of rule in which power depends not on popular legitimacy but on the coercive force of the political authorities.

The reason why we highlight the importance of adhering to democratic procedures and institutional arrangements becomes apparent when we turn to the second category of democracy that we use in this book. In mixed systems, a façade of democratic institutions often conceals numerous practices that violate some core features of democracy. As a general matter, although there is usually greater legal protection of citizen rights and liberties in mixed systems than in authoritarian regimes—there is considerably less than in consolidated democracies. The mixed systems that are covered in *Introduction to Comparative Politics* are Mexico and Russia.

How do we define authoritarian regimes—the third kind of political system in our typology? The simplest way is say that they lack most or even all of the features of a democracy. Thus, authoritarian regimes lack effective procedures for selecting political leaders through competitive elections based on universal suffrage; they include few institutionalized procedures for holding those with political power accountable to the citizens of the country; oppositional politics and dissent are severely restricted; people of different genders, racial groups, religions, and ethnicities do not enjoy equal rights; the legal system is highly politicized and the judiciary is not an independent branch of government capable of checking the power of the state or protecting the rights of citizens; and coercion and violence are part of the political process.

Clearly, then, authoritarian states are nondemocracies. But it isn't good social science to define something only by what it is not. The term *authoritarianism* refers to political systems in which power (or authority) is highly concentrated in a single individual, a small group of people, a single political party, ethnic group, region, or institution. Furthermore, those with power claim an exclusive right to govern and use various means, including force, to impose their will and policies on all who live under their authority.

As with states classified as democracies, there are an enormous variety of authoritarian regime types: communist party–states (e.g., China and Cuba), theocracies in which sovereign power is held by religious leaders and law is defined in religious terms (e.g., Iran), military governments (e.g., Thailand after the army overthrew the parliamentary government in 2014), absolute monarchies (e.g., Saudi Arabia), and personalistic dictatorships (e.g., Iraq under Saddam Hussein, North Korea under Kim Jong-un). Authoritarian regimes frequently claim that they embody a form of democracy, particularly in the contemporary era when the democratic idea seems so persuasive and powerful. For example, according to the Chinese Communist Party, the political system of the People's Republic of China is based on "socialist democracy," which it claims is superior to the "bourgeois democracy" of capitalist countries that favors the interests of wealthier citizens. But most political scientists would conclude that there is little substance to these claims and that in such states dictatorship far outweighs democracy. As the chapter on China will describe, the Communist Party monopolizes most decision making and its leaders are chosen by self-selection rather than popular election.

Nevertheless, even countries classified as authoritarian may include democratic values and practices. In Iran, a theocratic authoritarian regime, there are vigorously contested multiparty elections, although the extent of contestation is limited by Islamic clergy who ultimately exercise sovereign power. In China, a form of grassroots democracy has been implemented in the more than 600,000 rural villages where just under half of the population lives. Even though the Communist Party still oversees the process, China's rural dwellers now have some real choice when they elect their local leaders. Such democratic elements in Iran and China are certainly significant in understanding politics in those countries; however, they do not fundamentally alter the authoritarian character of the state.

Our categories of consolidated democracies, mixed systems, and authoritarian regimes are not airtight, and boundaries among categories are fluid. Some of the countries classified as mixed systems are experiencing such political turmoil that they could very well fall out of any category of democracy. Take Russia, for example, which we classify as a mixed system but whose trajectory in the last few years is in the authoritarian direction. Since Vladimir Putin's reelection as president in 2004, the Russian government has engaged in numerous undemocratic practices, including arbitrary detention and rigged trials of opponents, repeated violations of the constitution, and extensive political corruption. There are competitive but not fair elections, multiple parties but one dominant establishment party, terrible violations of across the board, not to mention dangerously bellicose foreign policy and blatant disregard for the sovereignty of Ukraine. We have kept Russia in the mixed system democratic camp for now because we recognize that a society like Russia may take several decades to transit to democracy, and setbacks are to be expected. But we are fully aware of the ominous tendencies that may move Russia into the authoritarian slot in our typology in the next edition of this book.

ORGANIZATION OF THE TEXT

We selected the countries for the case studies in this book for their significance in terms of our comparative themes and because they provide an extensive sample of types of political regimes, levels of economic development, and geographic regions. Although each of the country studies makes important comparative references, the studies primarily provide in-depth descriptions and analyses of the politics of individual countries. At the same time, the country studies have identical formats, with common section and subsection headings to help you make comparisons and explore similar themes across the various cases. And each chapter emphasizes the four themes that anchor analyses in ICP and enables you to engage in cross-country comparisons.

We also include a chapter on the European Union (EU), an organization grouping twenty-seven countries that seeks to promote the economic and political integration of member states. The EU is the foremost example of an attempt by states—often deeply at odds with each other in the past—to pool sovereignty in order to flourish in our globalized world. The organization of the chapter on the EU parallels the format of chapters on individual countries but is adapted to permit analysis of the particular features of this fascinating organization.

The following are brief summaries of the main sections and subsections of the country studies.

Focus Questions

- If you could choose one other country to study in a comparative politics course besides the thirteen included in this book, what would it be? Why?

- What would you like to know about politics in that country?

1: The Making of the Modern State

Section 1 in each chapter provides an overview of the forces that have shaped the state. We believe that understanding the contemporary politics of any country requires familiarity with the historical process of state formation. "Politics in Action" uses a specific event to illustrate an important political moment in the country's recent history and to highlight some of the critical political challenges it faces. "Geographic Setting" locates the country in its regional context and discusses the political implications of this setting. "Critical Junctures" looks at some of the major stages and decisive turning points in the state's development. This discussion should give you an idea of how the country assumed its current political shape and provide a sense of how relations between state and society have developed over time.

"The Four Themes and Country X" applies the text's key themes to the making of the modern state. How has the country's political development been affected by its place in position in the globalized world of states—its relative ability to control external events and its regional and global status? What are the political implications of the state's approach to governing the economy? What has been the country's experience with the democratic idea? What are the important bases of collective identity in the country, and how do they influence the country's politics? Section 1 ends by exploring "Themes and Comparison," that is, the broader significance of the country for the study of comparative politics.

2: Political Economy and Development

Section 2 analyzes the pattern of governing each country's economy, and it explores how economic development has affected political change. We locate this section toward the beginning of the country study because we believe that a country's economic profile has an important impact on its politics. Within this section, there are several subsections. "State and Economy" discusses the basic organization of the country's economic system and focuses on the role of the state and the role of markets in economic life. It also examines the relationship between the government and other economic actors. "Society and Economy" examines the social implications of the country's economic situation. It describes the state's social welfare policies, such as health care, housing, and pension programs. It asks who benefits from economic change and looks at how economic development creates or reinforces class, ethnic, gender, regional, or ideological in society. Section 2 closes by examining the country's relationship to "The Global Economy." How have international economic issues affected the domestic political agenda? How have patterns of trade and foreign investment changed over time? What is the country's relationship to regional and international economic organizations? To what degree has the country been able to influence multilateral policies?

3: Governance and Policy-Making

In Section 3, we describe the state's major government institutions and policy-making procedures. "Organization of the State" lays out the fundamental principles on which the political system and the distribution of political power are based, the country's constitution, key state institutions, and historical experience. The chapter also outlines the basic structure of the state, including the relationship among different levels and branches of government. "The Executive" encompasses the key offices (for example, presidents, prime ministers, communist party leaders) at the top of the political system, focusing on how they are selected and how they use their power to make policy. This subsection also analyzes the cabinet and the national bureaucracy, their relationship to the chief executive, and their role in policy-making. "Other State

Institutions" examines the military, the judiciary and the legal system, semipublic agencies, and subnational government. "The Policy-Making Process" summarizes how public policy gets made and implemented. It describes the roles of formal institutions and procedures, as well as informal aspects of policy-making, such as the influence of lobbyists and interest groups.

4: Representation and Participation

Section 4 focuses on the relationship between a country's state and society. How do different groups in society organize to further their political interests, how do they participate and get represented in the political system, and to what extent and how do they influence policy-making? Given the importance of the U.S. Congress in policy-making, American readers might expect to find the principal discussion of "The Legislature" in Section 3 ("Governance and Policy-Making") rather than Section 4. But the U.S. Congress is an exceptionally powerful legislature. In most other political systems, the executive dominates the policy process, even when it is ultimately responsible to the legislature (as is the case in parliamentary systems). In most countries other than the United States, the legislature functions primarily to represent and provide a forum for the political expression of various interests; it is only secondarily (and in some cases, such as China, only marginally) a policy-making body. Therefore, although this section does describe and assess the legislature's role in policy-making, its primary focus is on how the legislature represents or fails to represent different interests in society.

"Political Parties and the Party System" describes the overall organization of the party system and reviews the major parties. "Elections" discusses the election process and recent trends in electoral behavior. It also considers the significance of elections (or lack thereof) as a vehicle for citizen participation in politics and in bringing about changes in the government. "Political Culture, Citizenship, and Identity" examines how people perceive themselves as members of the political community: the nature and source of political values and attitudes, who is considered a citizen, and how different groups in society understand their relationship to the state. The topics covered may include political aspects of the educational system, the media, religion, and ethnicity. We also ask how globalization affects collective identities and collective action. "Interests, Social Movements, and Protests" discusses how groups in civil society pursue their political interests outside the party system. What is the relationship between the state and such organizations and movements? When and how do citizens engage in acts of protest? And how does the state respond when they do? The final subsection is about "The Political Impact of Technology" and assesses, for example, how the growth of the Internet and social media influence politics and how the state uses technology as an instrument of power.

5: Politics in Transition

In Section 5, we identify and analyze the major challenges confronting each country and revisit the book's four themes. "Political Challenges and Changing Agendas" lays out the major unresolved issues facing the country and how they may play

hegemony

The capacity to dominate the world of states and control the terms of trade and the alliance patterns in the global order.

out in the near future. Many of these challenges involve issues that have generated intense conflicts around the world in the recent period—globalization, economic distribution, collective identities, human rights, and civil liberties, the wars in Iraq and Afghanistan, and the consequences of America's exercise of global **hegemony**. "Youth Politics and the Generational Divide" is about how the concerns of the country's young people play out in political terms and shape the national agenda. "Politics in Comparative Perspective" highlights the implications of the country case for the study of comparative politics. How does the history—and how will the future—of the country influence developments in a regional and global context? What does this case study tell us about politics in other countries that have similar political systems or that face similar kinds of political challenges?

Key Terms, Suggested Readings, and Suggested Websites

In the margin of the text, we briefly define key terms, highlighted in bold in the text, that we consider especially important for students of comparative politics to know. The key words in each chapter are also listed at the end of the chapter and all key terms, with definitions, are included in the Glossary at the end of the book. Each chapter also has a list of books that reflect important current scholarship in the field and/or that we think would be interesting and accessible to undergraduates. This Introduction ends with suggested readings that survey the scope and methods of comparative politics and illuminate important issues in the field. We also include a set of websites, which will help you track developments and acquire timely information in the ever-changing world of comparative politics.

We realize that it is quite a challenge to begin a journey seeking to understand contemporary politics in countries around the globe. We hope that the timely information and thematic focus of *Introduction to Comparative Politics* will prepare and inspire you to explore further the often troubling, sometimes inspiring, and endlessly fascinating world of comparative politics.

Where Do You Stand?

Are you optimistic or pessimistic about the spread of democracy around the world? Why?

Do you think globalization will continue to erode the nation-state as the basic building block of politics in the world? Why or why not?

WHAT'S IN THE COMPARATIVE DATA CHARTS?

The following charts and tables present important factual and statistical information about each of the countries included in this book. We hope most of this information is self-explanatory, but a few points of clarification may be helpful.

The social and economic data mostly come from the CIA *World Factbook*, the World Bank *World Development Indicators*, and the United Nations *Human Development Report*, all of which are issued annually. These statistics are available at the following websites:

- https://www.cia.gov/library/publications/the-world-factbook/

- http://data.worldbank.org/
- http://hdr.undp.org/en/data

The data presented are as up-to-date as possible. Several important terms used in the data, including gross domestic product (GDP), gross national product (GNP), purchasing power parity (PPP), and Gini Index, are explained in the Glossary and/or the feature called "How Is Development Measured?" on page 15.

Total Geographic Area

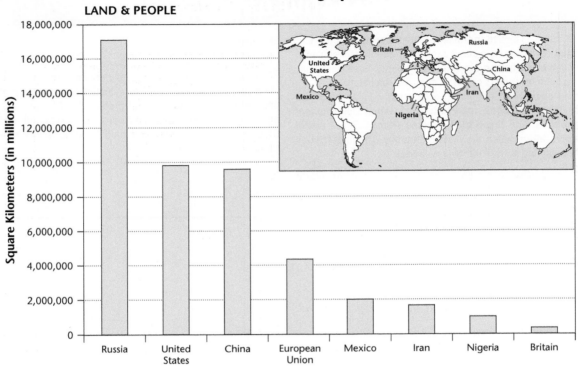

LAND & PEOPLE

	Britain	China	Iran
Official name	United Kingdom of Great Britain and Northern Ireland	People's Republic of China	Islamic Republic of Iran
Capital	London	Beijing	Teheran
Comparative size	Slightly smaller than Oregon	Slightly smaller than the United States	Slightly smaller than Alaska
Population growth per year	0.8%	0.5%	1.3%
Major ethnic groups	White 87.1%; Black 3.0%; Asian Indian 2.3%; Asian Pakistani 1.9%; other Asian 2.8%; mixed 2.0%; other 1.0%	Han Chinese 91.6%; other nationalities 8.4% (includes 55 ethnic minorities, such as Zhuang, Manchu, Hui, Miao, Uyghur, Yi, Mongol, Tibetan, and Korean)	Persian 61%; Azeri 16%; Kurd 10%; Arab 3%; Lur 6%; Baloch 2%; Arab 2%; Turkmen and Turkic 2%; other 1%
Major religions	Christian 71.6% Muslim 2.7%; Hindu 1%; other 1.6%; unspecified or none 23.1%	Buddhist 18.2%; Christian 5.1%; Muslim 1.8%; unaffiliated 52.2% Other 1.0% **Note:** officially atheist	Muslim 99.4% (Shia 90–95%, Sunni 5–10%); other 0.3% (includes Zoroastrian, Jewish, Christian, and Baha'i); unspecified 0.4%
Major languages	English The following are recognized regional languages: Scots, Scottish Gaelic Welsh, Irish, and Cornish	Standard Chinese or Mandarin based on the Beijing dialect; other major dialects include Cantonese and Shanghaiese. Also various minority languages; such as Tibetan and Mongolian	Persian 53%; Azeri and Turkic dialects 18%; Kurdish 10%; Gilaki and Mazandarani 7%; Luri 6%; Balochi 2%; Arabic 2%; other 2%

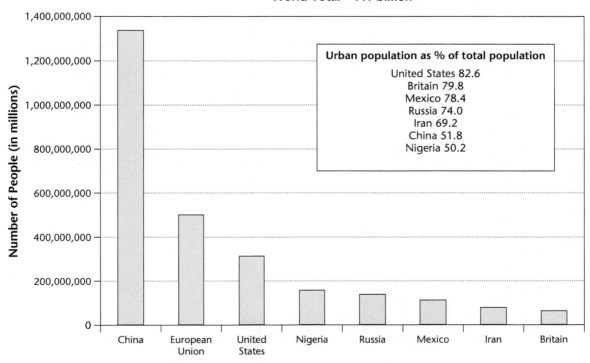

Total World Population (2014)
World Total = 7.1 billion

Number of People (in millions)

1,400,000,000
1,200,000,000
1,000,000,000
800,000,000
600,000,000
400,000,000
200,000,000
0

China, European Union, United States, Nigeria, Russia, Mexico, Iran, Britain

Urban population as % of total population

United States 82.6
Britain 79.8
Mexico 78.4
Russia 74.0
Iran 69.2
China 51.8
Nigeria 50.2

Mexico	Nigeria	Russia	United States
United Mexican States	Federal Republic of Nigeria	Russian Federation	United States of America
Mexico City	Abuja	Moscow	Washington, D.C.
Slightly less than three times the size of Texas	Slightly more than twice the size of California	Approximately 1.8 times the size of the United States	About half the size of Russia
1.2%	2.8%	0.4%	0.7%
Mestizo (Amerindian-Spanish) 60%; Amerindian or predominantly Amerindian 30%; White 9%; other 1%	More than 250 ethnic groups; the most populous and politically influential are Hausa and Fulani 29%, Yoruba 21%, Igbo (Ibo) 18%, Ijaw 10%	Russian 80.90%; Tatar 3.87%; Ukrainian 1.40%; Bashkir 1.15%; Chuvash 1.05%; Chechen 1.04%; other 10.59%	White 63.0%; Hispanic 13.9%; Black or African American 13.1%; Asian 5.1%; American Indian and Alaska Native 1.2%; Native Hawaiian and Other Pacific Islander 0.2%; two or more races 2.4%
Catholic 84.9%; Protestant 8.2%; none 4.9%; other 2.0%	Christian 50.8%; Muslim 48.8%; other .04%	Russian Orthodox 49.7%; Protestant 6.2%; Muslim 7.6%; Non-Religious 27.4%; Atheist 5.2%; Other 3.9%	Christian 78.40% (Evangelical Protestant churches 26.3%; Mainline Protestant 18.1%; Catholic 23.9%; Historically Black Churches 6.9%; Mormon 1.7%; Unaffiliated 16.10%; Jewish 1.70%; other faiths 2.90%; don't know/refused 0.80%
Spanish only 92.7%, Spanish and indigenous languages 5.7%, indigenous only 0.8%, unspecified 0.8%	English (official), Hausa, Yoruba, Igbo (Ibo), Fulani	Russian, many minority languages	Speak only English at home, 79.2%; speak only Spanish at home, 12.9%; speak only another language at home, 7.9%

Total Gross Domestic Product (GDP)

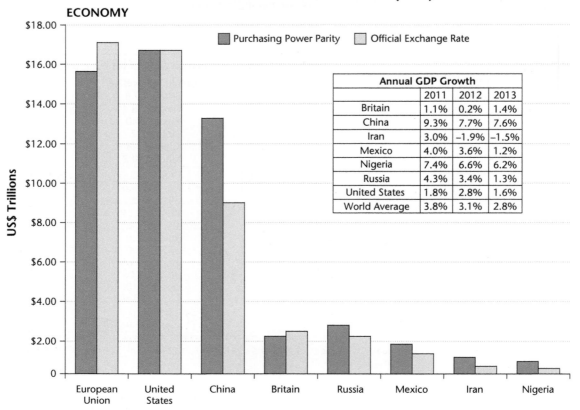

ECONOMY

Legend: ■ Purchasing Power Parity □ Official Exchange Rate

Y-axis (US$ Trillions): $18.00, $16.00, $14.00, $12.00, $10.00, $8.00, $6.00, $4.00, $2.00, 0

X-axis: European Union, United States, China, Britain, Russia, Mexico, Iran, Nigeria

Annual GDP Growth	2011	2012	2013
Britain	1.1%	0.2%	1.4%
China	9.3%	7.7%	7.6%
Iran	3.0%	–1.9%	–1.5%
Mexico	4.0%	3.6%	1.2%
Nigeria	7.4%	6.6%	6.2%
Russia	4.3%	3.4%	1.3%
United States	1.8%	2.8%	1.6%
World Average	3.8%	3.1%	2.8%

	Britain	China	Iran
GDP average annual growth: 2000–2013	1.7%	9.9%	3.8%
GDP *per capita* average annual growth			
2000–2013	1.1%	9.2%	2.6%
1990–1999	2.0%	8.8%	2.9%
1980–1989	2.3%	8.2%	–3.7%
1970–1979	2.3%	5.3%	2.9%
GDP composition by economic sector			
Agriculture	0.7%	9.7%	10.6%
Industry	20.5%	45.3%	44.9%
Services	78.9%	45.0%	44.5%
Labor force by occupation			
Agriculture	1.2%	34.8%	16.9%
Industry	18.9%	29.5%	34.4%
Services	78.9%	35.7%	48.7%
Foreign trade as % of GDP			
Exports	31.6%	27.3%	20.8%
Imports	33.8%	24.5%	12.7%
Inequality & poverty			
Household income or consumption by % share	3.4%	1.7%	2.6%
Poorest 10%	34.7%	30.0%	29.6%
Richest 10%	40.0	47.4	44.5
GINI Index *(0–100; higher = more unequal)*			
% of population in poverty			
National poverty line	14.0%	13.4%	18.7%
International poverty line (below $2/day)	–	27.2%	8.0%

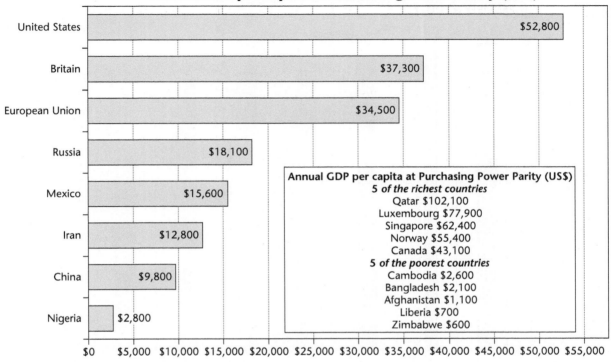

Annual GDP per capita at Purchasing Power Parity (US$)

United States	$52,800
Britain	$37,300
European Union	$34,500
Russia	$18,100
Mexico	$15,600
Iran	$12,800
China	$9,800
Nigeria	$2,800

Annual GDP per capita at Purchasing Power Parity (US$)
5 of the richest countries
Qatar $102,100
Luxembourg $77,900
Singapore $62,400
Norway $55,400
Canada $43,100
5 of the poorest countries
Cambodia $2,600
Bangladesh $2,100
Afghanistan $1,100
Liberia $700
Zimbabwe $600

Mexico	Nigeria	Russia	United States
1.9%	6.7%	4.9%	1.9%
1.0%	3.8%	5.0%	1.0%
1.7%	0.5%	4.8%	1.9%
0.1%	−1.8%	*Before collapse*	2.1%
3.3%	4.2%	*of Soviet Union*	2.3%
3.6%	30.9%	4.2%	1.1%
36.6%	43.0%	37.5%	19.5%
59.8%	26.0%	58.3%	79.4%
13.4%	70.0%	9.7%	1.6%
24.1%	10.0%	27.8%	16.7%
61.9%	20.0%	62.5 %	81.2%
32.9%	55.4%	29.4%	13.5%
34.5%	22.8%	22.1%	16.9%
2.0%	1.8%	5.7%	2.0%
37.5%	38.2%	42.4%	30.0%
47.2%	48.8%	42.0%	42%
52.3%	46.0%	11.0%	15.1%
4.5%	84.5%	–	–

Life Expectancy at Birth (Years)

SOCIETY & POLITY

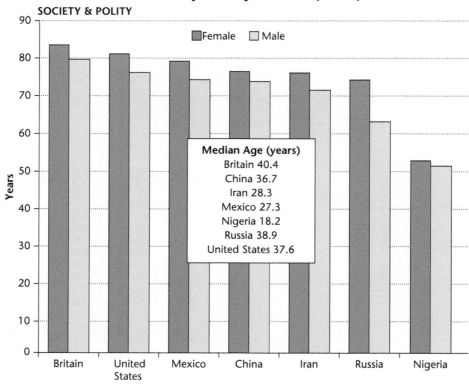

Median Age (years)
Britain 40.4
China 36.7
Iran 28.3
Mexico 27.3
Nigeria 18.2
Russia 38.9
United States 37.6

	Britain	China	Iran
EDUCATION			
Adult literacy (% of population age 15+)			
Female	99.0*	92.7	80.7
Male	99.0*	97.5	89.3
% age-eligible population in school			
Primary	99.6	99.4	99.6
Secondary	93.6	78.5	75.1
Tertiary	70.1	24.3	55.2
HEALTH			
Physicians per 1,000 population	2.8	1.8	0.9
Under 5 mortality rate/1,000 live births	4.8	14	17.6
Adolescent fertility (births per 1,000 women age 15–19)	25.8	8.5	31.6
Health spending per capita per year	$3609	$278	$346
OTHER			
Telephone lines (per 100 people)	52.9	20.2	37.6
Cell phones (per 100 people)	135.4	80.8	76.1
People using the Internet (%)	87.0	45.8	26.0
Households with a computer (%)	87.0	35.4	33.4
Households with a television set (%)	93.7	99.9	98.7
Motor vehicles (per 1,000 people)	519	83	200
Homicides per 100,000 population	1.2	1.0	3.0
Prison inmates per 100,000 total population	148.0 *England & Wales*	121.7	284
Women members of national legislature (%)			
• Lower house or single house	22.6	23.4	3.1
• Upper house (if any)	22.4		
Freedom House rating (1 = most free; 7= least free)	Free (1.0)	Not Free (6.5)	Not Free (5.5)
Economist Intelligence Unit Democracy Index (10 = most democratic)	Full Democracy (8.21)	Authoritarian Regime (3.00)	Authoritarian Regime (3.74)

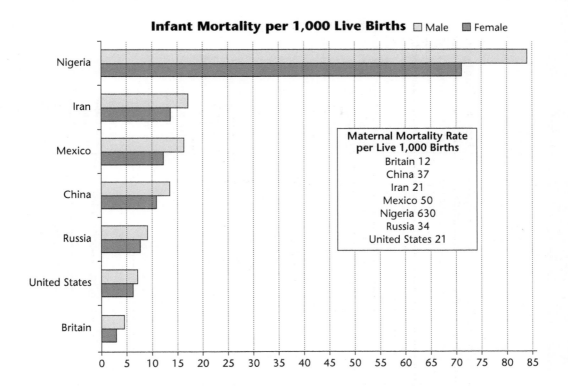

Infant Mortality per 1,000 Live Births ☐ Male ■ Female

Nigeria, Iran, Mexico, China, Russia, United States, Britain

Maternal Mortality Rate per Live 1,000 Births
Britain 12
China 37
Iran 21
Mexico 50
Nigeria 630
Russia 34
United States 21

Mexico	Nigeria	United States	Russia
92.3	50.4	99.0*	99.0*
94.8	72.1	99.0*	99.0*
98.1	58.8	96.5	92.5
69.9	25.8	90.9	74.7?
27.7	8.5	85.4	75.9
2.0	0.4	2.4	4.3
17.6	123.7	7.1	10.3
64.6	120.5	35.0	26.4
$620	$80	$8608	$807
16.7	0.25	44.4	30.1
83.4	66.8	89.0	182.3
38.4	32.9	81.0	53.3
32.2	9.3	75.6	57.1
93.7	42.5	94.5	98.6
275	31	797	293
23.7	12.2	4.7	9.7
201.2	32	715.4	495
37.4	6.7	18.3	13.6
34.4	6.4	20.0	8.0
Partly Free (3.0)	Partly Free (4.5)	Free (1.0)	Not Free (5.5)
Flawed Democracy (6.90)	Authoritarian Regime (3.77)	Full Democracy (8.11)	Authoritarian Regime (3.74)

* Developed countries have near universal adult *basic* literacy rates, but *functional* literacy among the working age population is lower. For example, in Britain it is 80% and the United States 86%.

COMPARATIVE RANKINGS

International organizations and research institutions have developed statistical methods to rate and rank different countries according to various categories of economic, social, political, and environmental performance. Such rankings can be controversial, but we think they provide an interesting approach to comparative analysis. Five examples of this approach are listed below. In addition to the countries included in this book (which are in bold), the top and bottom five countries in each of the rankings are also listed.

Human Development Index (HDI)

is a measure used by the United Nations to compare the overall level of well-being in countries around the world. It takes into account life expectancy, education, and the standard of living.

2012 HDI Rankings:

Very High Human Development

1. Norway
2. Australia
3. **United States**
4. Netherlands
5. Germany
26. **Britain**

High Human Development

18. **Britain**
19. **United States**
55. **Russia**
61. **Mexico**
76. **Iran**

Medium Human Development

101. **China**

Low Human Development

153. **Nigeria**
183. Burkino Faso
184. Chad
185. Mozambique
186. D.R. Congo
186. Niger

*http://hdr.undp.org/en/statistics
/hdi/ Identical numbers indicate
a tie in the rankings*

Global Gender Gap

measures the extent to which women have achieved equality with men in five critical areas: economic participation, economic opportunity, political empowerment, educational attainment, and health and well-being.

2013 Gender Gap Rankings:

1. Iceland
2. Finland
3. Norway
4. Sweden
5. Philippines
18. **Britain**
19. **United States**
61. **Russia**
68. **Mexico**
69. **China**
106. **Nigeria**
130. **Iran**
132. Mauritania
133. Syria
134. Chad
135. Pakistan
136. Yemen

*http://www.weforum.org
/issues/global-gender-gap*

Environmental Performance Index (EPI)

measures how close countries come to meeting specific benchmarks for national pollution control and natural resource management.

2014 EPI Rankings:

1. Switzerland
2. Luxemburg
3. Australia
4. Singapore
5. Czech Republic
12. **Britain**
33. **United States**
65. **Mexico**
73. **Russia**
83. **Iran**
134. **Nigeria**
118. **China**
174. Afghanistan
175. Lesotho
176. Haiti
177. Mali
178. Somalia

http://epi.yale.edu

International Corruption Perceptions Index (CPI)

defines corruption as the abuse of public office for private gain and measures the degree to which corruption is perceived to exist among a country's public officials and politicians.

2013 CPI Rankings:

1. Denmark
1. New Zealand
3. Finland
3. Sweden
5. Norway
14. **Britain**
19. **United States**
80. **China**
98. **Mexico**
127. **Russia**
144. **Iran**
144. **Nigeria**
173. South Sudan
174. Sudan
175. Afghanistan
175. North Korea
175. Somalia

*http://www.transparency.org
/Identical numbers indicate a
tie in the rankings*

Economist Intelligence Unit Democracy Index

categorizes four types of political systems based on five categories: electoral process and pluralism; civil liberties; the functioning of government; political participation; and political culture.

2013 Democracy Index:

Full Democracies

1. Norway
2. Sweden
3. Iceland
4. Denmark
5. New Zealand
16. **Britain**
21. **United States**

Flawed Democracies

51. **Mexico**

Authoritarian Regimes

120. **Nigeria**
122. **Russia**
142. **China**
158. **Iran**
163. Saudi Arabia
164. Syria
165. Chad
166. Guinea-Bissau
167. North Korea

http://www.eiu.com/public/

Key Terms

authoritarian regimes
bureaucracy
cabinet
causal theories
Cold War
collective identities
communist party–state
comparative politics
comparativist
consolidated democracies
Corruption Perceptions Index
country
critical juncture
democracy
democratic transition
dependent variable
dictatorships
distributional politics

Environmental Performance
   Index
executive
Freedom in the World Rating
Global Gender Gap
globalization
gross domestic product (GDP)
gross national product (GNP)
hegemony
Human Development Index
   (HDI)
independent variable
institutional design
International Monetary Fund
   (IMF)
judiciary
legislature
legitimacy

middle-level theory
mixed systems
nation-state
North American Free Trade
   Agreement (NAFTA)
political economy
purchasing power parity (PPP)
rational choice theory
social class
social movements
Social Progress Index
state
state formation
sustainable development
typology
World Bank
World Trade Organization
   (WTO)

Suggested Readings

Acemoglu, Daron, and James A. Robinson. *Why Nations Fail: The Origins of Power, Prosperity and Poverty*. New York: Crown Business, 2012.

della Porta, Donatella. *Mobilizing for Democracy: Comparing 1989 and 2011*. New York: Oxford University Press, 2014.

Diamond, Larry, Marc F. Plattner, and Philip J. Costopoulos, eds. *Debates on Democratization*. Baltimore: The Johns Hopkins University Press, 2010.

Hays, Jude C. *Globalization and the New Politics of Embedded Liberalism*. New York: Oxford University Press, 2009.

Krieger, Joel. *The Oxford Companion to Comparative Politics*. New York: Oxford University Press, 2013.

Levitsky, Steven R., and Lucan A. Way. *Competitive Authoritarianism: Hybrid Regimes after the Cold War*. New York: Cambridge University Press, 2010.

Nooruddin, Ifran. *Politics and Economic Development*. New York: Cambridge University Press, 2011.

Norris, Pippa. *Making Democratic Governance Work: How Regimes Shape Prosperity, Welfare, and Peace*. New York: Cambridge University Press, 2012.

Tarrow, Sidney. *Power in Movement*, 3rd ed. New York: Cambridge University Press, 2011.

Stepan, Alfred, Juan J. Linz, and Yogendra Yadav. *Crafting State-Nations: India and Other Multinational Democracies*. Baltimore: The Johns Hopkins University Press, 2011.

Suggested Websites

CIA World Factbook
https://www.cia.gov/library/publications
   /the-world-factbook

U.S. Bilateral Relations Fact Sheets
http://www.state.gov/r/pa/ei/bgn/

Election Guide (Consortium for Elections and Political
   Process Strengthening)
http://www.electionguide.org/

Freedom House
http://www.freedomhouse.org/

NationMaster
http://www.nationmaster.com/

Politics and Government Around the World
http://www.politicsresources.net/

2 Britain

Joel Krieger

Official Name: United Kingdom of Great Britain and Northern Ireland
Location: Western Europe
Capital City: London
Population (2014): 63.7 million
Size: 244,820 sq. km.; slightly smaller than Oregon

THE MAKING OF THE MODERN BRITISH STATE

SECTION 1

Politics in Action

The first woman prime minister in Western Europe, Margaret Thatcher, was also remarkable for being the first British prime minister to win three general elections in a row since Lord Liverpool in the nineteenth century. Born in 1925, the daughter of a shopkeeper in Grantham (Think: Downton Abbey), she studied chemistry at Oxford, then law. Winning the leadership of the Conservative Party in 1975 against the odds, Thatcher served as prime minister from 1979 to 1990, the longest continuous stretch as prime minister in the twentieth century and a very memorable one. Thatcher's leadership as prime minister marks a critical dividing line in postwar British politics. Like few others before or since she set the tone and redefined the goals of British politics. The Thatcher government inaugurated a decisively right-wing regime and set out to divide and conquer trade unions. New revelations in 2014 have revealed that Thatcher was so determined to defeat the miners during the epic strike in 1984 that she secretly considered using the military and declaring a state of emergency.

Focus Questions ▼

- How does its history of the empire still shape British politics today?

- Why did an electoral system designed to produce a stable single-party majority result in a Conservative–Liberal coalition government in 2010?

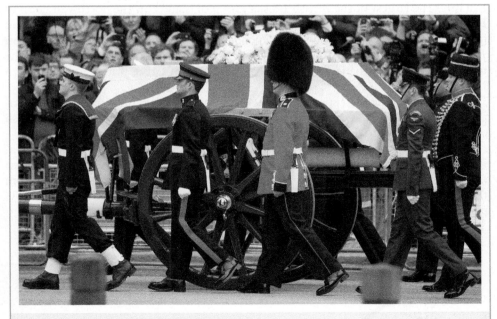

Margaret Thatcher's funeral procession.
Indigo/Getty Images

CHRONOLOGY of Modern Britain's Political Development

1832
Reform Act expands voting rights.

1945–1979
Establishment of British welfare state; dismantling of British Empire

1914–1918
World War I

| 1650 | 1700 | 1750 | 1800 | 1900 | 1940 | 1950 |

1688
Glorious Revolution establishes power of Parliament.

1939–1945
World War II

1929–1939
Great Depression

ca. 1750
Industrial Revolution begins in Britain.

1837–1901
Reign of Queen Victoria; height of British Empire

Despite all the trappings of a grandly staged funeral procession on a gun carriage when she died in 2013, with Queen Elizabeth in attendance, in London protesters on the left shouted slurs. Supporters decried President Obama's decision not to send any senior American officials to the funeral, despite Mrs. Thatcher's high-profile partnership with President Reagan and her role confronting the Soviet Union. The chant "Maggie, Maggie, Maggie, dead, dead, dead, dead!" could be heard as far away as Glasgow. (Thatcher never played well to the crowds in Glasgow.)

Geographic Setting

Britain is the largest of the British Isles, a group of islands off the northwest coast of Europe that encompasses England, Scotland, and Wales. The second-largest island includes Northern Ireland and the independent Republic of Ireland. The term *Great Britain* includes England, Wales, and Scotland, but not Northern Ireland. We use the term *Britain* as shorthand for the United Kingdom of Great Britain and Northern Ireland.

Covering an area of approximately 94,000 square miles, Britain is roughly two-thirds the area of Japan, or approximately half the area of France. In 2013 the British population was approximately 62 million.

As an island off the shore of Europe, Britain was for centuries less subject to invasion and conquest than its continental counterparts. This gave the country a sense of security. The separation has also made many Britons feel they are more apart from than an intrinsic part of Europe. This feeling complicates relations with Britain's EU partners.

1979–1990
Prime Minister Margaret Thatcher promotes "enterprise culture."

1997–2007
Prime Minister Tony Blair and Chancellor Gordon Brown lead New Labour in government.

2007
Gordon Brown becomes prime minister and promises to renew the party and the nation, but quickly loses support and credibility as the financial crisis deepens.

1970　　1990　　1995　　2000　　2005　　2010

2010
New Conservative–Liberal coalition government formed

1973
Britain joins the European Community.

2001
Under Blair's leadership, Britain "stands shoulder to shoulder" with America in war against terror.

Britain: Ethnicity

- Black 3.0%
- Asian/Indian 2.3%
- Asian/Pakistani 1.9%
- Asian/Other 2.8%
- Mixed 2.0%
- Other 1.0%
- White 87.1%

Britain: Religion

- None 25.7%
- Christian (includes Anglican, Roman Catholic, Presbyterian, Methodist) 59.5%
- Other 1.9%
- Unspecified 7.2%
- Hindu 1.3%
- Muslim 4.4%

British Currency
Pound (£)
International Designation: GBP
Exchange Rate (2013):
- 1 US$ = .639 GBP
- 1 GBP = 1.59 US$
50 GBP Note Design: Queen Elizabeth II (1926–)

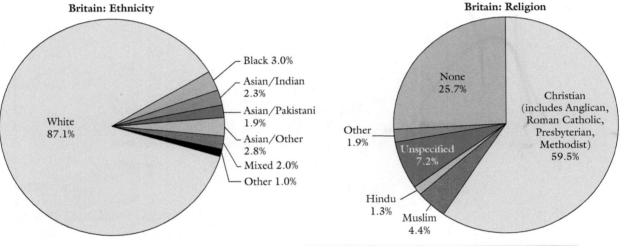

FIGURE 2.1 The British Nation at a Glance

Ben Molyneux/Alamy (for photo)

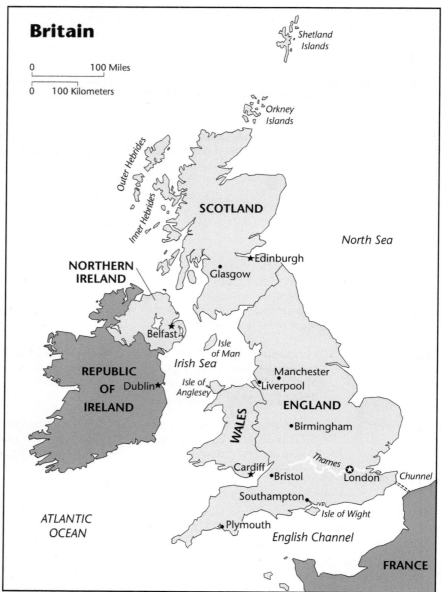

Critical Junctures

The Consolidation of the British State

The consolidation of the British state unified several kingdoms. After Duke William of Normandy defeated the English in the Battle of Hastings in 1066, the Norman monarchy eventually extended its authority throughout the British Isles, except for Scotland. In the sixteenth century, legislation unified England and Wales legally, politically, and administratively. Scotland and England remained separate kingdoms, until the Act of Union of 1707. After that, a common Parliament of Great Britain replaced the two separate parliaments of Scotland and of England and Wales.

Table 2.1	Political Organization
Political System	Parliamentary democracy, constitutional monarchy.
Regime History	Long constitutional history, origins subject to interpretation, usually dated from the seventeenth century or earlier.
Administrative Structure	Unitary state with fusion of powers. United Kingdom Parliament has supreme legislative, executive, and judicial authority. Limited powers have been transferred to representative bodies in Scotland, Wales, and Northern Ireland.
Executive	Prime minister (PM), answerable to House of Commons, subject to collective responsibility of the cabinet; member of Parliament who is leader of party or coalition that can control a majority in Commons (normally a single party but since 2010 as a two-party coalition [Conservative–Liberal Democrat]).
Legislature	Bicameral. House of Commons elected by single-member plurality system. Main legislative powers: to pass laws, provide for finance, scrutinize public administration and government policy. House of Lords, unelected upper house: limited powers to delay enactment of legislation and to recommend revisions. Since 2009, the judicial functions of parliament were transferred to the UK Supreme Court. Recent reforms eliminated voting rights for most hereditary peers.
Judiciary	Independent but with no power to judge the constitutionality of legislation or governmental conduct. UK Supreme Court, established in 2009, is the final court of appeal for all UK civil cases and criminal cases in England, Wales, and Northern Ireland.
Party System	Two-party dominant, with regional variation. Principal parties: Labour and Conservative; a center party (Liberal Democrat); and national parties in Scotland, Wales, and Northern Ireland; and United Kingdom Independence (UKIP).

© Cengage Learning®

Royal control increased after 1066, but the conduct of King John (1199–1216) fueled opposition from feudal barons. In 1215, they forced him to consent to a series of concessions that protected feudal landowners from abuses of royal power. These restrictions were embodied in the Magna Carta, a historic statement of the rights of a political community against the monarchical state. It has served as the inspiration for constitutions around the world that contain protections for citizens and groups from the arbitrary exercise of state power. In 1236, the term *Parliament* was first used officially for the gathering of feudal barons summoned by the king whenever he required their consent to special taxes. By the fifteenth century, Parliament had gained the right to make laws.

The Seventeenth-Century Settlement

By the sixteenth and seventeenth centuries Britain was embroiled in a complex interplay of religious conflicts, national rivalries, and struggles between rulers and Parliament. These conflicts erupted in the civil wars of the 1640s, and later forced the removal of James II in 1688. This was the last successful revolution in British history.

This "Glorious Revolution" of 1688 also resolved long-standing religious conflict. The replacement of the Roman Catholic James II by the Protestant William and

Mary ensured the dominance of the Church of England (or Anglican Church). To this day, the Church of England remains the established (official) church. By about 1700, a basic form of parliamentary democracy had emerged.

The Industrial Revolution and the British Empire

Industrial Revolution

A period of rapid and destabilizing social, economic, and political changes caused by the introduction of large-scale factory production, originating in England in the middle of the eighteenth century.

The Industrial Revolution from the mid-eighteenth century onward involved rapid expansion of manufacturing production and technological innovation. It also led to vast social and economic changes and created pressures to make the country more democratic. Britain's competitive edge also dominated the international order. The **Industrial Revolution** transformed the British state and society.

Despite a gradually improving standard of living throughout the English population in general, industrialization disrupted lives and shattered old ways of life. Many field laborers lost their jobs, and many small landholders were squeezed off the land.

The British Empire

hegemonic power

A state that can control the pattern of alliances and terms of the international order and often shapes domestic political developments in countries throughout the world.

Britain relied on imported raw materials, and by 1800, it sold the vast majority of finished goods overseas. Growth depended on foreign markets—not domestic consumption. This export orientation made economic growth much faster than an exclusively domestic orientation would have allowed.

Because Britain needed overseas trade, its leaders worked aggressively to secure markets and expand the empire. Backed by the British navy, international trade made England the dominant military and economic world power. Britain led the alliance that toppled Napoleon in the early nineteenth century, thus enabling the country to maintain its dominant position in the world.

By 1870, British trade represented nearly one-quarter of the world total (see Figure 2.2) and by 1900, Queen Victoria (1837–1901) ruled an empire that included 25 percent of the world's population, exercising direct colonial rule over 50 countries, including India and Nigeria. Britain also dominated an extensive economic empire—a worldwide network of independent states, including China, Iran, and Brazil. Britain ruled as a **hegemonic power**, controlling alliances and shaping domestic political developments in countries throughout the world.

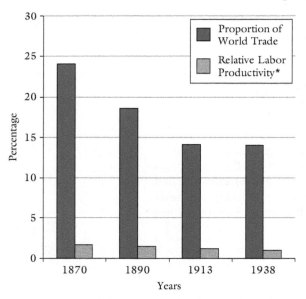

*As compared with the average rate of productivity in other members of the world economy.

FIGURE 2.2 World Trade and Relative Labor Productivity

Source: From AFTER HEGEMONY by Robert O. Keohane

Industrial Change and the Struggle for Voting Rights

The Industrial Revolution shifted economic power from landowners to businessmen and industrialists. The first important step toward democratization began in the late 1820s, when the propertied classes and increasing popular agitation pressed Parliament to expand the right to vote. With Parliament under considerable pressure, the Reform Act of 1832 extended the vote to a section of the (male) middle class.

The reform was narrow. Before 1832, less than 5 percent of the adult population could vote—afterward, only about 7 percent. The reform showed the strict property basis for political participation inflamed class-based tensions.

The Representation of the People Act of 1867 increased the electorate to 16 percent but left cities significantly underrepresented. The Franchise Act of 1884 nearly doubled the electorate. The Representation of the People Act of 1918 finally included nearly all adult men and women over age thirty. How slow a process was it? The struggle to extend the vote took place mostly without violence, but it lasted for centuries.

World Wars, Industrial Strife, and the Depression (1914–1945)

State involvement in the economy increased significantly during World War I (1914–1918). The state took control of numerous industries, including railways, mining, and shipping. It channeled resources into war production. After World War I, the state remained active in managing industry, but in a different way. Amid tremendous industrial disputes, the state fragmented the trade union movement and resisted demands for workers' control over production. This government manipulation of the economy openly contradicted the policy of laissez-faire (minimal government interference in the operation of economic markets) that generally characterizes Britain's approach to governing the economy.

welfare state

A set of public policies designed to provide for citizens' needs through direct or indirect provision of pensions, health care, unemployment insurance, and assistance to the poor.

Tensions between free-market principles and interventionist practices deepened with the Great Depression—1929 through much of the 1930s—and with World War II (1939–1945). Fear of depression and yearnings for a better life after the war transformed the role of the state and led to a period of unusual political harmony.

Collectivist Consensus (1945–1979)

The term *collectivism* describes the consensus in politics after World War II, when most Britons and all major political parties agreed that governments should work to narrow the gap between rich and poor, and provide for basic necessities through public education, national health care, and other policies of the welfare state (the set of policies designed to provide health care, pensions, unemployment benefits, and assistance to the poor). They also accepted state responsibility for economic growth and full employment. British people came to expect that the state should be responsible for economic growth and full employment. In time, however, economic downturn and political stagnation unraveled the consensus.

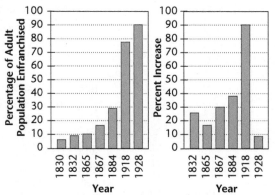

FIGURE 2.3 Expansion of Voting Rights
Expansion of the franchise in Britain was a gradual process. Despite reforms dating from the early nineteenth century, nearly universal adult suffrage was not achieved until 1928.

Source: From RASMUSSEN. The British Political Process, 1E. © 1993 Cengage Learning.

New Labour's Third Way

Under the leadership of Tony Blair from 1997 to 2007, the Labour Party was determined to modernize itself. Although its official name did not change, the party was rebranded "New Labour," promising a "third-way" alternative to Thatcherism and the collectivism of traditional Labour. New Labour rejected interest-based politics, in which unions and working people tended to vote for Labour and businesspeople and the more prosperous voted for the Conservatives. Labour won in 1997 with support from across the socioeconomic spectrum.

Early in their careers, Tony Blair and Gordon Brown formed an alliance as rising stars in the Labour Party. Blair pushed the party to modernize and expand its political base well beyond its heritage as a labor party. Brown became shadow chancellor (the opposition party's spokesman on the economy).

But after Labour took office, Blair and Brown became rivals rather than partners. Blair won a third electoral victory in May 2005. Due mainly to the war in Iraq, his parliamentary majority was slashed by nearly 100 seats. In June 2007 Blair resigned and Gordon Brown became prime minister.

A strong finance minister, Brown was not a nimble campaigner and was never able to get out from under the shadow cast by New Labour's role in the war in Iraq, a war that was extremely unpopular in the United Kingdom.

Brown's effectiveness as chancellor (finance minister) for ten years and his highly praised efforts to stabilize the global economy during the "Great Recession" was soon forgotten. Nor could Brown—or any prime minister—reduce the fear of sudden terrorist attacks that ordinary people in Britain have felt ever since bombs were set off in the London transport system on July 7, 2005 (in the United Kingdom referred to as 7/7).

The Conservative–Liberal Coalition

There is a familiar maxim: In politics, a week is a long time. If that is true, thirteen years is an eternity. Ever since the Conservatives held power in 1990, many of the core principles of New Labour's approach have become widely shared across much of the political spectrum. When the Conservatives elected David Cameron as their party leader in 2005, he took the party in a familiar mainstream direction, appealing directly to youth for political support and championing modernization and pragmatism. Young (he was born in 1966), smart, and telegenic, Cameron seemed to consciously adopt, in both style and substance, much of Blair's early appeal, stealing the thunder of New Labour, and expanding the appeal of the Conservative Party by reaching out to youth and promoting agendas, such as climate change, citizen activism, and promises to reduce both the global development gap and the gap between rich and poor in the United Kingdom—issues that would have broad non-ideological appeal. As a result, when the May 2010 election produced what the British call a "hung parliament"—an outcome after a general election when no party can by itself control a majority of the seats in parliament—it was a stretch for the Conservatives and the Liberal Democrats to form a government, but it was not an unbridgeable gap.

The coalition government, like New Labour before it, has tried to capture the mood in Britain, by characterizing its governing objective as a commitment to reject ideological positions in favor of broad appeals to what Cameron and Clegg characterize as a radical, reforming government that attempts to blend the Conservative commitment to the dynamism of free markets with the Liberal Democrat commitment to decentralization. The result is captured in a new framework for governance, which the coalition partners call the "Big Society." The Big Society argues for wide-ranging initiatives to empower ordinary citizens to take control over their lives and shift the balance of power downward from the state to communities and individual citizens. Parents should be given the opportunity to start their own schools; citizens should be encouraged to take over the administration of post offices; to elect police commissioners; to recall MPs who violate the public trust. An innovative approach to governance in the United Kingdom, the Big Society is the "Big Idea"—the catchphrase and rebranding of politics demanded of all new governments in the United Kingdom. Thus far, the "Big Society" is, more than anything else, a catchphrase, but not yet a clear set of policies for encouraging local autonomy and citizen bottom-up activism, viewed by Conservatives as a much-needed corrective to New Labour's tendency toward the concentration of power away from the center, despite lip service to a governing vision create citizen stakeholders and devolve power away from the central government.

Critics have expressed skepticism about the Big Society, and supporters have not yet been able to clearly define what it means in policy terms or how to implement Big Society policies effectively. At a time when severe cuts in public spending demanded a rollback of government, it remains unclear whether the Big Society is a defining vision that will drive the agenda of a strong, stable, and effective coalition government, or that it will be remembered as a catchphrase that could not paper over the difficulties that a government would face once it was committed to making the broad, deep, and increasingly unpopular cuts demanded by the "great recession" that began in 2008. The challenges are all the greater for a young, untested, and divided government, which faces the special challenges of coalition government that emerged from the 2010 general election. Note that one-party government is very much the rule in Britain. How unusual is coalition government? Note that the last formal coalition government before 2010 was the wartime coalition government led by Winston Churchill, the indomitable leader who saved Britain from the Nazi juggernaut. It is no great insult to observe that David Cameron is no Winston Churchill. Who could be? As we will discuss throughout this chapter, these are very challenging times for any British government. The challenges are especially daunting in the case of a coalition government, which must contend with crosscutting pressures to keep the coalition intact—and must bring along an electorate that is instinctively uneasy about—if not hostile to—the very idea of coalition government. We are speaking about Britain, a country with the longest tradition of parliamentary democracy, and a populace that is inclined to privilege tradition and the British way of doing things over institutional change and the uncertainty that brings.

The Four Themes and Britain

Britain in a Globalized World of States

The first theme analyzes how a country's position in the globalizing world of states influences its ability to manage domestic and international challenges. A weaker international standing makes it difficult for a country to control international events or insulate itself from external pressures. Britain's ability to control the terms of trade and master political alliances during the nineteenth century confirms this maxim, but times have changed.

Through gradual decolonization Britain fell to second-tier status. Its formal empire shrank between the two world wars (1919–1939) as the "white dominions" of Canada, Australia, and New Zealand gained independence. In Britain's Asian, Middle Eastern, and African colonies, pressure for political reforms that would lead to independence deepened during World War II and afterward. Beginning with the formal independence of India and Pakistan in 1947, an enormous empire dissolved in less than twenty years. Finally, in 1997, Britain returned the commercially vibrant crown colony of Hong Kong to China. The process of decolonization ended Britain's position as a dominant player in world politics.

Is Britain a world power or just a middle-of-the-pack country in Europe? Maybe both. On the one hand, resulting from its role in World War II, Britain sits as a permanent member of the United Nations Security Council and a leading member of the world's select club of nuclear powers. On the other hand, Britain almost always plays second fiddle in its special relationship to the United States, which has exposed British foreign policy to extraordinary pressures, especially since 9/11. British governments also face persistent challenges in their dealings with the EU. Many countries in Europe, but not Britain, have adopted a common currency, the euro. Can Britain afford to remain aloof from such fast-paced changes of economic integration?

PROFILE

David Cameron

Christopher Furlong/ WPA Pool/Getty Images

The King's Speech is a charming award-winning movie on both sides of the Atlantic, based on a true story about how an Australian speech therapist secretly aided King George VI, a stutterer, enabling him to speak quite clearly and forcefully over the radio—a remarkable technological innovation at the time—to rally the British people to stand together against Hitler's fascism as World War II erupted. As *The Economist*, an influential weekly noted, it is a movie with deep political–cultural resonance:

> "There are some lessons here for Britain's present rulers. This is a prickly, conservative and proud nation, in which grandeur must be offset with displays of humanity: David Cameron, a privileged chap who has suffered tragedies in his private life, knows this already."*

Born in 1966, in London, Cameron was brought up in Berkshire, a historic county near Oxford and the royal residence, Windsor Castle. He is the son of a stockbroker and followed generations of Cameron males who attended Eton, the historic boarding school for the privileged elite, and then Oxford, where he studied Politics, Philosophy, and Economics (PPE). Cameron graduated in 1988 with a first-class honors degree, a signal achievement affording great and lasting status.

A journalist once asked Cameron, just before he became leader of the Conservative Party in 2005, if he thought his pedigree and elite schooling would hurt him politically. Cameron sighed mightily and then offered a very revealing reply. "I don't know. You can try to be logical about it and say the upside is a terrific education, the downside is the label that gets attached and mentioned in every article," replied Cameron. "Or you can just think to yourself: I am what I am. That is what I had, I am very grateful for it."**

Cameron's elite education and step-by-step rise to political leadership from MP (member of parliament) to member of the Conservative Party research department, to opposition spokesman (member of the shadow cabinet with increasingly significant portfolios), to leader of the Conservative Party is very traditional, if unusually rapid. Nevertheless Cameron represents a new brand of Conservative, a "third-way" conservative who has tried to steal much of the thunder from Tony Blair, whom admirers liken to John Kennedy, and who characterizes himself as a compassionate conservative. If Cameron can lead Britain successfully through the tough economic and political times he inherited from New Labour in 2010, he will have achieved a lasting place in modern British politics—and he will have earned it the hard way.

MAKING CONNECTIONS Do you think David Cameron's elite pedigree is an asset or a hindrance to leadership of the nation in hard economic times?

*Bagehot, *The Economist*. January 15, 2011, p. 62 (Economist.com/ blogs/Bagehot)

**Francis Elliott and James Hanning, *Cameron: The Rise of the New Conservative*, London: Harper Perennial, 2009, p. 25.

A second theme examines the strategies employed in governing the economy. Since the dawn of Britain's Industrial Revolution, prosperity at home has relied on superior competitiveness abroad. This is even truer today with intensified international competition and global production. Will Britain's "less-is-more" laissez-faire approach to economic governance, invigorated by partnerships between the state and key competitive businesses, sustain economic growth and competitiveness in a global context?

Our third theme assesses the potent political influence of the democratic idea, the universal appeal of core values associated with parliamentary democracy as practiced first in the United Kingdom. Even in Britain, issues about democratic governance, citizen participation, and constitutional reform have been renewed with considerable force. What are the implications of the election of May 2010 for democracy in Britain? In a sense no party won the election, but Labour was soundly defeated. The Liberal Democrats won five seats fewer than they had won in 2005 (down from 62 to 57), but won the opportunity to be the junior partner in the Conservative–Liberal Democrat coalition government; and the Conservatives, with 36.1 percent of the vote, a mere 3.7 percent increase over 2005, were unable to form a government on their own, but won the right to be responsible for shepherding the country through political uncertainty and a moment of severe economic challenges. The highly unusual outcome—the first peacetime coalition in 70 years—guarantees that 2010 will be remembered as a remarkable election, but the consequences for the democratic idea in Britain will take longer to tally.

The traditionally respected royal family, which has been rocked by improprieties, including tax scandals and infidelity over the past two decades, has seized on the marriage of Prince William as a moment of redemption. Few reject the monarchy outright, but questions about the finances and decorum of the monarchy have placed on the agenda broader issues about citizen control over government and constitutional reform. That William of Wales is now the knight in shining armor coming to the rescue of the royal family provides a graphic reminder that long-settled issues about the constitutional form and unity of the state have not been put to rest. Can the interests of England, Wales, Scotland, and Northern Ireland be balanced within a single nation-state?

The fourth theme, the politics of collective identity, considers how individuals define themselves politically through group attachments, come together to pursue political goals, and face their status as political insiders or outsiders. Through the immigration of former colonial subjects to the United Kingdom, decolonization created a multiracial and multiethnic society. Issues of race, ethnicity, and cultural identity have challenged the long-standing British values of tolerance and consensus. The concept of "Britishness"—what the country stands for and who makes up the political community—has come into question, especially since 9/11 and the bombings of the London transport system by British Muslims in July 2005.

Themes and Comparisons

Britain was the first nation to industrialize. For much of the nineteenth century, the British Empire was the world's dominant power, with a vast network of colonies. Britain was also the first nation to develop an effective parliamentary democracy.

British politics is often studied as a model of representative government. Named after the building that houses the British legislature in London, the **Westminster model** emphasizes that democracy rests on the supreme authority of a legislature—in Britain's

laissez-faire

A term taken from the French, which means "to let do," it refers to the pattern in which state management is limited to such matters as enforcing contracts and protecting property rights, while private market forces are free to operate with only minimal state regulation.

Westminster model

A form of democracy based on the supreme authority of Parliament and the accountability of its elected representatives; named after the Parliament building in London.

case, the Parliament. Finally, Britain has served as a model of gradual and peaceful evolution of democratic government in a world where transitions to democracy are often turbulent, interrupted, and uncertain.

Where Do You Stand?

Was Margaret Thatcher just what the doctor ordered to jump-start the British economy—or was she too divisive and ideological?

Tony Blair and Gordon Brown reinvented the modern Labour Party, severing its ties with the working class and emphasizing a cross-class coalition, which often seemed to tilt toward business. In this era of occupy movements and huge income inequality should Labour return to its historic roots?

POLITICAL ECONOMY AND DEVELOPMENT

▼ Focus Questions

- What are the similarities and what are the differences in New Labour's approach to governing the economy compared to that of Margaret Thatcher and John Major?

- What are the key elements of the coalition government's approach to economic management in the post-2008 context?

The pressures of global competitiveness and the perceived advantages of a minimalist government have encouraged the adoption in many countries of neoliberal approaches to economic management. A legacy from Thatcher's Britain, **neoliberalism** was a key feature of Tony Blair's and Gordon Brown's New Labour government. Its policies aimed to promote free competition, interfere with entrepreneurs and managers as little as possible, and create a business-friendly environment to attract foreign investment and spur innovation. Given that New Labour had long accepted the core principles of neoliberalism, the differences in economic policy between New Labour and the Conservative–Liberal coalition reflected changed circumstances—the economic crisis driven by the recession of 2008—more than ideological shifts.

State and Economy

In the 1980s, economic growth in Britain was low and unemployment high. Britain was routinely called the "sick man of Europe." But from the mid-1990s to the "Great Recession" of 2008, Britain avoided the high unemployment and recession of many EU nations. The UK economy has run on a "two-track" pattern of growth. A strong service sector (especially in financial services) offset a much weaker industrial sector. Until the global downturn of fall 2008, the British economy exhibited overall strength. With low unemployment, low interest rates, low inflation, and sustained growth, the UK performance was one of the best among the leading industrial economies. Weeks before the collapse of Lehman brothers heralded the Great Recession, Brown warned at a meeting of Eurozone countries that the collapse of the U.S. housing market and the Great Recession to follow could be blamed on America, but insisted that global problems required coordinated global solutions. Thus far neither Britain nor other European economies have stepped up to the plate.

With the transition in 2010 from a New Labour to a Conservative–Liberal government, the policy orientation did not change at a stroke. Neoliberalism drove the economic policy of New Labour and, as a result, the economic performance of the

neoliberalism

A term used to describe government policies aiming to promote free competition among business firms within the market, including reduced governmental regulation and social spending.

UK economy today remains oriented to a patchwork neoliberal approach. Two central dimensions, economic management and social policy, capture the new role of the state and show how limited this new state role really is, partly by design and partly by the sheer force of changes demanded by the recession.

Economic Management Like all other states, the British state intervenes in economic life, sometimes with considerable force. However, the British state has generally limited its role to broad policy instruments that influence the economy generally (**macroeconomic policy**). How has the orientation of economic policy evolved during the postwar period?

The Consensus Era After World War II, the unity inspired by shared suffering during the war and the need to rebuild the country crystallized the collectivist consensus. The state broadened and deepened its responsibilities for the economy.

The state assumed direct ownership of key industries. It also accepted the responsibility to secure low levels of unemployment (a policy of full employment), expand social services, maintain a steady rate of growth (increase economic output or GDP), keep prices stable, and achieve desirable balance-of-payments and exchange rates. The approach is called Keynesian demand management, or **Keynesianism** (named after the British economist John Maynard Keynes, 1883–1946).

Before Thatcher became leader of the Conservative Party in 1975, Conservative leaders generally accepted the collectivist consensus. By the 1970s, however, Britain was suffering economically without growth and with growing political discontent. Investments declined, and trade union agitation increased. Industrial unrest in the winter of 1978–1979 dramatized Labour's inability to manage the trade unions. It seemed as if everyone was on strike. Strikes by truckers disrupted fuel supplies. Strikes by train-drivers disrupted intercity commerce and visits to granny. Some ambulance drivers refused to respond to emergency calls. Grave diggers refused to bury the dead. Thatcher came to power a few months later in May 1979. What was dubbed "the winter of discontent" destroyed Britain's collectivist consensus and discredited the Keynesian welfare state.

Thatcherite Policy Orientation The economic orientations of Thatcher and John Major, her successor, rejected Keynesianism. **Monetarism** emerged as the new economic doctrine. It assumed that there is a "natural rate of unemployment" determined by the labor market itself. State intervention to steer the economy should be limited to a few steps to foster appropriate rates of growth in the money supply and keep inflation low. Monetarism reflected a radical change from the postwar consensus regarding economic management. Not only was active government intervention considered unnecessary; it was seen as undesirable and destabilizing.

New Labour's Economic Policy Approach Gordon Brown as chancellor—and later as prime minister—insisted on establishing a sound economy. He was determined to reassure international markets that the British economy was built on a platform of stability (low debt, low deficit, low inflation) and that the Labour government could be counted on to run a tight financial ship. Only after he turned the public debt into a surplus did the "iron chancellor" reinvent himself as a more conventional Labour chancellor. Even then, Brown used economic growth to increase spending (rather than cut taxes).

macroeconomic policy

Policy intended to shape the overall economic system by concentrating on policy targets such as inflation and growth.

Keynesianism

Named after British economist John Maynard Keynes, an approach to economic policy in which state economic policies are used to regulate the economy to achieve stable economic growth.

monetarism

An approach to economic policy that assumes a natural rate of unemployment, determined by the labor market, and rejects the instruments of government spending to run budgetary deficits for stimulating the economy and creating jobs.

Artist: Chris Riddell. Published in The
Observer, 13 Nov 2011. http://www
.cartoons.ac.uk/record-request/95507.
British Cartoon archive Kent

Brown claimed that since capital is international, mobile, and not subject to control, industrial policy and planning are futile if they focus on the domestic economy alone. Instead, government should improve the quality of labor through education and training, maintain labor market flexibility, and attract investment to Britain. Strict control of inflation and tough limits on public expenditure would promote both employment and investment opportunities. Economic policy should increase competitive strength through government–business partnerships and efforts to improve the skill of the workforce and therefore the competitiveness of British industry.

The Coalition Government's Economic Policy Approach The centerpiece of the coalition government's approach to economic policy is its overarching commitment to deficit reduction as the necessary precondition for stabilizing the economy. Very soon after taking office, the coalition government engaged in a comprehensive spending review and a predictably harsh retrospective critique of the state of the economy they inherited from New Labour. To say the least, Britain's chancellor of the exchequer (finance minister) George Osborne cast significant doubt on the way New Labour handled public finances. Cameron's speech to the Tory Party conference in October 2010 lambasted Labour, characterizing the result of Labour's economic policy and the urgent need for debt reduction this way:

> Back in May, we inherited public finances that can only be described as cata-strophic.... This year, we're going to spend 43 billion pounds (68 billion dollars) on interest payments alone ... not to pay off the debt—just to stand still.... That's why we have acted decisively—to stop pouring so much of your hard-earned money down the drain.

Key cuts announced by the chancellor, which are scheduled to be in effect for four years, include cuts in government subsidies for public housing, increases in the age for pensions, a reduction in child benefits for middle-class families, a general reduction of about 10 percent in a range of social protection and welfare benefits, and a cut of roughly 20 percent in public spending across the board. Of course, the new economic course set by the coalition government spurred considerable controversy. Osborne insisted that the budget was "guided fairness, reform," while Labour critics characterized it as "a reckless gamble with people's livelihoods," and a threat to any economic recovery. On balance, the cuts were viewed as both necessary and regressive, hitting those in the lower end of the income distribution harder than those who are better off.

Social Policy

Historically, in the United Kingdom welfare state provisions have interfered relatively little in the workings of the market, and policy-makers do not see the reduction of group inequalities as the proper goal of the welfare state. In fact, through changes in government there has been considerable continuity across the period of postwar consensus, despite differences in perspectives on the welfare state. The collectivist era enshrined the welfare state. Thatcher assailed the principles of the welfare state but accepted many of the policies as increased need triggered expanding welfare state budgets. New Labour attempted to link social expenditures to improving skills, making everyone a stakeholder in society, and tried hard—with only limited success—to turn social policy into an instrument for improving education, skills, and competitiveness.

In comparative European terms, the UK welfare state has offered few comprehensive services, and the policies are not very generous. At the same time—and the one exception—the National Health Service (NHS) provides comprehensive and universal medical care and has long been championed as the jewel in the crown of the welfare state in Britain, an exception to the rule in ordinary times because it provides fine, low cost medical care to all British citizens as a matter of right. Despite periodic infusions of cash to temporarily stabilize the NHS, the NHS is chronically underfunded, general practitioners are woefully underpaid, and the NHS faces some of the same challenges, which the Affordable Care Act in the United States is facing, such as the excessive use of emergency rooms and insufficient access to primary care physicians. According to a recent report of the European Commission, Britain has fewer doctors per capita than nearly all the other countries in the EU.

Society and Economy

New Labour rejected both the cutbacks in social provisions of Conservative governments that seemed mean-spirited as well as the egalitarian traditions of Britain's collectivist era that emphasized entitlements or what in the United States is called "tax-and-spend liberalism." Instead, New Labour focused its social policy on training and broader social investment as a more positive third-way alternative.

New Labour emphasized efficiencies and attempted to break welfare dependency. Its effort to identify comprehensive solutions to society's ills and reduce the tendency for government to let marginalized individuals fall by the wayside captures the third-way orientation of the New Labour project.

The economic upturn that began in 1992, combined with Major's moderating effects on the Thatcherite social policy agenda narrowed inequality in the mid-1990s. Attention to social exclusion in its many forms, and strong rates of growth were good omens for narrowing the gap between rich and poor. But even before the "Great Recession" of 2008 and despite New Labour's commitment to producing a more egalitarian society and reducing poverty, it has proven very difficult to achieve success.

A 2007 report by UNICEF compared twenty-one wealthy countries (members of the OECD) on their success in securing the well-being of children along six dimensions. Both the United States and the United Kingdom were in the bottom third for five of the six dimensions under review. In the summary table that presents the overall rankings, the United Kingdom came in dead last, just behind the United States. Despite repeated high visibility commitments by New Labour to eliminate childhood poverty, they were unable to make any sustained headway toward that laudable goal.

In a market-driven economy, it is extremely difficult for governments to effectively pursue targeted goals such as eliminating childhood poverty. The government may have the will, but it doesn't have the way (the policy instruments or the strategic capacity) to meet such goals. That said, the United Kingdom has moved up in the rankings since 2007, having risen from last place in 2000/2001 to a middle-of-the-pack position (sixteenth) in 2013, close to Portugal and the Czech Republic—not auspicious perhaps but, at least, in the middle, not the bottom of the rankings.

Inequality and Ethnic Minorities

Ethnic minorities disproportionately suffer diminished opportunity in the United Kingdom. Despite the common and often disparaging reference to ethnic minority individuals as "immigrants," members of ethnic minority groups are increasingly native-born. Today, fully one-third of the children born in England and Wales have at least one foreign-born parent. Americans are accustomed to characterizing themselves with pride as a nation of immigrants, but in empirical terms it is probably more appropriate to characterize Britain as a nation of immigrants—in fact, Britain is positioned to become the most ethnically diverse Western nation by 2050. Unfortunately, this does not mean that Britain has resolved the challenges of social exclusion and marginalization of its ethnic minority members.

Ethnic minority individuals, particularly young men, are subject to unequal treatment by the police and considerable physical harassment by citizens. They have experienced cultural isolation as well as marginalization in the educational system, job training, housing, and labor markets. There is considerable concern about the apparent rise in racially motivated crime in major metropolitan areas with significant ethnic diversity.

Poor rates of economic success reinforce the sense of isolation and distinct collective identities. Variations among ethnic minority communities are quite considerable, however, and there are some noteworthy success stories. For example, among men of African, Asian, Chinese, and Indian descent, the proportional representation in the managerial and professional ranks is actually higher than that for white men (although they are much less likely to be senior managers in large firms). Also, Britons of South Asian, especially Indian, descent enjoy a high rate of entrepreneurship. Nevertheless, the experiences faced by ethnic minorities remain grim, as is the case for younger workers. Minority individuals are twice as likely to be unemployed than whites. Government data indicate that in 2013 the gap in the unemployment rate for ethnic minority youth compared to whites rose to 13 percent as the average unemployment rate for young people in all minority groups hit 37 percent. The jobless rate for young Bangladeshi and Pakistani workers was 46 percent and the rate for young blacks was 45 percent. As if these data were not sufficiently concerning, the trend suggests even harder times ahead, since ethnic minorities are overrepresented in public sector jobs in health care and social work—which face significant cutbacks due to austerity measures.[1]

Inequality and Women

According to data from the Office of National Statistics (ONS) released in December 2013, for the first time in 5 years the gender pay gap has widened, reversing what had been a period of steady progress in narrowing the gap. Based on median hourly earnings for full-time workers the differential between men and women increased last year from 9.5 percent to 10 percent—and that is only part of the story. If all employees, including those in part-time work are included, the gender gap increased to just under 20 percent. In addition the gap is expected to widen as public sector cuts increase the number and percentage of women into the private sector—where the gender gap is greater than in the public sector. At the same time, a survey by a highly regarded management group concludes that a woman can be expected to earn roughly $678,000 less than a man over her career. Nor is the gender gap in economic rewards the only expression of gender bias in Britain. Despite the legal recognition of equality between women and men, and the growing empowerment of women in nearly all spheres of social and political life in the United Kingdom, readily observable differences in the treatment and experiences of women and men persist—and as every student reading this text knows instinctively, the terrain of gender in every society produces complicated and crosscutting evidence about the role of women in society. On the one hand, girls and young women routinely out-perform boys and young men at every educational level, yet more men than women are in the workforce (although the gap is narrowing).[2] Where family dynamics and cultural habits intercede, however, gender divisions remain strong. Women who work are far more likely than their male counterparts to work part-time (56–57 percent), compared to 86–87 percent for men, while women are far more likely to shoulder the additional burdens of childcare, eldercare, and housework, but recent UK policy has favorably impacted women's role. In 2013 the government implemented policies to provide early learning facilities for the 20 percent most disadvantaged 2-year-olds and in 2014 introduced early learning facilities for roughly 40 percent of all 2-year-olds. Clearly these policies reduce the strain on women (and increasing numbers of men) who juggle the responsibilities of work and family.

Environmental Issues

In Britain, as in much of America, extreme weather events in 2013–2014 have pro-voked intense debate about environmental issues. Britons have suffered through the worst storm and tidal surges in 60 years on the North Sea coastline, floods ruining Christmas. The most intense and unremitting rainfall in Somerset and Dorset in 250 years has inspired intensified and increasingly politicized hostile debate within the government and in the scientific community about the role of climate change in the rash of floods and storms.

More generally, the British public has expressed increasing concern about a vari-ety of environmental issues including acid rain, as pollution from coal-fired power plants endanger animals and plants. There is concern also about fracking, which involves drilling holes deep into the ground and then using high-pressure liquid to fracture shale rocks to release gas trapped inside. Environmentalists have strongly criticized the practice, warning of health risks to those in the surrounding area and the effect the method would have on surrounding areas. They have claimed it could have dire effects over the public's health. At the same time, Britain has environmen-talists who have long raised concerns about the safety of the food supply. Concerns have been raised about contaminated beef, the use of pesticides, the risk of salmonella, and the potential risks of genetically modified (GM) food. Environmental policy is hotly contested in the United Kingdom, perhaps most dramatically in the case of "climategate" in 2009, when scientists at the University of East Anglia were accused of manipulating data to overstate the dangers of climate change. In 2012 the UK government produced the first of what are intended to be 5-year climate risk assess-ment reports. In general, environmental policy has reflected a cross-party consensus, although Labour has been accused by critics of an urban bias, which played into the view of some that British governments, regardless of party, are slow and ineffective when it comes to addressing the needs of rural areas, a view exacerbated in 2013–2014 by the slow and ineffective response to extreme weather. Politicians have been accused of becoming little more than "flood tourists" who have visited the scenes of devastation in droves, producing endless photo opportunities, while the environ-ment agency responsible for flood protection and river management has been roundly criticized as ineffectual. These historic floods have provoked produced tension with rural interests, most significantly with the countryside alliance, a broad-based and extremely effective organization to promote traditional hunting and shooting, especially hunting with hounds, which was outlawed in 2005. In general there remains a tension between a growing desire of many in Britain, including Prime Minister Cameron, to "think Green" and the anti-regulatory bias that makes effective environmental policy more difficult, despite the professed cross-party commitment to effective environmental policy.

Britain in the Global Economy

foreign direct investment

Ownership of or investment in cross-border enterprises in which the investor plays a direct managerial role.

Foreign direct investment (FDI) favors national systems, like those of Britain (and the United States), that rely mostly on private contractual and market-driven arrangements. Because of low costs, a business-friendly political climate, government-sponsored financial incentives, reduced trade union power, and a large pool of potential nonunionized recruits, the United Kingdom is a highly regarded location in Europe for FDI. In 2013 Britain scored eighth globally in foreign direct investment inflows.

The United Kingdom scores well in international comparisons of microeconomic competitiveness and growth competitiveness. It has also achieved significant competitive success in particular pockets of science-based high technology industries. Even before the Great Recession, the picture of UK global competitiveness, however, was clouded by weak industrial performance.

Gordon Brown's Britain preached a globalization-friendly model of flexible labor markets throughout EU Europe, and its success in boosting Britain's economic performance in comparison with the rest of Europe won some reluctant admirers.

Under New Labour, Britain achieved an enviable record of growth, low inflation, and low unemployment in part because of its sustained commitment to attract foreign investment and to assume an outward-looking competitive profile. Of course, that international market-driven orientation of the British economy, combined with a hands-off antiregulatory approach exposed Britain to enormous risk and a very severe downturn, with reverberating political consequences, when the global recession engulfed Britain in 2008. Until the great recession, the British economy exhibited an enviable growth model that was fueled by ready access to consumer credit and by the simultaneous "fool's paradise" of low interest rates, inflated housing values, low inflation, and highly questionable lending practices.[3]

Under the woeful conditions that the coalition government faced from their first days in office, their options for governing the economy are very limited. Rejecting the temptation to stimulate the economy through government spending, budgetary cuts are the first, second, and third priority, and effective economic management will be a daunting challenge. Government leaders are resolute and plain-spoken about the challenges they face and in the early going have impressed many by their willingness to insist on radical cuts and tight budgetary control across the board. This is bitter medicine, but if they can maintain popular support and keep their coalition afloat, they may yet have an opportunity to benefit from the recovery they anticipate around the middle of the decade. The governor of the Bank of England, Mark Carney, a Canadian, a former executive at Goldman Sachs, and the first non-Briton to head the bank that governs the city of London, the United Kingdom's equivalent to Wall Street, is determined to end 5 years of stagnation, and keep Britain's interest rates low, if possible, below 7 percent. Broadly speaking this aligns the Bank of England and America's Federal Reserve.

Where Do You Stand?

Will Blair be more remembered for the successes of New Labour or the tragic failure of the war in Iraq?

Will Cameron's tough stance on austerity turn around the British economy or wreck the coalition government?

GOVERNANCE AND POLICY-MAKING

SECTION **3**

Britain's constitution is notable for two features: its form and its age. Britain lacks a formal written constitution in the usual sense. There is no single unified and authoritative text (like the U.S. Constitution) that has special status above ordinary law and can be amended only by special procedures. Rather, the British constitution is a combination of statutory law (mainly acts of Parliament), common law, convention, and authoritative interpretations. Although it is often said that Britain has an unwritten constitution, this is not accurate. Authoritative legal treatises are written, of course, as are the much more significant acts of Parliament that define crucial elements of the political system. These acts define the powers of Parliament and its relationship with the monarchy, the rights governing the relationship between state and citizen, the relationship of constituent nations to the United Kingdom, the relationship of the United Kingdom to the EU, and many other rights and legal arrangements. In fact, "What distinguishes the British constitution from others is not that it is unwritten, but rather that it is part written and uncodified."[4]

The conventions and acts of Parliament with constitutional implications began at least as early as the seventeenth century, notably with the Bill of Rights of 1689, which helped define the relationship between the monarchy and Parliament. "Britain's constitution presents a paradox," a British scholar of constitutional history has observed. "We live in a modern world but inhabit a pre-modern, indeed, ancient, constitution."[5]

Constitutional authorities have accepted the structure and principles of many areas of government for so long that the very appeal to convention itself has enormous cultural force. Thus, widely agreed-on rules of conduct, rather than law or U.S.-style checks and balances, set the limits of governmental power. Absolute principles of government are few, but those that exist are fundamental to the organization of the state and central to governance, policy-making, and patterns of representation. It will become clear, however, that even the most time-encrusted principles of Britain's ancient constitutional traditions are subject to quick and potentially radical changes.

Organization of the State

The core of the British system is **parliamentary sovereignty**: Parliament can make or overturn any law; the executive, the judiciary, and the throne do not have any authority to restrict, veto, or otherwise overturn parliamentary action. In a classic **parliamentary democracy**, the prime minister is answerable to the House of Commons (the elected element of Parliament) and may be dismissed by it. That said, by joining the European Economic Community in 1973 (now known as the European Union), Parliament

Focus Questions ▼

- What are the strengths and weaknesses of parliamentary democracy?

- How has the devolution of powers from the UK Parliament to Wales, Scotland, and Northern Ireland changed both the organizing principles of the state and politics in the United Kingdom?

parliamentary sovereignty

The doctrine that grants the legislature the power to make or overturn any law and permits no veto or judicial review.

parliamentary democracy

System of government in which the chief executive is answerable to the legislature and may be dismissed by it.

accepted significant limitations on its power to act. It acknowledged that European law has force in the United Kingdom without requiring parliamentary assent and that European law overrides British law. Parliament has accepted the authority of the European Court of Justice (ECJ) to resolve jurisdictional disputes. To complete the circle, the ECJ has confirmed its right to suspend acts of Parliament.

Second, Britain has long been a **unitary state**. By contrast to the United States, where powers not delegated to the national government are reserved for the states, no powers are reserved constitutionally for subcentral units of government in the United Kingdom. However, the Labour government of Tony Blair introduced a far-reaching program of constitutional reform that created a quasi-federal system. Specified powers have been delegated (the British prefer to say *devolved*) to legislative bodies in Scotland and Wales, and to Northern Ireland as well, now that the long-standing conflict there seems settled. In addition, powers have been redistributed from the Westminster Parliament to an authority governing London with a directly elected mayor. As part of New Labour's constitutional reform agenda, regional development agencies (RDAs), which are appointed bodies, were set up in 1999 to enhance development plans for regions throughout the United Kingdom.

Third, Britain has a system of **fusion of powers** at the national level: Parliament is the supreme legislative, executive, and judicial authority and includes the monarch as well as the House of Commons and the House of Lords. The fusion of legislature and executive is also expressed in the function and personnel of the cabinet. U.S. presidents can direct or ignore their cabinets, which have no constitutionally mandated function, but the British cabinet bears enormous constitutional responsibility. Through collective decision making, the cabinet—and not an independent prime minister—shapes, directs, and takes responsibility for government. This core principle, **cabinet government**, however, may at critical junctures be observed more in principle than in practice. Particularly with strong prime ministers, such as Thatcher and Blair, who can rally—or bully—the cabinet, power gravitates to the prime minister.

Britain is a **constitutional monarchy**. The Crown passes by hereditary succession, but the government or state officials must exercise nearly all powers of the Crown. Parliamentary sovereignty, parliamentary democracy, and cabinet government form the core of the British or Westminster model of government.

unitary state

In contrast to a federal system, a system of government in which no powers are reserved for subnational units of government.

fusion of powers

A constitutional principle that merges the authority of branches of government, in contrast to the principle of separation of powers.

cabinet government

A system of government in which most executive power is held by the cabinet, headed by a prime minister.

constitutional monarchy

System of government in which the head of state ascends by heredity but is limited in powers and constrained by the provisions of a constitution.

The Executive

The term *cabinet government* emphasizes the key functions that the cabinet exercises: responsibility for policy-making, supreme control of government, and coordination of all government departments. However, the term does not capture the full range of executive institutions nor the scale and complexity of operations. Nor does it capture the realities of a system in which power invariably flows upward to the prime minister. In addition, the executive reaches well beyond the cabinet. It extends from ministries (departments) and ministers to the civil service in one direction, and to Parliament (as we shall see in Section 4) in the other direction.

Cabinet Government

After a general election, the Crown invites the leader of the party that emerges from the election with control of a majority of seats in the House of Commons to form a government and serve as prime minister. The prime minister selects approximately two dozen ministers for the cabinet. Senior cabinet posts include the Foreign Office (equivalent to the U.S. secretary of state), the Home Office (ministry of justice or attorney general), and the chancellor of the exchequer (finance minister). Unlike the French Constitution, which prohibits a cabinet minister from serving in the legislature, British constitutional tradition *requires* overlapping membership between Parliament and cabinet. A member of the cabinet must be either a member of parliament (MP) or less commonly, a member of the House of Lords.

The cabinet room at 10 Downing Street (the prime minister's official residence) is a place of intrigue as well as deliberation. From the prime minister's viewpoint, the cabinet may appear as loyal followers or as ideological combatants, potential challengers for party leadership, and parochial advocates for pet programs that run counter to the overall objectives of the government. By contrast, the convention of collective responsibility normally unifies the cabinet. In principle, the prime minister must gain the support of a majority of the cabinet for a range of significant decisions, notably the budget and the legislative program.

The only other constitutionally mandated mechanism for checking the prime minister is the government's defeat on a vote of no confidence in the House of Commons (discussed further in Section 4). Since the defeat of a government by parliament is rare and politically dangerous, the cabinet remains the only routine check on the prime minister.

Margaret Thatcher often attempted to galvanize loyalists in the cabinet and either marginalize or expel detractors. In the end, her treatment of the cabinet, which stretched British constitutional conventions, helped inspire the movement to unseat her as party leader. John Major returned to a more consultative approach.

Tony Blair, like Thatcher, narrowed the scope of collective responsibility. The prime minister, a few key cabinet members, and a handful of advisers made many important policy decisions in smaller unofficial gatherings. Under Blair, cabinet meetings were usually less than an hour and could not seriously take up (much less resolve) policy differences.

The decision to go to war in Iraq underscored the cabinet's weakened capacity to exercise constitutional checks and balances. Blair and his close aides seemed skeptical about the effectiveness and centrality of the cabinet as well as cabinet committees. Blair preferred to coordinate strategically important policy areas through highly politicized special units in the Cabinet Office.

How does David Cameron run his cabinet? Carefully, no doubt, since he presides over a potentially unstable coalition in which one wrong move could bring down the government. On balance, cabinet government represents a durable and effective formula for governance, although the United Kingdom has very little experience with coalition governments. The cabinet operates within a broader cabinet system, or core executive (see Figure 2.4), and the prime minister holds or controls many of the levers of power in the core executive. Because the prime minister is the head of the cabinet, his or her office helps develop policy, coordinates operations, and functions as a liaison with the media, the party, interest groups, and Parliament.

The cabinet is supported by a set of institutions that help formulate policy, coordinate operations, and facilitate the support for government policy. Acting within a context set by the fusion of legislature and executive, the prime minister enjoys a great opportunity for decisive leadership that is lacking in a system of checks and balances and separation of powers among the branches of government.

Cabinet committees (comprising ministers) and official committees (made up of civil servants) supplement the work of the cabinet. In addition, the treasury plays an important coordinating role through its budgetary control. The cabinet office supports day-to-day operations. Leaders in both the Commons and the Lords, the *whips*, smooth the passage of legislation sponsored by the government. Given that the government always has a working majority (except when the government declares

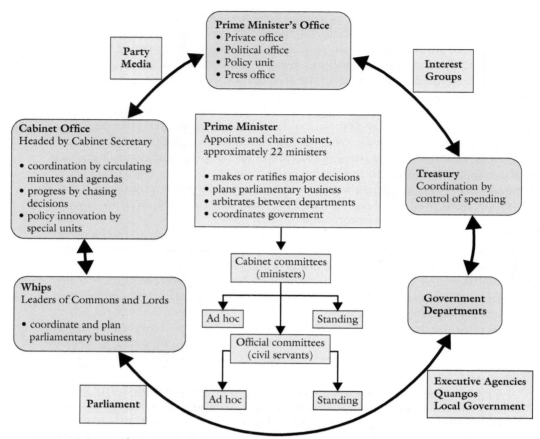

FIGURE 2.4 The Cabinet System
The cabinet is supported by a set of institutions that help formulate policy, coordinate operations, and facilitate the support for government policy. Acting within a context set by the fusion of legislature and executive, the prime minister enjoys a great opportunity for decisive leadership that is lacking in a system of checks and balances and separation of powers among the branches of government.

a "free vote," which signals that a matter is either too controversial or too inconsequential to be introduced on behalf of the government), the outcome of a vote is seldom in doubt.

Because the cabinet system and the core executive concentrate power at the top, London does not suffer from Washington-style gridlock. The risk in the United Kingdom is the opposite danger of excessive concentration of power by a prime minister who is prepared to manipulate cabinet and flout the conventions of collective responsibility.

Bureaucracy and Civil Service

Policy-making may appear to be increasingly concentrated in the prime minister's hands. When viewed from Whitehall (the London street where key UK units of government and administration are located), however, the executive may appear to be dominated by its vast administrative agencies. The range and complexity of state policy-making mean that the cabinet's authority must be shared with a vast set of unelected officials. Government departments are directed by members of the cabinet.

Ministers are assisted by a very senior career civil servant, called a permanent secretary, who has chief administrative responsibility for running a department. Other senior civil servants, including deputy secretaries and undersecretaries, assist the permanent secretaries. In addition, the minister reaches into his or her department to appoint a principal private secretary, an up-and-coming civil servant who assists the minister as gatekeeper and liaison with senior civil servants.

Since nearly all legislation is introduced on behalf of the government and presented as the policy directive of a ministry, civil servants in Britain do much of the work of conceptualizing and refining legislation. (In the United States committee staffers in the Congress often do this work.) Civil servants, more than ministers, assume operational duties.

As a result of the ongoing modernization of Whitehall, the civil service has been downsized and given a new corporate structure. Few at the top of these agencies (agency

---

THE U.S. CONNECTION

Comparing the U.S. Presidential System to the British Parliamentary System

Political scientists—especially those engaged in comparative politics—often discuss how the design of political institutions affects political outcomes.

Among the institutional differences that matter most is the distinction between presidential systems such as the United States and parliamentary systems such as the United Kingdom.

In a presidential system, the legislature and executive are *independent*. Both the legislature and the chief executive have their own fixed schedule for election and their own political mandate. Legislators and presidents have been elected independently of each other. They have different constituencies and often have different political agendas. Each may even gain credibility and support by opposing the other. In presidential systems the agenda and the authority of the president are often compromised when the president and the majority of legislators are from different parties—in fact this is the rule, rather than the exception in the United States and in many other presidential systems. Stalemates on key items of legislation are common. Between presidential elections, it is very difficult to remove a president, even one who has very little popular support or is suspected of acting unconstitutionally. It requires impeachment, which, in turn, requires a finding of extraordinary misconduct and a strong majority vote in the legislature.

Prime ministers, in contrast, must enjoy the support of the majority of the legislature to achieve office—and they must preserve that support to stay in office, since prime ministers and their governments can fall if they lose a vote of no confidence in the legislature. Furthermore, in a parliamentary system the timing of elections is typically not fixed

(although the Cameron government has modified this rule). When riding high, the prime minister can call for a new election in an effort to win a new mandate and a deeper majority in parliament. When in trouble, a prime minister can be sent packing in an instant through a vote of no confidence.

In a parliamentary system like Britain's, because the legislators and prime minister sink or swim together, they tend to cooperate and work through differences. In a presidential system like America's, because the legislature and executive are mutually independent—one can swim, while the other sinks—the tendency for finger pointing and stalemate is much greater.

But the distinctions should not be exaggerated. Powerful prime ministers such as Thatcher and Blair were routinely criticized for being too presidential. And in Britain, the threat a prime minister faces of losing office through a vote of no confidence has all but disappeared—it has happened only once in more than 80 years. In fact, if recent history is a good predictor, an American president is more likely to face a bill of impeachment than a British prime minister is to face a serious vote of no confidence.

MAKING CONNECTIONS Is a parliamentary system more or less effective than a presidential system?

The analysis draws heavily from Alfred Stepan, with Cindy Skatch, "Constitutional Frameworks and Democratic Consolidation: Parliamentarism versus Presidentialism," in Mark Kesselman and Joel Krieger, eds., *Readings in Comparative Politics: Political Challenges and Changing Agendas* (Boston: Houghton Mifflin, 2006), pp. 284–293.

chief executives) are traditional career civil servants. There is growing concern that the increasing importance of special advisers (who are both political policy advisers and civil servants) is eroding the impartiality of civil servants. Key special advisers played critical roles in making the case in the famous "dodgy dossier" of September 2002 alleging that the threat of weapons of mass destruction justified regime change in Iraq.

Public and Semipublic Institutions

Like other countries, Britain has institutionalized "semipublic" agencies, which are sanctioned by the state but without direct democratic oversight. Examples include nationalized industries and nondepartmental public bodies.

Nationalized Industries The nationalization of basic industries—such as coal, iron and steel, gas and electricity supply—was a central objective of the Labour government's program during the postwar collectivist era. By the end of the Thatcher era the idea of public ownership had clearly run out of steam and most of these giant state enterprises were privatized, that is, sold to private large-scale investors or sold in small units to ordinary citizens, as was the case with British Telecom, the communications giant. More than 50 percent of the BT shares were sold to the public. When thinking of expanding state functions, we can look to a set of semipublic administrative organizations.

Nondepartmental Public Bodies Since the 1970s, an increasing number of administrative functions have been transferred to bodies that are typically part of the state in terms of funding, function, and appointment of staff, but operate at arm's length from ministers.

These nondepartmental public bodies (NDPBs) are better known as quasi-nongovernmental organizations or **quangos**. They take responsibility for specific functions and can combine governmental and private sector expertise. At the same time, they enable ministers to distance themselves from controversial areas of policy.

Alongside quangos, in recent years the government has looked for ways to expand the investment of the private sector in capital projects such as hospitals and schools. Thus New Labour continued the private finance initiative (PFI) it inherited from the Conservatives as a key part of its signature modernization program and as a way to revitalize public services. The results are controversial: Critics and supporters disagree about the quality of services provided and about whether taxpayers win or lose by the financial arrangements. In addition, the tendency of PFI initiatives to blur the line between public and private raise important and controversial issues.[6]

quangos

Acronym for *quasi-nongovernmental organizations,* the term used in Britain for nonelected bodies that are outside traditional governmental departments or local authorities.

Other State Institutions

The Military and the Police

Those involved in security and law enforcement have enjoyed a rare measure of popular support in Britain. Constitutional tradition and professionalism distance the British police and military officers from politics.

In the case of the military, British policy since the Cold War remains focused on a gradually redefined set of North Atlantic Treaty Organization (NATO) commitments. Still ranked among the top five military powers in the world, Britain retains a global presence. In 1999, the United Kingdom strongly backed NATO's Kosovo campaign and pressed for ground troops. According to Blair, global interdependence rendered isolationism obsolete and inspired a commitment to a new ethical dimension in foreign policy. Throughout the war in Iraq and its bloody aftermath, Blair persistently sought to characterize Iraq as an extension of Kosovo, an effort to liberate Muslims from brutal dictatorships, whether Serbia's Milosevic or Iraq's Saddam Hussein. Until Blair's decision to support the American plan to shift the main venue of the war on terror from Afghanistan to Iraq, the use of the military in international conflicts generated little opposition. It may be that the Iraq war is the exception that proves the rule that the United Kingdom can play an important role in the world of states, including the use of force, when justified, without losing public support. In 2011, the Cameron government played a leading role in the international effort, endorsed by the U.N. Security Council, to protect civilians and enhance the cause of rebels fighting the regime of Libyan dictator Muammar Gaddafi. In the early stages, Cameron enjoyed strong support for his decision to participate in the international coalition. In August 2013, however, despite strong pressure from the United States and Cameron's best efforts, parliament refused to authorize use of force to quell the violence in Syria.

The police have traditionally operated as independent local forces throughout the country. Since the 1980s, the police have witnessed growth in government control, centralization, and level of political use. During the coal miners' strike of 1984–1985, the police operated to an unprecedented, perhaps unlawful, degree as a national force coordinated through Scotland Yard (London police headquarters). Police menaced strikers and hindered miners from participating in strike support activities. This partisan use of the police in an industrial dispute flew in the face of constitutional traditions and offended some police officers and officials. During the 1990s, concerns about police conduct focused on police–community relations. These included race relations, corruption, and the interrogation and treatment of people held in custody.

The Judiciary

In Britain, the principle of parliamentary sovereignty has limited the role of the judiciary. Courts have no power to judge the constitutionality of legislative acts (**judicial review**). They can only determine whether policy directives or administrative acts violate common law or an act of Parliament. Hence, the British judiciary is generally less politicized and influential than its U.S. counterpart.

Jurists, however, have participated in the wider political debate outside court. They have headed royal commissions on the conduct of industrial relations, the struggle in Northern Ireland riots in Britain's inner cities, and the suspicious death of a UN weapons inspector who challenged Blair's case for the war in Iraq.

In recent years Britain has witnessed dramatic institutional changes in law and the administration of justice, most notably with the 2009 creation of the UK Supreme Court, which serves as the highest court of appeal, removing that authority from the House of Lords.

As a member of the EU, Britain is bound to abide by the European Court of Justice (ECJ). For example, with the passage of the Human Rights Act in 1998, Britain is required to comply with the European Convention on Human Rights (ECHR). Also, the adoption of the ECHR forced Britain to curtail discrimination against gays in the military.

Subnational Government

The United Kingdom is a state comprising distinct nations (England, Scotland, Wales, and Northern Ireland). Because the British political framework has traditionally been

judicial review

The ability of a high court to nullify actions by the executive and legislative branches of government that in its judgment violate the constitution.

unitary, not federal, for centuries, no formal powers devolved to either the nations within the United Kingdom or to subnational (really subcentral or sub-UK) units as in the United States, Germany, or India. Historically, the UK Parliament asserted authority over all political units in the United Kingdom. No powers were reserved for any other units of government: There are no states, and no powers were reserved for nations within the United Kingdom, or for local government. Even so, nations were a significant aspect of collective identities in the United Kingdom, often exerting a powerful hold on their members. For many, to be Scottish or Welsh or English or Northern Irish was a core source of identity that created a sense of commonality and shared fates among members. Nations were not political units. But that is no longer true.

Recent constitutional reforms have introduced important modifications in the organizing principles of the United Kingdom. After referendums in Wales and Scotland in 1997, and in Northern Ireland, which is part of the United Kingdom, and in the Republic of Ireland (an independent country) in 1998, Tony Blair's Labour government introduced a set of power-sharing arrangements (what the British call "devolution") to govern the arrangements among the UK Westminster Parliament, the Welsh Assembly, the Northern Ireland Assembly, and the Scottish Parliament. And by the time you are reading this passage, a referendum on Scottish independence may have ratified the creation of an independent Scotland.

In general, the UK government retains responsibility for all policy areas that have not been devolved, and that are the traditional domain of nation-states. Westminster controls security and foreign policy, economic policy, trade, defense, and social security for the United Kingdom as a whole, except where it doesn't; that is, where specific powers have been ceded to Scotland, Northern Ireland, or Wales.

Of all the devolved nations and regions within the United Kingdom, Scotland and the Scottish government enjoy the most robust powers. Whereas Wales and Northern Ireland have relatively limited independent authority and have legislative arenas called assemblies, Scotland has a parliament, and the Scottish government is responsible for crucial areas of policy, including education, health, and the administration of justice. Clearly, devolution involves both an element of federalism and a carefully crafted compromise. The UK Parliament is still the mother of all parliaments, but it has some potentially restive offspring!

It is important to note that every power devolved from the UK Parliament to the Scottish Parliament or the Welsh or Northern Ireland assembly chips away at the very core of parliamentary sovereignty that lies at the heart of the Westminster model. Devolution has also sparked a controversy about the asymmetry in voting rights that devolution produces.

What right should a Scottish MP have to vote on laws that might relate to England or Wales, while English and Welsh MPs cannot vote on some matters related to Scotland, in areas where policy had been devolved from the Westminster Parliament to the Scottish Parliament?

Devolution within England is also part of the reform process. Regional Development Agencies (RDAs) were introduced throughout England in 1999 to facilitate economic development at the regional level. Even though they are unelected bodies with no statutory authority, they have opened the door to popular mobilization in the long term for elected regional assemblies. In addition, the Blair government placed changes in the governance of London on the fast track. The introduction of a directly elected mayor of London in May 2000 marked an important reform, leading to the direct election of mayors in other major cities, such as Birmingham and putting into practice a process of decentralizing power.

The Policy-Making Process

Parliamentary sovereignty is the core constitutional principle of the British political system. But for policy-making and policy implementation, the focus is not on Westminster but rather on Whitehall.

In the United Kingdom Parliament has little direct participation in policy-making. Policy-making emerges primarily from within the executive. There, decision-making is strongly influenced by policy communities—informal networks with extensive knowledge, access, and personal connections to those responsible for policy. In this private hothouse environment, civil servants, ministers, and members of the policy communities work through informal ties. A cooperative style develops as the ministry becomes an advocate for key players and as civil servants come perhaps to overidentify the public good with the advancement of policy within their area of responsibility.

This cozy insider-only policy process has been challenged by the delegation of more and more authority to the EU. Both ministers and senior civil servants spend a great deal of time in EU policy deliberations and are constrained both directly and indirectly by the EU agenda and directives. More than 80 percent of the rules governing economic life in Britain are determined by the EU. Decisions by the EU Council of Finance Ministers and the European Central Bank shape British macroeconomic, monetary, and fiscal policies in significant ways. Even foreign and security policy are not immune from EU influences. The increasing Europeanization of policy-making has been and promises to further become one of the most interesting and potentially transformative developments in British politics.

Where Do You Stand?

Which is a more effective form of government: American checks and balances or British parliamentary democracy?

Does the strength of the cabinet and the power of the prime minister risk turning Britain into an elective dictatorship?

REPRESENTATION AND PARTICIPATION

SECTION **4**

As discussed in Section 3, parliamentary sovereignty is the core constitutional principle defining the role of the legislature and, in a sense, the whole system of British government. The executive or judiciary can set no act of Parliament aside, nor is any Parliament bound by the actions of any previous Parliament. Nevertheless, in practice, the control exerted by the House of Commons (or Commons)—the lower of the two houses of Parliament and by far the more powerful—is not unlimited. This section investigates the powers and role of Parliament, both Commons and Lords. It also looks at the party system, elections, and contemporary currents in British political culture, citizenship, and identity. We close by offering an analysis of surprising new directions in political participation and social protest.

Focus Questions ▽

- What are the political implications of the Conservative–Liberal coalition government?

- What are the constitutional implications of the Conservative–Liberal government?

The Legislature

Today, the Commons does not really legislate in a meaningful way. Its real function is to assent to government legislation, since (with rare exceptions such as the present coalition government) a single governing party has a majority of the seats and can control the legislative agenda and pass legislation at will. In addition, the balance of effective oversight of policy has shifted from the legislature to executive agencies.

The House of Commons

The House of Commons, the lower house of Parliament, with 650 seats at the time of the 2010 election, exercises the main legislative power in Britain. Along with the two unelected elements of Parliament, the Crown and the House of Lords, the Commons has three main functions: (1) to pass laws, (2) to provide finances for the state by authorizing taxation, and (3) to review and scrutinize public administration and government policy.

In practical terms, the Commons has a limited legislative function. Nevertheless, it serves a very important democratic role. It provides a highly visible arena for policy debate and the partisan collision of political worldviews. The flash of rhetorical skills brings drama to Westminster. One crucial element of drama, however, is nearly always missing. The outcome is seldom in doubt. MPs from the governing party (or as now, members of the Conservative–Liberal coalition) who consider rebelling against the leader of their respective parties or challenge the terms of the coalition agreement are understandably reluctant in a close and critical vote to force a general election. This would place their jobs in jeopardy. Only once since the defeat of Ramsay MacDonald's government in 1924 has a government been brought down by a defeat in the Commons (in 1979). Today, the balance of institutional power has shifted from Parliament to the governing party (or at present parties backing the coalition) and the executive.

The Legislative Process

Bills must be introduced in the Commons and the Lords, although approval by the Lords is not required. Ideas for legislation come from political parties, pressure groups, think tanks, the prime minister's policy unit, or government departments. Proposed legislation, on behalf of the government, is then drafted by civil servants, circulated within Whitehall, approved by the cabinet, and then refined by the office of Parliamentary Counsel.

In the Commons the bill usually comes to the floor three times. The bill is formally *read* upon introduction, printed, distributed, debated in general terms, and after an interval, given a *second reading*, followed by a vote. The bill then undergoes detailed review by a standing committee reflecting the overall party balance. It then goes through a report stage during which new amendments may be introduced. In the *third reading*, the bill is considered in final form (and voted on) without debate.

A bill passed in the Commons follows a parallel path in the Lords. There the bill is either accepted without change, amended, or rejected. The Lords passes bills concerning taxation or budgetary matters without alteration, but can add technical and editorial amendments to other bills (if approved by the Commons) to add clarity and precision. Finally, it receives royal assent (which is only a formality) and becomes an Act of Parliament.

The House of Lords

Traditionally the House of Lords (or Lords) was a wholly unelected body that was comprised of hereditary peers (nobility of the rank of duke, marquis, earl, viscount, or baron), and life peers (appointed on the recommendation of the prime minister or the recently institutionalized House of Lords Appointment Commission). The Lords also includes the archbishops of Canterbury and York and some two-dozen other bishops and archbishops of the Church of England. As part of a gradual reform agenda, in 1999, the right of all hereditary peers to sit and vote in the Lords was curtailed, and that right limited to 92, pending further reform. In 2014 there were about 760 members eligible to take part in the work of the House of Lords.

The Lords serves mainly as a chamber of revision, providing expertise in redrafting legislation, with the power to suggest amendments to legislation in the Commons. The Lords can debate, refine, and delay—but not block—legislation. For example, in 2006, to protect the civil liberties of British Muslims the Lords persuaded the Commons to water down a bill that prohibited incitement to violence, on the grounds that the bill might unfairly be used to target Muslim clerics. It is interesting that when it comes to parliamentary reform more attention has been paid in recent years to reform of the Lords—an issue that has repeatedly deadlocked with multiple versions of reform in play, including the possibility of an elected upper chamber, which would bear some kinship to the U.S. Senate. Increasingly the Lords engaged in unruly and inconclusive debate, challenging the coalition government on a variety of governance and substantive matters, for example, displaying firm resistance to reforms in the National Health Service and welfare benefits. It appears that in what might be the waning days of the House of Lords, members seem inclined to go out with a bang, not a whimper.

Reforms in Behavior

There have been a number of changes in the House of Common, which, ironically, have been tamer than the potential changes afoot in the House of Lords. Since the 1970s, backbenchers (MPs of the governing party who have no governmental office and rank-and-file opposition members) have been markedly less deferential. A backbench rebellion against the Major government's EU policy in 1993, which was viewed by Thatcherites as dangerously pro-European, weakened the prime minister considerably and divided the party. In addition, one-third of Labour MPs defected on key votes authorizing the use of force in Iraq in 2003—an historic rebellion.

Structural Changes: Parliamentary Committees

In addition to the standing committees that routinely review bills, in 1979 the Commons extended the number and responsibilities of select committees, which help Parliament exert control over the executive by examining specific policies or aspects of administration.

The most controversial select committees monitor the major departments and ministries. Select committees hold hearings, take written and oral testimony, and question senior civil servants and ministers. Their reports have included strong policy recommendations at odds with government policy. These reforms have complicated the role of the civil service. Civil servants have been required to testify in a manner that may damage their ministers, revealing official culpability or flawed judgments. More significant has been a tawdry scandal that has affected all the major parties concerning fraudulent claims by MPs (including ministers) for travel expenses and expenses for upkeep of extravagant homes away from London—in some cases, homes occupied by their lovers. The practice of fiddling expense accounts was widespread and improprieties over expense accounts in some cases resulted in jail time.

Political Parties and the Party System

Britain is often referred to as a two-party system, but as the 2010 election makes clear, that is a misnomer. It is true that from 1945 until the 2010 election, only leaders of the Labour or Conservative parties had served as prime ministers. And Conservative and Labour have been very closely matched. From 1945 through 2005, the Conservative and Labour parties each won eight general elections. In addition, throughout the postwar period, these two parties have routinely divided at least 85 percent of the seats in the Commons. But since the 1980s the Liberal Democrats (Lib Dems) have become an important alternative. Britain also has several national parties: the Scottish National Party (SNP) in Scotland and the Plaid Cymru in Wales as well as a roster of parties competing in Northern Ireland.

The Labour Party

Fifty years ago, those not engaged in manual labor voted Conservative three times more commonly than they did Labour. More than two out of three manual workers, by contrast, voted Labour. Britain then conformed to one classic pattern of a Western European party system: a two-class/two-party system.

Since the mid-1970s significant changes have developed in the party system, for example, the decline in class-based voting. It has also seen growing disaffection with even the moderate social democracy associated with the Keynesian welfare state and Labourism. The Labour Party suffered from divisions between its trade unionist and parliamentary elements, constitutional wrangling over the power of trade unions to determine party policy at annual conferences, and disputes over how the leader would be selected. Divisions spilled over into foreign policy issues.

The 1980s and 1990s witnessed relative harmony within the party. Moderate trade union and parliamentary leadership agreed on major policy issues. Labour became a moderate center-left party. Under the leadership of Tony Blair, Labour was rebranded as "New Labour," although its formal name remained the Labour Party. After the party's defeat in the 2010 election, two close-knit brothers who had served in the cabinet, David Miliband with close ties to Blair as foreign minister, and Ed Miliband with close ties to Brown and former Secretary of State for Climate Change, were the top contenders to succeed Gordon Brown. In a dramatic contest for leadership of the Labour Party in September 2010, Ed Miliband, the younger brother, prevailed in a very close election, signaling a turn away from New Labour and an effort to turn the party in a more progressive direction, without returning to "Old Labour." Miliband has tried with only moderate success to rally the base, particularly among trade unionists and public sector employees who are feeling the pinch the hardest under the austerity policies of the Coalition government.

The Conservative Party

The Conservative Party dates back to the eighteenth century. Its pragmatism, flexibility, and organizational capabilities have made it one of the most successful and, at times, innovative center-right parties in Europe.

In 2003, the combative and experienced Michael Howard took over as party leader. For a time, the Conservatives seemed revitalized. But it was not easy for Howard to translate his assured performances from the front bench in Parliament into popular support, as effective opposition to New Labour proved elusive. In fact, Conservatives made far less trouble for Labour Prime Minister Tony Blair on Iraq than did members of the Labour Party. Despite an energetic campaign in 2005, one likely to be remembered for the Conservatives' playing of the race and ethnicity card, electoral defeat led to his quick resignation. In December 2005, the Conservatives elected David Cameron as party leader in a landslide.

Cameron wasted little time in reorienting the party, modernizing its appeal, and reaching out beyond its traditional core values. He acknowledged that New Labour had been right in understanding the mood of Britain and right, also, to insist on achieving both social justice and economic success. Cameron promised to reduce poverty both in Britain and globally, take on climate change as a priority, and ensure security from terrorism. A testament to Blair's success, Cameron worked hard to reposition the Conservatives as a reforming more centrist party that could compete effectively with post-Blair New Labour across the economic and social spectrum.

Liberal Democrats

Through the 1970s, the Liberal Party was the only centrist challenger to the Labour and Conservative parties. Since the 1980s, a changing roster of centrist parties posed an increasingly significant threat to the two-party dominance of Conservative and Labour. In 1981, the Social Democratic Party (SDP) formed out of a split within the Labour Party. After the Conservative victory in 1987, the Liberal Party and most of the SDP merged to form the Social and Liberal Democratic Party (now called the Liberal Democrats or Lib Dems), which quickly emerged as a major political player.

In the 2001 general election the party increased its vote tally by nearly one-fifth and won fifty-two seats, the most since 1929. This success positioned the party as a potentially powerful center-left critic of New Labour. That said, at least until Blair's fortunes declined, Labour did not make it easy for them. As the Blair government began to spend massively to improve education and health care—an approach that would come to haunt them later—it narrowed the range of policy issues on which the Liberal Democrats could challenge New Labour. Party leader Charles Kennedy won the political gamble in spring 2003 by opposing the war in Iraq. But it was not easy to take electoral advantage of Blair's political weakness. For a time, the fortunes of the Liberal Dems declined. In December 2007, after two leadership turnovers, Nick Clegg, a 40-year-old ex-journalist and former member of the European Parliament, took over leadership of the Liberal Democrats. Clegg and his party faced an uphill battle to make the Lib Dems a serious contender in time for the 2010 election. But the country's fatigue with New Labour, post-9/11 and post-7/7 concerns about the erosion of civil liberties that played to the party's strength, and Clegg's energetic and confident leadership—in fall 2008 Clegg launched a campaign to knock on 1 million doors to connect with ordinary citizens—quickly catapulted the Liberal Democrats into serious contention. Today, in the context of the unfamiliar terrain of a coalition government, many are concerned that the two-party system is eroding. Some anticipate the emergence of a two-and-and-a-half party system, which may be evolving into a more fluid multiparty system, with an enhanced role for less mainstream parties. This prospect provokes considerable handwringing, notably with reference to the far-right British National Party, which placed their first members in the European Parliament in 2009 and UKIP (The United Kingdom Independent Party), which, drawing on a deep reservoir of Britain's Euroskepticism, pushed Labour into third place. Despite a broad but apparently not deep commitment to a green Britain, the Green Party performed badly, winning only one seat while the BNP and UKIP secured no seats in 2010. In comparative European terms, radical right parties have not had the success in Britain that they have enjoyed elsewhere.

Elections

British general elections are exclusively for seats in the House of Commons. The prime minister is not directly elected as prime minister but as a member of Parliament (MP) from a single constituency (electoral district). The Queen invites the leader of the party that can control a majority in the Commons to become prime minister. Constituencies vary widely in size, but the average number of voters remains roughly comparable. (In the 2010 election, the average number of voters in each constituency was roughly 68,000.)

Traditionally, Parliament had a maximum life of five years, with no fixed term. The 2010 coalition agreement proposed a fixed term of five years subject to dissolution by a 55 percent vote of members of parliament.

The Electoral System and the 2010 Election

Election for representatives in the Commons (members of Parliament, or MPs) is by a "first-past-the-post" principle in each constituency. In this single-member plurality system, the candidate who receives the most votes is elected. There is no requirement of a majority and no element of proportional representation (a system in which each party is given a percentage of seats in a representative assembly roughly comparable to its percentage of the popular vote).

This winner-take-all electoral system tends to exaggerate the size of the victory of the largest party and to reduce the influence of regionally dispersed lesser parties. This system is praised for increasing the chances that a party or coalition of parties will gain a majority of parliamentary seats and therefore form a stable government. Critics of the electoral system charge that it does not give adequate representation to minority opinion.

Contrary to the typical tendency of the winner-take-all electoral system, the 2010 election resulted in a **hung parliament** (a situation after an election when no single party comprises a majority in the Commons). Only after a quick set of negotiations, could an arrangement be found to form a coalition government. Thus, 2010 is one for the record books. On the one hand, it was the exception that proves the rule. Ordinarily Britain exhibits a stable two-party-dominant system (Conservative and Labour), with support for a third party (Liberal Democrat) spread widely across the country, but spread too thinly for the party to win a substantial number of seats. The Liberal Democrats needed an exceptional stroke of luck to buck the trend—and they got it in 2010.

hung parliament

A situation after an election when no single party comprises a majority in the Commons.

FIGURE 2.5 Comparison of Number of Seats Won by Conservative versus Labour in UK General Elections from 1945 to 2010

Source: http://ukpolitical.info.

The campaign by the Tories peaked early, failed to inspire, and could not convince the electorate that they had the experience or were equipped to handle the enormous challenges of the economic downturn. With Blair fatigue, an unpopular successor in Gordon Brown, and a failing economy, New Labour never really stood a chance to win the election outright. The first televised debates ever in UK politics certainly enlivened the campaign. They also initially fueled a surge in popularity for the telegenic and media-savvy Liberal Democratic leader, Nick Clegg, who stole the show in the first debate. In fact, for a time, "Cleggmania" produced polls showing the Lib Dems with an unprecedented one-third of the electorate behind them. For a brief moment, Britain enjoyed the unlikely spectacle of a three-party contest, but one in which Labour never really had a chance.

With a two-party dominant party system, the UK electoral system tends to produce a stable single-party government. That observation seems less certain now than it did before 2010, but it will take more than one hung parliament to make observers think that the UK party system has been fundamentally transformed into a multi-party system.

It is not clear whether the 2010 election returns signal the beginning of a critical realignment in the electoral system, but most observers recognize some grounds for improvement. For a start, the electoral system raises questions about representation and fairness. Like other winner-take-all systems, a close second place in a constituency (as in a U.S. electoral district) is simply a loss. The system reduces the competitiveness of smaller parties, like the Lib Dems, with diffuse pockets of support across the country.

In 2010 the Liberal Democrats with 23 percent of the vote won 57 seats. Labour with 29 percent of the vote won 258 seats. The Conservatives with 36.1 percent of the vote won 306 seats. Thus, the Liberal Democrats achieved a share of the vote that was roughly two-thirds that of the Conservatives, but won roughly one-fifth of the seats won by the Tories. Such are the benefits of an electoral system to the victor (as well as the second major party).

Is there any wonder why more than anything else the Liberal Democrats want what neither major party would give them: a change in the electoral system to proportional representation (PR), where the number of seats allocated to parties in Parliament would closely approximate the proportion of votes cast for a given party? PR would be a game changer, catapulting the Lib Dems into major party status and making them a potential kingmaker, tipping the balance in many close general elections to either the Conservatives or Labour. For that very reason, it is unlikely that such a fundamental change in the electoral system will be introduced any time soon. But parliamentary sovereignty means that any time there is a political will to change the electoral system, the electoral system can be changed by Parliament.

Under the terms of the 2010 coalition agreement, a referendum was held in May 2011 as follows: At present the United Kingdom uses the "first-past-the-post" system to elect MPs to the House of Commons. Should the "a vote" system be used instead (a system in which voters rank preferences among candidates)? If no candidate receives a majority of first-preference votes, then second-preference votes of the candidate who finished last are redistributed, and the process is continued until a candidate achieves a majority. The coalition agreement called for a referendum on exactly this question—and the referendum failed, preserving the first-past-the-post system.

Gender, Ethnicity, and Representation

The party and electoral systems contribute to the creation of a Parliament that has been and remains a bastion of white men, but it is becoming more diverse. The

2010 election produced a record number of ethnic minority MPs, with 27 elected, nearly double the number in 2005. Moreover there were a set of firsts: Labour's first Muslim female MP and first African MP; and for the Conservatives, their first Asian female MP. Also a record percentage of women were elected in 2010 (21.5 percent, up from 19.8 percent in 2005). But this increase is hardly a surge, and in comparative terms the United Kingdom has a long way to go when it comes to women's representation: It ranks 73rd in the world in female representation. Despite the general trend of increased representation of women and minorities, they remain substantially underrepresented in Parliament.

Trends in Electoral Behavior

Recent general elections have deepened geographic and regional fragmentation. British political scientist Ivor Crewe has referred to the emergence of two two-party systems: (1) Competition between the Conservative and Labour parties dominates contests in English urban and northern seats, and (2) Conservative-center party competition dominates England's rural and southern seats. A third two-party competition has emerged in Scotland, where Labour competes with the Scottish National Party.[7,9]

The national (that is regional) parties have challenged two-party dominance since the 1970s, but with only limited results. The Scottish National Party (SNP) was founded in 1934 and its Welsh counterpart, the Plaid Cymru, in 1925. The 2010 election showed the strength of Labour in Scotland, where it won 41 seats and 42 percent of the Scottish popular vote, an improvement over 2005. The Lib Dems came in a distant second with 11 seats, the SNP won six seats. The election demonstrated once more that the Conservatives have very little traction in Scotland. They walked away with a single seat. In Wales, the Conservatives fared better, gaining five more seats than they had won in 2005 for a total of eight seats at Westminster. The Plaid Cymru won three seats, one more than in 2005. Although Labour lost four seats compared to 2005, they walked away with a very strong showing, winning 26 out of 40 seats. The right-wing populist UK Independence party was the big winner in Britain in the European parliament elections in 2014. It won no seats but transformed the future electoral map in Britain, winning 27.5 percent of the ballots. It won 161 English council seats (up from a total of 30 seats combined in 2009 and 2012). By contrast none of the major parties did well. Labour fared better than the Conservatives, although below their expectations. The Liberal Democrats lost ten of their 11 seats in the EP and 310 council seats. The Conservatives benefited from Cameron's warnings of low expectations. With UKIP strongest in traditional Conservative constituencies it seems likely that UKIP's older, more conservative, more rural whiter conservative base may significantly challenge Tory electoral bastions in the years ahead. We will return to the increasingly dramatic and significant politics of the nations within the United Kingdom, notably Scotland, in Section 5.

Political Culture, Citizenship, and Identity

In their study of the ideals and values that shape political behavior, political scientists Gabriel Almond and Sidney Verba wrote that the civic (or political) culture in Britain was characterized by trust, deference to authority, and pragmatism.[8,10] But the 1970s became a crucial turning point in British political culture and group identities that challenged this view.

During the 1970s, the long years of economic decline culminated in economic reversals in the standard of living for many Britons. Also for many, the historic bonds of occupational and social class grew weaker. Both union membership and popularity declined. At the same time, a growing number of conservative think tanks and mass-circulation newspapers worked hard to erode support for the welfare state. New social movements such as feminism, antinuclear activism, and environmentalism challenged basic tenets of British political culture. Identities based on race and ethnicity, gender, and sexual orientation gained significance. These trends fragmented the political map and inspired a shift to the right.

Thatcher's ascent reflected these changes in political culture, identities, and values. Thatcherism rejected collectivism, the redistribution of resources from rich to poor, and state responsibility for full employment. It considered individual property rights more important than the social rights claimed by all citizens in the welfare state. Thatcherism set the stage in cultural terms for the new Labour consolidation of neoliberalism and the core political–cultural orientation in Britain.

Social Class

A key change in political culture in the last quarter-century has been the weakening of bonds grounded in the experience of labor. During the Thatcher era, the traditional values of "an honest day's work for an honest day's pay" and solidarity among coworkers were derided as "rigidities" that reduced competitiveness—a perspective that has continued through New Labour and the coalition government .

Being "tough on the unions" was a core premise of New Labour and a view that the Conservative-led coalition government has powerfully reinforced. In the context of the aggressive cuts in public spending, it looks like very tough days ahead for unions, particularly public sector unions, which have become a lightning rod, not only in the United Kingdom, but in the United States as well, for governments looking to cut budgets—and blame somebody for the need to make cuts. Collective bargaining has been largely relegated to declining private sector industries and the public sector.[9,11] Strike rates in the United Kingdom have generally been below the average of both the OECD and the EU in recent decades.

National Identity

Decolonization has created a multiethnic Britain. National identity has become especially complicated. Questions about fragmented sovereignty within the context of the EU, the commingled histories of four nations (England, Scotland, Wales, and Ireland/Northern Ireland), and the interplay of race and nationality have created doubts about British identity that run deep. Ethnicity, intra-UK territorial attachments, Europeanization, and globalization are complicating national identity. Can Britain foster a more inclusive sense of British identity?

Nearly 8 percent of the people who live in Britain are of African, African-Caribbean, or Asian descent. The authors of a landmark study of multiethnic Britain explained: "Many communities overlap; all affect and are affected by others. More and more people have multiple identities—they are Welsh Europeans, Pakistani Yorkshirewomen, Glaswegian Muslims, English Jews, and black British. Many enjoy this complexity but also experience conflicting loyalties."[10,12]

Despite many success stories, ethnic minority communities have experienced police insensitivity, problems in access to the best public housing, hate crimes, and accusations that they are not truly British if they do not root for the English cricket team. In addition, harsh criticism is directed at immigrants and asylum seekers. Since this criticism comes in the wake of intense scrutiny of the Muslim community after 9/11 and 7/7, it contributes to the alienation of the ethnic minority community, particularly among some groups of Muslim citizens. Ordinary law-abiding Muslims have experienced intensified mistrust and intimidation. But it is also true that Muslim university graduates are assuming leading roles in the professions and that dozens of Muslim city counselors have been elected across the country.

Interest Groups, Social Movements, and Protest

In recent years, partly in response to globalization, political protest has been on the rise. Protesters demand more accountability and transparency in the operations of powerful international trade and development agencies. For example, in 1999 London became the site of protests timed to correspond with the Seattle meeting of the World Trade Organization (WTO). The London demonstration generated some 100,000 protesters.

The intensity of environmental activism has taken off with the growing attention to genetically modified (GM) crops in the late 1990s. In November 1999, the government announced a ban on commercially grown GM crops in Britain.

A quite different kind of activism spread to the countryside among a population not usually known for political protest. Farmers had been badly hurt by the "mad cow disease" crisis in 1996 and saw an urban bias at play in New Labour and the growing threat to fox hunting. They launched massive protests, and, even after a law banning the hunt went into effect in 2005, they kept up the heat with legal challenges.

A series of antiwar rallies were held in London before the United Kingdom and the United States launched the Iraq war. In September 2002, a huge protest rally was organized in London, led by the Stop the War Coalition and the Muslim Association of Britain. Both within the United Kingdom and among observers of British politics and society, many still endorse the view that British culture is characterized by pragmatism, trust, and deference to authority. This may be true, but the persistence of a wide range of protest movements, including reverberating protests in 2011 against the very significant cuts introduced by the Conservative–Liberal Democrat coalition government qualifies this story.

The Political Impact of Technology

Two recent developments have underscored the impact of technology on British politics. In a scandal that is still reverberating with global implications, a parliamentary committee released a report in 2012, disclosing that Rupert Murdoch, the Australian media mogul whose companies in 2011 accounted for the second largest media holdings in the world including the prestigious *Times of London* and *The Wall Street Journal* engaged in hacking. The hacking scandal, which involved the use of sophisticated electronic technologies to hack into emails and voice mails for the purpose of breaking major news stories ahead of the competition, created collateral damage for many news organizations and high-flying politicians. The scandal also implicated Tony Blair at a trial exposing the scandal, when it was revealed that the former prime minister secretly offered to advise the Murdoch empire as the scandal erupted—a scandal that besmirched reputations among members of Parliament in all three major parties and extended to allegations of corruption and kickbacks by senior police officials. Potentially more significant in this era of governmental use of sophisticated and often secret surveillance of ordinary citizens, it has been revealed that Government Communications Headquarters (GCHQ), the UK surveillance agency, has collected millions of webcam images in bulk from Yahoo users, some of which may have revealed pornographic images.

Where Do You Stand?

Is perpetual surveillance too high a price to be for security?

Nearly everyone in Britain wants Britain to go green. Why is the support for a Green Party so weak?

BRITISH POLITICS IN TRANSITION

SECTION 5

Political Challenges and Changing Agendas

On July 7, 2005, four British suicide bombers, all Muslims, detonated a set of coordinated attacks on the London transport system during morning rush hour. Three bombs went off in quick succession on the London underground (subway) and one, an hour later, on a double-decker bus nearby. Fifty-six people were killed including the al-Qaeda–linked suicide bombers, and some 700 people were injured. The mayor and most inhabitants of the city, often invoking imagery of stoic Londoners withstanding the German blitz during World War II, remained calm and determined in the face of these devastating attacks. They insisted that London would remain an open and cosmopolitan city as it had been for centuries. And then the other shoe dropped.

Two weeks after 7/7, an entirely innocent Brazilian electrician, unconnected to the bombings, was shot dead by police who were under enormous pressure to prevent further attacks and mistakenly considered him responsible for the suicide attacks. The victim was traveling from his apartment to a job in Northwest London when he was killed. He was chased into a London subway station by roughly twenty police officers, where he was cornered, tripped, and shot seven times in the head and once in the shoulder. He was wearing a thick coat that, in the jittery aftermath of 7/7, raised suspicions that he might be hiding a suicide belt. He ran from the police when ordered to stop. A Brazilian could be mistaken for a person of Pakistani or Jamaican or Middle Eastern descent, as were the 7/7 bombers. Coming on the heels of 7/7, this tragic accident underscores how tense everyone is about security from terror attack and how race and ethnicity probably blinded even well-trained police officers into making an awful mistake.

As our democratic idea theme suggests, no democracy, however secure it may be, is ever a finished project. Even in Britain, with its centuries-old constitutional

Focus Questions ?

- Is Britain best understood as four nations or one?

- How well is Britain's ancient political system adjusting to contemporary challenges?

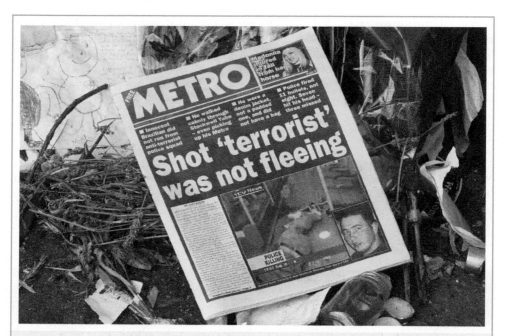

The murder of an innocent Brazilian electrician by police officers shortly after 7/7 raised new and troubling questions about security and about ethnic and racial tension in Britain.

Alessandro Abbonizio/AFP/Getty Images

settlement and secure institutional framework, issues about democratic governance and citizens' participation remain unresolved.

Constitutional Reform

Questions about the role of the monarchy and the House of Lords have long been simmering on Britain's political agenda. Why should the House of Commons share sovereignty with the House of Lords? What is the role of the monarchy—a very expensive institution and one subject to periodic scandals—in a modern political system? In addition, the balance of power among constitutionally critical institutions raises important questions about a democratic deficit at the heart of the Westminster model. Britain's executive easily overpowers Parliament. Its strength in relation to the legislature may be greater than in any other democracy. Add to these concerns the prime minister's tendency to bypass the cabinet on crucial decisions and the bias in the electoral system that privileges the two dominant parties. Consider how tumultuous and volatile the contemporary political moment in Britain has become. The British have very little experience with coalition governments, and yet they presently have one. Moreover, not only is the capacity of the party system to produce the familiar one-party leadership in doubt, but the electoral system is under scrutiny and subject to potential change. The May 2011 referendum on the voting system—a key element in the coalition agreement—produced a decisive vote to preserve the United Kingdom's current system for electing MPs, but managed to upset the apple cart anyway. The Labour leader, Ed Miliband, who supported the "Alternative Vote" system, was chastened by its resounding defeat by the electorate, and by losses in Scotland in local government elections. But the outcome was even worse for Liberal Democrat leader, Nick Clegg, for whom electoral reform was a calling card issue and a key part of the Liberal Democrat rationale for joining the coalition government. As the dust settled on the referendum on the UK voting system, held on the same day as local elections throughout the United Kingdom, the fate of Clegg and the ultimate future of the coalition remained uncertain.

Identities in Flux

The relatively small scale of the ethnic minority community limits the political impact of the most divisive issues concerning collective identities. It is probably in this area that rigidities in the British political system most severely challenge principles of democracy and tolerance. Given Britain's single-member, simple-plurality electoral system, and no proportional representation, minority representation in Parliament remains very low. There are deep-seated social attitudes that no government can easily transform.

The issues of immigration, refugees, and asylum still inspire a fear of multiculturalism among white Britons. Since the London bombings by British Muslims on 7/7 that killed fifty-six people, intense scrutiny has been focused on the Muslim community, which faces endless finger pointing and harassment. According to police, the number of hate crimes primarily affecting Muslims soared 600 percent in the weeks after the bombings. Then, in 2007, Salman Rushdie, whose book, *The Satanic Verses*, had offended many Muslims around the world and forced him into hiding in the face of a formal death threat from Iranian religious leaders, was knighted by the Queen. The honor accorded Rushdie was widely held to be an affront to the Muslim community in Britain. There is increasing concern across the political spectrum that Britain needs to find a way to deepen the ties of shared political culture and values that hold society together as well as to ensure security.

But finger pointing at the Muslim community has intensified since 9/11 and 7/7, and positions are hardening against multiculturalism. In February 2011, Prime Minister Cameron explicitly challenged the long-standing cross-party support for multiculturalism at a high-visibility security conference in Munich. Cameron condemned a culture of "hands-off" tolerance in the United Kingdom and in Europe. He criticized immigrants, and particularly Muslims (whom he seemed to define as immigrants whatever their immigration status) for leading lives apart from mainstream society. In strong terms, he warned of the dangers of multicultural policy, which made it possible for Islamic militants to radicalize Muslim youth, some of whom were likely to become terrorists. And he concluded that Europe had to defeat terrorism at home, not exclusively by the use of force elsewhere, for example, in Afghanistan.

With the war in Iraq viewed across the political spectrum as a debacle forged by the thoughtless application of the special relationship, Cameron tried hard to recalibrate the special relationship by broadening its meaning to extend beyond its historic U.S.-UK definition and to include other key allies and critical trading partners with special historic ties to the United Kingdom, for example, India.

Youth Politics and the Generational Divide

It comes as no surprise but with considerable concern and regret that the recession that began in 2008 has produced a huge generational divide. Imagine that you were born in Britain between 1980 and 1990. If that were you, bad luck. It would

GLOBAL CONNECTION

Britain and the Legacies of Empire

At its height during the reign of Queen Victoria (1837–1901), the British Empire encompassed fully one-quarter of the world's population and exerted direct colonial rule over some four-dozen countries scattered across the globe. In a stunning reversal of Britain's global status and fortunes, the empire fell apart in the half-century of decolonization between the independence of India in 1947 and the return of Hong Kong to China in 1997. Apart from a few scattered dependencies, the sun finally set on the British Empire, but the legacies of empire lived on to shape its relationship to the world of states in important ways.

The end of empire did not bring the end of great power aspirations for Britain, but it shifted the emphasis as the British role in the globalizing world of states has been shaped by its determination to view its "special relationship*" with the United States as a dominant framework for foreign policy and global leadership, even at the expense of a full commitment to economic integration with and leadership in the European Union.

With the end of empire it was inevitable that the special relationship between the United Kingdom and the United States would become a relationship between unequal partners. As a result, U.S. interests have tended to exert a tremendous magnetic pull on British foreign policy, to the relative neglect of European partnerships and broader international influences.

Before 9/11 New Labour stood for a coherent and progressive foreign policy framework, one that linked globalization to a growing UK commitment to narrow the development gap and in the words of Robin Cook, Blair's first foreign secretary, "to be a force for good" in the world. The Kosovo war created the context for Blair's explicit linkage of globalization with foreign and security policy.

Blair's "doctrine of international community" gave new weight to the notion of global interdependence by asserting a responsibility to use military force when necessary to achieve humanitarian objectives and contain catastrophic human rights abuses. This doctrine, as well as Blair's Atlanticist leanings, conditioned his response to 9/11 and subsequently his determination to bring the United Kingdom into the war in Iraq.

But in the days following 9/11, the powerful attraction of the Atlantic Alliance, with Blair's distinctive inflections, took an irresistible hold over British foreign policy. At this critical juncture, several elements came together to forge the decision to support the U.S. administration, even when the venue of the war on terror changed from Afghanistan to Iraq:

1. A fear that if the United States were left to fight the war on terror by itself, then unilateralist forces in Washington would be strengthened, and the world would be worse off.[11]
2. Blair's conviction that Iraq should be understood, like Kosovo, as an exercise in humanitarian intervention to save Muslims from catastrophic human rights abuses.[12]
3. A particular reading of the special relationship that made it imperative that the United Kingdom support the U.S. war in Iraq, viewing it as a necessary part of the global war on terror.

In Blair's doctrine of international community, the reverberations of empire were unmistakable. The civilizing mission of empire and the right of the metropolitan power to use force against the weaker dependent or failed states were both understood as an exercise of humanitarian intervention. And the use of force, however it was justified, represented an exercise in great power politics. How will the Conservative–Liberal government under the leadership of David Cameron recast the United Kingdom's role in the world of states? It seems likely that the Liberal Democrats will be more inclined to align British interests with Europe, while the Tories will remain in the Euroskeptic camp, aloof from further integration with Europe, especially so long as many of the European economies remain troubled. Perhaps to allay European concerns as well as that of his coalition partners, Cameron's first trip abroad as prime minister was to Paris and Berlin. Equally revealing, to emphasize his concerns about security, Afghani president Hamid Karzai was the first foreign leader to meet Cameron as prime minister, and at a joint press conference with Karzai at the White House, President Obama was quick to confirm "the extraordinary special relationship between the United States and Great Britain." As a sign of the times and the shifting power among British allies, Cameron has also made clear that he regards a "new special relationship with India" as a critical element in UK foreign relations and trade policy. With a proliferation of "special relationships" it may be time to wonder if the United States is still the United Kingdom's BFF (Best Friends Forever) or just one of several special relationships.

MAKING CONNECTIONS Does the special relationship enhance Britain's standing in a globalizing world of states or lock Britain in to a set of problems not of its own making but rather determined in Washington?

*Definitions of key terms in this boxed feature appear in the Glossary, which begins on p. 411.

be very difficult for you to get a job. Unemployment for university graduates in your generation's shoes is close to 20 percent. For dropouts the unemployment rate is close to 50 percent. Hardly anyone can get a loan to finance their mortgage. Train fare for getting to work has eaten up roughly 8 percent of your income; the gas bill has gone up 15 percent a year. Although the cost of university/college in the United Kingdom is not nearly as high as it is in the United States, the costs have increased substantially, which produced riots outside parliament when tuition fees were tripled in 2010. Rents have been hitting record highs. If you were a young Briton in your 40s and with a job and starter house with a low mortgage, recession has barely hurt your life style. For those in retirement or facing retirement, record low interest rates have reduced their monthly income. The generation retiring today can complain that their pensions are squeezed, but many are the beneficiaries of traditional pension plans that guaranteed two-thirds salary in retirement.

British Politics in Comparative Perspective

Until the Asian financial crisis that began in 1997, it was an axiom of comparative politics that economic success required a style of economic governance that Britain lacks. Many argued that innovation and competitiveness in the new global economy required the strategic coordination of the economy by an interventionist state. But the United Kingdom escaped the recession that plagued the rest of Europe for much of the 1990s. Britain also outperformed most major world economies until the "Great Recession" of 2008 signaled a decisive downturn in Britain's economic fortunes.

In many countries throughout the world, politicians have been looking for an economic model that can sustain competitiveness while improving the plight of the socially excluded. For this reason, New Labour's third way—a political orientation designed to transcend left and right in favor of practical and effective policies—was carefully watched for more than ten years. Observers saw in New Labour a historic intellectual and political realignment, not only in Britain, but in Clinton's America and Cardoso's (and later Lula's) Brazil. Ten years is a very long time in politics, and for ten years it looked as if New Labour had found a way to mold a new political orientation that combined a sophisticated approach to competitiveness in the global economy with a pragmatic anti-ideological approach to governance. But in time, the bloom most decidedly came off the rose of New Labour, which could never recover from the war in Iraq. The electorate grew tired of Blair and never warmed up to Brown. When the financial and economic crisis struck in 2008, Britain was among the hardest hit of the core European economies.

Where Do You Stand?

Is Britain important enough and functioning well enough today to stand alongside the United States as one of the two great models of democratic government?

With Putin's Russia on the ascendant, America looking inward, and the EU facing tremendous economic and institutional challenges, is there an opportunity for Britain to play a greater role in a globalizing world of states?

Chapter Summary

Consider the decline of Britain's historic laissez-faire economic model, its refusal to participate in the Eurozone, and the unresolved legacies of empire, reflected in tumultuous debates and recriminations over race, ethnicity, and the meaning of "Britishness." Add to those tensions the surprising constitutional and institutional uncertainty about the role of the Commons and the Lords; and the possibility that Britons might have to get used to coalition governments and an independent Scotland; and perhaps a series of referendums on UK voting systems.

It is fair to say that Britain is experiencing a period of uncertainty across all four of our core themes as challenging as anything the country has experienced for generations.

Undoubtedly people in Britain today sense that the nation is divided on multiple fronts and, measured against the historic achievements of parliamentary democracy, empire, and Industrial Revolution—that Britain is in decline, with little confidence that renewal is in the cards.

Since 2008, Britain has been facing daunting challenges. Almost inevitably, economic downturn produces political challenges, but it also creates opportunities for change and renewal. A new generation of untested leadership in all the major political parties and, most importantly, at the helm of the coalition government will produce new political challenges, innovative policy directions, new approaches to solving old problems, and occasional policy U-turns. Will the coalition hold or will the strains and challenges of governing shatter the coalition of convenience between the Conservatives and Liberal Democrats? Across the globe, many electorates are asking for effective pragmatic leadership in hard times. If the

United Kingdom's coalition government, which came to office almost by accident and in very difficult times, stays intact and effectively manages from the center, it may last long enough to benefit both from the resourcefulness of an electorate and a country that is not easily daunted and from a rising economic tide. If that happens, it may build on the New Labour legacy of government judged on effectiveness, not ideology, and enjoy a long run in office. If not, the British distaste for coalition government will be confirmed. Perhaps more important for the future of the United Kingdom is the very basis of the union measured against the real possibility of a profound and fundamental institutional change with unknown consequences for the fate of Britain.

In September 2014, a referendum was held on the straightforward question: "Should Scotland be an independent country?" An incredible 97% of eligible voters registered to vote—a remarkable indication of the intensity of feelings on all sides. Polls leading up to the referendum indicated the prospect of an extremely close result. In the end, the "No" votes scored a rather decisive victory (55.3%), with the "Yes" vote tally at 44.7 %. The United Kingdom preserved its historic constitutional design, but at some cost. To secure the "No" vote, the leaders of all three Westminster parties, David Cameron, Nick Clegg, and Ed Miliband, promised extensive new powers to the Scottish parliament in regard to taxing, spending, and social welfare benefits. Within days of the referendum, prime minister Cameron also introduced plans to limit the voting rights of Scottish MPs on English issues, a sign that the referendum only began what seems likely to be an extended period of constitutional uncertainty.

Key Terms

cabinet government	judicial review	parliamentary sovereignty
constitutional monarchy	Keynesianism	quangos
foreign direct investment	laissez-faire	special relationship
fusion of powers	macroeconomic policy	unitary state
hegemonic power	monetarism	welfare state
hung parliament	neoliberalism	Westminster model
Industrial Revolution	parliamentary democracy	

Suggested Readings

Bogdanor, Vernon. *The Coalition and the Constitution.* Oxford: Hart, 2011.

Brown, Gordon. *Beyond the Crash: Overcoming the First Crisis of Globalization.* New York: Free Press, 2010.

Elliott, Francis, and James Hanning. *Cameron: The Rise of the New Conservative.* Harper: 2009.

Flinders, Matthew V. *The Oxford Handbook of British Politics.* Oxford: Oxford University Press, 2011.

Howell, Chris. *Trade Unions and the State: The Construction of Industrial Relations Institutions in Britain, 1890–2000*. Princeton: Princeton University Press, 2005.

Kumar, Krishan. *The Making of English National Identity*. Cambridge: Cambridge University Press, 2003.

McLean, Iain. *Scotland's Choices: The Referendum and What Happens after It*. Edinburgh: Edinburgh University Press, 2013.

Modood, Tariq. *Multicultural Politics: Racism, Ethnicity, and Muslims in Britain*. Minneapolis: University of Minnesota Press, 2005.

Modood, Tariq. *Still Not Easy Being British: Struggles for a Multicultural Citizenship*. Stoke-on-Trent, UK: Trentham, 2010.

Parekh, Bhiku, et al., *The Future of Multi-Ethnic Britain: The Parekh Report*. London: Profile Books, 2000.

Thompson, E. P. *The Making of the English Working Class*. New York: Vintage, 1966.

Thompson, Noel. *Political Economy and the Labour Party*, 2nd ed. London and New York: Routledge, 2006.

Suggested Websites

The official UK government website
www.direct.gov.uk

The UK Parliament
www.parliament.uk

BBC
www.bbc.co.uk

The UK cabinet office
www.cabinet-office.gov.uk

Ipsos-Market & Opinion Research International (Mori)
Britain's leading polling organization
http://www.ipsos-mori.com/

The Scottish Parliament
www.scottish.parliament.uk

The Welsh Assembly Government
http://wales.gov.uk/

3 The United States

Louis DeSipio

Official Name: United States of America

Location: North America, between Canada and Mexico

Capital City: Washington, D.C.

Population (2014): 318.9 million

Size: 9,826,630 sq. km.; about half the size of South America; slightly larger than China

AP Images/Moshe Bursuker

© Cengage Learning®

THE MAKING OF THE MODERN AMERICAN STATE

Barack Obama's election in 2008 saw the largest presidential victory margin in recent elections (a margin not repeated in 2012). His 2008 victory was accompanied by increases in the size of the Democratic majorities in the U.S. House and Senate. Having one party in control of both houses of Congress and the presidency was unusual in contemporary politics. The sizes of Democratic majorities in the House and Senate were also substantial. Obama used these majorities to pass a series of major bills including two economic stimulus bills, the Affordable Care Act (ACA) (discussed later), civil rights legislation focusing on workplace discrimination, and reform of the financial services industry. The Senate also confirmed two members of the U.S. Supreme Court nominated by President Obama.

The 2010 and 2012 elections changed the balance of political power in Washington and reduced the likelihood that the Obama administration would be able to continue to promote its agenda. Democratic losses in 2010 in the U.S. House gave control of that body to the Republicans. Democrats maintained a slight majority in the U.S. Senate, but not a sufficient majority to overcome Republican filibusters (a parliamentary procedure to slow debate) on major issues. The divided government of the period after 2010 is more the norm in contemporary U.S. politics and limits the ability of the United States to execute its responsibilities among the globalized world of states or to its own citizens.

Focus Questions ▽

- Based on your reading of the issues that led to the previous critical outcomes and their resolutions, what do you think will be the trigger of the next critical juncture and its outcome?

- How does geographic setting shape the governing structures that have emerged in the United States over the past 225 years?

Politics in Action

In 2013, the U.S. federal government shut down for sixteen days and ceased most of its routine activities. This shutdown resulted from the failure of the U.S. Congress to fulfill its constitutional responsibility and pass an appropriations bill to fund the federal government for the president's review. This failure resulted from a deep-seated disagreement between the Republican-controlled U.S. House of Representatives and the Democrat-controlled U.S. Senate. In the past, most disagreements like this were resolved with short-term appropriations bills that allowed the government to continue to operate while Congress worked out its differences. In 2013, however, some Republican leaders—including members of the Tea Party caucus (discussed later)—felt that it was better to pass no bill and shut down the government than to compromise with Democrats and the president.

Such behavior made little sense to many in the United States. The president's approval ratings improved throughout the shutdown. It made even less sense to U.S. allies and other nations who look to the United States for global military and economic leadership. During the shutdown, U.S. embassies and consulates had to partially close and U.S. economic support for other countries stopped.

After sixteen days, cooler heads prevailed and Congress passed an appropriations bill. Although there were certainly some short-term economic costs to the country and the global economy from the congressional bickering, the long-term consequence is probably greater. The United States showed how the design of U.S. national government is structured to impede policy-making, particularly in political eras like the present in which the division between the two parties is narrow. With the shutdown,

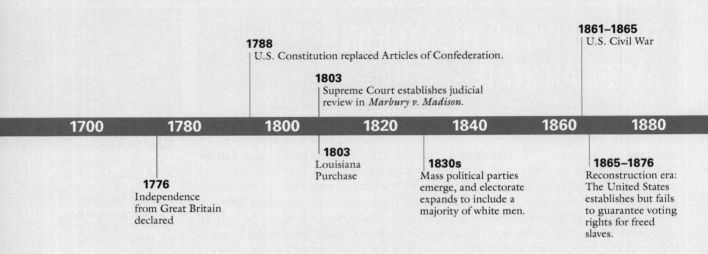

1788
U.S. Constitution replaced Articles of Confederation.

1803
Supreme Court establishes judicial review in *Marbury v. Madison*.

1861–1865
U.S. Civil War

1700　1780　1800　1820　1840　1860　1880

1776
Independence from Great Britain declared

1803
Louisiana Purchase

1830s
Mass political parties emerge, and electorate expands to include a majority of white men.

1865–1876
Reconstruction era: The United States establishes but fails to guarantee voting rights for freed slaves.

the United States sent a signal to its own citizens and the world that it cannot always be relied upon to fulfill its role as a global leader. A longer shutdown would undoubtedly have had a more profoundly negative effect on the global economy and the authority with which the United States can speak on international affairs.

For many in the United States, the effect was somewhat more muted because of another feature in the constitutional design—**federalism**. The primary contact between most U.S. residents and government is with their state and local governments. Federalism is a system of governance with twin sovereigns—the federal government and state governments in the case of the United States. A short-term shutdown of the federal government does not lead to any change in the activities of state governments. A longer-term shutdown would likely impede state government functioning as in implementing many federal programs and expecting the federal government to pay for these programs, something it could not do if shutdown.

Geographic Setting

The United States occupy nearly half of North America. Its only two neighbors, Mexico and Canada, do not present a military threat and are linked in a comprehensive trade agreement: the North American Free Trade Agreement (NAFTA). U.S. territory is rich in natural resources, arable land, navigable rivers, and protected ports. This abundance has led Americans to assume they will always have enough resources to meet national needs. Finally, the United States has always had low population densities and has served as a magnet for international migration.

European colonization led to the eventual unification of the territory that became the United States under one government and the expansion of that territory from the Atlantic to the Pacific Oceans. This process began in the early 1500s and reached its peak in the nineteenth century, when rapid population expansion was reinforced by an imperialist national ideology (**manifest destiny**) to expand all the way to the Pacific. Native Americans were pushed aside. The United States experimented with colonialism around 1900, annexing Hawaii, Guam, the Northern Marianas Islands, and Puerto Rico.

Puerto Rico is a colony of the United States with limited autonomy in trade and foreign policy. Puerto Ricans are U.S. citizens by birth and can travel freely to the

federalism

A system of governance in which political authority is shared between the national government and regional or state governments. The powers of each level of government are usually specified in a federal constitution.

manifest destiny

The public philosophy in the nineteenth century that the United States was not only entitled but also destined to occupy territory from the Atlantic to the Pacific.

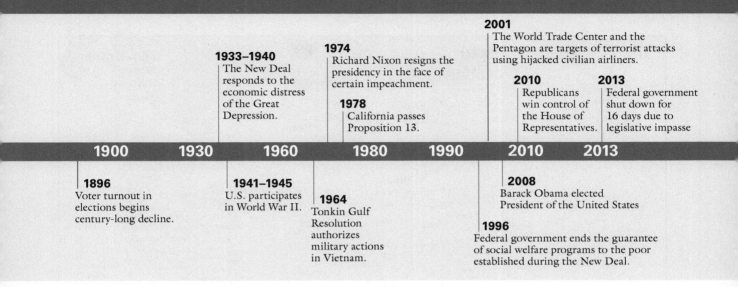

1933–1940
The New Deal responds to the economic distress of the Great Depression.

1974
Richard Nixon resigns the presidency in the face of certain impeachment.

1978
California passes Proposition 13.

2001
The World Trade Center and the Pentagon are targets of terrorist attacks using hijacked civilian airliners.

2010
Republicans win control of the House of Representatives.

2013
Federal government shut down for 16 days due to legislative impasse

1900   1930   1960   1980   1990   2010   2013

1896
Voter turnout in elections begins century-long decline.

1941–1945
U.S. participates in World War II.

1964
Tonkin Gulf Resolution authorizes military actions in Vietnam.

2008
Barack Obama elected President of the United States

1996
Federal government ends the guarantee of social welfare programs to the poor established during the New Deal.

United States. Although some in Puerto Rico seek independence, most want either a continuation of Commonwealth status or statehood. Guam is an "unincorporated territory" (a U.S. territory that is not on the road to statehood and does not have all of the protections of the U.S. Constitution).

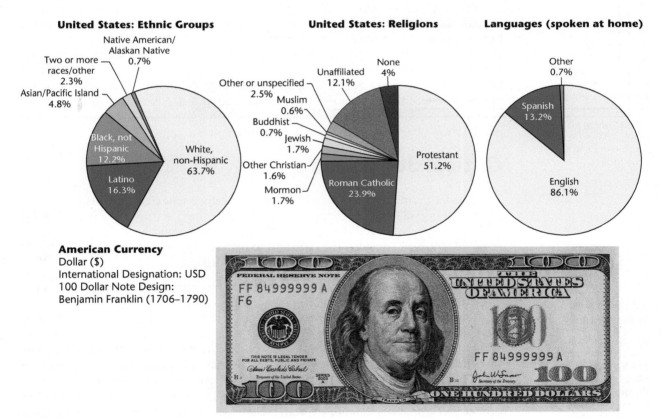

United States: Ethnic Groups
- Native American/Alaskan Native 0.7%
- Two or more races/other 2.3%
- Asian/Pacific Island 4.8%
- Black, not Hispanic 12.2%
- Latino 16.3%
- White, non-Hispanic 63.7%

United States: Religions
- None 4%
- Unaffiliated 12.1%
- Other or unspecified 2.5%
- Muslim 0.6%
- Buddhist 0.7%
- Jewish 1.7%
- Other Christian 1.6%
- Mormon 1.7%
- Roman Catholic 23.9%
- Protestant 51.2%

Languages (spoken at home)
- Other 0.7%
- Spanish 13.2%
- English 86.1%

American Currency
Dollar ($)
International Designation: USD
100 Dollar Note Design:
Benjamin Franklin (1706–1790)

FIGURE 3.1 The American Nation at a Glance

© Sai Yeung Chan/Shutterstock.com (for photo)

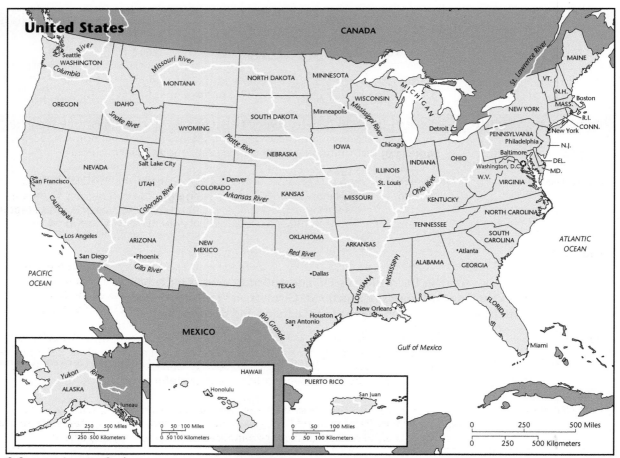

© Cengage Learning®

Critical Junctures

The first four critical junctures in U.S. political history appeared at points when mass discontent organized itself enough to change governing institutions or relationships. Each juncture challenged dominant ideas about who should have a voice in democratic government and what the relationship between government and citizen should be. Four periods of focused popular demand are explored here:

1. From the beginning of the American Revolution through the ratification of the Constitution and Bill of Rights
2. The Civil War and Reconstruction
3. The New Deal
4. The contemporary period of routinely divided national government and frequent shifts in which party controlled the presidency, the Senate, and the House of Representatives that began with the 1968 national elections

The Revolutionary Era (1773–1789)

Mass and elite discontent with British colonial rule sparked the American Revolution and the signing of the **Declaration of Independence**. Mass interests wanted to keep

Declaration of Independence

The document asserting that the British colonies in what is now the United States had declared themselves independent from Great Britain. The Declaration of Independence was signed in Philadelphia on July 4, 1776.

Table 3.1	Political Organization
Political System	Presidential system.
Regime History	Representative democracy, usually dated from the signing of the Declaration of Independence (1776) or the Constitution (1787).
Administrative Structure	Federalism, with powers shared between the national government and the fifty state governments; separation of powers at the level of the national government among legislative, executive, and judicial branches.
Executive	President, "directly" elected (with Electoral College that officially elects president and vice president) for four-year term; the cabinet is an advisory group of heads of major federal agencies and other senior officials selected by president to aid in decision making but with no formal authority.
Legislature	Bicameral. Congress composed of a lower house (House of Representatives) of 435 members serving two-year terms and an upper house (Senate) of 100 members (two from each state) serving six-year terms; elected in single-member districts (or, in the case of the Senate, states) by simple plurality (some states require a majority of voters).
Judiciary	Supreme Court with nine justices nominated by president and confirmed by Senate, with life tenure; has specified original and appellate jurisdiction and exercises the power of judicial review (can declare acts of the legislature and executive unconstitutional and therefore null and void).
Party System	Essentially two-party system (Republican and Democrat), with relatively weak and fractionalized parties; more than in most representative democracies, the personal following of candidates remains very important.

government close to home, in each colony, and wanted each colony to have substantial independence from the others. Elite interests advocated a national government with control over foreign policy, national assumption of state Revolutionary War debts, and the ability to establish national rules for commerce.

Mass interests won the first round of this battle. From 1777 to 1788, the **Articles of Confederation** governed the nation. Because the national government could not implement foreign or domestic policy, raise taxes, or regulate trade between the states without the cooperation of the individual states, elite interests gained support for replacing the Articles with the Constitution. The limited powers of the national government under the Articles rested in a legislature, but the states had to ratify most key decisions. States also established their own foreign policies, often different from each other. They also established their own fiscal policies and financed state budgets through extensive borrowing.

The Constitution maintained most power with the states but granted the federal (or national) government authority over commerce and foreign and military policy. It also gave the federal government a source of financing independent of the states. And, most important, it created a president, who had powers independent of the legislature. The Constitution delegated specific, but limited, powers to the national government. These included establishing post offices and roads, coining money, promoting the progress of science, raising and supporting an army and a navy, and

Articles of Confederation

The first governing document of the United States, agreed to in 1777 and ratified in 1781. The Articles concentrated most powers in the states and made the national government dependent on voluntary contributions of the states.

establishing a uniform rule of naturalization. These powers (Article I, Section 8 of the Constitution) tended to give the federal government the power to create a national economy. Finally, the Constitution limited citizens' voice in government. Presidents were elected indirectly, through the Electoral College, a body of political insiders from each state who are elected on election day and meet the following month to formally elect the president. Members of the Senate were originally elected by state legislatures. Only the members of the House of Representatives were elected by the people, but the states determined who could vote for members of the House. At first, only property-holding men held the vote in most states. By the 1840s, most white adult men could vote. Women did not receive voting rights nationally until 1920.

As popular support for ratifying the Constitution grew, many who had supported the Articles of Confederation made a new demand: The newly drafted U.S. Constitution should include enumerated protections for individuals from governmental power. Meeting this demand for a **Bill of Rights** was necessary to ensure the ratification of the Constitution. Because federal judges had to interpret these rights, the federal courts later played a growing role in the national government, particularly in the twentieth century.

Bill of Rights

The first ten amendments to the U.S. Constitution (ratified in 1791), which established limits on the actions of government. Initially, the Bill of Rights limited only the federal government. The Fourteenth Amendment and subsequent judicial rulings extended the provisions of the Bill of Rights to the states.

The Civil War and Reconstruction (1861–1876)

The morality of slavery convulsed the nation before the war, but the war itself began over the question of whether the states or the national government should be dominant. Many states believed they could reject specific federal laws. Any time Congress threatened to pass legislation to restrict slavery in the South, one or more southern state legislatures would threaten to nullify it. Many believed that if any state could nullify federal laws, the union would be put at risk. The Civil War resolved this issue in favor of the indivisibility of the union. The war also established an enforceable national citizenship to supplement state citizenship, which had existed even before the Constitution.[1] Establishing national citizenship began a slow process that culminated in the New Deal, as citizens looked to the federal government to meet their basic needs in times of national crisis.

To establish full citizenship for the freed slaves, Congress revisited the question of individual liberties and citizenship. These post–Civil War debates on the relationship of citizens to the national government established several important principles in the Fourteenth Amendment to the Constitution (1868). First, it extended the protections of the Bill of Rights to cover actions by states as well as by the federal government. Second, it extended citizenship to all persons born in the United States. This made U.S. citizens of freed slaves and also guaranteed that U.S.-born children of immigrants who migrated would become U.S. citizens at birth. Third, Congress sought to establish some federal regulation of voting and to grant the vote to African Americans. When the federal government failed to continue enforcing black voting rights, African Americans, particularly in the South, could not routinely exercise the vote until the Voting Rights Act in 1965. These fundamental guarantees that ensure electoral opportunities today limit prerogatives recognized as the states' responsibilities in the Constitution.

The New Deal Era (1933–1940)

The third critical juncture in U.S. political development was the New Deal, the Roosevelt administration's response to the economic crisis of the Great Depression. The federal government tapped its constitutional powers to regulate interstate commerce in order to vastly expand federal regulation of business. It also established a nationally guaranteed safety net, which included such programs as **Social Security** to provide monthly payments to the elderly who had worked and programs to provide housing for the working poor and food subsidies for children in poor households. The federal government also subsidized agriculture and protected farmers against the cyclical nature of demand. The legislative and judicial battles to establish such policies represent a fundamental expansion of the role of the federal government.

The federal government now asserted dominance over the states in delivering services to the people. Equally important, during the New Deal the presidency asserted dominance over the Congress in policy-making. The New Deal president, Franklin D. Roosevelt, found powers that no previous president had exercised. All post–New Deal presidents remain much more powerful than any of their predecessors, except perhaps for Abraham Lincoln, who served during the Civil War. Beginning in the 1960s, however, Congress began to challenge growth in executive power. Although the New Deal programs represented a significant change from the policies that preceded the Great Depression, they also reflected underlying American political values (see Section 4). Even in the New Deal era, class-based politics was kept to a minimum.

As the Depression came to a close, the United States geared up for its involvement in World War II. Although the United States had previously been involved in international conflicts beyond its borders, the experience of World War II was different at the beginning of U.S. involvement and at the end. The United States entered the war after U.S. territory was attacked. After the war, the United States was at the center of a multilateral strategy to contain the Soviet Union.

Divided Government, Frequently Shifting Partisan Dominance, and Political Contestation of the Scope of Government (1968 to the Present)

The fourth critical juncture, which began with the 1968 presidential election, is ongoing today. This critical juncture has two dimensions. First, the national government has been routinely divided between the two political parties with dominance of each branch of government shifting regularly. This division exacerbates the inefficiency that was designed into the American constitutional order and increases popular distrust of government (see Section 3).

In 1968 Richard Nixon (a California Republican) became president. Through Nixon's term and that of his Republican successor, Gerald Ford, the Democrats maintained control of both houses of Congress. In the period since 1968, one of the parties has controlled the presidency, the U.S. Senate, *and* the U.S. House of Representatives only five times. The Democrats controlled all three from 1977 to 1980, from 1993 to 1994, and from 2009 to 2010. The Republicans controlled all three from late January to June 2001 and again from 2003 to 2007. One party has replaced the other in the presidency five times since 1968. This division of the federal government between the parties and the routine shift in party control of the Congress or the presidency slow government response to controversial policy issues.

The second ongoing dimension of the contemporary critical juncture emerges from the apparent inefficiency caused by divided government. Many in the United States began to question the steady increase in the scope of governmental services. The electoral roots of this popular discontent can be found in the passage of Proposition 13 by California voters in 1978, which limited California's ability to increase **property taxes**.

Social Security

National systems of contributory and noncontributory benefits to provide assistance for the elderly, sick, disabled, unemployed, and others similarly in need of assistance. The specific coverage of social security, a key component of the welfare state, varies by country.

property taxes

Taxes levied by local governments on the assessed value of property. Property taxes are the primary way in which local jurisdictions in the United States pay for the costs of primary and secondary education. Because the value of property varies dramatically from neighborhood to neighborhood, the funding available for schools—and the quality of education—also varies from place to place.

The passage of Proposition 13 began an era that continues today, in which many citizens reject the expansion of government.

Popular discontent in the contemporary era is not limited to taxes; it also focuses on the scope of government. This period saw popular mobilization to reshape government's involvement in "values" issues, such as abortion, same-sex marriage, and the role of religion. Advocates on all sides of these issues want government to protect their interests, while condemning government for allegedly promoting the interests of groups with opposing positions. Ultimately, the courts become the venue to shape government policies on social issues.

While divided government had become the norm in 1968, the division became even more razor thin in the late 1990s. Each election raises the possibility of a switch in partisan control of the Senate or the House and the intense focus of both parties and **interest groups** on winning the handful of seats that could switch from one party to the other.

interest groups

Organizations that seek to represent the interests—usually economic—of their members in dealings with the government. Important examples are associations representing people with specific occupations, business interests, racial and ethnic groups, or age groups in society.

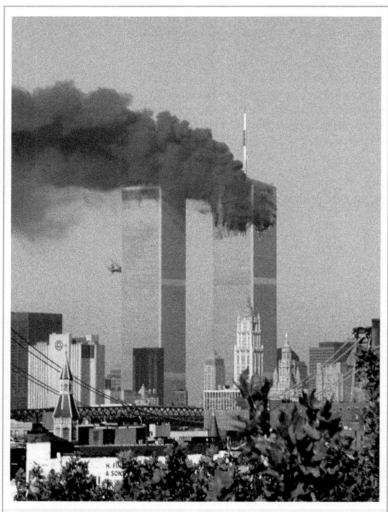

A jet crashes into the World Trade Center on September 11, 2001.
Source: AP Images/Moshe Bursuker.

September 11, 2001, and Its Aftermath

It is in this environment that the United States responded to the terrorist attacks of September 11. Initially, Congress and the populace rallied behind the president to increase the scope of federal law enforcement powers and to provide financial assistance for New York City, the families of the victims of the attack, and the airlines.

Popular support for President Bush and his administration's initial efforts to respond to the challenges of September 11 continued as the administration prepared for an invasion of Afghanistan. The United States also experienced a period of international support immediately following the September 11, 2001, attacks. In addition to immediate offers of humanitarian assistance, initial U.S. military responses to the attacks won widespread backing around the world.

The initial domestic cohesion and international support for the United States dissipated quickly. U.S. efforts to extend the war on terrorism to Iraq became the focus of many of the objections to growing U.S. power and unilateralism in international affairs.

Domestically, Bush saw steadily declining popular support. A sizeable minority of the U.S. population opposed the U.S. invasion of Iraq without the support of the United Nations or other international bodies. This opposition grew in the period after the military phase of the war ended when it became evident that the peace would be harder fought than the war. Bush's policies and overall stridency in domestic and foreign policy returned the country to the near-even partisan division that had characterized the country in the 1990s.

The Four Themes and the United States

The United States in a Globalized World of States

The constitutional structure of the U.S. government may now be at a disadvantage relative to other governing systems that can react more quickly and decisively to societal needs and shifts in public opinion. In parliamentary systems, even when they are burdened by the compromises necessary to maintain coalition governments, prime ministers can exercise power in a way that a U.S. president or Congress can never expect to do. In the United States, elections are held on a regular cycle, regardless of the popularity of the president. The presidency and Congress are routinely controlled by the two opposing parties. Federalism further slows government action.

Until the New Deal and World War II, the United States pursued a contradictory policy toward the rest of the world of states: It sought isolation from international politics but unfettered access to international markets. World War II changed the first of these stances, at least at elite levels (see Section 2): The United States sought to shape international relations through multilateral organizations and military force. It designed the multilateral organizations so that it could have a disproportionate voice (for example, in the United Nations Security Council). With the end of the Cold War, some now call for a reduced role of the U.S. government in the world of states or, at a minimum, a greater willingness to use a unilateral response to international military crises. This decline in mass interest in the U.S. role in the world among some U.S. citizens in the decade since the 9/11 attacks and the wars in Iraq and Afghanistan reflects the fact that foreign policy has never been central to the evolution of U.S. politics and governance.

Governing the Economy

The conflict between the president and Congress, the centralization of federal power in the twentieth century, and the growing concern about the cost and scope of government represent the central challenge to predicting the future direction of U.S. politics. Each part of this conflict speaks to questions of how much the United States and the states should regulate the economy. There will be no quick resolution; the Constitution slows resolution by creating a system of federalism and **separation of powers** (see Section 3).

The federal government and the states have sought to manage the economy by building domestic manufacturing, exploiting the nation's natural resources, and regulating the banking sector, while interfering little in the conduct of business (see Section 2). This hands-off attitude toward economic regulation can come at a price.

The Democratic Idea

The democratic idea in the U.S. context was one of an indirect, representative democracy with checks on democratically elected leaders. The emergence of a

separation of powers

An organization of political institutions within the state in which the executive, legislature, and judiciary have autonomous powers and no one branch dominates the others. This is the common pattern in presidential systems, as opposed to parliamentary systems, in which there is a fusion of powers.

strong national government after the New Deal era meant that national coalitions could often focus their demands on a single federal government, rather than always having to target a host of state governments as well. The decline in mediating institutions that can channel these demands reduces the ability of individual citizens to influence the national government (see Section 4). In the contemporary era, however, many in U.S. society challenge the size and scope of the federal government and seek a return to the state-focused polity that characterized the United States before the New Deal.

The Politics of Collective Identity

As a nation of immigrants, the United States must unite immigrants and descendants of immigrants from Europe, Africa, Latin America, and Asia with the established U.S. population. Previous waves of immigrants experienced only one to two generations of political and societal exclusion. Whether today's immigrants (particularly those who enter the United States without legal immigrant status) experience the same relatively rapid acculturation remains an open question. Preliminary evidence indicates that the process may be even quicker for immigrants who possess skills and education but slower for those who do not.[2] The United States has never fully remedied its longest-lasting difference in collective identities with full economic and political incorporation of African Americans, which was central to the Civil War and Reconstruction era and remains a challenge to today's U.S. politics.

Themes and Comparisons

single-member-plurality (SMP) electoral system

An electoral system in which candidates run for a single seat from a specific geographic district. The winner is the person who receives the most votes, whether or not they amount to a majority. SMP systems, unlike systems of proportional representation, increase the likelihood that two national coalition parties will form.

Scholars of U.S. politics have always had to come to terms with the idea of American exceptionalism—the idea that the United States is unique and cannot easily be compared to other countries. In several respects, the United States *could* be considered exceptional: Its geography and natural resources offer it advantages that few other nations can match; its experience with mass representative democracy is longer than that of other nations; it has been able to expand the citizenry beyond the descendants of the original citizens; and U.S. society has been much less divided by class than have the societies of other states.[3]

The U.S. Constitution, for all of its limitations, has served as the model for the constitutions of many newly independent nations. Some form of separation of powers (see Section 3) has become the norm in democratic states. Similarly, district-based and **single-member-plurality (SMP) electoral systems** (see Section 4) have been widely adapted to reduce conflict in multiethnic states, of which the United States was the first large-scale example. Through its active role in multilateral institutions, the United States also attempts to impose its will on other nations.

Where Do You Stand?

The balance between the powers of the federal and state governments has shifted considerably. Where should the balance of power rest for different government responsibilities?

Can the United States afford to continue to be the world's policeman?

POLITICAL ECONOMY AND DEVELOPMENT

State and Economy

When national leaders present the accomplishments of the United States, they often claim that by governing the economy less, the United States allows the private economy to thrive. In this simplified version of this story, the private sector is the engine of national growth, and this private sector is most successful when left alone by government. Economic success, then, is tied to the **free market**—*the absence of government regulation* and the opportunity for entrepreneurs to build the nation's economy.

Relative to other advanced democracies, the U.S. economy is much less regulated. The U.S. government has traditionally taken a laissez-faire attitude toward economic actors. This absence of regulation allowed for the creation and expansion of many new types of production that subsequently spread throughout the world, but it also can come at a cost. U.S. policy-makers cede power to private actors who are not concerned with the impact of their activities on the broader economy, such as the mortgage lenders who built the subprime lending industry or the investment banks that bought the subprime loans.

The Constitution reserves for the federal government authority to regulate *inter*-state commerce and commerce with foreign nations. As a result, state and local governments are limited in their ability to shape the economy. Over time, however, states have established the ability to regulate workplace conditions as part of their **police powers** or of jurisdiction over public health and safety.

Except for agriculture, higher education, and some defense-related industries, the size of various sectors of the economy is almost entirely the result of the free market. The federal government does try to incubate some new industries, but it primarily uses grants to private agencies—often universities—to accomplish this end. The United States also occasionally supports ailing industries.

Since the New Deal, the federal government has guaranteed minimum prices for most agricultural commodities and has sought to protect agriculture by paying farmers to leave some land fallow. It has also considerably reduced the costs of production and risks associated with agriculture by providing subsidized crop insurance, canals and aqueducts to transport water, and flood control projects. It has subsidized the sale of U.S. agricultural products abroad and purchased some surplus agricultural production for storage and distribution in the United States. Although a less explicit form of subsidy, weak regulation of U.S. immigration laws has ensured a reliable, inexpensive labor supply.

The federal government has also limited its own ability to regulate the economy. With the formation of the **Federal Reserve Board** in 1913, it removed control of the money supply from elected officeholders. Today, unelected leaders on the Federal Reserve Board, many with ties to the banking industry, control the volume of money in the economy and the key interest rates that determine the rates at which banks lend money to businesses and individuals. As the United States slid toward recession in 2008, the Federal Reserve was the central U.S. policy-making agency seeking to avert recession. It provided direct subsidies and low-cost loans to banks, allowing

free market

A system in which government regulation of the economy is absent or limited. Relative to other advanced democracies, the United States has traditionally had less market regulation.

police powers

Powers that are traditionally held by the states to regulate public safety and welfare. Police powers are the form of interaction with government that citizens most often experience. Even with the growth in federal government powers in the twentieth century, police powers remain the primary responsibility of the states and localities.

Federal Reserve Board

The U.S. central bank established by Congress in 1913 to regulate the banking industry and the money supply. Although the president appoints the chair of the board of governors (with Senate approval), the board operates largely independently.

them to survive. The Federal Reserve also purchased government bonds owned by banks to keep interest rates low in the expectation that the banks would use their newly available cash to lend to private borrowers. Congressional challenges to the Federal Reserve's autonomy raise concerns among other nations that the United States will be less able to act as a global banker and lender of last resort in the future.

The U.S. government does not regulate the flow of capital. As a result, many large U.S.-based firms have evolved into multinational corporations, removing themselves from a great deal of U.S. government regulation and taxation.

It is important to recognize that from the nation's earliest days, the federal government promoted agriculture and industry, spurred exports, and (more recently) sought to stabilize the domestic and international economy. These promotional efforts included tariffs, which sought to disadvantage products that competed with U.S. manufactures; roads and canals, so that U.S.-produced goods could be brought to market cheaply and quickly; the distribution of federally owned lands in the West to individuals and to railroads, so that the land could contribute to national economic activity; and large-scale immigration, so that capital would have people to produce and consume goods (see Section 3). Efforts to promote U.S. industry often came at the expense of individual citizens, who are less able to organize and make demands of government. Tariffs, for example, kept prices high for domestic consumers.

Through much of the nation's history, the United States used its diplomatic and military resources to establish and maintain markets for U.S.-produced commodities and manufactured goods abroad. The United States, for example, uses its position in the world economy and on multilateral lending institutions to open markets, provide loans for nations facing economic distress, and protect some U.S.-produced goods from foreign competition. Despite national rhetoric to the contrary, the United States has consistently promoted economic development, though not by regulating production or spurring specific industries.

The U.S. economy has increasingly come to rely on two unintentional forms of international subsidy. First, it has built up a steadily increasing international trade deficit. In other words, the United States has bought much more abroad than it has sold. Although some aspects of these trade deficits could well reflect a strength in the U.S. economy (for example, being able to purchase goods produced inexpensively abroad), continuing deficits of this level act as a downward pressure on the U.S. dollar (see Figure 3.2). Slowing this downward pressure for the time being is

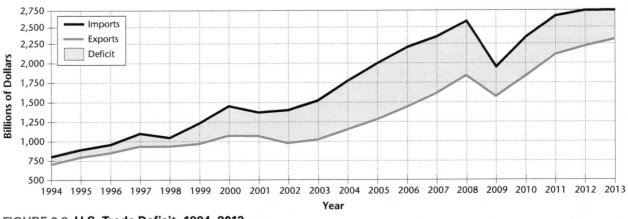

FIGURE 3.2 U.S. Trade Deficit, 1994–2013

Source: U.S. Bureau of the Census. 2014. "U.S. Trade in Goods and Services—Balance of Payments (BOP) Basis," http://www.census.gov/foreign-trade/statistics/historical/gands.pdf (accessed March 9, 2014).

the second form of international subsidy: The U.S. dollar is the international reserve currency. This means that many nations and individual investors keep their reserves (their savings) in dollars. By doing this, they keep demand for the dollar up, reducing the downward pressure that comes from trade deficits. The euro, the European common currency, however, is increasingly serving as a reserve currency. The long-term stability of the U.S. economy and the value of the dollar as a reserve currency are being challenged by an increasing national debt (discussed later in this chapter) and market concerns about unfunded liabilities in federal and state pension, health care, and insurance programs.

In the twentieth century, the U.S. government took on new responsibilities to protect citizens and to tax businesses, in part, to provide government-mandated services for workers. The government also expanded regulation of workplace safety, pension systems, and other worker–management relations issues (see Section 3). Despite this expansion of the government role in providing protections to workers, the United States offers fewer guarantees to its workers than do other advanced democracies.

The public sector has traditionally been smaller in the United States than in other advanced democracies. Nevertheless, the U.S. government and the states conduct activities that many believe could be better conducted by the private sector. The federal government operates hospitals for veterans, provides water and electrical power to Appalachian states, manages lands in the West and Alaska, runs the civilian air traffic control system, and, after September 11, manages passenger and luggage screening at commercial airports. Roads have traditionally been built and maintained by the state and federal governments, and waterways have been kept navigable (and open to recreational use) by the federal government.

Often left out of the story of the development of the U.S. economy is the role of its natural resources and the environment. The nation's territory is diverse in terms of natural resources and environments, stretching from tropical to arctic. The territory includes arable land that can produce more than enough year round for the domestic market as well as for extensive exports. The United States has protected ports and navigable rivers, and few enemies can challenge U.S. control over these transportation resources. For more than a century, it was able to expand trade while not investing in a large standing military to defend its trade routes.

Society and Economy

The United States adheres more strictly to its laissez-faire ideology in terms of the outcomes of the economic system. The distribution of income and wealth is much more unequal in the United States than in other advanced democracies, and that gap has been steadily widening over the past 30 years. In 2012, the top 5 percent alone earned more than 22.3 percent of the total amount earned (see Figure 3.3). Wide differences exist between women and men and between racial groups. Women, on average, earned $14,000 annually less than men. Non-Hispanic whites earned an average of $44,000 in 2012 compared to $48,000 for Asian Americans, $31,000 for blacks, and $29,000 for Hispanics.

The United States has tolerated these conditions and sees them as an incentive for people at the lower end of the economic spectrum. Wealth and income have become more skewed since 1980. The mere mention in an election of the class implications of a policy, particularly tax policy, will usually lead to the charge of fomenting class warfare.

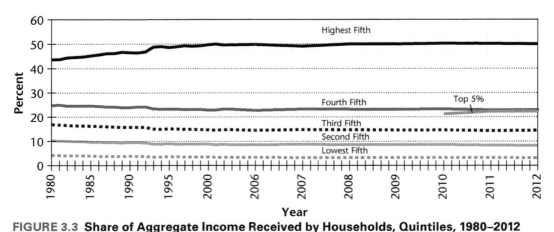

FIGURE 3.3 Share of Aggregate Income Received by Households, Quintiles, 1980–2012

Source: U.S. Bureau of the Census. 2013. "Historical Income Table—Households" Table H-2. Share of Aggregate Income Received by Each Fifth and Top 5 Percent of Households. http://www.census.gov/hhes /www/income/data/historical/household/index.html (accessed March 9, 2014).

Federal income taxation of individuals is progressive, with higher-income people paying a higher share of their income in taxes. Rates range from 0 percent for individuals with incomes less than $8,925 to 39.6 percent for individuals with incomes exceeding approximately $406,750. The progressive nature of federal taxes is reduced considerably by two factors. Upper-income taxpayers receive a much higher share of their income from investments, which are taxed at lower rates. Second, all taxpayers with salary income are subject to a regressive tax for Social Security and disability benefits. The tax for Social Security and Medicare is currently 7.65 percent paid by the worker and 7.65 percent paid by the employer. The Social Security share of this tax is imposed only on the first $117,000 of income and not at all on higher incomes.

State and local taxes tend to be much less progressive. Most states levy a sales tax. This is a flat tax, ranging between 2.9 and 8.25 percent depending on the state. Many states levy a state income tax. No state has an income tax that is as progressive as the federal income tax. The final major form of individual taxation is property taxes. Governments in the United States have increasingly supplemented taxes with user fees charged for the provision of specific services.

Thus, the gap between rich and poor in the United States is not remedied by progressive taxation. This gap might well have led to the emergence of class-based political movements, but immigration policy, which also promoted economic development, focused workers' attention away from class and toward cultural differences that reduced the salience of class divisions in U.S. society. Unions, which could also have promoted class-based politics and focused workers' attentions on income inequalities, have traditionally been weak in the United States. This weakness reflects individual-level antipathy toward unions, but also state and federal laws that limit the abilities of unions to organize and collectively bargain.

The U.S. economy could not have grown without the importation of immigrant labor. The United States has generally sought to remedy labor shortages with policies that encouraged migration. Today, the United States is one of just four countries that allow large-scale migration of those who do not already have a cultural tie to the receiving nation. Immigration to the United States numbers approximately 1,100,000 people annually, who immigrate under the provisions of the law to a permanent status that allows for eventual eligibility for U.S. citizenship (see Figure 3.4).[4]

Until the economy soured in 2008, these legal immigrants were joined by as many as 500,000 additional unauthorized migrants annually.[5]

Although the United States tolerates the unequal distribution of income and wealth, in the twentieth century, it intervened directly in the free market to establish protections for workers and, to a lesser degree, to guarantee the welfare of the most disadvantaged in the society. The programs for workers, which are primarily **distributive policies**, receive much more public support than do programs to assist the poor, which are primarily **redistributive policies**. Distributive policies allocate resources into an area that policy-makers perceive needs to be promoted without a significant impact on income or wealth distribution. Redistributive policies take resources from one person or group in society and allocate them to a more disadvantaged group in the society. Most worker benefits, such as health insurance, childcare, and pensions, are provided by private employers, if they are provided at all, but are regulated by the government.

Best known among the federal programs aimed toward workers is Social Security, which taxes workers and their employers to pay for benefits for retired and disabled workers (and nonworker spouses). In the past, retirees almost always received more than they had paid into the system (a form of intergenerational redistribution), but it will take significant reforms to guarantee that this outcome continues when today's workers reach retirement age. Actuarial estimates indicate that the Social Security Trust Fund will be exhausted in 2033 if there are no changes to the tax used to pay for Social Security or the benefit rates or age of eligibility. Medicare—the government health plan for the elderly—will run out of funds in 2024. The U.S. government faces the dilemma of having to lower benefits for each of these programs, raising taxes, or paying benefits out of general revenues. Changing the tax basis of Social Security and Medicare now (or lowering benefits now) would delay this point of reckoning.

distributive policies

Policies that allocate state resources into an area that lawmakers perceive needs to be promoted. For example, leaders today believe that students should have access to the Internet. In order to accomplish this goal, telephone users are being taxed to provide money for schools to establish connections to the Internet.

redistributive policies

Policies that take resources from one person or group in society and allocate them to a different, usually more disadvantaged, group. The United States has traditionally opposed redistributive policies to the disadvantaged.

[a]Until 1867, the federal government recorded as immigrants only people who arrived at seaports.

[b]These figures include recipients of legalization under the Immigration Reform and Control Act of 1986 who immigrated to the United States prior to 1982 but were recorded as having entered in the year in which they received permanent residence.

FIGURE 3.4 Immigration to the United States, 1821–2010

Source: Adopted from DeSipio, Louis, and Rodolfo O. de la Garza, *Making Americans/ Remaking America: Immigration* and Immigrant Policy (Boulder, CO: Westview Press, 1998), Table 2.1.

In 2010, in response to growing numbers of uninsured Americans and spiraling health care costs, Congress created a new national health care program for U.S. citizens and permanent residents—the Affordable Care Act. The ACA is largely distributive in nature with some additional subsidies (redistribution) for low-income individuals. It builds on the private health insurance that many Americans receive through their employers or unions. The ACA will not be fully implemented until 2020 at the earliest; it is controversial for several reasons. Some fear that it will undermine the incentive for employers, particularly small employers, to provide insurance. Governments would then have to provide a higher share of insurance and assume costs currently paid by employers. Others resent that government is not more central to the provision of insurance and that private insurance, with its overhead costs and quest for profits, will absorb health care expenditures that could go to providing better treatments. When the national health care bill was debated, some in Congress called for government to replace the role of private insurers (the so-called single-payer option). States are concerned that they will have to provide insurance to residents who are not otherwise able to get private insurance and that they will have to assume at least 10 percent of the costs of providing this insurance (the federal government will pay the rest). Finally, some feel that the new mandate that all Americans have health insurance or be fined violates the Constitution (the Supreme Court rejected this assertion in 2013).

The government also established a minimum wage and a bureaucratic mechanism to enforce this wage. Some states and localities have established higher minimum wages than the federal minimum wage.

The states regulate worker–employer relations through unemployment insurance and insurance against workplace injuries. Benefits and eligibility requirements vary dramatically by state, although the federal governmental mandates that all workers be eligible for twenty-six weeks of unemployment benefits (assuming the worker has been employed for more than six months).

Beginning in the 1930s, the United States also established social welfare programs to assist the economically disadvantaged. As one would expect in a system organized around the free market, these programs have never been as broad-based or as socially accepted as in other economies. The states administered these programs—which provide food, health care, housing assistance, some job training, and some cash assistance to the poor—with a combination of federal and state funds. Eligibility and benefit levels varied dramatically from state to state.

In today's economy, public benefits and public employment are increasingly limited to U.S. citizens. Over time, these policies could enhance differences between the non-Hispanic white and black populations, on the one hand, and ethnic groups with large shares of immigrants, such as Latinos and Asian Americans, on the other.

Both the federal and state governments are facing gaps between income and expenditures. The federal government can continue to run a large annual deficit. The sum of these deficits—the national debt—totals nearly $17.5 trillion. Most states do not have this option and must either raise revenues or cut services annually.

Deficits can have a salutary effect on the national economy during weak economic times because the federal government can more easily borrow and then spend this money to stimulate the economy and support individuals who are out of work. In the long run, however, this federal debt absorbs money that could be invested in private sector activities and will slow national economic growth. In 2014, the federal government will pay approximately $233 billion in interest on its debt, an amount that will increase considerably when interest rates rise.

Environmental Issues

One area in which the United States has taken a limited role in regulating the activities of private actors in the American economy is environmental regulation. When the environment first became an issue in international politics, the United States took aggressive action to clean the air and the nation's oceans and navigable waterways. In each of these regulatory areas, federal legislation had dramatic impacts. Emissions standards have made the air much healthier, even in the nation's most car-focused cities. Waterways that were dangerous to the touch are now open to swimming. New lands were added to the national park system.[6] The visible successes of the early environmental **regulations** reduced the salience of environmental issues. These 1970s-era environmental regulations have not been followed by a continuing national commitment to environmentalism.

The United States has fewer environmental regulations than other advanced democracies and has been less willing to engage in multilateral agreements on environmental issues than on issues such as international security and economic cooperation. The United States, for example, is a signatory to the Kyoto Protocols to limit climate change (primarily through the reduction of greenhouse gases), but the treaty was never ratified by the U.S. Senate and is nonbinding on the United States. At least nine U.S. states and 740 U.S. cities have passed emissions caps that broadly follow Kyoto guidelines (though often less rapidly than Kyoto would mandate). Unlike an international treaty, however, these state and city efforts can be amended with a majority vote in a legislature and are more difficult to enforce.

Early in his term, President Obama proposed "cap and trade" energy regulation that would have set limits on carbon emissions while allowing factories and other carbon emitters to sell unused carbon emissions to create incentives for conversion to renewable energy sources. Despite some early bipartisan support, this legislation ultimately failed, losing support from all Senate Republicans and some Democrats.

Environmental issues are not central to the agendas of either U.S. political party. In an era of routinely divided government (see Section 4), new legislation to protect the environment is unlikely to pass in the U.S. Congress. Using his executive authority, President Obama has expanded the number of national parks and wilderness areas.

regulations

The rules that explain the implementation of laws. When the legislature passes a law, it sets broad principles for implementation; how the law is actually implemented is determined by regulations written by executive branch agencies. The regulation-writing process allows interested parties to influence the eventual shape of the law in practice.

The United States in the Global Economy

Since colonial times, the United States has been linked to world trade. By the late twentieth century, the United States had vastly expanded its role in international finance and was an importer of goods produced abroad (often in low-wage countries that could produce goods less expensively than U.S. factories) as well as an exporter of agricultural products.

After World War II, the United States reversed its traditional isolationism to take a leading role in regulating the international economy. The increasing interdependence of global economies was the result, in part, of conscious efforts by world leaders at the end of World War II, through the Bretton Woods Agreement, to establish and fund multinational lending institutions. Chief among these institutions were the World Bank and the International Monetary Fund. Since their establishment in the 1940s, they have been supplemented by a network of international lending and regulatory agencies and regional trading agreements.

The United States is also part of regional trading networks, such as NAFTA with Canada and Mexico. After its passage, the United States also entered into an agreement with neighboring countries in the Caribbean to reduce tariffs on many goods.

The U.S. government plays a central role in the international political economy. It achieves this through its domination of international lending agencies and regional defense and trade organizations. But these efforts are ultimately limited by domestic politics. Thus, while presidents may promote an international agenda, Congress often limits the funding for international organizations. The United States then appears to many outside the country as a hesitant and sometimes resentful economic leader.

In recent years, another multilateral institution has emerged that can potentially challenge U.S. economic dominance. The European Union (EU) is much more than a trading alliance. It is an organization of twenty-seven European nations with growing international influence. Eighteen EU members share a common currency, the euro. As the euro came into widespread use, the dollar faced its first challenge in many years as the world's dominant trading currency.

The United States also funds binational international lending through such agencies as the Export-Import Bank and the Overseas Private Investment Corporation. These agencies make loans to countries and private businesses to purchase goods and services from U.S.-owned businesses. The United States also provides grants and loans to allies to further U.S. strategic and foreign policy objectives or for humanitarian reasons.

"Well, they look pretty undocumented to me."

Immigration has been central to the development of the United States economy from its earliest days. Native populations have long been suspicious of the newcomers.

J.B. Handelsman The New Yorker Collection/The Cartoon Bank

THE GLOBAL CONNECTION

Arizona SB 1070 and U.S. Relations with Mexico

Many issues divide the United States and Mexico: trade disputes, migration, drug smuggling and violence, and gun smuggling among others. In 2010, Arizona added to this list. Reflecting popular concerns over Congress's failure to reform immigration, it passed a law requiring police to verify the legal immigration status of people arrested or detained by the police. The law, SB 1070, also criminalized giving assistance to an unauthorized alien, such as allowing a unauthorized immigrant family member to live in your home.

Many in the United States were concerned by these requirements. Under the Constitution, regulation of immigration is an enumerated power of the federal government. Aside from this constitutional concern, many raised concerns of racial profiling. Would police in Arizona verify the legal status of all people detained or just of those who were Latino or Asian American? Mexico also objected

to SB 1070 asserting that its nationals will be subject to harassment in Arizona. In 2012, the Supreme Court held much of SB 1070 to be unconstitutional, but left in place provisions that allowed for immigration status checks during law enforcement activities.

Arizona's enactment of the law made it more difficult for the U.S. government to negotiate with Mexico on issues of joint importance. SB 1070 demonstrates the inherent difficulty in a federalist system for the making of foreign policy. Ultimately, the United States cannot prevent any state from passing legislation that can muddy binational relations.

MAKING CONNECTIONS Should the regulation of immigrants be a state responsibility like other police powers or federal responsibility related to the establishment of national immigration policy?

The United States has slowly, and grudgingly, adapted to a world where it can no longer simply assert its central role. Thus, the U.S. government and, more slowly, the American people have seen their problems and needs from a global perspective. The separation of powers between the executive and legislative branches, and the local constituencies of members of Congress, ensures continuing resistance to this new international role (see The Global Connection: Arizona SB 1070 and U.S. relations with Mexico).

Where Do You Stand?

What services and protections should the United States guarantee to each of its citizens?

The United States has seen its national debt grow dramatically over the past decade and will probably not be able to rely on borrowing at comparable levels in the future. Should taxes be raised to meet the level of federal expenditures or should programs be cut? If you believe that programs should be cut, which programs should be cut?

GOVERNANCE AND POLICY-MAKING

SECTION 3

Organization of the State

The U.S. Constitution was drafted in 1787 and ratified the following year. The Constitution established a central government that was independent of the states but left the states most of their preexisting powers (particularly police powers and public

▼ Focus Questions

- How have twentieth-century presidents been able to expand these powers of the presidency?

- Can citizens more effectively influence the policy-making process through anti-party movements like the Tea Party or through traditional mainstream party mobilization?

safety). Although it had limited powers, the new U.S. government exercised powers over commerce and foreign policy that were denied to the states.

The Constitution has been amended twenty-seven times since 1787. The first ten of these amendments (ratified in 1791) make up the Bill of Rights, the set of protections of individual rights that were a necessary compromise to ensure that the Constitution was ratified. The remaining seventeen amendments have extended democratic election practices and changed procedural deficiencies in the original Constitution that came to be perceived as inconsistent with democratic practice. Examples of amendments to extend democratic election practices are the extension of the vote to women and to citizens between the ages of eighteen and twenty (the Nineteenth and Twenty-Sixth Amendments, respectively) or the prohibition of poll taxes, a tax that had to be paid before an individual could vote (the Twenty-Fourth Amendment). Changes to procedural deficiencies included linking presidential and vice presidential candidates on a single ticket, replacing a system where the candidate with the most votes in the Electoral College won the presidency and the second-place candidate won the vice presidency (the Twelfth Amendment), and establishing procedures to replace a president who becomes incapacitated (the Twenty-Fifth Amendment).

Each amendment requires three-quarters of the states to agree to the change. Although the Constitution allows states to initiate amendments, all twenty-seven have resulted from amendments initially ratified by Congress. When Congress initiates an amendment to the Constitution, two-thirds of the members of the House and the Senate must vote in favor of the amendment before it is sent to the states. States set their own procedures for ratifying constitutional amendments

Two guiding principles anchor the American system of government: federalism and separation of powers.[7]

Federalism is the division of authority between multiple levels of government in the United States, between the federal and state governments. Separation of powers is an effort to set government against itself by vesting separate branches with independent powers so that any one branch cannot permanently dominate the others.

These two characteristics of American government—federalism and separation of powers—were necessary compromises to guarantee the ratification of the Constitution. They are more than compromises, however. They reflect a conscious desire by the constitutional framers to limit the federal government's ability to control citizens' lives. To limit what they perceived as an inevitable tyranny of majorities over numerical minorities, the framers designed a system that set each part of government against all the other parts. Each branch of the federal government could limit the independent action of the other two branches, and the federal government and the states could limit each other.

Federalism and separation of powers have a consequence that could not be fully anticipated by the framers of the Constitution: U.S. government is designed to be inefficient. Because each part of government is set against all others, policy-making is difficult. No single leader or branch of government can unequivocally dominate policy-making as the prime minister can in a parliamentary system. Although a consensus across branches of government can sometimes appear in times of national challenge, such as in the period immediately after the 9/11 attacks, this commonality of purpose quickly dissolves as each branch of government seeks to protect its prerogatives and position in the policy-making process.

Federalism establishes multiple sovereigns. A citizen of the United States is simultaneously a national citizen and a citizen of one of the states. Each citizen has responsibilities to each of these sovereigns and can be held accountable to the laws of each. Over the nation's history, the balance of power has shifted, with the federal government gaining power relative to the states, but to this day, states remain responsible for many parts of citizens' lives and act in these areas independently of the federal government.

Many powers traditionally reserved to the states have shifted to the federal government. The most rapid of these shifts occurred during the New Deal, when the federal government tapped its commerce regulation powers to create a wide range of programs to address the economic and social needs of the people. In part, the court challenges to the ACA focused on the questions of federalism: whether Congress had the authority to mandate individual health coverage or to require the states to establish insurance pools for their residents who could not buy insurance from private insurers as part of Congress's authority to regulate interstate commerce.

The second organizing principle of American government is separation of powers. Each of the three branches of the federal government—the executive, the legislative (see Section 4), and the judiciary—shares in the responsibilities of governing and has some oversight over the other branches. In order to enact a law, for example, Congress must pass the law, and the president must sign it. The president can block the action of Congress by vetoing the law. Congress can override the president's veto through a two-thirds vote in both houses of Congress. The courts can review the constitutionality of laws passed by Congress and signed by the president. Congress and the states acting in unison can reverse a Supreme Court ruling on the constitutionality of a law by passing a constitutional amendment by two-thirds votes in each house that is subsequently ratified by three-quarters of the states. The Senate must ratify senior appointments to the executive branch, including members of the cabinet, as well as federal judges. The president nominates these judges, and Congress sets their salaries and much of their jurisdiction (except in constitutional matters). In sum, separation of powers allows each branch to limit the others and prevents any one branch from carrying out its responsibilities without the others' cooperation. It also allows for the phenomenon of divided government in which different political parties control the executive and legislative branches of government. This complexity encourages an ongoing competition for political power.

The Executive

The Presidency

The American presidency has grown dramatically in power since the nation's first days. The president, who is indirectly elected, serves a fixed four-year term and is limited to two terms by a constitutional amendment ratified in 1951. The president is both head of state and head of government.

Through much of U.S. political history, the president was not at the center of the federal government. Quite the contrary: The Constitution established Congress as the central branch of government and relegated the president to a much more poorly defined role whose primary responsibilities are administering programs designed and funded by Congress. Even now, the structural weaknesses of the presidency remain. The president must receive ongoing support from Congress to implement his agenda. But the president cannot control Congress except to the degree that public opinion (and, to a much lesser degree, party loyalty) encourages members of Congress to support the president. U.S. presidents are far weaker than prime ministers in parliamentary systems; they can, however, stay in office long after they have lost popular support.

The president is the commander-in-chief of the military and may grant pardons, make treaties (with the approval of two-thirds of the Senate), and make senior appointments to the executive branch and to judicial posts (again with the Senate's concurrence). The president is required to provide an annual state of the union report to Congress and may call Congress into session. Finally, the president manages the bureaucracy, which at the time of the Constitution's ratification was small but has subsequently grown in size and responsibility. In terms of formal powers, the president is far weaker than Congress.

With one exception, presidents until the turn of the twentieth century did not add considerably to the delegated powers. The exception was Abraham Lincoln, who dominated Congress during the Civil War. His example was one that twentieth-century presidents followed. He became a national leader and was able to establish his own power base directly in the citizenry. Lincoln realized that each member of Congress depended on a local constituency (a district or state), and he labeled their activities as being local or sectional. Lincoln created a national power base for the presidency by presenting himself as the only national political leader, an important position during the Civil War. He had an advantage in being commander-in-chief during wartime; however, the foundation of his power was not the military but his connection to the people.

In the twentieth century, presidents discovered that they had a previously untapped resource. Beginning with Theodore Roosevelt, twentieth-century presidents used the office of the president as a bully pulpit to speak to the nation and propose public policies that met national needs. No member of Congress or the Senate could claim a similar national constituency.

Later in the twentieth century, presidents found a new power. As the role of the federal government expanded, they managed a much larger federal bureaucracy that provided services used by nearly all citizens. Thus, a program like Social Security connects most citizens to the executive branch. Beginning with the New Deal, presidents proposed programs that expanded the federal bureaucracy and, consequently, the connection between the people and the president. Some congressional opposition to the ACA focused on the creation of another program that linked the individual welfare of all Americans to an executive branch program.

Finally, twentieth-century presidents learned another important lesson from the experience of Abraham Lincoln. The president has an authority over the military that places the office at the center of policy-making in military and international affairs. Thus, in the period from World War II to the collapse of the Soviet Union, the presidency gained strength from the widely perceived need for a single decision-maker.

Although the presidency gained powers in the twentieth century, the office remains structurally weak relative to Congress. Presidential power is particularly undercut by the norm of divided government: Presidents have little power over Congresses controlled by the other party. Since Congress retains the power to appropriate funds, the president must ultimately yield to its will on the design and implementation of policy.

Until the election of Barack Obama, all presidents had been white men. All but one (John F. Kennedy) have been Protestant. In today's politics having served as a governor works to a candidate's advantage. Despite a common assumption, only four vice presidents have been elected to the presidency immediately at the end of their terms. It is more common for vice presidents to move to the presidency on the death of the president.

PROFILE

Barack Obama

Source: Official White House Photo by Pete Souza.

Barack Obama's 2008 and 2012 elections to the presidency surprised many observers of U.S. society and politics. Obama self-identifies as, and is understood to be, African American in a society that has persistently discriminated against blacks. Many observers felt that this would prevent many white Americans from supporting his candidacy. In the end, the majority of white voters opposed Obama, but his victory was sealed by strong support from African Americans, Latinos, and Asian Americans. Obama's African roots come from his father, who migrated to the United States as a student in the early 1960s.

Obama's preparation for his candidacy and for the presidency included service as a community organizer and later as a civil rights attorney. On many other dimensions, Obama shared characteristics with people recently elected to the presidency. He is trained as a lawyer, is married, and held elective office at the time of his candidacy.

President Obama began his administration facing greater challenges than most of his predecessors. The United States was engaged in two ground wars abroad as well as the war on terrorism. Obama's resources to address these international challenges were limited by a collapse in the global economy that worsened in the months before his election. A collapse in the financial services sector spurred a recession that more than doubled unemployment rates and the federal deficit. Personal bankruptcies and home foreclosures grew to new record levels.

During his first two years in office, President Obama had a resource that few of his predecessors did—sizeable Democratic majorities in the Senate and House of Representatives. The result was an ambitious agenda that saw the passage of more major pieces of legislation than any president since Lyndon Johnson had been able to pass, including: the ACA, two economic stimulus bills to help the nation recover from the recession, a bill to regulate the financial services industry, ratification of an arms control treaty with Russia, the end of the military's restrictions on gay and lesbian service members, civil rights legislation focusing on the workplace, and the confirmation of two Supreme Court justices, one of whom was the first Latino on the high court.

MAKING CONNECTIONS President Obama's first two years in office saw many legislative successes. What resources did Obama have to achieve his goals? What limits do presidents face?

The Cabinet and the Bureaucracy

To manage the U.S. government, the president appoints (and the Senate confirms) senior administrators to key executive branch departments. The chief officers at each of the core departments make up the president's cabinet. The U.S. cabinet has no legal standing, and presidents frequently use it only at a symbolic level. The president is also free to extend membership to other senior appointed officials (such as the U.S. ambassador to the United Nations), so the number of cabinet members fluctuates from administration to administration.

The senior officers of the executive branch agencies manage a workforce of approximately 2.2 million civilian civil servants (the bureaucracy). Although formally part of the executive branch, the bureaucracy must also be responsive to Congress. The presidential appointees who lead the federal agencies establish broad policy objectives and propose budgets that can expand or contract the responsibilities of executive-branch offices. Congress must approve these budgets, and it uses this financial oversight to encourage bureaucrats to behave as their congressional monitors wish.

Arguably, the inability of either Congress or the president to control the bureaucracy fully should give it some independence. But the bureaucracy as a rule does not have the resources to collect information and shape the laws that guide its operations.

Interest groups have steadily filled this informational role, but the information comes at a cost. Bureaucracies often develop symbiotic relations with the interests that they should be regulating. The interest groups have more access to Congress and can shape the operations of the regulatory agencies. These **iron triangle relationships** (among a private interest group, a congressional committee or subcommittee overseeing the policy in question, and a federal agency implementing the policy) often exclude new players who represent alternative views on how policies should be implemented. Without an independent source of authority, the bureaucracy must depend on both the elected branches and also on interest groups.

iron triangle relationships

A term coined by students of American politics to refer to the relationships of mutual support formed by particular government agencies, members of congressional committees or subcommittees, and interest groups in various policy areas.

Other State Institutions

Besides the presidency and the Congress (see Section 4), several other institutions are central to the operation of U.S. government: the military, national security agencies, the judiciary, and state and local governments.

The Military

The U.S. Army, Navy, Marine Corps, Coast Guard, and Air Force include approximately 1.4 million active-duty personnel plus an additional 900,000 reserve and national guard troops. The president is commander-in-chief of the U.S. military, but on a day-to-day basis, U.S. forces serve under the command of a nonpolitical officer corps.

Because of the unique geographic resources of the United States, the military has had to dedicate few of its resources to defending U.S. territory. Beginning with the new U.S. geopolitical role after World War II, the military was given new responsibilities to support U.S. multilateral and regional defense agreements.

The United States increasingly looks to its allies to support U.S. military objectives abroad. In preparation for war with Iraq, U.S. military leaders designed an invasion force of 130,000, with 100,000 ground troops and the remainder in support positions abroad. These 100,000 U.S. military ground troops were supported by at least 15,000 British ground troops. They were supplemented by approximately 160,000 contractors.[8]

Many of the traditional responsibilities of the military, such as support of troops and specialized technical activities, have been transferred to reserve units and to private firms who work under contract to the Defense Department. Reserve troops are now called to active duty more frequently. They were required to serve multiple long-term commitments in Iraq and Afghanistan and were prohibited from leaving the reserves at the end of their commitments.

With the increased expectations for the military came increased reliance on defense technologies. U.S. nuclear weapons, intelligence technologies, and space-based defense technologies, as well as the maintenance of conventional weaponry and troop support, have significantly raised the cost of maintaining the military. This has led to ongoing national debates about the cost of the military and whether defense resources should go to technology or for troops. Industries have emerged to provide goods and services to the military. Proposals to cut defense spending often face opposition from these industries.

National Security Agencies

The September 11, 2001, attacks focused the attention of policy-makers on domestic security. Agencies with responsibility in this area had been dispersed throughout the federal government. They were now concentrated in the Department of Homeland Security under a single cabinet secretary. Although it took somewhat longer, intelligence-gathering agencies were placed under the administrative control of a director of national intelligence. Funding for domestic security and international intelligence gathering increased by approximately one-third.

Legislation passed in the months after September 11, 2001, also subjected U.S. citizens and permanent residents to greater levels of government scrutiny and to potential violations of civil rights. The Bush administration asserted (and the courts rejected) a position that suspected terrorists could be seized and held indefinitely, without charges.

The Judiciary

Of the three branches of federal government, the courts are the most poorly defined in the Constitution. Initially, it was unclear what check the courts had on other branches of government. Equally important, the courts were quite dependent on the president, who appointed judges, and on Congress, which approved the nomination of judges and set the jurisdictional authority of the courts.

In 1803, the Supreme Court established the foundation for a more substantial role in federal policy-making. It ruled in *Marbury v. Madison* that the courts inherently had the right to review the constitutionality of the laws. This ruling, though used rarely in the nineteenth century, gave the judiciary a central place in the system of **checks and balances**.

Even with the power of judicial review, the judicial branch remained weaker than the other branches. In addition to Congress's ability to establish court jurisdiction in nonconstitutional cases and the president's ability to fill the courts with people of his choosing, the courts have other weaknesses. They must rely on the executive branch to enforce their decisions. Enforcement proves particularly difficult when a court's rulings are not in line with public opinion, such as when the courts ruled that busing should be used as a tool to accomplish racial integration in the schools.

Beginning in the second half of the twentieth century, the federal courts gained power relative to the other branches of government. In part, this came from expanding the rules of standing so that groups as well as individuals could challenge laws, policies, or government actions and by maintaining longer jurisdiction over cases as a tool to establish limited enforcement abilities. The courts also gained relative power because of the expansion of federal regulatory policy. Unclear laws and regulations, often requiring technical expertise to implement, placed the courts at the center of many policy debates. The courts have also gained power because they became a venue for individuals and groups whose interests were neglected by the democratically elected institutions but who could make claims based on constitutional guarantees of civil rights or civil liberties. African Americans, for example, received favorable rulings from federal courts before Congress and the president responded to their demands. Since the 9/11 attacks, the executive branch and majorities in Congress showed that they were willing to limit individual rights in a search for collective security. Courts—including the Supreme Court—have been more cautious.

The power of the courts ultimately rests with their ability to persuade the citizenry that their procedures are fair and their judgments are based on the Constitution and the law. This may become more difficult in the future as the courts and particularly the Supreme Court have moved steadily to the ideological right. Analysis in 2010, at the time of the retirement of longtime Justice John Paul Stevens, demonstrated that each of the current nine justices is more conservative than his or

Marbury v. Madison

The 1803 U.S. Supreme Court ruling that the federal courts inherently had the authority to review the constitutionality of laws passed by Congress and signed by the president. The ruling, initially used sparingly, placed the courts centrally in the system of checks and balances.

checks and balances

A governmental system of divided authority in which coequal branches can restrain each other's actions. For example, the U.S. president must sign legislation passed by Congress for it to become law. If the president vetoes a bill, Congress can override that veto by a two-thirds vote of the Senate and the House of Representatives.

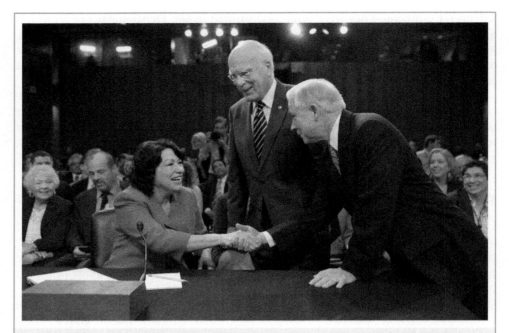

Supreme Court nominee Sonia Sotomayor prepares to testify before the Senate Judiciary Committee as part of her confirmation process.

AP Images/J. Scott Applewhite

her predecessor on the Court and that majority opinions have become more conservative, on average, than under any of the three previous chief justices. With the courts increasingly involved in contentious national issues, the Senate has taken its role in reviewing appointments more seriously and has slowed the confirmation of appointees, leaving some judicial circuits severely short of judges.

The steady increase in judicial power in the twentieth century should not obscure the fundamental weaknesses of the courts relative to the elected branches. The courts are more dependent on the elected branches than the elected branches are on them.

Subnational Government

State governments serve as an important part of government in the United States. Their responsibilities include providing services to people more directly than does the federal government. Most important among these is education, which has always been a state and local responsibility in the United States.

States and localities are able to experiment with new policies. If a policy fails in a single state, the cost is much lower than if the entire country had undertaken a new policy that eventually failed. Successes in one state, however, can be copied in others or nationally.

In addition to state governments, citizens pay taxes to, and receive services from, local governments that include counties, cities, and districts for special services such as water and fire protection, and townships. These local entities have a different relationship to the states, however, than do states to the federal government. The local entities are statutory creations of the state and can be altered or eliminated by the state (and are not a form of federalism).

Local governments provide many of the direct services that the citizenry receives from the government. Because states and localities have different resources (often based on local property taxes) and different visions of the responsibilities of government, people in the United States may receive vastly different versions of the same government service, depending simply on where they live.

The Policy-Making Process

Because of separation of powers and constitutional limits on each branch of government, the federal policy-making process has no clear starting or ending point. Instead, citizens and organized interests have multiple points of entry and can fight outcomes through multiple points of attack. Without centralization, policies often conflict with each other. The United States, for example, subsidizes tobacco cultivation but seeks to hamper tobacco companies from selling cigarettes through high taxes, health warnings, and limits on advertising. Federalism further complicates policy-making. Each state sets policy in many areas, and states often have contradictory policies. In sum, policy advocates have many venues in which to propose new policies or to change existing policies: congressional committees, individual members of Congress, executive-branch regulatory agencies, state governments, and, in some states, direct ballot initiatives.

With so many entrance points, there are equally many points at which policies can be blocked. Once Congress passes a law, executive-branch agencies must issue regulations to explain specifically how the law will be implemented. Subtle changes can be inserted as part of this process. On controversial issues, senior political appointees set policy for the writing of regulations.

Furthermore, people or interest groups that feel disadvantaged by the regulations can fight regulations in the courts. They also can contest the law itself, if they can find a way to claim that the law is unconstitutional or conflicts with another law or with state government responsibilities. Once a policy is in place, it can be opposed or undermined by creating a competing policy in another agency or at the state level.

The Constitution gives no guidance about the origins and outcomes of policy initiatives. The president must present an annual report to Congress on the state of the nation. This has evolved into an organized set of policy proposals. Without presidential leadership in policy-making, Congress partially filled the void. Enumerated powers in the Constitution direct Congress to take action in specific policy areas, such as establishing a post office or building public roads. Once Congress established committees to increase its efficiency (see Section 4), these committees offered forums for discussion of narrow policy. These committees, however, are not mandated in the Constitution and are changed to reflect the policy needs of each era. Thus, while presidents can propose policies (and implement them), only Congress has the ability to deliberate about policy and pass it into law.

Beginning in the 1970s some federal courts experimented with initiating policy as a way of maintaining jurisdiction in cases brought before them. These efforts, such as court-mandated control over state prison or mental health care systems, spurred much national controversy and caused the judiciary to decline in public opinion. Today, the courts are much more likely to block or reshape policies than to initiate them.

Without any clear starting point, individual citizens have great difficulty when they seek to advocate a new policy. Into this void have come extragovernmental institutions, some with narrow interests and some promoting collective interests.

Prominent or wealthy individuals or groups can get Congress's or the president's attention through campaign contributions and other types of influence.

Mediating institutions have also emerged to represent mass interests. Political parties organize citizen demands and channel them to political leaders. The parties balance the needs of various interests in society and come as close as any other group in society to presenting comprehensive policy proposals (often summarized in the parties' platforms). Group-based interests also organize to make narrow demands. In the twentieth century, as both federal and state governments began to implement more widespread distributive and redistributive policies, more organized interest groups appeared. These interest groups have become the dominant form of mediating institution in U.S. politics (see Section 4). Unlike political parties, however, interest groups represent only a single issue or group of narrowly related issues.

Where Do You Stand?

With the new role assumed by the United States among the globalized world of states after World War II, could the United States be led by the presidency of the nineteenth century envisioned in the Constitution?

Separation of powers and federalism impede the policy-making process in the United States relative to other nations. What constitutional changes would you propose to improve the policy-making process in the United States?

SECTION 4

REPRESENTATION AND PARTICIPATION

Focus Questions

- How do Congress's constitutional powers and its organizational structure ensure that it is the most powerful branch of the U.S. government?

- Who votes and who doesn't in U.S. politics? Why?

The Legislature

Of the three branches in the federal government, the founders envisioned that Congress would be at the center and would be the most powerful. They concentrated the most important powers in it and were most explicit about its responsibilities. For most of the nation's history, their expectations for the powers of Congress have been met.

One of the most important compromises of the Constitutional Convention involved the structure of Congress. States with large populations wanted seats in the national legislature to be allocated based on population. Small states feared they would be at a disadvantage under this system and wanted each state to have equal representation. The compromise was a **bicameral** system with two houses, one allocated by population—the House of Representatives—and the other with equal representation for each state—the Senate. This compromise has remained largely uncontested for the past 225 years despite the growing gap in population between large and small states. The senatorial vote of each resident of Wyoming has sixty-six times the impact of each Californian.

The two legislative bodies are structured differently. The House has 435 members and is designed to be more responsive to the popular will. Terms are short (two years), and the districts are smaller than Senate seats except in the smallest states. The average House seat has approximately 716,000 constituents and will continue to grow. The Senate has 100 members and is designed to be more deliberative, with six-year, staggered terms. Although unlikely, it is possible every two years to vote out an entire House of Representatives; the Senate could see only one-third of its members unseated during any election year.

Membership in the U.S. House of Representatives is more diverse than the people who have held the presidency, although most members are white male Protestants. In the 112th Congress (2013–2015), approximately 19 percent of House members were women, 10 percent were African American, 7 percent were Latino, and 2 percent were Asian American. Most members, regardless of gender, race, or ethnicity, are highly educated professionals. Law is the most common profession. The Senate is less racially diverse but has a comparable share of women to the House: Two African Americans, three Latinos, two Asian Americans, and twenty women served in the Senate in 2014.

The two central powers of Congress are legislation and oversight. For a bill to become law, it must be passed in the same form by both the House and the Senate and signed by the president. Equally important, Congress has the ability to monitor the implementation of laws that it passes. Since it continues to control the appropriation of funds for programs each year, Congress can oversee programs being administered by the executive branch and shape their implementation through allocations of money or by rewriting the law.

Congress has organized itself to increase its efficiency. Discussion and debate take place primarily in committees and subcommittees. The committee system permits each member to specialize in specific areas of public policy. Committees are organized topically, and members often seek to serve on committees that are of particular interest to their constituencies—for instance, a member of Congress from a rural area may seek to serve on the Agriculture Committee. All members seek to serve on committees that have broad oversight of a wide range of government activities, such as the Appropriations Committee, through which all spending bills must pass. Specialization allows each member to have some influence while not requiring that she or he know the substance of all facets of government.

For a bill to become law, it must be reviewed by the committee and subcommittee that have responsibility for the substantive area that it covers. When a member proposes a bill, it goes to a committee based on its subject matter and usually never gets any further. In each session, relatively few bills receive hearings before a subcommittee or committee. The House and Senate leadership (the Speaker of the House, the Senate Majority Leader, and committee chairs) are central to deciding which bills receive hearings. If the bill receives support from the committee, it must then be debated by the body as a whole. In the House, this may never occur because that institution has another roadblock: the Rules Committee, which determines what can be debated on the floor and under what terms. Only in the Senate can debate be unlimited (although it can be limited by cloture, a vote of sixty senators to limit debate). These hierarchical structures strengthen the powers granted to the House and the Senate in the Constitution because they allow Congress to act efficiently and to use its powers to investigate federal programs, even though it does not administer them. As a result, Congress places itself at the center of the policy-making process. This specialization and hierarchy ensure that congressional leaders are more central to the design and oversight of policy than are members of European parliaments.

This tension between the constitutional powers of Congress and the national focus on the president as the national leader became evident in the federal government's response to the 9/11 attacks. Initially, President Bush shaped the public

bicameral

A legislative body with two houses, such as the U.S. Senate and the U.S. House of Representatives. Just as the U.S. Constitution divides responsibilities between the branches of the federal government and between the federal government and the states, it divides legislative responsibilities between the Senate and the House.

policy response. As Bush administration policies evolved and the response came to focus on structural changes in the federal government, however, Congress began to reassert its constitutional prerogatives. Congress also ensured that the National Commission on Terrorist Attacks on the United States, unofficially known as the 9/11 Commission, would be formed, funded, and given sufficient time to conduct its investigation and write its report. The commission documented executive-branch intelligence-gathering failures and provided the political pressure necessary to force the Bush administration to create a new federal official—the Director of National Intelligence—who would oversee most U.S. intelligence-gathering agencies.

Congressional oversight of presidential leadership in the U.S. response to September 11 and the wars in Afghanistan and Iraq demonstrate that Congress has not yielded as the president gained power. It passed legislation to undermine presidential power and, equally important, applied its authority to investigate federal programs to weaken the presidency. These investigations of presidents and their senior appointees weaken the connection between the presidency and the people and weaken not just the presidents as individuals, but also the presidency as an office.

Political Parties and the Party System

The roots of two-party politics can be found both in the nation's political culture and in the legal structures that govern elections. The Democrats can trace their origins to the 1800 election, while the Republicans first appeared in 1854. Despite the fact that today's parties have consistently competed against each other, the coalitions that support them (and which they, in turn, serve) have changed continually.

Today, the Republicans depend on a coalition of upper-income voters, social conservatives, small-business owners, residents of rural areas, and evangelical Christians. They receive more support from men than from women and are strongest in the South and the Mountain West.

The Republicans have tried to make inroads in minority communities but have been largely unsuccessful, with the exception of Cuban Americans and some Asian American groups (see Table 3.2). For Republicans to win Latino (or African American) votes on a wider scale, the party would have to be willing to alienate some core Republican constituencies.

The contemporary Democratic coalition includes urban populations, the elderly, racial and ethnic minorities, workers in export-oriented businesses, unionized labor, and, increasingly, working women. Suburban voters have increasingly joined the Democratic coalition. Today's Democrats are concentrated in the Northeast and on the West Coast. The Democrats have built a steady advantage among women voters.

Democratic partisanship grew steadily over the Bush years and declined slightly in the first Obama term. In 2014, Democrats made up 30 percent of the electorate, Republicans 23 percent, and Independents 45 percent. Although the Independents have seen the most growth over the past two decades, they tend to lean reliably toward one party or the other. When these "leaners" are accounted for, the Democrats maintain the advantage—roughly 47 percent to 40 percent. Generally, Democrats, who are more likely to be poor, less educated, and younger than Republican voters, are less likely to turn out on Election Day, particularly in "off-year" (nonpresidential) elections. After the 2012 election, the Republicans controlled governorships in twenty-nine states, and the Democrats controlled twenty-one. In 2014, the Republicans hold a majority of seats in the House of Representatives (234 to 199, with two vacancies). Democrats hold the majority in the Senate (55 to 45).

Table 3.2	Democratic Party Share of Two-Party Vote, Presidential Elections 1992–2012					
	1992 Percent	**1996 Percent**	**2000 Percent**	**2004 Percent**	**2008 Percent**	**2012 Percent**
Whites	49.4	48.3	43.8	41.4	43.9	39
Blacks	89.2	87.5	91.8	88.9	96.0	93
Hispanics	70.9	77.4	68.4	56.6	68.9	71
Asian Americans	36.0	47.3	56.8	56.0	63.9	73

Note: These calculations exclude votes for candidates other than Democratic and Republican candidates.
Source: Author's calculations based on *New York Times.* 2008. "Election Results 2008." http://elections
.nytimes.com/2008/results/president/national-exit-polls.html (accessed February 15, 2010) and *New York
Times.* 2012. "President Exit Polls." http://elections.nytimes.com/2012/results/president/exit-polls?action=
click&module=Search&region=searchResults%230&version=&url=http%3A%2F%2Fquery.nytimes.com%2
Fsearch%2Fsitesearch%2F%23%2F2012%2Belection%2Bpoll%2F (accessed March 9, 2014).

These majorities will likely be in flux for the next several elections. The electorate is much more evenly divided than the U.S. House or the governorships suggest; both saw Democratic gains in 2006, 2008, and 2012 and gains for the Republicans in 2010. Of the two parties, the Republicans have a more fragile coalition. Beginning in the 1990s, internal conflicts grew in the Republican Party. Moral conservatives and fiscal conservatives each wanted the party to focus on their interests and jettison the others' issues as a way of expanding the party's base of support. In 2010, this division manifested itself in the emergence of the Tea Party activists who sought to move the Republican Party to the right out of concerns that the federal government was spending too much and usurping powers that should be held by the states (see U.S. Connection: The Tea Party).

These party divisions lead to speculation that new parties might emerge. But the political culture of the United States dampens the likelihood that a faction of one of the parties will break off and form a party that competes in election after election. Instead, two coalitional parties are the norm, an unusual pattern among advanced democracies.

Electoral law reinforces this situation. Most U.S. elections are conducted under a single-member-plurality election system in district-based elections. Single-member district-based elections reward coalitional parties and diminish opportunities for single-issue parties or narrowly focused parties, such as the Green Party or the Tea Party, should it break off from the Republican Party. Broad coalitional parties can contest seats in election after election, while smaller parties in the United States are likely to dissolve after several defeats.

There are more than 600,000 elected offices in the United States. To compete regularly in even a small percentage of these, a party must have a national presence and a national infrastructure. Most third parties fail long before they are able to compete in more than a few hundred races.

Finally, the heterogeneity of the U.S. population and the range of regional needs and interests rewards parties that can form coalitions prior to elections, as does a system with just two political parties. The Constitution-driven inefficiency of the U.S. government

U.S. CONNECTION

The Tea Party

The 2010 U.S. elections saw the emergence of a new political movement—the Tea Party. Despite its name, it is a social movement not a party, and largely organizes within the Republican Party. Tea Party activism emerged in response to anger in the electorate over federal government spending and growing federal budget deficits, to Federal Reserve actions to support the banking sector and to keep interest rates low, and to the enactment of the ACA. Tea Party activism is highly decentralized, so there is no single Tea Party, and it rejects centralized leadership.

Various Tea Party organizations and chapters endorsed candidates for the House of Representatives and Senate in the 2010, 2012, and 2014 elections. In several cases, Tea Party candidates defeated the preferred candidates of Republican leaders in party primaries. Although the Tea Party saw some major victories in the U.S. House of Representatives, several Tea Party candidates who defeated establishment Republicans in primaries went on to defeat in the general election. Had the mainstream Republicans been their party's candidate in 2010 or 2012, it is likely that they would have won the general election. Had all won, Republicans would have controlled the Senate in 2011 and 2013.

Today's Tea Party reflects the latest in a long line of U.S. populist movements that appear in eras when the national government is perceived to be distant and out of touch. Over time, its energy will likely dissipate. Its rejection of formal organization and leadership structures make it difficult to sustain the high levels of citizen involvement seen in the period leading up to the 2010 and 2012 elections. That said, it will undoubtedly be a force in the 2014 and 2016 elections. Candidates for the 2016 Republican presidential nomination will need to win support from the activists who have been mobilized by the Tea Party movement and local Tea Party members will challenge incumbent moderate Republicans in party primaries. Whether or not the Tea Party survives as an independent movement, its organizing principles of reducing the size and scope of the federal government will likely be part of U.S. political debates for the foreseeable future.

MAKING CONNECTIONS What groups in the U.S. electorate does the Tea Party movement speak to and mobilize? Are these groups likely to be a larger or smaller share of the overall electorate twenty years from now?

would become all the more dramatic if multiple parties (rather than two that must, by their nature, be coalitions) were competing in legislatures to shape outcomes.

Elections

As an example of its commitment to democratic norms, the United States points to the frequency of elections and the range of offices filled through elections. Unlike the case in parliamentary systems, these elections are conducted on a regular schedule: presidential elections every four years, Senate elections every six years, House of Representatives elections every two years. States and localities set the terms of state and local offices, but almost all have fixed terms.

Fundamental to understanding U.S. elections is federalism. States set the rules for conducting elections and for who can participate and how votes are counted. When the country was founded, this authority was almost complete, since the Constitution said little about elections. At the country's founding, most states limited electoral participation to white male landholders. By the 1830s, many states had eliminated the property-holding requirement, in part in response to the emergence of competitive political parties that sought to build membership.

Further expansion of the U.S. electorate required the intervention of the federal government and amendment of the Constitution to reduce state authority in determining voter eligibility. The first of the efforts to nationalize electoral rules was initially a failure. This was the effort to extend the franchise to African Americans after the Civil

War through the Fourteenth and Fifteenth Amendments. More successful was the Nineteenth Amendment, ratified in 1920, which extended the vote to women.[9] The Civil War amendments finally had an impact with the passage of the Voting Rights Act (VRA) in 1965, which secured African Americans access to the ballot box. In 1975, Congress extended the VRA to other ethnic and racial groups who had previously seen their right to vote abridged because of their origin or ancestry—Hispanics, Asian Americans, Native Americans, and Alaskan Natives. In 1971, the Twenty-Sixth Amendment gave the vote to all citizens aged eighteen and older.

States continue to regulate individual participation in elections through their control of voter registration. In most advanced democracies, the national government is responsible for voter registration rather than the individual. Individual registration prescreens potential voters to ensure they meet the state's requirements for voting: residence in the jurisdiction for a set amount of time and, in many states, the absence of felony convictions. While this may appear minimal and necessary to prevent voter fraud such as an individual's voting multiple times in the same election, the requirement to register in advance of the election prevents many from being able to vote.[10]

There is a second consequence of federalism on U.S. elections: The responsibility for holding elections, deciding which nonfederal offices are filled through elections, and determining how long nonfederal officeholders will serve before again having to be elected is the responsibility of the states and, if the states delegate the power, to localities. Thus, a local office that is elected in one state could be an appointed office in another. Terms for state and local offices, such as governors, vary. Elections are held at different points throughout the year. Finally, federalism shapes elections by delegating to the states responsibilities for determining how votes are collected and how they are counted, even in elections to national office.

What are the consequences of this federalist system of elections? At a minimum, it leads to confusion and burnout among potential voters. Many voters are unaware of elections that are not held on the same schedule as national elections. Others who are aware become overloaded with electoral responsibilities in jurisdictions that have frequent elections and so choose not to vote in local races.

One result of this decentralized system with a legacy of group-based exclusion is that increasing numbers of citizens do not vote. In the late 1800s, for example, turn-out in national elections exceeded 80 percent of those eligible to vote, and the poor participated at rates comparable to the rich. By 1996, turnout in the presidential election dropped below 50 percent (returning to 62 percent in 2012). In state and local races, turnouts in the range of 10 to 20 percent are the norm. Perhaps more important, turnout varies dramatically among different groups in society. The poor are less likely to vote than the rich, the young less likely than the old, and the less educated less likely than the more educated.[11] Because blacks and Hispanics are more likely to be young, poor, and have lower levels of formal education, they are less likely to vote than are whites. Hence, political institutions are less likely to hear their demands and respond to their needs.

These class- and age-driven differences in participation are not entirely the result of federalism and variation in the rules for individual participation and the conduct of elections. Declining party competitiveness

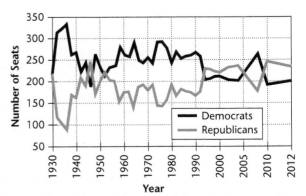

FIGURE 3.5 Party Control of the U.S. House of Representatives, 1930–2012

Source: U.S. House of Representatives, Office of the Clerk. 2013. "Party Divisions of the House of Representatives (1789 to Present)." http://clerk.house.gov/art_history /house_history/partyDiv.html (accessed March 9, 2014).

at the state level also plays a role. Nevertheless, the steady elimination of formal group-based exclusion has been replaced by the marginalization of the majority of some groups, such as Asian Americans and Hispanics. The United States has yet to live up to its democratic ideals.

This declining participation should not obscure the dramatic changes in leadership and issues addressed that result from elections (see Figure 3.5). In 2006, the Democrats regained control of the Senate and House of Representatives and elected the first woman to serve as Speaker of the House (Nancy Pelosi). In 2010, the Republicans gained control of the House as well as many governorships and state house majorities. These Republican majorities in many state governments allowed them to guide redistricting that determined congressional and state legislative seats for the remainder of the decade.

Political Culture, Citizenship, and Identity

The United States is a large country with distinct regional cultures, ongoing immigration leading to distinct languages and cultures, class divisions, and a history of denying many Americans their civil rights. Despite these cleavages, the United States has maintained almost from its first days a set of core political values that has served to unify the majority of the citizenry. These values are liberty, equality, and democracy.

Liberty, as it is used in discussions of U.S. political culture, refers to liberty from restrictions imposed by government. A tangible form of this notion of liberty appears in the Bill of Rights, which provides for the rights of free speech, free assembly, free practice of religion, and the absence of cruel and unusual punishment. Support for liberty takes a second form: support for economic liberty and free enterprise. Property and contract rights are protected at several places in the Constitution. Furthermore, Congress is empowered to regulate commerce.

Clearly, these liberties are not mutually exclusive. But protections of the Bill of Rights often conflict with each other: Economic liberties reward some in the society at the cost of economic opportunities for others. Nevertheless, the idea that citizens should be free to pursue their beliefs and their economic objectives with only limited government interference has been a unifying element in U.S. political culture.

Equality is the second unifying American political value. In the Declaration of Independence, it is "self-evident" that "all men are created equal." At various times in the nation's history, women, Native Americans, African Americans, Mexican Americans, Chinese Americans, Japanese Americans, and naturalized citizens have been excluded from membership in the polity and, consequently, from access to this equality. But each of the excluded groups, such as African Americans during the civil rights movement, used the widespread belief in equality to organize and demand that the United States live up to its ideals.

It is important to observe what this belief in equality is not. The equality that has long been sought is equality of opportunity, not equality of result, such as that sought in the communist states. There is support for the notion that people should have an equal opportunity to compete for economic rewards, not that they should end up at the same point.

The final unifying value is representative democracy. Throughout the nation's history, there has been a belief that government is legitimate only to the degree that it reflects the popular will. As with the notion of equality, the pool of citizens whose voices should be heard has changed over time, from white male property holders at

"Warning: offer void in some states."

State regulation of marriage ensures that same-sex marriage rulings that apply to one state do not immediately translate into a national policy recognizing same-sex marriage.

Christopher Weyant The New Yorker Collection/The Cartoon Bank

the time of the founding to most citizen adults today (convicted felons are excluded from the franchise in many states).

The United States has never had a national religion and, at times in the nation's history, conflicts between Protestants and Catholics have been divisive. In contemporary society, division over religion is more between those for whom religion provides routine guidance in politics and social interactions and those for whom religion is a private matter that does not shape political activities.

In 2013, 50 percent of U.S. adults were Protestant, 24 percent were Roman Catholic, and 2 percent were Jewish or Mormon. Less than 1 percent were Muslim. Nearly 17 percent of U.S. adults reported no religious preference. Despite the fact that there is no national religion in the United States, religion plays a more central role in U.S. politics than it does in the politics of European democracies. Moral issues—such as abortion and LGBTQ rights—guide the votes of a sizeable minority of the population. Many elected leaders are overt in their religiosity to a degree that would not be acceptable in European politics (and would not have been in U.S. politics as recently as thirty years ago).

Values are very much at the heart of contemporary political debates. Leaders have marshaled these values throughout the nation's history to reduce potential cleavages in U.S. society. Since the United States cannot look to a common ethnicity of its people (as, for example, Germany can), to a sovereign with a historical tie to the citizenry (as in a monarchy like the United Kingdom), or to a purported common religion or ideology among its citizens (as does Iran or Cuba), the belief in these values has been used to unify the diverse peoples of the United States.[12]

Interest Groups, Social Movements, and Protest

In the United States, political participation has long included activities other than elections and party politics. In the nation's story about its origins, protest proves central; the Revolution was spurred by acts of civil disobedience such as the Boston Tea Party. Similarly, protest and social movements repeatedly forced the United States to live up to its democratic ideals. From the woman's suffrage movement of the nineteenth century to the civil rights movement of the 1950s and 1960s, people defined as being outside the democratic community organized to demand that they be included.

These protest movements have also been able to tap the willingness of Americans to become involved in collective action. This voluntarism and civic involvement have long been identified as stronger in the U.S. democracy than in other advanced democracies.

In recent years, however, observers of U.S. politics have noted a decline in civic involvement, a decline that has also appeared in the other advanced democracies. Although social movements remain, they have become much more driven by elites than were their predecessors. Voluntarism and civic involvement have declined, and the likelihood of participation has followed the patterns of voting, with the more educated, wealthier, and older generally more likely to volunteer and be civically engaged.[13] This decline in civic involvement in U.S. politics has serious long-term implications for society. As civic involvement declines, Americans talk about politics less with their peers and have a lessened sense that they can shape political outcomes. They are less likely to be part of networks that allow for collective political action. Political scientist Robert Putnam has identified this as the "bowling alone" phenomenon in which social capital—the networks of relationships with norms of behavior, trust, and cooperation that increase the likelihood that society will function effectively—is in decline.[14] Americans traditionally had many social venues, such as bowling leagues, where they had an outlet to talk about politics and, potentially, to organize when they were frustrated with political outcomes. There are fewer of these today (people are busier, have more job responsibilities, and spend more time watching television). The decline in civic engagement has led to reduced political efficacy and greater frustration with the course of politics.

Protest, of course, remains an option for people who feel neglected by the political order. In 2006, for example, as many as 5 million immigrants, their families, and their supporters took to the streets to protest anti-immigrant legislation in the U.S. House of Representatives. Mass protests such as these, however, are very much the exception. Despite the fact that many in the United States oppose immigration at current levels, the social movement organizations that have formed to promote this cause—most notably the Minuteman organization—have rarely been able to generate much mass participation. National polling indicates that for the population as a whole—who neither joined the street protests nor the militias—immigration is an area of continuing concern. Each of the last five Congresses has sought to reform immigration in a comprehensive manner, but has failed, suggesting that neither the street protests, nor the anti-immigrant militias were of sufficient gravity or organization to pressure Congress into action on immigration.

The twentieth century saw the rise of a new form of organized political activity: interest groups. Like political parties and candidates for office, these organizations try to influence the outcome of public policy by influencing policy-makers. They differ, however, in that they are usually organized to influence a single issue or a tightly related group of issues. Also unlike social movements, they rely on money and professional staff rather than on committed volunteers. Interest groups increased in prominence as the federal and state governments increasingly implemented distributive and redistributive policies. Beginning in the 1970s, a specialized form of interest group, the **political action committee (PAC)**, appeared to evade restrictions on corporations and organized labor to make financial contributions to political candidates and political parties.

Interest groups are so numerous in U.S. politics that it is not possible to even venture a guess as to their number. They include national organizations, such as the National Rifle Association, as well as local groups, such as associations of library patrons who seek to influence city council appropriations. They include mass organizations, such as the American Association of Retired Persons, and very narrow interests, such as oil producers seeking to defend tax protections for their industry.

Although interest groups and PACs are now much more common than social movements in U.S. politics, they do not replace one key function traditionally fulfilled by the social movements, which seek to establish accountability between citizens and government. Interest groups by definition protect the needs of a cohesive group in the society and demand that government allocate resources in a way that benefits the interests of that group. They usually include as members people who already receive rewards from government or are seeking new benefits. Their membership, then, tends to include more socially, financially, and educationally advantaged members of U.S. society. There is no place in the network of interest groups for individuals who are outside the democratic community or whose voices are ignored by the polity. The key role that social movements and protest have played in U.S. politics is being replaced by a more elite and more government-focused form of political organization.

political action committee (PAC)

A narrow form of interest group that seeks to influence policy by making contributions to candidates and parties in U.S. politics.

The Political Impact of Technology

An open question for scholars of U.S. politics is the degree to which technology, and particularly social media, can serve as a resource to share political information and to mobilize those who are not fully engaged in civic and political life, in other words to counter the growing bowling alone phenomenon. Social media ensure that most Americans are in more frequent contact with friends, family, and colleagues than they have been in the recent past. Just as a bowling league did once, this contact can allow for the easy transfer of political information and the subtle (and, sometimes, not so subtle) encouragement to participate.

Candidates, parties, and interest groups are certainly aware of technology's potential value in generating more mass engagement. The 2008 and 2012 Obama campaigns, for example, focused an unprecedented effort on using social media, both in the party primaries and the general election. Analysts credit these efforts with turning out higher than expected turnout from young voters and for the high levels of support they gave to Obama. Few candidates (or parties or interest groups) can delicate the level of resources and cutting-edge technologies that the Obama campaign did. Future campaigns (and social movement activism and interest group activity) will find new strategies—and probably more effective strategies—to use technology to reach potential supporters, but this process will generally be slower than the development of new communications technologies.

Technology, however, should not be seen as a panacea for reinvigorating community engagement in U.S. civic and political life. Not all in society have equal access to technologies and some of the gaps in access to technology overlap with the groups least likely to participate in politics. Ultimately, technology is a means to communicate and it is up to leaders to develop a message that will resonate with potential supporters, however that message is delivered.

Where Do You Stand?

The nation's founders wanted the U.S. Congress at the center of government and the policy-making process. Would you give it the same powers and responsibilities if you were writing the Constitution today? Why or why not?

Should voting in U.S. national elections be made mandatory?

SECTION 5

UNITED STATES POLITICS IN TRANSITION

▼ Focus Questions

- In what ways can effective mediating institutions overcome the roadblocks to governance built into the U.S. Constitution?

- How has the U.S. role in global governance and global institutions changed in the period since World War II?

The election of Barack Obama signaled a significant transition for U.S. electoral politics. Had only non-Hispanic whites voted, John McCain and Mitt Romney would have easily won the presidency. Obama's victories should not, however, obscure the fact that the U.S. electorate has a dramatically lower share of minority participants than does the population as a whole. Latinos, for example, made up 17 percent of the population in 2012, but just 8 percent of the electorate; Asian Americans made up 5 percent of the population and 3 percent of the electorate.

Without question, some of these gaps will narrow over time. Minority populations tend to be younger, for example, than non-Hispanic whites, and voting increases with age. The minority voting gap, nevertheless, presents an ongoing challenge for the American democracy, one that will likely grow in the short term. The gap is even greater in the states with large minority populations. At the state level, the pool of regular voters is dominated by older upper-income white voters; this population is more resistant to pay for the services needed by many of the minority nonvoters, such as K–12 education, social services, and adult education. Candidates and office holders, however, often speak to the needs of voters over the societal need to ensure that all Americans have access to the resources they need to succeed.

Political Challenges and Changing Agendas

The United States today faces some familiar and some new challenges that result from the nation's new place in the world of states. Primary among the continuing challenges is the need to live up to its own definition of the democratic idea and to balance this goal of representative government elected through mass participation with the divergent economic outcomes that result from its laissez-faire approach to governing the economy. The United States must address these challenges with a system of government that was designed to impede the actions of government and a citizenry that expects much of government but frequently does not trust it to serve popular needs.

The United States has assumed a relatively new role and set of responsibilities in the world of states, at least new as far as the past seventy years; U.S. governing institutions must now respond not just to their own people, but more broadly to an international political order that is increasingly interconnected and seeks rapid responses to international security, political, and economic crises. The institutional arrangements of U.S. government hamper quick responses and increase the likelihood of parochial responses that the rest of the world can hear as isolationism or unilateralism. These institutional arrangements are reinforced by a citizenry that for the most part cares little about foreign policy (except when war threatens), expects quick and often painless solutions to international crises, and has little respect, and sometimes open animosity, for multinational political and economic institutions such as the UN and the IMF. Despite the citizenry's continued focus on domestic concerns, U.S. jobs and national economic well-being are increasingly connected to international markets and to the willingness of governments and individuals to buy U.S. bonds. Over time, many in the United States may come to resent this economic integration.

Economics is not the only role that the United States plays in the world of states, as has been brought home in the period since the 9/11 attacks. Although the citizenry has demonstrated a willingness to pay the financial cost of a global military, it has been much less willing to sacrifice lives. As a result, U.S. leaders must continually balance their military objectives and responsibilities to allies and international organizations with an inability to commit U.S. forces to conflicts that might lead to substantial casualties.

This tension between U.S. reliance on a global economic order among developed nations and a willingness to pursue a unilateral military and defense policy appeared repeatedly after the 9/11 attacks. The initial approach of national leaders as well as the citizenry was to pursue military actions against Afghanistan and Iraq alone if necessary. Although alliances formed for each military engagement, this threat of unilateral action made the building of long-term multilateral alliances all the more difficult.

In addition to its economic and military roles, the United States exports its culture and language throughout the world. This process contributes to economic development in the United States; equally important, it places the United States at the center of an increasingly homogenizing international culture. But this process also creates hostility in countries that want to defend their national and local cultures.

The substantial changes in the U.S. connections to the world of states have not been matched by equally dramatic changes in the U.S. role in governing the economy. Laissez-faire governance continues. The United States tolerates income and wealth disparities greater than those of other advanced democracies. Business is less regulated and less taxed in the United States than in other democracies. Few in the polity contest this system of economic regulation.

Since the Great Depression, the United States has seen an expansion of redistributive programs to assist the poor. In the period of divided government, however, the United States has reduced its commitment to assisting the poor and has established time limits for any individual to collect benefits. It seems highly unlikely that the United States will develop targeted programs to assist citizens in need that compare to those of other advanced democracies.

Distributive programs targeted to the middle class, such as Social Security, Medicare, and college student loans, have also been implemented in the twentieth century. These have much more support among voters and are harder to undermine, even if they challenge traditional laissez-faire approaches. The costs of these programs, however, are putting an increasing long-term burden on the federal budget and, because of deficit spending, on the national economy. There is little political will to deal with these long-term costs. Divided government, with routinely shifting Democratic and Republican majorities, adds to this complexity; each party must treat each election as the opportunity to reenter the majority.

The U.S. government faces a challenge to its sense of its own democratic idea that is more dramatic than that faced by other advanced democracies. The 62 percent of the electorate who turned out in 2012 represented a slight decline from 2008. Turnout in non–presidential-year elections is even lower—approximately 42 percent in 2010. Participation is not spread evenly across the population: older, more affluent, and more educated citizens are much more likely to vote than are the young, the less educated, and the poor. Elected representatives are receiving less guidance from a narrower subset of the people.

The breadth of nonelectoral politics is also narrowing. Previous study of the United States found rich networks of community-based organizations, voluntary organizations, and other forms of nonelectoral political activity. Community politics in the United States, however, began to decline in the 1950s (roughly when electoral turnout began to decline) and appears to be at record lows today.

The politics of collective identities has always been central to U.S. politics because the country has been a recipient of large numbers of immigrants through much of its history. Each wave of immigrants has differed from its predecessors in terms of culture and religion. These differences forced the country to redefine itself in order to live up to its democratic idea. The "old" group of each era also perceived the "new" group as a threat to the political values of the nation. Today, Asian and Hispanic immigrants are seen as a challenge by the descendants of European immigrants.

The United States has experienced a long period of sustained high levels of immigration since 1965. The current period of high immigration has seen higher levels of overall immigration than the previous period of sustained high immigration (beginning after the Civil War and extending to the 1920s). Many in Congress today are proposing legislation to further deter undocumented migration, but there have been few proposals to reduce the opportunities for legal immigration.

Without strong political parties, mediating institutions, and nonelectoral community politics, the political integration of these immigrants and their children may stall. The preliminary evidence is that naturalization rates are increasing, but that naturalized citizens vote and participate in other forms of politics at lower levels than comparably situated U.S.-born citizens. If these patterns continue, the United States faces a new risk: Contemporary immigrants and their children may not be represented in the political order, even when these immigrants become U.S. citizens.

In the past, institutional arrangements and mediating institutions could partly overcome the weaknesses of the U.S. constitutional system. Congress dominated the executive until the New Deal era, after which the president dominated Congress until Watergate. This institutional dominance reflected the framers' intent through the Great Depression and after, at least in terms of the dominance of one branch. It is unclear that the framers envisioned a system where two, and occasionally all three, branches of government would compete for dominance and where the Congress and the presidency would be routinely controlled by different political parties.

Mediating institutions once played a role that they cannot tackle today. Once the political parties formed as mass institutions in the 1830s, they served a necessary role in unifying popular opinion and forcing elite compromise. Today, parties are in decline and have been replaced by a distinct type of mediating institution that does not seek compromise across issues and instead promotes narrow interests. Interest groups connect the citizenry to political institutions, but they only advance a narrow agenda.

The United States faces the same challenges it has always faced, and it is still limited by a governing system that seeks to inhibit government activity. In the past, it has overcome these challenges when citizens participated actively, often working through mediating institutions and mobilizing new groups to active political participation. With citizen participation becoming more selective and mediating institutions less broadly based, the United States will have trouble facing challenges. Because of our central position in the world economy, if we cannot meet our challenges, the whole world will suffer with us.

Youth Politics and the Generational Divide

Increasingly, the group asked to resolve these tensions in American governance, define the place of the United States in the world, and pay for the long-term costs of underfunded social welfare programs for the elderly are today's young adults and those who are not yet of voting age. This youth population is a very different population along many dimensions than today's likely voters. The under-30 population in the United States is much more likely to be non-white and more likely to be either an immigrant or the child of an immigrant. They are much less likely to live in rural areas than is today's electorate and (at least for those who are in their 20s) are likely to have higher levels of formal education. Perhaps most troubling for a nation like the United States that premises its legitimacy on the democratic idea, the youth population has a high share of long-term unauthorized immigrants who have no way to adjust their immigration status (and only limited connections to their countries of birth).

The differences between today's youth population and older members of U.S. society are not simply compositional. Today's young adults have come of age in an era of sustained economic uncertainty and geopolitical change. They have grown up in a world in which the United States was attacked on September 11, 2001; the threat of global terror has shaped their understandings of safety and the role of government in their lives. Their likely future participatory and partisan trajectories and their understandings of the U.S. role in the world are not yet fully formed (particularly for those under 18). It is safe to say that based on composition and experiences alone, however, that they will be very different from today's voters and leaders in terms of the issues that shape their connection to politics and their expectations for what government can realistically deliver.

Ultimately, the position of today's youth in tomorrow's politics will depend on the degree to which they organize, that political institutions mobilize them, and they feel that government is responsive to their needs. Youth are probably most affected by the bowling alone phenomenon, so they have lower than average rates of civic and electoral participation. The Obama campaigns made clear than youth can be better mobilized. Even without specific mobilization, today's youth will likely follow the paths of previous generations and increase their civic and political engagement as they age. The incentive for institutions to mobilize today's youth will only increase in the future as today's regular participants die off. While the nearly even partisan divide impedes governance, it creates a huge incentive to educate the citizenry and mobilize supporters. Young adults already benefit from this environment and, so far at least, have served as a resource for the Democrats. Finally, today's youth need to feel a sense of political efficacy, that government is responsive to them. Evidence suggests that young adults are somewhat less efficacious, but they share the American values discussed here and will increasingly want to have their voices heard as they and their families come to seek more from government in order to thrive in U.S. society.

United States Politics in Comparative Perspective

From the perspective of the study of comparative politics, the United States may well remain an enigma. Its size, wealth, unique experiences with immigration, history of political isolation from the world, and reliance on separation of powers and federalism do not have clear parallels among other advanced democracies. This distinctness comes through perhaps most clearly in the way the United States engages its international political responsibilities. While the president has traditionally directed the scope of U.S. foreign policy, Congress, as it reasserts power relative to the president, will likely play an increasing role. Members of Congress, who represent narrow geographic districts and are more directly connected to mass interests, are less likely to take an internationalist perspective than the president does. When Congress speaks on international issues, it is often with multiple voices, including some that oppose U.S. involvement in multilateral organizations. This conflict over control and direction of foreign policy has increased since the end of the Cold War.

The relationship of the United States to Cuba offers an example. Since the Cuban revolution (1959), the United States has not recognized Cuba and has imposed economic sanctions in an effort to remove Fidel and, now, Raul Castro from power and to encourage economic reforms. Increasingly, however, interests in the United States across the ideological spectrum (agricultural producers, recent Cuban émigrés, the travel and tourism industry, and liberals who never supported the sanctions) have sought to expand opportunities for trade with Cuba. These efforts, however, have been effectively blocked by Cuban American leaders, who raise the prospect of Cuban American voters fleeing a candidate who supports a change in policy, and by Cuban American members of Congress who use leadership positions to slow policy change. In the 112th Congress (2011–2013), Cuban American Ileana Ros-Lehtinen chaired the U.S. House Foreign Affairs Committee. Her position on the committee and in the Republican leadership blocked any change in U.S. economic sanctions on Cuba.

The impact of the constitutionally mandated structural and institutional weaknesses of U.S. government is not limited to the American people. The United States plays a dominant role in the world economy, as well as a central political role in international organizations. Thus, the inefficiencies and multiple entry points into U.S. policy-making shape the ability of the United States to respond to crises and develop coherent long-term policies in conjunction with its allies. In 1998, for example, as the world economy declined, the president, with the support of the chair of the Federal Reserve, proposed that the United States increase its contribution to the IMF by $18 billion. Congress initially balked at this request for several reasons, none of which were apparent to the U.S. allies. While the power of intransigence and horse trading makes sense to analysts of U.S. politics, analysts abroad cannot so easily understand the seeming failure of the United States to act in a time of crisis. Eventually Congress passed the added IMF appropriation.

In sum, despite its central role in the international economic system and in multilateral organizations, the United States often remains reluctant to embrace fully the international system that it helped shape. This hesitancy appears despite the active role of U.S. economic interests abroad and the importance of international trade to the U.S. economy. The United States does not hesitate to impose its will abroad when it perceives its security threatened, or when it perceives that the rules made by the international organizations undermine its economic or political interests. Thus, despite its central role in the world of states, the United States is sometimes a hesitant leader. The post–9/11 world makes this a much more difficult position to sustain. The challenge of the contemporary era is not states—as it was in the Cold War era—but instead international non–state-based networks. These cannot so easily be controlled through economic dominance and multilateral political alliances. As the United States faces the new challenges of a post–9/11 world, it must again reexamine the degree to which it is willing to act unilaterally and to pay the price for global concern about its occasional unilateralism.

Where Do You Stand?

Thinking about likely changes to demographic composition of the United States and the electorate over the next fifty years, do you expect the United States to have more or less engagement in the globalized world of states in the future? Why?

Should the United States rely on its geographic isolation and economic power to reduce its leadership role in the multilateral organizations that it helped create after World War II?

Chapter Summary

The U.S. democratic model remains a powerful force in the world of nations. It has survived for over two centuries and has adapted to the pressures of an increasingly globalized world. It faces the ongoing challenge of meeting the demands of its citizens and other nations with a system of governance designed over two centuries ago to limit government and to set the institutions of government against each other. Reinforcing this challenge is the stark partisan division in the populace that has emerged over the past twenty years. This division came to a head in the 2013 federal government shutdown.

Mass organization can significantly change the focus and direction of government. In recent elections, however, coalitions on the left (2008) and on the right (2010) have emerged victorious each offering a vision of change that resonates with and mobilizes different segments of the electorate. The constitutional system may slow the influence of this mass mobilization on policy-making, but ensures that the citizenry's voice will be heard every two years and that governing institutions will change to reflect changing demands among voters and other organized interests in U.S. society.

This internal debate over the size and scope of the U.S. government presents an ongoing challenge for the globalized world of states. The long-term health of the U.S. economy (and consequently U.S. society) requires the health of the global economy. Frequent changes in the leadership role that the United States is willing to play in the world and its willingness to work with multinational institutions that it created make it harder in the long run for the United States to maintain the role of a global leader that it has occupied since the end of World War II.

Key Terms

Articles of Confederation	Declaration of Independence	free market
bicameral	distributive policies	interest groups
Bill of Rights	Federal Reserve Board	iron triangle relationships
checks and balances	federalism	manifest destiny

Marbury v. Madison
police powers
political action committee (PAC)
property taxes

redistributive policies
regulations
separation of powers

single-member-plurality (SMP)
electoral system
social security

Suggested Readings

Amar, Akhil Reed. *The Bill of Rights: Creation and Reconstruction*. New Haven, CT: Yale University Press, 1998.

Dawson, Michael C. *Black Visions: The Roots of Contemporary African-American Political Ideologies*. Chicago: University of Chicago Press, 2002.

Deering, Christopher J., and Steven S. Smith. *Committees in Congress*, 3rd ed. Washington, DC: Congressional Quarterly Books, 1997.

The Federalist Papers. Edited by Clinton Rossiter. New York, Mentor, 1961.

Hartz, Louis. *The Liberal Tradition in America*. New York: Harvest/HBJ, 1955.

Judis, John B., and Ruy Teixeira. *The Emerging Democratic Majority*. New York: Scribner, 2002.

Kupchan, Charles. *The End of the American Era: U.S. Foreign Policy and the Geopolitics of the Twenty-First Century*. New York: Knopf, 2002.

Verba, Sidney, Kay Lehman Schlozman, and Henry Brady. *Voice and Equality: Civic Voluntarism in American Politics*. Cambridge: Harvard University Press, 1995.

Wilson, Woodrow. *Congressional Government: A Study in American Politics*. Baltimore: Johns Hopkins University Press, 1885.

Zolberg, Aristide. *A Nation by Design: Immigration Policy in the Fashioning of America*. Cambridge: Harvard University Press, 2006.

Suggested Websites

The 9/11 Commission Report
http://www.gpoaccess.gov/911/index.html

Find Law—Cases and Codes: U.S. Constitution
findlaw.com/casecode/constitution/

New York Times
www.nytimes.com

Thomas—Legislative Information from the Library of Congress
thomas.loc.gov

U.S. Census Bureau
www.census.gov

White House
www.whitehouse.gov

4 European Union

George Ross

Official Name: European Union

Location: Comprised of twenty-eight countries in Western and Eastern Europe

Capital City: Brussels (Belgium)

Population (2014): 505 million

Size: 4,234,782 sq. km; less than one-half the size of the United States

1950
Schuman Plan for European Coal and Steel Community includes France, Germany, Italy, Belgium, the Netherlands, and Luxembourg.

1957
"Original six" agree to Rome Treaty creating European Economic Community.

1971 and after
EEC economic difficulties after United States ends Bretton Woods exchange rate regime; oil shocks.

1989
Fall of Berlin Wall, leading to German unification and end of Cold War

1965
Treaty unites ECSC, EEC, and Euratom in "European Communities."

1973
Enlargement to United Kingdom, Ireland, Denmark

1981
Greece joins EC.

1950	1965	1970	1975	1980	1985	1990

1945–1948
Europe devastated; Cold War and Marshall Plan

1965
French precipitate "empty chair crisis," leads to "Luxembourg compromise."

1979
European Monetary System (EMS) begins; direct elections to the European Parliament

1986
Spain and Portugal join.

1985
Commission White Paper on Completing the Single Market, Single European Act

1961
French President de Gaulle vetoes British EEC application.

1975
European Council founded (summits of state and government heads)

THE MAKING OF THE EUROPEAN UNION

▼ Focus Questions

- Why would the economic problems of the 1970s cause a retreat into "Eurosclerosis"?

- How did the end of the Cold War affect prospects for European integration?

Politics in Action

On May 9, 1950, French Foreign Minister Robert Schuman proposed that France and Germany, plus any other democratic nation in Western Europe that wanted to join, should establish a transnational "community" to govern the coal and steel industries. France and Germany had been at war, or preparing for war, for most of the twentieth century, at huge cost. Schuman's announcement spoke to deeper issues:

> World peace cannot be safeguarded without creative efforts.... The contribution that an organized and vital Europe can bring to civilization is indispensable to the maintenance of peaceful relations.... Europe will not be made all at once, nor ... in a single holistic construction: it will be built by concrete achievements that will create solidarity in facts. To assemble European nations first demands that opposition between France and Germany be eliminated.... (first paragraph of the Schuman declaration, of May 9, 1950)

Robert Schuman came from Lorraine, a battleground area between France and Germany. Konrad Adenauer, first chancellor of the German Federal Republic

1997
Treaty of Amsterdam—creates European Employment Strategy, movement toward Central and Eastern European enlargement

2007
Fiftieth Anniversary of EU; climate change and energy security package, Lisbon Treaty adopted, containing most of ECT institutional reforms

2005
French and Dutch refuse to ratify European Constitutional Treaty in referendums.

2008
Irish vote against ratifying Lisbon Reform Treaty. Global financial crisis hits EU.

2002
European Convention

1995	2000	2003	2005	2008	2010

1995
Sweden, Finland, and Austria join.

2000
Treaty of Nice—flawed weak institutional reform for eastern enlargement; Lisbon Strategy—reform plan to confront globalization and make EU the world's leading "knowledge economy" by 2010

2004
European Constitutional Treaty (ECT) approved by European Council, paving the way for ten Central and Eastern European countries plus Cyprus and Malta to join EU in 2005–2007 (fifth enlargement)

2010–2014
Crisis of sovereign debt in Eurozone, beginning with Greece, then Ireland. Member states have difficulty reaching effective agreement on remedies and redesign of EMU.

1991
Maastricht Treaty on European Union, initiating Economic and Monetary Union, "co-decision," intergovernmental pillars on Justice and Home Affairs and Common Foreign and Security Policy

2009
Second Irish referendum on Lisbon Treaty passes and treaty comes into effect. EU fails to influence Copenhagen UN Climate Change Conference.

and eager participant in the new European Coal and Steel Community (ECSC), had been mayor of Cologne before Hitler put him into Buchenwald prison. The primary author of the "Schuman plan" was Jean Monnet, a brilliant networker and technocrat who then headed France's economic planning commission. Leaders in the other ECSC countries were also veterans of war-making determined to change Europe.

Sixty-five years later, after huge efforts the European Union, direct descendant of the ECSC, has become something that its creators could never have imagined. There were six original ECSC members. Now there are twenty-eight EU members, over 500 million citizens, and the world's largest open market. The EU was built in peace, around democracy, and with respect for the rule of law.

Critical Junctures

European integration is a unique construction built by European states seeking peace. It quickly took on economic forms and expanded into other areas of its members' sovereignty but without weakening their national identities. This "new" Europe has grown in response to changing international conditions, rarely resting and always innovating, often in ways that outsiders have had difficulty understanding.

Integration emerged after World War II, a cataclysmic event in which tens of millions of Europeans perished. The war had broken the appeal of antidemocratic regimes that had earlier come to power and brought democratic ideals and sweeping social reforms. At this point the United States, the United Kingdom, France, and the Union of Soviet Socialist Republics (USSR) jointly occupied Germany and were determined to prevent anything like Nazism from recurring. The war left Europe economically devastated, however, without money to rebuild.

The Union of Soviet Socialist Republics and the United States, wartime allies, became enemies after 1945, leading to the Cold War and communist-dominated "Peoples' Republics" in eastern Europe. In the west, national efforts plus Marshall Plan help from the United States jump-started reconstruction. Overwhelming American military power made war between Western European countries inconceivable, and the North Atlantic Treaty Organization (NATO) provided territorial defense under American hegemony. Economic integration was paramount to removing the threat of war, however. If different national markets could be tied together, economic interests might in time acquire stakes in peaceful resolution of differences. This was the process begun by the European Coal and Steel Community (ECSC). The ECSC established a centrally regulated market of the coal and steel industries of six Western European countries, the traditional enemies, Germany and France, plus Italy, Belgium, the Netherlands, and Luxembourg, around a common European authority.

The six ECSC countries became more committed to European integration than anyone anticipated and in 1957 signed the Treaty of Rome creating a European Economic Community (EEC, or "Common Market") to abolish economic borders between them. The EEC started precisely when postwar economic reconstruction opened a period of prosperity. It supplemented national economies by creating a customs-free area between them, allowing national manufacturing firms to export more, plus a Common Agricultural Policy (CAP) to stimulate agricultural modernization. The EEC's external tariff imposed uniform duties on goods imported into the common market, sheltering EEC members from the international market and, in particular, from some of the economic power of the United States. Mass production, consumerism, and full employment followed, and EEC states redistributed some of their economic growth through national social programs for health care, housing, pensions, and education that were backed by social groups that had long been politically excluded. These EEC "postwar settlements" founded enduring representative democracy in much of Western Europe.

International economic turmoil in the 1970s ended this happy situation. EEC members—nine after the United Kingdom, Denmark, and Ireland joined in 1973—then faced home-grown inflation, oil shocks, and "stagflation," a combination of high inflation and low growth. They made things worse by their different national policies that endangered the EEC customs-free area and added to the exchange-rate fluctuations that followed the American ending of its Bretton Woods commitments to back the dollar by gold. Growth disappeared, Europe lost competitiveness, and unemployment returned. In an era characterized by "Eurosclerosis," an inability to move forward because of disagreements among member states brought European integration to a halt and endangered the Common Market. For a brief period after 1985 the EEC found new energy after member states agreed to "complete the single market" and create a Europe-wide "space without borders." The period culminated in the Treaty on European Union (TEU, ratified in 1993) when the EEC became the EU and its members agreed to form an **Economic and Monetary Union** (EMU, a Europe-wide monetary policy and single currency), build a **Common Foreign and Security Policy (CFSP)**, and begin cooperation in **Justice and Home Affairs (JHA)** to facilitate free movement of people within EU borders. These large new commitments also brought institutional changes, in particular increased powers for the European Parliament.

Economic and Monetary Union

The 1991 Maastricht Treaty federalized EU monetary policy, created a European Central Bank and founded the Eurozone and its single currency, the euro.

Common Foreign and Security Policy (CFSP)

Commitment in the Maastricht Treaty for deeper cooperation in international affairs and defense.

Justice and Home Affairs (JHA)

Engagements to make legal and regulatory changes to allow free movement of EU citizens throughout the EU.

The post-Maastricht EU saw international conditions change dramatically again. Globalization came rapidly, fueled in part by new technologies that shrunk the manufacturing jobs that had been the key to earlier prosperity. European industrial production began migrating to lower labor cost areas elsewhere. The United States was already way ahead of the EEC in creating a new "knowledge economy."

The end of the Cold War posed new daunting challenges. After 1989, the EU had to rethink its security positions, beginning unhappily by its clumsy response to brutal warfare in the Balkans. Deciding what to do with the formerly communist countries of Central and Eastern Europe (CEECs) was another puzzle. Beginning in 1989 the EU sent aid, negotiated freer trade, and encouraged countries to apply for EU membership, but it was not until the later 1990s that it undertook the process of incorporating the CEECs, encouraging new democracy, organizing economic interdependencies, and transferring resources to help foster modernization. The prospect of enlargement also forced the EU to think seriously about remodeling its institutions.

Facing such challenges, Europeans turned inward. The EU was becoming more intrusive, eastern enlargement was confusing, and many Europeans felt they had not been adequately consulted and that there was an EU "democratic deficit." The Union then embarked on a decade-long effort to rebuild EU institutions to cope with newcomers, a process that proved difficult and painful. A first effort, the 2001 Nice Treaty, produced tensions between larger and smaller countries. Leaders then decided to sponsor wide-ranging public debate in a "European Convention" that in 2004 produced an ambitious "European Constitutional Treaty." When the new treaty was sent out for ratification, however, it was rejected in 2005 referendums by both the French and the Dutch. It took several years more before leaders hammered out an amended proposal that led to the 2009 **Lisbon Treaty**. The institutional changes that the new treaty initiated were put immediately to the test by the global financial collapse in 2007–2008, which threatened several Eurozone countries with national bankruptcy, beginning with Greece in 2009–2010. The EU then entered a deep crisis mode.

Themes and Comparisons

EU politics obliges EU member states to accept shrinking national sovereignty, making the EU the most significant modern workshop at transcending a world of independent states. Europe's states, earlier producers of world wars, learned to produce peace, economic success, and high levels of cooperation while maintaining their identities in a context of cultural diversity. The principal implications of the EU for comparative politics lie here. We are accustomed to thinking about a world of sovereign states interacting and competing with one another. By its very successes the EU transcends traditional assumptions of comparative politics, because it is based on cooperative decision making among governments. Its founders recognized that intergovernmental cooperation needed new institutions. The EU was endowed with a Commission with exclusive powers to propose legislation and a Court that could build a body of binding European-level law. Then came a directly elected **European Parliament** that "co-decided" proposed legislation as the representative of European peoples alongside the Council of Ministers that represented national governments. More recently, the institutional structure has

Lisbon Treaty

After a decade of efforts to redesign EU institutions in light of enlargement to Central and Eastern Europe, the treaty created new positions of the President of the European Council and High Representative for foreign and security policy and increased the powers of the European Council and European Parliament.

European Parliament

The Parliament of the European Union, which meets in Strasbourg and Brussels, "co-decides" EU law with the Council of Ministers, but it cannot initiate legislation.

European Council

The European Council is a regular summit meeting of heads of state and government, under an appointed president, to find grand strategies for resolving EU problems and delineating paths into the future.

been supplemented by the **European Council**, a regular summit of member state leaders that provides general strategy. The product is a political system that bears little resemblance to anything we know at a national level, an "unidentified flying political object."

Because the EU is not a state, and because of its unique institutions, understanding its role and function in a world of states is not easy. The EU mediates among national states primarily in economic governance. But it also mediates between its members and the broader globalized world in some areas. In foreign policy, EU members agree that some questions are to be handled by the EU and others remain national. Members that were great powers such as Britain and France insist on the capacity to act independently. On international trade, however, the EU Commission negotiates everything of significance, making the EU a significant global power in global trade. The EU has assumed its largest roles in market-building and regulating, in breaking down economic barriers, including the free circulation of people, legislating and enforcing rules to build a "single" market, and then setting up the Economic and Monetary Union (EMU). Once rules are legislated, the Commission monitors and enforces compliance. The politically independent European Central Bank (ECB) takes responsibility for EMU monetary policy. The EU has little power over national social spending (pensions, education, health care), the largest component of national budgets.

In the immediate postwar period European integration consolidated democracy and the rule of law in western European countries whose democratic pasts had been fragile. As the EEC enlarged in the 1980s, welcoming formerly authoritarian southern European countries (Spain, Greece, and Portugal), it insisted that they undertake reforms to demonstrate their democratic commitments. A decade later, when the time came to welcome the formerly communist countries of central and eastern Europe, the EU stipulated that candidate countries had to prove commitments to democracy, possess an effective judiciary dedicated to the rule of law, and establish a competitive modern market economy. Aspirants for EU membership had always been obliged to accept and adopt all of the norms, laws, and procedures of the European "club" they wanted to join, but the "Fifth enlargement" to the east refined this process by developing direct apprenticeships in democratic practices. Finally, as the contemporary EU began to reach beyond its own borders as an international actor in trade promotion, humanitarian aid and peace-keeping, environmental policy, and classical foreign policy, it presented itself as a "normative Europe" spreading its democratic DNA abroad.

The EU's politics of collective identity are works in progress. The EU has always made efforts to *combine* existing national identities with growing European identity. Since the 1993 Maastricht Treaty these efforts have institutionalized coexistence between national and European citizenships, each with specific rights and duties. There has been endless discussion about what being "European" means, however, and the larger the EU, the more the disagreement.

The EU has indeed been a massive force for peace on the European continent, but now that lasting European peace has been achieved, citizens take it for granted. There is an EU flag, anthem, passport and many EU programs designed to build European identity. To choose but one, the Erasmus program has subsidized millions of European students to study outside their own countries as a way of promoting their educational progress and deepening "European-ness." In the economic realm, as businesses and workers have participated in the EU's huge internal market, they became more "European." But becoming French, British, German, and so forth were historical projects that took centuries. We cannot expect ordinary Europeans to embrace dual identities, one old, national, and familiar, and one new, European, and unclear, with ease or rapidly.

The EU has played an enormous rule in making Europe fully democratic and has united the European continent, both historic firsts. Yet, as Jacques Delors, president of the European Commission from 1985–1995 often observed, "people do not fall in love with a single market." The EU is difficult for ordinary Europeans to understand, steeped as they are in their native lands, particularly since the EU's policy backbone has been in matters of economic governance that are often difficult to penetrate. In addition, the EU has often been a convenient scapegoat for national politicians to blame for policies that national citizens do not like. Its moments of popular success have come when its policies have been experienced by citizens as providing real benefits. Depending on the popularity of policy outputs is precarious, however, because European public policies, like national ones, are often redistributive, satisfying some but upsetting others. Convincing citizens that European integration brings broad public benefits is a hard job, therefore, even if it may be the key to the EU's futures.

Where Do You Stand?

Being part of a fervent national community is a fundamental part of a person's identity. Is it dangerous to tamper with this, as the EU has done?

Should the EU become a state? What kind of a state?

POLITICS AND ECONOMICS IN THE DEVELOPMENT OF THE EUROPEAN UNION

SECTION 2

State and Economy: EU Economic Governance

A combination of international politics, national and local issues, and political creativity launched European integration, but economics quickly became the heart of things. Integration began as an ingenious plan to integrate coal and steel sectors in six continental western European countries under Cold War pressure. The movement for integration proved powerful enough to create the EEC "common market" in industrial and agricultural goods. Delegating sovereignty raised large issues, however, such as deciding what to delegate and how to administer what had been delegated.

Starting in the Cold War

The United States and the United Kingdom, concerned with rebuilding international trade after World War II, designed the Bretton Woods system. The United States committed to support the dollar with gold, there would be a World Bank to

Focus Questions

- What have been the relative weights of international and European-domestic factors in the development of the EU?

- How would you assess the changing balance between "supranational" and member state institutions in EU history?

help fund postwar rebuilding, an International Monetary Fund (IMF) to stabilize international trading, and the General Agreement on Tariffs and Trade (GATT) to promote freer trade. Before a war-devastated, penniless Europe could trade, however, it had to rebuild. The Americans, worried about European political stability, responded with the Marshall Plan (1947) that provided billions of dollars to reconstruct European economies, coinciding with the outbreak of Cold War. In its central and eastern European sphere of influence, the USSR established "popular democracies" backed by Soviet troops. With Paris only a few hundred miles from a million Soviet troops and the political power of communists in some Western European countries, Americans feared that a Soviet westward offensive would be difficult to stop. Cold War rearmament indirectly spurred European integration. The United States pressed Western European nations to rearm through NATO, which would provide American-led western European territorial defense. It then decided to rehabilitate, rather than punish, postwar Germany, leading in 1949 to a new German Federal Republic (FRG). The Americans then insisted that this new FRG be rearmed.

Europeans knew that they needed to cease periodic bloodbaths, perhaps by integration. But what should European integration be? Federalists wanted a United States of Europe. "Intergovernmentalists" pressed for a method in which national states would retain power and make decisions. Their debates led to the Council of Europe, a human rights organization, but not to integration. Europe's immediate problem was to end chronic conflict between France and Germany. The French, overrun by the Germans three times in seventy-five years, initially wanted to fragment post–Nazi Germany and neutralize its heavy industrial power, goals that stood in the way of American insistence on rehabilitating Germany. The French leader closest to the German problem was Jean Monnet, who faced American pressure for a less punitive French policy on Germany. Monnet proposed integrating the French and German coal and steel industries in a European Coal and Steel Community, an idea that quickly became the "Schuman plan," when it was taken up by Robert Schuman, French foreign minister. The "original six," France, Germany, Luxembourg, the Netherlands, Belgium, and Italy (the British refused to participate), signed the ECSC treaty in 1951 and the new Community began in July 1952.

Monnet thought that integration could best begin with practical solutions to practical problems, fitting with his idea that transnational integration of coal and steel could prevent the rebirth of nationalistic German heavy industry. Monnet also thought that the interdependence of modern economies might mean that economic cooperation in coal and steel could spread into new areas. France and Germany were willing to accept the ECSC because both knew that the United States would impose a less attractive plan. French public opinion, deeply hostile to Germany after the war, might accept the ECSC because it promised to neutralize German threats. German industrial interests needed larger markets to grow. The ECSC that resulted had an appointed high authority to propose rules and policies that a Council of Ministers would then vote up or down. It also had an appointed parliamentary-like assembly that had to be consulted, but had little power. Finally, a Court of Justice could review ECSC processes and decisions for their conformity with the ECSC treaty.

Despite the 1954 failure of a more ambitious Monnet proposal for a European Defense Community (EDC), the idea of European integration had staying power. In Messina, Italy, in 1955, the ECSC six committed to a European atomic energy agency, another Monnet idea, plus a European Common Market, brainchild of the

Dutch and Belgians. The Treaties of Rome in 1957 established Euratom and the European Economic Community (EEC). The French wanted Euratom but were less enthusiastic about the Common Market, while the Germans knew that a trade liberalizing Common Market would help their economy grow and give legitimacy to the new FRG. The French eventually accepted the EEC in exchange for a common agricultural policy. The United Kingdom, which had not joined the ECSC, once again stayed outside, betting on a parallel European Free Trade Area (EFTA) that would not share sovereignty.

At its core, the Common Market was a customs union removing internal trade barriers for industrial goods with ambitions to end "obstacles to freedom of movement for persons, services, and capital," a common external tariff, and unified trade policies toward third countries. The treaty's other objectives included common antitrust, agricultural, and transport policies. On Common Market matters, member states were to harmonize their legal systems. There were also provisions for a European Social Fund, a European Investment Bank to help less prosperous regions, and association arrangements that allowed access to the Common Market for overseas ex-colonies. In institutional terms, there was an appointed **European Commission**, sited in Brussels—a subdued copy of the ECSC's high authority—with exclusive power to propose laws and rules, implement policy, and safeguard the treaty. A Council of Ministers representing each national government and coordinated by a presidency rotating every six months, was the EEC "legislature" that decided on Commission proposals. There was also a European Parliament, appointed rather than elected, empowered to bring suits before the ECJ against other EEC institutions for "failure to act" on Treaty commitments and pose questions to which the Commission had to respond, but not much more. Finally, there was a **European Court of Justice** (ECJ) to adjudicate in those areas where the Rome Treaty gave EEC law precedence over national statutes.

The Commission's job was to carve space from member state sovereignty to build the Common Market, and some countries objected when it tried to do this. Because the Commission was appointed, critics attacked it as an unelected "Brussels bureaucracy." And because the Council of Ministers acted behind diplomatic secrecy, it was criticized for lack of transparency. The European Court of Justice was vulnerable to those who opposed "judge-made law." Behind this there was disagreement about what the new EEC should be, often from France. French President Charles de Gaulle twice vetoed British applications for membership (in 1963 and 1967) because the United Kingdom was not sufficiently "European" (meaning too close to the United States) and paralyzed the Council of Ministers in the 1965 "empty chair" crisis to block Commission power-grabbing and prevent the shift from unanimity to **qualified majority voting** (which would allow some member states to be outvoted) foreseen in the Rome EEC Treaty. When the Commission proposed a liberal Common Agricultural Policy (CAP) that threatened French and German agricultural subsidies, it was replaced by a French-inspired plan that was protectionist and subsidized farmers at the expense of consumers and taxpayers. Commission attempts to promote common transport, regional, and industrial policies came to little, despite the goals of the Rome Treaty. The young EEC survived because it floated on buoyant economic conditions. Emulating the American model of consumerism and mass production, Western Europeans enjoyed new cars on new roads, household appliances for their new houses, seaside holidays, and television, built on an impressive 5 percent average economic growth of EEC member states in the 1960s. Internal EEC trade grew even faster.

European Commission

The EU executive, which has a legal monopoly on proposing EU legislation and overseeing its implementation as "guardian of the treaties."

European Court of Justice

EU Supreme Court that decides the legality of EU legislation and its implementation.

qualified majority voting

Method in the Council of Ministers for deciding most EU legislation that weights member state voting power depending upon size and defining how many votes constitute a majority.

Crisis and Renewal: 1970–1993

The 1969 Hague Summit of EEC leaders set out ambitious plans for more market opening, enlarging to new members, greater EEC budgetary powers, foreign policy coordination, and Economic and Monetary Union (EMU). The British, Irish, and Danes then joined in 1973. The EEC, which had initially depended on direct funding from its members, also acquired new revenues from agricultural levies, import duties, and national value-added taxes. An energetic future seemed ahead, but international storm clouds appeared. The United States, threatened by trade deficits, ended its commitment to the Bretton Woods dollar/gold standard, allowing the dollar to "float" against other currencies and fluctuating exchange rates that caused havoc in the international monetary system, making economic prediction difficult, slowing trade growth, and tempting governments to use revaluations as trading weapons. At the same moment oil price shocks engineered by OPEC in response to the 1973 Yom Kippur war caused inflation to spike in energy-dependent Western Europe—a gesture that OPEC repeated in 1979.

Conditions became treacherous for the multicurrency EEC. Member states reneged on economic and monetary union. Profits and investment declined. EEC industry began to lose competitive advantage. "Stagflation"—simultaneous inflation, sluggish growth, and rising unemployment, led to cutbacks in social programs and precarious public finances. Divergent national responses made things worse. Germany restructured in a context of stable prices. After 1981 France's new Socialist administration pursued statist inflationary policies. Margaret Thatcher's Britain went its own harsh liberal reforming way.

By the early 1980s European integration was in danger. Decision making was paralyzed by budget disputes, in particular by the United Kingdom, which had paid too high a price to join, demanding their money back. Greece, which joined in 1981, immediately demanded that the EEC cough up more development aid. Non-tariff barrier protectionism caused the Common Market to clog up. The infrequent EEC-level responses to problems came mainly from summits of leaders (after 1974 called the European Council) that proposed direct elections to the European Parliament, held for the first time in 1979, and a new European Monetary System (EMS), to limit currency fluctuations. Observers began commenting about "Eurosclerosis."

In early 1985 the new Commission President Jacques Delors asked the European Parliament, "… is it presumptuous to … remove all the borders inside Europe between now and 1992 …?" Then, after the Commission produced its White Paper on Completing the Internal Market replete with three hundred new market-opening measures, the EEC began to stir again. Internal border posts would disappear, cross-border formalities simplified, common European product standards developed, value-added and excise taxation harmonized, and other obstacles to cross-border trade removed, allowing the free movement in the EEC of goods, services, and capital. National leaders then called an "intergovernmental conference" (IGC) in May 1985, which produced the Single European Act (SEA, ratified in 1987). The SEA tied the single-market program to qualified Council majority voting, leaving unanimity for only the most sensitive matters (fiscal policy, external border controls, the movement of people, and workers' rights). It also empowered the European Parliament to propose amendments and expanded the EU's prerogatives to enhance regional development ("economic and social cohesion"), research and development, and environmental policy. It legally acknowledged the European Council (summits of government heads) and European Political Cooperation (foreign policy coordination), both of which had been unofficial earlier. Last but not least, the new treaty anticipated monetary integration. The single-market program played to political realities. The Germans wanted new European trade. The French wanted to enhance their diplomatic power and help domestic reforms move forward. The British favored liberalization and deregulation in principle. Big business wanted a single market. Organized labor, less enthusiastic about the single market for fear of "social dumping" (companies relocating to find lower overhead costs), was seduced by promises of new "social dialogue" between Euro-level "social partners."

The Delors Commission, after profoundly reforming the EU's budgeting methods and innovating in regional development funding, then turned to economic and monetary union. A blue ribbon Committee led by Delors and of central bankers proposed a federal monetary policy, a European Central Bank, a single currency, and open capital movement. EMU, the committee claimed, could make intra-European factor costs more transparent, reduce transaction costs, prod Europe's financial sector to restructure, make wages better reflect national productivity, bring national budgetary and fiscal policies closer to economic fundamentals, and give governments new reasons for needed economic reforms.

The drive to EMU culminated in the **Maastricht Treaty**, ratified in 1993. Agreement was helped by German unification. Germany had been reluctant about EMU, but its unification scared other Europeans, and the German government agreed to EMU to reassure them. In exchange, however, Germany demanded their kind of EMU, one that guaranteed price stability and national financial responsibility. The French, whose hope had been to use EMU to constrain German monetary power, gave in to a final bargain that proposed stiff "convergence criteria" obliging EMU applicants to lower budget deficits to 3 percent and longer-term debt to 60 percent of GDP. EU members that reached these targets would be eligible to join the new EMU on January 1, 1999.

The negotiations were complicated by Belgian and German insistence on parallel talks about "political union" (leading to the new title of "European Union"). Political union included a common EU foreign and security policy (CFSP), greater democratization and more power for the European Parliament, and more efficient, coherent institutions. "Justice and home affairs" (JHA)—matters relating to the free circulation of people—sought to broaden existing "Schengen" open border policies to all EU states and coordinate police information and action on "Europeanized" crime. Maastricht also established EU citizenship and common immigration and asylum policies. By far the most significant institutional result, however, was "co-decision" in which the European Parliament got equal weight to the Council of Ministers deciding Community legislation plus the right to vote on the membership of Commissions. There was a hitch, however. Negotiators deemed that the CFSP and JHA were too important for the traditional "community method" of decision making (Commission proposals, Council and Parliament decisions, and ECJ review) and insisted on separate intergovernmental "pillars" with unanimity decision rules.

Maastricht Treaty

Treaty renegotiations (ratified in 1993) that gave the EU its present name, created the EMU and the CFSP, and granted the European Parliament power to "co-decide" EU legislation.

Globalization and the EU

The years after Maastricht were meant to consolidate the new treaty's innovations, but things proved much more complicated. The GATT Uruguay Round, the first to include agricultural trade, came to a head just after Maastricht and would have failed without a 1992 CAP reform. The EU and the United States then transformed the GATT into the World Trade Organization. In Europe itself, however, citizens worried that EU changes had been too rapid and far-reaching, something that first appeared in difficulties ratifying Maastricht. The Danes voted against the treaty—approving it later after concessions, and a French referendum in September 1992 passed by only 1 percent. Then followed a sharp economic down-turn due to European monetary problems just when the single-market program, which led employers to shed labor, was worsening unemployment. After the down-turn, member states faced difficult growth compressing preparations for the EMU membership deadline in 1998—the 3 percent deficit and 60 percent debt criteria in particular.

In 1993 the Delors Commission tried to remobilize the EU with a new White Paper on *Growth, Competitiveness, and Employment* that sounded alarms about glo-balization and suggested changes in EU economic governance. The EU's interna-tional competitive position was worsening, it argued, and this necessitated labor market and educational changes, more flexible social policies, and new attention to productivity. EU members refused to follow the Commission's lead, however. Citizens were unenthusiastic, while governments opposed the EU debt programs the Commission wanted. The Union enlarged again in 1995 to include Austria, Sweden, and Finland (the Norwegians voted against membership for the second time), all against new incursions into their sovereignty. Finally, the Germans, skeptical about some eventual EMU members, imposed a Stability and Growth Pact (SGP, incorpo-rated into the treaty of Amsterdam in 1997) to continue EMU convergence targets, and relative austerity, after EMU began.

In autumn 1989 Europe had been divided so long that most thought that this was permanent, but when the Berlin Wall came down in November, divisions abruptly ended. The Commission welcomed German unification, even if British Prime Minister Thatcher and French President Mitterrand had reservations. Helping ex-socialist societies of Central and Eastern Europe to democratize and modernize, and, perhaps, eventually join the EU, was a big challenge, first of all to hopes for

GLOBAL CONNECTION

The EU's International Connections

The EU has been a formidably successful organiza-tion committed to market economics, standing with the United States in promoting an open world trading sys-tem. It worries seriously about terrorism, failed states, how to help poor countries develop, promoting the rule of law, holding repressive dictators to account, and fitting newcomers like China, India, Brazil, Russia, and South Africa into a peaceful world order. The EU has been deeply devoted to multilateral approaches to international affairs, a highly positive approach in a globalizing world where integrating and giving voice to different countries has been a wise way forward. The EU, the largest market in the world, is central to inter-national commerce. It is also one of the world's largest fully democratized regions, as well as the world's leading development aid donor and a pioneer in humanitarian aid and crisis management. Recent globalization has been a profound challenge, however. The EU's members sought, usually successfully, to build strong industrial econo-mies and protective social policies to allow its citizens to better themselves through education and growing incomes and live secure lives. Globalization has brought new competition from emerging markets with compara-tive advantages in lower labor and social policy costs, as well as financial volatility. The EU has tried to persuade its member states to adapt to these challenges. Whether or not it will succeed is not yet clear.

MAKING CONNECTIONS What dimensions of globalization most challenge the EU and its members?

a common EU foreign and security policy. The end of the Cold War found most EU members ready to confront a Soviet invasion as the Soviet Union was dying, but before they had time to reconsider their defense preparations, the Yugoslav Federation disintegrated. Belgrade launched brutal campaigns—the word *genocide* may be appropriate—against Croatia in 1990, and then against Bosnia-Herzegovina. The first European wars since 1945 were greeted by Euro-posturing—solemn statements, high-powered delegations, economic sanctions, and handwringing that made little difference. It took American brokerage to stop war in Bosnia. The lesson was clear. The United States could make credible threats and call shots, while Europe's threats were hollow.

Later in the 1990s the EU began to respond. Evasive wording on CFSP was clarified in the 1997 Amsterdam Treaty to help circumvent the vetoes inherent in Maastricht's confusing decision rules. Amsterdam also created a "Mr. CFSP" to lead the CFSP process. Squabbling with the United States over NATO was moderated with new arrangements for the EU to share some NATO assets, provided that EU ambitions remained modest. By the turn of the century the EU had a small military planning staff and new goals for international peace-keeping and crisis management, and a new goal of portraying the EU as a different, gentler and more humane military actor.

A different problem arose about what to do about the formerly communist countries of Central and Eastern Europe (CEECs). In the early 1990s, the EU began coordinating to them through a PHARE program that soon became the EU's major instrument to help CEECs to build infrastructure, business, education, training, and research, and fund new environmental protection. The 1993 Copenhagen European Council then declared that the EU was "conditionally" willing to accept new members if they built stable democratic institutions (the rule of law, human rights, and minority rights), a functioning market economy, and the capacities to cope with competitive pressures inside the EU. Past EU experience obliged new applicants to conform to an *acquis communautaire*, by 2000 an accumulation of 80,000 plus pages of EU rights, obligations, and processes touching every corner of applicants' lives. Enlarging thus involved massive reforms that imposed Western European norms. A detailed "pre-accession strategy" came in 1994, including regular meetings, preparing for the single market, and new policies on infrastructure, environmental policy, CFSP, and justice and home affairs. The strategy worked better in some CEECs than others, with problems in Hungary, Romania, and Bulgaria.

Ten new members joined the EU in 2005 (eight CEECs plus Cyprus and Malta), followed in 2007 by Bulgaria and Romania. The joy of the moment was tempered, however. To make an EU of twenty-seven members work (28 after Croatia joined in 2013), EU institutions had to be redesigned because what had worked, more or less, for six or nine, might have become a crowd shouting in a football stadium at twenty-seven. But changing EU institutions was not simple, however, because it upset existing power relationships. The result was a decade of debates that few citizens could follow, national referendum defeats on new treaty texts (Ireland 2002 and 2008, France and the Netherlands 2005), and much acrimony and confusion. Finally, in 2009 the Treaty of Lisbon was adopted.

The Great Recession and the Euro zone Crisis

By 2009 the EU faced the worst economic crisis since the Great Depression of the 1930s, originating in the financial sector and symbolized by the 2008 bankruptcy of Lehman Brothers in New York. Anglo-American risk-defying financial innovation had already spread widely in the EU, however. The Great Recession brought credit freezes, negative growth, mass unemployment, declining government revenues, and rising costs. The United States and EU leaders agreed that failing banks needed to be saved to provide credit supplies and that stimulus plans could help jump-start the real economy again. Central banks, including the new ECB, supplied liquidity to re-oil the financial machinery. The EU also advocated re-regulation of the global financial sector, through the G-20. All this helped avoid the worst, but the damage went very deep.

In the fall of 2009, George Papandreou, the new Prime Minister of Greece, confessed that his predecessors had lied about his country's budget deficit—double what had earlier been announced. Thus did the greatest crisis in EU history open. International bond markets, fearing Greek default, then raised interest rates on future borrowing, confronting the EU with stark choices. Should EMU member states help Greece or should Greece be allowed to default and leave the Euro zone, perhaps creating new and potentially disastrous problems?

Decisions about what to do would be made by the Euro group of EMU members and the European Council, the EU's strategic decision-maker since Maastricht. Both were inter-governmental, meaning that governments had to bargain in processes that were slow, cumbersome, and guaranteeing that the preferences of stronger member states would shape decisions. Germany, initially reluctant to help Greece, shifted its position once it realized that the existence of the Euro was threatened and agreed to conditional loans to Greece from a temporary European Financial Solidarity Facility (EFSF), armed with €750 billion from the EU budget, EMU member states, and the International Monetary Fund. The first Greek loan was not large enough, however, and its high interest rates worsened Greece's debt and its conditions were draconian. Greece had to reduce its deficit to 3 percent by 2014, cut public sector pay, increase taxes, freeze pensions, lower wages, reform labor markets, and privatize, a package that led to widespread Greek social protest. The loan did not calm the situation and the crisis spread to Ireland and Portugal, who had to borrow with the same harsh conditions. Germany was the powerhouse in this bargaining.

The crisis showed that Maastricht's EMU architecture and rules needed restructuring. During the first EMU decade, EMU members had regularly disregarded the rules, which were not backed by serious sanctions in any case. The Maastricht negotiators had anticipated that EMU members would converge economically, but the opposite happened. Finally, there were no provisions for emergencies or to aid EMU members in trouble. Germany insisted throughout on strict policies obliging bailout countries (Ireland, Portugal, and Greece, plus Spain and Italy in partial ways) to impose harsh "internal devaluations," monitored by a *Troika* of Commission, ECB, and IMF officials. The major goal of EMU reconstruction became more effective central controls over member state fiscal practices. Members had to submit budgets for EU-level scrutiny before they were nationally voted, with stronger, more detailed monitoring of national fiscal policies, quasi-automatic sanctioning for bad behavior, and new regulations for the financial sector. A 2011 "Euro Plus Pact" pledged member states to control wage growth, raise retirement ages, reduce payroll taxes on labor, and observe new EU debt and deficit rules, backed by stiff penalties for noncompliance. German insistence also produced private sector involvement (bondholder liability) for restructuring bailout country debt. Then in 2012 a "Treaty on Stability, Coordination, and Governance" enjoined signatories to make national balanced budget commitments—the "golden rule." Finally, members were committed to set up a "Banking Union" to exercise ECB supervisory control over most EMU banks, a new "resolution" authority to deal with failing banks, and an EMU deposit insurance system.

Every choice brought trade-offs between those who bargained for national goals and international financial interests, above all bond holders seeking favorable terms. What with miscalculations, myriad political tensions, and tawdry back-room deals, crisis after crisis ensued. At one point the *Economist*'s cover labeled EU and EMU leaders as a "gang that couldn't shoot straight." The interest rates of the 2010 Greek bailout deal were too high and repayment schedules too rapid, worsening Greece's debt problems and necessitating more Greek loans. A German proposal for "haircuts" on expected bond returns (that is, agreements to for financial interests to take far less than a hundred cents on the dollar) upset the ECB and caused new market agitation. Later discussions about a second Greek loan went on for months and helped to spread the crisis to Italy and Spain. In November 2011, French and German intervention helped fire Greek Prime Minister Papandreou and Italian Premier Berlusconi and replace them with EU-influenced technocrats, an experiment that did little to help economically but deeply angered Greeks and Italians. In 2013, when called upon to bail out Cyprus, EU leaders botched things by calling for deep haircuts even for small depositors.

Hesitations about moving to a banking union unsettled the situation again. By 2013 the crisis had calmed, mainly because of the ECB's policies. Calmer bond markets were to be distinguished from disgruntled EU citizens, however. Euro zone policies of harsh sacrifice and redistributive reform badly tarnished the EU's legitimacy. "Internal devaluations" left citizens in borrowing countries in protracted austerity and insecurity. They experienced negative economic growth and very high unemployment (25 percent in Spain in 2012, 19 percent in Greece, 14 percent in Ireland, 13 percent in Portugal). Long-standing labor market rules were changed at the expense of trade unions. Minimum wages and unit labor costs declined, social programs cut back, public sector employment slashed, and inequality, poverty, and social exclusion shot up. Finally, generalized European recession in 2013, the product of Euro zone austerity policies, made things even worse. The intergovernmental ways in which decisions were made also hurt EU legitimacy, mainly because some EU member states, Germany in the first instance, decided policies that were experienced by those hurt as an unpleasant and unwelcome imposition from outside. Issues of democratic legitimacy are less about statistics than about how groups of citizens understand events, however. Favorable opinions of the EU have declined, with the trends stronger in the most crisis-affected countries. In mid-2013, a majority thought that the worst was yet to come and worried about their own employment prospects. According to one report only 28 percent believed that European integration had helped their economies. Loss of confidence in the EU was particularly strong among younger people.

Where Do You Stand?

Does EU-style transnational cooperation in response to large economic challenges inevitably create profound political problems?

Some EU countries do better than others economically, even in crises as threatening as the recent global financial collapse. Why?

EU GOVERNANCE

- To what degree does the EU provide lessons for governance on a global scale?

- Why might citizens have trouble identifying with EU institutions?

community method

The EU method of making decisions in which the European Commission proposes, the Council of Ministers and European Parliament decide, and the European Court of Justice reviews European law.

The Maze of EU Institutions

In 1648, exhausted from the Thirty Years War, Europeans founded the Westphalian state system. The results over centuries were strong, powerful states—each with its own language, identity, and ways of doing things—that were rivals and sometimes fought one another. Sixty plus years ago, some of these states began to create what would become the European Union. Their experiment began tentatively, in particular areas, with members warily keeping most of their powers. The new institutions they built were not "statelike," but built to govern particular things. These institutions persist today, making the EU a unique and complex system of multilevel governance.

For much of its life, the EU has been primarily a triangle of **community method** institutions including the European Commission, the Council of (national) Ministers, and the European Parliament. As the EU matured, however, complexities blurred this model. Beginning in the 1970s, the European Council, regular summit meetings of heads of state and government, slowly became the EU's longer-term strategist and decision-maker of last resort. The 1993 Maastricht Treaty on European Union then expanded the Union's scope into new areas such as foreign policy, defense and security, criminal justice, and immigration. These new areas lay

🪪 PROFILE

AP Images/Cornelius Poppe/NTB Scanpix/Pool

Jose Manuel Barroso, Herman Van Rompuy, Martin Schulz

The EU was awarded the 2012 Nobel Peace Prize because of its record in preserving European peace and because the Nobel Committee hoped to encourage EU leaders to work harder to surmount the Euro zone crisis. When the award was announced, however, no one knew which leader of which EU institution should go to Oslo. In the event, three of them, Jose Manuel Barroso—Commission President, Martin Schulz—President of the European Parliament, and Herman Van Rompuy—European Council President, mounted the stage together. Behind this lay serious questions. What was the "true" nature of the EU, and where was its institutional heart? Everyone could agree that the EU was central to European economic governance, sharing the job with its members. And everyone knew that the EU's prerogatives had

grown substantially beyond economic governance, although there were arguments about how much, where, and whether it was good thing. The three presidents on the Oslo stage stood for three different axes of government. The European Commission represented the regulatory governance ideals of Jean Monnet, one of the EU's main founding fathers. The European Parliament represented federalist ideals and the hope that eventually the EU might become something like a European state. The European Council of heads of state and government represented another ideal, that of a confederation of states in which important decisions were reached by intergovernmental bargaining. In fact, the EU was an unsteady mixture of all three.

MAKING CONNECTIONS Think about the reasons behind the complexity of the EU's institutions. What differences have this complexity made?

at the core of national sovereignty, however, and EU leaders initially decided that the Community institutional "triangle" was not the best place for them, opting instead for intergovernmental "pillars." Since then, the EU Community "triangle" has dealt with most things, but institutional power has steadily shifted toward the intergovernmental European Council and the member states. Before entering such complexities, however, we must first describe the EU's major institutions.

The European Commission

The 1957 Rome treaties gave the European Commission three prerogatives: It alone could propose Community legislation in the form of regulations, directives, and recommendations (laws binding on all members in the same terms, laws that have to be transposed into national legal codes, plus nonbinding "soft law"). Next, as the EU's executive, it supervised the implementation of Community policy. Finally, it was the "guardian" of the EU treaties, seeing to the observation of EU law and, if needed, bringing member states and private bodies before the European Court of Justice to oblige them to follow. On a different plane, its main job has been to help overcome the difficulties that national governments have in reconciling their differences by devising projects and ideas that express common European interests and goad member states to make collective commitments. It has been most successful when key member states—often France and Germany—agree that greater integration is desirable and encourage a strong Commission President. When key member states have wanted a weak Commission, as they have since 1995, they have appointed a weak Commission President. Since 2005, member states have also agreed that the Commission President, preferably a former prime minister, should share the political leanings of the majority in the most recently elected European Parliament.

The Commission can initiate proposals only where the EU treaties explicitly allow it. It does have some policy competencies where it behaves much like a federal government, however. It administers EU competition (antitrust) policies, the Common Agricultural Policy (CAP), proposes rules for and administers the European single market, and manages plans to help the EU's poorer regions to develop. It also has a key role in European environmental policy and helps design European-level research and development programs. It draws up the draft EU budget, even if the draft is always rewritten by member states. Internationally, it represents the Union in trade matters and, until 2009, when the Lisbon Treaty created a High Representative Foreign and Security policy, in some international organizations, plus manages foreign aid programs and supervises EU diplomatic delegations.

Commissioners are appointed by member state governments for five-year terms coinciding with the electoral life of the European Parliament. The 2004–2007 enlargement gave each member state one commissioner, making twenty-eight in all today, too many for the number of important Commission jobs. The Commission has a president, nominated by the European Council and approved by the Parliament, plus several vice presidents who oversee different clusters of activities. Commissioners work together in a "college" in which each commissioner, whatever his or her specific tasks, participates equally in all decisions. The Commission president exerts influence from assigning specific tasks to commissioners and by "presiding" over the Commission and planning its agenda. Each commissioner politically supervises one or several of the Commission's "services" (General Directorates or DGs), but does not have completely independent powers over them, since tasks are undertaken in accordance with programmatic lines to which the entire Commission has agreed. Despite its reputation as a formidable "Brussels bureaucracy," the total Brussels-EU

European single market

Official title of the EU's barrier-free economic space created after 1985.

administration, of which the Commission is the largest part, is small, around 30,000 people—about the number in a mid-sized European city, and only a minority are real "Eurocrats," the "A-grade" officers. Such A-level posts are carefully allocated to member state nationals. Each major Commission service is headed by a general director, the Commission's highest administrative post. Commission jobs are interesting and well paid (A-level jobs, the top of the ladder, range from around $150,000 to over $250,000 yearly, have numerous perks, and are exempt from national taxes, even if the EU itself taxes them lightly).

The Commission's most important job is to design policy proposals and get them passed by the Council of Ministers and the European Parliament. It rarely proposes from scratch, however, and in most cases translates the desires of others, particularly the European Council, and the requirements of international agreements. The Commission thus spends much time sounding out politicians, national ministries, and other Euro-level institutions for openings to act. It is also the object of intense lobbying, mainly because its most important tasks involve economic governance. The implementation of most Community measures is left to the administrations of member states.

The Council of Ministers

The original EU system was relatively simple. Where the EU could act legally, the Commission proposed, and the Council of (national) Ministers disposed. The European Parliament had to be "consulted," but lacked real power. The European Court of Justice could then review decisions and proceedings to ensure conformity with the EU's treaties. Things changed rapidly beginning in the 1980s, however. The Single European Act allowed the Parliament to propose amendments, and it became a "co-decider" with the Council in the Maastricht Treaty. Maastricht also introduced two new intergovernmental "pillars" for CFSP and "justice and home affairs" that initially fell almost completely outside the Community. The 2009 Lisbon Treaty "communitized" most of what these pillars did, but progress at this has been slow.

For two decades, after a crisis precipitated by France in the 1960s, the Council decided unanimously on anything any member deemed in its vital national interest. The SEA (1987) opened quality majority voting (QMV) on almost everything in the program for completing the single market. The Maastricht, Amsterdam, and Nice Treaties extended QMV, but not to everything. The 2009 Lisbon Treaty replaced QMV with a "double majority" formula on most matters that required both a majority (55 percent) of member states with a majority (65 percent) of the EU population for approval.

The Council of Ministers, along with the European Council, is where member states express their preferences and negotiate. Composed of national ministers empowered to deal with European issues, its most important job is passing European laws. It also legally concludes international agreements for the EU, approves the EU budget (with the Parliament), and decides some issues in the CFSP and Justice and Home Affairs areas. A powerful Committee of Permanent Representatives (or COREPER), composed of member state ambassadors to the EU, does much of the preliminary work for the Council. COREPER, which relies on preliminary sorting of issues by 150–200 working committees composed of national civil servants, also coordinates high-level functional committees, including the political and security committee that prepares CFSP, a special agriculture committee, a trade committee, a committee for justice and home affairs matters, and an economic and financial committee.

The Council of Ministers traditionally worked behind closed doors. Except for leaks, the public never really knew what debates took place, what alternatives were considered, and the positions of different countries. Worries about legitimacy led to efforts to open the proceedings, however, including television broadcasts showing parts of meetings and public announcements of certain votes, although because the Council usually works on consensus rather than voting, this is less important than it seems. Inside knowledge remains limited because much of the Council's work is done in bilateral and multilateral discussions before things close to decision. Shrouding deliberations in diplomatic secrecy has facilitated the wheeling and dealing that can lead to decisions and allowed national governments to obscure their responsibility especially when they have had serious redistributive effects at national level. The 2009 Lisbon Treaty obliged the Council's actual decision-making sessions to be open, however, so some change is occurring.

Up until the Lisbon Treaty, the Council was organized by a presidency that rotated among member states every six months, which coordinated Council–Parliament interactions, including the "conciliation committees" for co-decision, and submitted the Council's annual program to the Parliament. It also prepared and presided European Council summits and spoke for the EU on foreign policy (excepting trade). After Maastricht, CFSP and JHA broadened the presidency's role, since it also coordinated the new noncommunity "pillars" where decisions were taken intergovernmentally. The member state that held the presidency also played the role of power broker, coalition builder, and program initiator. The presidency was not always effective, however, and sometimes there were leadership discontinuities, poor preparation, and ineptitude.

The European Council

Enlargement to twenty-seven members led the 2009 Lisbon Treaty to establish a president of the European Council. Prior to this, the European Council had been a summit reunion of heads of state and government plus one other minister (usually the foreign minister), the Council secretary-general, and the Commission president and secretary-general, that met twice during each six-month Council presidency. The relative intimacy of its meetings was meant to encourage open discussion on important matters of EU strategy. The final hours of intense work produced a "Presidency Conclusion," which provided the European Council's decisions, intentions, and goals. The importance of the European Council is clear from a partial list of its conclusions (see Table 4.1).

The European Council president—the first was Herman von Rompuy, a former Belgian Prime Minister—serves for a two-and-one-half-year, once renewable, term. The Lisbon Treaty hoped to create a powerful new personal symbol of the EU and a more effective administrative leader than the rotating Council presidency had been. Lisbon also provided for a new M/Mme CFSP—Catherine Ashton was the first—to represent the EU internationally, consolidate the EU's different and divided foreign policy operations, and establish a new EU "External Action" (diplomatic) service. The Council of Ministers and the European Council rely on a 2,000-strong secretariat (several hundred A-level administrators), with a staff for the secretary-general, legal services, and seven general directorates. The Council secretary-general, with an international focus, and his assistant, who focuses on EU domestic matters, are important officials.

The European Parliament

The European Parliament (EP) lives a vagabond existence between Strasbourg, France, where it holds its plenary sessions, and Brussels, where it meets in groups

Table 4.1	Major Conclusions of Recent European Councils
European Council	**Product(s)**
Fontainebleau, 1984	Solved "British check" issue; Spain and Portugal; admitted appointment of Jacques Delors
Milan, 1985	Approved "1992" White Paper; decided intergovernmental conference leading to SEA
Brussels, 1987	Adopted first Delors budgetary package (reform of structural funds)
Madrid, 1989	Accepted Delors report on EMU
Dublin, 1990	Decided German East-West reunification within the EU
Maastricht, 1991	Maastricht Treaty
Edinburgh, 1992	Decided enlargement to European Free Trade Association countries
Essen, 1994	Began discussing enlargement to CEECs
Dublin, 1996	EMU Stability and Growth Pact
Amsterdam, 1997	Amsterdam Treaty
Berlin, 1999	Approved Agenda 2000 budgetary package to facilitate enlargement
Lisbon, 2000	Lisbon Strategy on competitiveness and knowledge society
Nice, 2000	Nice Treaty
Laeken, 2001	Called European Convention
Brussels, 2003	Ten countries signed treaty to join EU
Brussels, 2004	Agreement on new Constitutional Treaty derived from Convention
Brussels, 2005	New budgetary package for 2007–2013
Brussels, 2007	Adopted proposals on energy, the environment, and global warming. Agreement on Lisbon Treaty
Brussels, 2007	Initial EU responses to Great Recession
2010–2013	Grappled with Eurozone crisis
2013	New budgetary package for 2014–2020

and committees. Since 1979 the Parliament has been directly elected. (Table 4.2 shows the allocation of seats among member states as of 2014.) Candidates run on national party tickets and then, if elected, their national political groups usually join European-level party coalitions. Elections to the EP are meant to encourage debate between aspiring leaders and voters about future European policies, raise levels of political education and consciousness about European integration, and reinforce EU solidarities and identity. Up to now, however, votes for the EP have been second-order national elections, treated by national politicians more as important indicators of the relative strength of national parties than as important EU events.

The EP elects its president and executive bureau for two-and-one-half-year terms. The presidency has usually alternated between a Socialist and a Christian Democrat, most often the two largest groups. After the 2009 elections the presidential term was divided between a Polish Christian Democrat, who served until 2012, and a German Social Democrat who served until the 2014 elections. The president presides

Table 4.2	European Parliament, Seats per Country 2014 (alphabetical order of country's name in its own language)		
Country	**2014**	**Country**	**2014**
Belgium	21	Lithuania	11
Bulgaria	17	Luxembourg	6
Cyprus	6	Malta	6
Croatia	11	Netherlands	26
Czech Rep	21	Austria	18
Denmark	13	Poland	51
Germany	96	Portugal	21
Greece	21	Romania	32
Spain	54	Slovakia	13
Estonia	6	Slovenia	8
France	74	Finland	13
Hungary	21	Sweden	20
Ireland	11	United Kingdom	73
Italy	73		
Latvia	8	TOTAL	751

over parliamentary sessions, participates in periodic inter-institutional discussions with Commission and Council counterparts, and addresses member state leaders at European Council summits. The bulk of Parliament's work is done by seventeen permanent committees, which produce detailed reports in their functional areas, making them target for an army of lobbyists.

In the early years the Parliament was only "consulted" by the Commission, but it has slowly become more important. In the 1970s it won power over the Community's budget and discovered that it could delay decisions by juggling the required time limits for delivering its opinions. The real shift began in 1987, however, when the Single European Act (SEA) instituted a "cooperation" (amending) procedure for most single-market legislation, soon replaced at Maastricht by "co-decision," a term to be taken literally, because Parliament and the Council "co-decide" on Commission proposals as if they were two separate legislative houses. Each reads and sometimes amends Commission proposals twice. Then, if they do not agree, the proposal goes to a "conciliation committee" of the Council and Parliament. If the committee can agree, the measure goes back to Council and Parliament for a "third reading" when it is usually approved. Parliament also possesses "assenting" power over applications from prospective new members, international treaties, EMU arrangements, multiyear regional fund programs, and its own electoral procedures. In addition, the Rome Treaty gave Parliament the right to bring the Commission and Council before the ECJ for "failure to act" where the treaty seemed to oblige them to, supplemented later by a right to sue if the Council infringed on its powers. The Parliament also must approve the Commission's annual budget proposal and "discharge" completed budget years (retrospective auditing).

Growing parliamentary influence has been good for the EU. Parliaments are most effective when they pursue specific political platforms, as happens nationally when they deliberate proposals from elected governments. The EP has no right of legislative initiative, however, and deals with, but can only react to, proposals from the Commission. The Lisbon Treaty added new "yellow card" linkages between EU institutions and national parliaments, which allow the latter to indicate whether they believe an EU legislative proposal violates subsidiarity, the principle that decisions should be made at the lowest and least centralized competent authority. The Lisbon Treaty also established a citizen initiative procedure by which at least a million citizens across several member states can petition EU institutions to take up a specific piece of legislation, provided that it is legally within the remit of EU treaties. But none of these reforms have resolved a challenge at the heart of the EU—how to make ordinary citizens accredit the EU's legitimacy.

The Eurozone crisis was an earthquake that caused political aftershocks in the May 2014 European Parliament (EP) elections. The crisis multiplied protest and support for populist parties on the right and the left, and not only those hardest hit by the austerity policies. Anti-EU passions reinforced the existing political repertories of unconventional political forces, whether statist protectionism on the left or right-wing anti-immigrant xenophobia.

Low turnout for EP elections traditionally favoured protest voting, even if the result was usually a majority from traditional center-left and center-right parties. The 2014 election was a test of new Eurosceptic strength, however. Turnout was stable (43.09%), but the center-left and center-right parties did less well than in the past. The European People's Party (EPP; conservatives and Christian Democrats) remained the largest party group, but lost 6.6% of its 2009 vote (to 29.4%, down from 36%) and 44 seats (to 221). The Socialists and Democrats (S&D) gained 0.6% (25.6% from 25%) and 9 new seats (to 192). Alliance of Liberals and Democrats for Europe

subsidiarity

Principle consecrated by the 1991 Maastricht Treaty that the EU should seek decision making at the level of the lowest effective jurisdiction.

citizen initiative

Clause in 2009 Lisbon Treaty allowing citizens to propose referendums to initiate EU legislation, provided 1 million legal signatures have been obtained in a "significant number" of different EU member states.

lost 2.7% (8.7% from 11.4%) and 17 seats. Finally, anti-EU and antisystem candidates won more than 20% of votes and seats. The UK Independence Party, the French *Front National*, and the Danish Peoples' Party, in the intolerant right, along with new left Syriza in Greece, made breakthroughs while anti-EU rebels of all stripes did well.

What did this mean for the EP? Reduced support for the center-right EPP and the center-left S&D compels them to combine to create majorities, implying more compromise. Eurosceptical newcomers will make a great deal of noise, but because they disagree among themselves, the noise will be cacophonic. In addition, because of these disagreements, it is difficult for Eurosceptic parties to ally enough to form the official parliamentary groups that give greater access to financing, staffing, speaking time, and EP committees. Whether rebel voices grow louder and more coherent will depend on how the EU proceeds as the economic crisis eases, if it eases. If employment levels rise and growth returns, Eurosceptic threats could moderate. If austerity, low growth, and economic despair persist, there could be deeper political troubles.

The 2014 EP elections produced an additional aftershock, however. In their campaigns, the larger EP parties invoked a clause in the Lisbon Treaty enjoining member states to "take into account" EP election results in the choice of the next President of the European Commission and presented "leading candidates" for this presidency, in the hope of forcing the European Council to appoint the candidate from the party with the most votes, the EPP's Jean-Claude Juncker, ex-Prime Minister of Luxembourg and former chair of the Eurogroup. The broader goal was to connect the Commission presidency with electoral results to politicize and further legitimate the Commission while frustrating claims of the intergovernmental European Council's to be the EU's final decision maker. Member state leaders responded with a serious row. British Prime Minister Cameron, faced with a major Eurosceptic challenge inside his own party and committed to negotiating a repatriation of powers from the EU before an "in or out" national referendum in 2017, denounced Juncker as "too federalist" and forcefully stated that member states, not voters in EP elections, were the legitimate base of the EU. German Chancellor Merkel, whose Social Democratic Grand Coalition partner had been central in the "leading candidate" campaign, eventually came out for Juncker, leading many of Cameron's earlier allies to retreat and a European Council vote for Juncker. The decision did little to resolve uncertainty about the EU's future, however. How far would the Euro-parliamentary challenge to intergovernmental power in the EU actually go? Would it help citizens to see the "Community method" as more democratic?

The European Court of Justice

European law is based on the treaties that member states have signed over six decades, and EU action must spring from this "treaty base." European law is only part of the laws of European Union member states, but where it exists, it is superior to, and supersedes, their laws. The European Court of Justice (ECJ), born in the ECSC, has been the key to making this happen. The Court, located in Luxembourg, is composed of twenty-eight justices (one from each member state) and eight advocates-general. The advocates-general review cases and provide legal opinion to the justices but do not rule on fundamental legal matters. The Court can sit in plenary session when it wishes, but must do so when dealing with matters brought before it by a Community institution or member state. Otherwise, it subdivides its work into "chambers" (of three and five judges each), any one of which may refer matters to the full Court. The ECJ's decisions are binding on member states and their citizens. The Court's huge workload led the SEA to establish of a

Tribunal of First Instance, known since the Lisbon Treaty as the General Court (composed of one judge for each member state, each with six-year terms). The General Court covers complex matters of fact in litigation brought by individuals and companies. Its decisions concerning questions of law (but not fact) can be appealed to the full ECJ.

The ECJ can strike down laws from member states and EU institutions when it judges them contrary to the treaties and, in so doing, interprets the treaties and makes EU law with its rulings. Cases get to the ECJ in many ways. The most significant is "preliminary ruling" in which a national court, presented with a case that may involve European law, forwards it to the ECJ for advice, which then usually settles the matter. Next are "annulment proceedings" in which a European institution, government, or individual can ask the court to rule on the legality of European legislation and other EU measures. A third path involves the Commission or a member state asking the ECJ to decide whether or not a member state has failed to fulfill its EU legal obligations ("treaty infringement proceeding"). Member states, other EU institutions, or individuals may also bring cases against a particular institution for "failure to act" when it ought to have done so. Cases for damages against Community institutions are considered as well. Member states and EU institutions may ask for rulings on the compatibility of international agreements with EU law. In general, ECJ rulings have been central in the evolution of European integration as Table 4.3, listing landmark cases, shows. The 2009 Lisbon Treaty established an EU Charter

Table 4.3	Significant Decisions of the European Court of Justice
Decision	**Importance**
Van Gend and Loos, 1963	Ruled that the Community constituted a new order of international law, whose subjects were member states and their nationals, derived from limitations of sovereignty by member states.
Costa v. ENE, 1964	Central in establishing the supremacy of EU law itself.
Van Duyn v. Home Office, 1974	Gave individuals the same right to employment in another member state as nationals of that state.
Defrenne v. Sabena, 1976	Based upon Article 119 of the Rome Treaty enjoining equal treatment of men and women in employment. The case opened initiatives attenuating gender discrimination in EU labor markets.
Cassis de Dijon, 1979	Member states must accept goods from other member states on the principle of mutual recognition, assuming that all members have reasonable product standards.
Vereniging Bond van Adverteerders v. the Netherlands State, 1988	Obliged member states to open up national telecommunications services to competition.
Bosman, 1995	Made illegal local club rules and restrictions on the employment of football players, opening international movement for professional athletes.

of Fundamental Rights (with the United Kingdom, Poland, and the Czech Republic securing opt-outs), which is promoting substantial new litigation, particularly by individuals invoking Charter provisions to settle grievances. The Court will be called upon to decide their claims, implying a significant extension of EU jurisprudence.

Other Institutions

The EU has several other institutions. In Brussels there also two important "advisory committees": An Economic and Social Committee with delegates from business, labor, and other professions and a Committee of the Regions with representatives from the EU's regions. Both review and submit opinions on pending EU legislation and, informally, are useful places for organized interests to network and connect with the Commission, Council, and Parliament. There is also an official Court of Auditors that reviews EU spending, and a European Investment Bank that mobilizes investment loans for regional planning and development purposes. Finally, there are now thirty-three "community agencies" scattered across the member states (each member state has a claim) that work on informational and regulatory matters, from fish stocks and plant variety, Europol, maritime security, health and safety at work, disease prevention and control, the environment, food safety, railways, and many more.

Where Do You Stand?

EU institutions are much more difficult to understand than those of most democratic national states, to the detriment of European integration. If true, why?

Imagine you are a European trying to make sense of all this. Would you throw up your hands and revert to your national identity or would you dive headlong into the brave new world of Europe?

THE EU AND ITS POLICIES

SECTION 4

Focus Questions

- Why does the EU have so many legitimacy problems?

- Is there a place for the EU as a new kind of "soft power" international actor?

The EU can only work where members have agreed by treaty to do so. The EU has grown because EU policy cooperation in one area has sometimes spilled over into others, as Jean Monnet had hoped. Sometimes spillover has happened via classic "community method" market building. Sometimes the Commission has quasi-governmental roles, as in Competition Policy, or, to a lesser degree, in agricultural policy. EU governance can also be federal, but not in a "community method" way, as with EMU. In many areas governance prerogatives are shared between EU and national levels. In some the EU, without formal power, can influence governance through soft law.

Building a European Market

The most important thing the EU has done has been integrating many national markets into one. After the Rome Treaties it built a "common market" customs-free area where manufactured goods could move freely, plus a common agricultural policy. The "community method" and the Commission's power to propose legislation were at this market-building core. After the first decades, however, it was clear that other problems needed resolving before the market was truly open. People could not circulate freely across borders, goods stalled in trucks at customs posts while drivers filed endless forms, professionals had difficulty working in other countries, financial and services markets remained national, and national sales taxes discouraged trade. In the 1970s, when economic times got tougher, members set up new nontariff barriers to trade.

The 1985 program to complete the single-market and open a "space without borders" revived, and may have saved, European integration. The program liberalized and deregulated national markets, promoted new trade between EU members and, ultimately, created one European market and economy. To do this, it established uniform standards and norms, stiffer competition rules and environmental policies, and integrated some forms of taxation. For example, when the EU enlarged to poorer countries, it devised new regional development policies to help them. Finally, pledges to establish fully the "four freedoms" of goods, services, capital, and people movement had to be fulfilled.

Initially, under the guidance of the commissioner for the internal market, the single-market program drafted proposals after consulting widely with interests, committees, national-level administrations, the Committee of Permanent Representatives (COREPER), and other bodies. The European Parliament, its new power of amendment in hand, examined these proposals, and the Council of Ministers made final decisions by new QMV procedures. The last step was for member states to "transpose" the new rules into national legal codes. One of the more daunting tasks was harmonizing technical standards and norms. When this had been tried earlier, multilateral negotiations often failed. The single-market program proposed instead to proceed by "mutual recognition" following the ECJ's 1979 *Cassis de Dijon* ruling that goods legally marketed in any member state should circulate freely throughout the EU as long as minimum standards were upheld. Last but not least, VAT (value-added) taxes had to be harmonized to prevent different levels and types of national taxes from distorting competition within the single market.

After 1992, the target date for completing the single-market program, change did not stop, but what remained was harder to do. Members disagreed, particularly about liberalizing the service sector—70 percent of European economic activity. The Union changed intellectual property laws; harmonized taxation on savings; liberalized public procurement; opened up telecoms, electricity, and gas provision to greater competition; and made it easier for service businesses to set up in other countries. Beginning in 1999, the Commission also proposed a major action plan to harmonize rules and open markets in securities, banking, and insurance. Opening up service markets was controversial, however, and protest about a 2005 Services Directive was central in referendums that defeated the proposed European Constitutional Treaty. Public services have been a particular problem. There has always been recognition that public services in health, education, public transportation, post offices, and utilities were different from grocery stores and law firms, but economic conditions change, and so have ideas about public services. Postal services, challenged by private delivery firms like FedEx and UPS and the Internet, have been privatizing. National pricing and access restrictions for what had once been "natural monopolies" (airlines, electricity, gas, and telecoms) needed lowering. It is not hard to foresee challenges to the public nature of health care and education in the future.

Single-market progress has often been blocked by entrenched special interests in national professional associations, powerful banks and financial service firms, employers, and unions. Enlargement to twenty-eight members brought the task of insuring that existing market rules and regulations were applied. The free movement of people has stirred deep national anxieties about immigration. Still, the Commission has calculated that the single market had increased EU GDP by 1.8 percent, created 2.5 million more jobs, increased exports and imports, lowered utility prices, and enhanced consumer choice.

Competition Policy

There would have been little point in opening the European market if companies and countries could then limit competition within it. The Rome Treaty declared that measures should be taken so that "competition in the internal market is not distorted" and granted the European Commission responsibility for this. Competition policy has since become one of the Commission's rare federal competencies, subject only to ECJ review. The Commission traditionally has done most of Europe's big antitrust work, leaving only small cases to national authorities. Anticompetitive firm behaviors—cartels, trusts, and monopolies—can be outlawed when judged to be against European interests, and since 1989, the Commission has overseen mergers and more recently played a key role in deregulating public utilities.

The Commission's antitrust powers are both negative—preventing illegal behavior—and positive—regulating and authorizing. Its Competition DG works with lawyers and economists who monitor company conditions, the business press, and market developments. It can request information from firms and carry out investigations, including "dawn raids" to obtain company documents. Because mergers in other parts of the world can have market-limiting effects in Europe, the Commission's merger control operations have international scope and DG Comp is among the most powerful competition authorities in the world. Its investigations of potential violations often end informally after the threat of sanctions leads to successful negotiations. But when informal dealing fails, the Commission may levy substantial fines. It ruled against Microsoft's practice of "bundling" software programs in Windows, for example, initially fining it €500 million and then fining it later even more for noncompliance. EU procedures for merger control involve proactive economic and legal judgments about how a proposed merger could restrain trade. Perhaps the most spectacular case occurred in 2001, when the Commission blocked an avionics merger between General Electric and Honeywell, even after U.S. authorities had already approved. More often, mergers go through after company plans are reformulated to meet DG Comp's concerns.

The issue of state aid to companies is more difficult because national companies, jobs, and votes are at stake and some member states have traditions of state-centered industrial policy. While the Commission uses its power to prevent state subsidies that could impair markets from working, it has also allowed state aid for projects such as well-defined one-off industrial restructuring in industries hurt by recessions or world market shifts. This power has been extensively used in the Great Recession and Euro zone crisis, almost always with the proviso that subsidies are phased out once crisis conditions are over. It has also allowed subsidies for large projects that might enhance the European market, like the English Channel tunnel, and to shore up regions hit by natural disasters.

EU competition policy is constantly evolving. National as well as corporate players push back and insist on their right to use instruments such as subsidies to promote social cohesion, economic growth, and job creation. The ECJ has also slapped down DG COMP when it has occasionally done its work badly. In recent years the

Commission has decentralized competition policy matters below a certain threshold of importance to national authorities, but following European rules.

Agriculture

The Rome Treaty proposed a Common Market for agricultural as well as manufactured products. The original Common Agricultural Policy (CAP) was a strange market, however, with price supports administered by the Commission to keep Community prices for agricultural goods higher than they might have been otherwise in the interests of food security and modernizing European agriculture. After only a few years, it had begun to encourage farmers to overproduce, overuse chemical fertilizers, pollute, and damage water tables. But farmers had been shrewd enough to build powerful groups and alliances with national agriculture ministers in order to protect the policy from reformers. The CAP, the largest single EU budget item, became redistributive from taxpayers and consumers to farmers and also moved a great deal of money from country to country, giving some members more than others. The CAP's incentives to produce more created surpluses that necessitated expensive EU-funded storage facilities and dumping on the international market. Finally, as economies of scale grew, there were disproportional additional transfers to larger, more efficient producers.

The CAP made DG Agriculture the largest administrative unit in Brussels. For much of the CAP's existence hundreds of technocrats measured carrots, rented barns, sold surpluses the world over, and proposed prices for a huge range of products that the Council of Ministers voted on by QMV (with the Parliament marginalized until the Lisbon Treaty). Because the DG proposed prices and regulations, it was heavily lobbied by farmers' organizations. Highly regulated markets also tempted fraud, leading DG Agriculture to police farmers to see that they actually produced what they claimed. Each product area had its own management committee, with the entire system tracked by an intergovernmental committee on agriculture, but implementation was left largely to member states, monitored by the Commission.

Reforming the CAP began not long after the CAP itself. "Net contributor" member states like Great Britain and the Netherlands disliked subsidizing French beet-sugar conglomerates and well-off Danes. The CAP's costs grew so fast that they threatened to crowd out other EU activities and discredit European integration. In response, cost control began in the 1980s and land "set asides" and direct income support came in 1992 and have since accelerated. There has been a lessening of EU international dumping, if not enough to satisfy farm producers elsewhere. Fitting the CAP to Eastern European agriculture has been another challenge. Making new member states full CAP participants, particularly Poland and its plethora of small farmers, might have expanded the budget more than anyone wanted. The result, Poles ended up with less than they expected and western farmers hung onto their benefits.

In tough negotiations about the EU's 2007–2013 budget package, the CAP, defended by the French, became part of the negotiating endgame. No one won much, but the CAP budget lost least. As had traditionally been the case, CAP reforms were made by raising the budget to placate farmers for incremental changes. More recently, budgets have been kept at a nominally steady state but slowly declining as a percentage of the EU budget. "Decoupling" CAP subsidies from price supports and shifting spending to rural development left the CAP budget more vulnerable in 2014, however, when a new EU budgetary package began. Farmers are a dwindling and aging part of EU population and the long CAP saga may be coming to an end.

Regional Development

Financing regional development through the "structural funds" is the EU's largest budgetary item after agriculture and an expression of solidarity between better-off and less-developed regions. There was recognition about regional development in the Rome Treaty, mainly to help Italy with its underdeveloped south. Then, after the EU enlarged in 1973 to the United Kingdom, Denmark, and Ireland, a European Regional Development Fund (ERDF) was created to help distressed and undeveloped areas. Enlargement in the 1980s to poorer countries like Greece in 1981, then Spain and Portugal in 1986, necessitated greater efforts and the SEA made "economic and social cohesion" a new common policy. The 1988 reform of the structural funds doubled financing over five years, with another doubling in the 1990s.

EU regional development prioritizes specific objectives and promotes "partnership" between the Commission (which vets projects and administers them) and national and regional levels, which must come up with cofinancing—the so-called principle of additionality. The priorities developed in the later 1980s were to assist underdeveloped regions (75 percent of the structural fund budget), help restructure deindustrialized regions, enhance skills and combat long-term and youth unemployment, and aid rural areas. The money went to multiannual, multitask, and multiregional programs, mainly in areas where average income was 75 percent or less than the EU average. The Maastricht Treaty added a "cohesion fund" to compensate Greece, Ireland, Portugal, and Spain for participation in the EU's environmental and transport policies. Enlargement to the CEECs has reshaped regional development policies, however, because the new members were almost all below the 75 percent threshold. By rights they should have received most of the money, but this did not happen immediately because older member states wanted to continue receiving what they had earlier.

THE EU BUDGET: A SIGNIFICANCE TEST?

In 2013 the EU spent €150.9 billion in the general categories shown in the table below. While this may seem large, it is only 1 percent of the GDP of its member states, whose national budgets are incomparably larger (44.5 percent of GDP on average). The budget grew through the 1980s and 1990s, stabilized, and has declined slightly recently, as member states try to keep the EU on a tighter leash. Many EU policies also entail large national spending. Almost all western EU members contribute more to the budget than they get back and poorer countries are "net beneficiaries." The EU budgetary process has two steps. The first is intergovernmental negotiation every five years on multiyear "financial perspectives"—a new deal was negotiated in 2013 for 2014–2020. The second involves annual European Parliamentary review of yearly budgets and EP "discharge" (approval) of the books after the year is completed.

Spending Category 2013	Billion Euros
Sustainable Growth, of which 77 percent is for regional development, the rest R&D and life-long education	70.5
Natural Resources, of which 90+ percent is for agriculture and rural development, the rest fisheries and climate change policy	60.1
Citizenship, Liberty, Security and Justice (Maastricht's JHA)	2.1
EU as a global player (CFSP, aid, development cooperation)	9.5
Administration	8.4
Total	150.9

The cumulative effects of EU regional programs are hard to calculate. Amounts given to any particular country are small in absolute terms, but can add up to 4 percent to local investment, particularly in infrastructural projects that might not have been affordable. Some, like Ireland and Spain, were spectacularly successful until the Great Recession, while others upgraded a great deal. The funds have also provided incentives to avoid "races to the bottom" through the use of cheap labor and minimalist social policies. Another bonus has been that regional levels of government have developed stakes in European integration and increased purchasing power in poorer areas is used to buy goods and services from the rest of the EU. The structural funds also provide incentives for reform. The CEECs, for example, with incomes of less than 40 percent of EU average, needed the money, and to get it they had to develop administrative capacity to absorb it productively. Funding improvement in roads, railroads, energy provision, telecommunications, airports, and ports brings rapid returns. But the biggest payoff, proven by experiences in Spain, Portugal, and Greece and the CEECs, all emerging from authoritarian regimes, is that EU regional development can help consolidate the rule of law and greater democracy. Finally, when countries have been reluctant to invest enough in such capacities, the threat of withholding structural funds—as recently for Romania and Bulgaria—can be sobering.

The Euro and EMU

Economic and Monetary Union (EMU), decided at Maastricht, began in 1999. Its importance for the EU, both positively and negatively, cannot be overestimated. For business, a single currency means more transparent costs and economic indicators. Ordinary Europeans and foreign tourists no longer have to exchange money every time they cross a border. Most importantly, the EU has built a single market that would have been hard pressed to manage fluctuations among national currencies if EMU and the euro had not been invented. EMU has done a very good job at maintaining price stability. In light of the Eurozone crisis, however, the record has been mixed.

How did EMU work prior to 2007–2008? Maastricht created a European System of Central Banks that included all member state central banks and charged it with maintaining price stability, designing and implementing EU monetary policy, managing foreign exchanges, holding reserves, and operating payments systems. Its core, very federal, institution is the European Central Bank (ECB) with a powerful president and six-member executive board plus a governing council of central bank governors from all EMU members. Located in Frankfurt, Germany, the ECB is statutorily independent from political influence. Its most important job is achieving price stability, defined as an inflation rate of 2 percent a year or less and tracked by targeting money supply and inflation levels and adjusting EMU-wide interest rates.

All EU members excepting those with explicit opt-outs (the UK and Denmark) were expected to join EMU eventually, but only those who have met Maastricht's convergence criteria have joined. EMU officially thus started at eleven members in 1999—now eighteen—and the ECB made its philosophy clear from the beginning. If some members had problems, it was their own fault and most likely caused by selfish market actors and imprudent governments. Economic growth in 1998–2000 allowed the ECB to dispel worries that its dedication to price stability might stifle new growth. Major early criticisms were that it had problems communicating and that the new euro fluctuated too much. The 1997 Stability and Growth Pact (reformed in 2005) bound EMU members to budgetary deficits of less than 3 percent, but after 2000 more than half of EMU members stopped observing this, indicating something amiss. EMU's "one size fits all" monetary policy lowered interest rates to smaller and poorer economies like those of Greece, Ireland, Portugal, and Spain, providing them with a windfall that encouraged debt-based development strategies that often fed housing bubbles.

EMU "federalized" monetary policy, but its members retained national taxing, spending, and budgeting. A "Eurogroup" of EMU finance ministers tried to promote coherence in these areas across the Euro zone, but with few tools to oblige members to comply. The absence of cooperative economic and financial governance helped create the situation that eventually exploded in the Euro zone crisis. As discussed earlier, the crisis demanded a reconfiguration of EMU's architecture involving a substantial increase in central oversight of national fiscal and budgetary policies backed by new enforcement powers, increasing the power of the ECB as policy-maker and regulator and the Commission as monitor and enforcer. The ECB performed well during the crisis, both as a tough negotiator in crisis summits and, most important, by implementing "nonstandard measures" such as providing funds to commercial banks at low interest rates to keep credit flowing, buying up bank debt, and buying up national debt on secondary markets, in all providing liquidity to the financial sector and member states that otherwise would not have been available. A pledge made by ECB President Mario Draghi in 2012 to "do what it takes," that is, to continue such policies, was widely credited as the turning point that finally calmed crisis.

Shared Policies

The EU is a mixed system of public policy-making. In some areas the EU has strong, "vertical" powers that directly shape national policies. In others it has more limited, "horizontal" power to generate ideas, set examples, delineate best practices, provide seed money, and cajole, but national policy-making remains central. The precise division of shared labor is determined by EU treaties and in the concept of "subsidiarity" written into Maastricht, according to which the public interest is best served when policy is undertaken at the lowest appropriate level.

Globalization and Competitiveness

To respond to globalization the EU has most often used its "horizontal" powers. EU policies to promote economic competitiveness stretch to the beginning of the European Coal and Steel Community (ECSC). Since then, the EU has often been involved in helping to reconfigure troubled industries and regions, providing financial aid, retraining, and temporary trade protection. Many of these actions were to ease the pain of regional deindustrialization. By the 1990s, however, EU focus had turned toward investment in high-end innovation.

Six decades ago Europe was far behind the United States, and the ECSC and Common Market were Western Europe's catch-up tools. After the economic difficulties of the 1970s, the United States jumped ahead again, while Japan and the Asian Tigers came onto the scene. The single-market program and EMU were meant to prevent Europe from falling behind, but the United States moved forward again in the 1990s, propelled by its financial power and vanguard position in information technology, while China, India, and other low-cost newcomers began gobbling up manufacturing markets in which Europe had earlier specialized. Today's EU Europe of 500 million people is the richest single market in the world, but it is not at the top of the league in economic competitiveness.

Key new areas like research and technological development (R&D) and industrial policy remain primarily national issues, but the EU can provide incentives for new cooperation. In the early 1980s, the EU began funding high-tech R&D, particularly for research in electronics. The SEA and the Maastricht Treaty allowed more EU activity in research and technological development to complement member states' efforts. The 2000 Lisbon European Council then called for the creation of a "European Research Area" that would raise spending on R&D—primarily national, but also EU-level—to 3 percent of EU GDP by 2010, a target still not met. The flagship vehicles for EU R&D have been multiyear research "framework programs" drawn up by the Commission and approved by the Council, designed to work with, rather than substitute for, national policies. The 2000 Lisbon strategy sought greater cooperation and convergence among member states around general European goals. Budgets have been relatively small—in the just-completed Sixth Plan the budget was €17.5 billion, and efforts have been hindered by national rivalries, but there has been greater European focus and coherence. One significant product has been trans-European scientific networks. The EU has also invested in areas of immediate trans-European importance—infrastructure, environmental research, and health and food safety, for example. There have also been major European "industrial policy" innovations in mobile phones, space technologies, and satellites that have "Europeanized" standards and helped security policy and air transport.

The 2000 "Lisbon Agenda" sought to make EU Europe the world's most advanced "knowledge economy" by 2010, by which point the EU was also to have restored full employment and preserved Europe's "social model"—welfare states and labor market policies—through reform. The Lisbon program also included new infrastructure, environmental policies for sustainable development, and upgraded "citizen competence" through education and training. The Lisbon architects, anticipating problems of cooperation, proposed an "open method of coordination" (OMC) that involved setting general European goals, encouraging member states to hold regular and open national discussions about achieving them, identifying best practices, building up comparative indicators of progress, and publicizing successes and failures—naming and shaming—from Brussels. The hope was that in the absence of harder tools, "soft law" would work. It did not, however, and in 2004–2005, the Barroso Commission refocused efforts more narrowly on structural reforms and liberalization, retreating from the OMC and reassigning responsibilities to member states. Proposals to open energy markets were hindered by opposition from national energy monopolies, making it difficult for the EU to have a European energy policy. Brussels moved on chemicals regulation (REACH) and climate change while talking a great deal about lightening its regulatory hand, but results have been limited. After a decade, consensus was that the Lisbon strategy fell short because it depended on voluntary coordination by member states.

By 2010 it was clear that reform was going on, but not enough, and the financial crises had set things back considerably. Unemployment had risen, and the EU was far from becoming the world's leading knowledge economy. But by then the EU was looking forward to its new "2020" strategy to follow the Lisbon project. Europe 2020 was a more modest affair—raising the employment rate that had dropped in the crisis, finally reaching Lisbon's 3 percent R&D target, reducing greenhouse gas and finding new non-carbon energy sources, and reducing school dropout and poverty rates.

Social Policy

Social policy best illustrates the EU's multilevel governance and subsidiarity issues. The EU has some influence to exhort countries, but little direct power, because welfare state and employment policies are national. The Treaty of Rome narrowly limited the EU to matters of labor market mobility within the common market, some occupational training, and equal opportunity for men and women. It created a European Social Fund with the vague purposes of making "the employment of workers easier, increasing their geographical and occupational mobility within the Community." In general, however, the great variety of social policy regimes within the EU today reflects the variety of its members, who protect their systems well.

Concern with inequality in the workplace between men and women translated into an article in the 1957 Rome Treaty, requiring "equal treatment." EU Europe has since developed progressive programs for advancing women's rights. The SEA added workplace health and safety to EU-level social policy prerogatives out of anticipation that lower national rules might be a source of comparative advantage. The SEA also included an article stating that "the Commission shall endeavor to develop the dialogue between management and labor at European ... level." This was elaborated into a "Social Chapter" at Maastricht and led to EU social policy directives on working time, consultative European Works Councils, parental leave, and "atypical work" (part-time and short-term contracts). By the later 1990s, however, member states had lost enthusiasm for EU social policy, and emphasis shifted to decentralized "soft" procedures and the open method of coordination (OMC) in the European Employment Strategy in the 1997 Amsterdam Treaty, followed by wider use of OMC to promote change in pensions, poverty policy, and other matters. By 2011 there were signs that the European Employment Strategy was helping, but OMC had by then been abandoned in other areas. Despite "soft" activities, the EU's direct influence over social policy has remained very limited.

Environmental Policy

When environmental issues exploded into the public consciousness in the 1960s and 1970s, they seemed a perfect fit for EU action. Acid rain, air and water pollution, transporting dangerous materials, protecting biodiversity, and managing the externalities of industrial development were problems that did not respect borders. The likelihood of EU action was enhanced by the political success of "green movements" in key EU countries like Germany, the Netherlands, and France. When in 1972 a member state summit invited the Commission to work in the environmental policy area, it responded eagerly, passing legislation including legal recognition of the "polluter pays" principle, promoting codes of conduct through "green labels" on products, requiring environmental impact assessments for large projects, and testing and grading beach water safety. Since then, the Commission and its DG Environment have proposed six ambitious multiyear environmental action programs, and are currently working on another. The EU's conversion to strong environmentalism was strengthened in the early 1980s after the European Parliament urged that environmental policy be placed in European Treaties. The Single European Act then established EU competence via a formula that enshrined subsidiarity.

The EU rapidly committed to transnational environmental protection, signing conventions on the Mediterranean and Antarctic, and by the later 1980s the Commission and many heads of state, attuned to growing awareness of climate change, decided to place the EU on the front line out of conviction that climate change could only be confronted globally and because they saw it a good issue to enhance the EU's image as a "soft power" international player. The EU then became a leader in promoting sustainable development with several large initiatives that began with its signature of the UN Framework Convention on Climate Change at Rio in 1992. It was also central in negotiating the Kyoto Protocol, and perhaps more important, in bringing it into legal operation. The EU cap-and-trade scheme for limiting greenhouse gas emissions quickly became the world's most advanced, albeit not without problems. In 2007–2008 it committed to a very ambitious "20-20-20" program that promised to cut EU greenhouse gas emissions by 20 percent, reach 20 percent use of renewable energy, and become 20 percent more energy efficient by 2020. This program imposed significant constraints on member states and was advertised as a "smart development" response to slow economic growth.

The 20-20-20 program was also meant to help launch a successor to the Kyoto Protocol. The 2009 UN Copenhagen climate change negotiations demonstrated how easily EU attempts to lead multilateral climate negotiating could be ignored, however. The EU brought 20-20-20 to the table and promised even more if others agreed to follow in an ambitious post-Kyoto bargain. Copenhagen ended with a very weak deal struck by the United States and China, with the EU on the sidelines, however, a resounding slap in the face for its climate change strategy. EU leaders had overestimated the openings for "soft-power" leadership on the environment. Moralizing had obvious limits, but more important was that multilateral negotiating had changed. Even with a new American president, there was no chance that the U.S. Congress would accept a new treaty modeled on EU objectives. Emerging market powers like China, India, Brazil, and others insisted on being heard. Some, like China, expressed willingness to undertake national actions but opposed binding international commitments in the name of sovereignty. Others, including African leaders, were unwilling to commit to new constraints unless the wealthy world agreed to subsidize the costs of climate change regulation. There was also suspicion that western-led pleading on climate change were in part new ways to deprive economic newcomers of comparative cost advantages just as they started to modernize.

This setback was followed by internal problems. It was unfortunate, but significant, that the EU had been able to band together to try to force the pace at Copenhagen but had never agreed on a coordinated energy policy itself. Europe was heavily dependent on imported energy, particularly oil and gas, but the EU's member states had chosen different strategies to cope with this, from North sea oil and gas Russian oil and gas that Germany and others sourced, expensive nuclear power, as in France, to "fracking," all variations on a go-it-alone theme prompted by needs to nail down present and future energy supplies. This led to a wide disparity in energy costs, even if most EU members paid a great deal more than other industrial countries for energy. The global financial collapse and the Eurozone crisis made things worse. High unemployment, low growth, and squeezed government revenue streams made it much harder for national governments to ask citizens to make sacrifices to mitigate climate change. The consequences have been new disagreements and confusion that have further deflated EU claims of global leadership and lowered EU ambitions on climate change issues.

Intergovernmental Europe

The EU's scope has grown substantially, encroaching ever more on national sovereignty. This has been especially true of Justice and Home Affairs (JHA) and the Common Foreign and Security Policy (CFSP), both hived off into two new intergovernmental pillars by the Maastricht Treaty to allow governments alone to control the pace of change. The 1997 Amsterdam Treaty the 2009 Lisbon Treaty both pledged to integrate these pillars further into the "community method." Movement has been slow, however.

Justice and Home Affairs

The Rome Treaty proclaimed "free movement of people" as a goal, but the EU did not do much about it for decades. After the single-market program made serious new commitment to opening borders, it became inevitable that organized crime—drug dealers, human traffickers, money launderers, and terrorists, and other evildoers—would "Europeanize" along with legitimate business. In the absence of new EU cooperation on visas, identification, asylum policy, and enhanced control at external borders, individual EU states would have been in the dark about who was wandering around and what they might be doing. On top of this, without increased legal cooperation, freedom of movement would leave perfectly respectable EU citizens faced with a bewildering array of national civil laws and baffled about their rights.

The issues were real, and even before the EU took them up, ad hoc groups of member states formed organizations on specific problems such as drugs and human trafficking. But it was the Schengen Group in the 1980s—originally France, Germany, and the Benelux countries, that first removed internal border crossings to allow free movement of their citizens. The Justice and Home Affairs (JHA) clauses at Maastricht were meant to bring these areas together in an intergovernmental pillar outside the community method—leaving only parts of visa policy a "community" matter. Detailed JHA business was done by COREPER and the Council of Ministers (via the K.4 Committee) with help from committees of national experts on immigration and asylum, police and customs cooperation, plus judicial cooperation on civil and criminal matters. Even though JHA decisions had to be made unanimously, there was considerable JHA activity in the 1990s. Europol built up police cooperation among EU member states, gathering, pooling, and circulating intelligence and information. JHA also built up data bases about the **Schengen area**, customs, asylum-seeking, and stolen property, even before the Amsterdam Treaty incorporated the full Schengen *acquis*.

Intergovernmentalism was slow, in part because ministers were secretive and zealously protected national interests. The 1997 Treaty of Amsterdam thus agreed to shift some JHA matters to the "Community Method" and qualified-majority voting, including asylum, parts of immigration, judicial cooperation in civil matters with cross-border implications, and common procedures at EU external borders. There was also a new *passarelle* clause that allowed member states, if they were unanimous, to shift new areas toward the community method and QMV. Highly sensitive matters of police and judicial cooperation remained intergovernmental, however. Amsterdam also committed the EU to build an "area of freedom, security, and justice." The change was meant to shift emphasis from mysterious intergovernmental police activities toward the rights of EU citizens and legal visitors (along with growing harshness for immigrants, part of a general shift in national political focus). Maastricht made citizens of EU member states automatic EU citizens, with equal rights of movement, residence, voting in European elections, and diplomatic protection abroad, and a broader Charter of Fundamental Rights was legalized in the 2009 Lisbon Treaty (with British, Polish, and Czech opt-outs). Amsterdam also proposed policy harmonization through "mutual recognition," better transnational

Schengen area

EU area, named after small city in Luxembourg, where freedom of transnational movement without border controls was first agreed in 1985. Schengen now includes all EU members except Romania, Bulgaria, Croatia, the United Kingdom and, Ireland. It also includes non-EU countries Norway, Iceland, and Switzerland.

readability of national policies, and more international cooperation on civil law matters like divorce and alimony, child visitation, and financial problems such as debt and bankruptcy.

Matters of the police, interior ministers, and criminal law have been difficult to follow because of closed doors and secretive actors, but there are now a number of monitoring and information agencies on drugs, discrimination, and fraud. There are also a European Police College, a European Police Chiefs Task force, and Eurojust, an organization of senior justice officials to facilitate cross-border prosecutions. After 2004 a common European arrest warrant has superseded complicated national extradition proceedings. Europol's antiterrorist coverage and budget were already expanding prior to 9/11 and grew substantially thereafter. There have been serious recent terrorist incidents in the EU as elsewhere, in Madrid in 2004 and London in 2005, for example. But there have been few American complaints about lack of European counterterrorist cooperation, meaning that Europeans have been doing a good job. On the other hand, American NSA spying, which includes the EU's leaders, has opened a serious rift with the EU.

The 2009 Lisbon Treaty further "communitarized" JHA by moving border and asylum control issues and minimal rules about crime and punishment for certain cross-border crimes (terrorism, drugs and arms trafficking, money laundering, sexual exploitation of women, cyber-crime) to qualified majority voting, co-decision, and ECJ review. The Lisbon Treaty also promised an increase in the speed and effectiveness of legal cooperation, in particular because of "mutual recognition" in which member states accepted the decisions of one another as valid. Passports and identity cards, family law, and further Europeanization of criminal law remained intergovernmental, however, to be decided only unanimously.

There are growing clouds over the spirit, if not the letter, of JHA, however. Immigration is a heated issue among across the EU, and citizens usually include internal economic migration from new EU members westward and economic migrants from the EU south in their grievances, which have grown because of unemployment and insecurity from recent conditions of economic crisis. These pressures have created an elite balancing act between defending the rights of Europeans, including free movement and the human rights of migrants, and recognizing anti-immigrant pressures that are sometimes openly xenophobic. The 2011–2012 Arab spring turned illegal immigration in the Mediterranean region into panic flight, overwhelming the EU's practical ability to cope with the surge of refugees. Then French President Sarkozy and Italian Premier Berlusconi both advocated limiting free movement inside the EU for non-EU citizens, a cry echoed by the Danish prime minister who even shut down the Danish border with Germany for a few days. There has also been widespread agitation and repressive responses to Roma migration. This may mean that JHA has been too effective and is feeding growing Euroscepticism.

Foreign and Security Policy

When Jacques Delors was Commission president, he often asked, rhetorically, whether the EU was happy being a "big Switzerland," an economic giant and foreign policy dwarf. The question remains pertinent. The EU has been an important actor in international trade from the beginning and as it grew became an "economic giant." But American hegemony and NATO kept it distant from important security matters and the diverging foreign policy goals of larger members prevented serious foreign policy action. After the Cold War, the Maastricht Treaty created another intergovernmental

THE U.S. CONNECTION

The EU and the United States have had a long, sometimes quarrelsome, but intimate history. Without American policies after World War II European integration would not have begun, but American leaders were persistently annoyed with the early EU. The French were a bother about NATO and European defense, the Germans with *Ostpolitik*, the Common Agricultural Policy threatened American food exports, and there was wrangling about competition policy and exchange rates. U.S. governments favored European integration, but hoped for an obedient "special relationship" like that with Britain rather than what emerged. As the EU revived in the 1980s, the United States thought it too slow to copy American neoliberalism and too eager to keep its social programs. The EU persisted with Economic and Monetary Union despite the scepticism of American leaders who also believed that the Common Foreign and Security Policy could threaten NATO. Trade conflicts,

exemplified by a long dispute about bananas that pit an EU determined to protect its former colonies against gigantic, politically influential American agro-corporations whose bananas actually came from Central and Latin America, were chronic. Larger U.S.-EU conflicts such as the EU's divided response to the Iraq war left bitter tastes. The EU's antitrust policies annoyed big American corporations and NSA spying on EU leaders annoyed European politicians. The picture changes if we step back, however. The United States and the EU have stood side-by-side on things that count like democracy, the rule of law, the need for open and free societies, human rights, and opposition to illiberal dictatorships.

MAKING CONNECTIONS The EU and the United States have always been close friends and faithful allies. Why has their connection been so fraught with controversy?

pillar for the new CFSP. Did the post–Cold War world demand a larger European international footprint? Many thought it did.

The EU is very important in international trade, and because of globalization, trade policy will structure world events for years to come. EU trade policy begins with a general mandate from the Council of Ministers that is then administered by the Commission and carried out by the International Trade Commissioner. The EU privileges its trade positions for "ACP" (African, Caribbean, Pacific) countries whose relationships are regulated separately, but open trade has also been extended to most of the world's poorer countries via free trade in "anything but arms." The EU has been more open to developing countries than other rich parts of the world, with agriculture a large exception. Of late, issues that were outside earlier trade talks such as health, environmental, and labor standards, public procurement, and intellectual property rights, are on the table because the EU has put them there. Private diplomacy by European economic interests and a lively international civil society composed of protest groups and nongovernmental organizations (NGOs) are also recent facts of life. Together with the United States, the EU engineered the Doha Development Round, the first WTO trade negotiations, aimed at bringing the poorest developing societies into global trade. Rapid development in Asia and Latin America has created other threats to established northern interests, however. The Doha Round has fallen far short of EU hopes, but trade diplomacy remains central to EU foreign policy. Most recently, post-Doha, the EU has sought new bilateral trade treaties such as that recently concluded with Canada, meant in part to be a door-opener to new negotiations with the United States. International trade policy will continue to be a bumpy, but essential, road for the EU.

Is the EU still a security dwarf in a world where global summits, bombs, and big battalions remain fundamental? At Maastricht, where the EU's CFSP originated, participants knew that cooperation would be difficult and that intergovernmentalism implied slow progress. They nonetheless had hopes that the Western European Union (WEU), a European defense arrangement originating in the 1940s, might grow to become the Union's defense arm. Europe's incoherence toward the former Yugoslavia in the 1990s demonstrated how difficult the issues were. Reflections then led to official focus on the WEU "Petersberg tasks" of humanitarian intervention and peacekeeping, which called for combat-ready, properly equipped European forces to manage crises in and outside Europe. The first challenge was building rapid-response capacities. The 1997 Amsterdam Treaty discussion of a "European Security and Defense Identity" included planning operations in the Council of Ministers, the appointment of a High Representative for CFS, and empowerment of the Council to develop common strategies. In December of that year, the French and British met in St. Malo and issued a "Joint Declaration on European Defense" to create "… the capacity for autonomous action, backed up by credible military forces, the means to decide to use them, and a readiness to do so." This new determination was reinforced by what happened over Kosovo, where the United States called, and fired, most of NATO's shots to deter Serbian brutality.

The December 1999 Helsinki European Council announced "headline goals" for 2003 of a 60,000 man rapid-reaction force for crisis management, peace-keeping, and humanitarian aid that could be deployed within sixty days and stay for a full year, backed by warplanes and ships. The Council of Ministers then created mechanisms to plan and control these forces that included a Council Politics and Security Committee (COPS), an EU Military Committee that included the military chiefs of EU members, and a Brussels general staff of 150. Helsinki also underlined EU "determination to develop an autonomous capacity to take decisions and, where NATO as a whole is not engaged, to launch and conduct EU-led military operations in response to international crises." As a result, the EU took on new, if limited, military duties. By 2003, however, the new European Security Strategy had downsized the Helsinki goals to fifteen battalion-sized battle groups, mobilizable, with tactical support, in five days and able to operate for thirty days. This was not a "European army," for which neither money nor political commitment existed, but nonetheless a coordinated commitment for particular kinds of missions. More coordination and integration of the European defense industry was also needed, but this threatened national jobs and vested interests. The number of ready EU battalions is now close to full capacity, and there has been new investment in high-tech fighter planes, smarter weapons, new airlift capacity (the Airbus A400), and new satellites.

Since 2003 the EU has been involved in fourteen civilian, six military, and three mixed missions on three different continents, sometimes moving "out of area" in contingents of a few hundred. On the civilian side, the EU took over policing in Bosnia and Herzegovina from the UN, monitored elections in East Timor in 2005, worked in Iraq, Afghanistan, Palestine, and Moldova-Ukraine, and sent 3,000 people to help develop the rule of law in Kosovo in 2008. Militarily, it has engaged in joint missions with NATO in Macedonia and Bosnia and Herzogovina and, by itself, it has engaged in a 1,500-troop emergency mission to Goma in the Democratic Republic of Congo to calm a very troubled region, and in 2006 EUFOR RD Congo calmed Kinshasa during elections. More recently the EU has intervened in Chad and the Central African Republic in 2009, and been the mainstay of anti-piracy patrolling off Somalia.

Even tentative EU initiatives in defense and security inevitably spilled over into relations with the United States. Long arguments in the 1990s over the role of NATO ended up in an agreement in which the United States will give the EU access to some NATO assets for limited kinds of action, as long as NATO remains predominant, something that the EU's renunciation of the WEU facilitated. A French journalist has noted that Americans and Europeans "indulge in incompatible dreams. The U.S. wants to be number one.... Europeans want to keep the U.S. as the ultimate insurance policy as they evolve towards a common identity." The meaning of this became clearer after September 11, 2001. Europeans immediately and unanimously expressed massive support and sympathy for Americans, did all they could to assist U.S. intelligence services to beef up European counterterrorism, and EU member states fully participated in the U.S.-led NATO expedition to Afghanistan. Deep disagreements emerged over Iraq, however. When the United States decided to invade, the French and Germans were deeply opposed, while the British marched to Baghdad along with Spain, Italy, Portugal and several CEEC then-applicant EU members, in G. W. Bush's "coalition of the willing."

European nations, especially old imperial powers, have long-standing divergent foreign policy goals. Smaller EU countries worried about domination in security matters by bigger ones. Some, like Sweden, Finland, and Austria, had earlier been neutral. Others, like many CEECs, were strongly pro-American because of what the United States had stood for in the Cold War. The term "common foreign policy" thus could not mean a *single* European policy that would replace everything member states did. Building on long years of European Political Cooperation—constant diplomatic communication that could, on occasion, lead to joint statements—the Maastricht CFSP ambitions were more modest, demonstrated by Maastricht's intergovernmental pillar and Lisbon's "communitization" that left large matters for unanimity decision making. In the years since the turn of the century the EU has invested in "soft power" foreign policy areas like international environmental politics, partly because EU leaders were seeking new issues where the EU could agree and then take a global lead. EU enlargement itself has been "soft" foreign policy. The EU "club" has proved attractive to neighbors, and the prospect of joining has pushed many to democratize, commit to the rule of law, and cooperate for the European greater good, a process documented in the histories of Greece, Spain, and Portugal in the 1980s and formerly communist CEECs more recently. The EU has also tried this approach to offer partial benefits such as trade and development aid to "near neighbors" to the east (Turkey, the Ukraine, and others), and Mediterranean countries, but progress has not been smooth. The EU and Turkey continue to dance around one another without progress toward Turkish membership. A "Mediterranean Union" promoted by French president Sarkozy disappeared in the dust of the Arab spring. The EU's "neighborhood" policy has more recently run up against the brash toughness of Vladimir Putin in Ukraine, against which EU "soft power" was ineffective, particularly because member states were divided over its use.

EU humanitarian and development aid is part of this "soft" approach. The EU, long in the aid business, has expanded and concentrated its approaches. There is now a European Development Fund directed to ACP countries, special regional aid programs directed to the very poorest countries, a cluster of humanitarian aid programs often used to co-finance worthy NGO activities in poorer parts of the world, and sophisticated humanitarian aid operations for areas hit by natural disasters, population displacement, and deadly conflict. The EU (the Union and its member states taken together) gives 50 percent of the world's development aid, and is now more problem-targeted and conditional, seeking out infrastructure projects (transportation, water supply, schools, health care), trying to leverage its aid into better administration and governance in recipient countries.

The EU's "big Switzerland" position has never really been a contrast between muscular America and weakling EU. As a heavyweight in trade, environmental and sustainable development, a significant promoter of democratization, a well-equipped expert in humanitarian aid and crisis management, and a major player in the international exchange rate regime, the EU is difficult to overlook internationally. By smart bomb and big battalion measures, however, the EU remains a small power. Whether and how this will change in a perilous world that is becoming more "multipolar" is unforeseeable. The 2009 Lisbon Treaty created a new institutional foundation in foreign and security policy. The new High Representative for CFSP, Baroness Ashton, was "double hatted" as president of the CFSP Council in the Council of Ministers and vice president of the Commission and charged with combining the different and often rival administrative bodies presently dealing in foreign affairs, energizing the Council's fledgling security groups, developing a new EU diplomatic service out of disparate EU and national units, and being the public face for EU diplomacy. She has needed lots of energy and good fortune to get started, and the going so far has been tough.

Where Do You Stand?

The EU's institutional system seems to be too complicated to understand and does not work very well. Can the EU survive and thrive?

The EU institutions may not be democratically legitimate enough to sustain the EU's policies. What institutional changes might help to change this?

SECTION 5

EURO-POLITICS IN TRANSITION

▼ Focus Questions

- Why has adding new members to the EU caused so much difficulty?

- How can we explain the recent "retreat" of EU member states from commitment to European integration?

Eurozone crisis

Crisis of sovereign debt within Eurozone that broke out after 2009 that led to frantic emergency efforts by Eurozone members and the European Council to bail out Greece, Ireland, and Portugal and reconfigure EMU rules.

Analogies between the biographies of people and political systems are sometimes useful. The EU is now a "young adult" compared to many Western states. Young adulthood is often a perilous moment both for humans and states, however. The bloom is off initial patriotic and identity enthusiasms. Generations have changed and the facts of what went before have been forgotten. The less-than-glorious practices of real politics have started to puncture the rhetoric of happy talk. Finally, conflicts that obscured in the foundational period break through. At the EU's present age, the United States was moving toward the Civil War, the Soviet Union toward the gerontocratic stagnation that would lead to its demise, and Italy and Germany after World War I were embracing fascism. Young adulthood is often a time of crisis, and so it has been for the European Union.

The EU'S recent years have been tumultuous. Maastricht's new policies in foreign affairs and defense, internal affairs, the environment, market liberalization, and monetary union, at a moment when the EU was doubling its membership—have brought changes that EU citizens have often misunderstood and disliked. Economic globalization has challenged the EU's economy and destabilized its social contracts. The joys of uniting post–Cold War Europe were obscured by the conflictual reform of the EU's institutions to welcome new Central and Eastern European members. Last, but far from least, the Great Recession and **Eurozone crisis** put the EU in economic harm's way. The EU is in transition, and there is great uncertainty about what will come next.

The EU's problems defining new foreign and defense policies should not have been surprising. The CFSP was meant to coexist with those of member states rather than replace them. Member states continued to prioritize their own interests and goals, as seen in responses to the invasion of Iraq, policies toward Russia (of great importance in the energy realm), attitudes toward NATO and the United States, and responses to the risings in North Africa and the Middle East. The slow accretion of EU savoir-faire in peace-keeping and crisis management and military matters has run up against a world of hard-nosed territorial defense and force projection that remains resolutely national and coordinated by the United States and NATO. Rhetorical announcements about the nobility of the EU's "soft power" foreign policy DNA failed at the 2009 UN Copenhagen Climate Change

The EU's stars are out of line after the Eurozone crisis. Is there a way forward?

Martin Sutovec/Cagle Cartoons

Conference, had limited effects in the EU's "neighborhoods" in the eastern European borderlands, the Mediterranean, and the Middle East, and have been overwhelmed by economic globalization and new international multipolarity. The 2009 Lisbon Treaty's appointment of a Mr./Ms./Mrs. CFSP to establish order from the EU's existing dispersion of foreign, defense, development, and humanitarian aid policies has proceeded very slowly.

The institutional reforms connected with enlargement to the CEECS were turbulent because they opened a Pandora's box of reshuffling the relative power of different EU institutions and member states. The 2000 Nice Treaty that threatened smaller member states was rejected by the Irish in a 2002 referendum. There followed a European Convention in which delegates from EU institutions, member states, and civil society debated for almost two years before producing a European Constitutional Treaty (ECT). The ECT was then submitted for ratification in 2005 and rejected in French and Dutch referendums. Two years later the most important parts of the ECT were rewritten into a new treaty and then rejected by the Irish in another referendum. Leaders then cajoled the Irish to vote again and this time they approved, allowing the Lisbon Treaty to come into effect in 2009. This decade-long debate about EU institutions persuaded many citizens that the EU was not working very well. Declining turnout in elections to the European Parliament has been another sign of the EU's waning popularity

European economic fortunes greatly contributed to citizen skepticism. The EU's first period had seen high economic growth, full employment, and positive life changes. Its more recent programs have been sold as remedies for the lowered growth and higher unemployment in the globalization era. Although EU members had varying records of success and failure, promises made had not been redeemed even before the disasters of the Great Recession and the Eurozone crisis led to harsh and protracted austerity, very high unemployment, and unwanted social reforms, plunged the EU into a second recession, further tarnished the EU's already shaky legitimacy, deepened the EU's North-South divisions, and divided Eurozone from non-EMU countries.

The EU that had helped bring peace and prosperity seemed further and further in the past. In the present, many citizens sense that the EU is far away, top-down and bureaucratic, and not very effective at solving their problems. When asked about the EU, or asked to vote for a European Parliament they had trouble making sense of, they responded with negativity or indifference much more than they had in the past. Their puzzlement was connected, first of all, to lack of transparency and ineffectiveness in the EU's institutions. The "community method" seemed technocratic, depoliticizing, and baffling. More recently, it had receded in favor of a new intergovernmental confederalism led by the European Council that worked too slowly and clearly favored the preferences of more powerful EU members. Citizen negativity was also connected to EU responses to globalization. In the 1990s the EU had decided to be proactive and promote reform at all levels. Many Europeans, accustomed to middle-class lifestyles and extensive social protection, perceived this as threatening. Worse still, the new strategies did not rejuvenate European economic energies, restore growth, and alleviate unemployment. The global financial crisis that exploded in 2007–2008 accentuated widespread and growing citizen pessimism. The European integration experiment had always lived from crisis to crisis, often responding well. Its future could depend on how well it could distance itself from the financial crisis and rebuild its credibility.

Despite all this, the young adult European Union has been a fabulous success, well beyond any of its founders' dreams. It has bound together nations that earlier had gone regularly to war. Yet for younger generations that have not experienced European war, this is a fading memory. The EU has gone far beyond its original concerns in economic governance into European citizenship, monetary policy, foreign affairs, environmental regulation, and unifying Europe politically after the Cold War. Yet these changes have often caused greater uncertainty and confusion, particularly as success at economic governance became more difficult to achieve with the advance of globalization. The EU proved over and over again that multilateral negotiations between sovereign states in carefully designed and innovative institutions could build lasting and growing cooperation. It created European interests and identities where neither had existed. Its different citizens are unquestionably more comfortable with one another and more "European" than ever. But the EU remains an "unidentified political object," a strange combination of federation and confederation that does not resemble a state and is badly understood by citizens. It has coexisted with sovereign states that have learned to share power with others when cooperation made more sense than clinging to sovereignty, but this coexistence has had many rocky moments. The present period is one of the rockiest. The EU has a good record at responding to vast changes in the lives and social orders of its members and the international system. In a world filled with turbulence this is truly extraordinary, but today's uncertainty is very troubling.

Where Do You Stand?

Enlargement of the EU to include almost all European countries, ex-communist central and eastern European ones in particular, was bound to bring new difficulties. What are the most important of these difficulties, how has the EU responded to them, and how well have these responses worked?

The Eurozone crisis has left the EU in a difficult situation. EU member states are at odds, many citizens are unhappy, and economic conditions are not promising. How might the EU rekindly public enthusiasm for the cause of integration?

Key Terms

citizen initiative
Common Foreign and Security
    Policy
community method
Economic and Monetary Union
    (EMU)
European Commission

European Council
European Court of Justice
European Parliament
European single market
Eurozone crisis
Justice and Home Affairs (JHA)
Lisbon Treaty

Maastricht Treaty
qualified majority voting
Schengen area
subsidiarity

Suggested Readings

Bastasin, Carlo. *Saving Europe: How National Politics Nearly Destroyed the Euro* Washington Brookings, 2012.

Cini, Michelle and Nieves Perez-Solorzano Borragan. *European Union Politics,* 3rd ed. Oxford: Oxford University Press, 2010.

Dinan, Desmond. *Ever Closer Union*, 4th ed. Boulder: Lynne Rienner, 2010.

Eichengreen, Barry. *The European Economy Since 1945.* Princeton: Princeton University Press, 2007.

Kassim, Hussein, John Peterson, Michael W. Bauer, and Sara Connolly. *The European Commission in the 21st Century.* New York: Oxford University Press, 2013.

Rosamond, Ben. *Theories of European Integration.* Basingstoke, England: Palgrave, 2000.

Ross, George. *The European Union and Its Crises seen through the Eyes of the Brussels Elite.* Houndsworth: Palgrave-Macmillan, 2011.

_____. *Jacques Delors and European Integration.* Cambridge: Polity, 1995.

Scharpf, Fritz. *Governing in Europe: Effective and Democratic.* Oxford: Oxford University Press, 1999.

Wallace, Helen, Mark A. Pollack, and Alasdair Young, eds. *Policy-Making in the European Union*, 6th ed. New York: Oxford University Press, 2010.

Suggested Websites

Delegation of the European Commission to the USA
www.eurunion.org

European Union, official Brussels site
www.europa.eu

Bruegel, a good site for EU economics
www.bruegel.org

EUobserver, excellent daily EU bulletin from centrist-liberal group in the European Parliament
www.EUObserver.com

Notre Europe-Institut Jacques Delors (Paris); includes many documents in English
www.notre-europe.eu/en/

5 Mexico

Halbert Jones

Official Name: United Mexican States (Estados Unidos Mexicanos)

Location: Southern North America

Capital City: Mexico City

Population (2014): 120.3 million

Size: 1,972,550 sq. km.; slightly less than three times the size of Texas

AP Images/Gregory Bull

© Cengage Learning®

THE MAKING OF THE MODERN MEXICAN STATE

Politics in Action

Early on the morning of February 22, 2014, Mexican marines raided an apartment in the Pacific resort of Mazatlán and detained Joaquín Guzmán, the powerful head of the Sinaloa drug cartel. Known as "El Chapo"—or "Shorty"—on account of his diminutive stature, Guzmán had built a massive fortune over several decades through his control of the flow of narcotics through Mexico and into the United States. His escape from a maximum-security prison in 2001 and his success in evading arrest for more than a decade thereafter made him a symbol of the weaknesses and shortcomings of the Mexican state. After running his criminal empire from a lavish jail cell for several years, Guzmán bribed his way out of prison, and even after President Felipe Calderón launched an offensive against the cartels in 2006, he managed to stay at least one step ahead of the authorities. Mexicans were left to wonder if the security forces simply could not find "El Chapo" or if corrupt officials were allowing him to remain free. Neither scenario gave citizens much cause for confidence in their leaders. Guzmán's arrest therefore had considerable symbolic importance as an indication that the Mexican government has both the will and the capacity to uphold the rule of law.

Successes like the capture of "El Chapo" have helped to counter exaggerated fears, voiced as Calderón's campaign against the cartels triggered intense violence in some parts of the country, that Mexico was in danger of becoming a "failed state." Nonetheless, the threats posed by criminal organizations both to public safety and to the authority of the government remain major preoccupations for Mexican leaders. Although Enrique Peña Nieto, Mexico's president since 2012, would prefer to focus the attention of the world and of his people on his country's economic potential rather than on security issues, he was obliged in January 2014 to assert federal control over law enforcement operations in the state of Michoacán, where the rise of vigilante groups in opposition to a local cartel had led to concerns about the absence or ineffectiveness of the legitimately constituted authorities. While Mexican officials face the need to develop institutions that can take on criminal elements and win the trust of Mexican citizens, unfortunately the activities of drug trafficking organizations are likely to remain a challenge for Mexico for as long as there is a large market for illegal narcotics next door in the United States.

Meanwhile, President Peña Nieto has sought since taking office to demonstrate that the Mexican government is capable of bold and effective action in other areas. His election in July 2012 as the candidate of the Institutional Revolutionary Party (PRI) was a milestone in Mexican history. The PRI dominated the country's politics for most of the twentieth century, but when it lost the presidency to an opposition party in 2000, many observers doubted that it would ever recover. However, after more than a decade of legislative paralysis, and as the country reeled from drug-related violence that had claimed some 60,000 lives over six years, voters turned again

Focus Questions ▽

- In what ways have the critical junctures of Mexican history grown out of the country's relations with other countries, especially the United States?

- What factors contributed to Mexico's democratic transition at the end of the twentieth century?

1810–1821
War of independence from Spain

1876–1911
Dictatorship of Porfirio Diaz

1917
Mexican Constitution

1934–1940
Presidency of Lázaro Cárdenas; entrenchment of corporatist state

| 1500 | 1830 | 1860 | 1890 | 1920 | 1950 | 1980 |

1521
Spaniards led by Hernán Cortés capture the Aztec capital, initiating three centuries of colonial rule.

1929
Plutarco Elías Calles founds PRI.

1968
Massacre of Tlatelolco; an unknown number of protesting students killed.

1910–1920
Mexican Revolution

to the PRI in the 2012 presidential election. To overcome the structural difficulties created by partisan divisions in the legislature, the new president signed an accord with party leaders that committed them to an ambitious program of reforms. The impact of these changes will be felt for years to come, and as these measures are being drafted and implemented, the dynamics of Mexican politics are being redefined. A long-ruling, formerly authoritarian party is learning to govern in the context of the competitive, multiparty system that has taken shape over the past several decades. To understand how Mexican politics is likely to evolve in the future, it will be necessary to study closely the development and structure of this system.

Geographic Setting

Mexico includes coastal plains, high plateaus, fertile valleys, rain forests, and deserts within an area slightly less than three times the size of Texas. Two imposing mountain ranges run the length of Mexico: the Sierra Madre Occidental to the west and the Sierra Madre Oriental to the east. Mexico's geography has made communication and transportation between regions difficult and infrastructure expensive. Mountainous terrain limits large-scale commercial agriculture to irrigated fields in the north, while the center and south produce a wide variety of crops on small farms. The country is rich in oil, silver, and other natural resources, but it has long struggled to manage those resources wisely.

Mexico is the second-largest nation in Latin America after Portuguese-speaking Brazil and the largest Spanish-speaking nation in the world. Sixty percent of the population is *mestizo*, or people of mixed indigenous and Spanish ancestry. About 30 percent of the population claim descent from Mexico's original inhabitants, although only 6.5 percent speak an indigenous language. The largest **indigenous groups** are the Maya in the south and the Náhuatl in the central regions, with well over 1 million members each. Although Mexicans take great pride in their nation's pre-Columbian heritage, issues of race and class divide society.

mestizo

A person of mixed white, indigenous, and sometimes African descent.

indigenous groups

Population descended from the original inhabitants of the Americas, present prior to the Spanish Conquest.

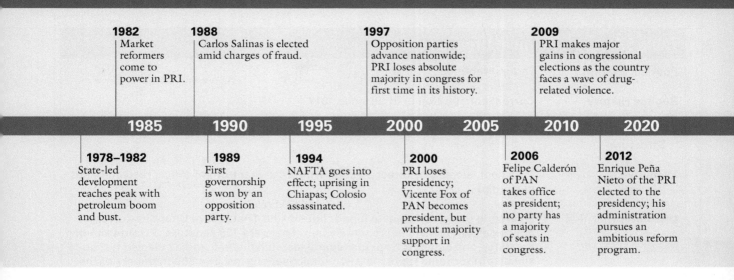

1982 Market reformers come to power in PRI.

1988 Carlos Salinas is elected amid charges of fraud.

1997 Opposition parties advance nationwide; PRI loses absolute majority in congress for first time in its history.

2009 PRI makes major gains in congressional elections as the country faces a wave of drug-related violence.

1985   1990   1995   2000   2005   2010   2020

1978–1982 State-led development reaches peak with petroleum boom and bust.

1989 First governorship is won by an opposition party.

1994 NAFTA goes into effect; uprising in Chiapas; Colosio assassinated.

2000 PRI loses presidency; Vicente Fox of PAN becomes president, but without majority support in congress.

2006 Felipe Calderón of PAN takes office as president; no party has a majority of seats in congress.

2012 Enrique Peña Nieto of the PRI elected to the presidency; his administration pursues an ambitious reform program.

Mexico: Religions

Jehovah's Witnesses 1.4%
Pentecostal 1.6%
Other Evangelical Churches 5.0%
Other 1.9%
None 4.7%
Unspecified 2.7%
Roman Catholic 82.7%

Mexico: Ethnic Groups

Other 1%
White 9%
Indigenous or predominantly indigenous 30%
Mestizo 60% (Indigenous-Spanish)

Mexico: Languages

Spanish and indigenous languages 5.7%
Indigenous only 0.8%
Unspecified 0.8%
Spanish only 92.7%

Mexican Currency

Peso ($)
International Designation: MXN
Exchange Rate (2014): 1 US$ = 13.09 MXN
500 Peso Note Design: Diego Rivera (1886–1957), painter and husband of artist Frida Kahlo (1907–1954; pictured on the reverse)

FIGURE 5.1 The Mexican Nation at a Glance

Javier Correa/Alamy (for photo)

Table 5.1	Political Organization
Political System	Federal republic
Regime History	Current constitution in force since 1917
Administrative Structure	Federal system with thirty-one states and a federal district (Mexico City)
Executive	President, elected by direct election with a six-year term of office; reelection not permitted
Legislature	Bicameral Congress. Senate (upper house) and Chamber of Deputies (lower house); elections held every three years. There are 128 senators, 3 from each of the thirty-one states, 3 from the federal (capital) district, and 32 elected nationally by proportional representation for six-year terms. The 500 members of the Chamber of Deputies are elected for three-year terms from 300 electoral districts, 300 by simple majority vote and 200 by proportional representation.
Judiciary	Independent federal and state court system headed by a Supreme Court with eleven justices appointed by the president and approved by the Senate.
Party System	Multiparty system. One-party dominant (Institutional Revolutionary Party) system from 1929 until 2000. Major parties: National Action Party, Institutional Revolutionary Party, and the Party of the Democratic Revolution.

Mexico became a largely urban country in the second half of the twentieth century, and Mexico City is one of the world's largest metropolitan areas, with about 20 million inhabitants. Migration both within and beyond Mexico's borders has become a major issue. Greater economic opportunities in the industrial cities of the north lead many women and men to seek work there in the *maquiladoras*, or assembly industries. Many job seekers continue on to the United States. On Mexico's southern border, many thousands of Central Americans look for better prospects in Mexico and beyond.

maquiladoras

Factories that produce goods for export, often located along the U.S.–Mexican border.

Critical Junctures

Independence, Instability, and Dictatorship (1810–1910)

After a small band of Spanish forces led by Hernán Cortés toppled the Aztec Empire in 1521, Spain ruled Mexico for three centuries. Colonial policy was designed to extract wealth from New Spain, as the territory was known, ensuring that economic benefits flowed to the mother country.

In 1810, a parish priest in central Mexico named Miguel Hidalgo began the first of a series of wars for independence. Although independence was gained in 1821, Mexico struggled to create a stable government for decades afterward. Liberals and conservatives, monarchists and republicans, and federalists and centralists were all engaged in the battle to shape the new nation's future. Between 1833 and 1855, thirty-six presidential administrations came to power, and in many regions, local strongmen, or *caudillos*, exercised more authority than the national government.

caudillos

Charismatic populist leaders, usually with a military background, who use patronage and draw upon personal loyalties to dominate a region or a nation.

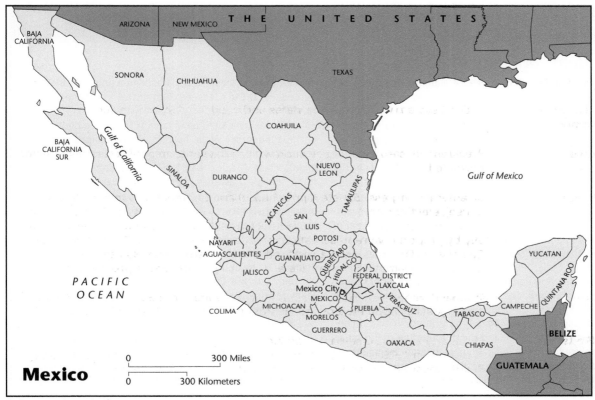

© Cengage Learning®

During this chaotic period, Mexico lost half its territory. Central America rejected rule from Mexico City in 1823, and the northern territory of Texas won independence in 1836. After Texas became a U.S. state in 1845, a border dispute led the United States to declare war on Mexico in 1846. U.S. forces invaded the country and occupied Mexico City. An 1848 treaty recognized the loss of Texas and gave the United States title to what later became the states of New Mexico, Utah, Nevada, Arizona, California, and part of Colorado for about $18 million, leaving a legacy of deep resentment toward the United States.

After the war, liberals and conservatives continued their struggle over issues of political and economic order. The Constitution of 1857 incorporated many of the goals of the liberals, such as a somewhat democratic government, a bill of rights, and limitations on the power of the Roman Catholic Church. In 1861, Spain, Great Britain, and France occupied Veracruz to collect debts owed by Mexico. The French army continued on to Mexico City, where it installed a European prince as the Emperor Maximilian (1864–1867). Conservatives welcomed this respite from liberal rule. Benito Juárez returned to the presidency in 1867 after defeating and executing Maximilian. Juárez is still hailed in Mexico today as an early proponent of more democratic government.

In 1876, a popular retired general named Porfirio Díaz came to power. He established a dictatorship—known as the *Porfiriato*—that lasted thirty-four years and was at first welcomed by many because it brought sustained stability to the country.

Díaz imposed an authoritarian system to create political order and economic progress. Over time, he relied increasingly on a small clique of advisers, known as

GLOBAL CONNECTION

Conquest or Encounter?

The year 1519, when the Spanish conqueror Hernán Cortés arrived on the shores of the Yucatán Peninsula, is often considered the starting point of Mexican political history. The land that was to become Mexico was home to extensive and complex indigenous civilizations that were advanced in agriculture, architecture, and political and economic organization. By 1519, diverse groups had fallen under the power of the militaristic Aztec Empire, which extended throughout what is today central and southern Mexico.

Cortés and the colonial masters who came after him subjected indigenous groups to forced labor; robbed them of gold, silver, and land; and introduced flora and fauna from Europe that destroyed long-existing ecosystems. They also brought alien forms of property rights and authority relationships, a religion that viewed indigenous practices as the devil's work, and an economy based on mining and cattle—all of which soon overwhelmed existing structures of social and economic organization. Within a century, wars, exploitation, and the introduction of European diseases reduced the indigenous population from an estimated 25 million to 1 million or fewer. Even so, the Spanish never constituted more than a small percentage of the total population, and massive racial mixing among the Indians, Europeans, and to a lesser extent Africans produced a new *raza*, or *mestizo* race.

What does it mean to be Mexican? Is one the conquered or the conqueror? While celebrating indigenous achievements in food, culture, the arts, and ancient civilization, middle-class Mexico has the contradictory sense that to be "Indian" nowadays is to be backward. But perhaps the situation is changing, with the upsurge of indigenous movements from both the grassroots and the international level striving to promote ethnic pride, defend rights, and foster the teaching of Indian languages.

The collision of two worlds still resonates. Is Mexico colonial or modern? Third or First World? Southern or Northern? Is the United States an ally or a conqueror? Many Mexicans at once welcome and fear full integration into the global economy, asking themselves: Is globalization a new form of conquest?

MAKING CONNECTIONS How does Mexico's experience as a colony of Spain compare with the history of other countries that once were part of European empires?

---

científicos (scientists), who wanted to adopt European technologies and values to modernize the country. Díaz and the *científicos* encouraged foreign investment and presided over a period of rapid growth and development. Social tensions grew, however, as many poorer Mexicans found themselves forced off their lands, and as many members of the middle and upper classes came to resent the Porfirians' monopoly on political power.

The Revolution of 1910 and the Sonoran Dynasty (1910–1934)

The most formative event in the country's modern history was the Revolution of 1910, which ended the *Porfiriato* and was the first great social revolution of the twentieth century. The revolution was fought by a variety of forces for a variety of reasons, which made the consolidation of power that followed as significant as the revolution itself.

Díaz had promised an open election for president, and in 1910, Francisco Madero presented himself as a candidate. Madero and his reform-minded allies hoped that a new class of politically ambitious citizens would move into positions of power. When this opposition swelled, Díaz tried to repress growing dissent, but the clamor for change forced him into exile. Madero was elected in 1911, but he was soon using the military to put down revolts by reformers and reactionaries alike. When Madero was assassinated during a **coup d'état** in 1913, political order collapsed.

coup d'état

A forceful, extra-constitutional action resulting in the removal of an existing government.

At the same time that middle-class reformers struggled to displace Díaz, a peasant revolt that focused on land claims erupted in central and southern regions. This revolt had roots in legislation that made it easy for wealthy landowners and ranchers to claim the lands of peasant villagers. Villagers joined forces under a variety of local leaders. The most famous was Emiliano Zapata. His manifesto, the Plan de Ayala, became the cornerstone of the radical agrarian reform that became part of the Constitution of 1917.

In the north, the governor of Coahuila, Venustiano Carranza, placed himself at the head of an army that pledged to restore constitutional governance after Madero's murder, while Francisco (Pancho) Villa's forces combined military maneuvers with banditry, looting, and warlordism. In 1916, troops from the United States entered Mexico to punish Villa for an attack on U.S. territory. The presence of U.S. troops on Mexican soil resulted in increased hostility toward the United States.

The Mexican Constitution of 1917 was forged out of the diverse and often conflicting interests of the various factions that arose during the 1910 Revolution. It established a formal set of political institutions and guaranteed citizens a range of progressive social and economic rights: agrarian reform, social security, the right to organize in unions, a minimum wage, an eight-hour workday, profit sharing for workers, a secular public education system, and universal male suffrage. Despite these socially advanced provisions, the constitution did not provide suffrage for women, who had to wait until 1953 to vote in local elections and 1958 to vote in national elections. To limit the power of foreign investors, restrictions were placed on the ability of non-Mexicans to own land or exploit natural resources. Numerous articles severely limited the power of the Catholic Church, long a target of liberals who wanted Mexico to be a secular state. Despite such noble sentiments, violence continued as competing leaders sought to assert power and displace their rivals.

Power was gradually consolidated in the hands of a group of revolutionary leaders from the north of the country. Known as the Sonoran Dynasty, after their home state of Sonora, these leaders were committed to a capitalist model of economic development. Eventually, one of the Sonorans, Plutarco Elías Calles, emerged as the *jefe máximo*, or supreme leader. After his presidential term (1924–1928), Calles managed to select and dominate his successors from 1929 to 1934.

In 1929, Calles brought together many of the most powerful contenders for leadership to create a political party. The bargain he offered was simple: Contenders for power would accommodate each other's interests in the expectation that without political violence, the country would prosper and they would be able to reap the benefits of even greater power and economic spoils. For the next seven decades, Calles's bargain ensured nonviolent conflict resolution among elites and the uninterrupted rule of the Institutional Revolutionary Party (PRI) in national politics.

Lázaro Cárdenas, Agrarian Reform, and the Workers (1934–1940)

In 1934, Calles handpicked Lázaro Cárdenas as the official candidate for the presidency. He fully anticipated that Cárdenas would go along with his behind-the-scenes management of the country. To his surprise, Cárdenas executed a virtual coup that established his own supremacy.[1] Even more unexpectedly, Cárdenas mobilized peasants and workers in pursuit of the more radical goals of the revolution. During his administration, more than 49 million acres of land were distributed, nearly twice as much as had been parceled out by all the previous postrevolutionary governments combined. Most of these lands were distributed in the form of *ejidos* (collective land grants) to peasant groups. Recipients of these grants provided an enduring base of

ejido

Land granted by Mexican government to an organized group of peasants.

support for the government. Cárdenas also encouraged workers to form unions to demand higher wages and better working conditions. In 1938, he wrested the petroleum industry from foreign investors and placed it under government control.

During the Cárdenas years (1934–1940), the bulk of the Mexican population was incorporated into the political system. Organizations of peasants and workers, middle-class groups, and the military were added to the official party. In addition, Cárdenas's presidency witnessed a great expansion of the role of the state as the government encouraged investment in industrialization, provided credit to agriculture, and created infrastructure.

The Politics of Rapid Development (1940–1982)

In the decades that followed, Cárdenas's successors used the institutions he created to counteract his reforms. Gradually, the PRI developed a huge patronage machine, characterized by extensive chains of personal relationships based on the exchange of favors. These exchange relationships, known as clientelism, became the cement that built loyalty to the PRI and the political system.

PROFILE

Lázaro Cárdenas

As president from 1934 to 1940, Lázaro Cárdenas arguably did more than any other Mexican leader to make possible the longevity of the political system that emerged from the Revolution of 1910. Through his reforms, Cárdenas won the loyalty and admiration of many Mexicans, convincing them of the legitimacy of the revolutionary regime.

Cárdenas was very much a product of the Revolution. Born in 1895 in the small town of Jiquilpan, Michoacán, he was only 15 years old when fighting broke out in 1910. As armed groups marched across west-central Mexico, the young Cárdenas joined the revolutionary forces, leaving behind the printshop where he had been working to support his widowed mother and seven siblings. Thanks to his literacy and penmanship, he received a commission as an officer on the staff of a local commander, and he rose quickly through the ranks. As part of the Constitutionalist Army, Cárdenas served under General Plutarco Elías Calles, a mentor who would later become a rival.

While on campaign, Cárdenas became more deeply aware of the hardships endured by Mexico's indigenous and rural populations and of their struggles for land. Later, in the 1920s, as the regional military commander in the country's most important oil-producing zone, he saw how foreign companies disregarded local regulations and flouted Mexican sovereignty. These experiences played a significant role in shaping his political outlook.

After serving as governor of his native state (1928–1932) and in the cabinet as defense minister (1933), Cárdenas was selected by his old patron Calles as the ruling party's presidential candidate in the 1934 elections. After taking office, however, Cárdenas shook off his predecessor's influence and launched wide-ranging reforms. His policies made him unpopular with business leaders, landowners, and social conservatives, but many more Mexicans felt that he was the first president to concern himself with their well-being. Cárdenas also won widespread admiration for his personal honesty and morality.

After stepping down from the presidency, Cárdenas watched with concern as subsequent administrations turned to the right, adopting more conservative policies even as they continued to claim to represent the ideals of the Revolution. The venerable ex-president sought to use his standing within the PRI and in Mexican society to press for more progressive policies. In the early 1960s, for example, he praised Fidel Castro's Cuban Revolution and signaled his support for renewed reform within Mexico. Nonetheless, he ultimately remained loyal to the system he had played such an important role in constructing.

Though Lázaro Cárdenas died in 1970, his name continues to carry great weight. Both the PRI and the PRD—founded by his son Cuauhtémoc—lay claim to his legacy, and countless Mexicans identify Cárdenas as the president they admire most.

MAKING CONNECTIONS Given his role in the nationalization of the oil industry, what effect might Cárdenas's iconic status have on current debates in Mexico over the future of the energy sector?

This kind of political control reoriented the country's development away from the egalitarian social goals of the 1930s toward a development strategy in which the state actively encouraged industrialization and the accumulation of wealth. Growth rates were high from the 1940s through the 1960s, but protests against the regime's authoritarian tendencies were beginning to arise by 1968, when government forces brutally suppressed a student movement in the capital's Tlatelolco district. Moreover, by the 1970s, Mexico's economic strategy was faltering.

Just as the economy faced a crisis in the mid-1970s, vast new amounts of oil were discovered in the Gulf of Mexico. Soon, extensive public investment programs were fueling rapid growth in virtually every sector of the economy. The boom was short-lived, however. International petroleum prices plunged in the early 1980s, forcing Mexico to default on its national debt in 1982 and plunging the country into a deep economic downturn.

Crisis and Reform (1982–2000)

This crisis led two presidents, Miguel de la Madrid (1982–1988) and Carlos Salinas (1988–1994), to introduce the first major reversal of the country's development strategy since the 1940s. New policies were put in place to limit the government's role in the economy and to reduce barriers to international trade. This period marked the beginning of a new effort to integrate Mexico into the global economy. In 1993, President Salinas signed the North American Free Trade Agreement (NAFTA), which committed Mexico, the United States, and Canada to the elimination of trade barriers between them. These economic reforms were a turning point for Mexico and meant that the country's future development would be closely tied to international economic conditions.

After a "lost decade" of stagnant growth following the 1982 default, the economic volatility that continued to afflict the country through much of the 1990s came to be accompanied by worrying signs of political instability. In 1994, a guerrilla movement, the Zapatista Army of National Liberation (EZLN), seized four towns in the southern state of Chiapas. The group demanded land, democracy, indigenous rights, and the immediate repeal of NAFTA. Many citizens throughout the country openly supported the aims of the rebels. Following close on the heels of the rebellion came the assassination of the PRI's presidential candidate, Luis Donaldo Colosio, an event that shocked all citizens and shook the political elite deeply.

With the election of replacement candidate Ernesto Zedillo in August 1994, the PRI remained in power, but these shocks provoked widespread disillusionment and frustration with the political system. At the same time, reforms to the country's electoral processes and institutions made it easier for opposition groups to challenge the ruling party and gave the public greater confidence in the fairness of elections. In 1997, for the first time in modern Mexican history, the PRI lost its majority in the lower house of the national congress. The 2000 election of Vicente Fox as the first non-PRI president in seven decades was the culmination of this electoral revolution.

Since 2000: Mexico as a Multiparty Democracy

After taking office in December 2000, Vicente Fox found it difficult to bring about the changes that he had promised to the Mexican people. Proposals for reform went down to defeat, and the president was subjected to catcalls and heckling when he made his annual reports to the congress. The difficulties faced by Fox as he attempted to implement his ambitious agenda arose in part because he and his administration lacked experience. However, a bigger problem for the president was that he lacked the compliant congressional majority and the close relationship with his party that his PRI predecessors had enjoyed.

With his legislative agenda stalled, Fox hoped that achievements in international policy would enhance his prestige at home. He was particularly hopeful that a close connection with the U.S. president, George W. Bush, would facilitate important breakthroughs in relations with the United States. The events of September 11, 2001, dramatically changed the outlook, however. The terrorist attacks on the United States led officials in Washington to seek to strengthen border security and to shift much of their attention away from Mexico and Latin America and toward Afghanistan and the Middle East. As a result, Mexican hopes for an agreement under which a greater number of their citizens would legally be able to migrate to and work in the United States were dashed. Thus, Fox found both his domestic and international policy priorities largely blocked.

As Fox's term in office came to a close, his National Action Party (PAN) turned to Felipe Calderón as its candidate in the 2006 presidential election. His main opponent was Andrés Manuel López Obrador of the Party of the Democratic Revolution (PRD). When Calderón won by a small margin, López Obrador refused to concede defeat. This defiant response had the unintended effect of dividing the opposition and allowing Calderón to consolidate his hold on power. By far the greatest challenge Mexico faced as Calderón took office was the increasing cost of fighting the war on drugs and organized crime. The new president relied on the army and federal police to launch military offensives against drug cartels throughout the country. Calderón secured the support of the United States for his strategy through the Mérida Initiative, which offered U.S. security assistance to Mexico and to Central American countries fighting transnational criminal organizations. The offensive resulted in the apprehension or killing of many leading drug traffickers, but it also touched off a wave of violence that has claimed tens of thousands of lives, damaged the country's image abroad, and undermined the confidence of many Mexicans in the ability of their government to maintain order and assure their safety.

In recent years, Mexican authorities have moved forcefully against the country's drug-trafficking organizations, which had amassed considerable resources through their criminal activities.

SUSANA GONZALEZ/dpa/Corbis

In the 2012 presidential election, Mexicans turned to the PRI in the hope that the party that had maintained stability in the country for so many years would be able to control the violence and govern effectively. Voters chose Enrique Peña Nieto, the young former governor of the state of Mexico, over the PRD's López Obrador and Josefina Vázquez Mota of the PAN (the first female presidential candidate nominated by a major party). López Obrador again made allegations of electoral fraud, but in contrast to the situation after the very close election of 2006, official results showed that Peña Nieto had won by a clear margin. Another orderly and peaceful transfer of power between parties, this time from the PAN back to the PRI, took place on December 1, 2012.

The return of the formerly dominant party to the presidency did not amount to a restoration of the old political system, however. Unlike his PRI predecessors, Peña Nieto faced a divided legislature and a citizenry that had become accustomed to questioning presidential authority and to having its say. To overcome the partisan divisions in congress that had created so many problems for Fox and Calderón, Peña Nieto moved quickly to capitalize on his mandate, entering into a "Pact for Mexico" with the major party leaders to press ahead on needed reforms. The agenda has included an overhaul of the education system, a revamping of tax policy, and—perhaps most controversially in a country in which Cárdenas's expropriation of the oil industry is remembered as a national triumph—the opening of the energy sector to foreign investment. Though the new administration has so far been successful in steering many of its initiatives through the legislative process, it has also faced intense protests. The fate of its program and of its approach to governing Mexico therefore remains to be determined.

The Four Themes and Mexico

Mexico in a Globalized World of States

Mexico's history has been deeply marked by its place in the world economy, its interactions with foreign powers, and its weakness relative to its powerful neighbor to the north. Through much of the nineteenth century, it faced pressure and intervention not just from the United States but also from European powers seeking to dominate the country. When stability was finally achieved under Porfirio Díaz, it was foreign investment that fueled development and growth, even as foreign domination of some sectors of the economy contributed to the resentments that would explode in the Revolution of 1910. Through much of the twentieth century, Mexico sought to protect its interests by developing its own industries to serve a domestic market and by asserting its economic and ideological independence from the world's great powers. After the early 1980s, the government rejected this position in favor of rapid integration into the global economy.

Since taking the strategic decision to open its economy, Mexico has embraced the opportunities and confronted the challenges presented by globalization. Mexican leaders calculated that by securing access to the vast U.S. and Canadian markets, they would allow the country to maintain a competitive position in an increasingly interconnected global economy. NAFTA did lead to a dramatic rise in the level of trade between Mexico and its North American neighbors, but the increased exposure to the world economy also left Mexico more vulnerable to abrupt shifts in international capital flows and to financial crises. After one such crisis hit at the end of 1994, for example, the Mexican economy contracted sharply, inflation soared, and taxes rose while wages were frozen. Mexico was likewise deeply affected by the global economic crisis of 2008, largely because of its strong links with the hard-hit U.S. economy.

Governing the Economy

Mexico's development from the 1930s to the 1980s was marked by extensive government engagement in the economy. During this period, the country industrialized and became primarily urban. At the same time, the living conditions of most

Mexicans improved, and standards of health, longevity, and education grew. Yet, along with these achievements, development strategies led to industrial and agricultural sectors that were often inefficient and overly protected by government, inequalities in the distribution of income and opportunities increased, and growth was threatened by a combination of domestic policies and international economic conditions. In the 1980s, the earlier model of development collapsed in crisis, and more market-oriented policies have significantly reduced the role of government in the economy and opened the country up to global economic forces. Yet growth has been slow under the new policies and inequalities have increased further. The larger questions of whether the current development strategy can generate growth, whether Mexican products can find profitable markets overseas, whether investors can create job opportunities for millions of unemployed and part-time workers, and whether the confidence of those investors can be maintained over the longer term continue to challenge the country.

The Democratic Idea

The Mexican people's pursuit of the ideal of democratic governance has been another important historical theme. Indeed, Madero launched the Revolution of 1910 with a call for "effective suffrage" and competitive elections, and his slogans were adopted by the postrevolutionary regime. Under the PRI, however, the country opted not for true democracy but for representation through government-mediated organizations within a **corporatist state**, in which interest groups became an institutionalized part of state structure rather than an independent source of advocacy. Although the democratic forms specified in the constitution were observed, the ruling party dominated the electoral process at all levels of government, and opposition groups were co-opted, marginalized, or (as a last resort) repressed. The system was referred to as a "perfect dictatorship," because of its ability to perpetuate itself and maintain stability, generally without having to resort to violence.

Over the last several decades of the twentieth century, however, the legitimacy of PRI rule was increasingly called into question. Demands for a more democratic system led to electoral reforms and the emergence of a more open political landscape. In the more competitive political environment that developed as a result, opposition parties won governorships, seats in congress, and, in 2000, the presidency. Though the PRI returned to power (via the ballot box) in 2012, democratic practices are now well established. However, many Mexicans are frustrated that democratic governance has not delivered security and sustained growth. The country's future stability depends on the ability of a more democratic system to guarantee public safety and provide economic opportunities.

The Politics of Collective Identity

A fundamental underlying strength of the Mexican nation is a strong sense of identity forged through more than two centuries of resistance to foreign interventions and invasions and through the shared experience of the Mexican Revolution. Mexico's identity is also strongly reinforced by the country's proximity to the United States. Though commercial links, migration, popular culture, and many other forces tie Mexico closely to the "colossus of the north," Mexicans are keenly aware of what sets them apart from their American neighbors, and they are determined to maintain their own traditions and values.

corporatist state

A state in which interest groups become an institutionalized part of the state structure.

While patriotism and a common cultural background bind together citizens from all walks of life, Mexican society is also marked by deep divisions. The EZLN's 1994 rebellion reflected the fact that rural Mexico in general, the south of the country in particular, and indigenous groups most of all had been left behind by policies promoting industrial development and integration into the world economy. Huge disparities in the distribution of wealth and income also create potentially explosive divisions between economic and social classes throughout the country. Though the PRI was able to maintain stability by using patronage and clientelism to mediate between a diverse range of interest groups for decades, in a more democratic system political appeals directed at particular classes might well become increasingly effective.

Themes and Comparisons

Mexico's modern history resembles that of Russia and China in that it has been framed by a social revolution that overturned the preexisting order, but the ideology that drove the Mexican revolutionary process was not communism. Instead, the Revolution of 1910 reflected concerns that arose from social conditions and historical experiences that were particular to Mexico. A diverse, often fractious revolutionary coalition called for democratic government, social justice, and national control of the country's resources. In the years after the revolution, the state created conditions for political and social peace. By incorporating peasants and workers into party and government institutions, by providing benefits to low-income groups during the 1930s, and by presiding over considerable economic growth after 1940, the regime became widely accepted as legitimate. In a world of developing nations wracked by political turmoil, military coups, and regime changes, the PRI established a strong state with enduring institutions. The party presided over decades of political stability and sustained (if unequally distributed) growth. Only in the face of economic crisis did this system begin to crumble toward the end of the twentieth century.

By moving since the 1980s to develop a more open and competitive political system, while embracing globalization as a development strategy, Mexico has followed a path chosen by a number of other Latin American nations, such as Brazil and Chile. Unlike those countries, though, Mexico made a transition away from civilian authoritarian rule rather than military dictatorship, and the democratic nature of the institutions provided for in the 1917 constitution meant that no major reform was required to bring about a change in regime. In the twenty-first century, the Mexican government is more transparent and accountable to its citizens than it was in the past, and there is much greater scope than before for **civil society** activism and for independent political activity. Mexicans value the new opportunities for political participation that they have won, but they have discovered that democratic institutions do not necessarily provide more efficient and effective governance. The rise of drug cartels as a significant threat to public security in recent years has also shaken Mexicans' confidence in their institutions. Though these criminal organizations do not pursue explicitly political ends in the way that guerrilla insurgencies and terrorist groups in other nations might, their wealth and the powerful economic forces that sustain them make them in some ways harder to fight. Given the capacity that these groups have to corrupt public officials and to carry out acts of violence, Mexicans fear the influence they might have on their country's politics. Finally, though Mexico has achieved an impressive degree of industrialization and economic development, it

civil society

Refers to the space occupied by voluntary associations outside the state, for example, professional associations (lawyers, doctors, teachers), trade unions, student and women's groups, religious bodies, and other voluntary association groups.

continues to face the challenge of overcoming deep inequalities between regions and social classes and of providing opportunities for millions of citizens living in poverty.

Where Do You Stand?

How would you assess the meaning and legacy of the Mexican Revolution? To what extent were the promises of the revolution fulfilled?

In recent years, both the resiliency and the fragility of the Mexican state have been on display, as the country has experienced both a peaceful political transition to competitive democracy and a wave of violence as the government has confronted criminal organizations. Do you see Mexico's institutions as fundamentally strong or fundamentally weak?

SECTION 2 — POLITICAL ECONOMY AND DEVELOPMENT

▼ Focus Questions

- What accounts for the Mexican government's decision to seek greater integration into the global economy?

- In what ways have global linkages helped or harmed the lives of various social groups?

state capitalism

An economic system that is primarily capitalistic but in which there is some degree of government ownership of the means of production.

State and Economy

In light of the central role played by the Mexican state in the development of the national economy over the course of more than a century, a more thorough discussion of that history is necessary to understand the relationship between state and economy today.

During the *Porfiriato* (1876–1911), policy-makers believed that Mexico could grow rich by exporting raw materials. Their efforts to attract international investment encouraged a major boom in the production and export of products such as henequin (for making rope), coffee, cacao (cocoa beans), cattle, oil, silver, and gold. Soon, the country had become so attractive to foreign investors that large amounts of land, the country's petroleum, its railroad network, and its mining wealth were largely controlled by foreigners. Nationalist reaction against these foreign interests played a significant role in the tensions that produced the Revolution of 1910.

After the revolution, this nationalism combined with a sense of social justice inspired by revolutionary leaders such as Zapata. The country adopted a strategy in which the government guided industrial and agricultural development. This development strategy, often called **state capitalism**, relied heavily on government actions to encourage private investment and reduce risks for private entrepreneurs. At the same time, many came to believe that Mexico should begin to manufacture the goods that it was then importing.

Import Substitution and Its Consequences

Between 1940 and 1982, Mexico pursued a form of state capitalism and a model of development known import substitution industrialization (ISI). Like Brazil and other Latin American countries during the same period, the government provided incentives and assistance to promote industries that would supply the domestic market.

Between 1940 and 1950, GDP grew at an annual average of 6.7 percent, while manufacturing increased at an average of 8.1 percent. In the 1950s, manufacturing

Table 5.2	**Mexican Development, 1940–2010**						
	1940	**1950**	**1960**	**1970**	**1980**	**1990**	**2010**
Population (millions)	19.8	26.3	38.0	52.8	70.4	88.5	117.9
Life expectancy (years)	–	51.6	58.6	62.6	67.4	68.9	76.7
Infant mortality (per 1,000 live births)	–	–	86.3	70.9	49.9	42.6	14.7
Illiteracy (% of population age 15 and over)	–	42.5	34.5	25.0	16.0	12.7	6.9
Urban population (% of total)	–	–	50.7	59.0	66.4	72.6	77.8
Economically active population in agriculture (% of total)	–	58.3	55.1	44.0	36.6	22.0	13.1
	1940–1949	**1950–1959**	**1960–1969**	**1970–1979**	**1980–1989**	**1990–1999**	**2000–2009**
GDP growth rate (average annual percent)	6.7	5.8	7.6	6.4	1.6	3.4	1.3
Per capita GDP growth rate	–	–	3.7	3.3	–0.1	1.6	0.3

Sources: World Bank, World Development Indicators; Central Intelligence Agency.

achieved an average of 7.3 percent growth annually, and in the 1960s, that figure rose to 10.1 percent. Agricultural production also grew as new areas were brought under cultivation and new technologies were adopted on large farms. Even the poorest Mexicans believed that their lives were improving, and key statistical indicators reflected a real rise in standards of living (see Table 5.2). So impressive was Mexico's economic performance that it was referred to internationally as the "Mexican Miracle."

During this period, business elites, unionized workers, and wealthy commercial farmers benefitted from state policies and provided a strong base of support for the apparently successful ISI model. Government policies eventually limited the potential for further growth, however.[2] Industrialists who received subsidies and were protected from competition had few incentives to produce efficiently. The domestic market was also limited by poverty; many Mexicans could not afford the sophisticated manufactured products the country would need to produce in order to keep growing under the import substitution model.

Indeed, as the economy grew, many were left behind. The ranks of the urban poor grew steadily, particularly from the 1960s. By 1970, a large proportion of Mexico City's population was living in inner-city tenements or squatter settlements surrounding the city.[2] Mexico developed a sizable informal sector—workers who produced and sold goods and services at the margin of the economic system and faced extreme insecurity.

Also left behind in the country's development after 1940 were peasant farmers. Their lands were often the least fertile, plot sizes were minuscule, and access to markets was impeded by poor transportation and exploitive middlemen. Increasing disparities in rural and urban incomes, coupled with high population growth rates, contributed to the emergence of rural guerrilla movements and student protests in the mid- and late 1960s.

Sowing the Oil and Reaping a Crisis

In the early 1970s, Mexico faced the threat of social crisis brought on by rural poverty, chaotic urbanization, high population growth, and the questioning of political legitimacy. The government responded by investing in infrastructure and public industries, regulating the flow of foreign capital, and increasing social spending. It was spending much more than it generated, causing the public debt to grow rapidly.

Just as the seriousness of this unsustainable economic situation was being recognized, vast new finds of oil came to the rescue. Between 1978 and 1982, Mexico became a major oil exporter. The government embarked on a policy to "sow the oil" in the economy and "administer the abundance" with vast investment projects in virtually all sectors and with major new initiatives to reduce poverty and deal with declining agricultural productivity.

Oil accounted for almost four-fifths of the country's exports, causing the economy to be extremely vulnerable to changes in oil prices. And change they did. Global overproduction led to a steep drop in petroleum prices in 1982. At the same time, access to foreign credit dried up. In August 1982, the government announced that the country could not pay the interest on its foreign debt, triggering a crisis that reverberated around the world.

The economic crisis had several important implications for structures of power and privilege in Mexico. The crisis convinced even the most diehard believers that import substitution created inefficiencies in production, failed to generate sufficient employment, cost the government far too much in subsidies, and ultimately increased dependency on industrialized countries. In addition, the power of privileged interest groups and their ability to influence government policy declined.

A wide variety of interests began to organize outside the PRI to demand that government do something about the situation. Massive earthquakes in Mexico City in September 1985 proved to be a watershed for Mexican society. Severely disappointed by the government's failure to respond to the disaster, hundreds of communities organized rescue efforts, soup kitchens, shelters, and rehabilitation initiatives. A surging sense of political empowerment developed, as groups long accustomed to dependence on government learned that they could solve their problems better without it.[3]

The elections of 1988 became a focus for protest against the economic dislocation caused by the crisis and the political powerlessness that most citizens felt. For the first time in decades, the PRI was challenged by the increased popularity of opposition political parties, one of them headed by Cuauhtémoc Cárdenas, the son of the country's most revered president. When the votes were counted, it was announced that Carlos Salinas, the PRI candidate, had received a bare majority of 50.7 percent, as opposition parties claimed widespread electoral fraud.

New Strategies: Structural Reforms and NAFTA

Between 1988 and 1994, the mutually dependent relationship between industry and government was weakened as new free-market policies were put in place. Deregulation gave the private sector more freedom to pursue economic activities and less reason to seek special favors from government. The private sector also came to control much more of the economy as the government sold off state enterprises as part of its reform program. In the countryside, a constitutional revision made it possible for *ejidos* to be divided into individually owned plots; this made farmers less dependent on government but more vulnerable to losing their land.

Among the farthest-reaching initiatives was the North American Free Trade Agreement (NAFTA). This agreement with Canada and the United States created the basis for gradual introduction of free trade among the three countries. However, the liberalization of the Mexican economy and opening of its markets to foreign competition increased Mexico's vulnerability to changes in international economic conditions. These factors, as well as mismanaged economic policies, led to a major economic crisis for the country at the end of 1994 and profound recession in 1995. NAFTA has meant that the fate of the Mexican economy is increasingly linked to the health of the U.S. economy.

The Mexican Economy Today

Under the influence of NAFTA, the Mexican economy has become increasingly oriented toward production for the North American market, and the manufacturing sector in particular has grown in importance. In addition to the traditional *maquiladora* industries along the northern border, Mexico is taking advantage of the large number of engineers trained by its universities to develop more advanced industries. Querétaro, in central Mexico, for example, is emerging as a center for the aerospace industry. The country also plays an integral part in a manufacturing process for automobiles that has become continental in scale, with parts from the United States, Canada, and Mexico moving between plants in the three countries as new cars are assembled. These developments give the country an economic profile that is quite distinct from that of many of its Latin American neighbors, many of which still rely more heavily on exports of agricultural products and raw materials.

remittances

Funds sent by migrants working abroad to family members in their home countries.

Remittances reflect another close economic link with the United States. Mexican migrants abroad sent some $22 billion home to relatives in 2013, with 98 percent of those funds coming from the United States (see The U.S. Connection: Mexican Migration to the United States). This sum represents 2 percent of Mexico's GDP, not an insignificant figure, and though the volume of remittances has declined somewhat since the economic crisis of 2008, these transfers provide a vital economic lifeline to many communities in central and southern Mexico, some of which send almost all of their adult men to the United States to work.[4]

Oil production also remains important to the economy, particularly since the national petroleum company, PEMEX, continues to provide a substantial proportion of government revenues. However, the government's reliance on oil revenues

THE U.S. CONNECTION

Mexican Migration to the United States

Mexicans began moving to the United States in substantial numbers late in the nineteenth century, and their ranks grew as many fled the conditions created by the Revolution of 1910. Most settled in the border states of California and Texas, where they joined preexisting Mexican communities that had been there since the days when the American southwest had been part of Mexico. Even greater numbers of migrants began to arrive during World War II, when the U.S. government allowed Mexican workers, known as *braceros*, to enter the country to help provide much-needed manpower for strategic production efforts. After the *bracero* program came to an end in 1964, Mexicans continued to seek work in the United States, despite the fact that most then had to enter the country illegally.

To a large extent, the U.S. government informally tolerated the employment of undocumented migrants until the 1980s, when policy-makers came under pressure to assert control over the border. The 1986 Immigration Reform and Control Act (IRCA) allowed migrants who had been in the United States for a long period of time to gain legal residency rights, but it called for tighter controls on immigration in the future. IRCA and subsequent efforts to deter illegal immigration turned a pattern of seasonal migration into a flow of migrants that settled permanently north of the border. Before 1986, most Mexican migrant workers left their families at home and worked in the United States for only a few months at a time before returning to their country with the money they had earned. The money that these migrants send back to Mexico helps to sustain not just their own families but entire regions that have been left behind by the migrants who gained amnesty under IRCA and then sent for their families to join them, creating a more permanent immigrant community. Also, as increased vigilance and new barriers making the crossing of the border more difficult, more of the migrants who arrived in the United States decided to remain there rather than risk apprehension by traveling back and forth

between the two countries. High-profile efforts to patrol the border around urban areas such as San Diego and El Paso led migrants to use more remote crossing points, and although the number of Mexicans who died trying to reach the United States rose as many attempted to travel through the desolate deserts of Arizona, the overall rate of illegal immigration was not affected by the government's crackdown.

In the 1990s and 2000s, growing Mexican communities in the United States spread into areas such as North Carolina, Georgia, Arkansas, and Iowa, where few Mexicans had lived before. They also became increasingly mobilized politically as they organized to resist anti-immigrant voter initiatives such as Proposition 187 in California in 1994 and Proposition 200 in Arizona in 2004, both of which threatened to cut off social services for undocumented migrants. At the same time, their political importance in Mexico has reached unprecedented heights as officials at all levels of government there recognize the critical importance to the Mexican economy of the remittances received from migrants working in other countries. Mexican governors, mayors, and federal officials now regularly visit representatives of migrant groups in the United States, often seeking their support and funding for projects at home. Moreover, a 1996 law allowing Mexicans to hold dual citizenship makes it possible for many Mexican migrants to have a voice in the governance of both the country of their birth as well as the country where they now reside. In 2005, Mexican legislators finally approved a system under which registered Mexican voters living abroad could participate in federal elections. Although levels of electoral participation by Mexicans abroad have so far been relatively modest, this huge group could play a decisive role in future contests.

MAKING CONNECTIONS How might debates over immigration policies in the United States affect the politics and foreign relations of Mexico?

has starved the state oil monopoly of the capital it would need to invest in new technologies and seek out new deposits. As the output of existing oilfields has begun to decline, the politically sensitive question of reform in the energy sector has therefore become unavoidable. Peña Nieto's energy reform will allow foreign companies to enter into joint ventures in Mexico with PEMEX, a development that could revitalize the sector but could also inflame nationalist resentments if Mexico is not seen to benefit from new discoveries.

Society and Economy

Mexico's economic development has had a significant impact on social conditions in the country. Overall, standards of living and quality of life rose markedly after the 1940s. Provision of health and education services expanded until government cutbacks on social expenditures in the early 1980s and has been extended further in recent years as modest economic growth has resumed. Among the most important consequences of economic growth was the development of a large middle class, most of whom live in Mexico's numerous large cities.

These achievements reflect well on the ability of the economy to increase social well-being in the country. But in terms of standard indicators of social development—infant mortality, literacy, and life expectancy—Mexico fell behind a number of Latin American countries that grew less rapidly but provided more effectively for their populations. Costa Rica, Colombia, Argentina, Chile, and Uruguay had lower over-all growth but greater social development in the period after 1940. These countries paid more attention to the distribution of the benefits of growth than did Mexico.

In part, because of the specific way in which Mexico has pursued economic growth, there is also a regional dimension to disparities in social development. The northern areas of the country are significantly better off than the southern and central areas. In the north, large commercial farms using modern technologies grow fruits, vegetables, and grains for export. Moreover, urban industrial centers such as Monterrey and Tijuana provide steady employment for skilled and unskilled labor. Along the border, *maquiladoras* provide many jobs, particularly for young women who are seeking some escape from the burdens of rural life or the constraints of traditional family life.

In the southern and central regions of the country, the population is denser, the terrain more difficult, and the number of farmers eking out subsistence greater. Investment in irrigation and transportation infrastructure has been lacking in many areas. Most of the 26 million Mexicans who continue to live in rural areas, and most of the country's remaining indigenous groups live in the southern regions, often in remote zones where they have been forgotten by government programs and exploited by regional bosses for generations.

The general economic crisis of the 1980s had an impact on social conditions in Mexico as well. Wages declined by about half, and unemployment soared as businesses collapsed and the government laid off workers. The informal sector expanded rapidly. Here, people manage to make a living by hawking chewing gum, umbrellas, candy, shoelaces, and many other items in the street; jumping in front of cars at stoplights to wash windshields and sell newspapers; producing and repairing cheap consumer goods; and selling services on a daily or hourly basis. The economic crisis also reduced the quality and availability of social services, as the government imposed austerity measures. Though economic recovery has been slow and fitful in recent decades, the Mexican government has begun to fill the void left by cuts in social spending during the depths of the crisis. Recent years have seen the launch of successful programs that provide vastly expanded access to basic health care and cash grants to poor families that keep their children in school.

Environmental Issues

With its varied landscapes, including long coastlines, extensive coral reefs, towering mountain peaks, tropical rain forests, and arid deserts, Mexico is a country of tremendous biodiversity, with many fragile ecosystems that have been badly damaged by insensitive economic development. Though a tradition of conservation stretches back at least to the 1930s, when Lázaro Cárdenas established a national park system, for many years the pursuit of economic development and industrialization was given priority over the enforcement of environmental regulations. One result was that Mexico City became one of the most polluted cities in the world, and in some rural areas oil exploitation left devastating environmental damage.[5]

When residents of Mexico City and other parts of the country began to mobilize outside of the PRI in the 1980s to pressure the government to address the issues that mattered most to their communities, environmental concerns were an important item on their agenda, and much stricter controls on automobile and industrial emissions have helped to make the capital's air more breathable since that time. As Mexico has sought a place in the global economy since the late 1980s, pressure from abroad also played a vital role in bringing about a strengthening of the state's commitment to environmental protection. When critics of NAFTA threatened to block the agreement in the United States on the grounds that Mexico failed to live up to international environmental standards, the Mexican government signed onto side agreements providing for greater environmental oversight in order to secure the ratification of the free-trade accord. The government also signalled that it was assigning greater importance to environmental concerns by creating a ministry for the environment and natural resources in 1994; more than coincidentally, the new cabinet department came into existence in the same year that NAFTA went into effect.

Although many concerns remain, the will and the capacity of the Mexican state to act to protect the environment have been significantly enhanced over the past two decades. Moreover, in an increasingly interconnected world, Mexican civil society organizations with an interest in these issues have benefitted greatly from the connections they have developed with international networks of environmental groups.

Mexico in the Global Economy

The crisis that began in 1982 altered Mexico's international economic policies. In response to that crisis, the government relaxed restrictions on the ability of foreigners to own property, reduced and eliminated tariffs, and did away with most import licenses. Foreign investment was courted in the hope of increasing the manufacture of goods for export. The government also introduced a series of incentives to encourage the private sector to produce goods for export. In 1986, Mexico joined the General Agreement on Tariffs and Trade (GATT), a multilateral agreement that sought to promote freer trade among countries and that later became the basis for the World Trade Organization (WTO). In the 1990s and 2000s, Mexico signed trade pacts with many countries in Latin America, Europe, and elsewhere.

The government's effort to pursue a more outward-oriented development strategy culminated in the ratification of NAFTA in 1993, with gradual implementation beginning on January 1, 1994. In 2013, 77.6 percent of the country's exports were sent to the United States, and 50.1 percent of its imports came from that country, making Mexico's northern neighbor its most important trading partner by a wide margin.[6] Access to the U.S. market is essential to Mexico and to domestic and foreign investors. NAFTA signaled a new period in U.S.–Mexican relations by making closer integration of the two economies a certainty.

NAFTA also entails risks for Mexico. Domestic producers worry about competition from U.S. firms. Farmers worry that Mexican crops cannot compete effectively with those grown in the United States; for example, peasant producers of corn and beans have been hard hit by the availability of lower-priced U.S.-grown grains.[7] In addition, many believe that embracing free trade with Canada and the United States indicates a loss of sovereignty. Certainly, Mexico's economic situation is now more vulnerable to the ebb and flow of economic conditions in the U.S. economy. Indeed, after the United States plunged into a deep recession in 2008, Mexico's economy contracted by more than 7 percent, despite the fact that the crisis was not of its own making. Moreover, some in Mexico are also concerned with evidence of "cultural imperialism" as U.S. movies, music, fashions, and lifestyles increasingly influence consumers. Indeed, for Mexico, which has traditionally feared the power of the United States in its domestic affairs, internationalization of political and economic relationships poses particularly difficult problems of adjustment.

On the other hand, the United States, newly aware of the importance of the Mexican economy to its own economic growth and concerned about instability on its southern border, hammered together a $50 billion economic assistance program composed of U.S., European, and IMF commitments to support its neighbor when economic crisis struck in 1994. The Mexican government imposed a new stabilization package that contained austerity measures, higher interest rates, and limits on wages. Remarkably, by 1998, Mexico had paid off all of its obligations to the United States.

Globalization is also stripping Mexico of some of the secrecy that traditionally surrounded government decision making, electoral processes, and efforts to deal with political dissent. International attention increasingly focuses on the country, and investors want clear information on what is occurring in the economy. The government can no longer respond to events such as the peasant rebellion in Chiapas, alleged electoral fraud, or the management of exchange rates without considering how such actions will be perceived in Tokyo, Frankfurt, London, or Washington.

Where Do You Stand?

Mexico is recognized by investors as an important emerging economy, but can its development strategy be considered a success when some regions of the country and some economic sectors are being left behind? What can be done to address the disparities being exacerbated by uneven growth?

Taking into account the full range of effects that NAFTA has had on Mexico, do you think the free trade agreement has been good or bad for the country?

GOVERNANCE AND POLICY-MAKING

SECTION **3**

Organization of the State

Under the Constitution of 1917, Mexico's political institutions resemble those of the United States. There are three branches of government, and a set of checks and balances limits the power of each. The congress is composed of the Senate and the

- In what ways does the actual exercise of state power differ from the model outlined in the constitution? What are the main reasons for these discrepancies?

- To what extent is federalism a reality in Mexico today? How is power divided between administrations at the national, state, and local levels?

sexenio

The six-year term in office of Mexican presidents.

Chamber of Deputies. One hundred twenty-eight senators are elected, three from each of the country's thirty-one states; three from the Federal District, which contains the capital, Mexico City; and another thirty-two elected nationally by proportional representation (PR). The **500** members of the Chamber of Deputies are elected from **300** electoral districts—300 by simple majority vote and 200 by proportional representation. State and local governments are also elected. The president, governors, and senators are elected for six years, an important institutional feature of Mexican politics referred to as the *sexenio*. Congressional deputies (representatives in the lower house) and municipal officials are elected for three years.

In practice, the Mexican system is very different from that of the United States. The constitution is a long document that can be easily amended. It lays out the structure of government and guarantees a wide range of human rights, including familiar ones such as freedom of speech and protection under the law, but also economic and social rights such as the right to a job and the right to health care. In practice, these rights do not reach all of the population. Although there has been some decentralization, the political system is still much more centralized than that of the United States. Since the democratic transition of 2000, congress has become more active as a decision-making arena and as a check on presidential power, but the executive remains central to initiating policy and managing political conflict.

The Executive

The President and the Cabinet

The presidency is the central institution of governance and policy-making in Mexico. Until the 1990s, the incumbent president always selected who would run as the PRI's next presidential candidate, appointed officials to all positions of power in the government and the party, and often named the candidates who almost automatically won elections as governors, senators, deputies, and local officials.[8] Even after the transition to a more competitive political system, the president continues to set the broad outlines of policy for the administration and has numerous resources to ensure that those policy preferences are adopted. Until the mid-1970s, Mexican presidents were considered above criticism in national politics and revered as symbols of national progress and well-being. While the crises of the 1980s and 1990s diminished presidential prestige, the extent of presidential power remains a legacy of the long period of PRI dominance.

Mexican presidents have a set of formal powers that allows them to initiate legislation, lead in foreign policy, create government agencies, make policy by decree or through administrative regulations and procedures, and appoint a wide range of public officials. More importantly, informal powers allow them to exert considerable control. The president manages a vast patronage machine for filling positions in government and initiates legislation and policies that were, until recently, routinely approved by the congress.

Mexican presidents, though powerful, are not omnipotent. They must, for example, abide by a deeply held constitutional norm by stepping down at the end of their term, and they must adhere to tradition by removing themselves from the political limelight to allow their successors to assume full presidential leadership. All presidents, regardless of party, must demonstrate their loyalty to the myths and symbols of Mexican nationalism, and they must make a rhetorical commitment to social justice and sovereignty in international affairs.

President Enrique Peña Nieto (left) is congratulated by his predecessor, Felipe Calderón, at his inauguration on December 1, 2012.

AP Images/Alexandre Meneghini

In the 1990s, President Zedillo gave up a number of the traditional powers of the presidency. He announced, for example, that he would not select his PRI successor but would leave it up to the party to determine its candidate. This created considerable tension as the PRI had to take on unaccustomed roles and as politicians sought to fill the void left by the "abandonment" of presidential power. Fox, Calderón, and Peña Nieto inherited a system in which the president is expected to set the policies and determine the priorities for a very wide range of government activity, yet needs a strong party in congress and experienced people in his administration to enact legislation and implement policies.

Until the democratic transition of 2000, presidents were almost always members of the outgoing president's cabinet. With the victory of the PAN in 2000, this long tradition came to an end. Prior to running for president, Vicente Fox had been in business and had served as the governor of the state of Guanajuato. Calderón, although he had served briefly as energy minister, was not the candidate within the PAN that Fox had initially favored. In this respect, Calderón's victory in 2006 continued a trend toward greater independence of parties from presidential preferences. As the PRI candidate in 2012, Peña Nieto obviously had not served in the cabinets of Fox or Calderón; instead, he had just completed a term as the governor of the populous state of Mexico, which includes many of the suburbs of Mexico City. His candidacy reflected the prominence that state governors had attained in the PRI during the years that the party had been out of power at the national level.

Mexican presidents since the mid-1970s have had impressive educational credentials and have tended to be trained in economics and management rather than in the traditional field of law. Most presidents since López Portillo have had postgraduate training at elite institutions in the United States. By the 1980s, a topic of

technocrats

Career-minded bureaucrats who administer public policy according to a technical rather than a political rationale.

great debate in political circles was the extent to which a divide between *políticos* (politicians) and *técnicos* (technocrats) had emerged within the national political elite. Having studied law and attended Mexican universities, Peña Nieto's educational background differs from that of his immediate predecessors.

Once elected, the president moves quickly to name a cabinet. Before 2000, he usually selected those with whom he had worked over the years as he rose to political prominence. He also used cabinet posts to ensure a broad coalition of support; he might, for example, appoint people with close ties to the labor movement, business interests, or some of the regional strongholds of the PRI. Only in rare exceptions were cabinet officials not active members of the party. When the PAN assumed the presidency, the selection of cabinet members became more difficult. Until then, the PAN had elected officials only to a few state and local governments and to a relatively small number of seats in congress. As a consequence, the range of people with executive experience to whom Fox could turn was limited. He appointed U.S.-trained economists for his economic team and business executives for many other important posts. Few of these appointees had close ties to the PAN or prior experience in government. By contrast, Calderón filled his cabinet positions with longtime members of the PAN who had a longer history of political engagement, but after so many years in opposition, many of these appointees also lacked extensive experience in government. Over the years, few women have been selected for ministry-level posts. Initially, they only presided over agencies with limited influence over decision making, like the ministries of tourism and fisheries. More recently, however, women have served as foreign minister and as attorney general. Peña Nieto has followed the traditions of the PRI by naming a number of aides from his term as governor of Mexico state, as well as allies from key regions, to his cabinet. At the same time, he has looked beyond his party to fill some posts. He named Rosario Robles, a woman and the former president of the left-of-center Party of the Democratic Revolution (PRD), as minister for social development, and he appointed a member of Calderón's cabinet as foreign minister.

The president has the authority to fill numerous other high-level positions, which allows him to provide policy direction and keep tabs on what is occurring throughout the government. The range of appointments that a chief executive can make means that the beginning of each administration is characterized by extensive turnover of positions. Progress on the president's policy agenda can therefore be slow toward the beginning of each *sexenio* as newly appointed officials learn the ropes and assemble their staff, though this effect was not noticeable during Peña Nieto's very active first year in office. The president's power to make appointments allows him to build a team of like-minded officials in government and ensure their loyalty.

The Bureaucracy

Mexico's executive branch is large and powerful. Almost 1.5 million people work in the federal bureaucracy, most of them in Mexico City. An additional 1 million work in state-owned industries and semiautonomous agencies of the government. State and local governments employ over 1.5 million people.

Officials at lower levels in the bureaucracy are unionized and protected by legislation that gives them job security and a range of benefits. At middle and upper levels, most officials are called "confidence employees"; they serve as long as their bosses have confidence in them. These officials have been personally appointed by their superiors at the outset of an administration. Their modest salaries are compensated for by the significant power that they can have over public affairs. For aspiring young professionals, a career in government is often attractive because of the challenge of dealing with important problems on a daily basis. Some employees also benefit from opportunities to take bribes or use other means to promote their personal interests.

The Parastatal Sector

The parastatal sector—composed of semiautonomous or autonomous government agencies, many of which produce goods and services—was extremely large and powerful in Mexico prior to the 1990s. As part of its post-1940 development strategy, the government engaged in numerous activities that in other countries are carried out by the private sector. Thus, until the Salinas administration, the country's largest steel mill was state-owned, as were the largest fertilizer producer, sugar mills, and airlines. In addition, the national electricity board still produces energy, which it supplies to industries at subsidized prices. The state-owned petroleum company, PEMEX, grew to enormous proportions in the 1970s and 1980s under the impact of the oil boom. NAFIN, a state investment corporation, provides a considerable amount of investment capital for the country. At one point, a state marketing board called CONASUPO was responsible for the importation and purchase of the country's basic food supplies, and in the 1970s, it played a major role in distributing food, credit, and farm implements in rural areas.

This large parastatal sector was significantly trimmed by the economic policy reforms that began in the 1980s. Concerted efforts were then made to privatize many of these enterprises, including the telephone company, the national airlines, and the nationalized banks. Many strategic industries thus passed into a small number of private hands, and much of the banking sector came under the control of foreign corporations. However, some core components of the parastatal sector will likely remain in government hands for the foreseeable future because an influential bloc of nationalist political actors insists on the symbolic importance of public ownership of key industries. For example, even with reforms taking effect to allow foreign investment in the energy sector, PEMEX is likely to remain a state enterprise with a key position in the petroleum industry.

Other State Institutions

The Military

Mexico is one of only a few countries in the developing world, particularly in Latin America, to have successfully marginalized the military from centers of political power. Although former military leaders dominated Mexican politics during the decades immediately after the Revolution of 1910, Calles and Cárdenas laid the groundwork for civilian rule by introducing the practice of rotating regional military commands so that generals could not build up geographic bases of power. In addition, postrevolutionary leaders made an implicit bargain with the military leaders by providing them with opportunities to engage in business so that they did not look to political office as a way of gaining economic power. After 1946, the military no longer had institutional representation within the PRI and became clearly subordinate to civilian control. No military officer has held the presidency since that time.

This does not mean that the military has operated outside politics. It has been called in from time to time to deal with domestic unrest: in rural areas in the 1960s, in Mexico City and other cities to repress student protest movements in 1968, and in

Chiapas beginning in 1994. When the PAN government made it possible for citizens to gain greater access to government information, it was discovered that the military had been involved in political repression, torture, and killing in the 1970s and 1980s. The scandal created by such revelations lowered its reputation, though polls show that Mexicans continue to have more confidence in the armed forces than many other institutions, including the police forces, which are widely regarded as corrupt and ineffective.

In recent years, the military has been heavily involved in efforts to combat drug trafficking, and rumors have at times arisen about deals struck between military officials and drug barons. The military continues to be used to fight drug cartels and organized crime. In some regions particularly hard-hit by drug-related violence, the military took over many policing functions. Though the army is seen as less corrupt than many of the local police forces they have replaced, concerns about their ongoing presence on the streets of Mexican cities have arisen, particularly as allegations of civil and human rights violations by soldiers have emerged in some areas.

Whenever the military is called in to resolve domestic conflicts, some Mexicans become concerned that the institution is becoming politicized and may come to play a larger role in political decision making. Thus far, such fears have not been realized, and many believe that as long as civilian administrations are able to maintain the country's tradition of stability, the military will not intervene directly in politics.

The Judiciary

Unlike Anglo-American legal systems, Mexico's law derives from the Roman and Napoleonic tradition and is highly formalized. Because Mexican law tends to be very explicit and because there are no punitive damages allowed in court cases, there are fewer lawsuits than in the United States. One important exception to this is the *amparo* (protection), whereby individual citizens may ask for a writ of protection, claiming that their constitutional rights have been violated by specific government actions or laws.

There are both federal and state courts in Mexico. The federal system is composed of the Supreme Court, which decides the most important cases; circuit courts, which take cases on appeal; and district courts, where cases enter the system. As in the United States, Supreme Court justices are nominated by the president and approved by the Senate. Since most of the important laws in Mexico are federal, state courts have played a subordinate role. This is changing, however. As Mexican states become more independent from the federal government, state law has been experiencing tremendous growth. In addition, there are many important specialized federal courts, such as labor courts, military courts, and electoral courts.

Like other government institutions in Mexico, the judiciary was for many decades politically, though not constitutionally, subordinate to the executive. The courts occasionally slowed the actions of government by issuing *amparos*; however, in almost every case in which the power of the state was at stake, the courts ruled on the side of the government. The Zedillo administration tried to change this by emphasizing the rule of law over that of powerful individuals. Increasing interest in human rights issues by citizens' groups and the media added pressure to the courts to play a stronger role in protecting basic freedoms.

Although the judicial system remains the weakest branch of government, reforms continue to be proposed. In 2008, in response to concern for the rights of defendants who fall victim to police and prosecutorial misconduct, constitutional amendments called for the introduction of public trials with oral testimony and the presumption of innocence. When fully implemented, the reforms will represent one of the most significant changes to the judiciary in modern Mexican history. The northern state of Chihuahua was the first to adopt the new system, but the new procedures have been controversial there, and progress elsewhere in the country has been slow.

Subnational Government

As with many other aspects of the Mexican political system, regional and local government in Mexico is quite different from what is described in the constitution. Under Mexico's federal system, each state has its own constitution, executive, unicameral legislature, and judiciary. Municipalities (equivalent to U.S. counties) are governed by popularly elected mayors and councils. But most state and municipal governments are poor. Most of the funds they command are transferred to them from the central government, and they have little legal or administrative capacity to raise their own revenue. States and localities also suffer greatly from the lack of well-trained and well-paid public officials. As at the national level, many jobs in state and local governments are distributed as political patronage, but even officials who are motivated to be responsive to local needs are generally ill equipped to do so. In light of these weaknesses, it is not surprising that local governments have been particularly susceptible to the ability of wealthy, heavily armed drug cartels to corrupt and intimidate public officials, especially in poor and remote regions.

Since the early 1990s, the government has made several serious efforts to decentralize and devolve more power to state and local governments. At times, governors and mayors have resisted such initiatives because they meant that regional and local governments would have to manage much more complex activities and be the focus of demands from public sector workers and their unions. Local governments were also worried that they would be unable to acquire the budgetary resources necessary to carry out their new responsibilities.

Until 1989, all governors were from the PRI, but since then politics at the state level has become competitive in almost every region of the country. During the 25 years since the first PAN governor took office in Baja California, approximately three-quarters of Mexico's states have had at least one non-PRI administration. Municipalities have also increasingly been the focus of authentic party competition. As opposition parties came to control these levels of government, they were challenged to improve services such as police protection, garbage collection, sanitation, and education. PRI-dominated governments have also tried to improve their performance because they are now more threatened by the possibility of losing elections.

The Policy-Making Process

The Mexican system is very dependent on the quality of its leadership and on presidential understanding of how economic and social policies can affect the development of the country. As indicated throughout this chapter, the president's single six-year term of office, the *sexenio*, is an important fact of political life in Mexico. New presidents can introduce extensive change in positions within the government. They are able to bring in "their" people, who build teams of "their" people within ministries, agencies, and party networks. This generally provides the president with a group of high- and middle-level officials who share the same general orientation toward public policy and are motivated to carry out his goals. When the PRI was the dominant party, these officials believed that in following presidential leadership, they enhanced their chances for upward political mobility. In such a context, even under a single party, it was likely that changes in public policies could be introduced every six years, creating innovation or discontinuity, or both.

Together with the bureaucracy, the president is the focal point of policy formulation and political management. Until 1997, the legislature always had a PRI majority and acted as a rubber stamp for presidentially sponsored legislation. Since then, the congress has proven to be a more active policy-maker, blocking and forcing the negotiation of legislation, and even introducing its own bills. The president's skills in negotiating, managing the opposition, using the media to acquire public support, and maneuvering within the bureaucracy can be important in ensuring that his program is fully endorsed.

Significant limits on presidential power occur when policy is being implemented. At times, policies are not implemented because public officials at the lower levels disagree with them or make deals with affected interests in order to benefit personally. This is the case, for example, with taxes that remain uncollected because individuals or corporations bribe officials to overlook them. In other cases, lower-level officials may lack the capacity to implement some policies, such as those directed toward improving education or rural development services. For various reasons, Mexican presidents cannot always deliver on their intentions. Traditionally, Mexican citizens have blamed lower-level officials for such slippage, but exempting the president from responsibility for what does or does not occur during his watch has become much less common since the 1970s.

Where Do You Stand?

Should Mexico lift its constitutional ban on presidential reelection, as a number of other Latin American countries have done in recent years? Would having to face the voters for reelection make officials more accountable, or might allowing them to stay in office for more than one term open the door to a return to authoritarianism?

With the decline in the deference given to presidential preferences in recent years, more voices have been heard and taken into account as policies have been formulated, but the process has become more contentious and less efficient. On balance then, is it good for Mexico that the authority of the president has diminished over the past two decades?

SECTION 4

REPRESENTATION AND PARTICIPATION

How do citizen interests get represented in Mexican politics, given the high degree of centralization, presidentialism, and, until recently, single-party domination? Is it possible for ordinary citizens to make demands on government and influence public policy? In fact, Mexico has had a relatively peaceful history since the revolution, in part because the political system offers some channels for representation and participation. Throughout this long history, the political system has emphasized compromise among contending elites, behind-the-scenes conflict resolution, and distribution of political rewards to those willing to play by the formal and informal rules of the game. It has also responded, if only reluctantly and defensively, to demands for change.

Often, citizens are best able to interact with the government through a variety of informal means rather than through the formal processes of elections, campaigns, and interest group lobbying. Interacting with government through the personal mechanisms of clientelism usually means that the government retains the upper hand in deciding which interests to respond to and which to ignore. For many interests, this has meant "incorporation without power."[9] Increasingly, however, Mexican citizens are organizing to alter this situation, and the advent of truly competitive elections has increased the possibility that citizens who organize can gain some response from government.

The Legislature

Students in the United States are frequently asked to study complex charts explaining how a bill becomes a law because the formal process of lawmaking affects the content of legislation. Under the old reign of the PRI in Mexico, while there were formal rules that prescribed such a process, studying them would not have been useful for understanding how the legislature worked. Because of the overwhelming dominance of the ruling party, opposition to presidential initiatives by Mexico's two-chamber legislature, the Senate and the Chamber of Deputies, was rarely heard. If representatives did not agree with policies they were asked to approve, they counted on the fact that policy implementation was flexible and allowed for after-the-fact bending of the rules or disregard of measures that were harmful to important interests.

Representation in congress has become more diverse since the end of the 1980s. Between 1988 and 2006, the PRI's grip on the legislature steadily weakened. By the end of that period, the party had fewer representatives in the Chamber of Deputies than either of its two main rivals. The PRI subsequently made large gains in midterm legislative elections in 2009, and it is once again the largest party in the both houses of congress, but today the legislature is divided between strong PRI, PAN, and PRD blocs, with no single party able to dominate proceedings. In large part because the PRI has lost its stranglehold on congressional representation, the role of

Focus Questions ▽

• Since the early 1980s, how has the balance of power shifted between the legislative and executive branches of government? How do these shifts correspond to changes in the overall political landscape?

• What are the power bases of the main political parties in Mexican politics? What factors made it possible for the PAN to unseat the long-dominant PRI in 2000? What accounts for the success of the PRI in returning to power in 2012?

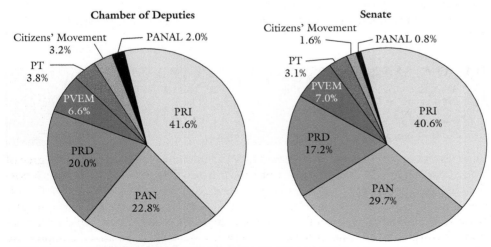

FIGURE 5.2 Congressional Representation by Party, 2014

Source: CIA World Factbook, www.cia.gov/library/publications/the-world-factbook/geos/mx.html#Govt; see also www.senado.gob.mx and www.camaradediputados.gob.mx.

the legislature in the policy process has been strengthened considerably since the late 1990s.[10] The cost of greater power sharing between the executive and the legislature, however, has been a slow-down in the policy process. The biggest change, therefore, has been that the congress has evolved from a rubber-stamp institution to one that must be negotiated with by the executive branch.

Political Parties and the Party System

Even under the long reign of the PRI, a number of political parties existed in Mexico. By the mid-1980s, some of them were attracting more political support, a trend that continued into the 1990s and 2000s (see Table 5.3). Electoral reforms introduced by the PRI administrations between the 1970s and the 1990s made it easier for opposition parties to contest and win elections. In 1990, an electoral commission was

Table 5.3	Voting for Major Parties in Presidential Elections, 1934–2012			
Year	Votes for PRI Candidate	Votes for PAN Candidate	Votes for PRD Candidate	Voter Turnout (% of eligible adults)
1934	98.2	—	—	53.6
1940	93.9	—	—	57.5
1946	77.9	—	—	42.6
1952	74.3	7.8	—	57.9
1958	90.4	9.4	—	49.4
1964	88.8	11.1	—	54.1
1970	83.3	13.9	—	63.9
1976	93.6	—	—	29.6
1982	71.0	15.7	—	66.1
1988	50.7	16.8	31.0	49.4
1994	50.1	26.7	16.6	77.3
2000	36.1	42.5	16.6	64.0
2006	22.3	35.9	35.3	58.6
2012	38.2	25.4	31.6	63.1

Source: From *Comparative Politics Today: A World View*, 4th ed., Gabriel Almond and G. Bingham Powell, Jr. © 1988. Reprinted by permission of Addison-Wesley Educational Publishers, Inc. For 1988: *El Universal*, "Resultados Electorales," graficos.eluniversal .com.mx/tablas/presidente/presidentes.htm. For 1994: Instituto Federal Electoral, *Estadística de las Elecciones Federales de 1994, Compendio de Resultados* (México, D.F., 1995). For 2000–2012: Instituto Federal Electoral, www.ife.org.mx.

created to regulate campaigns and elections, and in 1996 it became fully independent of the government. Now all parties receive funding from the government and have access to the media.

The PRI

Mexico's Institutional Revolutionary Party (PRI) was founded by a coalition of political elites who agreed that it was preferable to work out their conflicts within an overarching structure of compromise than to continue to resort to violence. In the 1930s, the forerunner of the PRI (the party operated under different names until 1946) incorporated a wide array of interests, becoming a mass-based party that drew support from all classes in the population. Over seven decades, its principal activities were to generate support for the government, organize the electorate to vote for its candidates, and distribute jobs and resources in return for loyalty to the system.

Until the 1990s, party organization was based largely on the corporatist representation of class interests. Labor was represented within party councils by the Confederation of Mexican Workers (CTM), which included industry-based unions at local, regional, and national levels. Peasants were represented by the National Peasant Confederation (CNC), an organization of *ejido* and peasant unions and regional associations. The so-called popular sector, comprising small businesses, community-based groups, and public employees, had less internal cohesion but was represented by the National Confederation of Popular Organizations (CNOP). Of the three, the CTM was consistently the best organized and most powerful. Traditionally, the PRI's strongest support came from the countryside, where *ejidatarios* and independent small farmers were dependent on rewards of land or jobs. As the country became more urbanized, the support base provided by rural communities remained important to the PRI, but produced many fewer votes than were necessary to keep the party in power.

Within its corporatist structures, the PRI functioned through extended networks that distributed public resources—particularly jobs, land, development projects, and access to public services—to lower-level activists who controlled votes at the local level. In this system, those with ambitions to hold public office or positions within the PRI put together networks of supporters from above (patrons), to whom they delivered votes, and supporters from below (clients), who traded allegiance for access to public resources. For well over half a century, this system worked extremely well. PRI candidates won by overwhelming majorities until the 1980s. Of course, electoral fraud and the ability to distribute government largesse are central explanations for these numbers, but they also attest to an extremely well-organized party.

By the 1980s, new generations of voters were less beholden to patronage-style politics and much more willing to question the party's dominance, and the PRI began to be challenged by parties to the right and left. Outcomes were hotly contested by the opposition, which claimed fraudulent electoral practices. As the PRI faced greater competition from other parties and continued to suffer from declining popularity, efforts were made to restructure and reform it. Party conventions were introduced in an effort to democratize the internal workings of the party, and some states and localities began to hold primaries to select PRI candidates, a significant departure from the old system of selection by party bosses.

After the PRI lost the presidency in 2000, the party faced a difficult future. At the dawn of the twenty-first century, Mexico's voters were younger, better educated, and more middle class than they were during the period of PRI dominance. They were also more likely to live in urban areas than they were in the days of the party's greatest success. With the vast majority of the country's population living in cities, the PRI faced the challenge of winning the support of more urban voters.

Nonetheless, the PRI remained a strong political force. It did not, as some predicted, dissolve once it lost the ability to control the presidency. As one of the largest blocs in a divided congress between 2000 and 2012, PRI representatives could often exercise significant control over the legislative agenda. Just as importantly, the party continued to control most subnational governments, and state governors emerged as some of the most influential figures in the party. The PRI is still the only party that has a presence in every region of the country, and after the violence and legislative gridlock of recent years, some Mexicans clearly hope that the party will be able to draw upon its long experience in government to offer a greater degree of order and stability.

The PAN

anticlericalism

Opposition to the power of churches or clergy in politics. In some countries, for example, France and Mexico, this opposition has focused on the role of the Catholic Church in politics.

The National Action Party (PAN) was founded in 1939 to represent interests opposed to the centralization and **anticlericalism** of the PRI. It was established by those who believed that the country needed more than one strong political party and that opposition parties should oppose the PRI through legal and constitutional actions. Historically, this party has been strongest in northern states, where it has drawn upon a regional tradition of resistance to central authority. It has also been primarily an urban party of the middle class and is closely identified with the private sector. The PAN has traditionally campaigned on a platform endorsing greater regional autonomy, less government intervention in the economy, reduced regulation of business, clean and fair elections, rapprochement with the Catholic Church, and support for private and religious education. When PRI governments of the 1980s and 1990s moved toward market-friendly and export-oriented policies, the policy differences between the two parties were significantly reduced. Nevertheless, a major difference of perspectives about religion continued to characterize the two parties.

For many years, the PAN was able to elect only about 10 percent of all deputies to the national congress and to capture control of just a few municipal governments. Beginning in the 1980s, it was able to take advantage both of the damage done to the PRI by economic crises and the opportunities provided by political reforms to increase its power. A PAN candidate was elected as the first opposition state governor in many years in 1989, and the party built up a sizeable bloc in both houses of congress during the 1990s. The PAN's victory in the 2000 presidential election was a historic breakthrough. Its triumph that year and in 2006 made the PAN the nation's governing party for 12 years.

In nominating Vicente Fox for the presidency in 2000, the party was taking an unusual step, for Fox was not a long-standing member of the party. Many party insiders considered him to be an opportunistic newcomer. Though Fox won the presidential election, the PAN organization was weak and not at all united in backing him. His inability to capitalize on his electoral victory and push forward a more ambitious package of reforms allowed the party insiders to regain control of the nominating process and advance the candidacy of Felipe Calderón in 2006. Unlike Fox, he was a lifelong member of the PAN and was the son of one of the PAN's founding members. In 2012, the party nominated a former education and social development minister, Josefina Vázquez Mota, as its presidential candidate. Her third-place showing indicated the country was ready for a change, and though the party continues to hold several governorships and the second-largest number of seats in both houses of congress, the PAN has struggled since its defeat to overcome internal divisions over its future.

The PRD

Another group that has played a key role in the construction of a more competitive political system in Mexico is the Party of the Democratic Revolution (PRD), which emerged in the late 1980s as a populist, nationalist, and leftist alternative to the PRI. Its candidate in the 1988, 1994, and 2000 elections was Cuauhtémoc Cárdenas, the son of Mexico's most revered president. In the 1988 elections, Cárdenas was officially credited with winning 31.1 percent of the vote. He benefited from massive political defection from the PRI and garnered support from workers disaffected with the boss-dominated unions, as well as from peasants who remembered his father's concern for the welfare of the poor.

Even while the votes were being counted, the party began to denounce widespread electoral fraud and claim that Cárdenas would have won if the election had been honest. The party challenged a number of vote counts in the courts and walked out on the inaugural speech given by the PRI's Salinas. Considerable public opinion supported the party's challenge. After the 1988 elections, then, it seemed that the PRD was a strong contender to become Mexico's second-most-powerful party. It was expected to have a real chance in future years to challenge the PRI's "right" to the presidency.

Nevertheless, in the aftermath of these elections, the party was plagued by internal divisions over its platform, leadership, organizational structure, and election strategy. By 1994, it still lagged far behind the PRI and the PAN in establishing and maintaining the local constituency organizations needed to mobilize votes and monitor the election process. In addition, the PRD found it difficult to define an appropriate left-of-center alternative to the market-oriented policies carried out by the government. In the 1994 and 2000 elections, Cárdenas won less than 17 percent of the vote.

Under the leadership of a successful grassroots mobilizer named Andrés Manuel López Obrador, who was elected to head the party in 1996 and who subsequently served as mayor of Mexico City, the PRD began to stage a turnaround. PRD administrations in several states, many municipalities, and, most importantly, in the Federal District, showed that the party could take on the challenges of governance. Under López Obrador, the PRD's prospects for the 2006 elections looked good. Indeed, for most of 2005, polls indicated that López Obrador was the clear favorite to win the presidency. In early 2006, however, Calderón was able to shift the focus of his campaign and raise fears that a López Obrador presidency would threaten the stability of Mexico's economy. The election was hard fought and characterized by growing animosity. In the end, Calderón was able to win by a narrow margin. López Obrador refused to concede defeat and staged several protests, including a shadow inauguration where he declared himself the "legitimate" president of Mexico.

López Obrador's response to the outcome of the 2006 election split public opinion and created another debilitating divide in the PRD, this time between those who supported their candidate's claims and more pragmatic party leaders who favored looking to the future. These divisions deepened in the aftermath of the 2012 elections, when López Obrador again claimed fraud in the wake of his defeat. With some in the PRD signaling a willingness to work with the incoming Peña Nieto administration as a constructive opposition party, López Obrador took steps to break away and began the process of forming a new party, the National Regeneration Movement (MORENA). Though the PRD continues to govern the Federal District and a few states, the factionalism that has characterized the party make its future prospects uncertain.

Other Parties

There are a number of smaller parties that contest elections in Mexico. In 2014, the most important small parties were the Citizens' Movement, the Labor Party (PT), the Green Party (PVEM), and the New Alliance Party (PANAL). Since Mexican law requires parties to receive at least 2.5 percent of the vote to be able to compete in future elections, the long-term viability of some of these organizations is doubtful. Small parties, however, usually do win a few of the seats in the Chamber of Deputies and the Senate that are filled by proportional representation.

These small parties sometimes have an impact on national politics by forming alliances with the larger parties, either endorsing their candidates in national and state elections or backing a single slate of candidates for congress. For example, in 2012, the Citizens' Movement and the PT formed an alliance with the PRD to support the presidential candidacy of Andrés Manuel López Obrador, and the PRI and the PVEM jointly backed Peña Nieto. For its part, the New Alliance Party, generally seen as the political arm of the powerful national teachers' union, withdrew from the coalition supporting Peña Nieto and sought to influence the electoral process by nominating its own presidential candidate (who won just over 2 percent of the vote). The Green Party and the Citizens' Movement also hold one state governorship each, though in both cases their members were elected to office thanks to alliances with larger parties.

Elections

Each of the three main political parties draws voters from a wide and overlapping spectrum of the electorate. Nevertheless, a typical voter for the PRI is likely to be from a rural area or small town, to have less education, and to be older and poorer than voters for the other parties. A typical voter for the PAN is likely to be from a northern state, to live in an urban area, to be a middle-class professional, to have a comfortable lifestyle, and to have a high school or even a university education. A typical voter for the PRD is likely to be young, to be a political activist, to have an elementary or high school education, to live in one of the central states, and to live in a small town or an urban area. As we have seen, the support base for the PRI is the most vulnerable to economic and demographic changes in the country, though disillusionment with the status quo allowed the party to overcome this challenge in 2012.

Since 1994, elections have been more competitive and much fairer than they were during decades of PRI dominance, and subsequent congressional, state, and municipal elections reinforced the impression that electoral fraud is on the wane in many areas. The PAN's victory in 2000 substantially increased this impression. When López Obrador claimed in 2006 and 2012 that he had been robbed of victory, the legitimacy of the federal electoral authorities was questioned, but no evidence of wide-scale fraud or election tampering was uncovered.

Political Culture, Citizenship, and Identity

Most Mexicans have a deep familiarity with how their political system works and the ways in which they might be able to extract benefits from it. They understand the informal rules of the game in Mexican politics that have helped maintain political stability despite extensive inequalities in economic and political power. Clientelism has long been a form of participation in the sense that through their connections, many people, even the poorest, are able to interact with public officials and get something out of the political system. This kind of participation emphasizes how limited resources, such as access to health care, can be distributed in a way that provides maximum political payoff. This informal system is a fundamental reason that many Mexicans continued to vote for the PRI for so long. However, new ways of interacting with government are emerging, and they coexist along with the clientelistic style of the past. An increasing number of citizens are seeking to negotiate with the government on the basis of citizenship rights, not personal patron–client relationships.

As politics and elections became more open and competitive, the roles of public opinion and the mass media have become more important. Today, the media play an important role in forming public opinion in Mexico. As with other aspects of Mexican politics, the media began to become more independent in the 1980s, enjoying a "spring" of greater independence and diversity of opinion.[11] There are currently several major television networks in the country, and many citizens have access to global networks. The number of newspapers and news magazines is expanding, as is their circulation. To be sure, there is some concern that many of the most important and influential media outlets in the country are controlled by a small number of individuals and corporations. Also, violence against and intimidation of Mexican journalists by drug trafficking organizations has limited the ability of the press to report on the important issues raised in the context of the fight against organized crime in recent years. Nonetheless, citizens in Mexico today hear a much wider range of opinion and much greater reporting of debates about public policy and criticism of government than at any time previously.

Interest Groups, Social Movements, and Protest

The Mexican political system has long responded to groups of citizens through pragmatic **accommodation** to their interests. This is one important reason that political tensions among major interests have rarely escalated into the kind of serious conflict that can threaten stability. Where open conflict has occurred, it has generally been met with efforts to find some kind of compromise solution. Accommodation has been particularly apparent in response to the interests of business. Mexico's development strategy encouraged the growth of wealthy elites in commerce, finance, industry, and agriculture.

Labor has been similarly accommodated within the system. Wage levels for unionized workers grew fairly consistently between 1940 and 1982, when the economic crisis caused a significant drop in wages. At the same time, labor interests were attended to through concrete benefits and limitations on the rights of employers to discipline or dismiss workers. Union leaders controlled their rank and file in the interest of their own power to negotiate with government, but at the same time, they sought benefits for workers who continued to provide support for the PRI. The power of the union bosses has declined, in part because the unions are weaker than in the past, in part because union members are demanding greater democratization, and in part because the PRI no longer monopolizes political power. Likewise, in the countryside, rural organizations have gained greater independence from the government. Indigenous groups have also emerged to demand that government be responsive to their needs and respectful of their traditions.

accommodation

An informal agreement or settlement between the government and important interest groups in response to the interest groups' concerns for policy or program benefits.

Mexicans are accustomed to making demands on their leaders, and protest is an established feature of Mexican political culture. Here, protesters march into Mexico City's central square, the Zócalo.

AP Images/Gregory Bull

Despite the strong and controlling role of the PRI in Mexico's political history, the country also has a tradition of civic organizations that operate at community and local levels with considerable independence from politics. Urban popular movements, formed by low- and modest-income (popular) groups, gained renewed vitality in the 1980s.[12] When the economic crisis resulted in drastic reductions of social welfare spending and city services, working- and middle-class neighborhoods forged new coalitions and greatly expanded the national discussion of urban problems. The Mexico City earthquake of 1985 encouraged the formation of unprecedented numbers of grassroots movements in response to the slow and poorly managed relief efforts of the government. Subsequent elections provided these groups with significant opportunities to press candidates to respond to their needs.

Urban popular movements bring citizens together around needs and ideals that cut across class boundaries. Neighborhood improvement, the environment, local self-government, economic development, feminism, and professional identity have been among the factors that have forged links among these groups. Women have begun to mobilize in many cities to demand community services, equal pay, legal equality, and opportunities in business that have traditionally been denied to them.

Traditionally, much activism has focused on questions of economic redistribution rather than divisive social issues, but this has recently begun to change. Political issues that are commonly discussed in the United States, such as abortion and gay rights, have recently begun to be debated publicly in Mexico. In April 2007, the PRD-controlled legislative assembly of Mexico City voted to decriminalize abortions in the first trimester (in the rest of Mexico abortion continues to be illegal except in cases of rape or severe birth defects, although in fact gaining access to a legal abortion even under these circumstances is difficult). And in November 2006, the Federal District's PRD-led government legalized gay civil unions. Reflecting its background as a largely Catholic, socially conservative party, the PAN remains vehemently opposed to these measures. For example, in 2000 the PAN-dominated legislature of Guanajuato voted to ban abortion even in the case of rape, and established penalties of up to three years in prison for women who violated the law.

Although President Fox was opposed to abortion, he did attempt to distance himself from the Guanajuato law and for the most part avoided discussing contentious social and cultural subjects. But under his administration condom use was encouraged and a campaign against homophobia was launched. In 2004, he caused a furor within his own party when his administration approved the distribution of the morning-after pill in public clinics. These policies were denounced by Calderón, who came from a more traditionalist wing of his party. He vowed in his 2006 campaign to ban the use of this pill and openly expressed his opposition to abortion and gay rights. President Peña Nieto has so far largely sought to avoid confronting these contentious social issues. He has described himself as personally opposed to abortion but also opposed to its criminalization, and he has said that the question of same-sex unions should be left to Mexico's states.

The Political Impact of Technology

As in other countries, changes in communications technology over the past two decades or so have had a major impact on the ways in which citizens organize themselves and on the ways in which politicians and political parties seek to reach their constituents. Young, highly educated, and urban groups in particular are heavy users of social media, and even many poorer Mexicans and residents of smaller towns and rural areas have mobile telephones and some degree of access to the Internet. During the 2012 presidential campaign, therefore, all of the major candidates actively sought to attract Twitter followers and to project a positive image on Facebook. They also found themselves subject to embarrassment when footage of their gaffes on the campaign trail was circulated widely on social media. A viral video in which Peña Nieto struggled to name three books that had influenced him reinforced some voters' suspicion that the PRI candidate was not a deep thinker, and footage of Josefina Vázquez stumbling over prepared remarks damaged her efforts to make up ground in the polls.

Social media even gave rise to a movement that changed the narrative of the 2012 campaign for a time. After candidate Peña Nieto was confronted by protesters during an appearance at a Mexico City university in May 2012, the media reported that the protesters had been agitators from outside the campus rather than students at the institution, prompting 131 of the protesters to post a video online in which they displayed their university identification cards. Thousands of other social media users who also saw television and other media coverage of the campaign as biased toward Peña Nieto expressed their support by posting, "Yo soy 132," or "I am the 132nd [student]." The online movement led to marches and rallies, calling for a deepening of democracy in Mexico.

Communications technology has also taken on political significance in Mexican citizens' response to the drug-related violence that has affected the country in recent years. In regions in which local journalists were effectively silenced by threats from the cartels, some users of social media relied on that outlet to broadcast information on the danger posed by criminal activities in specific locations. When Twitter users in Veracruz circulated what turned out to be an inaccurate report of a shootout at a school, state authorities prosecuted them for terrorism. Though the governor issued a pardon in that case, the state legislature proceeded to pass a new law to make it a crime to use social media to undermine public order. Thus, the place of new communications technologies in Mexican politics and society continues to be negotiated and to evolve.

Where Do You Stand?

Through public funding and guaranteed broadcasting airtime, political parties in Mexico are given a privileged position as recognized vehicles for the representation of citizens' interests, but increasingly Mexicans are mobilizing for political change outside of party structures, through civil society organizations, popular movements, and social media. How should government policies respond to these developments?

Should public funding of political parties be curtailed, or would that simply create an opening for wealthy private interests to exert greater influence in politics?

SECTION 5

MEXICAN POLITICS IN TRANSITION

▼ Focus Questions

- What challenges does the process of globalization pose to Mexicans' strong sense of national identity?

- How successful has Mexico been in confronting the legacy of authoritarian rule? To what extent have recent administrations been able to make the government more accountable and transparent?

The Mexican political landscape has been transformed over the past twenty years, as a long period of dominance by a single party has given way to a competitive multiparty system. The country's institutions, leaders, and citizens are still adjusting to this ongoing process of change. While most Mexicans are proud that their political system has become more democratic, many also lament that the division of power between political parties and branches of government at times seems to make the state less efficient and possibly less able to address effectively the challenges of development and governance faced by Mexico.

One particularly dramatic illustration of how much Mexican politics has changed can be seen on September 1 of each year, when, in accordance with Article 69 of the Constitution, the executive branch delivers a report on the state of the nation to congress at the opening of its annual session. For decades, this date was known informally as the "Day of the President," as the ritual surrounding the address highlighted the prestige and authority of the chief executive. The president would don his ceremonial red, white, and green sash before traveling to the legislative chambers from the National Palace, the symbolic seat of power in Mexico since the days of the Spanish viceroys. While delivering his *informe* (report), the president could count on a respectful hearing from an attentive audience of deputies and senators who were overwhelmingly drawn from the ranks of his own party. Though the spectacle of the *informe* during the heyday of PRI dominance excluded dissenting voices, it projected an image of a strong, stable political system. Even in 1982, when President José López Portillo broke into tears while reporting on his failure to avert a debt crisis that sent the country into an economic tailspin, legislators dutifully applauded.

That deference to the president began to break down in 1988, however. After a contentious presidential election marred by allegations of fraud, a legislator who had broken away from the PRI to support opposition candidate Cuauhtémoc Cárdenas dared to interrupt President Miguel de la Madrid's speech. More recently, after members of the PRD charged that Felipe Calderón's election in 2006 was illegitimate, outgoing President Vicente Fox was prevented from even reaching the rostrum when he arrived to give his address on September 1 of that year. He complied with his constitutional mandate by submitting a printed copy of his report and then left the building without delivering his speech. In 2007, President Felipe Calderón likewise appeared before a deeply divided legislature only long enough to hand over a printed version of his *informe*, and new rules introduced in 2008 eliminated the requirement that the president deliver his report in person. Since then, the annual report of the executive branch has been transmitted by a government minister to the legislature, where representatives of the parties represented in Congress deliver a response. In 2013, plans for Peña Nieto to make a public presentation of his first *informe* at a large military parade ground had to be scaled back in the face of massive protests by a dissident teachers' union that had paralyzed Mexico City. Instead the president shared his report with a much smaller audience at his official residence. These incidents show how many more voices, besides the president's, are heard on important national issues in Mexico today, though to many the fact that the chief executive is no longer able to find a respectful audience for his report suggests that the capacity of the state has been diminished.

Political Challenges and Changing Agendas

As Mexicans adjust and adapt to the dramatic political transition of recent years, they are conscious that their nation faces many challenges, and they are struggling to build a political system that will be both democratic and effective. They are calling upon the state to be open about abuses of authority in the past and to protect citizens from such abuses in the future. They seek to address long-standing inequalities in Mexican society, in part by ensuring that women and ethnic minorities have access to economic opportunities and social services. They also hope to preserve Mexican identity while realizing the economic benefits of integration into global networks.

Mexico today provides a testing ground for the democratic idea in a state with a long history of authoritarian institutions. The democratic ideas of citizen rights to free speech and assembly, free and fair elections, and responsive government are major reasons that the power of the PRI came under so much attack beginning in the 1980s. As part of its commitment to delivering a sharp change from the practices of the past, the administration of Vicente Fox (2000–2006) pledged to make government more transparent and to improve the state of human rights in Mexico. In the past, the government had been able to limit knowledge of its repressive actions, use the court system to maintain the political peace, and intimidate those who objected to its actions. Fox appointed human rights activists to his cabinet and ordered that secret police and military files be opened to public scrutiny. He instructed government ministries to supply more information about their activities and about the rights that citizens have to various kinds of services. The government also sought to protect the rights of Mexicans abroad, and the United States and Mexico established a working group to improve human rights conditions for migrants.

The results of these actions have been dramatic. For the first time, Mexicans learned of cases of hundreds of people who had "disappeared" as a result of police and military actions. In addition, citizens have come forward to announce other disappearances, ones they were unwilling to report earlier because they feared reprisals. In 2002, former president Luis Echeverría was brought before prosecutors and questioned about government actions against political dissent in 1968 and 1971, a kind of accountability unheard of in the past. The National Human Rights Commission has been active in efforts to hold government officials accountable and to protect citizens from repetitions of the abuses of the past.

Yet challenges to human rights accountability remain. Opening up files and setting up systems for prosecuting abusers needs to be followed by actions to impose penalties on abusers. The Mexican judicial system is weak and has little experience in human rights cases. In addition, action on reports of disappearances, torture, and imprisonment has been slowed by disagreement about civil and military jurisdictions. Human rights activists claimed that police and military personnel, in particular, still had impunity from the laws, and human rights concerns have grown as the military has taken a more direct role in law enforcement in the context of the Calderón administration's effort to dismantle drug trafficking organizations. Human rights advocates point to recent alleged abuses by members of the armed forces and call for greater accountability from an institution that is still shielded from much civilian scrutiny. Although human rights are much more likely to be protected than in the past, the government still has a long way to go in safeguarding the rights of indigenous people, political dissidents, migrants, gays and lesbians, and poor people whose ability to use the judicial system is limited by poverty and lack of information.

Mexico is also confronting major challenges in adapting newly democratic institutions to reflect ethnic and religious diversity and to provide equity for women in economic and political affairs. The past two decades have witnessed the emergence of more organized and politically independent ethnic groups demanding justice and equality from government. These groups claim that they have suffered for nearly 500 years and that they are no longer willing to accept poverty and marginality as their lot. The Catholic Church, still the largest organized religion in the country, is losing members to Protestant sects that appeal particularly to the everyday concerns of poor Mexicans. Women are becoming more organized, but they still have a long way to go before their wages equal those of men or they have equal voice in political and economic decisions.

Another significant challenge for Mexico today is reconciling its strong sense of national identity with the strains placed on a country's sovereignty by the process of global economic integration. Mexicans define themselves in part through a set of historical events, symbols, and myths that focus on the country's troubled relationship with the United States. The myths of the Revolution of 1910 emphasize the uniqueness of the country in terms of its opposition to the capitalists and militarists of the northern country. This view stands in strong contrast to more recent perspectives touting the benefits of an internationally oriented economy and the undeniable post-NAFTA reality of information, culture, money, and people flowing back and forth across borders.

The country's sense of national identity is also affected by international migration. Every year, large numbers of Mexicans enter the United States as workers. Many return to their towns and villages with new values and new views of the world. Many stay in the United States, where Hispanics have become the largest ethnic minority population in the country. Although they may believe that Mexico is a better place to nurture strong family life and values, they are nevertheless strongly influenced by U.S. mass culture, including popular music, movies, television programs, fast food, and consumer goods.

The inability of the Mexican economy to create enough jobs pushes additional Mexicans to seek work in the United States, and the cash remittances that migrants abroad send home to their families and communities are now almost as important a source of income for Mexico as PEMEX's oil sales. However, the issues surrounding migration have become even more complex since the attacks of September 11, 2001. Hopes for a bilateral accord that would permit more Mexicans to enter and work in the United States legally evaporated after U.S. officials suddenly found themselves under greatly increased pressure to control the country's borders. Whether or not the U.S. government approves, the difference in wages between the United States and Mexico will persist for a long time, which implies that migration will also persist.

There is disagreement about how to respond to the economic challenges that Mexico faces. Much of the debate surrounds the question of what integration into a competitive international economy really means. For some, it represents the final abandonment of Mexico's sovereignty. For others, it is the basis on which future prosperity must be built. Those who are critical of the market-based, outward-oriented development strategy are concerned about its impact on workers, peasants, and national identities. They argue that the state has abandoned its responsibilities to protect the poor from shortcomings of the market and to provide for their basic needs. They believe that U.S. and Canadian investors have come to Mexico only to find low-wage labor for industrial empires located elsewhere. They see little benefit in further industrial development based on importation of foreign-made parts, their assembly in Mexico, and their export to other markets. Those who favor closer integration with Canada and the United States acknowledge that some foreign investment does not promote technological advances or move the workforce into higher-paying and more skilled jobs. They emphasize, however, that most investment will occur because Mexico has a relatively well-educated population, the capacity to absorb modern technology, and a large internal market for industrial goods.

Inequality represents another daunting challenge for Mexican society. While elites enjoy the benefits of sumptuous lifestyles, education at the best U.S. universities for their children, and luxury travel throughout the world, large numbers of Mexicans remain ill-educated, poorly served with health care, and distant from the security of knowing that their basic needs will be met. As in the United States, some argue that the best solutions to these problems are economic growth and expanded employment. They believe that the achievement of prosperity through integration into the global economy will benefit everyone in the long run. For this to occur, however, they insist that education will have to be improved and made more appropriate for developing a well-prepared workforce. From their perspective, the solution to poverty and injustice is fairly clear: more and better jobs and improved education.

For those critical of the development path on which Mexico embarked in the 1980s and 1990s, the problems of poverty and inequity are more complex. Solutions involve understanding the diverse causes of poverty, including not only lack of jobs and poor education but also exploitation, geographic isolation, and discriminatory laws and practices, as well as the disruptive impact of migration, urbanization, and the tensions of modern life. In the past, Mexicans looked to government for social welfare benefits, but their provision was deeply flawed by inefficiency and political manipulation. Thus, although many continue to believe that it is the responsibility of government to ensure that citizens are well educated, healthy, and able to make the most of their potential, the populace is deeply suspicious of the government's capacity to provide such conditions fairly and efficiently.

Youth Politics and the Generational Divide

Young people have long played a central role in driving political change in Mexico. The student movement of 1968 helped to begin the process of questioning the legitimacy of PRI rule, and younger voters played a disproportionally important part in bringing about the democratic transition of 2000. The younger generation is also heavily overrepresented in the social media world from which future political campaigns and initiatives are likely to arise, as the "Yo soy 132" movement did in 2012.

Another fundamental reason for the importance of young people in Mexican politics is that they currently account for a very high proportion of the country's population. Unlike Japan or many European countries, Mexico is not a rapidly aging country, with a large share of its population over 65. Instead, more than half of the population is under 30. This means that very many voters in the 2012 elections cast their ballots with little memory of the PRI's "perfect dictatorship." Having grown up in a democratic Mexico with a competitive political environment, these voters are perhaps unlikely to be interested in a return to the PRI's old style of politics, but the party preferences and affiliations of younger Mexicans remain to be defined. Given the demographic significance of Mexico's younger population, the development of those preferences will shape Mexican politics for a long time to come.

Mexican Politics in Comparative Perspective

Mexico faces many of the same challenges that beset other countries: creating equitable and effective democratic government, becoming integrated into a global economy, responding to complex social problems, and supporting increasing diversity without losing national identity. The legacies of its past, the tensions of the present, and the innovations of the future will no doubt evolve in ways that continue to be uniquely Mexican.

Mexico represents a pivotal case of political and economic transition for the developing world. If it can successfully bridge the gap between its past and its future and move from centralization to effective local governance, from regional vulnerability to global interdependence, and from the control of the few to the participation of the many, it will set a model for other countries that face the same kind of challenges.

Where Do You Stand?

Does Mexico offer lessons for other countries moving from authoritarian forms of governance to more democratic ones? What might Mexico learn from the experience of some of the other countries you are studying?

If you were a young person in Mexico today, what issues do you think would be most important to you? Which political party (if any) would you support, and why?

Chapter Summary

The Mexican political system is unique among developing countries in the extent to which it managed to institutionalize and maintain civilian political authority for a very long time. The country's development has been shaped by the revolutionary ideals that arose from its distinctive historical experience, by its proximity to the United States, and by its ongoing efforts to find a place in an interconnected global economy. Currently, Mexico is undergoing significant political change, transforming itself from a corporatist state to a democratic one. At the same time, Mexican society is experiencing high levels of violence as the state confronts drug trafficking organizations that represent a challenge to its authority and to the rule of law.

While Mexico's development from the 1930s to the 1980s was marked by extensive government engagement in the economy, since that time the country has opened its economy and pursued prosperity through market reforms and free trade. But while links with the U.S. economy have deepened, growth has been slow under the new policies. Industry and oil give the country a per capita income higher than those of most other developing nations, but the country suffers from great inequalities in how wealth is distributed, and poverty continues to be a grim reality for millions. The way the country promoted economic growth and industrialization is important in explaining why widespread poverty has persisted and why political power is not more equitably distributed.

On paper, Mexico's government resembles that of the United States, with three branches of government, checks and balances among them, and federalism defining the relationship between national, state, and local governments. In practice, however, the country developed a political system that concentrated most power in the hands of the president and the executive branch and managed political conflict through a dominant party. Much of the power of the president and the PRI was based on their capacity to use patronage to respond to political conflicts. This system is undergoing rapid change, as the legislature and court systems develop more independent roles, state and local governments acquire more independence, and multiple parties compete for power.

Mexico's democratic transition took place gradually, as Mexican citizens developed the capacity to question the dominance of the PRI regime and as the government introduced important changes that opened up opportunities for opposition parties to develop and for people to vote more easily for these parties. Since the election of 2000 demonstrated that a transition of power from a civilian authoritarian regime to a more democratic one could take place peacefully, Mexico has had considerable experience with democratic politics. This experience has been marked both by pride in the country's democratic path and frustration that democratic institutions have not been able to pass needed reforms, to create jobs, and to guarantee security.

What will the future bring? How much will the pressures for change affect the nature of the political system? In 1980, few people could have foreseen the extensive economic policy reforms and pressures for democracy that Mexico would experience in the next three decades. Few would have predicted the defeat of the PRI in the elections of 2000, much less its return to power in 2012. In considering the future of the country, it is important to remember that Mexico has a long tradition of relatively strong institutions. It is not a country that will easily slip into sustained political instability. Despite real challenges faced as Mexico confronts criminal organizations and seeks to reform its police forces and judicial system, the country is not in danger of collapse, as some outside observers have been tempted to suggest. A tradition of constitutional government, a strong presidency, a political system that has incorporated a wide range of interests, little military involvement in politics, and a deep sense of national identity—these are among the factors that need to be considered in understanding the political consequences of democratization, economic integration, and greater social equality in Mexico.

Key Terms

accommodation
anticlericalism
caudillos
civil society
corporatist state

coup d'état
ejidos
indigenous groups
maquiladoras
mestizo

remittances
sexenio
state capitalism
technocrats

Suggested Readings

Call, Wendy. *No Word for Welcome: The Mexican Village Faces the Global Economy.* Lincoln: University of Nebraska Press, 2011.

Camp, Roderic Ai. *The Metamorphosis of Leadership in a Democratic Mexico.* Oxford: Oxford University Press, 2010.

Davidow, Jeffrey. *The U.S. and Mexico: The Bear and the Porcupine.* Princeton, NJ: Markus Wiener Publishers, 2004.

Délano, Alexandra. *Mexico and its Diaspora in the United States: Policies of Emigration since 1848.* New York: Cambridge University Press, 2011.

Eisenstadt, Todd A. *Politics, Identity, and Mexico's Indigenous Rights Movements* (Cambridge Studies in Contentious Politics). New York: Cambridge University Press, 2011.

Grayson, George. *Mexico: Narco-Violence and a Failed State?* Piscataway, NJ: Transaction Publishers, 2009.

Henderson, Timothy J. *Beyond Borders: A History of Mexican Migration to the United States.* New York: Wiley-Blackwell, 2011.

Preston, Julia, and Samuel Dillon. *Opening Mexico: The Making of a Democracy.* New York: Farrar, Straus and Giroux, 2004.

Selee, Andrew, and Jacqueline Peschard. *Mexico's Democratic Challenges: Politics, Government, and Society.* Stanford, CA: Stanford University Press, 2010.

Speed, Shannon. *Rights in Rebellion: Indigenous Struggle and Human Rights in Chiapas.* Stanford, CA: Stanford University Press, 2007.

Suggested Websites

Office of the President (in Spanish and English)
www.presidencia.gob.mx

Secretariat of Foreign Relations (in Spanish and English)
www.sre.gob.mx

Mexican Embassy to the United States
http://embamex.sre.gob.mx/usa/

Office of Mexican Affairs, U.S. Department of State
http://www.state.gov/p/wha/ci/mx/

The Mexico Project, National Security Archive
www2.gwu.edu/~nsarchiv/mexico

6 Nigeria

Darren Kew and Peter Lewis

Official Name: Federal Republic of Nigeria

Location: Western Africa

Capital City: Abuja

Population (2014): 177.2 million

Size: 923,768 sq. km.; slightly more than twice the size of California

1960
Independence. Nigeria consists of three regions under a Westminster parliamentary model. Abubakar Tafawa Balewa, a northerner, is the first prime minister.

January 1966
Civilian government deposed in coup. General Aguiyi Ironsi, an Igbo, becomes head of state.

1967–1970
Biafran civil war

July 1975
Military coup deposes Gowan; led by General Murtala Muhammed, a northerner.

February 1976
Murtala Muhammed assassinated in failed coup led by Middle Belt minorities. Muhammed's second-in-command, General Olusegun Obasanjo, a Yoruba, assumes power.

October 1979
Elections held. A majority in both houses is won by NPN, led by northern/Hausa-Fulani groups. Alhaji Shehu Shagari is elected Nigeria's first executive president.

June 12, 1993
Moshood Abiola wins presidential elections, but Babangida annuls the election eleven days later.

July–September 1994
Prodemocracy strike by the major oil union, NUPENG, cuts Nigeria's oil production by an estimated 25 percent. Sympathy strikes ensue, followed by arrests of political and civic leaders.

1960	1965	1970	1975	1980	1985	1990	1995

July 1966
Countercoup is led by General Yakubu Gowan (an Anga, from the Middle Belt) with aid from northern groups.

November 1993
Defense Minister General Sani Abacha seizes power in a coup. Two years later he announces a three-year transition to civilian rule, which he manipulates to have himself nominated for president in 1998.

August 1993
Babangida installs Ernest Shonekan as "interim civilian president" until new presidential elections could be held later that autumn.

August 1985
Buhari is overthrown by General Ibrahim B. Babangida, a Middle Belt Muslim, in a palace coup. Babangida promises a return to democracy by 1990, a date he delays five times before being forced from office.

December 1983
Military coup led by General Muhammadu Buhari, a northerner

September 1978
New constitution completed, marking the adoption of the U.S. presidential model in a federation with 19 states

Spring 2002
The Supreme Court passes several landmark judgments, overturning a PDP-biased 2001 electoral law, and ruling on the control of offshore oil and gas resources. In November the Court opens the legal door for more parties to be registered.

April–May 2007
The ruling PDP again takes a vast majority of election victories across the nation amid a deeply compromised process. Umaru Musa Yar'Adua becomes president. Yar'Adua promises reform, but spends his first year trying to solidify his tenuous hold on power.

June 1998
General Abacha dies; succeeded by General Abdulsalami Abubakar, a Middle Belt Muslim from Babangida's hometown. Abubakar releases nearly all political prisoners and installs a new transition program. Parties are allowed to form unhindered.

May 2006
President Obasanjo tries to amend the constitution to allow himself a third term in office, but is defeated by the National Assembly.

April 2011
Jonathan wins the presidential election despite opposition from Northern factions for violating an informal ethnic rotation principle. The PDP again takes the majority of contests, but improved elections under a reformist chairman allow opposition parties to make some inroads.

February 2015
Nationwide elections are scheduled, promising a titanic struggle between the PDP and APC at all levels of government.

1999	2000	2005	2007	2011	2012	2020

1999
Former head of state Olusegun Obansanjo and his party, the Peoples Democratic Party (PDP), sweep the presidential and National Assembly elections, adding to their majority control of state and local government seats. The federation now contains thirty-six states.

November 1999
Zamfara state in the north is the first of twelve to institute the *shari'a* criminal code, resulting in Muslim-Christian communal conflicts in several of these states over the next two years. That same month, President Obasanjo sends the army to the Niger Delta town of Odi to root out local militias, leveling the town in the process. The military remains engaged in regular skirmishes with Niger Delta militias throughout the next decade, until President Yar'Adua reaches an agreement with the militants and offers them amnesty in 2009.

August 2002
The National Assembly begins impeachment proceedings against President Obasanjo over budgetary issues. The matter ends by November, with the president apologizing.

2011
A formerly minor Islamist movement, dubbed Boko Haram by the media, resurfaces with even greater tactical sophistication in the northeast after being crushed by the military in 2009, and launches a stunning bombing campaign across the northeast, even striking the UN headquarters in Abuja. President Jonathan declares a state of emergency in three northeast states in 2013, and a military counteroffensive hems the insurgency inside its core area of operations around Borno and Yobe states, but military scorched-earth tactics result in heavy civilian casualties.

May 2010
President Yar'Adua dies in office, after several months incapacitated in a Saudi hospital. Vice President Goodluck Jonathan assumes the presidency.

2013
The four main opposition parties merge to form the All Progressives Congress (APC), creating the first major threat to PDP rule since the start of the Fourth Republic in 1999. Six PDP governors defect, giving the APC control of nearly have the state governments and federal House seats, and a majority in the federal Senate.

January 2012
Massive public demonstrations, which civil society activists call Occupy Nigeria, peacefully fill the streets of Lagos, Kano, Abuja, and other major urban areas to protest the president's removal of a fuel price subsidy. Social media plays a key role for the organizers, many of who are from the nation's growing middle class professionals. Trade unions, however, form the key muscle for strikes that bring the nation to a standstill for two weeks, and when the unions agree to a partial restoration of the fuel subsidy, the demonstrations collapse.

THE MAKING OF THE MODERN NIGERIAN STATE

▼ Focus Questions

- What are some of the key impacts that colonialism and military rule left on the development of the Nigerian state?

- What role has ethnicity played in the development of Nigeria's political parties, and in the collapse of Nigeria's First Republic and descent into civil war?

Politics in Action

In late November 2009, President Umaru Musa Yar'Adua collapsed for at least the third time since coming to office in 2007 from an ailment that he had never fully explained to the nation. He was rushed unconscious to a hospital in Saudi Arabia, and only his wife and a handful of his closest advisors saw him directly. For over three months, Nigerians had no direct evidence that their president was conscious or alive, and even his own ministers and a delegation of senators were refused access. Government activity at the federal level ground to a halt.

Shockingly, for the first two months, neither the National Assembly nor the cabinet raised any public concern that the nation in effect had no president. The First Lady and the president's inner circle released occasional statements that the president was recovering well, but prevented any direct contact with him and blocked all attempts to have Vice President Jonathan step in as acting president as the constitution directs. Finally, under both international pressure and the threat of a military coup, the National Assembly declared Jonathan Acting President in February 2010. President Yar'Adua returned to the country shortly thereafter, but was clearly too ill to govern, and he passed away in May 2010. Goodluck Jonathan then was sworn in as president.

The fact that Nigeria could persist for months without a functioning president, during which time his wife and a few advisors could seek to run the country themselves—and that they would go largely unchallenged—speaks volumes about the state of the nation's politics. Democratization in Nigeria—15 years after the exit of the military from power—has yet to produce good governance. Instead, authoritarian rule has given way to competitive oligarchy, in which an increasingly greedy, oil-rich political elite fight to expand their power, while more than 90 percent of Nigerians struggle to survive on less than two U.S. dollars per day. This impoverished majority is so disenfranchised by the state that their president could disappear for months, and a small cabal could hold the nation hostage, without much public outcry.

Under the surface of this fiasco, however, were some important signs that a decade of democracy has had some impact. First and foremost, throughout the crisis, as opposition grew it insisted on the constitution as the framework for resolving the dispute. Ultimately, elites turned to the National Assembly, not the military, and military leaders rejected pressure from some junior officers to stage a coup.

Nigeria thus encapsulates many characteristics that more broadly identify Africa, as the young democracy faces the challenge of managing the country's contentious ethnic and religious diversity in conditions of scarcity and weak institutions, while facing the constant struggle between **authoritarian** and democratic governance, the push for development amidst persistent underdevelopment, the burden of public corruption, and the pressure for accountability. Nigeria, like most other African countries, has sought to create a viable nation-state out of the incoherence created by its

authoritarian

A system of rule in which power depends not on popular legitimacy but on the coercive force of the political authorities.

colonial borders. More than 250 competing ethnic groups, crosscut by two major religious traditions, have repeatedly clashed over economic and political resources. The result: a Nigeria with low levels of popular legitimacy and **accountability**, and a persistent inability to meet the most basic needs of its citizens. Nigeria today remains an **unfinished state** characterized by instabilities and uncertainties. Will Nigeria return to the discredited path of authoritarianism and greater underdevelopment, or will the civilian leadership rise to achieve a consolidated democracy and sustainable growth?

Geographic Setting

Nigeria, with 160 million people inhabiting 356,669 square miles, is the most populous nation in Africa. A center of West African regional trade, culture, and military strength, Nigeria borders four countries—Benin, Niger, Chad, and Cameroon. Nigeria, like nearly all African states, is barely over a half-century old.

Nigeria was a British colony from 1914 until 1960. Nigeria's boundaries had little to do with the borders of the precolonial African societies, and merely marked the point

accountability

A government's responsibility to its population, usually by periodic popular elections, transparent fiscal practices, and by parliament's having the power to dismiss the government by passing a motion of no confidence. In a political system characterized by accountability, the major actions taken by government must be known and understood by the citizenry.

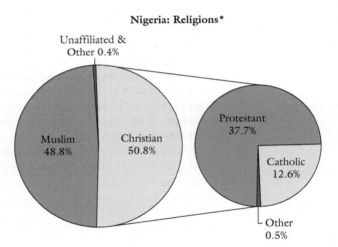

Languages: English (official), Hausa, Yoruba, Igho (Ibo), Fulani, 100–200 additional indigenous

Nigerian Currency

Niara (₦)
International Designation: NGN
Exchange Rate (2010): 1 US$ = 150.88 NGN
500 Naira Note Design: Aliyu Mai-Bornu
(1919–1970) and Clement Isong (1920–2000),
economists and governors of the Central Bank
of Nigeria

FIGURE 6.1 The Nigerian Nation at a Glance
© iStockphoto.com/Johnny Greig (for photo)

Table 6.1	Political Organization
Political System	Federal republic
Regime History	Democratic government took office in May 1999, after sixteen years of military rule. The most recent national elections were held in 2011.
Administrative Structure	Nigeria is a federation of thirty-six states, plus the Federal Capital Territory (FCT) in Abuja. The three tiers of government are federal, state, and local. Actual power is centralized under the presidency and the governors.
Executive	U.S.-style presidential system, under Goodluck Jonathan
Legislature	A bicameral civilian legislature was elected in April 2011. The 109 senators are elected on the basis of equal representation: three from each state, and one from the FCT. The 360 members of the House of Representatives are elected from single-member districts.
Judiciary	Federal, state, and local court system, headed by the Federal Court of Appeal and the Supreme Court, which consists of fifteen appointed associate justices and the chief justice. States may establish a system of Islamic law (*shari'a*) for cases involving only Muslims in customary disputes (divorce, property, etc.). Most Nigerian states feature such courts, which share a Federal Court of Appeal in Abuja. Non-Muslim states may also set up customary courts, based on local traditional jurisprudence. Secular courts retain supreme jurisdiction if conflict arises between customary and secular courts.
Party System	Nearly fifty parties have been registered by the Nigerian electoral commission since 2002. The largest are the People's Democratic Party (PDP) and the All Progressives Congress (APC), which together control all but two states of the federation. PDP won the presidency and a slight majority of governorships, but defections from the PDP have given the APC control of the Senate.

unfinished state

A state characterized by instabilities and uncertainties that may render it susceptible to collapse as a coherent entity.

where British influence ended and French began. Britain ruled northern and southern Nigeria as two separate colonies until 1914, when it amalgamated its Northern and Southern Protectorates. In short, Nigeria was an arbitrary creation reflecting British colonial interests. This forced union of myriad African cultures and ruling entities under one political roof remains a central feature of Nigerian political life today.

Nigeria is a hub of regional activity. Its population is nearly 60 percent of West Africa's total. Nigeria's gross domestic product (GDP) typically represents more than half of the total GDP for the entire subregion. It is one of the few countries in the world that is evenly divided religiously, half Muslim and half Christian.

Nigeria includes six imprecisely defined "zones." The Hausa, Nigeria's largest ethnic group, dominate the northwest (or "core North"). The northeast consists of minority groups, the largest of whom are the Kanuri. Both northern regions are predominantly Muslim. The Middle Belt includes minority groups, both Muslim and Christian. The southwest is dominated by the country's second-largest ethnic group, the Yoruba, who are approximately 40 percent Muslim, 50 percent Christian (primarily Protestant), and 10 percent practitioners of Yoruba traditional beliefs. The southeast is the Igbo homeland, Nigeria's third largest group, who are primarily Christian. Between the Yoruba and Igbo regions is the southern minority zone, which stretches across the Niger Delta areas and east along the coast as far as Cameroon.

Critical Junctures

Nigeria's recent history reflects influences from the precolonial period, the crucial changes caused by British colonialism, the postcolonial alternation of military and civilian rule, and the economic collapse from 1980 to 2000, caused by political corruption and overreliance on the oil industry, which has been reinforced by the post–2003 oil boom.

The Precolonial Period (800–1900)

In contrast to the forest belt to the south, the more open terrain in the north, with its need for irrigation, encouraged the early growth of centralized states. Such states from the eighth century included Kanem-Bornu and the Hausa states. Another attempt at state formation led to the Jukun kingdom, which by the end of the seventeenth century was a subject state of the Bornu Empire.

Trade across the Sahara Desert with northern Africa shaped developments in the savanna areas of north. Trade brought material benefits as well as Arabic education and Islam, which gradually replaced traditional spiritual, political, and social practices. In 1808, the Fulani, from lands west of modern Nigeria, fought a holy war (*jihad*), and established the Sokoto Caliphate, which used Islam and a common

jihad

Literally "struggle." Although often used to mean armed struggle against unbelievers, it can also mean to fight against sociopolitical corruption or a spiritual struggle for self-improvement.

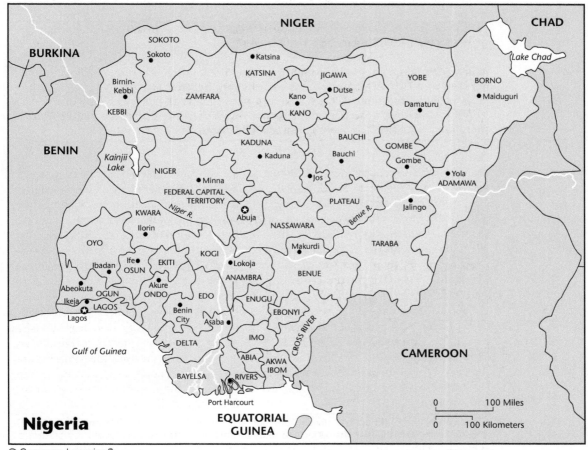

Nigeria

© Cengage Learning®

language, Hausa, to unify the disparate groups in the north. The Fulani Empire held sway until British colonial authority was imposed on northern Nigeria by 1900.

Toward the southern edge of the savanna, politics generally followed kinship lines. Political authority was so diffuse that later Western contacts described them as "stateless," or acephalous societies. Because such groups as the Tiv lacked complex political hierarchies, they escaped much of the upheaval experienced under colonialism by the centralized states, and retained much of their autonomy.

Southern Nigeria included the highly centralized Yoruba empires and the kingdoms of Oyo and Ife; the Edo kingdom of Benin in the Midwest; the acephalous societies of the Igbo to the east; and the trading city-states of the Niger Delta and its hinterland, peopled by a wide range of ethnicities.

Several precolonial societies had democratic elements that might have led to more open and participatory polities had they not been interrupted by colonialism. Governance in the Yoruba and Igbo communities involved principles of accountability and representation. Among the Islamic communities of the north, political society was highly structured, reflecting local interpretations of Qur'anic principles. Leadership structures were considerably more hierarchical than those of the south, and women were typically consigned to subordinate political status. The Islamic Fulani Empire was a confederation in which the rulers, emirs, owed allegiance to the sultan, who was the temporal and spiritual head of the empire. The sultan's powers, in turn, were limited by his duty to observe Islamic principles.

acephalous societies

Literally "headless" societies. A number of traditional Nigerian societies, such as the Igbo in the precolonial period, lacked executive rulership as we have come to conceive of it. Instead, the villages and clans were governed by committee or consensus.

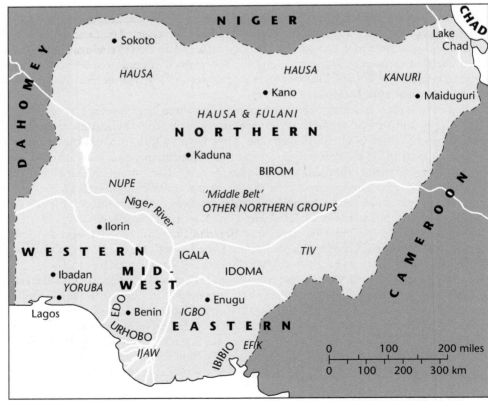

Nigeria under the First Republic, divided into four regions, with the massive Northern Region encompassing two-thirds of the nation's territory and more than half its population.

© Cengage Learning®

Colonial Rule and Its Impact (1860–1945)[1]

Competition for trade and empire drove the European imperial powers further into Africa. Colonial rule deepened the extraction of Nigeria's natural resources and the exploitation of Nigerian labor. Colonialism left its imprint on all aspects of Nigeria's political and economic systems.

Where centralized monarchies existed in the north, the British ruled through **indirect rule**, which allowed traditional structures to persist as subordinates to the British governor and a small administrative apparatus. With more dispersed kingships, as among the Yoruba, or in acephalous societies, particularly among the Igbo and other groups in the southeast, the colonizers either strengthened the authority of traditional chiefs and kings or appointed **warrant chiefs** (who ruled by warrant of the British Crown), weakening the previous practices of accountability and participation.

The British played off ethnic and social divisions to keep Nigerians from developing organized political resistance to colonial rule. When resistance did develop, the colonizers were not afraid to employ repressive tactics, even as late as the 1940s. Yet the British also promoted the foundations of a democratic political system. This dual standard left a conflicted democratic idea: formal democratic institutions within an authoritarian political culture. Colonialism also strengthened the collective identities of Nigeria's multiple ethnic groups by fostering political competition among them, primarily among the three largest: the Hausa, Yoruba, and Igbo.

Divisive Identities: Ethnic Politics under Colonialism (1945–1960)

Based on their experience under British rule, leaders of the anticolonial movement came to regard the state as an exploitative instrument. Its control became an opportunity to pursue personal and group interests rather than broad national interests. When the British began to negotiate a gradual exit from Nigeria, the semblance of unity among the anticolonial leaders soon evaporated. Intergroup political competition became increasingly fierce.

Nigerian leaders quickly turned to support. The three largest ethnic groups, the Hausa, Igbo, and Yoruba, though each a numeric minority, together comprise approximately two-thirds of Nigeria's population. They have long dominated the political process. By pitting ethnic groups against each other for purposes of divide and rule, and by structuring the administrative units of Nigeria based on ethnic groups, the British ensured that ethnicity would be the identification and mobilization.

With the encouragement of ambitious leaders, however, these groups took on a more political character. Nigeria's first political party, the National Council of Nigeria and the Cameroons (later the National Convention of Nigerian Citizens, NCNC), initially drew supporters from across Nigeria. As independence approached, however, elites began to divide along ethnic lines to mobilize support for their differing political agendas.

In 1954, the British divided Nigeria into a federation of three regions with elected governments. Each region soon fell under the domination of one of the major ethnic groups and their respective parties. The Northern Region came under the control of the Northern People's Congress (NPC), dominated by Hausa-Fulani elites. In the southern half of the country, the Western Region was controlled by the Action Group (AG), which was controlled by Yoruba elites. The Igbo, the numerically dominant group in the Eastern Region, were closely associated with the NCNC, which became the ruling party there.

Chief Obafemi Awolowo, leader of the AG, captured the sentiment of the times when he wrote in 1947, "Nigeria is not a nation. It is a mere geographical expression. There are no 'Nigerians' in the same sense as there are 'English,' 'Welsh,' or 'French.'

indirect rule

A term used to describe the British style of colonialism in Nigeria and India in which local traditional rulers and political structures were used to help support the colonial governing structure.

warrant chiefs

Leaders employed by the British colonial regime in Nigeria. A system in which "chiefs" were selected by the British to oversee certain legal matters and assist the colonial enterprise in governance and law enforcement in local areas.

The word 'Nigerian' is merely a distinctive appellation to distinguish those who live within the boundaries of Nigeria from those who do not."[2]

The First Republic (1960–1966)

The British granted Nigeria independence in 1960. Nigerians adopted the British Westminster model at the federal and regional levels, with the prime minister chosen by the majority party or coalition. Northerners came to dominate the federal government by virtue of their greater population. The ruling coalition for the first two years quickly turned into a northern-only grouping when the NPC achieved an outright majority in the legislature. Having benefited less from the economic, educational, and infrastructural benefits of colonialism, the northerners who dominated the First Republic set out to redistribute resources to their benefit. This NPC policy of "northernization" brought them into direct conflict with their southern counterparts, particularly the Yoruba-based AG and later the Igbo-dominated NCNC.

Precolonial Nigeria, showing the Sokoto Caliphate at its greatest extent in the early nineteenth century. The British conquest brought many nations under one roof.

© Cengage Learning®

Rivalries intensified as the NPC sat atop an absolute majority in the federal parliament with no need for its former coalition partner, the NCNC. Nnamdi Azikiwe, the NCNC leader who was also president in the First Republic (then a largely symbolic position), and Tafawa Balewa, the NPC prime minister, separately approached the military to ensure that if it came to conflict, they could count on its loyalty. Thus, "in the struggle for personal survival both men, perhaps inadvertently, made the armed forces aware that they had a political role to play."[3]

Civil War and Military Rule (1966–1979)

With significant encouragement from contending civilian leaders, a group of largely Igbo officers seized power in January 1966. General Aguiyi Ironsi, also an Igbo, was killed in a second coup in July 1966, which brought Yakubu Gowon, a Middle Belt Christian, to power as a consensus head of state among the non-Igbo coup plotters.[4]

Because many northern officials had been killed in the initial coup, a tremendous backlash against Igbos flared in several parts of the country. Ethnic violence sent many Igbos fleeing to their home region in the east. By 1967, the predominantly Igbo population of eastern Nigeria attempted to secede and form its own independent country, named Biafra. Gowon built a military-led government of national unity in what remained of Nigeria (the north and west) and, after a bloody three-year war of attrition and starvation tactics, defeated Biafra in January 1970. The conflict claimed at least a million deaths.

After the war, Gowon presided over a policy of national reconciliation, which proceeded fairly smoothly with the aid of growing oil revenues. Senior officers reaped the benefits of the global oil boom in 1973–1974, however, and corruption was widespread. Influenced by the unwillingness of the military elite to relinquish power and the spoils of office, Gowon postponed a return to civilian rule, and was overthrown in 1975 by Murtala Muhammad, who was assassinated before he could achieve a democratic transition. General Olusegun Obasanjo, Muhammad's second-in-command and successor, peacefully ceded power to an elected civilian government in 1979, which became known as the Second Republic. Obasanjo retired but would later reemerge as a civilian president in 1999.

The Second and Third Republics, and Predatory Military Rule (1979–1999)

The president of the 1979–1983 Second Republic, Shehu Shagari, and his ruling National Party of Nigeria (NPN, drawn largely from the First Republic's northern-dominated NPC), did little to reduce the mistrust between the various parts of the federation, or to stem rampant corruption. The NPN captured outright majorities in the 1983 state and national elections through

Olusegun Obasanjo ruled Nigeria first as military head of state from 1976 to 1979 and then as civilian president from 1999 to 2007. As president, he instituted a number of important reforms, but also tried—and failed—to change the constitution to extend his term in office.

Issouf Sanogo/Staff/AFP/Getty Images

massive fraud and violence. The last vestiges of popular tolerance dissipated, and a few months later the military, led by Major General Muhammadu Buhari, seized power.

When General Buhari refused to pledge a rapid return to democratic rule and failed to revive a plummeting economy, his popular support wavered, and in August 1985 General Ibrahim Babangida seized power. Babangida and his cohort quickly announced a transition to democratic rule, then stalled and subsequently annulled the presidential election of June 1993. In stark contrast to all prior elections, the 1993 election was relatively fair and was evidently won by Yoruba businessman Chief Moshood Abiola. The annulment provoked angry reactions from a population weary of postponed transitions, lingering military rule, and the deception of rulers. Babangida resigned, and his handpicked successor, Ernest Shonekan, led a weak civilian caretaker government. General Sani Abacha, who had been installed by Babangida as defense minister, soon seized power but delayed implementation, cracked down on opposition and civil liberties and fomented corruption on a massive scale. Only Abacha's sudden death in June 1998 saved the country from certain crisis. General Abdulsalami Abubakar, Abacha's successor, quickly established a new transition program and promptly handed power to an elected civilian government led by President Olusegun Obasanjo and the People's Democratic Party (PDP) in May 1999.

The Fourth Republic (1999 to the Present)

Obasanjo was called out of retirement by the leaders of the PDP to run for president. Obasanjo, although a Yoruba, handed over power as military head of state in 1979 to the northerner Shehu Shagari at the dawn of the Second Republic. The northern political establishment had concluded that Obasanjo was a Yoruba candidate they could trust. In addition, many perceived that an ex-military leader could better manage to keep the armed forces in the barracks once they left power.

Obasanjo claimed a broad mandate to arrest the nation's decline by reforming the state and economy. Within weeks, he electrified the nation by retiring all the military officers who had held positions of political power under previous military governments, seeing them as the most likely plotters of future coups.

Obasanjo targeted the oil sector for new management and lobbied foreign governments to forgive Nigeria's massive debts. The minimum wage was raised significantly, a "truth and reconciliation" commission was set up to address past abuses. Civil society groups thrived on renewed political freedom, corruption returned with a vengeance. Narrowly avoiding impeachment, Obasanjo secured renomination from his party (the PDP) in the 2003 elections, cutting deals with party barons, such that the PDP political machine succeeded while public confidence plummeted and reform was stymied. Faced with increasing political turmoil and social conflict, the president called a National Political Reform Conference in early 2005, which achieved little. The president chose a little-known, reclusive governor from the north with health problems to be his successor: Umaru Musa Yar'Adua of Katsina state.

Obasanjo misjudged both the Nigerian people and Yar'Adua. Despite local and international condemnation of the April 2007 polls, the public did not erupt, and Obasanjo had little choice but to hand over to leadership to Yar'Adua in May 2007. Instead of focusing on his campaign promises, Yar'Adua spent most of his energies solidifying his control of the PDP, which became a perpetual guiding principle of politics throughout this era. The president's sudden collapse and evacuation to Saudi Arabia in November 2009 showed that he was dying. Normal government activity all but ceased while a small circle of advisors usurped presidential powers and secured government contracts. International pressure grew. Coup threats surfaced. Finally Vice President Goodluck Jonathan, from the oil-rich Niger Delta, moved cautiously to assure Northern powerbrokers that they could work with him. His deft political efforts, backed in part by support from former President Obasanjo, ensured a smooth transition when President Yar'Adua at last passed away in May 2010.

Like Obasanjo and Yar'Adua, President Jonathan came to office without control of his own party, the PDP, and moved quickly to establish his control, using the largesse of Nigeria's massive state-controlled oil wealth. Within several months, he made clear his intention to run for president in April 2011. In stark contrast to his predecessors, however, President Jonathan pressed electoral reform.

The 2011 elections were much improved from the disastrous 2007 contests, but the PDP still utilized its massive resource advantages to buy votes. Expectations of cleaner elections sparked leading to over 800 deaths in post-election riots.

Many northern factions also remained antagonistic over the shift of power back to a southerner. This antagonism soon led to a massive struggle within the PDP, which the president eventually won, but at great cost. Six governors—five from the disgruntled northern bloc—decamped in 2013 for the new opposition party, the All Progressives Congress (APC). The APC had formed earlier in 2013 when leaders of the four main opposition parties recognized the limits of their smaller, largely regional parties, and sensed opportunity in the PDP's internal battles.

Jonathan took the oath of office in 2011 promising reforms, but his administration soon fell victim to massive corruption. A growing Islamist insurgency in the northeast, led by a group called Boko Haram, drew attention away from reform and development and toward increased security concerns and expenditures.

The Four Themes and Nigeria

Nigeria in a Globalized World of States

Federalism and democracy have been important strategies in the effort to build a coherent nation-state in Nigeria out of more than 250 different ethnic groups. The legacy of colonial rule and many years of military domination, however, left a nearly unitary system in federal guise: a system with an overly powerful central government surrounded by weak and largely economically dependent states.

When the military returned to the barracks in 1999, it left an overdeveloped executive arm at all levels of government—federal, state, and local—at the expense of weak legislative and judicial institutions. Unchecked executive power has encouraged the arbitrary exercise of authority and patronage politics, which sap the economy and undermine the rule of law of the national executive.

Nigeria in the Globalized World of States Nigeria, with its natural riches, has long been regarded as a potential political and economic giant of Africa. Nigerian leaders have long aspired to regional leadership, undertaking several peacekeeping operations and an ambitious diplomatic agenda—through the United Nations, the African Union, and on its own—to broker peace initiatives and to foster democracy in some instances. Recent efforts include Sudan's troubled Darfur region, Côte d'Ivoire, and Zimbabwe.

Governing Nigeria's Economy Nigeria's economy has largely depended on unpredictable oil revenues, sparse external loans, and aid. Owing to neglect of agriculture, Nigeria moved from self-sufficiency in basic foodstuffs in the mid-1960s to heavy dependence on imports less than twenty years later. Manufacturing activities, after a surge of investment by government and foreign firms in the 1970s, suffered from disinvestment for decades. Since 2003, however, this decline has reversed in the south—particularly Lagos—and many areas of the economy outside of oil also begin to expand rapidly. High oil and gas prices have spurred growth but done little to reduce poverty.

Democratic Ideas amid Colonialism and Military Rule The Nigerian colonial state was conceived and fashioned as **interventionist**, with administrative controls and significant ownership of the economy.

interventionist

An interventionist state acts vigorously to shape the performance of major sectors of the economy.

After independence in 1960, Nigeria's civilian and military rulers alike expanded the interventionist state. Although colonial rulers left Nigeria with the machinery of parliamentary democracy, they socialized the population to be passive subjects rather than responsive participants. Colonialism bequeathed an authoritarian legacy to independent Nigeria. Military rule continued this pattern from 1966 to 1979 and again from 1983 to 1999.

This dualism promoted two public realms to which individuals belonged: the communal realm, in which people identified by ethnic or subethnic groups (Igbo, Tiv, Yoruba, and others), and the civic realm in which citizenship was universal.[5] Nigerians came to view the state as the realm where resources were plundered (see Section 4). Morality was reserved for the ethnic or communal realm. Military rule reinforced this pattern and the democratic idea in Nigeria has also been filtered through deep regional divisions.

The south experienced the benefits and burdens of colonial occupation. The coastal location of Lagos, Calabar, and their surrounding regions made them important hubs for trade and shipping activity, around which the British built the necessary infrastructure—schools (promoting Christianity and Western education), roads, ports, and the like—and a large African civil service to facilitate colonialism. In northern Nigeria, the British used indirect rule and used local structures, left intact Islamic institutions, and prohibited Christian missionary activity. The north consequently received few infrastructural benefits, but its traditional administration was largely preserved.

Thus, at independence the south enjoyed the basis for a modern economy and exposure to democratic institutions, but the north remained largely agricultural and monarchical. Even throughout even the darkest days of military rule, these institutions persevered. Nigeria's incredible diversity continually demands involves constant processes to advances democracy promises.

Nigeria's Fragile Collective Identity This division between north and south is overlaid with hundreds of ethnic divisions across the nation, which military governments and civilians alike have been prone to manipulate for selfish ends. These many cultural divisions have been continually exacerbated by the triple threats of clientelism, corruption, and unstable authoritarian governing structures, which together stir up ethnic group competition and hinder economic potential.[6] Clientelism is the practice by which particular individuals or segments receive disproportionate policy benefits or political favors from a political patron, usually at the expense of the larger society. In Nigeria, patrons are often linked to clients by ethnic, religious, or other cultural ties, but these ties have generally benefited only a small elite. By fostering political competition along cultural lines, clientelism tends to undermine social trust and political stability, which are necessary conditions for economic growth.

Nevertheless, the idea of Nigeria has taken root among the country's ethnic groups over 50 years after independence. Most Nigerians enjoy many personal connections across ethnic and religious lines, and elites in both the north and the south have significant business activities throughout the country. Even so, ethnicity remains a critical flashpoint.

Themes and Comparisons

Nigeria is by far the largest country in Africa and among the ten most populous countries in the world. One out of every five black Africans is Nigerian. Unlike most other African countries, Nigeria has the human and material resources to overcome the vicious cycle of poverty and **autocracy**. Hopes for this breakthrough, however, have been regularly frustrated over five decades of independent rule.

autocracy

A government in which one or a few rulers has absolute power, thus, a dictatorship.

Nigeria remains the oldest surviving federation in Africa, and it has managed through much travail to maintain its fragile unity. That cohesion has come under increasing stress, however, and a major challenge is to ensure that Nigeria does not ultimately collapse. Nigeria's past failures to sustain democracy and economic development also render it an important case for the study of resource competition and the perils of corruption, and its experience demonstrates the interrelationship between democracy and development. Democracy and development depend on leadership, political culture, institutional autonomy, and the external economic climate; Nigeria has much to teach us on all these topics.

Where Do You Stand?

Many Nigerians feel that the British bringing together so many ethnicities and religions under one political roof was a terrible mistake, because the diversity is just too great for Nigeria to hold together as a single nation. Do you agree?

After all the problems caused by military rule, do you see any advantages to it? Why might it have been appealing?

POLITICAL ECONOMY AND DEVELOPMENT

SECTION 2

Colonialism bequeathed Nigeria an interventionist state, and governments after independence continued this pattern. The state became the central fixture in the Nigerian economy, stunting the private sector and encumbering industry and commerce. As the state began to unravel in the late 1980s and 1990s, leaders grew more predatory, plundering the petroleum sector, and preventing the nation's vast economic potential from being realized.

State and Economy

▼ **Focus Questions**

• What were some of the key impacts of the oil boom on Nigeria's political economy?

• What efforts has Nigeria made to try to address poverty and spur development?

The Nigerian state plays the central role in economic decision making. Most of the nation's revenues, and nearly all of its hard currency, are channeled through the government, which control these earnings, known as **rents**. Winning government contracts becomes a central economic activity, with lucrative results.[7] Those left out must try to survive on petty trade and subsistence agriculture (the informal sector economy) in which taxes and regulation rarely reach and accounts for about one-fifth of the entire Nigerian GDP.

Origins of Economic Decline

rents

Economic gains that do not compensate those who produced them and do not contribute to productivity, typically associated with government earnings that do not get channeled back into either investments or policies that benefit the public good. Pursuit of economic rents (or "rent-seeking") is profit seeking that takes the form of nonproductive economic activity.

In the colonial and immediate postcolonial periods, Nigeria's economy was centered on agricultural production for domestic consumption and export. Nigeria was self-sufficient in food production. In the 1960s, emphasis shifted to the development of nonfood export crops through large-scale enterprises.

Small farmers received scant government support. Food production suffered.[8] The Biafran War (1967–1970), severe drought, and the development of the petroleum industry reduced agricultural production, which plummeted from 80 percent of exports in 1960 to just 2 percent by 1980.[9] External debt skyrocketed, and corruption increased. The economic downturn of the 1980s created even greater incentives for government corruption. Within three years of seizing power in 1993, General Abacha allowed all of Nigeria's oil refineries to collapse, forcing this giant oil-exporting country into the absurd situation of having to import petroleum. Scam artists proliferated, especially on the Internet, which earned perhaps $100 million annually.

From 1985 to the Present: Deepening Economic Crisis and the Search for Solutions

structural adjustment program (SAP)

Programs established by the World Bank intended to alter and reform the economic structures of highly indebted Third World countries as a condition for receiving international loans. SAPs often involve the necessity for privatization, trade liberalization, and fiscal restraint, which typically requires the dismantling of social welfare systems.

Structural Adjustment The year 1985 marked a turning point for the Nigerian state and economy. Within a year of wresting power from General Buhari in August 1985, the Babangida regime developed an economic **structural adjustment program (SAP)** with the active support of the World Bank and the IMF (also referred to as the **international financial institutions**, or **IFIs**). The decision to embark on the SAP was made against a background of increasing economic constraints arising from the continued dependence of the economy on waning oil revenues, a growing debt burden, **balance of payments** difficulties, and lack of fiscal discipline.[10]

The large revenues arising from the oil windfall enabled the state to increase its involvement in direct production. Beginning in the 1970s, the government created a number of parastatals (state-owned enterprises; see Section 3), including large shares in major banks and other financial institutions, manufacturing, construction, agriculture, public utilities, and various services. Although the government has since sold many of its parastatals, the state remains the biggest employer as well as the most important source of revenue, even for the private sector.

Privatization, which is central to Nigeria's adjustment program, means that state-owned businesses would be sold to private (nonstate) investors, domestic or foreign to generate revenue and improve efficiency, but both domestic and foreign investors were for many years hesitant to risk significant capital in light of persistent instability, unpredictable economic policies, and endemic corruption. Recently, however, attractive areas such as telecommunications, utilities, and oil and gas are drawing significant foreign capital.

Economic Policy President Obasanjo opened his second term in office in 2003 with a renewed focus on economic reform and development. Nigeria stabilized its macroeconomic policy, restructured the banking sector, and established a new anticorruption agency, the Economic and Financial Crimes Commission (EFCC). Unfortunately, many of these ambitious goals were followed by lackluster implementation, and President Jonathan has continued this trend. Buoyant oil revenues have helped to spur the economy higher since 2003, but poverty has not significantly diminished.

Perhaps Obasanjo's greatest economic achievement was paying off most of Nigeria's heavy foreign debt (see Table 6.3). On taking office in 1999 he promptly undertook numerous visits to Europe, Asia, and the United States to urge the governments of those countries to forgive most of Nigeria's obligations. After persistent international lobbying, along with progress on economic reforms during Obasanjo's second term, Nigeria eventually secured an agreement for a substantial reduction of the country's debt. In June 2005, the Paris Club of official creditors approved a package of debt repayments, repurchases, and write-offs that reduced Nigeria's external debt by 90 percent.

international financial institutions (IFIs)

This term generally refers to the International Bank for Reconstruction and Development (the World Bank) and the International Monetary Fund (IMF), but can also include other international lending institutions.

balance of payments

An indicator of international flow of funds that shows the excess or deficit in total payments of all kinds between or among countries. Included in the calculation are exports and imports, grants, and international debt payments.

GLOBAL CONNECTION

From Vision 2010 to NEEDS

In the early 1990s, concerned with the nation's economic decline, a number of the larger Nigerian businesses and key multinational corporations decided to pursue new initiatives, including the first Economic Summit, a high-profile conference that advocated numerous policies to move Nigeria toward becoming an "emerging market" that could attract foreign investment along the lines of the high-performing states in Asia.

Through Vision 2010, the government pledged to adopt a package of business-promoting economic reforms, while business pledged to work toward certain growth targets consistent with governmental priorities in employment, taxation, community investment, and the like. Along with government and business leaders, key figures were invited to participate from nearly all sectors of society, including the press, nongovernmental organizations, youth groups, market women's associations, and others. Government-owned media followed Vision 2010's pronouncements with great fanfare, while the private media reviewed them with a healthy dose of skepticism regarding Abacha's intentions and the elitist nature of the exercise. Vision 2010's final report called for:

• Restoring democratic rule
• Restructuring and professionalizing the military

• Lowering the population growth rate
• Rebuilding education
• Meaningful privatization
• Diversifying the export base beyond oil
• Supporting intellectual property rights
• Central bank autonomy

Presidents Obasanjo and Yar'Adua both adopted the core goals of Vision 2010, announcing his own Vision 2020 and a Seven Point Agenda that included economic reforms. President Jonathan encompassed these in his own plan, called Vision 20:2020, which set many similar goals as the previous plans, and suffered similar problems of poor implementation.

MAKING CONNECTIONS What elements of Vision 2010 do you see evident in the economic policies of Nigerian presidents after 1999?

Source: Vision 2010 Final Report, September 1997; Federal Government of Nigeria, the *National Economic Empowerment and Development Strategy,* March 2004.

Table 6.2	Selected Economic Indicators, 1980–2009		
Years	Real GDP (in billions)	GDP %Growth	Inflation Rate % (CPI)
1980	64.2	4.2	9.97
1985	28.4	9.7	7.44
1990	28.5	8.2	7.36
1993	21.4	2.2	57.17
1995	28.1	2.5	72.84
1997	36.2	2.7	8.53
1999	34.8	1.1	6.62
2000	46	5.4	6.93
2001	48	3.1	18.87
2002	59.1	1.55	12.88
2003	67.7	10.3	14.03
2005	112.2	5.4	17.86
2007	165.9	6.45	5.38
2008	207.1	6	11.58
2009	173	5.6	11.54
2011	245.7	5.1	10.8
2012	262.6	6.7	12.2

Source: World Bank. Some data compiled by Evan Litwin and Mukesh Baral.

President Yar'Adua vowed to continue President Obasanjo's reforms, but made marginal progress. While this massive corruption around the oil industry has continued unabated, however, Nigeria's small private sector has been quietly expanding rapidly. Although the last three administrations have not followed through on the expansive development policies they promised, they have largely left much of the private sector to its own designs, and there has been a boom in the private sector and significant infrastructure development.

Social Welfare The continued decline in Nigeria's economic performance since the early 1980s has caused great suffering, and the recent rise of the private sector has yet to take a significant bite out of poverty for the majority of Nigerians.

Since 1986, there has been a marked deterioration in the quantity and quality of social services, complicated by a marked decline in household incomes. The SAP program and subsequent austerity measures emphasizing the reduction of state expenditures have forced cutbacks in spending on social welfare, Nigeria's provision of basic education, health care, and other social services—water, education, food, and shelter—remain woefully inadequate. In addition to the needless loss of countless lives to preventable and curable maladies, the nation is fighting to stave off an AIDS epidemic of catastrophic proportions. The government has made AIDS a secondary priority, leaving much of the initiative to a small group of courageous but underfunded nongovernmental organizations.

Society and Economy

Because the central government controls access to most resources and economic opportunities, the state has become the major focus for competition among ethnic, regional, religious, and class groups.[11]

Table 6.3	Nigeria's Total External Debt (millions of US$ at current prices and exchange rates)	
Years	**Total Debt /GDP**	**Total Debt Service/ Exports**
1977	8.73	1.04
1986	109.9	38.03
1996	88.97	14.79
1997	78.54	8.71
1999	83.76	7.54
2000	68.18	8.71
2001	64.67	12.9
2002	51.55	8.13
2003	51.16	5.96
2007	5.2	1.79
2008	5.55	0.67
2009	4.53	0.81
2012	18.37	.3

Source: World Bank. Recent data compiled by Evan Litwin and Mukesh Baral.

Ethnic and Religious Cleavages

Nigeria's ethnic relations have generated tensions that sap the country's economy of much-needed vitality.[12] The dominance of the Hausa, Igbo, and Yoruba in the country's national life, and the conflicts among political elites from these groups, distort economic affairs.

Government ineptitude (or outright manipulation), and growing Islamic and Christian assertion, have also heightened conflicts.[13] Christians have perceived past northern-dominated governments as being pro-Muslim in their management and distribution of scarce resources, some of which jeopardized the secular nature of the state. These fears have increased since 1999, when several northern states instituted expanded versions of the Islamic legal code, the *shari'a*. For their part, Muslims feared that President Obasanjo, a born-again Christian, tilted the balance of power and thus the distribution of economic benefits against the north, and such fears are again on the rise under President Jonathan, also a Christian. Economic decline has contributed to the rise of Christian and Muslim fundamentalisms, which have spread among unemployed youths and others in a society suffering under economic collapse.

Gender Differences

Although the Land Use Act of 1978 stated that all land in Nigeria is ultimately owned by the government, land tenure in Nigeria is still governed by traditional practice, which is largely patriarchal. Despite the fact that women, especially from the south and Middle Belt areas, have traditionally dominated agricultural production and form the bulk of agricultural producers, they are generally prevented from owning land, which remains the major means of production. Trading, in which women feature prominently, is also controlled in many areas by traditional chiefs and local government councilors, who are overwhelmingly male.

Women's associations in the past tended to be elitist, urban based, and mainly concerned with issues of trade, children, household welfare, and religion.[14] Women are grossly underrepresented at all levels of the governmental system; only 19 (of 469) national legislators are women.

Reflecting the historical economic and educational advantages of the south, women's interest organizations sprouted in southern Nigeria earlier than in the north. Although these groups initially focused generally on nonpolitical issues surrounding women's health and children's welfare, they are now also focusing on explicit political goals, such as getting more women into government and increasing funds available for education.

Environmental Issues

Northern Nigeria is located on the edge of the Sahel, the vast, semi-arid region just south of the Sahara desert that is farmable but often troubled with fragile water supplies. Although much of the north enjoys seasonal rains that come from the tropical southern part of Nigeria, the northern edges of the country have been suffering the growing effects of climate change, as water supplies dry up. Most dramatic has been the drying of Lake Chad in the northeast, which has shrunk to roughly a fifth of its size in the 1960s. As desertification pressures spread in the north, nomadic Fulani herdsman have been forced to move their cattle toward the more temperate south, causing growing numbers of local conflicts with farmers. These disputes can take on religious tones when the Fulani, who are predominantly Muslim, move into lands settled by Christian farmers.

The environment is also a major issue in the Niger Delta, but for a different reason. Here, years of pollution from the oil industry has killed off much of the local fish stock that communities in the region depended upon for their livelihoods, and gas flaring from the oil wells light up the night and make the air toxic to breathe. A small ethnic group in one of the oil-producing communities, the Ogoni, formed an environmental rights organization in 1990 that pushed for peaceful action to clean up the damage and give the Ogoni greater control over the oil wealth. The military, however, clamped down on the movement and hung its key leaders. Thereafter, protests across the region increased, and many turned violent, devolving into the militant insurgency that plagues the Niger Delta today.

Finally, Nigeria's environment faces growing pressures from the nation's population explosion. Sprawling megacities are stretching across Nigeria's urban areas, especially from the commercial hub of Lagos, whose entire urban stretch has absorbed as far as Ibadan to the north and is estimated to include over 20 million people. At the same time, Lagos is rapidly losing its coastline to the rising sea levels, putting increased pressure on the limited space.

Nigeria in the Global Economy

The Nigerian state has remained comparatively weak and dependent on foreign industrial and financial interests. The country's acute debt burden was dramatically reduced in 2005, but started growing again by 2014, and Nigeria is still reliant on the developed industrial economies for finance capital, production and information technologies, basic consumer items, and raw materials. Mismanagement, endemic corruption, and the vagaries of international commodity markets have squandered the country's economic potential. Apart from its standing in global energy markets, Nigeria receded to the margins of the global economy. The recent economic boom centered in Lagos has attracted increasing international investment, but this must be matched with serious development and anti-corruption policies at the federal level, which has so far been lacking.

Nigeria and the Regional Political Economy

Nigeria's aspirations to be a regional leader in Africa have not been dampened by its declining position in the global political economy. Nigeria was a major actor in the formation of the **Economic Community of West African States (ECOWAS)** in 1975 and has carried a disproportionately high financial and administrative burden for keeping the organization afloat. Under President Obasanjo's initiative, ECOWAS voted in 2000 to create a parliament and a single currency for the region as the

Economic Community of West African States (ECOWAS)

The West African regional organization, including fifteen member countries from Cape Verde in the west to Nigeria and Niger in the east.

THE U.S. CONNECTION

Much in Common

Since the 1970s Nigeria has had a strong relationship with the United States. Most of Nigeria's military governments during the Cold War aligned their foreign policies with the West, although they differed over South Africa, with Nigeria taking a strong anti-apartheid stance. Beginning with the Second Republic constitution, Nigeria closely modeled its presidential and federal systems on those of the United States, and Nigerian courts will occasionally turn to American jurisprudence for legal precedents. Since President Carter's visit to Nigeria in 1978, Washington has supported Nigerian efforts to liberalize and deepen democratic development.

Overwhelmingly, however, the key issue in U.S.–Nigerian relations has been oil. The United States buys roughly 8 percent of its petroleum imports from Nigeria and has repeatedly pushed Abuja to increase production of its "sweet crude," the especially high quality oil Nigeria offers. Nigeria also discovered massive gas reserves off its coasts. Nigeria's military governments used America's oil addiction to force it to moderate its pressure on Abuja to democratize. The civilian governments since 1999 have also largely ignored U.S. complaints over declining election quality, and the Yar'Adua administration cultivated ties with China after the United States suspended high-level diplomatic relations over the farcical 2007 elections.

Shortly thereafter, the Bush administration welcomed President Yar'Adua to Washington. President Jonathan, however, came to office in part with the help of U.S. pressure, and he has cultivated close ties with the Obama administration and featured his meetings with President Obama strongly in his 2011 and 2015 election campaigns.

Nigeria and the United States also share strong societal ties. Since the 1960s, Christian Nigerians have been avid consumers of American Pentecostalism, sprouting thousands of new churches over the years and infusing them with a uniquely Nigerian flare, such that many of these churches are now opening satellites in the United States and around the globe. In addition, a growing number of Nigerians have migrated to the United States, such that nearly 300,000 are now U.S. citizens. Since 2000, this diaspora has begun to exercise some influence over U.S. policy, and they have also used their financial resources to support development projects and exercise political influence in Nigeria.

MAKING CONNECTIONS Does American oil addiction give Nigeria more influence over the United States in the end?

next step toward a European Union–style integration. The currency was never implemented, but ECOWAS citizens are able to travel and trade across member state borders relatively freely.

Nigeria was also the largest contributor of troops to the West African peacekeeping force to Liberia from 1990 to 1997 to restore order and prevent the Liberian civil war from destabilizing the subregion. Nigeria under President Obasanjo also sought to mediate crises in Guinea-Bissau, Togo, and Ivory Coast, and in Darfur (Sudan), Congo, and Zimbabwe outside the ECOWAS region. President Jonathan has continued to support Nigerian peacekeeping commitments abroad, taking a particularly strong stand against the 2012 coup and Islamist rebellion in Mali through ECOWAS. The growing Boko Haram insurgency within Nigeria, however, has absorbed much of Nigeria's military resources since 2011 and left less for its international commitments.

Nigeria and the Political Economy of the West

Shortly after the 1973–1974 global oil crisis, Nigeria's oil wealth was perceived by the Nigerian elite as a source of strength.[15] By the 1980s, however, the global oil market had become a buyers' market. Thereafter, it became clear that Nigeria's dependence on oil was a source of weakness. The depth of Nigeria's international weakness became more evident with the adoption of structural adjustment in the mid-1980s. Given the enormity of the economic crisis, Nigeria was compelled to seek IMF/World Bank support to improve its balance of payments and facilitate economic restructuring and debt rescheduling, and it has had to accept direction from foreign agencies ever since.

Nigeria remains a highly visible and influential member of the Organization of Petroleum Exporting Countries (OPEC), selling on the average more than 2 million barrels of petroleum daily and contributing approximately 8 percent of U.S. oil imports. Nigeria's oil wealth and its great economic potential have tempered the resolve of Western nations in combating human rights and other abuses, notably during the Abacha period from 1993 to 1998.

The West has been supportive of the return of Nigerian leadership across Africa. Together with President Thabo Mbeki of South Africa, President Obasanjo was instrumental in convincing the continent's leaders to transform the OAU into the African Union (AU) in 2002, modeled on European-style processes to promote greater political integration across the continent.

Despite its considerable geopolitical resources, Nigeria's economic development profile remains harsh. Nigeria is listed very close to the bottom of the UNDP's Human Development Index (HDI), 153 out of 174, behind India and Tanzania. GDP per capita in 2014 was rising rapidly at $2258, but the wealth remains extremely poorly distributed, and less than 1 percent of GDP was recorded as public expenditures on education and health, respectively.

Where Do You Stand?

Has oil been a blessing or curse for the Nigerian economy?

Many Nigerians feel they have ample natural resources to develop the nation, but that they have been plagued with poor leadership to make it happen. Do you see evidence of this?

GOVERNANCE AND POLICY-MAKING

The rough edges of what has been called the "unfinished Nigerian state" appears in its institutions of governance and policy-making. What seemed like an endless political transition under the Babangida and Abacha regimes was rushed through in less than a year by their successor, Abdulsalami Abubakar. President Obasanjo thus inherited a government that was close to collapse, riddled with corruption, unable to perform basic tasks of governance, yet facing high public expectations to deliver rapid progress. He delivered some important economic reforms over his eight years as president, but he gradually succumbed to the "Big Man," prebendal style of corrupt clientelist networks, and tried to change the Constitution to allow himself to stay in power indefinitely. The Nigerian public, however, rejected his ambitions, providing his political opponents, civil society, and the media a strong base to mobilize and force him to leave in May 2007. President Yar'Adua, like Obasanjo, came to power without a client network of his own and immediately set out to build one. President Jonathan also took office without much of a network, and quickly turned Nigeria's massive state resources to the task of getting himself elected in 2011 and keeping control of the ruling party thereafter.

Focus Questions ▼

• What is the "National Question," and how have Nigerians tried to resolve it?

• What is prebendalism, and how has the "Big Man" problem played out in the civilian governments since 1999?

Organization of the State

The National Question and Constitutional Governance

After almost five decades as an independent nation, Nigerians are still debating the basic political structures of the country, who will rule and how, and in some quarters, if the country should even remain united. They call this fundamental governance issue the "national question." How is the country to be governed given its great diversity? What should be the institutional form of the government? How can all sections of the country work in harmony and none feel excluded or dominated by the others? Without clear answers to these questions, Nigeria has stumbled along since independence between democracy and constitutionalism, on the one hand, and military domination on the other. The May 2006 rejection of President Obasanjo's third-term gambit, and the fact that most elites insisted on a constitutional solution to the crisis over President Yar'Adua's incapacitation and death suggest, however, that Nigeria may have turned a corner in terms of a growing respect for constitutional rule.

Nigerian constitutions have suffered under little respect from military or civilian leaders, who have often been unwilling to observe legal and constitutional constraints. Governance and policy-making in this context are conducted within fragile institutions that are swamped by personal and partisan considerations.

Federalism and State Structure

Nigeria's First Republic experimented with the British-style parliamentary model, in which the prime minister is chosen directly from the legislative ranks. The First

Republic was relatively decentralized, with more political power vested in the three federal units: the Northern, Eastern, and Western Regions. The Second Republic constitution, which went into effect in 1979, adopted a U.S.-style presidential model. The Fourth Republic continues with the presidential model: a system with a strong executive who is constrained by a system of formal checks and balances on authority, a bicameral legislature, and an independent judicial branch charged with matters of law and constitutional interpretation.[16]

Like the United States, Nigeria also features a federal structure comprising 36 states and 774 local government units empowered, within limits, to enact their own laws. The judicial system also resembles that of the United States, with a network of local and appellate courts as well as state-level courts. Unlike the United States, however, Nigeria also allows customary law courts to function alongside the secular system, including *shari'a* courts in Muslim communities. Nigerian citizens have the right to choose which of these court systems that they wish to use, but if the disputants cannot agree, then the case goes to the secular courts by default.

In practice, however, military rule left an authoritarian political culture that remains despite the formal democratization of state structures. The control of oil wealth by this centralized command structure has further cemented economic and political control in the center, resulting in a skewed federalism in which states enjoy nominal powers, but in reality most are highly dependent on the central government. Another aspect of federalism in Nigeria has been the effort to arrive at some form of elite accommodation to moderate some of the more divisive aspects of cultural pluralism. The domination of federal governments from 1960 to 1999 by northern Nigerians led southern Nigerians, particularly Yoruba leaders, to demand a "power shift" of the presidency to the south in 1999, leading to the election of Olusegun Obasanjo. Northerners then demanded a shift back to the north in 2007, propelling Umaru Yar'Adua, a northern governor, into office. This ethnic rotation principle is not formally found in the constitution, but all the major political parties recognize it as a necessity. Moreover, the parties practice ethnic rotation at the state and local levels as well.[17]

A central issue in both the 2009–2010 crisis over Yar'Adua's incapacitation and the 2011 election of President Jonathan, a southerner from the Niger Delta, is that Jonathan's ascension has broken the ethnic rotation principle. Northern factions argued that under this rule the presidency should have stayed with them for two terms until 2015. These factions were, however, unable to unite and block Jonathan from winning the PDP nomination and election in 2011. Consequently, northern groups tried to wrest control of the PDP in 2012 from the president, and when they failed, they turned to the opposition in order to attempt to bring the presidency back to their region in 2015.

This informal norm of ethnic rotation has built upon an older, formal practice, known as "federal character." Federal character calls for ethnic quotas in government hiring practices, and was introduced into the public service and formally codified by the 1979 constitution. Although this principle is regarded by some as a positive Nigerian contribution to governance in a plural society, its application has also intensified some intergroup rivalries and conflicts. Some critics have argued that it is antidemocratic, encouraging elite bargaining at the expense of public votes. President Jonathan's breaking of this principle through his election in 2011 raised significant tensions in the PDP primaries and was partly responsible for the election riots that killed 800 people, and propelled northern factions of his party into the opposition by 2013.

The Executive

The Executive under Military Rule

The leadership styles among Nigeria's seven military heads of state varied widely but, in general, under military administrations, the president, or head of state, made appointments to most senior government positions.[18] Since the legislature was disbanded, major executive decisions (typically passed by decrees) were subject to the approval of a ruling council of high-level military officers, although by Abacha's time this council had become largely a rubber stamp for the ruler. Although the military became increasingly repressive, nearly all the juntas spoke of transiting to democracy in order to gain legitimacy.

Given the highly personalistic character of military politics, patron–client relationships flourished. The military pattern of organization, with one strongman at the top and echelons of subordinates below in a pyramid of top-down relationships, spread throughout Nigerian political culture and subcultures.

Having been politicized and divided by these patron–client relationships, the military was structurally weakened during its long years in power. While there have been reports of coup plots on a number of occasions during the Fourth Republic, especially during President Yar'Adua's final days, the military establishment has so far remained loyal and generally within its constitutional security roles.

President Obasanjo paid close attention to keeping the military professionally oriented—and in the barracks. U.S. military advisers and technical assistance were invited to redirect the Nigerian military toward regional peacekeeping expertise—and to keep them busy outside of politics. So far, this strategy has been effective, but the military remains a threat. Junior and senior officers threatened coups over the farcical 2007 elections and the refusal of Yar'Adua's advisors to hand power to Jonathan in 2009–2010, and could do so again if the 2015 election proves deeply contentious.

The Fourth Republic: The Obasanjo, Yar'Adua, and Jonathan Administrations

President Obasanjo's first six months in office were marked by initiatives to reform the armed forces, revitalize the economy, address public welfare, and improve standards of governance. The president sought to root out misconduct and inefficiency in the public sector. Soon, however, familiar patterns of clientelism and financial kickbacks for oil licenses resurfaced. Obasanjo proposed an anticorruption commission with sweeping statutory powers to investigate and prosecute public officials. Delayed in its establishment, the commission had little impact. A second anticorruption commission, however, the Economic and Financial Crimes Commission (EFCC), has since its founding in 2003 had an impressive record of indictments.

Nonetheless, a major impediment to reform came from the ruling party itself. The PDP is run by a collection of powerful politicians from Nigeria's early governments, many of whom grew rich from their complicity with the Babangida and Abacha juntas. With a difficult reelection bid in 2003, these fixers again delivered a victory for the president and the PDP, accomplished through massive fraud in a third of Nigeria's states and questionable practices in at least another third of the country.

After the 2003 election President Obasanjo appeared convinced that he needed to build his own prebendal network if he were to govern and if he were to pursue his ambition to stay in office past two terms. He and his supporters soon moved to gain control of the PDP, offering benefits for loyalty, and removing allies of rival Big Men in the party. The president then signaled the EFCC to investigate his rivals, arresting some and forcing others to support his plans. When Obasanjo's third-term amendment was quashed by the National Assembly in May 2006, the president then had himself named "Chairman for Life" of the PDP, with the power to eject anyone from the party, even his successor as president.

Not surprisingly, President Yar'Adua spent his first year in office trying to gain control over the PDP. He halted many of the last-minute privatizations of state assets into the hands of Obasanjo loyalists and replaced the chairman on the EFCC. The Yar'Adua administration also did nothing to prevent the National Assembly from instigating a series of investigations into the Obasanjo administration that unearthed massive corruption, including the discovery that more than $10 billion had been sunk into the power sector that had produced no results. President Yar'Adua also assisted many of the PDP governors—twelve of whom had their elections overturned by the courts—to retain their seats in rerun elections. By 2009, Yar'Adua had greater control of the PDP, and Obasanjo was on the decline. Yar'Adua's incapacitation later that year and death thereafter, however, reversed Obasanjo's fortunes, and he threw his support behind Goodluck Jonathan at the key moment when Yar'Adua loyalists were preventing him from becoming acting president.

With Obasanjo's support, Jonathan moved to build other alliances to gain influence in the PDP, particularly with the powerful state governors. Their support, bought with the massive resources in the hands of the presidency, won him the PDP nomination and swept him to victory in April 2011. As President Jonathan moved to take control of the PDP, however, his relationship soured with President Obasanjo, who then turned his support to Jonathan's opponents in the PDP. Within months, the party had divided, with six governors defecting in 2013 to the newly formed opposition party, the All Progressives Congress (APC).

These developments demonstrated the continuing deficits of legitimacy for the government as well as the democratic system. As Nigeria's political elites continue to flout the rules of the system, it is inevitable that patronage, coercion, and personal interest will drive policy more than the interests of the public. President Jonathan followed this pattern of "Big Man" prebendal politics—with one important exception: he appointed a credible chairman of the nation's electoral commission, Attahiru Jega. Jega had only a few months to prepare for the April 2011 election, but his reforms assured a more credible outcome than 2007, and hold the promise of significant change for 2015 as more reforms within the commission begin to take hold.

The Bureaucracy

As government was increasingly "Africanized" before independence, the bureaucracy became a way to reward individuals in the prebendal system (see below). Individuals were appointed on the basis of patronage, ethnic group, and regional origin rather than merit.

It is conservatively estimated that federal and state government personnel increased from 72,000 at independence to well over 1 million by the mid-1980s. The salaries of these bureaucrats presently consume roughly half of government expenditures. Several of President Obasanjo's progressive ministers undertook extensive reforms within their ministries, with some successes, but which the bureaucracy fought at every turn.

Semipublic Institutions

Among the largest components of the national administration in Nigeria are numerous state-owned enterprises, usually referred to as parastatals. In general, parastatals are established for several reasons. First, they are intended to furnish public facilities, including water, power, telecommunications, ports, and other transportation, at lower cost than private companies. Second, they were introduced to accelerate economic development by controlling the commanding heights of the economy, including steel production, petroleum and natural gas production, refining, petrochemicals, fertilizer, and certain areas of agriculture. Third, there is a nationalist dimension that relates to issues of sovereignty over sectors perceived sensitive for national security.

Prebendalism

Prebendalism is the disbursing of public offices and state rents to one's ethnic clients. It is an extreme form of clientelism that refers to the practice of mobilizing cultural and other sectional identities by political aspirants and officeholders for the purpose of corruptly appropriating state resources. Prebendalism is an established pattern of political behavior that justifies the pursuit of and the use of public office for the personal benefit of the officeholder and his clients. The official public purpose of the office becomes a secondary concern. As with clientelism, the officeholder's clients comprise a specific set of elites to which he is linked, typically by ethnic or religious ties. Thus, clients or supporters perpetuate the prebendal system in a pyramid fashion with a "Big Man" or "godfather" at the top and echelons of intermediate Big Men and clients below.[19]

prebendalism

Patterns of political behavior that rest on the justification that official state offices should be utilized for the personal benefit of officeholders as well as of their support group or clients.

Other State Institutions

Other institutions of governance and policy-making, including the federal judiciary and subnational governments (incorporating state and local courts), operate within the context of a strong central government dominated by a powerful chief executive.

The Judiciary

At one time, the Nigerian judiciary enjoyed relative autonomy from the executive arm. Aggrieved individuals and organizations could take the government to court and expect a judgment based on the merits of their case. This situation changed as each successive military government demonstrated a profound disdain for judicial practices, and eventually it undermined not only the autonomy but also the very integrity of the judiciary as a third branch of government.

The Buhari, Babangida, and Abacha regimes, in particular, issued a spate of repressive decrees disallowing judicial review. Through the executive's power of appointment of judicial officers to the high bench, as well as the executive's control of judicial budgets, the government came to dominate the courts. In addition, the once highly competent judiciary was undermined severely by declining standards of legal training and bribery. The decline of court independence reached a low in 1993 when the Supreme Court placed all actions of the military executive beyond judicial review. The detention and hanging of Ken Saro-Wiwa and eight other Ogoni activists in 1995 underscored the politicization and compromised state of the judicial system.

With the return of civilian rule in 1999, however, the courts have slowly begun to restore some independence and credibility. In early 2002, for instance, the Supreme Court passed two landmark judgments on election law and control of the vast offshore gas reserves. Since the farcical 2007 elections, the courts have overturned twelve gubernatorial races and a host of legislative contests, and the Supreme Court reviewed the 2007 and 2011 presidential elections as well.

State and Local Judiciaries The judiciaries at the state level are subordinate to the Federal Court of Appeal and the Supreme Court. Some of the states in the northern part of the country with large Muslim populations maintain a parallel court system based on the Islamic *shari'a* (religious law). Similarly, some states in the Middle Belt and southern part of the country have subsidiary courts based on customary law. Each of these maintains an appellate division. Otherwise, all courts of record in the country are based on the English common law tradition, and all courts are ultimately bound by decisions handed down by the Supreme Court.

How to apply the *shari'a* has been a source of continuing debate in Nigerian politics. For several years, some northern groups have participated in a movement to expand the application of *shari'a* law in predominantly Muslim areas of Nigeria, and some even have advocated that it be made the supreme law of the land. Prior to the establishment of the Fourth Republic, *shari'a* courts had jurisdiction only among Muslims in civil proceedings and in questions of Islamic personal law. In November 1999, however, the northern state of Zamfara instituted a version of the *shari'a* criminal code that included cutting off hands for stealing and stoning to death for those (especially women) who committed adultery. Eleven other northern states adopted the criminal code by 2001, prompting fears among Christian minorities in these states that the code might be applied to them. Two thousand people lost their lives in Kaduna in 2000 when the state installed the *shari'a* criminal code despite a population that is half Christian.

Although the *shari'a* criminal code appears to contradict Nigeria's officially secular constitution, President Obasanjo refused to challenge it, seeing the movement as a "fad." His refusal to challenge *shari'a* saved the nation from a deeply divisive policy debate and gave northern political and legal systems time to adjust. In fact, although the *shari'a* systems in these states have created more vehicles for patronage, they have also opened up new avenues for public action to press government for accountability and reform. In addition, women's groups mobilized against several questionable local *shari'a* court decisions to challenge them at the appellate level, winning landmark decisions that helped to extend women's legal protections under the code.

State and Local Government

Nigeria's centralization of oil revenues has fostered intense competition among local communities and states for access to national patronage. Most states would be insolvent without substantial support from the central government. About 90 percent of state incomes are received directly from the federal government, which includes a lump sum based on oil revenues, plus a percentage of oil income based on population. In all likelihood, only the states of Lagos, Rivers, and Kano could survive on their own. Despite attempted reforms, most local governments have degenerated into prebendal patronage outposts for the governors to dole out to loyalists. For the most part, they do little to address their governance responsibilities.

The federal, state, and local governments have the constitutional and legal powers to raise funds through taxes. However, Nigerians share an understandable unwillingness to pay taxes and fees to a government with such a poor record of delivering basic services. The result is a vicious cycle: government is sapped of

---

shari'a

Islamic law derived mostly from the Qur'an and the examples set by the Prophet Muhammad in the Sunnah.

resources and legitimacy and cannot adequately serve the people. Communities, in turn, are compelled to resort to self-help measures to protect these operations and thus withdraw further from the reach of the state. Very few individuals and organizations pay taxes, the most basic government functions are starved of resources.

The Policy-Making Process

Nigeria's prolonged experience with military rule has resulted in a policy process based more on top-down directives than on consultation, political debate, and legislation. A decade of democratic government has seen important changes, as the

---

 PROFILE

President Goodluck Jonathan

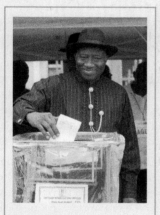

President Goodluck Jonathan, casting his vote in his Bayelsa state village and wearing a traditional hat common to many Niger Delta communities. He was elected vice president in 2007, named Acting President by the National Assembly on the incapacitation of President Yar'Adua in 2010, and elected president in 2011.

Pius Utomi Ekpei/AFP/ Getty Images

The story goes that President Jonathan's father, a canoe maker from Bayelsa state, had an innate sense that his son was born lucky, and so named him Goodluck. Whether the story is truth or legend, events certainly support its conclusion: fortune has so far smiled on the president, rocketing him from humble beginnings in the Niger Delta to the center of Nigerian politics. Jonathan worked as both a lecturer and an environmental official while finishing his Ph.D. in zoology. In 1998 he joined the PDP and won the office of deputy governor of Bayelsa state. He then became governor in 2005 when his predecessor was impeached for corruption. When President Obasanjo picked the little-known Yar'Adua as the 2007 presidential candidate for the PDP, he sought to balance the ticket with someone from the Niger Delta. The other regional governors—having been in office longer—were richer and deemed more powerful, so Obasanjo turned to Jonathan for the vice presidency. As President Yar'Adua's health failed, Jonathan found himself acting president in February 2010 and then president when Yar'Adua passed away in May 2010.

Given this quick ascent, the fact that the president chose a cautious approach based on continuity of the policies of his predecessors is not surprising. Unfortunately for Nigerians, however, President Jonathan has also continued the practices of promising bold policies and not implementing them, and of focusing his efforts on gaining control of the corrupt PDP machine. His administration is accused of levels of corruption higher than any of his predecessors. Bayelsa politics, where he started his ascent, is infamous for corruption and militant activity, and militias dynamited Jonathan's house the night he was elected vice president in 2007. His wife, Patience, was accused by the EFCC of money laundering in 2006 and forced to return $13.5 million, although she was never prosecuted, and her extravagant spending is a constant topic in the media, such as gold-plated iPhones for attendees at her daughter's wedding in 2014. His ambitions to be reelected in 2015 have split the PDP, such that power politics have dominated his tenure and sidelined most major policy initiatives. He did, however, name a respected civil society leader to head the electoral commission early in his time in office.

President Jonathan is the first Nigerian head of state to have a Facebook page (http://www.facebook.com/jonathangoodluck), and is even believed to take the time to write some of the postings himself.

MAKING CONNECTIONS What do you see as President Jonathan's most important contributions and failings so far?

legislatures, courts, and state governments have begun to force the presidency to negotiate its policies and work within a constitutional framework. But military rule and its "loyalty pyramids"[20] has left indelible marks on policy-making in Nigeria and its networks of corruption.[21]

Where Do You Stand?

The three presidents since 1999 all came to power promising reform, but soon succumbed to the dominant corrupt patterns of prebendalism set by the military years ago. Is corruption just too ingrained in Nigeria for any politician to resist?

Does Nigeria's parallel system of *shari'a* and customary courts alongside its secular ones seem like a good idea to accommodate the nation's diversity, or does it perpetuate ethnic and religious differences that divide the country?

SECTION 4

REPRESENTATION AND PARTICIPATION

▼ Focus Questions

- What have been the benefits and costs of the move from ethnic parties under the early republics to the multiethnic parties of the Fourth Republic?

- What role has civil society played in resisting military rule and voicing the public interest under civilian government?

Representation and participation are two vital components of modern democracies. Nigerian legislatures have commonly been sidelined or reduced to subservience by the powerful executive, while fraud, elite manipulation, and military interference have marred the formal party and electoral systems. Thus, we also emphasize unofficial methods of representation and participation through the institutions of civil society, which are sometimes more important than the formal institutions.

The Legislature

Nigeria's legislature has been a primary victim of the country's political instability. Legislative structures and processes historically suffered abuse, neglect, or peremptory suspension by the executive. Until the first coup in 1966, Nigeria operated its legislature along the lines of the British Westminster model, with an elected lower house and a smaller upper house composed of individuals selected by the executive. For the next thirteen years of military rule, a Supreme Military Council performed legislative functions by initiating and passing decrees at will. During the second period of civilian rule, 1979–1983, the bicameral legislature was introduced similar to the U.S. system, with a Senate and House of Representatives (together known as the National Assembly) consisting of elected members, which is the model still in use.

Election to the Senate is on the basis of equal state representation, with three senators from each of the thirty-six states, plus one senator from the federal capital territory, Abuja. The practice of equal representation in the Senate is identical to that of the United States, except that each Nigerian state elects three senators instead of two. Election to the Nigerian House of Representatives is also based on state representation but weighted to reflect the relative size of each state's population, again after the U.S. example. Only eight women were elected in 1999 to sit in the Fourth

Republic's National Assembly; by 2011 this number rose slightly to nineteen, but still constituting only 4 percent of the legislature's membership.

Political Parties and the Party System

An unfortunate legacy of the party and electoral systems after independence was that political parties were associated with particular ethnic groups.[22] The three-region federation created by the British, with one region for each of the three biggest ethnic groups (Hausa, Yoruba, and Igbo), created strong incentives for three parties—one dominated by each group—to form. This in turn fostered a strong perception of politics as an ethnically zero-sum (or winner-takes-all) struggle for access to scarce state resources. This encouraged the political and social fragmentation that ultimately destroyed the First Republic and undermined the Second Republic.

In addition to the three-region structure of the federation at independence, Nigeria's use of a first-past-the-post plurality electoral system produced legislative majorities for these three parties with strong ethnic identities. During subsequent democratic experiments, many of the newer parties could trace their roots to their predecessors in the first civilian regime. Consequently, parties were more attentive to the welfare of their ethnic groups than to the development of Nigeria as a whole. In a polity as potentially volatile as Nigeria, these tendencies intensified political polarization and resentment among the losers.

In the Second Republic, the leading parties shared the same ethnic and sectional support, and often the same leadership, as the parties that were prominent in the first civilian regime. In his maneuvering steps toward creating the civilian Third Republic, General Babangida announced a landmark decision in 1989 to establish only two political parties by decree.[23] The state provided initial start-up funds, wrote the constitutions and manifestos of these parties, and designed them to be "a little to the right and a little to the left," respectively, on the political–ideological spectrum. Interestingly, the elections that took place under these rules from 1990 to 1993 indicated that the two parties cut across the cleavages of ethnicity, regionalism, and religion, demonstrating the potential to move beyond ethnicity.[24] The Social Democratic Party (SDP), which emerged victorious in the 1993 national elections, was an impressive coalition of Second Republic party structures, including elements of the former UPN, NPP, PRP, and GNPP. The opposing National Republican Convention (NRC) was seen as having its roots in northern groups that were the core of the National Party of Nigeria (NPN).

Elections

Table 6.4 shows historical trends in electoral patterns and communal affiliations. As clearly outlined, northern-based parties dominated the first and second experiments with civilian rule. Given this background, it is significant that Moshood Abiola was able to win the presidency in 1993, the first time in Nigeria's history that a southerner electorally defeated a northerner. Abiola, a Yoruba Muslim, won a number of key states in the north, including the hometown of his opponent. Southerners therefore perceived the decision by the northern-dominated Babangida regime to annul the June 12 elections as a deliberate attempt by the military and northern interests to maintain their decades-long domination of the highest levels of government.

Table 6.4	Federal Election Results in Nigeria, 1959–2011

Presidential Election Results, 1979–2011

	Victor (% of the vote)	Leading Contender (% of the vote)
1979	Shehu Shagari, NPN (33.8)	Obafemi Awolowo, UPN (29.2)
1983	Shehu Shagari, NPN (47.3)	Obafemi Awolowo, UPN (31.1)
1993	M.K.O. Abiola, SDP (58.0)	Bashir Tofa, NRC (42.0)
1999	Olusegun Obasanjo, PDP (62.8)	Olu Falae, AD/APP alliance (37.2)
2003	Olusegun Obasanjo, PDP (61.9)	Mohammadu Buhari, ANPP (31.2)
2007	Umaru Yar'Adua, PDP (69.8)	Mohammadu Buhari, ANPP (18.7)
2011	Goodluck Jonathan, PDP (58.9)	Mohammadu Buhari, CDC (32.0)

Parties Controlling the Parliament/National Assembly (Both Houses) by Ethno-Regional Zone, First to Fourth Republics

		Northwest	North-Central	Northeast	Southwest	South-South	Southeast
First	1959	NPC	NPC (NEPU)	NPC	AG	AG	NCNC*
	1964–1965	NPC	NPC	NPC	NNDP* (AG)**	NNDP* (AG)**	NCNC
Second	1979	NPN	PRP (NPN, UPN)	GNPP (NPN)	UPN (NPN)	NPN (UPN)	NPP*
	1983	NPN	NPN (PRP)	NPN	UPN (NPN)	NPN	NPP**
Third	1992	NRC	SDP (NRC)	SDP (NRC)	SDP	NRC (SDP)	NRC
Fourth	1999	PDP (APP)	PDP	PDP (APP)	AD (PDP)	PDP (APP)	PDP
	2003	ANPP (PDP)	ANPP (PDP)	PDP (ANPP)	PDP AD	PDP (ANPP)	PDP (APGA)
	2007	ANPP (PDP)	PDP ANPP	PDP ANPP	PDP AC	PDP	PDP PPA
	2011	PDP CDC	PDP CDC	PDP ANPP	ACN PDP	PDP ACN	PDP ACN

Boldfaced: Ruling party
Italicized: Leading opposition
*: Coalition with ruling party
**: Coalition with opposition

(continued)

Table 6.4	(continued)

National Assembly and State-Level Elections

Senate	1999	2003
PDP	63	73
APP/ANPP	26	28
AD	20	6

House	1999	2003
PDP	214	213
APP/ANPP	77	95
AD	69	31
Other		7

Governorships	1999	2003
PDP	21	28
APP/ANPP	9	7
AD	6	1

State Houses of Assembly	1999	2003
PDP	23	28
APP/ANPP	8	7
AD	5	1

2007 election results:

Parties	House of Representatives		Senate	
	Votes %	Seats	Votes %	Seats
People's Democratic Party	54.5	223	53.7	76
All Nigeria People's Party	27.4	96	27.9	27
Action Congress	8.8	34	9.7	6
Others	2.8	7	2.7	–

Governorships		State Assemblies	
26	PDP	28	PDP
5	ANPP	5	ANPP
2	PPA	1	PPA
2	AC	2	AC
1	APGA		

2011 Elections

Party	House Votes %	House Seats	Senate Votes %	Senate Seats	Governorships	State Assemblies
PDP	54.4	152	62.4	53	23	26

(continued)

Table 6.4		(continued)				
ACN	19.0	53	21.2	18	6	5
CDC	11.1	31	7.1	6	1	0
Others	15.4	43	9.4	8	6	5

List of Acronyms Used in Table 6.4

AC (later ACN)	Action Congress (of Nigeria)	NPN	National Party of Nigeria
AG	Action Group	NPP	Nigerian People's Party
AD	Alliance for Democracy	NRC	National Republican Convention
ANPP	All Nigerian People's Party (formerly APP)	PPA	Progress People's Alliance
APGA	All People's Grand Alliance	PRP	People's Redemption Party
APP	All People's Party	PDP	People's Democratic Party
CDC	Congress for Democratic Change		
GNPP	Great Nigerian People's Party	SDP	Social Democratic Party
NAP	Nigerian Advance Party	UPN	Unity Party of Nigeria
NCNC	National Convention of Nigerian Citizens (formerly National Council of Nigeria and the Cameroons)		
NEPU	Northern Elements Progressive Union		
NNDP	Nigerian National Democratic Party		
NPC	Northern People's Congress		
NPF	Northern Progressive Front		

Old Roots and New Alignments: The PDP and the Other Parties of the Fourth Republic

Nigerians generally reacted with anger to General Abacha's 1993 coup and his subsequent banning of the SDP and NRC. With the unions crushed and Abiola in jail by the end of 1994, democracy deteriorated. In late 1996, the Abacha government registered only five parties,[25] all of which endorsed Abacha as president for elections scheduled in August 1998, and opposition increased. A group of former governors and political leaders from the north (many former NPN and PRP members) publicly petitioned Abacha not to run for president and human rights and prodemocracy groups protested. Even General Babangida voiced his opposition to Abacha's continuing as president. The only real obstacle to Abacha's plan for "self-succession" was whether the military would allow it.

The G-34, the prominent group of civilian leaders who had condemned Abacha's plans to perpetuate his power, created the People's Democratic Party (PDP) in late August, minus most of their Yoruba members, who joined the Alliance for Democracy

(AD). At least twenty more parties applied for certification to the electoral commission (INEC); many of them were truly grassroots movements, including a human rights organization and a trade union party.

To escape the ethnic-based parties of the First and Second Republics, INEC required that parties earn at least 5 percent of the votes in twenty-four of the thirty-six states in local government elections in order to advance to the later state and federal levels. This turned out to be an ingenious way of reducing the number of parties, while obliging viable parties to broaden their appeal. The only parties to meet INEC's requirements were the PDP, AD, and the All People's Party (APP). To assuage the Yoruba over Abiola's lost 1993 mandate, the PDP turned to retired General Obasanjo, who went on to defeat an AD/APP alliance candidate in the 1999 presidential contest.

The parties of the Fourth Republic are primarily alliances of convenience among prebendal Big Men from across Nigeria. Their sole purpose is to gain power. They have no ideological differences or policy platforms that distinguish them, such that politicians who lose in one party will frequently shift to another. Yet these parties do feature one terribly important innovation that distinguishes them from those of the First and Second Republics: the PDP, the old APP (later ANPP), and now the APC and other leading parties of the Fourth Republic are multiethnic. They rely on elite-centered structures established during previous civilian governments and transition programs, and demonstrate the cross-ethnic alliances that developed over the last quarter-century. The PDP includes core members of the northern established NPN, the northern progressive PRP, and the Igbo-dominated NPP of the Second Republic, as well as prominent politicians from the Niger Delta. The APP (later ANPP) was also a multiethnic collection, drawing from the Second Republic's GNPP, a party dominated by the northeastern-based Kanuri and groups from the Middle Belt, and also features politicians who had prominent roles in the Abacha-sponsored parties. The ANPP also included northwestern politicians of royal lineage, Igbo business moguls, and southern minority leaders. The AD, however, was as Yoruba-centered as its predecessors, the UPN in the Second Republic and the AG in the First Republic. The party would later pay at the polls for its lack of national appeal, however, and would join with breakaway factions of the PDP to form the Action Congress (AC, later ACN; see below). In 2013, the ANPP and ACN would join with two other opposition parties and six defecting governors from the PDP to form the APC, a truly multiethnic, national party to rival the PDP.

This rise of multiethnic political parties is one of the most significant democratic developments of the Fourth Republic. In multiethnic parties there is a strong incentive for politicians to bargain and bridge their ethnic differences *within* the party, so that they may then compete with the other parties in the system, which would preferably be multiethnic as well.[26] In Nigeria, ethnic divisions—supported by prebendal networks—still dominate national politics, but the multiethnic parties have at least done fairly well at bridging these many divides during election periods and at fostering a climate of compromise during particularly divisive national debates.

The main vehicle whereby other African countries like Ghana have begun to rise out this elite corruption trap is through the rise of a unified, viable political opposition. Prior to 2013, the two main opposition parties, the ANPP and AD (later ACN), never organized a working relationship or a serious policy challenge to the PDP, except in the weeks prior to elections. ANPP leaders generally preferred to work with the PDP in order to gain access to government largesse, and most of its governors actually left to join the PDP by 2010. The courts, however, overturned 2007 gubernatorial races in Edo, Osun, Ondo, Ekiti, Imo, and Abia, handing these seats to several opposition parties and bringing their total number of states to thirteen.

The PDP took power again in 2011 with a massive majority across Nigeria, controlling the presidency, twenty-three governorships and twenty-six state assemblies, and more than half of the seats of the National Assembly. Yet it was also a party in disarray, with its northern factions under pressure from outrage over President Jonathan's breaking of the ethnic rotation principle, and southern leaders like former President Obasanjo angered by Jonathan's efforts to seize control of the PDP. Sensing both the limits of their small parties and opportunity in the growing rebellion within the PDP, leaders of the ANPP, ACN, and two other parties, including 2003–2011 opposition presidential candidate (and former military head of state) Muhammahu Buhari, agreed to merge to form the All Progressives Congress (APC) in 2013. Within months, they had attracted six PDP governors to their alliance, bringing their total number of states controlled to sixteen, with a majority in the Senate and near parity with the PDP in the House. Thus, for the first time in the Fourth Republic, the opposition under the APC has a serious chance at unseating the PDP in the 2015 elections. Yet the APC, like the PDP, is largely an alliance of convenience among the powerful personal networks of its "Big Men" politicians, and it will hold together only so long as it serves the interests of these powerbrokers.

Political Culture, Citizenship, and Identity

Military rule left Nigeria with strong authoritarian influences in its political culture. Most of the younger politicians of the Fourth Republic came of age during military rule and learned the business of politics from Abacha, Babangida, and their military governors. Nigeria's deep democratic traditions discussed in Section 1 remain vibrant among the larger polity, but they are in constant tension with the values imbibed during years of governance when political problems were often solved by military dictate, power, and violence rather than by negotiation and respect for law. This tension was manifest in the irony that the leading presidential contenders in 2003 were all former military men, one of whom—Buhari—was the ringleader of the 1983 coup that overthrew the Second Republic. Perhaps symbolic of a growing shift in Nigerian political culture away from its authoritarian past, however, Umaru Yar'Adua was the nation's first university graduate to become president, and Goodluck Jonathan has a Ph.D. in zoology.

Modernity versus Traditionalism

The interaction of Western (colonial) elements with traditional (precolonial, African) practices has created the tensions of a modern sociopolitical system that rests uneasily on traditional foundations. Nigerians straddle two worlds, each undergoing constant evolution. On the one hand, the strong elements in communal societies that promoted accountability have been weakened by the intrusion of Western culture oriented toward individuality, and exacerbated by urbanization. On the other hand, the modern state has been unable to free itself fully from rival ethnic claims organized around narrow, exclusivist constituencies.

As a result, exclusivist identities continue to dominate Nigerian political culture and to define the nature of citizenship.[27] Individuals tend to identify with their immediate ethnic, regional, and religious groups rather than with state institutions, especially during moments of crisis. Entirely missing from the relationship between state and citizen in Nigeria is a fundamental reciprocity—a working social contract—based on the belief that there is a common interest that binds them.

Religion

Religion has been a persistent source of comfort and a basis for conflict throughout Nigerian history. Islam began to filter into northeast Nigeria in the eleventh and twelfth centuries, spread to Hausaland by the fifteenth century, and greatly expanded in the early nineteenth century. In the north, Islam first coexisted with, then gradually supplanted, indigenous religions. Christianity arrived in the early nineteenth century, but expanded rapidly through missionary activity in the south. The amalgamation of northern and southern Nigeria in 1914 brought together the two regions and their belief systems.

These religious cultures have consistently clashed over political issues such as the secular character of the state. The application of the *shari'a* criminal code in the northern states has been a focal point for these tensions. For many Muslims, the *shari'a* represents a way of life and supreme law that transcends secular and state law; for many Christians, the expansion of *shari'a* law threatens the secular nature of the Nigerian state and their position within it. The pull of religious versus national identity becomes even stronger in times of economic hardship.

The nation is now evenly divided between Muslims and Christians, and the Middle Belt states where the fault line runs have often been particularly volatile. Communal conflicts frequently erupt in these areas, often between Fulani herdsmen, who are Muslim, and farmers, who in some instances may be Christian, or between farmers of the two religions over control of land or access to public funds. In most of these instances, religion is not the source of the conflict, but once disputes ignite they can quickly engage religious identities.

A handful of violent Islamist and Christian fundamentalist groups, however, have become active in recent years, particularly in the northeast and the Middle Belt. Most violent among these has been the *Congregation of the People of Tradition for Proselytization and Jihad*, dubbed Boko Haram by the media, meaning "Western education is sinful," for the movement's rejection of the Western pedigrees of the Nigerian elite and the Western-created Nigerian state, manifest in its secular education system, that it views as corrupt and immoral. Boko Haram seeks to establish its idiosyncratic vision of an Islamist state in Nigeria and expresses common cause with global jihadist groups like al Qaeda. Much of its activities were focused in Borno and Yobe states in the northeast until 2011, at which point it received technical assistance from al Qaeda's Algerian affiliate and expanded its scope of operations across the northeast and north central region, attacking police stations and setting off bombs, including at the UN headquarters in Abuja. President Jonathan declared a state of emergency in three states, and a counteroffensive by the Nigerian military hemmed Boko Haram largely back within its Borno and Yobe base by 2014, but it remained capable of occasional attacks as far south as Abuja.

The Press

The plural nature of Nigerian society, with the potential to engender a shared political culture, can be seen in virtually all aspects of public life. The Nigerian press has long been one of the liveliest and most irreverent in Africa. The Abacha regime moved to stifle its independence, as had Babangida. In addition, members of the media are sometimes regarded as captives of ethnic and regional constituencies, a perception that has weakened their capacity to resist attacks on their rights and privileges. Significantly, much of the Nigerian press has been based in a Lagos-Ibadan axis in the southwestern part of Nigeria and has frequently been labeled "southern." Recently, however, independent television and radio stations have proliferated around the country, and forests of satellite towers now span Nigerian cities to support the boom in Internet cafés and telecommunications. Internet-based investigative journalists such as saharareporters.com have utilized the uncensored medium of the Internet to print stories that the mainstream newspapers have been afraid to publish, exposing the corrupt activities of some of Nigeria's biggest politicians.

Interest Groups, Social Movements, and Protest

Because the political machinery was in the hands of the military throughout the 1980s and 1990s, Nigerians sought alternative means of representation and protest. Historically, labor has played a significant role in Nigerian politics, as have student groups, women's organizations, and various radical and populist organizations. Business groups have frequently supported and colluded with corrupt civilian and military regimes. In the last year of the Abacha regime, however, even the business class, through mechanisms like Vision 2010, began to suggest an end to such arbitrary rule. The termination of military rule has seen civil society groups flourish across Nigeria.

Labor

Organized labor has played an important role in challenging governments during both the colonial and postcolonial eras in several African countries, Nigeria among them. Continuous military pressure throughout the 1980s and 1990s forced a decline in the independence and strength of organized labor in Nigerian politics. The Babangida regime implemented strategies of state corporatism designed to control and co-opt various social forces such as labor. When the leadership of the Nigerian Labour Congress (NLC), the umbrella confederation, took a vigorous stand against the government, the regime sacked the leaders and appointed conservative replacements. Prodemocracy strikes in mid-1994 by the National Petroleum Employees Union (NUPENG) and other sympathetic labor groups significantly reduced oil production and nearly brought the country to a halt, whereupon the Abacha regime arrested and disbanded its leadership.

The Nigerian labor movement has been vulnerable to reprisals by the state and private employers. The government has always been the biggest single employer of labor in Nigeria, as well as the recognized arbiter of industrial relations between employers and employees. Efforts by military regimes to centralize and co-opt the unions caused their militancy and impact to wane. Moreover, ethnic, regional, and religious divisions have often hampered labor solidarity, and these differences have been periodically manipulated by the state. Nevertheless, labor still claims an estimated 2 million members across Nigeria and remains one of the most potent forces in civil society. The unions have a great stake in the consolidation of constitutional rule in the Fourth Republic and the protections that allow them to organize and act freely on behalf of their members. The NLC has called national strikes on a number of occasions since 2000, typically over wages and fuel price hikes, including the Occupy Nigeria demonstrations of 2012 (see below).

The Business Community

Nigeria has a long history of entrepreneurialism and business development. This spirit is compromised by tendencies toward rent-seeking and the appropriation of state resources. Members of the Nigerian business class have been characterized as "pirate capitalists" because of the high level of corrupt practices and collusion with state officials.[28] Many wealthy individuals have served in the military or civilian governments, while others protect their access to state resources by sponsoring politicians or entering into business arrangements with bureaucrats.

Private interests have proven surprisingly resilient, as organized groups have emerged to represent the interests of the business class and to promote general economic development. There are numerous associations throughout Nigeria representing a broad variety of business activities and sectoral interests. National business associations, such as the Nigerian Association of Chambers of Commerce, Industry, Mines, and Agriculture (NACCIMA), the largest in the country, have taken an increasingly political stance, expressing their determination to protect their interests by advocating for better governance.

Other Social Groups

Student activism continues to be an important feature of Nigerian political life, and student unions have been major players in Nigerian politics since the 1960s. Since the 1990s, however, many universities have seen the rise of what are called "cults"— gangs of young men who are typically armed and sometimes do have cultish rituals associated with their groups. Many of these cultists "graduated" to join the militias and thugs of the politicians after 2000, while the cults are also often employed by elites for their power plays. In partial response to the cult phenomenon, religious movements have proliferated across Nigerian universities, providing students with an alternative way of life to these violent groups. Yet the religious groups on campuses have also provided vehicles for encouraging and recruiting both Christian and Muslim fundamentalists.

Overall, civil society groups are making substantial contributions to consolidating democracy in Nigeria. In particular, many groups have built good working relationships with the National Assembly and state legislatures, from which both sides have benefited. Their relationships with the political parties, however, remain distant. Nigeria's prospects for building a sustainable democracy during the Fourth Republic will depend, in part, on the willingness of many of these advocacy groups to increase their collaboration with the political parties, while avoiding cooptation and maintaining a high level of vigilance and activism.

The Political Impact of Technology

The dramatic rise of cellular phones in Nigeria since 2000—adding 100 million lines in a single decade—alongside a growing presence on the Internet have transformed the nation. Cellular phones are everywhere, including the latest models, and intense competition among service providers has produced ample coverage and one of the most efficient and lucrative industries in the country. The doubling in size of Nigeria's service sector during roughly the same period, as the nation's GDP grew on average over 6 percent annually since 2003, signals that the small but rapidly rising middle class is using this technology extensively.

Although middle-class professionals were using new technologies to monitor elections as early as 2003, the 2011 election marked an important watershed moment, as civil society activists used social media to track election violations across the country and plan a more extensive effort for 2015. Most impressive, however, were the protests that followed President Jonathan's removal of fuel subsidies in January 2012. In a movement inspired by the Arab Spring and Occupy Wall Street, thousands of Nigerians took to the streets for two weeks in what became known as Occupy Nigeria. Largely and loosely organized by concerned professionals working through social media sites like Facebook and Twitter, Occupy Nigeria brought peaceful demonstrations in cities across the nation, with the largest in Lagos, Abuja, and Kano, and within days attracted the attention of Nigerian Labour Congress (NLC), which in solidarity called for a general strike that brought economic activity to a halt.

Most impressively, the movement showed none of the ethnic, religious, or sectional elements so ever-present in Nigerian politics. In fact, interfaith cooperation was evident throughout, with breathtaking pictures of Christians forming a human shield around Muslims while they performed their required daily prayers, and Muslims escorting Christians to church, as just one example. What united the protesters was a common frustration with the massive corruption throughout Nigerian governance—a progressive agenda that seeks sweeping reform and broad-based development. The demonstrations collapsed after the NLC called off the strike as it reached a bargain with the Jonathan administration that restored half of the fuel subsidy, but many of the organizers continue to extend and consolidate their networks online, and promise to mobilize again at the next opportunity—most likely the 2015 elections.

Christians form a protective ring around Muslims while they conduct their afternoon prayers in Kano during Occupy Nigeria in 2012.

Ayemoba Godswill/Demotix/Demotix/Demotix/Corbis

What can the United States or other foreign governments do to support civil society groups and social media-based movements like Occupy Nigeria so they can transform Nigeria?

Do you agree that multiethnic parties are a good idea for political development? Can you think of examples from other countries that prove or disprove the point?

NIGERIAN POLITICS IN TRANSITION

SECTION 5

Despite the slow progress of the Fourth Republic, Nigerians overwhelmingly favor democratic government over military rule. About 70 percent of respondents in a recent survey said that they still prefer democracy to any other alternative, although popular frustration is growing with the slow pace of reform and continued corruption in politics.[29] This growing anger with the massive corruption is the one constant that transcends the nation, featuring strongly in the motives of groups as different as Boko Haram and the Niger Delta militias to Occupy Nigeria. Will democracy in Nigeria be consolidated sufficiently to meet minimal levels of public satisfaction, or will the nation again succumb to destructive authoritarian rule?

Nigerian politics must change in fundamental ways for democracy to become more stable and legitimate. First and foremost, the nation must turn from a system of politics dominated by "Big Men"—for all intents and purposes, a competitive oligarchy—to a more representative mode of politics that addresses the fundamental interests of the public. Second, Nigerians must conclusively settle the national question and commit to political arrangements that accommodate the nation's diversity. In short, Nigeria's Fourth Republic must find ways of moving beyond prebendal politics and develop a truly national political process in which mobilization and conflicts along ethnic, regional, and religious lines gradually diminish, and which can address Nigeria's true national crisis: poverty and underdevelopment.

Focus Questions

- What role can political opposition and civil society play in reversing prebendalism and the politics of the "Big Men"?

- What other reforms can help to settle the National Question and harness the strong democratic yearnings of the Nigerian public?

Political Challenges and Changing Agendas

Nigeria's fitful transition to democratic rule between 1985 and 1999 was inconclusive, largely because it was planned and directed from above. This approach contrasts sharply with the popular-based movements that unseated autocracies in Central and Eastern Europe or the Arab Spring. The military periodically made promises for democratic transition as a ploy to stabilize and legitimate their governments. General Abubakar dutifully handed power to the civilians in 1999, but only after ensuring that the military's interests would be protected under civilian rule and creating an overly powerful executive that reinforces prebendalism and its patronage system. The military's rapid transition program produced a tenuous, conflicted democratic government that faces daunting tasks of restoring key institutions, securing social stability, and reforming the economy. The continuing strength and influence of collective identities, defined on the basis of religion or ethnicity, are often more binding than national allegiances. The parasitic nature of the Nigerian economy is a further source of instability. Rent-seeking and other unproductive, often corrupt, business activities remain accepted norms of wealth accumulation.

Nonetheless, Nigerians are sowing seeds of change in all of these areas. Attitudes toward the military in government have shifted dramatically. Military attitudes themselves have changed significantly as well, as evidenced by the restraint shown by the armed forces during President Yar'Adua's incapacitation and long absence. The decline in the appeal of military rule can be attributed to the abysmal performances of the Babangida and Abacha regimes in economic oversight and governance. Many now recognize that the military, apart from its contributions to national security, is incapable of promoting economic and social progress in Nigeria. Yet frustrations with corruption and poor governance have grown to the point that others still see the military as possible solution, and may call on it to intervene in a future crisis, which could have catastrophic consequences. If, however, the armed forces can stay secure in their barracks, as still seems more likely, then the nature of the struggles among civilian political elites will decide the direction of political and economic change. Thus, democratic development may be advanced in the long run if stable coalitions appear over time in a manner that balances the power among contending groups, and if these key elites adapt to essential norms and rules of the political game.

Initially, members of the new political class confined their struggles within the constraints of the democratic system: using the courts, media, legislative struggles, and even legal expediencies such as impeachment. Political actors largely worked through formal institutions, contending openly and offsetting the power of a single group or faction. Since the 2003 elections, however, the political elite have also shown a growing willingness to use extra-systemic measures to forward their interests through election rigging, corruption, and militia-led violence. The Niger Delta has grown particularly violent, with increasingly well-armed militias that in some cases have shown a measure of independence from their political patrons. The rise of Boko Haram in the northeast has created an additional threat for the Nigerian state, which politicians have also been seeking to use for political gain.

The next critical step down the long road of democratic development for Nigeria is the creation of a viable, multiethnic opposition party that is also loyal, meaning that it plays by the rules of the system. Opposition parties help to reduce corruption in the system because they have an interest in exposing the misconduct of the ruling party, which in turn pressures them to restrain their own behavior. Furthermore, in order to unseat the ruling party and win elections, opposition parties need to engage the public to win their votes. In this manner, issues of interest to the public are engaged by the parties. This is the basis of the social contract: elites gain the privilege of power so long as they use it to promote the public interest.

The introduction of so many new parties after 2002 slowed the development of a viable, loyal opposition, further diluting it and allowing the PDP to govern largely unchecked. The PDP has also worked to absorb or co-opt opposition leaders when possible. The rise of the APC in 2013, however, at last offers a real chance for Nigeria to develop two national, multiethnic parties that can check and balance each other and offer the Nigerian public a serious alternative at the ballot box. If in their competition with each other the two parties reach out to civil society for support and vie for public attentions by offering real development policies they actually seek to implement, then Nigeria will finally turn the corner toward stability and growth, joining Ghana and other regional democratic leaders. Yet the political

Protests over federal exploitation of the oil-producing Niger Delta sparked a region-wide insurgency by 2003, with heavily armed militias engaged in both political disputes and criminal activities, cutting Nigeria's oil production by more than a quarter.

PIUS UTOMI EKPEI/AFP/Getty Images

bargains holding the APC together remain tenuous, and will face tremendous strain as the election approaches. Moreover, the moment when political opposition stands in striking distance of winning an election is one of the most dangerous points in political development, as ruling parties do not often give up power quietly. The PDP shows every intention of using rigging, bribery, and violence as in previous elections, and APC politicians are no strangers to these tactics either, raising the specter of massive instability and bloodshed for the 2015 contests if the situation spirals out of control. Meanwhile, the military watches closely from the sidelines.

The project of building a coherent nation-state out of competing nationalities remains unfinished. Ironically, because the parties of the Fourth Republic generally do not represent any particular ethnic interest—indeed, they do not represent any-one's interests except those of the leaders and their clients—ethnic associations and militias have risen to articulate ethnic-based grievances. Ethnic consciousness cannot—and should not—be eliminated from society, but ethnicity cannot be the main basis for political competition. If current ethnic mobilization can be contained within ethnic associations arguing over the agenda of the parties, then it can be managed. If, however, any of the ethnic associations captures one of the political parties or joins with the militias to foment separatism, instability will result. The same is true if the PDP comes to be seen as the Christian party of the south, and the APC the Muslim party of the north, which is a danger as the APC moves to nominate a northern Muslim presidential candidate to capitalize on the frustration there with President Jonathan. President Jonathan also stoked ethnic mobilization by convening a National Conference in March 2014, which was characterized primarily by the airing of ethnic and regional grievances. Meanwhile, the Niger Delta militias and Boko Haram have both threatened to divide the country.

Democratic development also requires further decentralization of power structures in Nigeria. The struggle on the part of the National Assembly and the state governors to wrest power from the presidency has advanced this process, as has the growing competence and role of the judiciary. Privatization of government parastatals could also reduce the power of the presidency over time, since it will no longer control all the primary sectors of the economy. A more decentralized system allows local problems to be solved within communities rather than involving national institutions and the accompanying interethnic competition. Decentralization also lowers the stakes for holding national offices, thereby reducing the destructive pressures on political competition and political office. The devolution of power and resources to smaller units, closer to their constituents, can substantially enhance the accountability of leaders and the transparency of government operations.

Civil society groups are the final link in democratic consolidation in Nigeria. These groups are critical players in connecting the Nigerian state to the Nigerian people. They aggregate and articulate popular interests into the policy realm, and they provide advocacy on behalf of their members. If the political parties are to reflect anything more than elite interests and clientelist rule, the parties must reach out and build alliances with the institutions of civil society. For opposition parties like APC to become a viable opposition movement capable of checking the power of the PDP, they will have to build alliances with civil society groups in order to mobilize large portions of the population, particularly labor unions. Foreign pressure also plays an important role in maintaining the quest for democracy and sustainable development. In recent years, major external forces have been more forthright in supporting civil society and democratization in Nigeria. The United States, Britain, and some member states of the European Union quite visibly exerted pressure on Babangida and Abacha to leave and applied modest sanctions in support of democracy. These same governments again pressed Nigerian leaders to name Jonathan acting president during the crisis over President Yar'Adua's incapacitation.

Nevertheless, the Western commitment to development and democracy in Africa is limited by the industrial powers' addiction to oil, which has blunted the impact of such pressure on Nigeria, and is now exacerbated by growing competition from China for energy resources. Much of the initiative for Africa's growth therefore needs to emerge from within. In Nigeria, such initiatives will depend on substantial changes in the way Nigerians do business. It will be necessary to develop a more sophisticated and far less corrupt form of capitalist enterprise and the development of entrepreneurial, particularly middle-class interests within Nigeria who will see their interests tied to the principles of democratic politics and economic initiative. Occupy Nigeria offers hope in this regard, signifying a rising progressive, multicultural movement of professionals seeking to fundamentally change the corrupt system.

Nigerian politics has been characterized by turmoil and periodic crises ever since the British relinquished colonial power. Over fifty years later, the country is still trying to piece together a fragile democracy, yet key signs of economic growth and political reform are at last on the horizon. Despite these positive trends, the nation continues to wrestle with overdependence of its economy on oil, enfeebled infrastructure and institutions, heightened sociopolitical tensions, an irresponsible elite, and an expanding mass culture of despondency and rage. Only responsible government combined with sustained civil society action can reverse this decline and restore the nation to what President Obasanjo called "the path to greatness."

Youth Politics and the Generational Divide

Much of this great choice between development or collapse facing Nigeria may well be decided by the nation's youth. With women averaging over five births each and yet a life expectancy of only 48 years, Nigeria's population is widely skewed toward youths, such that over 70 percent of Nigerians are under the age of 30, and over half are under the age of 19. At current rates, Nigeria's population is predicted to top 400 million by 2050, the fourth largest nation in the world that will be home to approximately 280 million or more youths under age 30.

The vast majority of these youths are and will be extremely poor, with more than half trying to eke out a living on less than a dollar per day. At least a fifth of them are officially unemployed, but the real figures are much worse, especially in the northern half of the country. A few are, however, wired into the global economy through cellular and Internet technology, and their numbers are growing along-side their political sophistication and organizing skills, which they demonstrated during Occupy Nigeria. Yet the fact that Nigeria is a youth-majority state under-lines another massive political divide growing in the country: the domination of its elders. Septuagenarian and older politicians still play powerful roles in both the PDP and APC, and wealthy men in their 50s and 60s dominate the presidency, National Assembly, and governorships. On the other hand, Boko Haram, the Niger Delta militias, and other anti-state actors are dominated by the young. Which way will Nigeria's new faces turn? Much will depend upon the ability of the political parties to engage youth in their ranks, and to produce serious policies that foster broad-based development that offers opportunity and hope to the massive younger generation that is now rising.

Nigerian Politics in Comparative Perspective

The study of Nigeria has important implications for the study of African politics and, more broadly, of comparative politics. The Nigerian case embodies a number of key themes and issues that can be generalized. We can learn much about how democratic regimes are established and consolidated by understanding Nigeria's pitfalls and travails. Analysis of the historical dynamics of Nigeria's ethnic conflict helps to identify institutional mechanisms that may be effective in reducing ethnic conflict in other states. We can also learn much about the necessary and sufficient conditions for economic development, and the particular liabilities of oil-dependent states.

A Globalizing World of States

Nigeria exists in two "worlds" of states: one in the global political economy and the other within Africa. Economically, Nigeria was thrust into the world economy in a position of weakness, first as a British colony and later as an independent nation. Despite its resources and the potential of oil to provide the investment capital needed to build a modern economy, Nigeria has grown weaker. It lost much of its international clout, and in place of the international respect it once enjoyed as a developing giant within Africa, the country became notorious throughout the 1990s for corruption, human rights abuses, and failed governance. The return of democracy and soaring oil prices have restored some of Nigeria's former stature, but its economic vulnerability and persistent corruption keep it a secondary player in the world of states.

The future of democracy, political stability, and economic renewal in other parts of Africa, and certainly in West Africa, will be greatly influenced for good or ill by unfolding events in Nigeria, the giant of the continent. Beyond the obvious demonstration effects, the economy of the West African subregion could be buoyed by substantial growth in the Nigerian economy. In addition, President Obasanjo conducted very active public diplomacy across Africa, seeking to resolve major conflicts, promote democracy, and improve trade. President Yar'Adua was far less active in foreign policy, and cultivated stronger ties with China. President Jonathan has strong ties with the United States, and took a strong stance against the 2012 coup and insurgency in Mali, but has not articulated a comprehensive African policy or further abroad.

Until recently, international political and business attention shifted elsewhere on the continent, focusing on such countries as South Africa, Botswana, and Ghana. Insurgency in the Niger Delta also meant that Nigeria has fallen behind Angola as the largest oil producer on the continent. Moreover, the Boko Haram insurgency has placed Nigeria under watch by Western security agencies as a base of operations for Islamist terror groups. Yet a decade of steady economic growth, focused primarily in the south, is attracting growing investment and business interest.

Governing the Economy

Nigeria provides important insights into the political economy of underdevelopment. At independence in 1960, Nigeria was stronger economically than its Southeast Asian counterparts Indonesia and Malaysia. Independent Nigeria appeared poised for growth, with a wealth of natural resources, a large population, and the presence of highly entrepreneurial groups in many regions of the country. Today, Nigeria is among the poorest countries in the world in terms of human development indicators, while many of its Asian counterparts have joined the ranks of the wealthy countries. One critical lesson Nigeria teaches is that a rich endowment of resources is not enough to ensure economic development. In fact, it may encourage rent-seeking behavior that undermines more productive activities.[30] Sound political and institutional development must come first.

Other variables are critically important, notably democratic stability and a capable developmental state. A developmentalist ethic, and an institutional structure to enforce it, can set limits to corrupt behavior and constrain the pursuit of short-term personal gain at the expense of national economic growth. Institutions vital to the pursuit of these objectives include a professional civil service, an independent judiciary, and a free press. Nigeria has had each of these, but they were gradually undermined and corrupted under military rule. The public "ethic" that has come to dominate Nigerian political economy has been prebendalism. Where corruption is unchecked, economic development suffers accordingly.

Nigeria also demonstrates that sustainable economic development requires sound economic policy. Without export diversification, commodity-exporting countries are buffeted by the price fluctuations of one or two main products. Nigeria, by contrast, has substituted one form of commodity dependence for another, and it has allowed its petroleum industry to overwhelm all other sectors of the economy, and only recently has the non-oil sector begun to revive. Nigeria even became a net importer of products (for example, palm oil and palm nuts) for which it was once a leading world producer. Nigeria is even in the absurd position of being unable to feed itself, despite rich agricultural lands. In comparative perspective, we can see that natural resource endowments can be tremendously beneficial. The United States, for example, has parlayed its endowments of agricultural, mineral, and energy resources into one of the world's most diversified modern economies. Meanwhile, Japan, which is by comparison poorly endowed with natural resources, has one of the strongest economies in the world, achieved in large part through its unique developmental strategies. Each of these examples illustrates the primacy of sound economic policies implemented through consolidated political systems.

The Democratic Idea

Many African countries have experienced transitions from authoritarian rule.[31] With the end of superpower competition in Africa and the withdrawal of external support for Africa's despots, many African societies experienced a resurgence of popular pressures for greater participation in political life and more open forms of governance. Decades of authoritarian, single-party, and military rule in Africa left a dismal record of political repression, human rights abuses, inequality, deteriorating governance, and failed economies. A handful of elites acquired large fortunes through wanton corruption. The exercise of postcolonial authoritarian rule in Africa has contributed to economic stagnation and decline. The difficulties of such countries as Cameroon, Togo, and Zimbabwe in achieving political transitions reflects, in large part, the ruling elites' unwillingness to cede control of the political instruments that made possible their self-enrichment.

Nigeria exemplifies the harsh reality of authoritarian and unaccountable governance. Nigerians have endured six military regimes, countless attempted coups, and a bloody civil war that claimed more than 1 million lives. They have also seen a once-prospering economy reduced to a near shambles. Today, democracy has become a greater imperative because only such a system provides the mechanisms to limit abuses of power and render governments accountable.

Collective Identities

Nigeria presents an important case in which to study the dangers of communal competition in a society with deep cultural divisions. How can multiethnic countries manage diversity? What institutional mechanisms can be employed to avert tragedies such as the 1967–1970 civil war or the continuing conflicts that have brought great suffering to Rwanda and the former Yugoslavia? This chapter has suggested institutional reforms such as multiethnic political parties, decentralization, and a strengthened federal system that can contribute to reducing tensions and minimizing conflict.

Insights from the Nigerian experience may explain why some federations persist, while identifying factors that can undermine them. Nigeria's complex social map, and its varied attempts to create a nation out of its highly diverse population, enhances our understanding of the politics of cultural pluralism and the difficulties of accommodating sectional interests under conditions of political and economic insecurity. Federal character in Nigeria has become a form of ethnic and regional favoritism and a tool for dispensing patronage. Yet the country has benefited in some ways from the attention devoted to creating state and local governments, and from giving people in different regions a sense of being stakeholders in the entity called Nigeria.

Where Do You Stand?

Are you convinced that a viable political opposition—perhaps the new APC—supported by civil society could put Nigeria on the path to development, or do you think that Boko Haram, the Niger Delta militias, and prebendal "Big Man" politics will eventually push Nigeria to collapse?

Should the United States and other countries be pushing for more and deeper democracy in Africa, or does the example of Nigeria suggest it is too difficult?

Chapter Summary

Colonialism forced many nations under one political roof, ensuring that ethnic divisions would dominate the nation's politics after independence in 1960, leading to collapse and civil war. Military rule for nearly 30 years after the war, greased by rents from the oil industry, reunified Nigeria under a federal system, but also fed the prebendal pattern that has corrupted the politics of the Fourth Republic.

Nigeria's challenges reflect the frustrated hopes of its people for a better life, stable government, and a democratic political order, while suggesting the potential contributions that this country could make to the African continent and the wider international arena. Such potential depends upon responsive and capable democratic governance. If Nigeria cannot reverse the corrupt, prebendal status quo, however, then the specter will remain of military entrepreneurs, or ethnic and religious extremists, plunging Nigeria into another cycle of coups, decline, and possibly collapse.

Key Terms

accountability
acephalous societies
authoritarian
autocracy
balance of payments
clientelism
indirect rule

international financial institutions (IFIs)
interventionist
jihad
legitimacy
prebendalism
rents

shari'a
structural adjustment program (SAP)
unfinished state
warrant chiefs

Suggested Readings

Agbaje, Adigun. *The Nigerian Press: Hegemony and the Social Construction of Legitimacy, 1960–1983.* Lewiston, NY: Edwin Mellen Press, 1992.

Diamond, Larry. *Class, Ethnicity and Democracy in Nigeria: The Failure of the First Republic.* London: Macmillan, 1988.

Decalo, Samuel. *Coups and Army Rule in Africa*, 2nd ed. New Haven: Yale University Press, 1990.

Falola, Toyin. *Violence in Nigeria: The Crisis of Religious Politics and Secular Ideologies.* Rochester, NY: University of Rochester Press, 1999.

Joseph, Richard A. *Democracy and Prebendal Politics in Nigeria: The Rise and Fall of the Second Republic.* Cambridge: Cambridge University Press, 1987.

Kew, Darren. "Nigerian elections and the neopatrimonial paradox: In search of the social contract," *Journal of Contemporary African Studies* 28, no. 4 (2010): 499–521.

Lewis, Peter M. "Endgame in Nigeria? The Politics of a Failed Democratic Transition." *African Affairs* 93 (1994): 323–340.

Lubeck, Paul. *Islam and Urban Labor in Northern Nigeria.* Cambridge: Cambridge University Press, 1987.

Osaghae, Eghosa. *Crippled Giant: Nigeria since Independence.* Bloomington: Indiana University Press, 1998.

Suberu, Rotimi. *Federalism and Ethnic Conflict in Nigeria.* Washington, DC: U.S. Institute of Peace, 2001.

Suggested Websites

British Broadcasting Corporation: A 2002 interview with President Obasanjo
news.bbc.co.uk/2/hi/talking_point/1800826.stm

Gamji: A collection of news stories from Nigerian newspapers, as well as opinion pieces and other news links
www.gamji.com

The Guardian, Nigeria's leading daily newspaper
www.ngrguardiannews.com

Human Rights Watch reports
hrw.org/doc/?t=africa&c=nigeri

International Institute for Democracy and Electoral Assistance
archive.idea.int/frontpage_nigeria.htm

Stanford University's Center for African Studies
http://africanstudies.stanford.edu/

7 The Russian Federation

Joan DeBardeleben

Official Name: Russian Federation (Rossiiskaia Federatsiia)

Location: Eastern Europe/Northern Asia

Capital City: Moscow

Population (2014): 142.5 million

Size: 17,075,200 sq. km.; approximately 1.8 times the size of the United States

THE MAKING OF THE MODERN RUSSIAN STATE

Politics in Action

On February 21, 2012, an unusual performance occurred in Christ the Savior Church in central Moscow. The punk rock group known as Pussy Riot displayed what it called a "punk prayer," protesting the Russian Orthodox Church's support for incumbent President Vladimir Putin in the upcoming presidential election. Formed in 2011, the group has described itself as feminist and in opposition to the Putin regime.[1] Although Pussy Riot had previously appeared at other venues, this performance elicited particular objection from the authorities, leading to the arrest and two-year sentencing of two members for "hooliganism, motivated by religious hatred." The ruling became a cause célèbre and focus of social media attention, interpreted as symbolic of the Kremlin's lack of tolerance of political opposition.

In December 2013, in a well-publicized move, the Russian legislative body (the State Duma) passed an amnesty law, supported by President Putin. Among those freed were the two imprisoned members of Pussy Riot. At a press conference following their release, the band members expressed continuing criticism of Putin, vowing

Focus Questions ▽

- What are the most important critical junctures in recent Russian history? In what ways was each juncture a reaction to a recurring problem in Russian history?

- What were Russia's principal challenges in the 1990s and how have they changed since the year 2000?

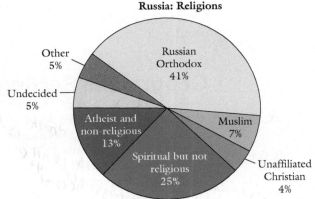

Russian Currency (₽)

Ruble
International Designation: RUB
Exchange Rate (2013):
- 1 US\$ = 31.8 RUB
- 1 RUB = 0.03 US\$
500 Ruble Design: Monument to Peter the Great

FIGURE 7.1 The Russian Nation at a Glance
© 4780322454/Shutterstock.com (for photo)

CHRONOLOGY of Soviet and Russian Political Development

1918–1928
Civil war, war communism, and the New Economic Policy

1929–1953
Stalin in power

1941–1945
Nazi Germany invades Soviet Union; "Great Patriotic War"

1965–1982
The Brezhnev era and bureaucratic consolidation

1982–1985
Leadership change after Brezhnev's death

| 1915 | 1925 | 1935 | 1945 | 1955 | 1965 | 1985 |

1929–1938
Collectivization and purges

1956–1964
The Khrushchev era and de-Stalinization

1985–1991
The Gorbachev era and *perestroika*

1917
The Bolshevik seizure of power

1953–1955
Leadership change after Stalin's death

to maintain the political struggle, with a particular focus on prisoners' rights. The amnesty, which also freed other regime critics, was widely interpreted as an effort to bolster the tarnished human rights reputation of the Russian government and head off potential boycotts of the Winter Olympics, to be held in Sochi, Russia, in February 2014.

The Pussy Riot incident became a powerful symbol of the efforts of the Russian leadership to steer a path between tight-handed political control, on the one hand, and concessions to international pressure, on the other. At the same time, increases in visible protest in Russia and often-successful efforts by the regime itself to mobilize domestic public opinion revealed deep cultural and political rifts plaguing the country.

Geographic Setting

After the Soviet Union broke up in 1991, fifteen newly independent states emerged on its territory. This section focuses on the Russian Federation, the largest successor state and the largest European country in population (142.5 million in mid-2014)[2] and, in area, the largest country in the world, spanning eleven time zones.

Russia underwent rapid industrialization and urbanization under Soviet rule. Only 18 percent of Russians lived in urban areas in 1917, at the time of the Russian Revolution; 73 percent do now. Less than 8 percent of Russia's land is arable, while 45 percent is forested. Russia is rich in natural resources, concentrated in western Siberia and northern Russia. These include minerals (even gold and diamonds), timber, oil, and natural gas, which now form the basis of Russia's economic wealth.

Before the communists took power in 1917, Russia's czarist empire extended east to the Pacific, south to the Caucasus Mountains and the Muslim areas of Central Asia, north to the Arctic Circle, and west into present-day Ukraine, eastern Poland, and the Baltic states. In the USSR the Russian Republic formed the core of a multiethnic state.

Timeline

1991
Collapse of the USSR and establishment of the Russian Federation as an independent state

1998
Financial crisis and devaluation of the ruble

2000–2008
Putin presidency, with recentralization of state power

2007–2008
Parliamentary and presidential elections establishing dominance of United Russia and smooth transition to the presidency of Dmitry Medvedev

1990   1995   2000   2005   2010   2015

1993
Adoption of the new Russian constitution by referendum; first (multiparty) parliamentary elections in the Russian Federation (December)

2004
Hostage-taking in Beslan, southern Russia; Putin announces new centralizing measures.

March 2014–
Russia takes control of the Ukrainian region of Crimea and annexes it to Russia.

March 2012–
Vladimir Putin elected as president, after a four-year break

1991–1999
Yeltsin presidency, with market and democratic reforms

December 2011–March 2012
State Duma elections and Presidential elections, and protest demonstrations

Russia's ethnic diversity and geographic scope have made it a hard country to govern. Currently Russia faces pockets of instability on several of its borders, most notably in eastern Ukraine (since early 2014), in Tajikistan and Afghanistan in Central Asia, and in Georgia and Azerbaijan in the south. Besides Ukraine, Russia's western neighbors include Belarus, and several member states of the European Union (EU), namely Finland, Estonia,

Table 7.1	Political Organization
Political System	Constitutionally a semi-presidential republic
Regime History	Re-formed as an independent state with the collapse of communist rule in December 1991; current constitution since December 1993.
Administrative Structure	Constitutionally a federal system, with eighty-three subnational governments, plus two regions annexed from neighboring Ukraine in 2014 that are not recognized by most Western countries as being part of Russia; politically centralized.
Executive	Dual executive (president and prime minister). Direct election of president; prime minister appointed by the president with the approval of the lower house of the parliament (State Duma).
Legislature	Bicameral. Upper house (Federation Council) appointed by heads of regional executive and representative organs. Lower house (*State Duma*) chosen by direct election, with mixed electoral system involving single-member districts and proportional representation for a total of 450 deputies. Powers include proposal and approval of legislation, approval of presidential appointees.
Judiciary	Independent constitutional court with nineteen justices, nominated by the president and approved by the Federation Council, holding twelve-year terms with possible renewal.
Party System	Dominant establishment party (United Russia) within a multi-party system

Latvia, Lithuania, and Poland. Located between Europe, the Islamic world, and Asia, Russia's regional sphere of influence is now disputed.

Critical Junctures

The Decline of the Russian Tsarist State and the Founding of the Soviet Union

patrimonial state

A system of governance in which the ruler treats the state as personal property (patrimony).

Until 1917, an autocratic system headed by the tsar ruled Russia. Russia had a patrimonial state that not only ruled the country but also owned the land.[3] The majority of the peasant population was tied to the nobles, the state, or the church (through serfdom). The serfs were emancipated in 1861 as a part of the tsar's effort to modernize Russia and to make it militarily competitive with the West.

The key impetus for industrialization came from the state and from foreign capital. Despite some reforms, workers became increasingly discontented, as did liberal intellectuals, students, and, later, peasants, in the face of Russia's defeat in the Russo-Japanese war and continued tsarist repression. Revolution broke out in 1905. The regime maintained control through repression and economic reform until March 1917, during the height of World War I, when revolution deposed the tsar and installed a moderate provisional government. In November, the Bolsheviks, led by Vladimir Lenin, overthrew that government.

The Bolshevik Revolution and the Establishment of Soviet Power (1917–1929)

The Bolsheviks were Marxists who believed their revolution reflected the political interests of the proletariat (working class). Most revolutionary leaders, however, were not workers, but came from a more educated and privileged stratum, the intelligentsia. Their slogan, "Land, Peace, and Bread," appealed to both the working class and the discontented peasantry—over 80 percent of Russia's population.

democratic centralism

A system of political organization developed by V. I. Lenin and practiced, with modifications, by all communist party-states. Its principles include a hierarchical party structure.

The Bolshevik strategy was based on two key ideas: democratic centralism and vanguardism. Democratic centralism mandated a hierarchical party structure in which leaders were, at least formally, elected from below, but strict discipline was required in implementing party decisions once they were made. The centralizing elements of democratic centralism took precedence over the democratic elements, as the party tried to insulate itself from informers of the tsarist forces and later from real and imagined threats to the new regime. The concept of a vanguard party governed the Bolsheviks' relations with broader social forces. Party leaders claimed to understand the interests of working people better than the people did themselves. Over time, this philosophy was used to justify virtually all actions of the party and the state it dominated.

vanguard party

A political party that claims to operate in the "true" interests of the group or class that it purports to represent, even if this understanding doesn't correspond to the expressed interests of the group itself.

In 1922 the Bolsheviks formed the Union of Soviet Socialist Republics (USSR); they were the first communist party to take state power. Prior to this, the Bolsheviks had faced an extended civil war (1918–1921), when they introduced war communism, which involved state control of key economic sectors and forcible requisitioning of grain from the peasants. The *Cheka*, the security arm of the regime, was strengthened, and restrictions were placed on other political groups. By 1921, the leadership had recognized the political costs of war communism. In an effort to accommodate the peasantry, the New Economic Policy (NEP) was introduced in 1921 and lasted until 1928. Under NEP, state control over the economy was loosened so that private enterprise and trade were revived. The state, however, retained control of large-scale industry.

Gradually, throughout the 1920s, the authoritarian strains of Bolshevik thinking eclipsed the democratic elements. Lacking a democratic tradition and bolstered by the vanguard ideology of the party, the Bolshevik leaders were plagued by internal struggles following Lenin's death in 1924. These conflicts culminated in the rise of Joseph Stalin and the demotion or exile of other prominent figures such as Leon Trotsky and Nikolai Bukharin. By 1929 all open opposition, even within the party itself, had been silenced.

The Bolshevik revolution also initiated a period of international isolation. Western countries were hardly pleased with the revolutionary developments, which led to expropriation of foreign holdings and which represented the first successful challenge to the international capitalist order. Some of Russia's former Western allies from World War I sent material aid and troops to oppose the new Bolshevik government during the civil war.

The Stalin Revolution (1929–1953)

From 1929 until his death in 1953, Joseph Stalin consolidated his power as Soviet leader. He brought changes to every aspect of Soviet life. The state became the engine for rapid economic development, with state ownership of virtually all economic assets. By 1935, over 90 percent of agricultural land had been taken from the peasants and made into state or collective farms. **Collectivization** was rationalized as a means of preventing the emergence of a new capitalist class in the countryside. It actually targeted the peasantry as a whole, leading to widespread famine and the death of millions. Rapid industrialization favored heavy industries, and consumer goods were neglected. Economic control operated through a complex but inefficient system of central economic planning, in which the state planning committee (Gosplan) set production targets for every enterprise in the country. People were uprooted from their traditional lives in the countryside and catapulted into the rhythm of urban industrial life. Media censorship and state control of the arts strangled creativity as well as political opposition. The party/state became the authoritative source of truth; anyone deviating from the authorized interpretation could be charged with treason.

Gradually, the party became subject to the personal whims of Stalin and his secret police. Overall, an estimated 5 percent of the Soviet population was arrested at one point or another under the Stalinist system, usually for no apparent cause. Forms of resistance were evasive rather than active. Peasants killed livestock to avoid giving it over to collective farms.

Isolation from the outside world was a key tool of the Stalinist system of power. But the policy had costs. While it shielded Soviet society from the Great Depression of the 1930s, the Soviet economy, protected from foreign competition, also failed to keep up with the rapid economic and technological transformation in the West.

In 1941, Nazi Germany invaded the Soviet Union, and Stalin joined the Allied powers. Casualties in the war were staggering, about 27 million people, including 19 million civilians. War sacrifices and heroism have remained powerful symbols of pride and unity for Russians up through the present day. After the war, the other Allied powers allowed the Soviet Union to absorb new territories into the USSR itself (these became the Soviet republics of Latvia, Lithuania, Estonia, Moldavia, and portions of western Ukraine). The Allies also implicitly granted the USSR free rein to shape the postwar governments and economies in East Germany, Poland, Hungary, Czechoslovakia, Yugoslavia, Bulgaria, and Romania. Western offers to include parts of the region in the Marshall Plan were rejected under pressure from the USSR. Local Communist parties gained control in each country. Only in Yugoslavia were

collectivization

A process undertaken in the Soviet Union under Stalin from 1929 into the early 1930s and in China under Mao in the 1950s, by which agricultural land was removed from private ownership and organized into large state and collective farms.

indigenous Communist forces sufficiently strong to hold power largely on their own and thus later to assert their independence from Moscow.

The USSR emerged as a global superpower as the Soviet sphere of influence encompassed large parts of Central and Eastern Europe. In 1947, the American president Harry Truman proclaimed a policy to contain further Soviet expansion (later known as the Truman Doctrine). In 1949, the North Atlantic Treaty Organization (NATO) was formed involving several West European countries, the United States, and Canada, to protect against potential Soviet aggression. In 1955 the Soviet Union initiated the Warsaw Pact in response. These events marked the beginning of the Cold War, characterized by tension and military competition between the two superpowers, leading to an escalating arms race that was particularly costly to the Soviet Union.

The Soviet Union isolated its satellite countries in Central and Eastern Europe from the West and tightened their economic and political integration with the USSR. Some countries within the Soviet bloc, however, had strong historic links to Western Europe (especially Czechoslovakia, Poland, and Hungary). Over time, these countries served not only as geographic buffers to direct Western contacts but also as conduits for Western influence.

Attempts at De-Stalinization (1953–1985)

Even the Soviet elite realized that Stalin's terror could be sustained only at great cost. The terror destroyed initiative and participation, and the unpredictability of Stalinist rule inhibited the rational formulation of policy. From Stalin's death in 1953 until the mid-1980s Soviet politics became more regularized and stable. Terror abated, but political controls remained in place, and efforts to isolate Soviet citizens from foreign influences continued.

In 1956, Nikita Khrushchev, the new party leader, embarked on a bold policy of de-Stalinization, rejecting terror as an instrument of political control. The secret police (KGB) was subordinated to the authority of the Communist Party of the Soviet Union (CPSU), and party meetings resumed on a regular basis. However, internal party structures remained highly centralized, and elections were uncontested. Khrushchev's successor, Leonid Brezhnev (party head 1964–1982), partially reversed Khrushchev's de-Stalinization efforts. Controls were tightened again in the cultural sphere. Individuals who expressed dissenting views through underground publishing or publication abroad were harassed, arrested, or exiled. However, unlike in the Stalinist period, the political repression was predictable. People generally knew when they were transgressing permitted limits of criticism.

From the late 1970s onward, an aging political leadership was increasingly ineffective at addressing mounting problems. Economic growth rates declined, living standards improved only minimally, and opportunities for upward career mobility declined. To maintain the Soviet Union's superpower status, resources were diverted to the military sector, gutting the consumer and agricultural spheres. An inefficient economic structure raised the costs of exploiting new natural resources. High pollution levels and alcoholism contributed to health problems. At the same time, liberalization in some Eastern European states and the telecommunications revolution made it increasingly difficult to shield the Soviet population from exposure to Western lifestyles and ideas. Among a certain critical portion of the population, aspirations were rising just as the capacity of the system to fulfill them was declining.

Russian Federation, February 2014

*'Yamal-Nenets (A Ok) and Khanty-Mansiisk (A Ok) are also part of Tyumen oblast.
**Nenetsia (A Ok) is also part of Arkhangel'sk oblast.

***Note: Hatching indicates that these regions are contested, as their inclusion in Russia is not recognized by large parts of the international community.

© Cengage Learning®

Perestroika and *Glasnost* (1985–1991)

Mikhail Gorbachev took office as a Communist Party leader in March 1985. He endorsed a reform program that centered around four important concepts intended to spur economic growth and bring political renewal. These were *perestroika* (economic restructuring), *glasnost* (openness), *demokratizatsiia* (a type of limited democratization), and "New Thinking" in foreign policy. Gorbachev's reform program was designed to adapt the communist system to new conditions rather than to usher in its demise.

The most divisive issues were economic policy and demands for republic autonomy. Only half of the Soviet population was ethnically Russian in 1989. Once Gorbachev opened the door to dissenting views, demands for national autonomy arose in some of the USSR's fifteen union republics. This occurred first in the three Baltic republics (Latvia, Lithuania, and Estonia), then in Ukraine, Georgia, Armenia, and Moldova, and finally in the Russian Republic itself. Gorbachev's efforts failed to bring consensus on a new federal system that could hold the country together.

Gorbachev's economic policies failed as well. Half-measures sent contradictory messages to enterprise directors, producing a drop in output and undermining established patterns that had kept the Soviet economy functioning, although inefficiently. To protect themselves, regions and union republics began to restrict exports to other regions, despite planning mandates. In "the war of laws," regional officials openly defied central directives.

Just as his domestic support was plummeting, Gorbachev was awarded the Nobel Peace Prize, in 1991. Under his New Thinking, the military buildup in the USSR was halted, important arms control agreements were ratified, and many controls on international contacts were lifted. In 1989, Gorbachev refused to prop up unpopular communist governments in the Soviet bloc in Central European countries. First in Hungary and Poland, then in the German Democratic Republic (East Germany) and Czechoslovakia, pressure from below pushed the communist parties out of power. To Gorbachev's dismay, the liberation of these countries fed the process of disintegration of the Soviet Union itself.

Collapse of the USSR and the Emergence of the Russian Federation (1991 to the Present)

In 1985 Mikhail Gorbachev drafted Boris Yeltsin into the leadership team as a nonvoting member of the USSR's top party organ, the Politburo. Ironically, Yeltsin later played a key role in the final demise of the Soviet Union. In June 1991 a popular election confirmed Yeltsin as president of the Russian Republic of the USSR (a post he had held since May of the previous year). In August 1991 a coalition of conservative figures attempted a coup d'état to halt Gorbachev's program to reform the Soviet system. While Gorbachev was held captive at his summer house (*dacha*), Boris Yeltsin climbed atop a tank loyal to the reform leadership and rallied opposition to the attempted coup. In December 1991, Yeltsin and the leaders of Ukrainian and Belorussian Republics declared the end of the Soviet Union, proposing to replace it by a loosely structured entity, the Commonwealth of Independent States.

As leader of the newly independent Russian Federation, Yeltsin took a more radical approach to reform than Gorbachev had done. He quickly proclaimed his commitment to Western-style democracy and market economic reform. However, that program was controversial and proved hard to implement. The executive and

---

glasnost

Gorbachev's policy of "openness," which involved an easing of controls on the media, arts, and public discussion.

legislative branches of the government also failed to reach consensus on the nature of a new Russian constitution; the result was a bloody showdown in October 1993, after Yeltsin disbanded what he considered to be an obstructive parliament and laid siege to its premises, the Russian White House. The president mandated new parliamentary elections and a referendum on a new constitution, which passed by a narrow margin in December 1993.

Yeltsin's radical economic reforms confronted Russians with an increasingly uncertain future marked by declining real wages, high inflation, and rising crime. Yeltsin's initial popularity was also marred by an extended military conflict to prevent Chechnya, a southern republic of Russia, from seceding from the country. Concern that separatism could spread to other regions was an important motivation for the military intervention. Despite these problems, with the help of an active public relations effort, Yeltsin was reelected president in 1996, winning 54 percent of the vote against the Communist Party candidate, Gennady Zyuganov, in a second round of voting. During his second term in office Yeltsin was plagued by poor health and continuing failed policies. In 1998 a major financial crisis added to his problems.

In 1999, Yeltsin appointed Vladimir Putin prime minister and when Yeltsin resigned as president in December 1999 Putin became Acting President. In presidential elections that followed in March 2000 Putin won a resounding victory. Putin benefited from auspicious conditions. In 1999 the economy began a period of sustained economic growth that lasted until the 2008–2009 global financial crisis. High international gas and oil prices fed tax dollars into the state's coffers.

Just as economic growth revived, worries about security increased. Instability associated with the Chechnya problem underlay a string of terrorist attacks, beginning in 1999. One particularly tragic event involved a hostage-taking on the first day of school (September 1, 2004) in the town of Beslan in southern Russia, which ended in tragedy, with more than 300 hostages killed—the majority children. Meanwhile, in March 2003, Russian authorities tried to set Chechnya on a track of

Opposition supporters stand in front of the stage during the "March of Millions" protest rally in Moscow, September 15, 2012.

MIKHAIL VOSKRESENSKY/Reuters /Landov

normalization, holding a referendum that would confirm Chechnya's status within the Russian Federation. However, intermittent violence continued.

Despite these problems, Putin recorded consistently high levels of popular support throughout his tenure and successfully managed the transition to his hand-picked successor as president, Dmitry Medvedev, who won the 2008 presidential elections handily. Putin introduced political reforms marked by increased political centralization, restrictions on political opposition, and the growing dominance of one political party, United Russia. Since 2000 Russia has been characterized by a drift to a form of soft authoritarianism, in which formal and informal mechanisms secure the dominance of the ruling group. When the economic-financial crisis took hold in 2008, a new source of insecurity arose. With the decline in oil and gas prices, Russia's main export commodities, the economic upturn was interrupted. In 2009 Russian President Medvedev announced a modernization program to address some of the imbalances in the Russian economy, but the momentum for reform proved to be weak. The December 2011 legislative elections reconfirmed the dominance of United Russia and elections in March 2012 reinstated Putin as president. However, charges of election fraud and unfair electoral conditions led to mass protests in major Russian cities and throughout the country.

soft authoritarianism

A system of political control in which a combination of formal and informal mechanisms ensure the dominance of a ruling group or dominant party, despite the existence of some forms of political competition and expressions of political opposition.

Themes and Comparisons

Following the collapse of the USSR in 1991, international support for the new reform-oriented government in Russia surged, with the proliferation of aid programs and international financial credits. However, in the 1990s, Russia's status as a world power waned, and the expansion of Western organizations (NATO, EU) to Russia's western border undermined its sphere of influence in Central and Eastern Europe. Russia's western neighbors began to look to Europe as a guidepost for the future. But Russia's economic recovery following 1998, the rise of energy prices, and Europe's dependence on imports of Russian energy resources fueled Russia's renewed international influence. Over time, despite American efforts to "reset" the relationship in a positive direction, tensions have reasserted themselves between Russia and the West. These have included differing position on issues such as the Syrian crisis, American intentions to install a missile shield in Central Europe to guard against a potential Iranian attack, and policies toward Russia's neighbors such as Ukraine and Georgia. In an effort to assert Russia's regional influence, in 2011 Putin announced the intent to create a Eurasian Union, as a counterpoint to the European Union; efforts have also increased to reinforce cooperation with other rising powers such as China. Shortly after the Sochi Olympics, in February 2014, a political crisis in neighboring Ukraine led to the removal of the Russia-leaning president, Victor Yanukovych, and put in place a pro-Western interim government; these changes elicited a Russian military takeover and quick annexation of Ukraine's southern region of Crimea, undoing much of the goodwill that Russia had won in hosting the Olympics. Western governments refused to recognize Russia's annexation of Crimea, and instituted sanctions to deter Russia from further violations of Ukraine's territorial sovereignty. In August 2014, Russia announced countersanctions that would restrict imports of some Western food products.

For nearly a decade after the collapse of the Soviet system, the Russian Federation was mired in a downward spiral of economic decline. After 1998, however, growth rates recovered, budget surpluses became routine, and the population experienced a marked increase in economic confidence. Questions arose, however, about the depth of the economic recovery. The temporary drop in energy prices associated with the 2008 financial crisis and ensuing global recession revealed that Russia's economic strategy, which relies heavily on the export of natural resources to support the state budget, makes the country vulnerable to fluctuations in the global economy. Although many important policy problems have been addressed, others remain unresolved, including inadequate levels of foreign investment, capital flight, continuing high levels of inequality, and a decline in the agricultural sector.

Concerns about the fate of Russian democracy have also become widespread in the West and have elicited increased public protests within Russia. While the constitution adopted in 1993 has gained a surprising level of public acceptance, domestic opponents express intensified concern that increasing centralization of power and institutional changes adopted after 2000 have undermined real political competition. The regime justifies these changes as necessary to ensure state capacity to govern and to secure continuing economic growth, but critics see Russia as moving in the direction of electoral authoritarianism, where political competition is "managed" by the president's office through a dominant political party, United Russia. High levels of corruption still pervade the Russian political and economic system, despite the proclaimed commitment of the political leadership to curtail them.

Finally, Russians continue to seek new forms of collective identity. The loss of superpower status, doubts about the appropriateness of Western economic and political models, and the absence of a widely accepted ideology have all contributed to uncertainty about what it means to be Russian. Russia itself suffers from internal divisions as well. Although overt separatism has been limited to the Republic of Chechnya, differing visions of collective identity have emerged in some of Russia's ethnic republics, particularly in Muslim areas. A revival of Russian nationalism, directed partly at the West and partly at non-Christian ethnic minority groups, is of increasing concern. Diverging views about gender roles and the legitimacy of diverse definitions of sexual orientation have become increasingly visible. A particular focus of international criticism relates to a Russian law passed in 2013 that imposes fines for "propagandizing" minors about nontraditional sexual relations.

Many countries have attempted a transition from authoritarian rule to democratic governance. In Russia's case, one of the most important factors affecting this process is the tradition of strong state control, stretching from tsarist times through the Soviet period, and now influencing present developments. In addition, the intertwined character of politics, economics, and ideology in the Soviet Union has made reform difficult. In effect, four transition processes were initiated simultaneously in the early 1990s: democratization, market reform, a redefinition of national identity, and integration into the world economy. Whereas other democratizing countries may have undergone one or two of these transitions, Russia initially tried to tackle all four at once. Because the former communist elites had no private wealth to fall back on, corrupt or illegal methods were sometimes used by Russia's emerging capitalist class to maintain former privileges. Citizens, confronted with economic decline and an ideological vacuum, have been susceptible to appeals to nationalism and for strong state control. No doubt, economic uncertainty has made the Russian public willing to accept strong leadership and limits on political expression that would be resisted in many Western countries. Russia's current "backsliding" from democratic development may, in part, reflect the difficulties of pursuing so many transitions at once.

Some countries rich in natural resources, such as Norway, have achieved sustained economic growth and stable democratic systems. In other cases, and this perhaps applies to Russia, such dependence on natural resource wealth has produced a "resource curse," leaving other economic sectors underdeveloped and uncompetitive, with the country highly vulnerable to global economic fluctuations. In the Russian case, the concentration of economic power associated with the natural resource sector has also fed high levels of inequality and corruption.

Where Do You Stand?

Mikhail Gorbachev was awarded the Nobel Peace Prize in 1991 and is credited in the West with having brought a peaceful end to Soviet rule. However, most Russians hold Gorbachev in low regard. How do you evaluate the historical significance of Gorbachev?

Is the centralization of power that has occurred under President Vladimir Putin justified in order to foster economic stability and stable government?

SECTION 2

POLITICAL ECONOMY AND DEVELOPMENT

▽ Focus Questions

- What were Russia's most difficult problems in moving from the Soviet command economy to a market economy?

- How have social policies changed in Russia since the Soviet period?

The collapse of the Soviet system in late 1991 ushered in a sea change, radically reducing the state's traditionally strong role in economic development and opening the Russian economy to foreign influence. However, the process of market reform that the Russian government pursued after 1991 brought with it an immediate dramatic decline in economic performance as well as fundamental changes in social relationships. After experiencing an unprecedented period of economic depression from 1991 to 1998, Russia experienced renewed economic growth, but this growth was built largely on the country's wealth of energy and natural resources. With the economic/financial crisis of 2008–2009, prices of oil and natural gas declined but recovered relatively quickly, avoiding major economic impacts. The Russian economy remains, however, highly dependent on natural resource exports, which introduces long-term economic risks. Under Vladimir Putin, the role of the state in key government sectors has been strengthened so that Russia's market economic system has distinctive features compared to Western systems. Extreme levels of social inequality and corruption also characterize the system.

State and Economy

In the Soviet period, land, factories, and all other important economic assets belonged to the state. Short- and long-term economic plans defined production goals, but these were frequently too ambitious. Except in the illegal black market and peasant market, prices were controlled by the state and production was unresponsive to demand.

The Soviet economic model registered some remarkable achievements: rapid industrialization, provision of social welfare and mass education, relatively low levels of inequality, and advances in key economic sectors such as the military and space industries. Nonetheless, over time, top-heavy Soviet planning could neither sustain rising prosperity at home nor deliver competitive products for export. Gorbachev's efforts to adapt Soviet economic structures to meet these challenges were largely unsuccessful.

Following the collapse of the USSR, Russian president Boris Yeltsin endorsed a more radical policy of **market reform**. Four main pillars of his program were (1) lifting price controls, (2) encouraging small private businesses and entrepreneurs, (3) privatizing most state-owned enterprises, and (4) opening the economy to international influences. In January 1992, price controls on most goods were loosened or removed entirely. As a result, the consumer price index increased by about 2,500 percent between December 1991 and December 1992. Real wages declined by 50 percent. Economic troubles continued throughout most of the 1990s.

Privatization in Russia was rapid compared to most other post-communist countries. By early 1994, 80 percent of medium-sized and large state enterprises in designated sectors of the economy had privatized; however, they often did not achieve the desired result of improving efficiency and competitiveness. The most widely adopted method, called **insider privatization**, hampered reform of business operations and reduced the expected gains of privatization. Managers, many of whom did not have the skills needed to operate in a market environment, were reluctant to lay off excess labor or resisted overtures by outside investors who might gain control of the enterprise. Some managers extracted personal profit from enterprise operations rather than investing available funds to improve production. Productivity and efficiency did not increase significantly; unprofitable firms continued to operate. When the sale of shares was opened to outside investors, many firms were unattractive because backward technology would require massive infusions of capital. Some of the more attractive enterprises fell into the hands of developing financial–industrial conglomerates that had acquired their wealth through positions of power or connections in the government. At the same time, new ventures, which were generally more efficient than former state firms, faced obstacles: confusing regulations, high taxes, lack of capital, and poor infrastructure (transport, banking, communications).

Reform of agriculture was even less satisfactory. Large joint-stock companies and associations of individual households were created on the basis of former state and collective farms. These privatized companies operated inefficiently, and agricultural output declined. Foreign food imports also undercut domestic producers, contributing to a downward spiral in agricultural investment and production.

A key obstacle to the success of the market reform agenda in the 1990s was the weakness of state institutions. Without an effective tax collection system, for instance, the government could not acquire revenues to pay its own bills on time, provide essential services to the population, and ensure a well-functioning economic infrastructure (such as transportation, energy, public utilities). A weak state meant inadequate regulation of the banking sector and poor enforcement of health, safety, and labor standards. As the state failed to carry out these functions, businesses took matters into their own hands, for example, by hiring private security services for protection, or by paying bribes. Ineffective government fed corruption and criminality.

The central state in Moscow also had difficulty exerting its authority in relation to regional officials and in the face of increasing power of business **oligarchs**. These wealthy individuals benefited from privatization and often wielded significant political influence. Diverse methods of laundering money to avoid taxes became widespread. Corruption involving government officials, the police, and operators abroad fed a rising crime rate. Rich foreigners, Russian bankers, and outspoken journalists became targets of the Russian mafia.

A financial crisis in August 1998 brought the situation to a head. Following a sharp upturn in 1996–1997, in August 1998 the Russian stock market lost over 90 percent of its value. The government defaulted on its bonds. Many Russian banks, holders of the government's short-term bonds, faced imminent bankruptcy. The

market reform

A strategy of economic transformation that involves reducing the role of the state in managing the economy and increasing the role of market forces.

insider privatization

The transformation of formerly state-owned enterprises into joint-stock companies or private enterprises in which majority control is in the hands of employees and/or managers.

oligarchs

A small group of powerful and wealthy individuals who gained ownership and control of important sectors of Russia's economy in the context of privatization of state assets in the 1990s.

Russians shop at the Apraksin Dvor market in St. Petersburg.

Yadid Levy/Alamy

government began to print more of the increasingly valueless rubles, threatening to undermine the ruble's value further and thus intensify the underlying financial crisis.

The government finally allowed a radical devaluation of the ruble. Within a two-week period, the ruble lost two-thirds of its value against the U.S. dollar, banks closed or allowed only limited withdrawals, supplies of imported goods decreased,

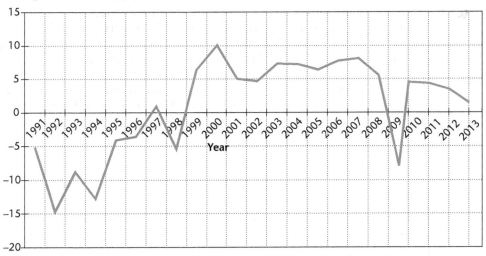

FIGURE 7.2 **Economic Decline and Recovery (gross domestic product), as percent of previous year**

Source: This figure is reproduced from *Introduction to Comparative Politics* (Cengage 6th edition, 2013) with addition of data from the Federal State Statistics Service of the Russian Federation website.

and business accounts were frozen—forcing some firms to lay off employees and others to close their doors. However, despite these effects, the 1998 financial crisis ushered in positive changes. First, the devalued ruble made Russian products more competitive with foreign imports. Firms were able to improve their products, put underused labor back to work, and thus increase productivity. The state budget benefited from improved tax revenues. Economic growth revived, beginning in 1999.

When Vladimir Putin became president in the year 2000, he set about strengthening the capacity of the state to maintain the growth impetus. He introduced a set of legislative reforms to spur recovery. A 13 percent flat income tax, deemed easier to enforce, was one very visible aspect of the package. A budget surplus replaced a deficit. By 2007 the Russian government had lowered its debt burden to 3 percent of GDP. Foreign reserves grew from just $12 billion (U.S.) in 1998 to about $500 billion (U.S.) in March 2008.[4] Putin also took measures to limit the power of economic oligarchs who used their financial positions to affect political outcomes. A prominent case involved Mikhail Khodorkovsky, the chief executive officer and major shareholder of the giant Russian oil company, Yukos. In 2003 Khodorkovsky was placed under arrest for fraud and tax evasion, and in May 2005 he was sentenced by a Russian court to nine years in prison. In December 2013 Khodorkovsky was pardoned and released from prison, a move that many observers interpreted as attempt to gain Western approval in the lead up to the February 2014 Winter Olympics in Sochi, Russia.

Despite Putin's successes in securing a revival of economic growth, corruption has remained a major obstacle to effective economic management. Transparency International's annual Corruption Perceptions index, based on a compilation of independent surveys, ranked Russia 127th out of the 177 countries surveyed in 2013,[5] indicating high levels of corruption and only a marginal improvement over previous ratings.

Society and Economy

The regime's social goals also produced some of the most marked achievements of the Soviet system. These achievements created a set of public expectations that continue to influence current policy choice. Benefits to the population in the Soviet period included free health care, low-cost access to essential goods and services, maternity leave (partially paid), child benefits, disability pensions, and mass education. In a short period of time, universal access to primary and secondary schooling led to nearly universal literacy under Soviet rule. Postsecondary education was free of charge, with state stipends provided to university students. Guaranteed employment and job security were other priorities. Almost all able-bodied adults, men and women alike, worked outside the home. Citizens received many social benefits through the workplace, and modest pensions were guaranteed by the state, ensuring a stable but minimal standard of living for retirement.

The Soviet system, however, was plagued by shortages and low-quality service. For example, advanced medical equipment was in limited supply. Sometimes under-the-table payments were required to prompt better-quality service. Many goods and services were scarce. Housing shortages restricted mobility and forced young families to share small apartments with parents. Productivity was low by international standards, and work discipline weak. Drunkenness and absenteeism were not unusual.

As a matter of state policy, wage differentials between the best- and worst-paid were lower than in Western countries. While having social benefits, this approach also reduced the incentive for outstanding achievements and innovation. Due to state ownership, individuals could not accumulate wealth in real estate, stocks, or businesses. Although political elites had access to scarce goods, higher-quality health care, travel, and vacation homes, these privileges were hidden from public view.

The Soviet experience led Russians to expect the state to ensure a social welfare network, but in the 1990s, budget constraints necessitated cutbacks, just when social needs were greatest. Although universal health care remained, higher-quality care and access to medicine depended more obviously on ability to pay. Benefits provided through the workplace were cut back, as businesses faced pressures to reduce costs. At the same time, some groups benefited from market reforms, including those with Western language skills and those employed in the natural resources, banking, and financial sectors. At the top of the scale are the super-wealthy, including people who appropriated benefits during the privatization process or engaged in successful business activity afterwards. However, losers have been more numerous. Poverty is highest among rural residents, the unemployed, children, the less educated, pensioners, and the disabled. As a result of low wage levels, the majority of those in poverty are the working poor.

Following the economic upturn that began in 1999, large differentials in income and wealth have persisted, but the portion of the population living below the subsistence level declined after 1999. In addition average real disposable income has increased. Beginning in 2000, levels of personal consumption began to rise, but many individuals still hold two to three jobs just to make ends meet. Social indicators of economic stress (such as a declining birthrate, suicide rate, and murder rate) began to decline after 2002, but only slowly. The economic-financial crisis of 2008–2009 introduced new economic uncertainties just when many Russians were beginning to feel that life was returning to normal.

In recent years, maintenance of existing levels of state support for social programs has been a contentious issue. Massive street demonstrations occurred in several Russian cities in early 2005 over changes to social welfare policy. Called "monetarization of social benefits," the reforms involved replacing certain services (such as public transport) that had been provided free to disadvantaged groups (pensioners, veterans, the disabled) with a modest monetary payment to the individual. Many Russians viewed the measures as involving direct reductions in social welfare benefits. After large-scale demonstrations, the government agreed to accompany the reforms by a modest increase in pensions and to restore subsidized transport. Learning from this experience the government has attempted to avoid cuts in social welfare measures and pensions since, even during the economic-financial crisis of 2008.

Russia saw a steady decline in population until 2009, mitigated to some extent by a positive inflow of immigrants, particularly from other former Soviet republics. Life expectancy in 2011 was estimated at 63 years for Russian men and 75 years for women, an improvement over the 1990s but still lower than in Western societies. Primary factors contributing to the high mortality rates include stress related to social and economic dislocation and unnatural causes of death (accidents, murders, suicides).

Both Putin and Medvedev introduced policies to encourage a rising birthrate, such as higher child support payments, and monetary and other benefits for women having two or more children. Birthrates had begun to rise already in 1999, so it is hard to know how much of the continuing increase is due to government policy. Although declining birthrates often accompany economic modernization, the extraordinary economic stresses of the 1990s exacerbated this tendency; the restoration of economic growth in the late l990s may have reduced the reluctance of many couples to have children, but the birthrate still is well below levels of the 1980s. Women continue to carry the bulk of domestic responsibilities while also working

Wearing shirts that read "Is something wrong? Give birth," Russian pensioners took part in a flash mob in Moscow's underground in May 2011. According
to organizers, the goal of the action was to encourage Russian women to get
pregnant and increase the nation's birthrate.

Denis Sinyakov/Landov

outside the home to boost family income. Many women take advantage of the permitted three-year maternity leave, which is only partially paid, but difficulties in
reconciling home and work duties no doubt contribute to low birthrates as well.

Russia's ethnic and regional diversity also has economic implications. Levels of
development vary greatly across the country's federal units, with major cities (such
as Moscow and St. Petersburg), as well as regions rich in natural resources, being the
most affluent.

Environmental Issues

In the Soviet period, an emphasis on economic growth at the expense of environmental protection resulted in high levels of air and water pollution, with associated
health problems. Inadequate technological safeguards and an insufficient regulatory
structure led to the disastrous nuclear accident at Chernobyl (now in Ukraine) in
1986, which produced long-lasting contamination of immense areas of agricultural
land in Ukraine, as well as in some areas of Russia. Following the Chernobyl accident, under Gorbachev's *glasnost* policy, citizen environmental awareness and activism increased, often associated with assertions of national identity in the various
republics of the USSR, including Russia. In 1988, under Gorbachev's leadership a
specific environmental protection agency was created.

Following the collapse of the USSR, the newly independent Russian state was preoccupied with other problems, in the face of the major economic downturn of the 1990s. The country's heavy economic reliance on resource-extraction industries brought with it higher than average environmental impacts. In May 2000, the State Committee for Environmental Protection (the successor to the environmental agency created in 1988) was abolished with most of its responsibilities moved to a new ministry (now called the Ministry of Natural Resources and Ecology). This model of mixing oversight of use and protection of nature in a single agency may be an indicator of the low priority assigned to environmental protection, as compared to resource use.

A particular priority for the European Union was to gain Russian ratification of the Kyoto Protocol, an international agreement to reduce greenhouse gas emissions and to address the dangers of climate change. Given the failure of the United States to support the agreement, Russia's signature was needed to put the agreement into effect. Russia ratified the Kyoto Protocol in 2004. However, this involved minimal commitment since Russia's greenhouse gas emission levels had decreased as a result of production downturns of the 1990s. In 2012 Russia declined further commitments under a second phase of the agreement. However, the proportion of global carbon emissions from Russia exceeds it relative share of the global population and GDP.[6] The relatively low utilization of renewable energy sources and highly inefficient use of energy in Russia suggest that Russia's environmental performance has clear avenues for improvement, and the Russian government has expressed support for such measures, even if their implementation has so far been weak.

Russia in the Global Economy

During the Soviet period, the economy was largely isolated from outside influences, as foreign trade was channeled through central state organs. However, things changed after 1991. Over time, the ruble was allowed to respond to market conditions, and firms were permitted to conclude agreements directly with foreign partners. Western governments and international organizations such as World Bank, the International Monetary Fund (IMF), and the European Union (EU) contributed substantial amounts of economic assistance, often in the form of repayable credits. After the August 1998 crisis, the Russian government defaulted, first on the ruble-denominated short-term debt, and then on the former Soviet debt. Since then, debt repayments have been made on time. In 2001, the government decided to forgo additional IMF credits. By 2005, it had paid off its IMF debt.

Russia has also become more open to foreign investment. However, levels still remain low compared to other East European countries, despite improvements since 2004. The inflow of West European investment capital was negatively affected by the financial and economic crisis there since 2008, and is likely to be negatively impacted in the future by the crisis over Ukraine and associated Western sanctions against Russia. Major sources of foreign direct investment since 2000 have been Germany, the United States, and Cyprus (mainly recycled Russian capital, previously exported for tax reasons), but foreign investors are, since 2006, prevented from gaining a majority share in certain sectors of the economy that are identified as of strategic importance. After an extended accession process, in 2012 Russia was admitted to the World Trade Organization (WTO). Initial adaptation costs have included difficulties in some sectors, such as the agricultural and food industries, due to increased competition, as well as lost tariff revenue. However, it is expected that in the medium to long run WTO membership will contribute significantly to economic growth.

The geographic focus of Russia's foreign trade activity has shifted markedly since the Soviet period. Whereas in 1994 Ukraine was Russia's most important trading partner, in 2011 the top spots were filled by Germany (11.0 percent of imports to Russia), the Netherlands (receiving 10.8 percent of Russian exports), and China (the largest source of Russian imports, 14 percent). Overall in 2012 the EU provided 34 percent of Russian imports and 45 percent of its exports, while imports from Russia were only 11.9 percent of the EU's total, with exports to Russia making up 7.3 percent. A substantial portion (about three-quarters) of Russia's export commodities to Europe are mineral resources (including energy resources), while about half of the EU's exports to Russia are machinery and transport equipment, resulting in an assymetrical trade relationship.[7] In the face of increased tensions with the West, Russia is seeking to increase energy exports to China.

Russia's position in the international political economy remains undetermined. With a highly skilled workforce, high levels of educational and scientific achievement, and a rich base of natural resources, Russia has many of the ingredients necessary to become a competitive and powerful force in the global economy. However, if the country's industrial capacity is not restored, reliance on natural resource exports will leave Russia vulnerable to global economic fluctuations in supply and demand.

GLOBAL CONNECTIONS

Russia and International Organizations

Russia has achieved membership in many international and regional organizations such the World Bank, the International Monetary Fund, the Council of Europe, and the World Trade Organization. In other cases, Russia has forged partnerships with organizations for which membership is currently not foreseen (e.g., the European Union or the North Atlantic Treaty Organization, NATO). Relations with three regional organizations are profiled here:

The European Union (*EU*). Russia has not expressed a desire to join the European Union, but in 1997 a ten-year Partnership and Cooperation Agreement (PCA) between the EU and Russia went into effect, setting the basis for a "strategic partnership." Discussions to renew the agreement are still underway. In 2003 the EU and Russia agreed on four "Common Spaces" of cooperation, relating to economic relations; common borders; external security; and research, education, and culture. In 2007 the EU and Russia initiated a process to facilitate the issuance of visas for Russians wishing to visit the EU, and in 2010 they announced a Modernization Partnership. The conflict over Ukraine in 2014 introduced a setback to progress in these and other areas.

The Council of Europe (distinct from the European Union) is the major European vehicle for the defense of human rights, enforced through the European Court of Human Rights (ECHR) in Strasbourg, France. Russia acceded to the organization in 1996 and ratified the European Convention on Human Rights in 1998. In joining the Council of Europe, Russia subjected itself to periodic reviews and to the judgments of the ECHR, along with a number of other obligations. Thousands of human rights cases involving Russia have been brought to the ECHR, many related to the Chechnya conflict, and most judgments have gone against Russia.

The North Atlantic Treaty Organization (*NATO*) was originally formed after World War II to safeguard its members on both sides of the Atlantic from the Soviet threat. Following the collapse of the communist system, NATO has had to rethink its mandate and the nature of potential threats. Among its redefined duties are crisis management, peacekeeping, opposing international terrorism, and prevention of nuclear proliferation. Since 1999 many countries of Central and Eastern Europe have been admitted as members. Russia has objected to the expansion of NATO at each step. Russia has, nonetheless, over time, developed a stronger working relationship with the organization, including the agreement on the NATO-Russia Founding Act on Mutual Relations in 1997, formation of the NATO-Russia Council in 2002, and, an agreement in November 2010 to undertake a Joint Review of 21st Century Common Security Challenges. The conflict over Ukraine in 2014 may undermine these efforts.

MAKING CONNECTIONS How has NATO enlargement affected Russia's relations with the West?

In 2010, about **69** percent of exports were mineral products (i.e., fuels and energy resources), whereas only about **5.7** percent were machinery and equipment, with other resources such as metals and timber making up a large part of the balance.[8] Furthermore, levels of capital investment and technological innovation have not been adequate to fuel increased productivity; even in the lucrative energy sector, experts doubt whether, without significant foreign involvement, Russian firms will be able to develop new reserves adequate to meet both domestic needs and contractual obligations to foreign (at this point mainly European) consumers. At the same time, its wealth in natural resources has given Russia advantages compared to its neighbors, since these expensive materials do not need to be imported. Ultimately, Russia's position in the global economy will depend on the ability of the country's leadership to address domestic economic challenges and to facilitate differentiation of the country's export base.

Where Do You Stand?

Do you think that a strong role for the state in economic affairs makes sense in Russia, given the country's history?

What measures do you think could be taken to bring corruption under control in Russia?

SECTION 3

GOVERNANCE AND POLICY-MAKING

▽ Focus Questions

• Why has the Russian leadership viewed centralization as necessary and what centralizing measures have been taken since 2000?

• What is the relationship between the prime minister and the president in Russia? How have the particular individuals who have filled these posts helped to shape this relationship?

In the 1990s the Russian leadership, under Boris Yeltsin, endorsed liberal democratic principles, and subsequent Russian presidents, both Vladimir Putin and Dmitry Medvedev, have reaffirmed their commitment to democracy. However, over time, the interpretation of how democratic governance should be interpreted to make it compatible with Russia's unique political tradition has become contested. Skeptics see Putin's measures to strengthen presidential power as undermining many of the Russian Federation's founding democratic principles. Protests reached a high point in late 2011 and early 2012, when large public demonstrations in Moscow and other major cities questioned the fairness of the legislative and presidential elections. In response, Vladimir Putin, reelected as president in March 2012 after a four-year interlude, endorsed a mix of concessions and heightened controls that elicited continuing debate about the fate of Russia's democratic experiment.

Organization of the State

In the Soviet period, before Gorbachev's reforms, top organs of the Communist Party of the Soviet Union (CPSU) dominated the state. The CPSU was hierarchical. Lower party bodies elected delegates to higher party organs, but elections were uncontested, and top organs determined candidates for lower party posts. The Politburo, the top party organ, was the real decision-making center. A larger body, the Central Committee, represented the broader political elite, including regional party leaders and representatives of various economic sectors. Alongside the CPSU were Soviet state structures, which formally resembled Western parliamentary systems but had little decision-making authority. The state bureaucracy had day-to-day responsibility in both the economic and political spheres but followed the party's directives in all matters. People holding high state positions were appointed through the *nomenklatura* system, which allowed the CPSU to fill key posts with politically reliable individuals. The Supreme Soviet, the parliament, was a rubber-stamp body.

The Soviet constitution was primarily symbolic, since many of its principles were ignored in practice. The constitution provided for legislative, executive, and judicial organs, but separation of powers was considered unnecessary because the CPSU claimed to represent the interests of society as a whole. When the constitution was violated (frequently), the courts had no independent authority to enforce or protect its provisions. Likewise, the Soviet federal system was phony, since all aspects of life were overseen by a highly centralized Communist Party. Nonetheless, the various subunits that existed within the Russian Republic of the USSR were carried over into the Russian Federation in an altered form.

Gorbachev introduced innovations into the Soviet political system: competitive elections, increased political pluralism, reduced Communist Party dominance, a revitalized legislative branch of government, and renegotiated terms for Soviet federalism. He also tried to bring the constitution into harmony with political reality. These changes moved the political system haltingly and unevenly closer to the liberal democratic systems of the West.

Likewise, even before the collapse of the USSR, political institutions began to change in the Russian Republic, which was only one of fifteen federal units that made up the Soviet Union. A new post of president was created, and on June 12, 1991, Boris Yeltsin was elected by direct popular vote as its first incumbent. Once the Russian Federation became independent in December 1991, a crucial turning point in its development was the adoption by referendum of a new Russian constitution in December 1993. This constitution provides the legal foundation for current state institutions and by now seems to have acquired broad-based popular legitimacy.

The document affirms many established principles of liberal democratic governance—competitive multiparty elections, separation of powers, an independent judiciary, federalism, and protection of individual civil liberties. At the same time, the president and executive branch are granted strong powers. Despite this, in reality, in the 1990s the state demonstrated only a weak capacity to govern, involving dysfunctional conflict between major institutions of government. Subnational governments demanded increased autonomy, even sovereignty, generating a process of negotiation and political conflict between the center and the regions that sometimes led to contradictions between regional and federal laws. The constitution made the executive dominant but still dependent on the agreement of the legislative branch to realize its programs. Under President Yeltsin, tension between the two branches of government was a persistent obstacle to effective governance. In addition, establishing real judicial independence remained a significant political challenge.

During Vladimir Putin's first term (2000–2008) the power of the presidency was augmented further in an effort to address the weakness of central state authority. Many observers feel, however, that Putin's centralizing measures have undermined the very checks and balances that were supposed to protect against reestablishment of authoritarian control. In addition, inadequate salaries, and lack of professionalism in the civil service have made it difficult to control widespread corruption and misuse of political power.

nomenklatura

A system of personnel selection in the Soviet period under which the Communist Party maintained control over the appointment of important officials in all spheres of social, economic, and political life.

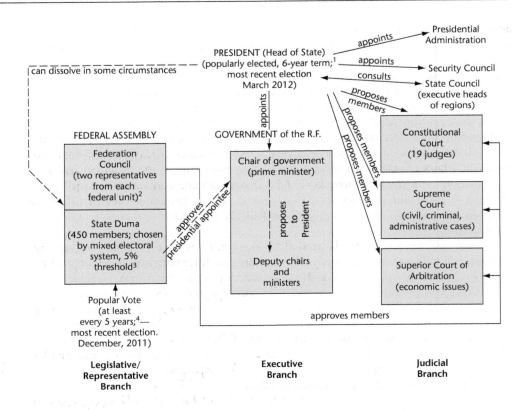

¹Before 2012 the term was 4 years.
²One representative appointed by the regional legislature and one by the regional excutive.
³Was a nationwide proportional representation system from 2007–2013, with 7% threshold. Until 2007 half of seats were chosen in single-member-districts and half by proportional representation with a 5% threshold.
⁴Prior to 2011–2012 the term was 4 years.

FIGURE 7.3 Political Institutions of the Russian Federation (R.F.) 2014

The Executive

The constitution establishes a semi-presidential system, formally resembling the French system but with stronger executive power. As in France, the executive itself has two heads (the president and the prime minister), introducing a potential context for intrastate tension. The president is also the head of state, and, except between 1998 and 2000 and between 2008 and 2012, this office held primary power. The prime minister, appointed by the president but approved by the lower house of the parliament (the State Duma, hereafter Duma), is the head of government. As a rule of thumb, the president has overseen foreign policy, relations with the regions, and the organs of state security, while the prime minister has focused his attention on the economy and related issues. However, with Yeltsin's continuing health problems in 1998 and 1999, operative power shifted in the direction of the prime minister. In December 1999, Yeltsin resigned from office, making the prime minister, Vladimir Putin, acting president until he was himself elected president in March 2000.

One of the president's most important powers is the authority to issue decrees, which Yeltsin used frequently for contentious issues. Although presidential decrees may not violate the constitution or specific legislation passed by the bicameral legislature, policy-making by decree allows the president to ignore an uncooperative or divided parliament. Yeltsin's decision in 1994, and again in 1999, to launch the offensive in Chechnya was not approved by either house of parliament. Under Putin and Medvedev the power of decree has been used more sparingly, partly because both leaders have had strong support in the legislature.

The president can also call a state of emergency, impose martial law, grant pardons, call referendums, and temporarily suspend actions of other state organs if he deems them to contradict the constitution or federal laws. Some of these actions must be confirmed by other state organs (such as the upper house of the parliament, the Federation Council). The president is commander-in-chief of the armed forces and conducts affairs of state with other nations. Impeachment of the president involves the two houses of the legislative body (the Duma and the Federation Council), the Supreme Court, and the Constitutional Court. If the president dies in office or becomes incapacitated, the prime minister fills the post until new presidential elections can be held.

The Russian government is headed by the prime minister, flanked by varying numbers of deputy prime ministers. The president's choice of prime minister must be approved by the Duma. During Yeltsin's presidency, six prime ministers held office, the longest being Viktor Chernomyrdin, from December 1992 until March 1998, and the final one being Vladimir Putin, appointed in August 1999. After becoming acting president in December 1999, Putin had three prime ministers (and one acting prime minister) during his first two terms of office. The first of these, Mikhail Kasyanov (May 2000 to February 2004), later became an outspoken opposition figure. Following his election as president in 2008, Medvedev selected Putin as his prime minister, with the roles reversed in 2012.

The prime minister can be removed by the Duma through two repeat votes of no confidence passed within a three-month period. Even in the 1990s when there was tension with President Yeltsin, the Duma was unable or unwilling to exercise this power, presumably in part because this action could lead to dissolution of the Duma itself. Until 2008, the prime minister was never the leader of the dominant party or coalition in the Duma. This changed when Putin became prime minister in 2008 because he was also elected as chairperson of the dominant party, United Russia, in that year.

The National Bureaucracy

The state's administrative structure includes twenty-one ministries, and some twenty federal services and agencies (as of January 2014). Based on an administrative reform adopted in 2004, ministries are concerned with policy functions or political aspects, whereas other state organs undertake monitoring functions or implementation, as well as providing services to the public. Many observers agree that these administrative reforms have not improved bureaucratic efficiency or government responsiveness.

Some government bodies (such as the Foreign Affairs Ministry, the Federal Security Service, and the Defense Ministry) report directly to the president. The president has created various advisory bodies that solicit input from important political and economic actors and also co-opt them into supporting government policies. The most important are the Security Council and the State Council. Formed in 1992, the Security Council advises the president in areas related to foreign policy and security (broadly conceived); its membership and size has varied over time, but has generally included heads of the so-called power ministries such as Defense and the Federal Security Service, as well as the other key ministers and government officials. The 2009 State Security Strategy of the Russian Federation accorded the Security

PROFILES

Vladimir Putin

President Vladimir Putin (right) with Prime Minister (and former President) Dmitry Medvedev (left).

AP Images/ITAR-TASS, Presidential Press Service, Vladimir Rodionov

Vladimir Putin, the current president, is no doubt the most powerful person in Russia; he has enjoyed a consistently high level of public support since his first election as president in March 2000, while at the same time being a controversial figure reviled by his critics for moving Russia in an authoritarian direction. For many ordinary Russians, Putin represents a reassertion of Russia's potential after painful years of economic decline, loss of international stature, and weak government in the 1990s. Projecting an image of masculine prowess, Putin has been captured in numerous alluring poses that contribute to his image of strength, for example while executing impressive judo moves, driving a three-wheeled Harley Davidson, and fishing topless in one of Russia's far-flung regions.

Putin was born in October 1952 in what is now St. Petersburg, Russia's second largest city. In the Soviet period, Putin pursued a career in the security services (the KGB) and was eventually assigned to duty in East Germany, where he remained until 1990 when the communist state there collapsed. Because of this career background, while in political office Putin has drawn many of his staff from the security forces.

Little known until 1999, Putin's rise to political prominence was swift and the rise in his popularity was equally meteoric. Upon returning to his home city of St. Petersburg in 1990, Putin gradually became involved in municipal government, moving to Moscow in 1996 to take up a political post. In 1999, Yeltsin appointed Putin prime minister and shortly thereafter acting president of the Russian Federation, when Yeltsin resigned from the presidential post. In February 2000 Putin won the presidential election with 56.7 percent of the vote, leaving his nearest competitor, Communist Party leader Gennady Zyuganov, behind with only 29 percent. Putin was reelected with over 71 percent of the vote in 2004.

Since the constitution limits a person to two consecutive terms as president, Putin hand-picked Dmitry Medvedev as the presidential candidate to succeed him for a four-year term from 2008 until 2012, but in September 2011 Putin and Medvedev announced that Putin, with Medvedev's support, would again seek the presidency in 2012. Putin reportedly indicated that the leadership deal had been arranged "several years back."[*] While parts of the Russian public did not react well to this preplanned "leadership swap," Putin was again elected president, this time for a six-year term, winning 63.6 percent of the vote.

Putin's domestic public approval rating has remained above 60 percent since the 2012 election, rising to above 80 percent in April 2014, a level most Western politicians would envy.[**] Some consider Putin to be a master tactician, who has managed to achieve a pragmatic mix of control and flexibility, weaving a political narrative that is contentious but persuasive to large parts of his domestic audience.

MAKING CONNECTIONS Why is Putin so popular with large parts of the Russian population?

[*] Reported by BBC World News, September 24, 2011.

[**]Levada Centre, Index of approval of the activities of Vladimir Putin and Dmitry Medevedev, http://www.levada.ru/indeksy (last accessed May 22, 2014).

Council a coordinating role in this area, but the body remains only advisory. The State Council, chaired by the president, was formed in September 2000 as part of Putin's attempt to redefine the role of regional leaders in federal decision making (see below) and includes the heads of Russia's constituent federal units. A smaller presidium, made up of seven of the regional heads selected by the president, meets monthly.

Ministers other than the prime minister do not require parliamentary approval. The prime minister makes recommendations to the president, who appoints these officials. Ministers and other agency heads are generally career bureaucrats who have risen through an appropriate ministry, although sometimes more clearly political appointments are made. Many agencies have been reorganized, often more than once. Sometimes restructuring signals particular leadership priorities. For example, in May 2008, Putin created a new Ministry of Energy, splitting off these functions from those of the Ministry of Industry and Trade. This move reflected the growing importance of this sector to Russia's economy.

Top leaders have also used restructuring to place their clients and allies in key positions. For example, Putin drew heavily on colleagues with whom he worked earlier in St. Petersburg or in the security establishment, referred to as *siloviki*, in staffing a variety of posts in his administration. **Clientelistic networks** continue to play a key role in both the presidential administration and other state organs. These linkages are similar to "old-boys' networks" in the West; they underscore the importance of personal loyalty and career ties between individuals as they rise in bureaucratic or political structures. While instituting a merit-based civil service system has been a state goal, it has not yet been achieved in reality. The Russian state bureaucracy continues to suffer low levels of public respect and continuing problems with corruption.

Despite efforts to reduce the size of the state bureaucracy during Putin's terms of office, its size increased substantially, in part through the creation of new federal agencies. As an apparent cost-cutting measure, in December 2010 Medvedev issued a presidential decree mandating further cuts in the size of the federal bureaucracy.

Public and Semipublic Institutions

In limited sectors of the economy, partial or complete state ownership has remained intact or even been restored after earlier privatization was carried out. Public or quasi-public ownership may take the form of direct state or municipal ownership of assets or majority control of shares in a "privatized" firm. Economic sectors more likely to involve public or semipublic ownership include telecommunications (the nonmobile telephone industry in particular), public transport (railways, municipal transport), the electronic media (television), and the energy sector. Prime examples from the energy sector are Gazprom, the natural gas monopoly, in which the federal government controls just over 50 percent of the shares, and Rosneft, operating in the petroleum industry, where the state owns nearly 70 percent. Several television channels are publicly owned. Indirect state influence is also realized through the dominant ownership share in many regional TV channels by Gazprom-Media, a subsidiary of the state-controlled natural gas company.

In other areas, such as education and health care, while some private facilities and institutions have emerged in recent years, these services are still primarily provided through tax-supported agencies. Some prestigious new private universities, often with Western economic support, have cropped up in major urban areas, but Russia's large historic universities remain public institutions. Likewise, a state-run medical care system assures basic care to all citizens, although private clinics and hospitals are increasingly servicing the more affluent parts of the population. In public transport, smaller private companies that provide shuttle and bus services have grown up alongside publicly owned transport networks. In general, public or semipublic agencies offer services at a lower price, but often also with lower quality.

Significant parts of the social infrastructure remain under public or semipublic control. In the Soviet period, many social services were administered to citizens through the workplace. These services included daycare, housing, medical care, and vacation facilities, as well as food services and some retail outlets. During the 1990s a process of divestiture resulted in the transfer of most of these assets and responsibilities to other institutions, either to private owners or, often, to municipalities. For

siloviki

Derived from the this refers to Russian word *sil*, meaning "force," this refers to Russian politicians and governmental officials drawn from the security and intelligence agencies, special forces, or the military, many of whom were recruited to important political posts under Vladimir Putin.

clientelistic networks

Informal systems of asymmetrical power in which a powerful patron (e.g., the president, prime minister, or governor) offers less powerful clients resources, benefits, or career advantages in return for support, loyalty, or services.

example, while many state- or enterprise-owned apartments were turned over to private ownership by their occupants, an important part of the country's housing stock was placed in municipal ownership.

Political authorities, including the president, are responsible for appointing executive officials in many public and semipublic institutions. This situation indicates a continuing close relationship between major economic institutions and the state, likely to remain in the future due to the Russian tradition of a strong state and the dismal economic results associated with privatization in the 1990s. Indicative of this trend, the overall share of GDP created in the non-state sector increased from 5 percent in 1991 to 70 percent in 1997, then fell from 70 percent in 1997 down to 65 percent in 2005–2006.[9]

Other State Institutions

The Judiciary

Concepts such as judicial independence and the rule of law were poorly understood in both pre-revolutionary Russia and the Soviet era. These concepts have, however, been embedded in the new Russian constitution and are, in principle, accepted both by the public and political elites. However, their implementation has been difficult and not wholly successful.

In Russia, a Constitutional Court was formed in 1991. Its decisions were binding, and in several cases even the president had to bow to its authority. After several controversial decisions, Yeltsin suspended the operations of the court in late 1993. However, the 1993 Russian constitution provided for a Constitutional Court again, with the power to adjudicate disputes on the constitutionality of federal and regional laws, as well as jurisdictional disputes between various political institutions. Judges are nominated by the president and approved by the Federation Council, a procedure that produced a political stalemate after the new constitution was adopted, so that the new court became functional only in 1995. Since 1995, the court has established itself as a vehicle for resolving conflicts involving the protection of individual rights and conformity of regional laws with constitutional requirements. The court has, however, been cautious in confronting the executive branch, and questions have been raised not only by critics but also by some justices themselves about the independence of the court from presidential influence.

Alongside the Constitutional Court is an extensive system of lower and appellate courts, with the Supreme Court at the pinnacle. These courts hear ordinary civil and criminal cases. In 1995, a system of commercial courts was also formed to hear cases dealing with issues related to privatization, taxes, and other commercial activities. The Federation Council must approve nominees for Supreme Court judgeships, and the constitution also grants the president power to appoint judges at other levels. Measures to shield judges from political pressures include criminal prosecution for attempting to influence a judge, protections from arbitrary dismissal, and improved salaries for judges. One innovation in the legal system has been the introduction of jury trials for some types of criminal offenses.

Subnational Governments

The collapse of the Soviet Union was precipitated by the demands of some union republics for more autonomy and, then, independence. After the Russian Federation became an independent state, the problem of constructing a viable federal structure resurfaced within Russia itself. Some of the federal units were very assertive in putting forth claims for autonomy or even sovereignty. The most extreme example is Chechnya, whose demand for independence led to a protracted civil war. The ethnic dimension complicates political relations with some other republics as well, particularly Tatarstan and Bashkortostan, which occupy relatively large territories in the center of the country and are of Islamic cultural background.

Putin's most controversial initiatives relating to Russia's regions were part of his attempt to strengthen what he termed the **power vertical**. This concept refers to an integrated structure of executive power from the presidential level down through to the local level. Critics have questioned whether this idea is consistent with federal principles, and others see it as undermining Russia's fledgling democratic system. A first step in creating the power vertical was the creation of seven, now nine, federal districts on top of the existing federal units. Although not designed to replace regional governments, the districts were intended to oversee the work of federal offices operating in these regions and to ensure compliance with federal laws and the constitution.

A second set of changes to create the power vertical involved a weakening of the independence of governors and republic heads (hereafter called governors). Beginning in 1996, the governors, along with the heads of each regional legislative body, sat as members of the upper house of the Russian parliament, the Federation Council. This arrangement gave the governors a direct voice in national legislative discussions and a presence in Moscow. In 2001, Putin gained approval for a revision to the composition of the Federation Council, removing regional executives. Now one regional representative is appointed by the regional executive and the other by the regional legislature. Some governors resisted this change, seeing it as an assault on their power. Putin made concessions to make the change more palatable, for example, giving governors the right to recall their representatives. The State Council was formed to try to assure the governors that they would retain some role in the federal policy-making arena.

power vertical

A term used by Vladimir Putin to describe a unified and hierarchical structure of executive power ranging from the national to the local level.

federal system

A political structure in which subnational units have significant independent powers; the powers of each level are usually specified in the federal constitution.

U.S. CONNECTION

Federalism Compared

Russia is a *federal system**, according to its constitution. This means that, at least in theory, powers are divided between the central government and Russia's constituent units. The number of federal units is disputed, as Russia claims to have eighty-five regions, including two regions in Crimea (Republic of Crimea and the city of Sevastopol), annexed from Ukraine in March 2014. However, most Western countries do not recognize the validity of the annexation.

In comparison to the American federal system, the Russian structure seems complicated. Some of Russia's federal units are called republics (21, or 22 including the Republic of Crimea), while others are *oblasts* (regions) (49), *krais* (territories) (6), one autonomous republic (1), autonomous *okrugs* (4), and cities of federal status (2, Moscow and St. Petersburg, or 3 with Sevastopol). Russia's size and

multiethnic population underlie this complexity. Because many ethnic groups are regionally concentrated in Russia, unlike in the United States, these groups form the basis for some federal units, notably the republics and okrugs, which are named after the ethnic groups that reside there.

In the 1990s, Russia's federal government had difficulty controlling what happened in the regions. Regional laws sometimes deviated from federal law. Bilateral treaties with the federal government granted some regional governments special privileges. During his term as president, Vladimir Putin put measures in place to ensure a greater degree of legal and political uniformity throughout the country.

Russia's federal units are represented in the upper house of the national legislature, the Federation Council. Just as the U.S. Senate includes two representatives from each state, in

(Continued)

Russia each region also has two delegates in this body; however, their method of selection has varied over time. In 1993 they were elected directly, as in the United States. From the mid-1990s, the governor and the head of each regional legislature themselves sat on the Federation Council. Now the members of the Federation Council are appointed, one by the region's governor and the other by the region's legislature.

Russia's federal units depend on funding from the central government to carry out many of their functions, especially in the field of social welfare. Other informal mechanisms, such as use of political patronage through the United Russia party, reduce the independence of the regional executives. Although Russia does have a constitutional court to resolve disputes over the jurisdictions of the federal government and the regions, unlike in the United States the constitution does not provide a strong basis for regional power, since it places many powers in the hands of the central government while most others are considered "shared" jurisdictions.

MAKING CONNECTIONS Have centralizing measures in Russia undermined the federal nature of Russia's political system?

*Definitions of key terms in this boxed feature appear in the Glossary, which begins on p. 698.

Following the Beslan terrorist attack in 2004, Putin identified corruption and ineffective leadership at the regional level as culprits in allowing terrorists to carry out the devastating school hostage taking. Accordingly, Putin proposed an additional reform that created the decisive element of central control over regional politics. This change eliminated the popular election of governors; rather, the president nominated them for approval by the regional legislature. The president's nominees were approved by the regional legislature in every case, usually with an overwhelming majority or even unanimously. In his first two years in office, Medvedev replaced eighteen incumbent governors in this way, apparently seeking individuals who would both be politically loyal and managerially competent.[10] Following the public protests against alleged fraud in the 2011 and 2012 elections, Medvedev proposed legislation reinstating gubernatorial elections, but with a "municipal filter" that requires a candidate's nomination to be supported by a certain number of local deputies or officials. The first elections under the law, held in October 2012 and September 2013, resulted in victories for the candidates of the dominant party, United Russia, in all cases. This outcome reflected both some restrictive features of the new law, informal mechanisms of influence exercised by the incumbent, and the failure of opposition forces to unite in support of viable candidates.

The distribution of tax revenues among the various levels of government has been another contentious issue. The Soviet state pursued a considerable degree of regional equalization, but regional differences have increased in the Russian Federation. Putin created a more regularized system for determining the distribution of revenues, taking account of both the regional tax base and differences in the needs of various regions (for instance, northern regions have higher expenses to maintain basic services). However, in fact, an increasing proportion of tax revenues are now controlled by Moscow, and regional governments are constantly faced with shortfalls in carrying out their major responsibilities, for example, in social policy. Economic disparities between rich and poor regions have reached dramatic proportions, with Moscow and areas rich in natural resources being the best off.

The Military and Security Organs

Because of Vladimir Putin's career background in the KGB, he drew many of his staff from this arena. Thus, while the formal status of the Federal Security Service (the successor to the KGB) has not changed, the security establishment has acquired increasing importance under Putin. A justification for the increasing role for security forces was a series of terrorist attacks, with targets including apartment buildings, schools, a popular Moscow theatre, public transport, and a Moscow airport. Attacks in Russia initially had indigenous roots in the separatist region of Chechnya, as terrorism was used by Chechen militants to counter Russian military efforts to defeat separatist forces. Over time, linkages between Russian terrorist groups and international Islamic fundamentalist organizations have become increasingly important. Since the September 11 attacks, cooperation between Russian and Western security agencies has increased.

Because many Russians are alarmed by the crime rate and terrorist bombings in the country, restrictions on civil liberties justified as guarding against the terrorist threat have not elicited strong popular concern. At the same time, there is widespread public cynicism about the honesty of the ordinary police. Many believe that payoffs can buy police cooperation in overlooking crimes or ordinary legal infractions such as traffic tickets.

The Soviet military once ranked second only to that of the United States. Russian defense spending declined in the 1990s, then increased again after 2000, but is still below Soviet levels. In 2012 military spending represented about 4.5 percent of GPD (roughly comparable to the proportion in the United States), but in absolute terms has risen due to economic growth following 1999. The Soviet and Russian military have never usurped civilian power. The Communist Party controlled military appointments and, during the August 1991 coup attempt, troops remained loyal to Yeltsin and Gorbachev, even though the Minister of Defense was among the coup plotters. Likewise, in October 1993, despite some apparent hesitancy in military circles, military units defended the government's position, this time firing on civilian protesters and shocking the country.

The political power and prestige of the military have suffered, in part as a result of its failure to deal effectively with Chechnya. Accordingly, the government increased the role of the Federal Security Service there instead of relying on the army alone. Reports of deteriorating conditions in some Russian nuclear arsenals have raised international concerns about nuclear security. The Russian Federation still maintains universal male conscription, but noncompliance and draftees rejected for health reasons have been persistent problems. In 2008 mandatory service was reduced from two years to one year; women have never been subject to the military draft. A law to permit alternative military service for conscientious objectors took effect in 2004. In 2013 the Defense Minister indicated that a military draft will remain necessary, alongside a professional army, but that soon draftees will not be used in combat.[11]

High crime rates indicate a low capacity of the state to provide legal security to its citizens. Thus, in addition to state security agencies, sometimes businesses and individuals turn to private security firms to provide protection. A network of intrigue and hidden relationships can make it hard to determine the boundaries of state involvement in the security sector, and the government's inability to enforce laws or to apprehend violators may create an impression of state involvement even where they may be none. A prominent example is the case of a former agent of the Russian Federal Security Service, Alexander Litvinenko, an outspoken critic of the Russian government, who took political asylum in the United Kingdom. In November 2006, Litvinenko was fatally poisoned in London with a rare radioactive isotope. On his deathbed, Litvinenko accused the Kremlin of being responsible for his death, an undocumented accusation. The United Kingdom's efforts to extradite Andrei Lugovoi, an ex-KGB agent and Russian politician, to stand trial for the murder were refused by the Russian government, citing a constitutional prohibition. The issue sparked tension between the two countries, including expulsion of diplomats on both sides. These kinds of incidents have generated an atmosphere reminiscent of Cold War spy novels.

The Policy-Making Process

Policy-making occurs both formally and informally. According to the constitution, the federal government, the president and his administration, regional legislatures, individual deputies, and some judicial bodies may propose legislation. In the Yeltsin era, conflict between the president and State Duma made policy-making contentious and fractious; under Putin and Medvedev, the State Duma has generally gone along with proposals made by the president and the government, and the proportion of legislation initiated by the executive branch has increased significantly.

In order for a bill to become law, it must be approved by both houses of the parliament in three readings and signed by the president. If the president vetoes the bill, it must be passed again in the same wording by a two-thirds majority of both houses in order to override the veto. Many policy proclamations have been made through presidential or governmental decrees, without formal consultation with the legislative branch. This decision-making process is much less visible and may involve closed-door bargaining rather than an open process of debate and consultation.

Informal groupings also have an important indirect impact on policy-making. During the Yeltsin period, business magnates were able to exert behind-the-scenes influence to gain benefits from the privatization of lucrative firms in sectors such as oil, media, and transport. Putin has attempted to reduce the direct political influence of these powerful economic figures, but at the cost of also reducing political competition.

A continuing problem is weak policy implementation. Under communist rule, the party's control over political appointments enforced at least some degree of conformity to central mandates. Under Yeltsin, fragmented and decentralized political power gave the executive branch few resources to ensure compliance. Pervasive corruption, including bribery and selective enforcement, hindered enforcement of policy decisions. Although Putin and Medvedev both have stated their commitment to restrict these types of irregularities, they continue to persist. However, the commitment to reestablishing order and a rule of law has been an important justification for the centralization of power.

Where Do You Stand?

Do you think a strong presidency, such as exists in Russia, is compatible with democracy? If the public supports such an arrangement, does that itself give it democratic legitimacy?

In a country as wide and diverse as Russia, is federalism a good idea, or is it likely to increase the risk of separatism and disunity?

SECTION 4

REPRESENTATION AND PARTICIPATION

civil society

A term that refers to the space occupied by voluntary associations outside the state, for example, professional associations, trade unions, and student groups.

Gorbachev's policies in the 1980s brought a dramatic change in the relationship between state and society, as *glasnost* sparked new public and private initiatives. Most restrictions on the formation of social organizations were lifted, and a large number of independent groups appeared. Hopes rose that these trends might indicate the emergence of **civil society**. Just a few years later, only a small stratum of Russian society was actually actively engaged; the demands of everyday life, cynicism about politics, and increasing controls on political opposition led many people to withdraw into private life. However, with hardships imposed by the economic crisis of 2008–2009 and allegations of election fraud in the December 2011 Duma elections, there is evidence of increasing political activism among a small but important sector of society.

The Legislature

The Federal Assembly came into being after the parliamentary elections of December 12, 1993, when the referendum ratifying the new Russian constitution was also approved. The upper house, the Federation Council, represents Russia's constituent federal units. The lower house, the State Duma (hereafter the Duma), has 450 members and involves a mixed electoral system (discussed below).

Within the Duma, factions unite deputies from the same party. In February 2013 there were four party factions representing the parties elected in the December 2011 vote; in January 2014, 237 (or 52.7 percent) of the 449 deputies in the State Duma were part of the faction of the dominant party, United Russia.[12] Other parties had, respectively 56 (Liberal Democratic Party of Russia), 92 (Communist Party of the Russian Federation), and 64 (A Just Russia) deputies. The Duma elects its own speaker (or chair); since December 2011, this has been Sergei Naryshkin of the United Russia party.

Compared to the communist period, deputies reflect less fully the demographic characteristics of the population at large. For example, in 1984, 33 percent of the members of the Supreme Soviet were women; after the 2007 Duma elections, 14 percent of deputies were women, but this dropped to 11 percent after the 2011 elections.[13] The underrepresentation of women, as well as of workers, in the present Duma indicates the extent to which Russian politics is primarily the domain of male elites.

The upper house of the Federal Assembly, the Federation Council, has two members from each of Russia's federal regions and republics. Many prominent businessmen are among the appointees, and in some cases the posts may be granted in exchange for political loyalty. Party factions do not play a significant role in the Federation Council. Deputies to the Federation Council, as well as to the Duma, are granted immunity from criminal prosecution.

The constitution grants parliament powers in the legislative and budgetary areas, but if there is conflict with the president or government, these powers can be exercised effectively only if parliament operates with a high degree of unity. In practice, the president can often override or bypass the parliament through mechanisms such as the veto of legislation or use of decrees. Each house of parliament has the authority to confirm certain presidential appointees. The Federation Council must also approve presidential decrees relating to martial law and state emergencies, as well as to deploying troops abroad.

Following electoral rebuffs in the 1993 and 1995 parliamentary elections, Yeltsin confronted a parliament that obstructed many of his proposed policies, but the parliament did not have the power or unity to offer a constructive alternative. Since the 2003 Duma election, however, parliament has cooperated with the president, since a majority of the deputies have been tied to the United Russia faction, closest to the president, and deputies from other parties have also often supported the president's initiatives. In general, the process of gaining Duma acceptance of government proposals has depended more on the authority of the president and on the particular configuration of power at the moment rather than on the presence of disciplined party accountability such as exists in some European countries.

mixed electoral system

A system of electoral representation in which a portion of the seats are selected in winner-take-all single-member districts, and a portion are allocated according to parties within multi-member constituencies, roughly in proportion to the votes each party receives in a popular election.

Society's ability to affect particular policy decisions through the legislative process is minimal. Parties in the parliament are isolated from the public at large, suffer low levels of popular respect, and the internal decision-making structures of parties are generally elite-dominated.

Political Parties and the Party System

One of the most important political changes following the collapse of communism was the shift from a single-party to a multiparty system. In the USSR, the Communist Party (CPSU) not only dominated state organs but also oversaw social institutions, such as the mass media, trade unions, youth groups, educational institutions, and professional associations. It defined the official ideology for the country, set the parameters for state censorship, and ensured that loyal supporters occupied all important offices. Approximately 10 percent of adults in the Soviet Union were party members, but there were no effective mechanisms to ensure accountability of the party leadership to its members.

As part of Gorbachev's reforms, national competitive elections were held in 1989, but new political parties were not formal participants in Russia until 1993. Since then, a confusing array of political organizations has run candidates in elections. For the December 2011 Duma elections only seven parties met conditions of legal registration. A change in the law governing political parties was adopted as a concession to popular protests after those elections; this loosened requirements for party registration. However, this has evoked concerns that one result might be fragmentation of opposition to United Russia.

In the 1990s, many parties formed around prominent individuals, making politics very personalistic. Furthermore, other than the Communist Party, Russian parties are young, so deeply rooted political identifications have not had time to develop. Finally, many citizens do not have a clear conception of how parties might represent their interests. In this context, image making is as important as programmatic positions, so parties appeal to transient voter sentiments.

While individual leaders play an important role in political life in Russia, some key issues have divided opinions in the post-1991 period. One such issue is economic policy. Nearly all political parties have mouthed support for creation of a market economy. However, communist/socialist groupings have been more muted in their enthusiasm and have argued for a continued state role in providing social protection and benefits for vulnerable parts of the population. The liberal/reform groupings, on the other hand, have advocated more rapid market reform, including privatization, free prices, and limited government spending. United Russia charts a middle ground, appealing to voters from a wide ideological spectrum.

Another dividing line relates to national identity. Nationalist/patriotic parties emphasize the defense of Russian interests over Westernization. They favor a strong military establishment and protection from foreign economic influence. Liberal/reform parties, on the other hand, advocate integration of Russia into the global market and the adoption of Western economic and political principles. Again, the United Russia party has articulated an intriguing combination of these viewpoints, with its leaders identifying Europe as the primary identity point for Russia, but at the same time insisting on Russia's role as a regional power, pursuing its own unique path of political and economic development. Ethnic and regional parties have not had a significant impact on the national electoral scene.

Table 7.2	Election Results and Seats in the Russian State Duma, 2007–2014					
Party	**Percent of 2007 party list vote**	**Percent of Duma seats 2007**	**Percent of party list vote 2011**	**Percent of Duma seats Feb 2014**	**Current party leader**
Centrist					
United Russia	64.3	70.0	49.3	52.7	Dmitri Medvedev (since 2012, Vladimir Putin 2007–2012)
A Just Russia	7.7	8.4	13.3	14.3	Sergey Mironov
Communist/Socialist					
Communist Party of the Russian Federation	11.6	12.7	19.2	20.5	Gennady Zyuganov
Nationalist/Patriotic					
Liberal Democratic Party of Russia	8.1	8.9	11.7	12.5	Vladimir Zhirinovksy
Patriots of Russia	0.9	0	1.0	0	Gennady Semigin
Liberal/Westernizing					
Yabloko	1.6	0	3.4	0	Sergey Mitrokhin
Union of Rightist Force/Just Cause	1.0	0	0.6	0	Viacheslav Maratkanov

Russian political parties do not fit neatly on a left–right spectrum. Nationalist sentiments crosscut economic ideologies, producing the following party tendencies:

- The traditional left, critical of market reform and often mildly nationalistic
- Centrist "parties of power," representing the political elite
- Liberal/reform forces, supporting assertive Western-type market reform and political norms
- Nationalist/patriotic forces, primarily concerned with identity issues and national self-assertion

The most important parties in all four groupings have not challenged the structure of the political system but have chosen to work within it. Since 2000, liberal/reform parties have been marginalized and are no longer represented in political institutions. Of the four parties represented in the State Duma, two are centrist (United Russia and A Just Russia). The second-strongest party after United Russia, the Communist Party of the Russian Federation, is a traditional left party. The fourth party, the Liberal Democratic Party of Russia, is nationalist/patriotic.

The Dominant Party: United Russia

dominant party

A political party that manages to maintain consistent control of a political system through formal and informal mechanisms of power, with or without strong support from the population.

Since 2003, one political party, United Russia, has taken on clear dominance. Its predecessor, the Unity Party, rose to prominence, together with Vladimir Putin, in the elections of 1999 and 2000. While the Unity Party gained 23.3 percent of the vote in Duma elections in 1999, United Russia received 37.6 percent in 2003, 64 percent in 2007, but just over 49 percent in 2011. In April 2008, at a party congress, United Russia's delegates unanimously approved creation of a custom-made post for Vladimir Putin as party chairman, but with his election as president in 2012, Dmitry Medvedev, who became prime minister, took over that position, keeping the presidency formally distinct from the party leadership.[14] In fact, United Russia has served as a major source of political support for Putin.

What explains United Russia's success? An important factor is the association with Putin, but the party has also built a political machine to generate persuasive incentives for regional elites. The party is truly a party of power, focused on winning to its side prominent people, including heads of Russia's regions, who then use their influence to further bolster the party's votes. The party has a rather poorly defined program, which emphasizes the uniqueness of the Russian approach (as distinct from Western models), an appeal to values of order and law, and a continued commitment to moderate reform. The question now facing the party is whether it has adequate institutional strength to impose accountability on its leaders and whether it can develop an organizational footing in society.

Other Parties Represented in the State Duma (2007–2011)

Many consider the Communist Party of the Russian Federation (CPRF) to be the only party that could be considered a real opposition force. The CPRF was by far the strongest parliamentary party after the 1995 elections, winning over one-third of the seats in the Duma. Since then its strength declined until 2011. With the second-strongest showing, after United Russia, in the 2011 Duma elections, the party's vote showed an increase from 11.6 percent in 2007 to 19.2 percent in 2011. The party defines its goals as being democracy, justice, equality, patriotism and internationalism, a combination of civic rights and duties, and socialist renewal. Primary among the party's concerns are the social costs of the market reform process.

The CPRF appears to represent those who have adapted less successfully to the radical and uncertain changes of recent years, as well as some individuals who remain committed to socialist ideals. Support for the party is especially strong among older Russians, the economically disadvantaged, and rural residents. The party's principal failures have been an inability to adapt its public position to attract significant numbers of new adherents, particularly among the young, as well as the absence of a charismatic and attractive political leader. Although one might expect Russia to offer fertile ground for social democratic sentiments like those that have been successful in the Scandinavian countries of Western Europe, the CPRF has not expanded its base of support, nor has it made room for a new social democratic party that could be more successful.

Two other parties were represented in the State Duma after the 2011 elections. The party called A Just Russia, founded in 2006, placed third, with 13.3 percent of the vote. Many observers consider that A Just Russia was formed with the Kremlin's support to demonstrate the competitive nature of Russia's electoral system, while undermining opposition parties that might pose a real threat to United Russia. The leadership espouses support for socialist principles, placing it to the left of United Russia on the political spectrum and offering a political magnet for dissatisfied supporters of the Communist Party. In highly exceptional cases, A Just Russia has been able to win mayoral elections in smaller cities; however, the party does not pose a real challenge to the position of United Russia and has generally supported the president and government.

The fourth party represented in the Duma, the Liberal Democratic Party of Russia (LDPR), is neither liberal nor particularly democratic in its platform; the party can be characterized as nationalist and populist. Its leadership openly appeals to the anti-Western sentiments that grew in the wake of Russia's decline from superpower status. Concern with the breakdown of law and order seems to rank high among its priorities. The party's leader, Vladimir Zhirinovsky, has garnered especially strong support among working-class men and military personnel. However, most often this party has not challenged the political establishment on important issues.

While these three parties, singly or combined, cannot challenge the power of United Russia, they have on occasion issued protests over what they consider to be unfair electoral procedures. For example, in October 2009 deputies from all three factions abandoned a session of the State Duma as a sign of protest against the results of regional elections, accusing United Russia of infringement of proper electoral procedures and demanding that the results be nullified. After consultations with the president, the demands were withdrawn.

The Liberal Democratic Parties: Marginalized

The liberal/reform parties (those that most strongly support Western economic and political values) have become marginalized since 2003, when they won only a handful of seats in the Duma. These groups have organized under a variety of party names since 1993, including Russia's Choice, the Union of Rightist Forces, and, most recently, Just Cause, as well as the Yabloko party. These parties have espoused a commitment to traditional liberal values, such as a limited economic role for the state, support for free-market principles, and the protection of individual rights and liberties. Prominent figures such as Boris Nemstov and Grigory Yavlinksy were visible and sometimes influential in the 1990s as representatives of reform policies, but they have since found it hard to build a stable and unified electoral base. Many Russians hold policies associated with these figures, such as rapid privatization and price increases, as responsible for Russia's economic decline in the 1990s. Often referred to as "democrats," their unpopularity also creates confusion as to what democracy really implies. An additional source of weakness has been their difficulty in running under a uniform and consistent party name or leadership figure. Mikhail Prokhorov, a Russian businessman and billionaire owner of the Brooklyn Jets, won support from a part of the liberal electorate in his bid for the presidency in 2012 (winning about 8 percent of the vote). He subsequently formed the party Civic Platform. Support for liberal/reform parties generally has been stronger among the young, the more highly educated, urban dwellers, and the well-off. Thus, ironically, those with the best prospects for succeeding in the new market economy have been the least successful in fashioning an effective political party to represent themselves.

Elections

Turnout in federal elections remains respectable, generally between 60 and 70 percent; it stood at 60 percent in the 2011 Duma election and close to 65 percent in the 2012 presidential vote, down from about 70 percent in 2008. National elections receive extensive media coverage, and campaign activities begin as long as a year in advance. The political leadership has also actively encouraged voter turnout, to give elections an appearance of legitimacy. Up until 2003, national elections since 1991 were generally considered to be reasonably fair and free. However, international observers have expressed serious concerns about the fairness of elections since 2003, related, for example, to slanted media coverage as well as electoral irregularities.

Until 2007, the electoral system for selecting the Duma combined proportional representation (with a 5 percent threshold) with winner-take-all districts. In addition, voters were given the explicit option of voting against all candidates or parties (4.7 percent chose this in 2003). In an interlude from 2007 until 2014, the single-member districts were abolished, so that all 450 deputies were elected on the basis of one national proportional representation district, with a minimum threshold for party representation raised to 7 percent. In February 2014 the electoral system was revised again, returning to a system similar to that which had existed prior to 2007; however, there are some additional requirements for registration of candidates in the winner-take-all districts. Parties are required to include regional representatives on their lists from across the country. A 2001 law on political parties created difficult thresholds for political parties to participate in elections, but these were relaxed in April 2012, so that now only 500 members are needed to register a party, although there must still be branches in half of Russia's federal regions. In 2006, national legislation removed the "against all" option from the ballot, but it was reinstated in 2012.

With the rapid ascent of United Russia since 1999, opposition parties have had difficulty offering an effective challenge to the dominant party. One reason is genuine popular support for Putin as well as the failure of the opposition parties to develop appealing programs or field attractive candidates. Media coverage has also strongly favored United Russia and the president. Administrative control measures and selective enforcement of laws have limited the scope of permissible political opposition, sometimes providing pretexts to disqualify opposition forces. In addition, the carrot-and-stick method has wooed regional elites, producing a bandwagon effect that builds on rewards for political loyalty.

Russia has yet to experience a real transfer of power from one political grouping to another, which some scholars consider a first step in consolidating democratic governance. Under the Russian constitution, presidential elections have been held every

Table 7.3	Russian Views on Political Systems														
	Nov97	Mar00	Mar03	Dec06	Nov07	Feb08	Feb09	Feb10	Feb11	Jan12	Jan13	Jan14
The Soviet one, which we had until the 1990s	38	42	48	35	35	24	38	34	33	29	36	39
The current system	11	11	18	26	17	36	25	28	19	20	17	19
Democracy like Western countries	28	26	22	16	19	15	18	20	23	29	22	21
Other	8	4	6	7	7	7	7	7	8	7	9	8
Hard to say	16	17	7	16	12	18	12	12	16	15	16	13

"What type of political system seems the best to you: the Soviet, the present system, or democracy of the type in Western countries?"

Source: Levada Center, http://www.levada.ru/24-02-2014/luchshaya-politicheskaya-i-ekonomicheskaya-sistema, accessed March 14, 2014.

four years, but beginning with the 2012 election the term is six years; the Duma mandate was extended from four to five years.

Political Culture, Citizenship, and Identity

Political culture can be a source of great continuity in the face of radical upheavals in the social and political spheres. Some attitudes toward government that prevailed in the Soviet period have endured with remarkable tenacity, including acceptance of strong political leadership and centralized power. At the same time, the Soviet development model glorified science, technology, industrialization, and urbanization; these values were superimposed on the traditional way of life of the largely rural population. When communism collapsed, Soviet ideology was discredited, and in the 1990s the government embraced Western political and economic values. Many citizens and intellectuals are skeptical of this "imported" culture, partly because it conflicts with other traditional civic values such as egalitarianism, collectivism, and a broad scope for state activity, and partly because it is viewed as an outside imposition. Public opinion surveys over time do, however, suggest at least general support for liberal democratic values such as an independent judiciary, a free press, basic civil liberties, and competitive elections, but at the same time a desire for strong political leadership. During Putin's presidency the leadership espoused a particular Russian concept of sovereign democracy, emphasizing the importance of adapting democratic principles to the Russian context.

sovereign democracy

A concept of democracy articulated by President Putin's political advisor, Vladimir Surkov, to communicate the idea that democracy in Russia should be adapted to Russian traditions and conditions rather than based on Western models.

In the USSR, just over 50 percent of the population was ethnically Russian. Since many ethnic minorities now reside in other Soviet successor states, according to the 2010 census Russians now make up 77.7 percent of the population of the Russian Federation. The largest minority group is the Tatars (3.7 percent), a traditionally Muslim group residing primarily in Tatarstan, one of Russia's republics. Other significant minorities are the neighboring Bashkirs (1.1 percent), various indigenous peoples of the Russian north, the many Muslim groups in the northern Caucasus region, and ethnic groups (such as Ukrainians and Armenians) of other former Soviet republics. There are over fifty languages spoken by at least 50,000 people in the Russian Federation,[15] although Russian is clearly the lingua franca. Some 25 million ethnic Russians reside outside of the Russian Federation in other former Soviet republics, which at times has provided a pretext for Russian intervention in regions adjacent to the country.

Because Russia is a multiethnic state, one important aspect of the state's search for identity relates to what it means to be Russian. The Russian language itself has two distinct words for Russian: *russkii*, which refers to an ethnicity, and *rossiiskii*, a broader civic concept referring to people of various ethnic backgrounds who make up the Russian citizenry. While the political foundation of the Russian Federation is based on a civic rather than ethnic definition of "Russianness," both anti-Semitic and anti-Muslim sentiments surface in everyday life. In recent years there have been increasing concerns about the rise of an exclusionary form of Russian nationalism among certain parts of the population. Official state policy, while explicitly opposing ethnic stereotypes, may, in some cases, have implicitly fed them.

Today, the Russian Orthodox Church appeals to many citizens who are looking for a replacement for the discredited values of the communist system. Although an important source of personal meaning and a strong social presence, religion has not emerged as a significant basis of political cleavage for ethnic Russians. A controversial law, directed primarily at Western proselytizers, was passed in 1997, making it harder for new religious groups to organize. Human rights advocates and foreign observers protested strongly, again raising questions about the depth of Russia's commitment to liberal democratic values.

Attitudes toward gender relations in Russia reflect traditional family values. It is generally assumed that women will carry the primary responsibility for child care and a certain standard of "femininity" is expected of women both inside and outside the workplace. Feminism is not popular in Russia, as many women consider it inconsistent with traditional notions of femininity or with accepted social roles for women. At the same time, a number of civil society organizations have sprung up to represent the interests of women; some of them advocate traditional policies to provide better social supports for mothers and families, while others challenge traditional gender roles and definitions.

Changing cultural norms affect gender relations in other ways as well. Images propagated in advertising and through the mass media often represent women as sex objects. Advertising also reinforces commercialized images of female beauty that may not correspond to cultural expectations or to healthy lifestyles. In the face of unemployment and the breakdown in traditional social linkages, increasing numbers of young women have turned to prostitution to make a living; HIV/AIDS rates are also increasing at a rapid rate, fueled by prostitution, low levels of information, and the rise of drug trafficking related to Russia's permeable eastern border.

Social class identity was a major theme in the Soviet period. The Bolshevik revolution was justified in the name of the working class, and the Communist Party of the Soviet Union claimed to be a working-class party. Because social class was a major part of the discredited Soviet ideology, in the post-communist period many Russians remain skeptical of claims made by politicians to represent the working class, and trade unions are weakly supported. Even the Communist Party of the Russian Federation does not now explicitly identify itself as a working-class party.

Interest Groups, Social Movements, and Protest

Since the collapse of the USSR, numerous political and social organizations have sprung up in every region of Russia, representing the interests of groups such as children, veterans, women, environmental advocates, pensioners, and the disabled. Many observers saw such blossoming activism as the foundation for a fledgling civil society that would nurture the new democratic institutions established since 1991. Despite limited resources and small staffs, these non-government organizations (NGOs) provided a potential source of independent political activity. However, there have been many obstacles to realizing this potential including inadequate resources and restrictions on their activities.

In January 2006 Putin signed legislation amending laws on public associations and noncommercial organizations. These controversial changes, protested widely by Western governments, placed new grounds for denying registration to such organizations, established new reporting requirements (particularly for organizations receiving funds from foreign sources), and increased government supervisory functions. Particular requirements are placed on foreign noncommercial nongovernmental organizations operating in Russia. A 2012 law requires NGOs that engage in political activity on the basis of foreign financing to register as "foreign agents" and submit to strict reporting requirements. Several Russian organizations have refused to comply;

some NGOs also filed a complaint with the European Court of Human Rights. The law reflects concern that foreign influence may spur political activism in the country that could challenge stability or the current structure of power.

At the same time, the government has attempted to channel public activism through official forums. These have included the Civic Forum, organized with government support in 2001, and more recently, the Public Chamber, created in 2005 by legislation proposed by the president. Based on voluntary participation by presidential appointees and representatives recommended by national and regional societal organizations, the organization is presented as a mechanism for public consultation and input, as well as a vehicle for creating public support for government policy. It likely involves an effort to co-opt public activists from more disruptive forms of self-expression, but also to mobilize the assistance of citizens' groups in delivering social services.

A variety of mass-based political organizations protest the current political direction of the government, but since 2007 the authorities have periodically tried to restrict use of public demonstrations and protests. The widespread protests that followed the 2011 Duma elections represented the most dramatic evidence of significant opposition sentiment in major urban centers. On December 10, 2011, an estimated 50,000 protesters participated, followed by equally large demonstrations leading up to the presidential election in March 2012. Just before a planned demonstration on June 12, 2012 (named the "march of millions"), Putin signed a new law that imposed high fines for participating in demonstrations that undermine public order or destroy public property; the homes of leading opposition figures were also searched.

In the context of the 2011-12 protests, new public figures emerged, the most notable being the 38-year-old anti-corruption blogger, Alexei Navalny. His depiction of United Russia as a "party of crooks and thieves" became an opposition rallying

The feminist rock punk group, Pussy Riot, undertakes a protest performance in Christ the Saviour Church, Moscow, in Feburary 2012

Aleshkovsky Mitya/Itar-Tass/ABACA/Newscom

call. After being arrested and convicted of alleged embezzlement that had occurred several years earlier, Navalny was sentenced to five years in prison. Surprisingly, Navalny was released pending an appeal and permitted to stand on the ballot in the newly reinstated Moscow mayoral race in October 2013. He won 27 percent of the vote against the incumbent mayor and Putin loyalist, Sergei Sobianin, who got just over 51 percent. In February 2014, Navalny was again placed under house arrest.

The official trade unions established under Soviet rule have survived under the title of the Federation of Independent Trade Unions (FITU). However, FITU has lost the confidence of large parts of the workforce. In some sectors, such as the coal industry, new independent trade unions have formed, mainly at the local level. Labor actions have, at various times, included spontaneous strikes, transport blockages, and even hunger strikes. Immediate concessions are often offered in response to such protests, but the underlying problems are rarely addressed. During the period of the financial-economic crisis that began in 2008, protests occurred across Russia, often focused on nonpayment of wages. More recently low wage levels have elicited some strikes. However, such local protest actions seem to be only weakly linked to the national political protests, referred to above, in Moscow and in other large cities.

The Political Impact of Technology

The media itself has an important impact on how interests are expressed. In the post-Soviet period, television has been the main source of news and political information for Russian citizens. Article 29 of the Russian constitution guarantees "freedom of the mass media" and prohibits censorship. However, Russia ranked 148th out of 179 countries in 2013 in terms of press freedom, according to *Reporters without Borders*.[16] A recent survey by a respected independent public opinion agency revealed that 69 percent of respondents acknowledged government censorship in the main Russian TV channels and 77 percent felt that a greater diversity of views expressed in TV media would be desirable.[17]

While much of the television coverage is subject to more or less direct influence by the government, some newspapers and independent journalists, as well as Internet sources, do offer a critical perspective on political developments. Independently minded journalists are exposed to significant risks due to the incapacity of the state to enforce law and order. An estimated fifty-two journalists have been murdered since 1992, making Russia the third-most-dangerous country for journalists in the world.[18] Many cases involved reporting in war-torn Chechnya; others are contract murders or assassinations

As in other countries, Internet usage has increased rapidly in the Russian Federation, and its use can have important political implications. In 2013 only 38 percent of survey respondents indicated that they did not make use of the Internet, and 37 percent reported using it almost every day, with 27 percent indicating use for finding news updates.[19] However, major uses of the Internet are social media and entertainment; the Russian corollary of Facebook, called *vKontake.ru*, is particularly popular with young people, as is the Russian Internet search engine Yandex. Internet use, as in other countries, is more widespread among the young. Contacts through social media and other Internet sources were important in mobilizing participation in demonstrations surrounding the 2011–2012 elections. Those who use the Internet to connect to opposition circles are often of a more critical political orientation, but the Internet has not provided a medium for creation of a sustained and unified opposition movement. Furthermore, the state has also made effective use of Internet communications to disseminate its interpretations of the news, [20] as well as creating relatively effective e-portals for government services.

The Russian government has also effectively used electronic media to project a positive image abroad through vehicles such as the global TV channel, RT (formerly Russia Today), and its associated Internet site (rt.com). In another widely publicized act, in August 2013 Russian authorities granted asylum to Edward Snowden, for whom the United States sought extradition in connection with Snowden's alleged release of classified security documents. Non-governmental sources in Russia have launched successful cyberattacks, most notably on a range of Estonian governmental and business sites in 2007, following an Estonian decision, sharply criticized by Russian authorities, to remove a pro-Soviet statue from central Tallinn.

While until recently government restrictions on domestic Internet usage have been minimal, in the context of the Sochi Olympics monitoring of e-communications was thorough-going, justified as needed to monitor security threats to the games. In early 2014, new legislation created instruments for closer monitoring of bloggers with large followings. More broadly Russian legislation provides security services with the authority to access citizens' online activity, as well as the obligation of Internet service providers to facilitate the collection of the information. As yet, this capacity has not been utilized in a systematic way to control opposition activities. The Internet still provides the attentive Russian public with access to a broad range of domestic and foreign opinion, even if most citizens do not utilize this opportunity to its full potential.

Where Do You Stand?

Is the Russian government justified in trying to limit the influence of foreign governments or international organizations on Russian domestic politics?

In a country with a history of radical ruptures, is it reasonable for the government to put limits on opposition protests in the name of stability and stable government?

SECTION 5
RUSSIAN POLITICS IN TRANSITION

Focus Questions

• What types of strategies has Russia pursued under Vladimir Putin's leadership in trying to reestablish itself as a regional and global power? How effective have these strategies been?

• What are the main challenges to political stability in Russia?

On March 1, 2014, the Russian Duma authorized President Putin to deploy military forces in Crimea, an autonomous region of the neighboring independent state of Ukraine, justified in order to protect the rights of Russians residing there. In the preceding days, Crimea had already effectively been brought under Russian military control due to the mobilization of forces of Russia's Black Sea Fleet based in Crimea under a long-term lease agreement with Ukraine. Russian control of the region was reinforced by the introduction of additional troops. A self-appointed pro-Russian regional government in Crimea held a contested referendum on March 16, with Russia's blessing, proposing that Crimea be annexed to Russia. Russia accepted Crimea into the Russian Federation the same week. The international community, especially the United States and the European Union, expressed sharp criticism of the Russian invasion and annexation, declaring it contrary to international law and the referendum illegal and invalid.

The Russian intervention was in response to a power turnover in Ukraine in late February 2014, which resulted from three months of massive popular demonstrations in Ukraine's capital, Kiev, against the incumbent president, Victor Yanukovych. Those protests were triggered by Yanukovych's decision, under heavy Russian pressure, to back away at the last minute from signing long-awaited free trade and association agreements with the European Union. When violence erupted, the crisis culminated in the collapse of Yanukovych's rule as he fled Ukraine. The new interim Ukrainian government, installed by the elected parliament, made a sharp pro-Western turn, with new presidential elections announced for May 25, 2014, which produced a clear victory for Petro Poroshenko, a pro-Western businessman. Moscow viewed events in Ukraine as undermining its efforts to draw Ukraine closer to Russia.

Russia's actions evoked a strong international reaction, as leaders of the United States, the European Union, and several European countries called upon Russia to refrain from violating Ukraine's territorial sovereignty Russia, along with the United States and the United Kingdom, had guaranteed that sovereignty in the 1994 Budapest Memorandum when Ukraine gave up its nuclear arsenal inherited from the Soviet period. Western governments and the EU instituted sanctions against Russia following the annexation of Crimea, claiming that Russia was continuing to foment unrest in eastern Ukraine by covertly encouraging takeovers of public buildings by armed separatist forces. The stationing of some 40,000 Russian troops near Ukraine's eastern border also fed fears that Russia might engage in further violations of Ukraine's territorial sovereignty. Although a portion of the troops were withdraw before the May 2014 election, Russia's actions fueled distrust of Russia in neighboring countries, and raised questions about the stability of the post-Soviet international order in Europe.

Political Challenges and Changing Agendas

Russia's future path continues to remain unclear. Will the country move "two steps forward, one step backward" toward a more democratic political system? Or is the country moving clearly in an authoritarian direction? Will Russia be able to reestablish a respected role as a regional and global power, to bring corruption under control, to establish trust in political institutions, and to diversify the economy? These are some of the key challenges facing the Russian Federation.

When the first edition of this book was published in 1996, five possible scenarios for Russia's future were presented:

1. A stable progression toward democratization
2. The gradual introduction of "soft authoritarianism"
3. A return to a more extreme authoritarianism of a quasi-fascist or communist variety
4. The disintegration of Russia into regional fiefdoms
5. Economic decline, civil war, and military expansionism

At the time of this writing, the "soft authoritarian" scenario seems to have taken hold; however, there are still significant forces that may move Russia back to a more democratic trajectory. Major questions also linger over Russia's regional and international aspirations in the wake of the 2014 events in Ukraine.

In the international sphere, Russia's flirtation with Westernization in the early 1990s produced ambiguous results, leading to a severe transitional recession and placing Russia in the position of a supplicant state requesting international credits and assistance from the West. Russia's protests against unpalatable international developments, such as NATO enlargement and NATO's bombing of Yugoslavia in

1999, revealed Moscow's underlying resentment against Western dominance, as well as the country's sense of powerlessness in affecting global developments. The events of September 11, 2001, however, provided an impetus for cooperative efforts in the battle against international terrorism, and Russia's economic revival imparted to the country a sense of greater power. Evidence of warmer relations included the formation of a NATO-Russia Council in May 2002, but new tensions arose around American withdrawal from the Anti-Ballistic Missile Treaty in 2002, Russian objections to the American incursion into Iraq in March 2003, American proposals to erect a missile defense system in Central Europe, a 2008 Russian incursion into Georgia, and most recently events surrounding developments in Ukraine in 2014.

One of Russia's main challenges has been to reestablish itself as a respected regional leader in neighboring countries, particularly those that were formerly part of the Soviet Union. The relationship to Ukraine has been fraught with particular difficulties. Ukraine's own internal political divisions have provided Russia with an opportunity to exert political leverage, as parts of the population desire closer ties with Russia, while others are oriented toward the West. Despite the country's declared aspiration for eventual membership in the European Union, Ukraine's economy remains closely linked to Russia's. Ukraine's role as a transit country for gas pipelines between Russia and the European Union has meant that tensions between Russia and Ukraine have sometimes led to the interruption of gas supplies to Western Europe.

The massive popular protests in Ukraine that followed the contested presidential election in 2004 (the Orange Revolution) elicited apprehension in Moscow, with Russia's leaders claiming they were nurtured by Western organizations. In February 2010 relations with Ukraine improved, as presidential elections in Ukraine saw the victory of the more pro-Russian candidate, Viktor Yanukovych, who subsequently concluded an agreement with Russia providing a twenty-five-year lease on a naval base in Ukraine's Crimea for use by Russia's Black Sea fleet in exchange for lower natural gas prices. However, as noted above, prospects for closer relations with the European Union in 2014 led Russia to increase the pressure on Ukraine to move closer to Russia, leading to an international crisis when Russia annexed Ukraine's region of Crimea. As a response to Russia's action, Ukraine and the European Union signed an Association Agreement in March 2014 and a comprehensive free trade agreement in June 2014, as the West strongly backed Ukraine's objections to Russia's move.

Relations with some other neighboring post-Soviet countries (e.g., Georgia) have been equally fraught with difficulties, as Russia has struggled to establish itself as a positive role model in the region. Efforts to form regional organizations to strengthen ties between these countries and Russia have taken a variety of forms. The largely ineffective Commonwealth of Independent States, formed in 1991 when the Soviet Union collapsed, was joined later by the Collective Security Treaty Organization (CSTO), the Eurasian Economic Forum, and the Shanghai Cooperation Organization (SCO, including China and the post-Soviet Central Asian states). Each of these organizations includes a subset of countries from the former Soviet space as members, but without Ukraine or Georgia. Most recently, Vladimir Putin announced the formation of the Eurasian Union, beginning with the formation of a Customs Union between Russia, Belarus and Kazakhstan. Putin's vision is for this to lead to more comprehensive integration, uniting several of the non-EU countries in the post-Soviet space under Russian leadership. However, concerns about Russian dominance and incompatibility with European aspirations have held back potential members, such as Ukraine, from signing on.

Russia's has also sought to establish itself as an equal partner with the United States and Europe. Following U.S. Secretary of State Clinton's effort to reset U.S.-Russian relations in March 2009, progress was made on key issues of conflict at a

FIGURE 7.4 Attitudes of the Russian Population to Foreign Countries
"Overall, how do you feel about the following at the current time?"

Source: Data from Levada Center, http://www.levada.ru/26-02-2014/otnoshenie-rossiyan-k-drugim
-stranam, accessed March 14, 2014.

NATO-Russia Summit in Lisbon in November 2010. In the face of the expiration of
the Strategic Arms Reduction Treaty in December 2009, a new agreement between the
United States and Russia went into effect in January 2011. However, the decision of
the United States to pursue installation of a missile defense system in Eastern Europe
(in response to potential Iranian action) has continued to irritate Russia. Until 2014,
progress in EU-Russia relations was more substantial, with a broad range of negotiating
platforms, and movement toward eased visa regulations and enhanced trade; however,
this process has largely halted in the face of the crisis over Crimea and the conflict in
eastern Ukraine. Nonetheless, Russia remains the most important source of Europe's
gas imports. However, experts believe that without increased Western investment
and technological know-how, Russia will not be able to develop untapped deposits
quickly enough to meet both domestic demands and export commitments. An major
agreement regarding future Russian gas exports to China, signed in May 2014, is an
indicator of Russia's intention of reducing its dependence on exports to Europe.

The 2008–2009 global financial-economic crisis sent a warning to Russia about the
dangers of an economy dependent on energy exports. A sharp drop in gas and oil prices
temporarily undercut the foundation of Russia's economic motor. From positive growth
rates in the previous ten years, Russia moved to a dramatic fall by the first quarter of
2009. Because energy prices recovered fairly quickly and Russian had reserve funds to
fall back on, the crisis did not push Russia back to the disastrous economic situation of
the 1990s, but the dramatic shift in economic performance may have reminded both
the Russian public and its leaders of the potential fragility of the economic recovery.

In November 2009 President Medvedev published a much-discussed article entitled "Go Russia" in which he called for a modernization program, primarily through
the development of high-technology sectors.[21] However, with Putin's return to the
presidency in 2012, the modernization program proved to be stillborn. Furthermore,
hopes that political liberalization might accompany efforts to diversify the economy
were also dashed. The continuing disjuncture between high personal support for
Putin alongside a continuing lack of confidence in the ability of political institutions to address the country's problems suggests that the legitimacy of the system is

still on thin ice. The more positive working relationship between the executive and legislative branches that emerged under the Medvedev-Putin tandem has been at the cost of permitting a real parliamentary opposition to function. Failed efforts to control corruption, mechanisms to exert control over the newly reinstated gubernatorial

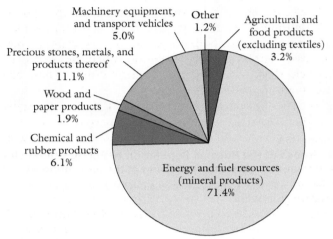

FIGURE 7.5 Structure of Russian Exports, 2012

Source: Data from the Russian State Statistical Service, *Russia in Figures 2013*, http://www.gks.ru/bgd/regl/b13_12/Main.htm, accessed 14 March 2014.

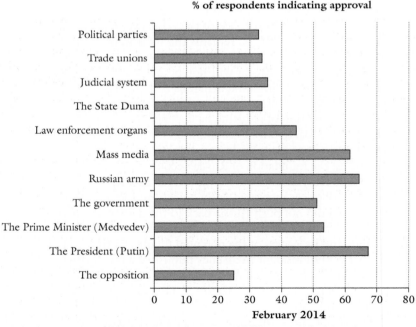

FIGURE 7.6 Approval Ratings of Various Offices and Institutions, % of Respondents Indicating Approval

Source: Data from the website of the Russian Public Opinion Research Center (VTsIOM), http://wciom.ru/ratings, accessed March 14, 2014.

elections and efforts to control political opposition already show signs of producing poor policy choices that may themselves reinforce public cynicism about the motives of politicians and the trustworthiness of institutions.

Despite changes in social consciousness, the formation of new political identities also remains unfinished business. Many people are still preoccupied by challenges of everyday life, with little time or energy to engage in new forms of collective action to address underlying problems. Under such circumstances, the appeal to nationalism and other basic sentiments can be powerful. The weakness of Russian intermediary organizations (interest groups, political parties, or associations) means that politicians can more easily appeal directly to emotions because people are not members of groups that help them to evaluate the political claims. These conditions reduce safeguards against authoritarian outcomes.

Nevertheless, the high level of education and increasing exposure to international media and the Internet may work in the opposite direction. Many Russians identify their country as part of Europe and its culture, an attitude echoed by the government. Exposure to alternative political systems and cultures may make people more critical of their own political system and seek opportunities to change it. Russia remains in what seems to be an extended period of transition. In the early 1990s, Russians frequently hoped for "normal conditions," that is, an escape from the shortages, insecurity, and political controls of the past. Now, "normality" has been redefined in less glowing terms than those conceived in the late 1980s. Russians seem to have a capability to adapt to change and uncertainty that North Americans find at once alluring, puzzling, and disturbing.

Youth Politics and the Generational Divide

Young people in Russia have grown up in political circumstances that differ dramatically from those that affected their parents. Whereas individuals born before 1970 (now middle-aged or older) were socialized during the period of communist rule, Russians between the ages of 18 and 30 had their formative experiences during a period of rapid political change following the collapse of the USSR. Whereas their elders were drawn into communist youth organizations and influenced by the dominance of a single party/state ideology, young people today are exposed to a wider range of political views, have greater freedom to travel abroad, and also have freer access to international contacts and viewpoints. These tendencies are reinforced even further by increased access to information through the Internet, which young people use more freely. It is, therefore, not surprising that age is associated with differing political orientations.

Generational experience also affects the ability to adapt. In the Soviet period, weak material incentives encouraged risk avoidance, low productivity, poor punctuality, absenteeism, lack of personal initiative, and a preference for security over achievement. However, young people in Russia are adapting to a new work environment. They are more flexible, in part due to their age, but also because of differing socialization experiences that have resulted in altered expectations. Consequently, they are inclined to support the market transition and are more oriented toward maximizing self-interest and demonstrating initiative. Nevertheless, many Russians of all age groups still question values underlying market reform, preferring an economy that is less profit driven and more oriented to equality and the collective good.

Despite generational differences, young people represent a wide range of political views in Russia, as elsewhere. A controversial phenomenon is the youth group, Nashi (Ours), formed in 2005. While claiming to oppose fascism in Russia, some observers see the group as nurturing intolerance and extremist sentiments. Nashi's goals include educating youth in Russian history and values, and forming volunteer groups to help maintain law and order. The group has been highly supportive of Putin, seeing him as a defender of Russia's national sovereignty. On the other hand, political critics of the Putin regime, such as those who initially participated in demonstrations in 2011, were disproportionately young, but over time they were joined by many middle-aged protesters. While support for Putin in the lead up to the presidential election of 2012 was relatively similar across age groups, those older than 40 were more likely to support the Communist Party, and more young people supported the non-establishment candidate, Mikhail Prokhorov. According to surveys carried out in December 2013, older respondents were far more likely to express regret about the collapse of the USSR (86 percent of those over 55, compared to only 24 percent of those 18–24).[22]

These indicators suggest that age does affect political orientations, but not strongly enough to predict a generational shift in voting patterns in the foreseeable future.

Russian Politics in Comparative Perspective

The way in which politics, economics, and ideology were intertwined in the Soviet period has profoundly affected the nature of political change in all of the former Soviet republics and generally has made the democratization process more difficult. How has Russia fared compared to some of the other post-communist systems that faced many of these same challenges, and what can we learn from these comparisons? A rule of thumb, simple as it seems, is that the further east one goes in the post-communist world, the more difficult and prolonged the transition period has been (with the exception of Belarus, which lies adjacent to the European Union but maintains an authoritarian system). This is partly because the more westerly countries of Central Europe that were outside the USSR (Poland, Hungary, Czech Republic, Slovakia), as well as the Baltic states (Estonia, Latvia, Lithuania), were able to accede to the European Union, producing a strong motivation to embark on fundamental reform. This illustrates the potentially powerful impact of international forces on domestic political developments, if domestic actors are receptive. Also these countries were under communist rule for a shorter period of time. In addition most of these countries had a history of closer ties and greater cultural exposure to Western Europe; ideas of liberalism, private property, and individualism were less foreign to citizens in countries such as Czechoslovakia, East Germany, Poland, and Hungary than in regions farther east, including Russia. Historical legacies and cultural differences do matter.

Russia's experience demonstrates the importance of strong political institutions if democracy is to be secured. Their weakness in the 1990s contributed to high levels of social dislocation, corruption, and personal stress, as well as to demographic decline and poor economic adaptation to the market. However, Russia's rich deposits of natural resources have sheltered it from difficulties facing some neighboring countries like Ukraine. At the same time, Russia's natural resource wealth has made it difficult to untangle economic and political power, reducing political accountability to the public. The "resource curse" produces economic hazards as well, including the so-called Dutch disease, in which heavy reliance on income from natural resource exports pushes the value of the currency up, making it more difficult for domestic producers to export successfully and feeding inflationary pressures.

In all of the post-Soviet states (except the Baltic states), the attempt to construct democratic political institutions has been characterized by repeated political crises, weak representation of popular interests, executive–legislative conflict, faltering efforts at constitutional revision, and corruption. In Russia, terrorist attacks persist, reinforcing a sense of insecurity and producing fertile ground for nationalist sentiments and a strong role for the security forces, which themselves enjoy a low level of popular legitimacy. Nonetheless, with the exception of the Chechnya conflict and its spillover into the neighboring areas in Russia's European south, Russia has escaped major domestic violence and civil war, unlike parts of the former Yugoslavia, Georgia, Moldova, the Central Asian state of Tajikistan, and, most recently, eastern Ukraine.

Will Russia be able to find a place for itself in the world of states that meets the expectations of its educated and sophisticated population? Even after the first decade of the new millennium, prospects are still unclear. One thing is certain: Russia will continue to be a key regional force in Europe and Asia by virtue of its size, its rich energy and resource base, its large and highly skilled population and its nuclear arsenal. However, Russia's leaders have had an ambivalent attitude toward accepting crucial norms that would underlie an effective and enduring partnership with the West.

If the Russian leadership gradually moves Russia on a path closer to liberal democratic development, then this may provide an example to other semiauthoritarian countries in Russia's neighborhood. On the other hand, if the continuation of existing authoritarian trends is associated with sustained economic growth and stability that benefits the majority of the population, then Russia may settle into an extended period of soft authoritarianism that reinforces the East–West divide, and that could, if not resisted by the political leadership, feed destructive nationalist tendencies. Finally, if the Russian leadership's insulation generates unpopular and ineffective policy outcomes, or if world energy prices trigger an economic downslide, this may stimulate a new process of reflection on Russia's future path and offer an opportunity for democratic forces to reassert themselves and find popular resonance.

Where Do You Stand?

Is Russia justified in taking strong action to assure that a neighboring country, such as Ukraine, stays within its "sphere of influence"?

Should Western countries make greater efforts to promote liberal democratic opposition groups in Russia?

Chapter Summary

Russian history has been characterized by a series of upheavals and changes that have often made life unpredictable and difficult for the citizen. The revolutions of 1917 replaced tsarist rule with a political system dominated by the Communist Party. In the Stalinist period, Communist rule involved a process of rapid industrialization, collectivization of agriculture, and purges of the party, followed by large losses of population associated with World War II. With the death of Stalin came another important transition, as Soviet politics was transformed into a more predictable system of bureaucratic authoritarianism, characterized by relative stability but without political competition or democratic control. The most recent transition, ushered in by the collapse of Communist Party rule in 1991, resulted in the emergence

of the Russian Federation as an independent state. When the Russian Federation was formed in 1991, new political structures needed to be constructed. A constitution was adopted in 1993, which involves a directly elected president with strong political powers.

Russia's political course since 1991 has been profoundly influenced by the fact that the country underwent simultaneous and radical transformations in four spheres: politics, economics, ideology, and geopolitical position in the world. Managing so much change in a short time has been difficult and has produced mixed results. Efforts to democratize the political system have been only partially successful, and experts disagree both about whether the political controls initiated by Putin were needed to ensure stability and under what conditions they might be reversed. In the economic sphere, after recovering from a period of deep economic decline in the 1990s, Russia's renewed growth depends largely on exports of energy and natural resources, making the country vulnerable to external shocks such as the 2008–2009 global crisis. The country faces the challenge of effectively using its natural resource wealth to rebuild other sectors of the economy. In terms of ideology, nationalism threatens to reinforce intolerance and undermine social unity. Continuing high levels of corruption also undermine popular confidence in state institutions. Whereas countries that have joined the European Union seem, for the most part, to have successfully established viable democratic systems with functioning market economies, other post-Soviet states in Eastern Europe and Central Asia face similar challenges to Russia's in consolidating democracy and market reform. Russia has sought to reassert its role as a regional and global force, but a revival of tension with the West in the face of Russia's annexation of Crimea and conflict over Ukraine threatens stability in Russia's neighborhood.

Key Terms

civil society	*glasnost*	patrimonial state
clientelistic networks	insider privatization	power vertical
collectivization	market reform	*siloviki*
democratic centralism	mixed electoral system	soft authoritarianism
dominant party	*nomenklatura*	sovereign democracy
federal system	oligarchs	vanguard party

Suggested Readings

Black, J. L. and Michael Johns, eds. *Russia After 2012: From Putin to Medvedev to Putin – Continuity, Change, or Revolution?* London and New York: Routledge, 2013.

Gel'man, Valdimir, and Cameron Ross, eds. *The Politics of Sub-National Authoritarianism in Russia.* Farnham, Surrey UK: Ashgate, 2010.

Hopf, Ted, ed. *Russia's European Choice.* New York: Palgrave MacMillan, 2008.

Hough, Jerry, and Merle Fainsod. *How the Soviet Union Is Governed.* Cambridge: Harvard University Press, 1979.

Ledeneva, Alena V. *Can Russia Modernize? Sistema, Power Networks and Informal Governance.* Cambridge: Cambridge University Press, 2013.

Mankoff, Jeffrey. *Russian Foreign Policy: The Return of Great Power Politics.* Lanham, MD: Rowman & Littlefield, 2012.

Oates, Sarah. *Revolution Stalled: The Political Limits of the Internet in the Post-Soviet Space.* Oxford: Oxford University Press, 2013.

Pipes, Richard. *Russia under the Old Regime.* New York: Scribner, 1974.

Remington, Thomas F. *Politics in Russia,* 7th ed. New Jersey: Pearson, 2012.

Sakwa, Richard. *Putin: Russia's Choice.* London and New York: Routledge, 2008.

Suggested Websites

The Carnegie Moscow Center
www.carnegie.ru/en/

Itar-TASS News Agency
http://en.itar-tass.com/

Johnson's Russia List
http://www.russialist.org/

Open Democracy (Russia)
http://www.opendemocracy.net/russia

Radio Free Europe/Radio Liberty
http://www.rferl.org/section/Russia/161.html

The Moscow News
www.mnweekly.ru

Russian Analytical Digest
http://www.laender-analysen.de/index .php?topic=russland&url=http://www.res.ethz.ch /analysis/rad/

Russia Today
rt.com

8 Iran

Ervand Abrahamian

Official Name: Islamic Republic of Iran (Jomhuri-ye Eslami-ye Iran)

Location: Middle East (West Asia)

Capital City: Tehran

Population (2014): 80.8 million

Size: approximately 1,648,000 sq. km.; slightly larger than Alaska

1925
Reza Khan establishes the Pahlavi dynasty.

1941–1945
Allied occupation of Iran during World War II

1953
CIA-supported coup overthrows Mossadeq.

1963
Shah launches "White Revolution."

1920　　1940　　1950　　1960　　1965　　1970　　1975

1921
Colonel Reza Khan's military coup

1941
Muhammad Reza Pahlavi becomes Shah of Iran.

1951
Nationalization of the oil industry by government of Prime Minister Mossadeq

1975
Shah establishes the Resurgence Party.

1905–1911
Constitutional Revolution

SECTION 1

THE MAKING OF THE MODERN IRANIAN STATE

ayatollah

Literally, "sign of God." A high-ranking cleric in Iran.

Politics in Action

In 2013, Iran with a resounding vote elected Dr. Hassan Rouhani president of the Islamic Republic. Rouhani is a middle-ranking religious cleric, not an **ayatollah**, and prefers to be addressed as Dr.—a title he has from a university in Scotland where he obtained a Ph.D. in constitutional law. He won the election running on a reform platform, promising to remedy a "sick economy," strengthen the rule of law, and, most important of all, improve relations with the West, especially over the nuclear stand-off with the United States. The 2013 election was in many ways a replay of previous ones. In 1997, Muhammad Khatami, another middle-ranking reform cleric, had been elected president in a landslide victory. He was reelected in 2001 again with a landslide victory. But in 2005, after deteriorations of relations with the United States, he had been replaced by an ultraconservative populist named Mahmoud Ahmadinejad. Ahmadinejad had retained the presidency in 2009 after a hotly disputed election. Iran may lack many features of a true democracy. But it certainly does not lack fiercely contested elections.

These very different electoral outcomes illustrate the contradictory political forces at work in the Islamic Republic of Iran. Iran is a mixture of **theocracy** and democracy. Its political system is based on both clerical authority and popular sovereignty, on the divine right of the clergy and the rights of the people, on concepts derived from early Islam and from modern democratic principles. Iran

Timeline

1979 | Islamic Revolution; Shah forced into exile; Iran becomes an Islamic Republic; Ayatollah Khomeini becomes Leader.

March 1980 | Elections for the First Islamic *Majles* (parliament). Subsequent Majles elections every four years

June 1981 | President Bani-Sadr ousted by Khomeini, replaced by Muhammad Ali Rajai

2005 | Ultraconservative Mahmoud Ahmadinejad elected president

2013 | Dr. Hassan Rouhani elected President on reform platform

1979 — 1980 — 1985 — 1990 — 2000 — 2005

1979–1981 | Hostage crisis—52 U.S. embassy employees held by radical students

December 1979 | Referendum on the Islamic constitution

October 1981 | Ayatollah Ali Khamenei elected president

January 1980 | Abol-Hassan Bani-Sadr elected president

1980–1988 | War with Iraq

1989 | Khomeini dies; Khamenei appointed Leader; Rafsanjani elected president (reelected in 1993)

1997 | Muhammad Khatami elected president on reform platform (reelected in 2001)

2009 | Ahmadinejad re-elected; large-scale protests against alleged electoral fraud take place in Tehran and other cities.

---

has regular elections for the presidency and the *Majles* (Parliament), but the clerically dominated **Guardian Council** determines who can run. The president is the formal head of the executive branch. But he can be overruled, even dismissed, by the chief cleric, the **Leader** known in the West as the **Supreme Leader**. The president appoints the minister of justice, but the whole judiciary is under the supervision of the chief judge, who is appointed directly by the Leader. The *Majles* is the legislature, but bills do not become law unless the Guardian Council deems them compatible with Islam and the Islamic constitution. Thus, the Guardian Council—formed of twelve senior judges with six appointed by the Leader and six jointly by the Majles and the chief judge—has considerable judicial as well as legislative authority.

Geographic Setting

Iran is three times the size of France, slightly larger than Alaska, and much larger than its immediate neighbors. Most of its territory is inhospitable to agriculture. Rain-fed agriculture is confined mostly to the northwest and the provinces along the Caspian Sea. Only pastoral nomads can survive in the semiarid zones and in the high mountain valleys. Thus, 67 percent of the total population of a little over 80 million is concentrated on 27 percent of the land—mostly in the Caspian region, in the northwest provinces, and in the cities of Tehran, Mashed, Isfahan, Tabriz, Shiraz, and Qom.

Iran is the second-largest oil producer in the Middle East and the fourth-largest in the world, and oil revenues have made Iran an urbanized and partly industrialized country. Nearly 70 percent of the population lives in urban centers; 84 percent of the labor force is employed in industry and services; 85 percent of adults are literate; life expectancy has reached over seventy-three years; and the majority of Iranians enjoy a standard of living well above that found in most of Asia and Africa. Iran can no longer be described as a typically poor developing country. It

theocracy

A state dominated by the clergy, who rule on the grounds that they are the only interpreters of God's will and law.

Majles

The Iranian parliament, from the Arabic term for "assembly."

Guardian Council

A committee created in the Iranian constitution to oversee the *Majles* (the parliament.

Leader/Supreme Leader

A cleric elected to be the head of the Islamic Republic of Iran.

is a middle-income country with a GDP per capita above that of Brazil and South Africa. Recent UN economic sanctions have caused considerable hardship but have not reduced its general standing.

Iran lies on the strategic crossroads between Central Asia and Turkey, between the Indian subcontinent and the Middle East, and between the Arabian Peninsula and the Caucasus Mountains, which are often considered a boundary between Europe and Asia. This has made the region vulnerable to invaders.

The population today reflects these historic invasions. Some 53 percent speak Persian (Farsi), an Indo-European language, as a first language; the remainder of the population primarily speaks eight other languages. Use of Persian, however, has dramatically increased in recent years because of successful literacy campaigns. Over 90 percent of the population can now communicate in Persian, the national language. Although Iran shares many religious and cultural features with the rest of the Islamic Middle East, its Persian heritage gives it a national identity distinct from that of the Arab and Turkish world. Iranians by no means consider themselves part of the Arab world.

Islam, with over 1 billion adherents, is the second-largest religion in the world after Christianity. Islam means literally "submission to God," and a Muslim is someone who has submitted to God—the same God that Jews and Christians worship. Islam has one central tenet: "There is only one God, and Muhammad is His Prophet." Muslims, in order to consider themselves faithful, need to perform the following four duties to the best of their ability: give to charity; pray every day facing Mecca, where Abraham is believed to have built the first place of worship; make a pilgrimage at least once in a lifetime to Mecca, which is located in modern Saudi Arabia; and fast during the daytime hours in the month of Ramadan to commemorate God's revelation of the Qur'an (Koran, or Holy Book) to the Prophet Muhammad. These four, together with the central tenet, are known as the Five Pillars of Islam.

From its earliest days, Islam has been divided into two major branches: Sunni, meaning literally "followers of tradition," and Shi'i, literally "partisans of Ali." Sunnis are by far in the majority worldwide. Shi'is constitute less than 10 percent of Muslims worldwide and are concentrated in Iran, southern Iraq, Bahrain, eastern Turkey, Azerbaijan, and southern Lebanon.

Although both branches accept the Five Pillars, they differ mostly over who should have succeeded the Prophet Muhammad (d. 632). The Sunnis recognized the early dynasties that ruled the Islamic empire with the exalted title of caliph ("Prophet's Deputy"). The Shi'is, however, argued that as soon as the Prophet died, his authority should have been passed on to Imam Ali, the Prophet's close companion, disciple, and son-in-law. They further argue that Imam Ali passed his authority to his direct male heirs, the third of whom, Imam Husayn, had been martyred fighting the Sunnis in 680, and the twelfth of whom had supposedly gone into hiding in 941.

The Shi'is are also known as Twelvers since they follow the Twelve Imams. They refer to the Twelfth Imam as the *Mahdi*, the Hidden Imam, and believe him to be the Messiah who will herald the end of the world. Furthermore, they argue that in his absence, the authority to interpret the *shari'a* (religious law) should be in the hands of the senior clerical scholars—the ayatollahs. Thus, from the beginning, the Shi'is harbored ambivalent attitudes toward the state, especially if the rulers were Sunnis or lacked genealogical links to the Twelve Imams. For Sunnis, the *shari'a* is based mostly on the Qur'an and the teachings of the Prophet. For Shi'is, it is based also on the teachings of the Twelve Imams.

Farsi

Persian word for the Persian language. Fars is a province in Central Iran.

Table 8.1	Political Organization
Political System	A mixture of democracy and theocracy (rule of the clergy) headed by a cleric with the title of the Leader.
Regime History	Islamic Republic since the 1979 Islamic Revolution.
Administrative Structure	Centralized administration with 30 provinces. The interior minister appoints the provincial governor-generals.
Executive	President and his cabinet. The president is chosen by the general electorate every four years and is limited to two terms. The president chooses his cabinet ministers, but they need to obtain the approval of the *Majles* (parliament).
Legislature	Unicameral. The *Majles*, formed of 290 seats, is elected every four years. It has multiple-member districts with the top runners in the elections taking the seats. Bills passed by the *Majles* do not become law unless they have the approval of the clerically dominated Council of Guardians.
Judiciary	A Chief Judge and a Supreme Court independent of the executive and legislature but appointed by the Leader.
Party System	The ruling clergy restricts most party and organizational activities.

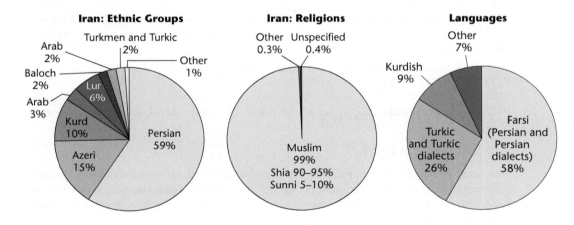

Iran: Ethnic Groups
Turkmen and Turkic 2%
Arab 2%
Other 1%
Baloch 2%
Lur 6%
Arab 3%
Kurd 10%
Azeri 15%
Persian 59%

Iran: Religions
Other 0.3%   Unspecified 0.4%
Muslim 99%
Shia 90–95%
Sunni 5–10%

Languages
Other 7%
Kurdish 9%
Turkic and Turkic dialects 26%
Farsi (Persian and Persian dialects) 58%

Iranian Currency

Rial (ریال)
International Designation: IRR
Exchange Rate (2013):
• 1 US$ = 18,517 IRR
• 1 IRR = 0 US$
100,000 Rial Note Design: Ayatollah Ruhollah Khomeini

FIGURE 8.1 The Iranian Nation at a Glance
© Oleg_Mit/Shutterstock.com (for photo)

© Cengage Learning®

Critical Junctures

The Safavids (1501–1722)

The Safavid dynasty conquered the territory that is now Iran in the sixteenth century and forcibly converted their subjects to Shi'ism, even though the vast majority had been Sunnis. By the mid-seventeenth century, Sunnism survived only among the tribal groups at the periphery.

Safavid Iran also contained small communities of Jews, Zoroastrians, and Christians. The Safavids tolerated religious minorities as long as they paid special taxes and accepted royal authority. According to Islam, Christians, Jews, and Zoroastrians were to be tolerated as legitimate **People of the Book**, because they were mentioned in the Holy **Qur'an** and possessed their own sacred texts: the Bible, the Torah, and the Avesta.

The Safavids governed through Persian scribes and Shi'i clerics as well as through tribal chiefs, large landowners, city merchants, guild elders, and urban ward leaders. Their army was formed mostly of tribal cavalry led by tribal chieftains. Safavid revenues came mostly from land taxes levied on the peasantry. The Safavids claimed absolute power, but they lacked a central state and had to cooperate with many semi-independent local leaders.

People of the Book

The Muslim term for recognized religious minorities, such as Christians, Jews, and Zoroastrians.

Qur'an

The Muslim Bible.

The Qajars (1794–1925)

In 1722 Afghan tribesmen invaded the capital. After a half-century of civil wars the Qajars—a Turkic-speaking Shi'i tribe—reconquered much of Iran. They moved the capital to Tehran and re-created the Safavid system of central manipulation and court administration. They also declared Shi'ism to be the state religion, even though they, unlike the Safavids, could not boast of genealogical links to the Twelve Imams. Since these new shahs, or kings, did not pretend to wear the Imam's mantle, Shi'i clerical leaders could claim to be the main interpreters of Islam.

Qajar rule coincided with the peak of European imperialism in the nineteenth century. The Russians seized parts of Central Asia and the Caucasus region from Iran and extracted major economic concessions. The British Imperial Bank won the monopoly to issue paper money. The Indo-European Telegraph Company got a contract to extend communication lines throughout the country. Exclusive rights to drill for oil in the southwest were sold to a British citizen. Iranians increasingly felt their whole country had been auctioned off.

These resentments led to the constitutional revolution of 1905–1909. The 1906 constitution introduced elections, separation of powers, a legislative assembly, and the concepts of popular sovereignty and the nation (*mellat*). It retained the monarchy, but centered political power in a national assembly called the *Majles*.

The constitution gave the *Majles* extensive authority over all laws, budgets, treaties, concessions, and the makeup of the cabinet. The ministers were accountable to the *Majles*, not to the shah. The constitution also included a bill of rights guaranteeing equality before the law, protection of life and property, and freedom of expression and association.

Shi'ism was declared Iran's official religion. Clerical courts continued to implement the *shari'a*. A Guardian Council of senior clerics elected by the *Majles* had veto power over parliamentary bills it deemed un-Islamic.

The initial euphoria soon gave way to deep disillusionment. Pressures from the European powers continued, and a devastating famine after World War I took some 1 million lives, almost 10 percent of the total population. Internal conflicts polarized the *Majles* into warring liberal and conservative factions. Liberals, mostly members of the intelligentsia, championed social reforms, especially the replacement of the *shari'a* with a modern legal code. Conservatives, led by landlords, tribal chiefs, and senior clerics, vehemently opposed such reforms, particularly land reform, women's rights, and the granting of full equality to religious minorities.

The central government, without any real army, bureaucracy, or tax-collecting machinery, could not administer the provinces. During World War I, Russia and Britain formally carved up Iran into three zones. Russia occupied the north, Britain the south. Iran was left with a small middle "neutral zone."

By 1921, Iran was in complete disarray. According to a British diplomat, the propertied classes, fearful of communism, were anxiously seeking "a savior on horseback."[1]

The Pahlavis (1925–1979)

In February 1921 Colonel Reza Khan carried out a coup d'état. He replaced the cabinet and consolidated power in his own hands. Four years later, he deposed the Qajars and crowned himself Shah-in-Shah—King of Kings—and established the Pahlavi dynasty. This was the first nontribal dynasty to rule the whole of Iran. During the next sixteen years, he systematically modernized the country by building almost from scratch a highly centralized state with a standing army and a large administrative bureaucracy.

Reza Shah ruled with an iron fist until 1941, when the British and the Soviets invaded Iran to stop Nazi Germany from establishing a foothold there. Reza Shah promptly abdicated in favor of his son, Muhammad Reza Shah, and went into exile, where he soon died. In the first twelve years of his reign, the young Shah retained control over the armed forces but had to tolerate a free press, an independent judiciary, competitive elections, assertive cabinet ministers, and boisterous parliaments. He also had to confront two vigorous political movements: the communist Tudeh (Masses) Party and the National Front, led by the charismatic Dr. Muhammad Mossadeq (1882–1967).

The Tudeh drew its support mostly from working-class trade unions. The National Front drew its support mainly from the salaried middle classes and campaigned to nationalize the British company that controlled the petroleum industry. Mossadeq also wanted to sever the Shah's links with the armed forces. In 1951, Mossadeq was elected prime minister and promptly nationalized the oil industry. The period of relative freedom, however, ended abruptly in 1953, when royalist army officers overthrew Mossadeq and installed the Shah with absolute power. The coup was financed by the U.S. Central Intelligence Agency (CIA) and the British. This intensified anti-British sentiment and created a deep distrust of the United States. It also made the Shah appear to be a foreign puppet.

The Pahlavi dynasty continued to build a highly centralized state. The armed forces grew from 40,000 in 1925 to 124,000 in 1941, and to 410,000 in 1979. The armed forces were supplemented by a pervasive secret police known as SAVAK.

Iran's bureaucracy expanded to twenty-one ministries employing over 300,000 civil servants in 1979. The Education Ministry grew twentyfold. The powerful Interior Ministry appointed provincial governors, town mayors, district superintendents, and village headmen; it could even rig *Majles* elections and create rubber-stamp parliaments.

The Justice Ministry supplanted the *shari'a* with a European-style civil code and the clerical courts with a modern judicial system culminating in a Supreme Court. The Transport Ministry built an impressive array of bridges, ports, highways, and railroads known as the Trans-Iranian Railway. The Ministry of Industries financed factories specializing in consumer goods. The Agricultural Ministry became prominent in 1963 when the Shah made land reform the centerpiece of his "White Revolution." This White Revolution was an effort to promote economic development and such social reform as extending the vote to women. It also created a Literacy Corps for the countryside. This White Revolution from above—encouraged by the United States—was a concerted attempt to forestall a communist-led Red Revolution from below. Thus, by the late 1970s, the state had set up a modern system of communications, initiated a minor industrial revolution, and extended its reach into even the most outlying villages.

The state also controlled the National and the Central Banks; the Industrial and Mining Development Bank; the Plan Organization in charge of economic policy; the national radio-television network; and most important, the National Iranian Oil Company.

The dynasty's founder, Reza Shah, had used coercion, confiscation, and diversion of irrigation water to make himself one of the largest landowners in the Middle East. This wealth transformed the Shah's imperial court into a large military-monied complex, providing work for thousands in its numerous palaces, hotels, casinos, charities, and beach resorts. This patronage system grew under his son, Muhammad Reza

Shah, particularly after he established his tax-exempt Pahlavi Foundation, which eventually controlled 207 large companies.

The Pahlavi drive for secularization, centralization, industrialization, and social development won some favor from the urban propertied classes. But arbitrary rule; the 1953 coup that overthrew a popular prime minister; the disregard for constitutional liberties; and the stifling of independent newspapers, political parties, and professional associations produced widespread resentment. The Pahlavi state, like the Safavids and the Qajars, hovered over, rather than embedded itself into, Iranian society.

In 1975, the Shah formed the Resurgence Party. He declared Iran a one-party state and threatened imprisonment and exile to those refusing to join the party. The Resurgence Party was designed to create yet another organizational link with the population, especially with the bazaars (traditional marketplaces), which, unlike the rest of society, had managed to retain their independent guilds and thus escape direct government control. The Resurgence Party promptly established its own bazaar guilds as well as newspapers, women's organizations, professional associations, and labor unions. It also prepared to create a Religious Corps to teach the peasants "true Islam."

bazaar

An urban marketplace where shops, workshops, small businesses, and export-importers are located.

The Islamic Revolution (1979)

These grievances were best summed up by an exile newspaper in Paris on the very eve of the 1979 revolution. In an article entitled "Fifty Years of Treason," it charged the Shah and his family with establishing a military dictatorship; collaborating with the CIA; trampling on the constitution; creating SAVAK, the secret police; rigging parliamentary elections; organizing a fascistic one-party state; taking over the religious establishment; and undermining national identity by disseminating Western culture. It also accused the regime of inducing millions of landless peasants to migrate into urban shantytowns; widening the gap between rich and poor; funneling money away from the middle-class bourgeoisie into the pockets of the wealthy comprador bourgeoisie (entrepreneurs linked to foreign companies and multinational corporations); wasting resources on bloated military budgets; and granting new capitulations to the West.

These grievances took sharper edge when the leading opposition cleric, Ayatollah Ruhollah Khomeini—exiled in Iraq—formulated a drastically new version of Shi'ism. His version of Shi'ism has often been labeled Islamic fundamentalism. It would be better to call it political Islam or even more accurately as Shi'i populism. The term *fundamentalism*, derived from American Protestantism, implies religious dogmatism, intellectual inflexibility and purity, political traditionalism, social conservatism, rejection of the modern world, and the literal interpretation of scriptural texts. While Khomeinism shares some of these characteristics, Khomeini was not so much a social conservative as a political revolutionary who used populist rhetoric to rally the population against a decadent elite.

political Islam

A term for the intermingling of Islam with politics and often used as a substitute for Islamic fundamentalism.

Khomeini was born in 1902 into a landed clerical family in central Iran. During the 1920s, he studied in the famous Fayzieh Seminary in Qom with the leading theologians of the day, most of whom were scrupulously apolitical. He taught at the seminary from the 1930s through the 1950s, avoiding politics even during the mass campaign to nationalize the British-owned oil company. His entry into politics did not come until 1963, when he, along with most other clerical leaders, denounced the White Revolution. Forced into exile, Khomeini taught at the Shi'i center of Najaf in Iraq from 1964 until 1978. During these years, Khomeini developed his own version of Shi'i populism by incorporating socioeconomic grievances into his sermons and denouncing not just the Shah but also the whole ruling class.

Khomeini denounced monarchies in general as part of the corrupt elite exploiting the oppressed masses. Oppressors were courtiers, large landowners, high-ranking military officers, wealthy foreign-connected capitalists, and millionaire palace dwellers. The oppressed were the masses, especially landless peasants, wage earners, bazaar shopkeepers, and shantytown dwellers.

jurist's guardianship

Khomeini's concept that the Iranian clergy should rule on the grounds that they are the divinely appointed guardians of both the law and the people.

Khomeini gave a radically new meaning to the old Shi'i term *velayat-e faqih* (jurist's guardianship). He argued that jurist's guardianship gave the senior clergy all-encompassing authority over the whole community, not just over widows, minors, and the mentally disabled (the previous interpretation). Only the senior clerics could understand the *shari'a*; the divine authority given to the Prophet and the Imams had been passed on to their spiritual heirs, the clergy. He further insisted the clergy were the people's true representatives, since they lived among them, listened to their problems, and shared their everyday joys and pains. He claimed that the Shah secretly planned to confiscate all religious endowment funds and replace Islamic values with "cultural imperialism."

In 1977–1978, the Shah tried to deal with a 20 percent rise in consumer prices and a 10 percent decline in oil revenues by cutting construction projects and declaring war against "profiteers," "hoarders," and "price gougers." Shopkeepers believed the Shah was diverting attention from court corruption and planning to replace them with government-run department stores. They also thought he was out to destroy the bazaar.

The Shah was also subjected to international pressure on the sensitive issue of human rights—from Amnesty International, the United Nations, and the Western press, as well as from the recently elected Carter administration in the United States. In 1977, the Shah gave the International Red Cross access to Iranian prisons and permitted political prisoners to have defense attorneys. This international pressure allowed the opposition to "breathe" again after decades of suffocation.[2]

This slight loosening of the reins sealed the fate of the Shah. Political parties, labor organizations, and professional associations—especially lawyers, writers, and university professors—regrouped after years of being banned. Bazaar guilds regained their independence. College, high school, and seminary students took to the streets—with each demonstration growing in size and vociferousness. On September 8, 1978, remembered in Iran as Black Friday, troops shot and killed a large but unknown number of unarmed civilians in central Tehran. This dramatically intensified popular hatred for the regime. By late 1978, general strikes throughout the country were bringing the whole economy to a halt. Oil workers vowed that they would not export petroleum until they had got rid of the "Shah and his forty thieves."[3]

pasdaran

Persian term for guards, used to refer to the army of Revolutionary Guards formed during Iran's Islamic Revolution.

In urban centers, local committees attached to the mosques and financed by the bazaars were distributing food to the needy, supplanting the police with militias known as *pasdaran* (Revolutionary Guards). They replaced the judicial system with ad hoc courts applying the *shari'a*. Anti-regime rallies were now attracting as many as 2 million protesters. Protesters demanded the abolition of the monarchy, the return of Khomeini, and the establishment of a republic that would preserve national independence and provide the downtrodden masses with decent wages, land, and a proper standard of living. The revolution was in full swing.

Although led by pro-Khomeini clerics, these mass rallies drew support from a broad variety of organizations: the National Front; the Lawyer's, Doctor's, and Women's associations; the communist Tudeh Party; the Fedayin, a Marxist guerrilla group; and the Mojahedin, a Muslim guerrilla group formed of lay intellectuals. The rallies also attracted students, from high schools and colleges, as well as shopkeepers and craftsmen from the bazaars. A secret Revolutionary Committee in Tehran coordinated protests throughout the country. This was one of the first revolutions to be televised worldwide. Many would later feel that these demonstrations inspired the 1980s revolutions that swept through Eastern Europe.

Confronted by this opposition and by increasing numbers of soldiers who were deserting to the opposition, the Shah decided to leave Iran. A year later, when he was in exile and dying of cancer, many speculated that he might have mastered the upheavals if he had been healthier, possessed a stronger personality, and received full support from the United States. But even a man with an iron will and full foreign backing would not have been able to deal with millions of angry demonstrators, massive general strikes, and debilitating desertions from his own armed forces.

On February 11, 1979, a few hours of street fighting provided the final blow to the fifty-four-year-old dynasty that claimed a 2,500-year-old heritage.

The Islamic Republic (1979 to the Present)

Returning home triumphant in the midst of the Iranian Revolution after the Shah was forced from power, Khomeini was declared the Imam and Leader of the new Islamic Republic. In the past, Iranian Shi'is, unlike the Arab Sunnis, had reserved the special term *Imam* only for Imam Ali and his eleven direct heirs, whom they deemed infallible, and, therefore, almost semidivine. For many Iranians in 1979, Khomeini was charismatic in the true sense of the word: a man with a special gift from God. Khomeini ruled as Imam and Leader of the Islamic Republic until his death in 1989.

Seven weeks after the February revolution, a nationwide referendum replaced the monarchy with an Islamic Republic. Liberal and lay supporters of Khomeini, including Mehdi Bazargan, his first prime minister, had hoped to offer the electorate the choice of a *democratic* Islamic Republic. But Khomeini overruled them. He declared the term was redundant since Islam itself was democratic. Khomeini was now hailed as the Leader of the Revolution, Founder of the Islamic Republic, Guide of the Oppressed Masses, Commander of the Armed Forces, and most potent of all, Imam of the Muslim World.

A new constitution was drawn up in late 1979 by the **Assembly of Experts** (*Majles-e Khebregan*). Although this seventy-three man assembly was elected by the general public, almost all secular organizations as well as clerics opposed to Khomeini boycotted the elections because the state media were controlled, independent papers had been banned, and voters were being intimidated by club-wielding vigilantes known as the *Hezbollahis* ("Partisans of God"). The vast majority of those elected were pro-Khomeini clerics, including forty *hojjat al-Islams* (middle-ranking clerics) and fifteen ayatollahs. They drafted a highly theocratic constitution vesting much authority in the hands of Khomeini in particular and the clergy in general—all this over the strong objections of Prime Minister Bazargan, who wanted a French-style presidential republic that would be Islamic in name but democratic in structure.

When Bazargan threatened to submit his own constitution to the public, television controlled by the clerics showed him shaking hands with U.S. policy-makers. Meanwhile, Khomeini denounced the U.S embassy as a "den of spies" plotting a repeat performance of the 1953 coup. This led to mass demonstrations, a break-in at the embassy, the seizure of dozens of American hostages, and eventually the resignation of Bazargan. Some suspect the hostage crisis had been engineered to undercut Bazargan.

Assembly of Experts

Group that nominates and can remove the Leader. The assembly is elected by the general electorate, but almost all its members are clerics.

Hezbollahis

Literally "partisans of God." In Iran, the term is used to describe religious vigilantes. In Lebanon, it is used to describe the Shi'i militia.

hojjat al-Islam

Literally, "the proof of Islam." In Iran, it means a medium-ranking cleric.

A month after the embassy break-in, Khomeini submitted the theocratic constitution to the public and declared that all citizens had a divine duty to vote; 99 percent of those voting endorsed it.

In the first decade after the revolution, a number of factors helped the clerics consolidate power. First, few people could challenge Khomeini's overwhelming charisma. Second, the invasion of Iran in 1980 by Saddam Hussein's Iraq rallied the Iranian population behind their endangered homeland. Third, international petroleum prices shot up, sustaining Iran's oil revenues. The price of a barrel of oil, which had hovered around $30 in 1979, jumped to over $50 by 1981. This enabled the new regime, despite war and revolution, to continue to finance existing development programs.

The second decade after the revolution brought the clerics serious problems. Khomeini's death in June 1989 removed his decisive presence. His successor, Ali Khamenei, lacked not only his charisma but also his scholastic credentials and seminary disciples. The 1988 UN-brokered cease-fire in the Iran-Iraq War ended the foreign danger. A drastic fall in world oil prices, which plunged to less than $10 a barrel by 1998, placed a sharp brake on economic development. Even more serious, by the late 1990s, the regime was facing a major ideological crisis, with many of Khomeini's followers, including some of his closest disciples, now stressing the importance of public participation over clerical hegemony, of political pluralism over theological conformity, and of civil society over state authority—in other words, of democracy over theocracy.

Iran after 9/11

The terrorist attacks in the United States on September 11, 2001, and the subsequent American invasions of Afghanistan in October 2001 and Iraq in March 2002, had

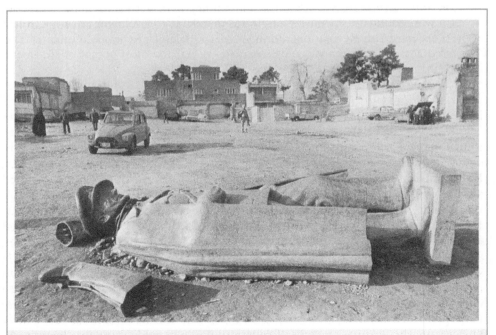

The Shah's statue on the ground, February 1979.
Abbas/Magnum Photos

profound consequences for Iran. At first, the American war on terror brought Iran and the United States closer together since Iran for years had seen both the Taliban and Saddam Hussein as its own mortal enemies. Saddam Hussein was hated for the obvious reason; he had waged an eight-year war on Iran. The Taliban was hated in part because it had massacred a large number of Shi'i Afghans; and in part because it was financed by Sunni Wahhabi fundamentalists in Saudi Arabia who consider Shi'ism as well as all innovations since the very beginnings of Islam to be unacceptable heresies. In fact, these Sunni fundamentalists consider Shi'is to be as bad if not worse than non-Muslim infidels. Not surprisingly, Iran helped the United States depose the Taliban in 2001. It also used its considerable influence among the Iraqi Shi'is to install a pro-American government in Baghdad in 2003. It offered the United States in 2003 a "grand bargain" to settle all major differences, including those over nuclear research, Israel, Lebanon, and the Persian Gulf.

These hopes, however, were soon dashed—first, because in his State of the Union address in January 2002, President George W. Bush named Iran (along with Iraq and North Korea) as part of an "Axis of Evil" supporting terrorism and developing weapons of mass destruction. Moreover, after the occupation of Iraq, the United States surrounded Iran with military bases in the Persian Gulf, Turkey, Azerbaijan, Georgia, Afghanistan, and Central Asia. Bush also refused to enter serious negotiations until Iran unconditionally stopped nuclear research. These hard-line actions played a major role in both undermining the Iran's liberal President Khatemi and paving the way for the electoral victory of the bellicose Ahmadinejad in 2005. Reformers did not want to be associated with an American administration that not only insisted Iran should not have a nuclear program but also aggressively advocated regime change in Tehran. For most Iranians, this again resurrected memories of the 1953 CIA coup. These issues increased tensions and brought Iran and the United States closer to a diplomatic, if not military, stand-off. The United States insisted—at least, until the election of President Obama—that it would not negotiate with Iran unless it stopped its nuclear enrichment program. Iran, in turn, insisted that its nuclear program had no military purpose and that it conformed to guidelines set by international treaties.

The Four Themes and Iran

Iran in a Globalized World of States

By denouncing the United States as an "arrogant imperialist," canceling military agreements with the West, and condoning the taking of U.S. diplomats as hostages, Khomeini asserted Iranian power in the region but also inadvertently prompted Saddam Hussein to launch the Iraq-Iran War in 1980.

Khomeini's policies made it difficult for his successors, including the current President Rouhani, from normalizing relations with the West. Khomeini had called for revolutions throughout the Muslim world, denouncing Arab rulers in the region, particularly in Saudi Arabia, as the "corrupt puppets of American imperialism." He strengthened Iran's navy and bought nuclear submarines from Russia. He launched a research program to build medium-range missiles and nuclear power—possibly even nuclear weapons. He denounced the proposals for Arab-Israeli negotiations over Palestine. He sent money as well as arms to Muslim dissidents abroad, particularly Shi'i groups in Lebanon, Iraq, and Afghanistan. He permitted the intelligence services to assassinate some one hundred exiled opposition leaders living in Western Europe. These policies isolated Iran not only from the United States but also from

THE GLOBAL CONNECTION

The Nuclear Power Issue

For Iran, nuclear technology—always defined as a "civilian program"—is a non-negotiable right of an independent nation, essential not only for its long-term energy needs but also to attain the hallmark of a developed country. It sees nuclear power as a matter of both sovereignty and modernity.

For the United States and the other Western powers, any nuclear technology—even for peaceful purposes—in the hands of Iran is fraught with many risks. They argue that such technology could be expanded into a weapons program, and nuclear weapons could then be used on Israel or passed on to "terrorist organizations." It seems that the only way to resolve the issue is for the West to accept Iran's civilian program, and Iran, in return, to provide verifiable guarantees that its program would not trespass into the military realm. Under the George W. Bush administration, negotiations broke down since the United States demanded that Iran cease forthwith all enrichment.

Furthermore, Iran's plans to develop nuclear power have been delayed because the United States has persuaded Europe not to transfer the technology needed to do so to Iran and by a successful joint U.S.-Israeli cyber-sabotage program that injected a software "worm" into the computers used to control the production of enriched uranium.

Under the Obama administration, the United States has implicitly accepted Iran's right to enrich so long as it provides verifiable guarantees that it would not enrich to the point of producing weapons. To pressure Iran to provide such guarantees, the Obama administration has persuaded the UN to place economic sanctions on Iran—especially on the Revolutionary Guards and elite members of the regime. In 2014, the Obama and the Rouhani administrations began serious negotiations to resolve these differences.

MAKING CONNECTIONS What are the main differences between Shi'i and Sunni Islam?

the European Community, human rights organizations, and the United Nations. Reforming presidents, especially Khatami and Rouhani, have done their best to rectify this damage.

The Islamic Republic is determined to remain dominant in the Persian Gulf and to play an important role in the world of states. It has one of the biggest but outdated conventional armies in the region, a large land mass, considerable human resources, a respectable gross domestic product (GDP), and vast oil production.

Governing the Economy

In the early years of the Islamic Republic in the 1980s, peasants continued to migrate to the cities because of the lack of both agricultural land and irrigation. Industry suffered from lack of investment capital. Inflation and unemployment were high. The population steadily increased, and real per capita income fell due to forces outside state control. To deal with these problems, some leaders favored state-interventionist strategies. Others advocated laissez-faire market-based strategies. Such differences over how to govern the economy are still being debated in Iran and are the source of much political contention.

The Democratic Idea

Khomeini argued that Islam and democracy were compatible since the vast majority of people in Iran respected the clerics as the true interpreters of the *shari'a*, and wanted them to oversee state officials. Islam and the democratic idea, however, appear less reconcilable now that much of the public has lost its enthusiasm for clerical rule. Khomeinism has divided into two divergent branches in Iran: political liberalism and clerical conservatism. These ideological currents, which will be discussed later in this chapter, are at the heart of Iranian politics today.

Democracy is based on the principles that all individuals are equal, especially before the law, and that all people have inalienable natural rights. The *shari'a* is based on inequalities—between men and women, between Muslims and non-Muslims, between legitimate minorities, known as the People of the Book, and illegitimate ones, known as unbelievers. Moderate clerics, however, advocate reforming the *shari'a* to make it compatible with individual freedoms and human rights.

The Politics of Collective Identity

The state emphasis on Shi'ism has to some extent alienated the 10 percent of Iranians who are Sunnis. In addition, the regime's insistence on a theocratic constitution antagonized some important clerics as well as lay secular Muslims, who lead most of the political parties. Similarly, the strong association of Shi'ism with the central, Persian-speaking regions of the country could alienate the important Turkic minority in Azerbaijan province. All of these trends put some strain on Iran's collective national identity.

Themes and Comparisons

The Khomeinist movement culminating in the 1979 revolution helped expand Islam from a personal religion concerned with the individual's relations with God into an all-encompassing ideology that dealt with political, legal, social, and economic matters as well as personal ones. The slogan of the revolution was "Islam is the Solution." This expanded interpretation of Islam became known as Islamism and political Islam. The direct product of this Islam is the creation of an Islamic Republic that is theocratic—a regime in which the clergy claim special authority on grounds that as experts on theology they have a better understanding of religion and therefore greater expertise than laymen in supervising the running of the state. This authority is based not on the claim they enjoy direct communications with God—they do not claim such privilege—but that they have scholarly knowledge of the scriptures and God's laws—the *shari'a*. This makes the Islamic Republic a unique political system in the modern world.

Islamism

The use of Islam as a political ideology. Similar to political Islam and Islamic fundamentalism.

Although this was the main contribution of the Islamic Republic to comparative politics, the reform movement of the 1990s and early 2000s did its best to counter it. The leading reformers, who label themselves the new Muslim intellectuals, argue that their intellectual fathers, the revolutionary generation, had mistakenly "bloated religion" and expanded it from personal ethics into an all-encompassing political ideology. In other words, they had turned faith into a total system of thought similar to twentieth-century European totalitarian ideologies—the other major isms. The new Muslim intellectuals set themselves the task of slimming down, narrowing, and lightening this overbloated system of thought. In short, they have turned away from Islamism back to a more conventional understanding of Islam.

It is this two contrasting interpretations of Islam that help explain the bitter conflict in contemporary Iran between reformers and conservatives, between so-called fundamentalists and liberal pragmatists, between supporters of Khatami-Rouhani and those of Ahmadinejad, between the generation that made the 1979 revolution and the new generation that came of age during the same revolution. They both consider themselves Islamic but have sharply different interpretations of Islam—especially when it comes to politics, including the relations with the West and the United States.

Where Do You Stand?

Some see revolutions as dawns of hope; others as unmitigated disasters. How would you assess the Iranian Revolution?

Some describe Khomeini as a conservative fundamentalist; others as a radical populist. How would you describe him?

POLITICAL ECONOMY AND DEVELOPMENT

State and Economy

▼ Focus Questions

- What impact did the Shah's economic policies have on Iranian society?

- What role do oil revenues play in integrating Iran into the global economy?

rentier state

A country that obtains much of its revenue from the export of oil or other natural resources.

British prospectors struck oil in Iran's Khuzistan province in 1908, and the British government in 1912 decided to fuel its navy with petroleum rather than coal. It also decided to buy most of its fuel from the Anglo-Iranian Oil Company. Iran's oil revenues increased modestly in the next four decades, reaching $16 million in 1951. After the nationalization of the oil industry in 1951 and the agreement with a consortium of U.S. and British companies in 1955, oil revenues rose steadily, from $34 million in 1955 to $5 billion in 1973 and, after the quadrupling of oil prices in 1974, to over $23 billion in 1976. Between 1953 and 1978, Iran's cumulative oil income came to over $100 billion.

Oil financed over 90 percent of imports and 80 percent of the annual budget and far surpassed total tax revenues. Oil also enabled Iran not to worry about feeding its population. Instead, it could undertake ambitious development programs that other states could carry out only if they squeezed scarce resources from their populations. In fact, oil revenues made Iran into a **rentier state**, a country that obtains a lucrative income by exporting raw materials or leasing out natural resources to foreign companies. Iran as well as Iraq, Algeria, and the Gulf states received enough money from their oil wells to be able to disregard their internal tax bases. The Iranian state thus became relatively independent of society. Society, in turn, had few inputs into the state. Little taxation meant little representation.

From the 1950s through the 1970s, Muhammad Reza Shah tried to encourage other exports and attract foreign investment into non-oil ventures. Despite some increase in carpet and pistachio exports, oil continued to dominate. In 1979, on the eve of the Islamic Revolution, oil still provided 97 percent of the country's foreign exchange. Foreign firms invested no more than $1 billion in Iran—and much of this was not in industry but in banking, trade, and insurance. In Iran, as in the rest of the Middle East, foreign investors were deterred by government corruption, labor costs, small internal markets, potential instability, and fear of confiscation.

Despite waste and corruption, there was significant growth in many modern sectors of the economy under the Shah. (See Table 8.2.) GNP grew at an average rate of 9.6 percent per year from 1960 to 1977. This made Iran one of the fastest-growing economies in the world. Land reform created over 644,000 moderately prosperous farms. The number of modern factories tripled. The Trans-Iranian Railway was completed. Roads were built connecting most villages with the provincial cities. Iran was seen as having started an economic "take-off" into modernization.

Iran's Economy under the Islamic Republic

Iran's main economic problem has been instability in the world oil market. Oil revenues, which continued to provide the state with much of its income, fell from $20 billion in 1978 to less than $10 billion in 1998. They did not improve until the early 2000s increasing to $17 billion in 2000, $44 billion in 2005, and over $55 billion per year by the late 2000s. This increase was due not to a rise in production—in fact, total production in 2005 was a third less than in 1975—but

Table 8.2	Industrial Production	
Product	1953	1977
Coal (tons)	200,000	900,000
Iron ore (tons)	5,000	930,000
Steel (tons)	—	275,000
Cement (tons)	53,000	4,300,000
Sugar (tons)	70,000	527,000
Tractors (no.)	—	7,700
Motor vehicles (no.)	—	109,000

Source: E. Abrahamian, "Structural Causes of the Iranian Revolution," *Middle East Research and Information Project*, no. 87 (May 1980), 22.

to the dramatic rise in the price of oil in the international market. A barrel of oil jumped from $14 in 1998 to $30 in 2000, $56 in 2005, and over $100 in 2013–14. Ironically, the impressive growth in private cars and public transport has strained the refineries and forced Iran to become more dependent on imported gasoline. What is more, the oil revenues enabled the government to allocate as much as $100 billion a year subsidizing essential goods such as bread, heating fuel, gasoline, sugar, rice, milk, and cooking oil. In 2011–14, it made bold moves trimming these subsidies, and, instead, giving cash directly to the poor.

Although contemporary Iran is awash in oil money, the country's economic situation has been complicated by a population explosion, the Iran–Iraq War, and the emigration of some 3 million Iranians. The annual population growth rate, which was 2.5 percent in the late 1970s, jumped to over 4 percent in the early 1980s, one of the highest rates in the world. The war with Iraq wrought on Iran as much as $600 billion in property damage and over 218,000 dead. The Islamic Revolution itself frightened many professionals and highly skilled technicians, as well as wealthy entrepreneurs, and industrialists into fleeing to the West.

The overall result was a twenty-year economic crisis lasting well into the late 1990s. The value of real incomes, including salaries and pensions, dropped by as much as 60 percent. Unemployment hit 20 percent; over two-thirds of entrants into the labor force could not find jobs. Peasants continued to flock to urban shantytowns. Tehran grew from 4.5 million to 12 million people. The total number of families living below the poverty level increased. By the late 1990s, over 9 million urban dwellers lived below the official poverty line.[4] Shortages in foreign exchange curtailed vital imports, even of essential manufactured goods. What is more, the regime that came to power advocating self-sufficiency now owed foreign banks and governments over $30 billion, forcing it to renegotiate foreign loans constantly. In the 2005 presidential elections, these problems helped explain the strong victory of Ahmadinejad, the conservative populist candidate. But the United States imposed sanctions on the Ahmadinejad administration compounded these economic problems, causing spiraling inflation, shortage of imported goods, and increasing brain drain to the West.

Nevertheless, the Islamic Republic has over the years scored some notable economic successes. The Reconstruction Ministry built 30,000 miles of paved roads, 40,000 schools, and 7,000 libraries. It brought electricity and running water to more than half of the country's 50,000 villages. The number of registered vehicles on the roads increased from 27,000 in 1990 to over 3 million in 2009. More dams and irrigation canals were built, and the Agricultural Ministry distributed some 630,000 hectares of confiscated arable land to peasants and gave farmers more favorable prices.

The government has exercised control over most of Iran's economy for the entire history of the Islamic Republic. Reformist president Khatami took steps to reduce the role of the state in governing the economy by allowing privatization in some sectors of the economy (including banking) and relaunching a stock market to sell shares of government businesses to private investors. Even Ayatollah Khamenei, the chief religious leader, and former conservative president Ahmadinejad have endorsed privatization. Ahmadinejad initiated a program to give "justice shares" of state-owned industries to low-income citizens. Nevertheless, about 70 percent of the Iranian economy continues to be under state control.

Society and Economy

During the Shah's reign, a huge amount of state investment went into social welfare. Enrollment in primary schools grew from fewer than 750,000 to over 4 million; in secondary schools from 121,000 to nearly 740,000; in vocational schools from 2,500 to nearly 230,000; and in universities from under 14,000 to more than 154,000. Between 1963 and 1977, the number of hospital beds increased from 24,126 to 48,000; medical clinics from 700 to 2,800; nurses from 1,969 to 4,105; and doctors from 4,500 to 12,750. These improvements, together with the elimination of epidemics and famines, lowered infant mortality and led to a population explosion.

The Shah's approach to development, however, increased his unpopularity with many sectors of Iranian society. The Shah believed that if economic growth benefited those who were already better off, some of the wealth would gradually trickle down to the lower levels of society. But these benefits got stuck at the top and never trickled down.

In fact, wealth trickled up: In 1972, the richest 20 percent of urban households accounted for 47.1 percent of total urban family expenditures; by 1977, it accounted for 55.5 percent. In 1972, the poorest 40 percent accounted for 16.7 percent of urban family expenditures; by 1977, this had dropped to 11.7 percent. In Iran's cities, the rich were getting richer, and the poor were getting poorer.

The new factories drew criticism that they were mere assembly plants that used inexpensive labor and were poor substitutes for real industrial development that would benefit the nation. The Shah's public health programs still left Iran with one of the worst doctor–patient ratios and child mortality rates in the Middle East. The per capita income in the richest provinces was ten times more than in the poorest ones. The ratio of urban to rural incomes was 5 to 1. Land reform created a small layer of prosperous farmers but left the vast majority of peasants landless or nearly landless (see Table 8.3). By the mid-1970s, Iran was one of the most unequal countries in the world.[5]

These inequalities created a **dual society**—on one side the modern sector, headed by elites with close ties to the oil state, on the other side the traditional sector, the clergy, the bazaar middle class, and the rural masses. Each sector, in turn, was sharply stratified into unequal classes (see Figure 8.2).

The upper class—the Pahlavi family, the court-connected entrepreneurs, the military officers, and the senior civil servants—made up less than 0.01 percent of the population. In the modern sector, the middle class—professionals, civil servants, salaried personnel, and college students—formed about 10 percent of the population. The bottom of the modern sector—the urban working class, factory workers, construction laborers, peddlers, and unemployed—constituted over 32 percent. In the traditional sector, the middle class—bazaar merchants, small retailers, shopkeepers, workshop owners, and well-to-do family farmers—made up 13 percent; the rural masses 45 percent.

Table 8.3	Land Ownership in 1977
Size (Hectares)	**Number of Owners**
200+	1,300
51–200	44,000
11–50	600,000
3–10	1,200,000
Landless	700,000

Note: One hectare is equal to approximately 2.47 acres.
Source: E. Abrahamian, "Structural Causes of the Iranian Revolution," *Middle East Research and Information Project,* no. 87 (May 1980).

These inequalities fueled resentments, which were expressed more in cultural and religious terms than in economic and class terms. Among the fiercest critics

dual society

A society and economy that are sharply divided into a traditional, usually poorer, and a modern, usually richer, sector.

Upper Class

Pahlavi Family; Court-Connected Entrepreneurs; Senior Civil Servants and Military Officers	0.1%

Middle Class

Traditional (Propertied)	13%	Modern (Salaried)	10%
Clerics Bazaaris Small Factory Owners Commercial Farmers		Professionals Civil Servants Office Employees College Students	

Lower Classes

Rural	45%	Urban	32%
Landed Peasants Near Landless Peasants Landless Peasants Unemployed		Industrial Workers Wage-Earners in Small Factories Domestic Servants Construction Workers Peddlers Unemployed	

FIGURE 8.2 Iran's Class Structures in the Mid-1970s.
Iranian society was divided sharply not only into horizontal classes, but also into vertical sectors—the modern and the transitional, the urban and the rural. This is known as a dual society.

was Jalal Al-e Ahmad (1923–1969). He argued that the ruling class was destroying Iran by mindlessly imitating the West; neglecting the peasantry; showing contempt for popular religion; worshipping mechanization, regimentation, and industrialization; and flooding the country with foreign ideas, tastes, luxury items, and mass-consumption goods. He stressed that developing countries such as Iran could survive this "plague" of Western imperialism only by returning to their cultural roots and developing a self-reliant society, especially a fully independent economy. Al-e Ahmad is deemed to be not only the main intellectual critic of the old order but also the founder of the "back to roots" movement that brought about the Islamic Revolution.

Al-e Ahmad's ideas were developed further by another young intellectual named Ali Shariati (1933–1977). Studying in Paris during the 1960s, Shariati was influenced by Marxist sociology, Catholic liberation theology, the Algerian revolution, and, most important, Frantz Fanon's *Wretched of the Earth* (1961), which urged colonial peoples to use violence to liberate themselves from imperial rule.

Shariati argued that history was a continuous struggle between oppressors and oppressed. Each class had its own interests, its own interpretations of religion, and its own sense of right and wrong. God periodically sent down prophets, such as Abraham, Moses, Jesus, and Muhammad. Muhammad had been sent to launch a dynamic community in "permanent revolution" toward the ultimate utopia: a perfectly classless society.

Although Muhammad's goal, claimed Shariati, had been betrayed by his illegitimate successors, his radical message had been preserved by the Shi'i Imams, especially by Imam Husayn, who had been martyred to show future generations that human beings had the moral duty to fight oppression in all places at all times. According to Shariati, the contemporary oppressors were the imperialists, the modern-day feudalists, the corrupt capitalists, and their hangers-on. He criticized the conservative clerics who had tried to transform revolutionary religion into an apolitical public opiate. Shariati died on the eve of the revolution, but his prolific works were so widely read and so influential that many felt that he, rather than Khomeini, was the true ideologue of the Islamic Revolution.

Despite setbacks in the 1980s, life improved for most Iranians in the 1990s. On the whole, the poor in Iran are better off now than their parents had been before the founding of the Islamic Republic. By the late 1990s, most independent farmers owned radios, televisions, refrigerators, and pickup trucks. The extension of social services narrowed the gap between town and country and between the urban poor and the middle classes. The adult literacy rate grew from 50 percent to 83 percent, and by 2000 the literacy rate among those in the six to twenty-nine age range hit 97 percent. The infant mortality rate has fallen from 104 per 1,000 in the mid-1970s to 39 per 1,000 in 2013. Life expectancy climbed from fifty-five years in 1979 to sixty-eight in 1993 and to seventy-three in 2013—one of the best in the Middle East. The UN estimates that by 2000, 94 percent of the population had access to health services and safe water.

The Islamic Republic also made major strides toward population control. At first, it closed down birth control clinics. But it reversed direction once the ministries responsible for social services felt the full impact of this growth. In 1989, the government declared that Islam favored healthy rather than large families and that one literate citizen was better than ten illiterate ones. It reopened birth control clinics, cut subsidies to large families, and announced that the ideal family should consist of no more than two children. It even took away social benefits from those having more than two children. The current population growth rate is 1.3 percent. The government is now toying with the idea of reversing policy and encouraging population growth.

Environmental Issues

Iran faces a horrendous environment problem. The ago-old problem of aridity and lack of regular rainfall has been compounded in recent years by a series of droughts and dry winters—most probably caused by climate change and global warming. Water levels have fallen; major rivers—such Sefid Rud in Isfahan—have turned into streams; and lakes such as Urmiah in Azerbaijan are drying up into ponds. The impressive numbers of dams built in the last fifty years have added to the problem since such concentrations of water inadvertently increase evaporation. These problems are prevalent throughout the Middle East and contribute to what is now known as the "Arab Spring"—especially in Syria.

The environmental issue comes in the form of a horrendous air pollution problem in Tehran where the city is flanked by a high mountain range that blocks the air currents and thus traps the polluted air. Much of this pollution comes from the increasing use of private cars. By 2000 Tehran had the reputation of having one of the world's worst air pollution problems. This problem has been further compounded by the recent UN sanctions. These sanctions have prevented Iran from importing properly refined gasoline. Instead, Iran has been producing its own poorly refined gasoline that seriously pollutes the air and endangers public health. The Department of Environment revealed that in 2013 some 45,000 deaths were directly or indirectly caused by air pollution. On a number of days the municipality warned citizens not to venture out unless they had to.

The environmental issue has been articulated by the reform movement—especially by the educated youth who supported President Khatami, the failed candidacy of Mousavi, and now President Rouhani. It is significant that Mousavi's supporters named their organization the Green Movement giving it a double meaning since green is traditionally the color of Shi'i Islam. There have also been public protests in Azerbaijan against the plight of Lake Urmiah.

Various administrations—both reform and conservative—have taken some measures to address the problem. They have channeled considerable resources into solar and nuclear energy—the avowed rational for the latter is that it will provide cleaner energy for industrial and home electrical use. They have supported reforestation and water conservation—especially in the cities. They have encouraged citizens in Tehran to use public transport especially city buses rather than private cars and taxis. What is more, they have built an extensive subway network in Tehran linking much of the suburbs—even the distant ones—to the central city. For the first time Tehran has a modern metro system worthy of the best ones in the West.

The core environmental problems, however, are harder to address. Car pollution will not diminish until vehicles and gasoline are cleaner. And these issues cannot be really addressed until the nuclear stand-off with the United States is resolved. And even more serious, the problem of increasing aridity and global warming cannot be addressed unless it is done on a worldwide scale. Iran, like other countries, is intimately interconnected with the rest of world—whether it likes it nor not.

Iran in the Global Economy

The integration of Iran into the world of states began in the latter half of the nineteenth century. Several factors account for this integration: concessions granted to the European powers; the Suez Canal and the Trans-Caspian railway; telegraph lines across Iran linking India with Britain; the outflow of capital from Europe after 1870; and, most important, the Industrial Revolution in Europe and the subsequent export

Organization of Petroleum Exporting Countries (OPEC)

An organization dedicated to achieving stability in the price of oil, avoiding price fluctuations, and generally furthering the interests of the member states.

resource curse

The concept that revenue derived from abundant natural resources, such as oil, often bring unforeseen ailments to countries.

of European manufactured goods to the rest of the world. In the nineteenth century, Iran's foreign trade increased tenfold.

Economic dependency resulted, a situation common in much of the developing world. Less-developed countries become too reliant on developed countries; poorer nations are vulnerable to sudden fluctuations in richer economies and dependent on the export of raw materials, whose prices often stagnate or decline, while prices for the manufactured products they import invariably increase.

Cash crops, especially cotton, tobacco, and opium, reduced the acreage for wheat and other edible grains in Iran. Many landowners stopped growing food and turned to commercial export crops. This led to disastrous famines in 1860, 1869–1872, 1880, and 1918–1920.

Furthermore, many local merchants, shopkeepers, and workshop owners in the bazaars now formed a national propertied middle class aware of their common interests against both the central government and the foreign powers. This new class awareness played an important role in Iran's constitutional revolution of 1905.

Under the Shah, Iran became the second-most-important member (after Saudi Arabia) of the **Organization of Petroleum Exporting Countries (OPEC)**; Iran could cast decisive votes for raising or moderating oil prices. At times, the Shah curried Western favor by moderating prices. At other times, he pushed for higher prices to finance his ambitious projects and military purchases. These purchases rapidly escalated once President Richard Nixon began to encourage U.S. allies to take a greater role in policing their regions. Moreover, Nixon's secretary of state, Henry Kissinger, argued that the United States should finance its ever-increasing oil imports, by exporting more military hardware to the Persian Gulf. Arms dealers joked that the Shah read their technical manuals the same way that some men read *Playboy*. The Shah's arms buying from the United States jumped from $135 million in 1970 to a peak of $5.7 billion in 1977. In addition to these vast military expenditures, the oil revenues had other unforeseen consequences: high labor costs; lack of incentives for competing industries; and the easy import of agricultural and manufactured goods. It is for this reason that some economists often describe oil as a **resource curse**.

This military might gave the Shah a reach well beyond his immediate boundaries. Iran occupied three small but strategically located Arab islands in the Strait of Hormuz, thus controlling the oil lifeline through the Persian Gulf but also creating distrust among his Arab neighbors. The Shah talked of establishing a presence well beyond the Gulf on the grounds that Iran's national interests reached into the Indian Ocean.

In the mid-1970s, the Shah dispatched troops to Oman to help the local sultan fight rebels. He offered Afghanistan $2 billion to break its then

The clerical regime relies on two crutches of power: the bayonet and the oil well.

Courtesy Mojahed (in exile).

close ties with the Soviet Union, a move that probably prompted the Soviets to intervene militarily in that country. A U.S. congressional report declared: "Iran in the 1970s was widely regarded as a significant regional, if not global, power. The United States relied on it, implicitly if not explicitly, to ensure the security and stability of the Persian Gulf sector and the flow of oil from the region to the industrialized Western world of Japan, Europe, and the United States, as well as to lesser powers elsewhere."[6]

These vast military expenditures, as well as the oil exports, tied Iran closely to the industrial countries of the West and to Japan. Iran was now importing millions of dollars' worth of rice, wheat, industrial tools, construction equipment, pharmaceuticals, tractors, pumps, and spare parts, the bulk of which came from the United States. Trade with neighboring and other developing countries was insignificant.

The oil revenues thus had major consequences for Iran's political economy, all of which paved the way for the Islamic Revolution. They allowed the Shah to pursue ambitious programs that inadvertently widened class and regional divisions within the dual society. They drastically raised public expectations without necessarily meeting them. They made the rentier state independent of society. Economic slowdowns in the industrial countries, however, could lead to a decline in their oil demands, which could diminish Iran's ability to buy such essential goods as food, medicine, and industrial spare parts.

One of the major promises made by the Islamic Revolution was to end this economic dependency on oil and the West. The radical followers of Ayatollah Khomeini, the founder of the Islamic Republic, once denounced foreign investors as imperialist exploiters and waxed eloquent about economic self-sufficiency.

But in 2002, Iran contemplated a dramatically new law permitting foreigners to own as much as 100 percent of any firm in the country, to repatriate profits, to be free of state meddling, and to have assurances against both arbitrary confiscations and high taxation. To maintain oil production, Iran needs new deep-drilling technology that can be found only in the West. This goes a long way toward explaining why the regime now is eager to attract foreign investment and to rejoin the world economy.

Where Do You Stand?

Some see Iran as divided into socioeconomic class. Others see it as a dual society divided into a modern and a traditional sector. How would you describe it?

Some see abundant oil revenues as a resource curse; others as a means for rapid development. Which description do you find more apt?

GOVERNANCE AND POLICY-MAKING

SECTION 3

Organization of the State

The political system of the Islamic Republic of Iran is unique. It is a theocracy with important democratic features. It is a theocracy (from the Greek, "divine rule") because the religious clerics control the most powerful political positions. But the system also contains elements of democracy with some high government officials, including the president, elected directly by the general public. All citizens, both male and female, over the age of eighteen now have the right to vote.

The state rests on the Islamic constitution implemented immediately after the 1979 revolution and amended between April and June 1989 during the last months of Khomeini's life by the Council for the Revision of the Constitution, which was handpicked by Khomeini himself. The final document is a highly complex mixture of theocracy and democracy.

The preamble affirms faith in God, Divine Justice, the Qur'an, the Day of Judgment, the Prophet Muhammad, the Twelve Imams, the eventual return of the Hidden Imam (the Mahdi), and, of course, Khomeini's doctrine of jurist's guardianship that gives supreme power to senior clergy. All laws, institutions, and state organizations must conform to these "divine principles."

The Executive

The Leader and Major Organizations of Clerical Power

The constitution named Khomeini to be the Leader for Life on the grounds that the public overwhelmingly recognized him as the "most just, pious, informed, brave, and enterprising" of the senior clerics—the grand ayatollahs. It further described him as the Leader of the Revolution, the Founder of the Islamic Republic, and, most important, the Imam of the Muslim Community. It stipulated that if no single Leader emerged after his death, then all his authority would be passed on to a leadership council of senior clerics.

After Khomeini's death in 1989, however, his followers distrusted the other senior clerics so much that they did not set up such a council. Instead, they elected one of their own, Ali Khamenei, a middle-ranking cleric, to be the new Leader.

Khamenei was born in 1939 in Mashed into a minor clerical family originally from Azerbaijan. He studied theology with Khomeini in Qom and was briefly imprisoned by the Shah's regime in 1962. Active in the anti-Shah opposition movement in 1978, he was given a series of influential positions immediately after the revolution, even though he held only the rank of *hojjat al-Islam*. He became Friday prayer leader of Tehran, head of the Revolutionary Guards, and, in the last years of Khomeini's life, president of the republic. After Khomeini's death, he was elevated to the rank of Leader even though he was neither a grand ayatollah nor a recognized senior expert on Islamic law. He had not even published a theological treatise. The government-controlled media, however, began to refer to him as an ayatollah. Some ardent followers even referred to him as a grand ayatollah qualified to guide the world's whole Shi'i community. After his elevation, he built a constituency among the regime's more diehard elements: traditionalist judges, conservative war veterans, and anti-liberal ideologues.

The Islamic Republic has often been described as a regime of the ayatollahs (high-ranking clerics). It could be more aptly called a regime of the *hojjat al-Islams* (middle-ranking clerics), since few senior clerics want to be associated with it. None of the grand ayatollahs and few of the ordinary ayatollahs subscribed to Khomeini's notion of jurist's guardianship. In fact, most disliked his radical populism and political activism.

The constitution gives wide-ranging powers to the Leader, who is elected now by an eighty-six member Assembly of Experts. As the vital link between the three branches of government, the Leader can mediate between the legislature, the executive, and the judiciary. He can "determine the interests of Islam," "supervise the implementation of general policy," and "set political guidelines for the Islamic Republic." He can eliminate presidential candidates and dismiss the duly elected president. He can grant amnesty. As commander-in-chief, he can mobilize the armed forces, declare war and peace, and convene the Supreme Military Council. He can appoint and dismiss the commanders of Revolutionary Guards as well as those of the regular army, navy, and air force.

The Leader has extensive power over the judicial system. He can nominate and remove the chief judge, the chief prosecutor, and the revolutionary tribunals. He can dismiss lower court judges. He also nominates six clerics to the powerful twelve-man Guardian Council, which can veto parliamentary bills. This Council has also obtained (through separate legislation) the right to review all candidates for elected office, including the presidency and the national legislature, the *Majles*. The other

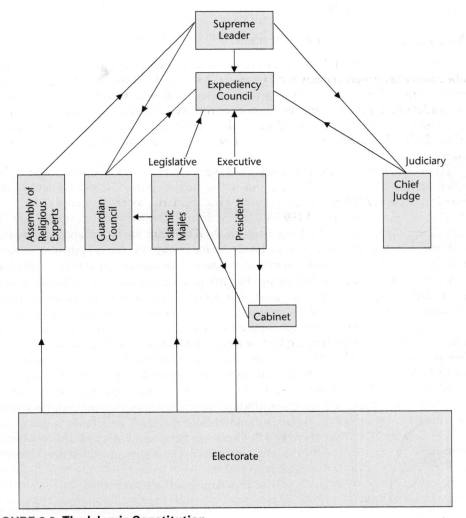

FIGURE 8.3 The Islamic Constitution
The general public elects the *Majles*, the president, and the Assembly of Experts. But the Leader and the Guardian Council decide who can compete in these elections.

Expediency Council

A committee set up in Iran to resolve differences between the *Majles* (parliament) and the Guardian Council.

Imam Jum'ehs

Prayer leaders in Iran's main urban mosques.

The Shah turning into Khomeini from an émigré newspaper.
Courtesy of Nashriyeh.

six members of the Guardian Council are jurists nominated by the chief judge and approved by the *Majles.* Furthermore, the Leader appoints more than two-thirds of the some fifty man **Expediency Council**, which has the authority to resolve differences between the Guardian Council and the *Majles* (the legislature) and to initiate laws on its own. This Council includes the most important personages in the Islamic Republic—the Guardian Council, the heads of the three branches of government, representatives of the cabinet, and individuals chosen by the Leader.

The Leader also fills a number of important non-government posts: the preachers (*Imam Jum'ehs*) at the main city mosques, the director of the national radio-television network, and the heads of the main religious endowments, especially the Foundation of the Oppressed (see below). By 2001, the Office of the Leader employed over six hundred in Tehran and had representatives in most sensitive institutions throughout the country. The Leader has obtained more constitutional powers than ever dreamed of by the Shah.

The Assembly of Experts is elected every eight years by the general public. Its members must have an advanced seminary degree, so it is packed with clerics. The Assembly has the right to oversee the work of the Leader and to dismiss him if he is found to be "mentally incapable of fulfilling his arduous duties." It has to meet at least once a year. Its deliberations are closed. In effect, the Assembly of Experts has become a second chamber to the *Majles*, the parliament of the Islamic Republic.

The Government Executive

The constitution of the Islamic Republic reserves important executive power for the president. The president is described as the highest state official after the Leader. The office is filled every four years through a national election. If a candidate does not win a majority of the vote in the first round of the election, a run-off chooses between the two top vote-getters. The president cannot serve more than two terms.

The constitution says the president must be a pious Shi'i faithful to the principles of the Islamic Republic, of Iranian origin, and between the ages of 25 and 75. The president must also demonstrate "administrative capacity and resourcefulness" and have "a good past record." There has been some dispute about whether the language used in the constitution restricts the presidency to males.

The president has the power to

- Conduct the country's internal and external policies, including signing all international treaties, laws, and agreements;
- Chair the National Security Council, which is responsible for defense matters;

- Draw up the annual budget, supervise economic matters, and chair the state planning and budget organization;
- Propose legislation to the *Majles*;
- Appoint cabinet ministers, with a parliamentary stipulation that the minister of intelligence (the state security agency) must be from the ranks of the clergy;
- Appoint most other senior officials, including provincial governors, ambassadors, and the directors of some of the large public organizations, such as the National Iranian Oil Company, the National Electricity Board, and the National Bank.

Iran has no single vice president. Instead the president may select " presidential deputies" to help with "constitutional duties." Often there are as many as ten such vice presidents. One is designated as the "first vice president." The others have specific responsibilities, such as presiding over veteran's, women's, or energy issues.

During the revolution, Khomeini often stressed that in his Islamic Republic trained officials and not clerics—also known as mullahs or akhunds—would administer the state. But in actual fact, four of the six presidents in the Islamic Republic have been clerics: Khamenei, Rafsanjani, Khatami, and now Rouhani. The first president, Abol-Hassan Bani-Sadr, a lay intellectual was ousted in 1981 precisely because he denounced the regime as "a dictatorship of the mullahtariat," comparing it to a communist-led "dictatorship of the proletariat." Ahmadinejad, the last lay president, was an urban planner, and was elected initially because of strong support from ultra-conservative clerics. But he eventually lost this support and was eased out of influence. He jeopardized this support by stressing the evangelical rather than the academic-theological side of Shi'i Islam. He insinuated that as a true believer he had privileged access to the hidden knowledge of the Hidden (Absent) Imam.

The Bureaucracy

As chief of the executive branch of the government, the president heads a huge bureaucracy. In fact, this bureaucracy continued to proliferate after the revolution, even though Khomeini had often criticized the Shah for having a bloated government. It expanded, for the most part, to provide jobs for the many college and high school graduates. On the eve of the revolution, the state ministries had 300,000 civil servants and 1 million employees. By the early 1990s, they had over 600,000 civil servants and 1.5 million employees.

Among the most important ministries of the Islamic Republic are Culture and Islamic Guidance, which has responsibility for controlling the media and enforcing "proper conduct" in public life; Intelligence, which has replaced the Shah's dreaded SAVAK as the main security organization; Heavy Industries, which manages the nationalized factories; and Reconstruction, which has the dual task of expanding social services and taking "true Islam" into the countryside. Its main mission is to build bridges, roads, schools, libraries, and mosques in the villages so that the peasantry will learn the basic principles of Islam. "The peasants," declared one cleric, "are so ignorant of true Islam that they even sleep next to their unclean sheep."[7]

The clergy dominate the bureaucracy as well as the presidency. They have monopolized the most sensitive ministries—Intelligence, Interior, Justice, and Culture and Islamic Guidance—and have given posts in other ministries to relatives and protégés. These ministers appear to be highly trained technocrats, sometimes with advanced degrees from the West. In fact, they are often fairly powerless individuals dependent on the powerful clergy—chosen by them, trusted by them, and invariably related to them.

Foundation of the Oppressed

A clerically controlled foundation set up after the revolution in Iran.

President Dr. Hassan Rouhani

President Rouhani with his foreign minister at the General Assembly meeting of the United Nations in 2013.

Chris Ratcliffe/Bloomberg /Getty Images

Hassan Rouhani, a consummate regime insider but running on a clearly moderate ticket, won an easy victory in the 2013 presidential elections. Born in 1948, he had grown up in a nonclerical household in a village a hundred miles east of Tehran. His father, surnamed Fereydun, was a carpenter-turned-farmer who had moved out of Tehran after World War II. At the age of twelve, Hassan enrolled in a seminary in Qum where he soon participated in anti-Shah activities and to confuse the police adopted the name Rouhani (literally meaning "Clerical"). Graduating from the seminary, he performed his military service and then enrolled in the Faculty of Law in Tehran University where he specialized in criminal justice. As the revolution began to unfold, he was one of the first young clerics to rush off to Paris to vow allegiance to Khomeini.

After the revolution, Rouhani held a series of high posts: as parliamentary deputy from his home province; as clerical representative on committees to reorganize the chiefs of staff and the radio-television network; as member of the Assembly of Experts and Expediency Council; as longstanding member of the National Security Council; as trouble-shooting ambassador to France, Syria, and North Korea; and, most important of all, President Khatami's chief nuclear negotiator with the United Nations and the United States. He had offered the UN a compromise solution that had been acceptable to most of the other parties, especially the United Kingdom, but had been rejected by the George W. Bush administration. After the Khatami era, he had headed the main think-tank for foreign policy named the Centre for Strategic Studies; had written a number of book on Islamic law; and somehow had managed to find time to complete a doctorate in law from Caledonian University in Glasgow.

He ran the 2013 election on a reform platform. He emphasized the need for "cautious realism," "moderation," "prudence," and "hope"; "economic well-being" and a higher standard of living; greater interaction with the outside world and "normalization of relations," especially with the United States and the West; as well as the importance of citizen's rights and gender equality. He took the previous Ahmadinejad administration to task—sometimes implicitly, sometimes explicitly—for "extremism"; for weakening the economy through mismanagement, inflation, and high unemployment; and bringing down on the nation the horrendous U.S.-UN sanctions by refusing to be more transparent on the nuclear program, by denying the Holocaust, and thereby by unnecessarily antagonizing the West. He was clearly courting voters who in previous elections had overwhelmingly supported political liberals like Khatami and economic reformers such as Rafsanjani. Not surprisingly, both Khatami and Rafsanjani enthusiastically endorsed Rouhani. For his part, the Leader remained above the fray—unlike the previous election when he had endorsed Ahmadinejad. He had probably concluded that the economic sanctions necessitated a more compromising foreign policy. His refusal to back the conservative candidates ensured that the revolutionary guards and the conservative clerical institutions would not interfere with the elections.

MAKING CONNECTIONS Why did Rouhani win the presidential elections in 2013?

Other State Institutions

The Judiciary

The constitution makes the judicial system the central pillar of the state, overshadowing the executive and the legislature. It also gives the Leader and the clergy wide-ranging powers over the judiciary. Laws are supposed to conform to the religious law, and the clergy are regarded as the ultimate interpreters of the *shari'a*. Bills passed by the *Majles* are reviewed by the Guardian Council to ensure that they conform to the *shari'a*. The minister of justice is chosen by the president but needs the approval of both the *Majles* and the chief judge.

The judicial system itself has been Islamized down to the district-court level, with seminary-trained jurists replacing university-educated judges. The Pahlavis purged the clergy from the judicial system; the Islamic Republic purged the university educated.

The penal code, the Retribution Law, is based on a reading of the *shari'a* that was so narrow that it prompted many modern-educated lawyers to resign in disgust, charging that it contradicted the United Nations Charter on Human Rights. It permits injured families to demand blood money on the biblical and Qur'anic principle of "an eye for an eye, a tooth for a tooth, a life for a life." It mandates the death penalty for a long list of "moral transgressions," including adultery, homosexuality, apostasy, drug trafficking, and habitual drinking. It sanctions stoning, live burials, and finger amputations. It divides the population into male and female and Muslims and non-Muslims and treats them unequally. For example, in court, the evidence of one male Muslim is equal to that of two female Muslims. The regime also passed a "law on banking without usury" to implement the *shari'a* ban on all forms of interest taking and interest giving.

Although the law was Islamized, the modern centralized judicial system established under the Shah was not dismantled. For years, Khomeini argued that in a truly Islamic society, the local *shari'a* judges would pronounce final verdicts without the intervention of the central authorities. Their verdicts would be swift and decisive. This, he insisted, was the true spirit of the *shari'a*. After the revolution, however, he discovered that the central state needed to retain ultimate control over the justice system, especially over life-and-death issues. Thus, the revolutionary regime retained the appeals system, the hierarchy of state courts, and the power to appoint and dismiss all judges. State interests took priority over the spirit of the *shari'a*—although religious authorities have ultimate control over the state.

Practical experience led the regime to gradually broaden the narrow interpretation of the *shari'a*. To permit the giving and taking of interest, without which modern economies would not function, the regime allowed banks to offer attractive rates as long as they avoided the taboo term *usury*. To meet public sensitivities as well as international objections, the courts rarely implemented the harsh penalties stipulated by the *shari'a*. They adopted the modern method of punishment, imprisonment, rather than the traditional one of corporal public punishment. By the early 1990s, those found guilty of breaking the law were treated much as they would be in the West: fined or imprisoned rather than flogged in the public square. Those found guilty of serious crimes, especially murder, armed violence, terrorism, and drug smuggling, were often hanged. Iran, after China, has the highest number of executions per year, and the highest per capita executions in the world. This has created a major issue for Iran at the UN.

The Military

The clergy have taken special measures to control Iran's armed forces—both the regular army of 370,000, including 220,000 conscripts, and the new forces formed of 120,000 Revolutionary Guards established immediately after 1979, and 200,000 volunteers in the Mobilization of the Oppressed (*Basej-e Mostazafin*), a volunteer militia created during the Iraqi war. The Leader, as commander-in-chief, appoints the chiefs of staff as well as the top commanders and the defense minister. He also places chaplains in military units to watch over regular officers. These chaplains act very much like the political commissars who once helped control the military in the Soviet Union and still do in China's People's Liberation Army.

After the revolution, the new regime purged the top ranks of the military, placed officers promoted from the ranks of the Revolutionary Guards in command positions over the regular divisions, and built up the Revolutionary Guards as a parallel force with its own uniforms, budgets, munitions factories, recruitment centers, and even small air force and navy. According to the constitution, the regular army defends the external borders, whereas the Revolutionary Guards protect the republic from internal enemies.

Political sentiments within the regular military remain unknown, if not ambivalent. In recent years, the *Basej* have been placed under the authority of the Revolutionary Guards. Although the military, especially the Revolutionary Guards, form an important pillar of the Islamic Republic, they consume only a small percentage of the annual budget. In fact, the republic spends far less on the armed forces than did the Shah. In the last years of the Shah's rule, military purchases accounted for 17 percent of the GDP; they now account for 2 percent. In 2012, Iran spent $6.2 billion on arms, whereas Turkey spent $18.1 billion, Saudi Arabia $21 billion, and the tiny United Arab Emirates $14.4 billion. It is this change of priorities that helps to explain how the Islamic Republic has been able to extend social services to the general population and has managed to survive for all these decades.

Subnational Government

Although Iran is a highly centralized unitary state, it is divided administratively into provinces, districts, subdistricts, townships, and villages. Provinces are headed by governors-general, districts by governors, subdistricts by lieutenant governors, towns by mayors, and villages by headmen.

The constitution declares that the management of local affairs in every village, town, district, and province will be under the supervision of councils whose members would be elected directly by the local population. It also declares that governors-general, governors, and other regional officials appointed by the Interior Ministry have to consult local councils.

Because of conservative opposition, no steps were actually taken to hold council elections until 1999 when Khatami, the new reform-minded president, insisted on holding the country's very first nationwide local elections. Over 300,000 candidates, including 5,000 women, competed for 11,000 council seats—3,900 in towns and 34,000 in villages. Khatami's supporters won a landslide victory taking 75 percent of the seats, including twelve of the fifteen in Tehran. The top vote getter in Tehran was Khatami's former interior minister, who had been impeached by the conservative *Majles* for issuing too many publishing licenses to reform-minded journals and newspapers. Conservatives did well in the 2003 local elections, due largely to widespread voter abstention, but moderates and reformers made a comeback in 2006 when the turnout was about 60 percent of voters. With the 2009 crackdown on the reforms now known as the Green Movement, the conservatives won. But with Rouhani's victory in 2013, the reformers are likely to make a comeback in the near future.

Semipublic Institutions

The Islamic Republic has set up a number of semipublic institutions. They include the Foundation of the Oppressed, the Alavi Foundation (named after Imam Ali), the Martyrs Foundation, the Pilgrimage Foundation, the Housing Foundation, the Foundation for the Publication of Imam Khomeini's Works, and the Fifteenth of Khordad Foundation, which commemorates the date (according to the Islamic calendar) of Khomeini's 1963 denunciation of the White Revolution. Although supposedly autonomous, these foundations are directed by clerics appointed personally by the Leader. According to some estimates, their annual income may be as much as half that of the government.[8] They are exempt from state taxes and are allocated foreign currencies, especially U.S. dollars, at highly favorable exchange rates subsidized by the oil revenues. Most of their assets are property confiscated from the old elite.

The largest of these institutions, the Foundation for the Oppressed, administers over 140 factories, 120 mines, 470 agribusinesses, and 100 construction companies. It also owns the country's two leading newspapers, *Ettela'at* and *Kayhan*. The Martyrs Foundation, in charge of helping war veterans, controls confiscated property that was not handed over to the Foundation for the Oppressed. It also receives an annual subsidy from the government. These foundations together control $12 billion in assets and employ over 400,000 people. The recent moves to "privatize" state enterprises have tended to strengthen these foundations since these semi-public organizations are well placed and well enough financed to be able to buy shares in these new companies. Their main competitors in winning government contracts and buying privatized enterprises have been the Revolutionary Guards. Indeed, "privatization" is a misleading term in the Iranian context since it invariably means transfer of state enterprises to semi-state foundations.

The Policy-Making Process

Policy-making in Iran is highly complex in part because of the cumbersome constitution and in part because factionalism within the ruling clergy has resulted in more amendments, which have made the original constitution even more complicated. Laws can originate in diverse places, and they can be modified by pressures from numerous directions. They can also be blocked by a wide variety of state institutions. In short, the policy-making process is highly fluid and diffuse, often reflecting the regime's factional divisions.

The clerics who destroyed Iran's old order remained united while building the new one. They were convinced that they alone had the divine mandate to govern. They followed the same leader, admired the same texts, cited the same potent symbols, remembered the same real and imaginary indignations under the Shah, and, most important, shared the same vested interest in preserving the Islamic Republic. Moreover, most had studied at the same seminaries and came from the same lower-middle-class backgrounds. Some were even related to each other through marriage and blood ties.

But once the constitution was in place, the same clerics drifted into two loose but identifiable blocs: the Society (*Majmu'eh*) of the Militant Clergy, and the Association (*Jam'eh*) of the Militant Clergy. The former can be described as statist reformers or populists, and the latter as laissez-faire (free-market) conservatives. The reformers hoped to consolidate lower-class support by using state power for redistributing wealth, eradicating unemployment, nationalizing enterprises, confiscating large estates, financing social programs, rationing and subsidizing essential goods, and placing price ceilings on essential consumer goods. In short, they espoused the creation of a comprehensive welfare state. The conservatives hoped to retain middle-class support, especially in the bazaars, by removing price controls, lowering business taxes, cutting red tape, encouraging private entrepreneurs, and balancing the budget, even at the cost of sacrificing subsidies and social programs. In recent years, the statist reformers have begun to emphasize the democratic over the theocratic features of the constitution, stressing the importance of individual rights, the rule of law, and government accountability to the electorate. In many ways, they have become

THE U.S. CONNECTION

Conservatives versus Liberals

In both the United States and Iran, conservative politicians—calling themselves "compassionate conservatives" in the United States and "principalists" in Iran—have a core base limited to less than 30 percent of the electorate. To win national elections, they have to reach out to others while continuing to energize their supporters to vote. To reach out, they both resort to patriotic and populist language—stressing "national security," accusing "weak-kneed liberals" for not standing up to foreign enemies, claiming to represent the "ordinary folks" and appealing to cultural values. In 2005, Ahmadinejad won the presidential elections in part because he presented himself as a "man of the people." He also won partly because his liberal opposition was badly divided. But the biggest reason for the conservative victory was probably because he projected himself as a tough patriot who could better defend the nation from foreign threats—especially after President George W. Bush named Iran as a member of the "Axis of Evil" in 2002 . Conversely, Rouhani won the 2013 elections by arguing that the conservative administration had stifled economic aspirations by unnecessarily antagonizing the United States, by underestimating the costs of UN sanctions, and by grossly mismanaging finances, especially through printing of money and thus causing of inflation. He held out the hope that normalization of relations with the United States would lead to improved standard of living.

MAKING CONNECTIONS Why has the nuclear issue become such a major problem between Iran and the United States?

like social democrats such as those in Britain's Labour Party. Since Khomeini had vehemently denounced liberalism as anti-Islamic, few describe themselves as liberals. They prefer the label reformers or progressives.

The conservatives in Iran were originally labeled middle-of-the-roaders and traditionalists. The statists were labeled progressives, seekers of new ideas, and Followers of the Imam's Line. The former liked to denounce the latter as extremists, leftists, and pro-Soviet Muslims. The latter denounced the free-marketers as medievalists, rightists, capitalists, mafia bazaaris, and pro-American Muslims. Both could bolster their arguments with apt quotes from Khomeini.

This polarization created a major policy-making gridlock, since the early Islamic *Majles* was dominated by the reformers, whereas the Guardian Council was controlled by the conservatives appointed by Khomeini. Between 1981 and 1987, over one hundred bills passed by the reformer-dominated *Majles* were vetoed by the Guardian Council on the grounds that they violated the *shari'a*, especially the sanctity of private property. The vetoed legislation included a labor law, land reform, nationalization of foreign trade, a progressive income tax, control over urban real estate transactions, and confiscation of the property of émigrés whom the courts had not yet found guilty of counterrevolutionary activities. Introduced by individual deputies or cabinet ministers, these bills had received quick passage because reformers controlled the crucial *Majles* committees and held a comfortable majority on the *Majles* floor. Some ultraconservatives had countered by encouraging the faithful not to pay taxes and instead to contribute to the grand ayatollahs of their choice. After all, they argued, one could find no mention of income tax anywhere in the *shari'a*.

Both sides cited the Islamic constitution to support their positions. The conservative free-marketers referred to the long list of clauses protecting private property, promising balanced budgets, and placing agriculture, small industry, and retail trade in the private sector. The reformers referred to an even longer list promising education, medicine, jobs, low-income housing, unemployment benefits, disability pay, interest-free loans, and the predominance of the public sector in the economy.

To break the gridlock, Khomeini boldly introduced into Shi'ism the Sunni Islamic concept of *maslahat*—that is, "public interest" and "reasons of state." Over the centuries, Shi'i clerics had denounced this as a Sunni notion designed to bolster illegitimate rulers. Khomeini now claimed that a truly Islamic state could safeguard the public interest by suspending important religious rulings, even over prayer, fasting, and the pilgrimage to Mecca. He declared public interest to be a primary ruling and the others mere secondary rulings. In other words, the state could overrule the views of the highest-ranking clerics. In the name of public interest, it could destroy mosques, confiscate private property, and cancel religious obligations. Khomeini added that the Islamic state had absolute authority, since the Prophet Muhammad had exercised absolute (*motalaq*) power, which he had passed on to the Imams and thus eventually to the Islamic Republic. Never before had a Shi'i religious leader claimed such powers for the state, especially at the expense of fellow clerics.

As a follow-up, Khomeini set up a new institution named the Expediency Council for Determining the Public Interest of the Islamic Order—known as the Expediency Council. He entrusted it with the task of resolving conflicts between the Islamic *Majles* and the Guardian Council. He packed it with thirteen clerics, including the president, the chief judge, the Speaker of the *Majles*, and six jurists from the Guardian Council. The Expediency Council eventually passed some of the more moderate bills favored by the reformers. These included a new income tax, banking legislation, and a much-disputed labor law providing workers in large factories with a minimum wage and some semblance of job security.

Constitutional amendments introduced after Khomeini's death institutionalized the Expediency Council. The new Leader could now not only name its members but also determine its tenure and jurisdiction. Not surprisingly, Khomeini's successor Khamenei, packed it with his supporters—none of them prominent grand ayatollahs. He also made its meetings secret and allowed it to promulgate new laws rather than restrict itself to resolving legislative differences between the Guardian Council and the *Majles*. The Expediency Council is now a secretive body that is accountable only to the Leader. It stands above the constitution. In this sense, it has become a powerful policy-making body rivaling the Islamic *Majles*, even though it did not exist in the original constitution.

maslahat

Arabic term for "expediency," "prudence," or "advisability," now used in Iran to refer to reasons of state or what is best for the Islamic Republic.

Where Do You Stand?

Iran is often described as a theocracy. Would you agree?

Khomeini claimed there were no contradictions between democracy and Islam. Would you agree?

REPRESENTATION AND PARTICIPATION

SECTION 4

Although the Islamic Republic is a theocracy, it incorporates some features of a democracy. According to the constitution, the voters directly choose the president and the Assembly of Experts, which in turn chooses the Leader. What is more, the elected legislature, the *Majles*, exercises considerable power. According to one of the founders of the regime, the *Majles* is the centerpiece of the Islamic constitution.[9]

▽ **Focus Questions**

• What are the powers and limitations of Iran's parliament?

• What social groups are most likely and least likely to support the Islamic Republic?

Another architect of the constitution has argued that the people, by carrying out the Islamic Revolution, implicitly favored a type of democracy confined within the boundaries of Islam and the guardianship of the jurist.[10] But another declared that if he had to choose between democracy and power of the clergy as specified in the concept of jurist's guardianship, he would not hesitate to choose the latter, since it came directly from God.[11] On the eve of the initial referendum, Khomeini himself declared: "This constitution, which the people will ratify, in no way contradicts democracy. Since the people love the clergy, have faith in the clergy, want to be guided by the clergy, it is only right that the supreme religious authority oversee the work of the [government] ministers to ensure that they don't make mistakes or go against the Qur'an."[12]

The Legislature

According to Iran's constitution, the *Majles* "represents the nation" and possesses many powers, including making or changing ordinary laws (with the approval of the Guardian Council), investigating and supervising all affairs of state, and approving or ousting the cabinet ministers. In describing this branch of government, the constitution uses the term *qanun* (statutes) rather than *shari'a* (divine law) so as to gloss over the fundamental question of whether legislation passed by the *Majles* is derived from God or the people. It accepts the reasoning that God creates divine law (*shari'a*) but elected representatives can draw up worldly statutes (*qanuns*).

The *Majles* has 290 members and is elected by citizens over the age of eighteen. It can pass *qanuns* as long as the Guardian Council deems them compatible with the *shari'a* and the constitution. It can choose, from a list drawn up by the chief judge, six of the twelve-man Guardian Council. It can investigate at will cabinet ministers, affairs of state, and public complaints against the executive and the judiciary. It can remove cabinet members—with the exception of the president—through a parliamentary vote of no confidence. It can withhold approval for government budgets, foreign loans, international treaties, and cabinet appointments. It can hold closed debates, provide members with immunity from arrest, and regulate its own internal workings, especially the committee system.

The *Majles* plays an important role in everyday politics. It has changed government budgets, criticized cabinet policies, modified development plans, and forced the president to replace some of his ministers. In 1992, 217 deputies circulated an open letter that explicitly emphasized the powers of the *Majles* and thereby implicitly downplayed those of the Leader. Likewise, the Speaker of the House in 2002 threatened to close down the whole *Majles* if the judiciary violated parliamentary immunity and arrested one of the liberal deputies.

Political Parties and the Party System

Iran's constitution guarantees citizens the right to organize parties, and a 1980 law permits the Interior Ministry to issue licenses to parties. But political parties were not encouraged until Khatami was elected president in 1997. Since then, three major parties have been active: the Islamic Iran Participation Front and the Islamic Labor Party, both formed by Khatami reformist supporters, and the more centrist Servants of Reconstruction created by *Hojjat al-Islam* Ali-Akbar Hashemi Rafsanjani, the former president and now chairman of the Expediency Council.

In general, formal parties are less important in Iranian politics than reformist and conservative coalitions and groups that form along ideological and policy lines. For example, former president Ahmadinejad had his initial power base in the Alliance of Builders of Islamic Iran, a coalition of several conservative political parties and organizations that delivered votes very effectively in local (2003), parliamentary (2004), and presidential (2005) elections.

According to the Interior Ministry, licenses have been granted to some seven hundred political, social, and cultural organizations, but all are led by people considered politically acceptable by the regime. Real political opposition has been forced into exile, mostly in Europe. The most important opposition groups are:

The Liberation Movement

Established in 1961 by Mehdi Bazargan, the Islamic Republic's first prime minister. Bazargan had been appointed premier in February 1979 by Khomeini himself, but had resigned in disgust ten months later when the Revolutionary Guards had permitted students to take over the U.S. embassy. The Liberation Movement is a moderate Islamic party. Despite its religious orientation, it is secular and favors the strict separation of mosque and state.

The National Front

Originating in the campaign to nationalize the country's oil resources in the early 1950s, the National Front remains committed to nationalism and secularism, the political ideals of Muhammad Mosaddeq, the prime minister who was overthrown in the CIA-supported coup in 1953. Because the conservative clergy feel threatened by the National Front's potential appeal, they have banned it.

The Mojahedin

Formed in 1971 as a guerrilla organization to fight the Shah's regime, the Mojahedin tried to synthesize Marxism and Islam. It interpreted Shi'i Islam as a radical religion favoring equality, social justice, martyrdom, and redistribution of wealth. Immediately after the revolution, the Mojahedin opposed the clerical regime and attracted a large following among students. The regime retaliated with mass executions forcing the Mojahedin to move their base of operations to Iraq. Not unexpectedly, the Mojahedin became associated with a national enemy and thereby lost much of its appeal.

The Fedayin

Also formed in 1971, the Fedayin modeled itself after the Marxist guerrilla movements of the 1960s in Latin America, especially those inspired by Che Guevara and the Cuban revolution. Losing more fighters than any other organization in the struggle against the Shah, the Fedayin came out of the revolution with great mystique and popular urban support. But it soon lost much of its strength because of massive government repression and a series of internal splits.

The Tudeh (Party of the Masses)

Established in 1941, the Tudeh is a mainstream, formerly pro-Soviet communist party. Although the Tudeh initially supported the Islamic Republic as a "popular anti-imperialist state," it was banned, and most of its organizers were executed during the 1980s. Some members now call for the overthrow of the regime; other call for its reform.

Elections

The constitution promises free elections. In practice, however, *Majles* elections, which are held every four years, have varied from relatively free but disorderly in the early days of the Islamic Republic to controlled and highly unfair in the middle years; back to relatively free, but orderly in the late 1990s; and back again to highly controlled—even rigged—in 2009. In 2013, however, they were surprisingly free permitting the victory of the reform candidate Rouhani. He won 52 percent of the vote, thus avoiding a run-off. His main rival, the well-known mayor of Tehran, obtained only 17 percent. The other four candidates—all well-known conservatives—mustered together no more than 30 percent. Ahmadinezad's candidate received a mere 11 percent. Rouhani's carried all the main cities with the exception of Qom with its large seminaries. He also carried the Sunni provinces as well as in his home Caspian region. Over 72 percent of the some 50 million eligible voters participated. The Islamic Republic needs such elections, especially with high voter turnout, to retain a modern form of political legitimacy.

In the 1980s, ballot boxes were placed in mosques with Revolutionary Guards supervising the voting. Neighborhood clerics were on hand to help illiterates complete their ballots. Club-wielding gangs assaulted regime opponents. Now electoral freedom is restricted by the government-controlled radio-television network, the main source of information for the vast majority of citizens. The Interior Ministry can ban dissident organizations, especially their newspapers on the grounds they are anti-Islamic. Moreover, the electoral law, based on a winner-take-all majority system rather than on proportional representation, is designed to minimize the voice of the opposition.

But the main obstacle to fair elections has been the Guardian Council with its powers to approve all candidates. For example, the Council excluded some 3,500 candidates (nearly half of the total) from running in the parliamentary elections of 2004 by questioning their loyalty to the concept of jurist's guardianship. The purge of reformers was facilitated both by President George W. Bush's labeling of Iran as a member of the global "Axis of Evil" in 2002 and by the American military occupation of Afghanistan and Iraq. Reluctant to rock the boat at a time of apparent and imminent "national danger," most reformers restrained themselves and withdrew from active politics. Not surprisingly, the conservatives won a hollow victory in the 2004 *Majles* elections. They received a clear majority of the seats, but the voter turnout was less than 51 percent, and in Tehran only 28 percent. This was the worst showing since 1979. For a regime that liked to boast about mass participation, this was seen as a major setback—even as a crisis of legitimacy. There was a bit of an upturn, to about 60 percent, in the turnout in both rounds of the presidential election of 2005. Still this was a sharp downturn from the more than 80 percent that had voted in the 1997 presidential contest that brought the reformist Khatami to power. The 2009 elections, by reactivating the reform movement, may well have produced another record turnout, but because of government interference in tallying the vote, the facts remain unclear.

Political Culture, Citizenship, and Identity

In theory, the Islamic Republic of Iran should be a highly viable state. After all, Shi'ism is the religion of both the state and the vast majority of the population. Shi'ism is the central component of Iranian popular culture. Also, the constitution guarantees basic rights to religious minorities as well as to individual citizens. All citizens, regardless of race, language, or religion, are promised the rights of free expression, worship, and organization. They are guaranteed freedom from arbitrary arrest, torture, and police surveillance.

The constitution extends additional rights to the recognized religious minorities: Christian Armenians, Christian Assyrians, Jews, and Zoroastrians. Although they form just 1 percent of the total population, they are allocated five *Majles* seats. They are permitted their own community organizations, including schools, their own places of worship, and their own family laws. The constitution, however, is ominously silent about Sunnis and Baha'is. Sunni Muslims are treated in theory as full citizens, but their actual status is not spelled out. Bahai'is, followers of a nineteenth-century preacher in Iran who emphasized the spiritual unity of all humankind, are considered heretics because their founder had proclaimed his own teachings to supersede that of not only the Old and New Testaments but also of the Qur'an and the Shi'i Imams. Moreover, some ultraconservative Shi'is deem Baha'is to be part of the "international Zionist conspiracy" on the grounds their main shrine is located in modern-day Israel. In fact, the shrine long predates the establishment of the state of Israel.

The constitution also gives guarantees to non-Persian speakers. Although 83 percent of the population understands Persian, thanks to the educational system, over 50 percent continue to speak non-Persian languages at home. The constitution promises them rights unprecedented in Iranian history. It states: "local and native languages can be used in the press, media, and schools." It also states that local populations have the right to elect provincial, town, and village councils. These councils can watch over the governors-general and the town mayors, as well as their educational, cultural, and social programs.

These generous promises have often been honored more in theory than in practice. The local councils—the chief institution that protected minorities—were not held until twenty years after the revolution. Subsidies to non-Persian publications and radio stations remain meager. Jews have been so harassed as "pro-Israeli Zionists" that more than half—40,000 out of 80,000—have left the country since the revolution. Armenian Christians had to end coeducational classes, adopt the government curriculum, and abide by Muslim dress codes, including the veil. The Christian population has declined from over 300,000 to fewer than 200,000.

The Baha'is, however, have borne the brunt of religious persecution. Their leaders have been executed as "heretics" and "imperialist spies." Adherents have been fired from their jobs, had their property confiscated, and been imprisoned and tortured to pressure them to convert to Islam. Their schools have been closed, their community property expropriated, and their shrines and cemeteries bulldozed. It is estimated that since the revolution, one-third of the 300,000 Baha'is have left Iran. The Baha'is, like the Jews and Armenians, have migrated mostly to Canada and the United States.

The Sunni population, which forms as much as 10 percent of the total, has its own reasons for being alienated from Iran's Islamic Republic. The state religion is Shi'ism, and high officials have to be Shi'i. Citizens must abide by Khomeini's concept of jurists' guardianship, a notion derived from Shi'ism. Few institutions cater to Sunni needs. There is not a single Sunni mosque in the whole of Tehran. It is not surprising that the newborn republic in 1979 faced most stiff opposition in regions inhabited by Sunni Kurds, Arabs, Baluchis, and Turkmans. It crushed the opposition by sending in Revolutionary Guards from the Persian Shi'i heartland of Isfahan, Shiraz, and Qom. Sunnis invariably now vote for reform candidates. For example, Rouhani won 81 percent of the vote in the Kurdish region of Baneh.

Azeris, who are Shi'i but not Persian speakers, are well integrated into Iran. In the past, the Azeris, who form 24 percent of the population and dwarf the other minorities, have not posed a serious problem to the state. They are part of the Shi'i community, and have prominent figures in the Shi'i hierarchy—most notably the current Leader, Khamenei. What is more, many Azeri merchants, professionals, and workers live and work throughout Iran.

But the 1991 creation of the Republic of Azerbaijan on Iran's northeastern border following the disintegration of the Soviet Union has raised new concerns, since some Azeris on both sides of the border have begun to talk of establishing a larger unified Azerbaijan. It is no accident that in the war between Azerbaijan and Armenia in the early 1990s, Iran favored the latter. So far, the concept of a unified Azerbaijan appears to have limited appeal among Iranian Azeris.

Interest Groups, Social Movements, and Protest

In the first two decades after its founding, the government of the Islamic Republic often violated its own constitution. It closed down newspapers, professional associations, labor unions, and political parties. It banned demonstrations and public meetings. It imprisoned tens of thousands without due process. It systematically tortured prisoners to extract false confessions and public recantations. And it executed some 25,000 political prisoners, most of them without due process of law. The United Nations, Amnesty International, and Human Rights Watch all took Iran to task for violating the UN Human Rights Charter as well its own Islamic constitution. Most victims were Kurds, military officers from the old regime, and leftists, especially members of the Mojahedin and Fedayin.

Although the violation of individual liberties affected the whole population, it aroused special resentment among three social groups: the modern middle class, educated women, and organized labor. The modern middle class, especially the intelligentsia, has been secular and even anticlerical ever since the 1905 revolution. Little love is lost between it and the Islamic Republic. Not surprisingly, the vast majority of those executed in the 1980s were teachers, engineers, professionals, and college students.

Educated women in Iran also harbor numerous grievances against the conservative clerics in the regime, especially in the judiciary. Although the Western press often dwells on the head-scarf, Iranian women consider the veil one of their less important problems. Given a choice, most would probably continue to wear it out of personal habit and national tradition. More important are work-related grievances: employment, job security, pay scales, promotions, maternity leave, and access to prestigious professions. Despite patriarchal attitudes held by the conservative clergy, educated women have become a major factor in Iranian society. They now form 60 percent of college students, 47 percent of doctors, 28 percent of government employees, and 33 percent of the general labor force, up from 8 percent in the 1980s. They have established their own organizations and journals reinterpreting Islam to conform

Executions in Kurdestan, 1979.
Jahangir Razmi/Magnum Photos

to modern notions of gender equality. Their main organization is known as the Women's One Million Signature Campaign. Women do serve on local councils and in the *Majles* (there are nine in the current parliament, 3.1 percent of the total). One grand ayatollah has even argued that they should be able to hold any job, including president, court judge, and even Leader.

Factory workers in Iran are another significant social group with serious grievances. Their concerns deal mostly with high unemployment, low wages, declining incomes, lack of decent housing, and an unsatisfactory labor law, which, while giving them mandatory holidays and some semblance of job security, denies them the right to call strikes and organize independent unions. Since 1979, wage earners have had a Workers' House—a government-influenced organization—and its affiliated newspaper, *Kar va Kargar* (*Work and Worker*), and since 1999 the Islamic Labor Party has represented their interests. In most years, the Workers' House flexes its political muscle by holding a May Day rally. In 1999, the rally began peacefully with a greeting from a woman reform deputy who had received the second-most votes in the 1996 Tehran municipal elections. But the rally turned into a protest when workers began to march to parliament denouncing conservatives who had spoken in favor of further watering down of the Labor Law. On May Day 2006, an estimated 10,000 workers marched to demand that the labor minister resign. Bus drivers in Tehran, who had been active in earlier protests, went on strike in January 2006 to protest the arrest and maltreatment of one of their leaders. Workers also protested the contested presidential elections of 2009 by participating in the mass demonstrations. The leader of the 2006 bus strike went into exile in Turkey and is now in North America.

The Political Impact of Technology

The regime places great importance on scientific, especially technological, education. It channels the top high school graduates into scientific fields, and generously nourishes Sharif University, the MIT of Iran—so much so that its top students are often recruited by North American universities even before graduating.

This interest is driven in part by security concern and in part by deep-seated cultural values. Such education provides not only the physicists needed for the nuclear projects and the lesser known space program, but also technicians to monitor the Internet and prevent cyber attacks on its nuclear installations. The desire to monitor the Internet and cell phones was greatly intensified after the 2009 mass protests over the presidential elections. The opposition made full use of the social media and cell phones—most urban households now have access to either cell phones or the Internet. The regime countered by making full use of the same to monitor and disrupt the opposition. Once the opposition had been crushed, many reformist journalists emigrated abroad where they started websites and blogs—often with the help of Western governments and NGOs. The security services in Iran have done their best to prevent citizens from gaining easy access to these sites.

The national culture also places great value on scientific education. Ever since the state set up an educational system, the top high school graduates have gravitated toward the sciences—not the arts and humanities. Science—and now nuclear science—is seen as the cutting edge of modernity. What is more, the prevalent view in Iran is that the Muslim Civilization had flourished in the distant past because of its scientific achievements, and, therefore, the key to recapturing the lost grandeur is through technology. When Reza Shah abolished traditional titles, college graduates with science-orientated degrees became generally known as "Engineers." Those with nonscientific ones became known as "Doctors." In recent years, a new title has appeared—that of Engineer Hojjat al-Islam—signifying the person has a science degree as well as a seminary education. We may well soon hear of His Excellency Engineer Grand Ayatollah.

Where Do You Stand?

The regime in Iran is known as the Islamic Republic. Would you describe it as more Islamic or republican?

The regime places great emphasis on elections. Why do you think it does so?

IRANIAN POLITICS IN TRANSITION

The recent mass demonstrations that brought down the presidents of Tunisia, Yemen, and Egypt have had repercussions in Iran. The Leader praised them claiming they replicated the Islamic Revolution of 1979 in Iran. The reform movement countered that these demonstrations were inspired by the 2009 protests against the rigged elections and that they showed such protests—if continued for length of time—could bring down other autocratic regimes. The Leader categorized Mubarek of Egypt and Bin Ali of Tunisia as versions of the Shah of Iran who was deposed by the Islamic Revolution of 1979. The reformers categorized Mubarek and Bin Ali as typical autocrats who rigged and manipulated elections. Despite these polemics, there are two major differences between Iran and these nearby countries. First, the latter, as well as the Shah, ultimately fell from power because of the defection of their armed forces. The former has survived in part because it retains the critical support of the armed forces. Second, the Islamic Republic—despite its democratic shortcomings—does hold regular elections. The others, however, had tried to transform republics into "hereditary republics"—an oxymoron that has enflamed public outrage.

Focus Questions ▽

• What are the most important challenges facing the Islamic Republic?

• In what ways is Iran different from other developing countries?

Political Challenges and Changing Agendas

Contemporary Iran faces both major internal and challenges. Internally, the Islamic Republic continues to struggle with the troubling question of how to combine theocracy with democracy, and clerical authority with mass participation. After several years, when Iran's reformers seemed to be on the political rise, the conservative clerics and their supporters, who already controlled the judiciary, took over the *Majles* in 2004 and the executive in 2009. In 2013, however, they lost the presidency to the moderate Rouhani and may well lose the *Majles* in the near future.

Many observers feel that the conservatives have lost touch with the grassroots of Iranian society and that their political base is probably less than 30 percent of the electorate. It is estimated that some 70 percent of the public favors the reformers, and that much of this majority, if not offered real choices, will, at a minimum, protest by staying home on election days. In fact, conservatives do best when the turnout is low, reformers benefit when it is high. The conservatives, including the Leader Khamenei, now face the challenge of how to maintain some semblance of legitimacy.

This challenge is troubling to the clerical leadership since the country has in recent decades gone through a profound transformation in political values, with much of the population embracing key aspects of the democratic idea including political pluralism, mass participation, civil society, human rights, and individual liberties. Even conservatives have begun to use such terms, openly describing themselves as "neoconservatives," "constructivists," and "pragmatists."

Meanwhile, those in the general public who feel excluded from national politics remain active in influential non-governmental organizations that make up an important part of Iranian civil society. The most visible of these is a human rights group headed by Shirin Ebadi, the winner of the Nobel Peace Prize in 2003. Ms. Ebadi has been a lawyer, judge (until the Islamic Republic barred women from holding such positions), writer, teacher, and prominent activist in the struggle to protect the rights of women and children. Even if excluded from the political arena, such activists will remain committed to using legal, nonviolent means to promote change. But they do not want to be associated with American projects for "regime change."

The development of the democratic idea in Iran has been constricted by theocracy. Some argue that Islam has made this inevitable. But Islam, like the other major religions, can be interpreted in ways that either promote or hinder democracy. Some interpretations of Islam stress the importance of justice, equality, and consultation as political principles. Islam also has a tradition of tolerating other religions, and the *shari'a* explicitly protects life, property, and honor. In practice, Islam has often separated politics from religion, government legal statutes from holy laws, spiritual affairs from worldly matters, and the state from the clerical establishment.

Moreover, theocracy in Iran originates not in Islam itself but in the very specific concept of the jurist's guardianship as developed by Khomeini. On the whole, Sunni Islam considers clerics to be theological scholars, not a special political class. This helps explain why the Iranian regime has found it difficult to export its revolution to other parts of the Muslim world. The failure of the democratic idea to take deeper root in Iran should be attributed less to anything intrinsic in Islam than to the combination of crises between 1979 and 1981 that allowed a particular group of clerics to come to power. Whether they remain in power depends not so much on Islamic values but on how they handle socioeconomic problems and especially the demands for political participation.

Politics in the Islamic Republic of Iran is sharply divided over the question of how to govern an economy beset by rising demands, wildly fluctuating petroleum revenues, and the nightmarish prospect that in the next two generations, the oil wells will run dry. Most clerics favor a rather conventional capitalist road to development, hoping to liberalize the market, privatize industry, attract foreign capital, and encourage the propertied classes to invest. Others envisage an equally conventional statist road to development, favoring central planning, government industries, price controls, high taxes, state subsidies, national self-reliance, and ambitious programs to eliminate poverty, illiteracy, slums, and unemployment. Some are hoping to find a third way, combining elements of state intervention with free enterprise.

Economic problems like those that undermined the monarchy could well undermine the Islamic Republic, particularly if there was another sharp drop in oil prices. The country's collective identity has also come under great strain in recent years. The emphasis on Shi'ism has antagonized Iran's Sunnis as well as its non-Muslim citizens. The emphasis on clerical Shi'ism has further alienated all secularists, including lay liberals and moderate nationalists, to say nothing of a large majority of Iranians who live abroad. Furthermore, the official emphasis on Khomeini's brand of Shi'ism has alienated those Shi'is who reject the whole notion of jurist's guardianship. The elevation of Khamenei as the Leader has also antagonized many early proponents of jurist's guardianship on the grounds that he lacks the scholarly qualifications to hold the position that embodies the sacred and secular power of the Islamic Republic.

Iran's ruling clerical regime has gradually eroded the broad social base that brought it to power in the Islamic Revolution nearly three decades ago. The country's collective identity, although strong in religious terms, is strained to some extent by other internal fault lines, especially those of class, ethnicity, gender, and political differences. Growing discontent may be expressed through apolitical channels, such as apathy, emigration, inward-looking religion, or even drug addiction. There is also a possibility that those seeking change may turn to radical action if they cannot attain their goals through legal reformist movement. Those who want to understand the possibilities for political change in Iran would do well to remember that the country produced two popular upheavals in the twentieth century that fundamentally transformed the political system: the constitutional (1905) and the Islamic (1979) revolutions.

The Islamic Republic's first attempt to enter the world of states as a militant force to spread its theocratic version of Islam proved counterproductive. This effort diverted scarce resources to the military and contributed to the disastrous war with Iraq. It drove Saudi Arabia and the Gulf sheikdoms into a closer relationship with the United States. It prompted the United States to isolate Iran, discouraged foreign investment, and prevented international organizations from extending economic assistance. Iran's militancy also alarmed nearby secular Islamic states such as Turkey, Tadzhikistan, and Azerbaijan. During the Khatami years, however, the regime managed to repair some of this damage. It won over many Arab states and established cordial relations with its neighbors. It also managed to repair some bridges to the European Community. This repair work, however, was seriously undone by the Ahmadinejad administration. The Rouhani administration is now trying to again repair the damage, return to Khatami's policies, and, if possible, normalize relations with the Gulf states, especially Saudi Arabia.

The major external challenge to the Islamic Republic comes from the United States. The George W. Bush administration, by naming Iran as a member of the "Axis of Evil" in 2002 and openly calling for "regime change" (and promoting such change by military means in neighboring Afghanistan and Iraq) dramatically increased pressures on Iran beyond those that already existed because of American economic sanctions, lack of diplomatic relations, and the successful barring of Iran from the World Trade Organization. The Bush administration accused Iran of sabotaging the Arab-Israeli peace process, helping terrorist organizations, especially Hamas in Palestine and Hezbollah in Lebanon, and "grossly violating" democratic and human rights of its own citizens. It also accused Iran of transforming its nuclear program into a nuclear weapons program and thus violating the UN Non-Proliferation Treaty.

The conservatives who then dominated Iranian politics were able to transform this external threat into a political asset. They intimidated many reformers into toning down their demands for domestic change, even silencing them, by declaring that the country was in danger, that the enemy was at the gates, and that any opposition to the government in such times would play into the hands of those who wanted to do harm to Iran. Political commentators even in the United States suspected that the Bush administration was seriously planning military action against Iran—perhaps a preemptive air strike against its nuclear reactors. Such suspicions fed rumors of war. Few Iranians are willing to appear unpatriotic by openly criticizing their government at a time of external danger.

The Obama administration has followed a more nuanced policy. Before his election, Obama offered an olive branch and implicitly accepted Iran's right to enrich uranium so long as it gave verifiable guarantees it would not produce nuclear weapons. After the election, he continued to hold out an olive branch but at the same time imposed through the UN stringent economic sanctions to bring Iran into serious negotiations. Such negotiations started in 2013—immediately after Rouhani's elections. Rouhani, who, as chief nuclear negotiator under Khatami, had himself earlier offered olive branches to Washington, quickly took up Obama's offer.

Both the Obama and the Rouhani administrations were eager for a compromise: the former because it did not want another war and was eager to wind down its entanglements in the Middle East; the latter in part because of the sanctions, in part because it had always favored transparency, and in part because its aim had always been not to develop actual nuclear weapons, but instead to attain the theoretical capacity to be able to develop such weapons in the long-term future if necessity ever required it—such as another Saddam Hussein invading Iran and unleashing weapons of mass destruction. To have such a capacity, Iran needs the scientific knowledge, the centrifuges, and the ability to enrich uranium to a high level required for weapons.

The negotiations are formally between Iran and the Permanent Five Members of UN Security Council plus 1 (United States, United Kingdom, France, Russia, and China, plus Germany). But in reality, they were between Iran and the United States. Behind closed doors negotiators tackled the hard technical issues of how much uranium Iran would be permitted to enrich, how many centrifuges it could retain, whether it could experiment with plutonium as well as uranium, and how much it would open up its facilities to UN inspections. The outline of a general settlement was there, but reaching a mutually satisfactory agreement will be a challenge.

Youth Politics and the Generational Divide

Iran's youth, especially college students, are a force to be reckoned with: Over half the current population was born after 1979 and as many as 1.15 million are enrolled in higher education. In 1999, eighteen different campuses, including Tehran University, erupted into mass demonstrations against the chief judge, who had closed down a reformist newspaper. Revolutionary Guards promptly occupied the campuses, killing or seriously injuring an unknown number of students. Again in late 2002, thousands of students protested the death sentence handed down to a reformist academic accused of insulting Islam. But in 2004, when the Guardian Council barred thousands of reformers from the parliamentary elections, the campuses remained quiet, partly out of fear, partly out of disenchantment with the reformers for failing to deliver on their promises, and partly because of the concern about the looming danger from the United States military presence in Iraq. Students, however, returned to active politics in large numbers during the 2009 presidential elections between Ahmadinejad and the reform candidates, and even more so in the mass demonstrations protesting these contested elections. Of course, they also played an important role in the 2013 election of Rouhani. Youth's major concern is the lack of jobs for the college educated. The "Brain Drain"—an international term coined to describe the exodus of professions from Iran in the 1960s—continues to plague twenty-first century Iran.

Iran, thus, has a generational gap similar to that in many developing and even developed counties. The young generation—especially college graduates—have difficulty finding appropriate jobs. They have to settle either for less suitable ones or emigrate to the West. They have difficulty buying or renting homes. They consequently delay leaving their parents and getting married. Despite these similarities with other parts of the world, Iran so far has not shown the typical symptoms of the generational conflict—conflicts over bread-and-butter issues as such pensions, medical benefits, and old-age care. Such concerns are easily alleviated by the abundant income coming from oil and the anticipated revenue expected from the untapped gas reserves. Oil—not youth—is expected to carry the "burden" of the older generation.

Iranian Politics in Comparative Perspective

Unlike most developing countries, Iran was never formally colonized by the European imperial powers and has always been independent. It is, in many ways, an old state with many institutions that date back to ancient times. Furthermore, while many other developing world states have weak connections with their societies, Iran has a religion that links the elite with the masses, the cities with the villages, the government with the citizenry. Shi'ism, as well as Iranian national identity, serves as social and cultural cement, which gives the population a strong collective identity.

Although Shi'ism gives Iran this asset, it also helps explain why the county is unique in the world in that it has a semi-theocratic state. Despite these theocratic features, Iran still has much in common with many other fast-developing countries in Asia and Latin American—especially Brazil, Mexico, Venezuela, India, and

Indonesia. In some ways, it is better off. It no longer fits the stereotype of the Third World. It has overcome the worst aspects of backwardness—dire poverty, hunger and malnutrition, illiteracy, highly infant mortality, high death rates, and low life expectancy. It has an impressive educational system, and with it a burgeoning middle class that feels quite at home in the modern world. It has large oil revenues and resources, and even larger gas reserves ready to be tapped—once UN sanctions are lifted and Iran return fully to the global economy. What is more, Iran—unlike some oil states such as Nigeria—has a functioning state that is capable of effectively distribution to the general population the benefits of the oil revenues as well as administering quite effectively the whole country. The Islamic Republic is by no mean a failed state.

Where Do You Stand?

Iran is often described with the neighboring countries, especially the Arab countries, as part and parcel of the Middle East. Would you agree with this description?

Iran's nuclear program has been very controversial in the international community. Do you think that Iran has good persuasive reasons to scale down this program?

Chapter Summary

The Iranian state—unlike many others in the Middle East—is viable and well established. It has a long history. Its official religion—Shi'ism—binds the elite with the masses, the government with the governed, the rulers with the ruled. Its ministries are embedded deep into society, providing multiple social services. It has substantial oil revenues, which, although fluctuating, provide the government the means to finance the ever-growing ministries. What is more, the recent past—especially the Islamic Revolution and the eight-year war with Iraq—has helped create a strong sense of national solidarity against the outside world—not just against the West but also much of the Sunni Muslim World.

It has often been said that oil is a resource curse of the producing countries. It has been blamed for creating "rentier states," "dual societies," autocratic governments, unpredictable budgets, and retardation of other economic activities. Although this may be true in some parts of the world, in Iran oil has been the main engine driving state development and social modernization. It is mainly due to oil that Iran enters the twenty-first century with a strong state and a fairly modernized society in which almost all citizens have access to schools, medical clinics, modern sanitation, piped water, electricity, radios, televisions, and basic consumer goods.

The clergy exercise authority over elected officials in three separate ways: the Leader, a cleric, supervises the three branches of government; the Guardian Council can veto legislation passed by parliament; and the same Council can vet all candidates running for high office. Despite these restrictions, the constitution—in theory—has the possibility of moving away from theocracy toward

democracy. After all, the constitution enshrines the public's right to elect parliament, president, and even the Leader. The constitution even endows the public with the authority to amend the constitution. The main obstacle to democracy is the vetting process, which grants ultimate power to the Leader, not the constitution itself.

The George W. Bush administration liked to denounce Iran as a "totalitarian state" tyrannized by unelected unpopular leaders. While Iran is no liberal democracy, it hardly fits the "totalitarian" category. The clergy, despite opposition from the intelligentsia, continue to rule in part because they still enjoy some legitimacy—especially among the bazaars, rural population, and urban poor; in part because they have brought economic benefits to the wider population; and in part because they have left some room for civil society and have permitted interest groups to function so long as they do not violate red lines and directly question the clergy's legitimacy. They have also been greatly helped by the perceived notion that the nation is under siege—even under imminent threat—from the United States.

Iran could meet its internal challenge by becoming more flexible, liberalizing, giving greater scope to civil society, and allowing more public participation and competitive elections—in short, strengthening the democratic as opposed to the theocratic features of the constitution. If it did so, it would transform itself closer to democracy. If it does not, it could freeze up, alienate the public, lose legitimacy, and thereby make itself vulnerable to destruction. Iran could also meet its external challenge by following a cautious foreign policy, going slow on its nuclear program, providing verifiable guarantees that it was not building nuclear weapons, toning down its rhetoric, and assuring its neighbors as well as the United States that it was a "normal state" uninterested in exporting revolution. If it does not, it could well end up with a confrontation with the United States—a confrontation that would be disastrous for both countries. A window of opportunity has now been opened up with the negotiations between the Obama and Rouhani administrations.

Key Terms

Assembly of Experts
ayatollah
bazaar
dual society
Expediency Council
Farsi
Foundation of the Oppressed
Guardian Council
Hezbollahis
hojjat al-Islam

Imam Jum'ehs
Islamism
jurist's guardianship
Leader/Supreme Leader
Majles
maslahat
Organization of Petroleum
　　Exporting Countries (OPEC)
pasdaran
People of the Book

political Islam
Qur'an
rentier state
resource curse
theocracy

Suggested Readings

Abrahamian, Ervand. *A History of Modern Iran*. New York: Cambridge University Press, 2008.
_____. *The Coup: 1953, The CIA, and the Roots of Modern U.S.-Iranian Relations*. New York: The New Press, 2013.
Beeman, William O. *The "Great Satan" vs. the "Mad Mullahs": How the United States and Iran Demonize Each Other*. New York: Praeger, 2005.
Ebadi, Shirin, and Azadeh Moaveni. *Iran Awakening: A Memoir of Revolution and Hope*. New York: Random House, 2006.
Gheissari, Ali, and Vali Nasr. *Democracy in Iran: History and the Quest for Liberty*. New York: Oxford University Press, 2006.

Keddie, Nikki. *Modern Iran: Roots and Results of Revolution*, updated ed. New Haven, CT: Yale University Press, 2006.
Moin, Baqer. *Khomeini: Life of the Ayatollah*. New York: Thomas Dunne Books, 2000.
Nafisi, Azar. *Reading Lolita in Tehran: A Memoir in Books*. New York: Random House, 2003.
Pollack, Kenneth. *The Persian Puzzle: The Conflict between Iran and America*. New York: Random House, 2005.
Satrapi, Marjaneh. *Persepolis*. New York: Pantheon, 2003.

Suggested Websites

University of Texas—Iran Maps
www.lib.utexas.edu/maps/iran.html

Columbia University—The Gulf/2000 Project's Map Collection
gulf2000.columbia.edu/maps.shtml

The Story of the Revolution, British Broadcasting Corporation
www.bbc.co.uk/persian/revolution

Iranian Mission to the United Nations
www.un.int/iran

Iran Report, Radio Free Europe
www.rferl.org/reports/iran-report

News Related to Iran
www.farsinews.net

www.onlinenewspapers.com/iran.htm

9 China

William A. Joseph

Official Name: People's Republic of China (Zhonghua Remin Gongheguo)

Location: East Asia

Capital City: Beijing

Population (2014): 1.35 billion

Size: 9,596,960 sq. km.; slightly smaller than the United States

1912
Sun Yat-sen founds the Nationalist Party (*Guomindang*) to oppose warlords who have seized power in the new republic.

1927
Civil war between Nationalists (now led by Chiang Kai-shek) and Communists begins.

1937
Japan invades China, marking the start of World War II in Asia.

| 1700 | 1900 | 1910 | 1920 | 1930 | 1940 | 1950 |

1911
Revolution led by Sun Yat-sen overthrows 2,000-year-old imperial system and establishes the Republic of China.

1921
Chinese Communist Party (CCP) is founded.

1934
Mao Zedong becomes leader of the CCP; formally elected chairman in 1943.

1949
Chinese Communists win the civil war and establish the People's Republic of China.

SECTION 1

THE MAKING OF THE MODERN CHINESE STATE

Focus Questions ▼

- How did the Communist Party come to power in China?

- How has China changed—and remained the same— since the Communist Party came to power?

Politics in Action

In the early morning hours of June 4, 1989, Chinese soldiers began an assault to clear pro-democracy demonstrators from Tiananmen Square in Beijing. One of the protestors described what happened when he and others joined hands on the outskirts of the square to form a human chain to halt the army's advance:

> …without warning, the troops opened fire on us. People cursed, screamed and ran. In no time, seventy or eighty people had collapsed all around me. Blood spattered all over, staining my clothes.

At a nearby intersection, he saw "several hundred bodies, mostly young people, including some children."

> As the army continued to move toward the square, an angry crowd of over ten thousand surged forward to surround the troops. This time the soldiers turned on the people with even greater brutality. The fusillades from machine guns were loud and clear. Because some of the bullets used were the kind that explode within the body, when they struck, the victims' intestines and brains spilled out. I saw four or five such bodies. They looked like disemboweled animal carcasses.[1]

By the time dawn broke, Tiananmen Square had indeed been cleared. A unknown number of civilians had been killed. In the days that followed, a wave of government repression spread throughout the country. Thousands of Chinese citizens were

1966–1976		
Great Proletarian Cultural Revolution		

1966–1976
Great Proletarian Cultural Revolution

1976
Mao Zedong dies.

1989
Tiananmen massacre

2002–2003
Hu Jintao succeeds Jiang as head of the CCP and president of the People's Republic of China; re-elected to those positions in 2007–2008.

1960	1970	1980	1990	2000	2010	2020

1958–1960
Great Leap Forward

1978
Deng Xiaoping becomes China's most powerful leader and launches the nation on the path toward rapid economic growth.

1997
Deng Xiaoping dies; Jiang Zemin becomes China's top leader.

2008
Hosts the Olympic Games in Beijing

2012–2013
Xi Jinping becomes head of the CCP and president of the PRC.

arrested for their participation in the demonstrations in Beijing and other cities, and there were several well-publicized executions.

June 4, 2014, marked the twenty-fifth anniversary of the Beijing massacre. In the weeks prior to that anniversary, dozens of political activists, artists, and lawyers were detained by the Chinese authorities to ensure that they would not try

Ethnic Groups

55 other nationalities, including Zhuang, Manchu, Hui, Miao, Uyghur, Mongal, Tibetan, and Korean, 8.5%

Han Chinese 91.5%

Major Ethnic Groups

Chinese Currency
Renminbi(RMB)("People's Currency"); also called yuan
International Designation: CNY
Exchange Rate (2013):
- 1 US$ = 6.1 CNY
- 1 CNY = 0.16 US$
100 RMB Note Design: Mao Zedong (1893–1976), Chairman of Chinese Communist Party (1943–1976)

Languages: Standard Chinese (Mandarin) based on the Beijing dialect; other major dialects include Cantonese and Shanghaiese. Also various minority languages, such as Tibetan and Mongolian.

Religions: Officially atheist; Buddhist 18.2%, Christian 5.1%, Muslim 1.8%, folk religion 21.9%, other .08%, unaffiliated 52.2%

FIGURE 9.1 The Chinese Nation at a Glance

© Cengage Learning® (for map)

© G2019/Shutterstock.com (for photo)

Table 9.1	Political Organization
Political System	Communist party–state; officially, a socialist state under the people's democratic dictatorship.
Regime History	Established in 1949 after the victory of the Chinese Communist Party (CCP) in the Chinese civil war.
Administrative Structure	Unitary system with twenty-two provinces, five autonomous regions, four centrally administrated municipalities, and two Special Administrative Regions (Hong Kong and Macao).
Executive	Premier (head of government) and president (head of state) formally elected by legislature, but only with approval of CCP leadership; the head of the CCP, the general secretary, is in effect the country's chief executive, and serves concurrently as president of the PRC.
Legislature	Unicameral National People's Congress; about 3,000 delegates elected indirectly from lower-level people's congresses for five-year terms. Largely a rubber-stamp body for Communist Party policies, although in recent years has become somewhat more active in policy-making.
Judiciary	A nationwide system of people's courts, which are constitutionally independent but, in fact, largely under the control of the CCP; a Supreme People's Court supervises the country's judicial system and is formally responsible to the National People's Congress, which also elects the court's president.
Party System	A one-party system, although in addition to the ruling Chinese Communist Party, there are eight politically insignificant "democratic" parties.

to commemorate it in any way. What happened in Tiananmen in 1989 cannot be mentioned in the press. It is not taught in schools. The Internet police scrub any reference to it in blogs and tweets. No official accounting of the number of dead has been given.

The People's Republic of China (PRC) has changed dramatically in many ways in the quarter century since so much blood was spilled on the streets of the country's capital. The country is much more prosperous and deeply integrated into the global economy. Its stature as a rising world power had increased enormously. The Chinese people enjoy greater economic, social, and cultural freedoms. In 1989, fewer than ten thousand Chinese students were studying abroad; by 2014 there were nearly 400,000.

But much has not changed. The Chinese Communist Party (CCP) still rules China with an iron political grip. Most people do not feel the coercive weight of that grip in their daily lives, but the party still crushes individual or collective action it judges as a challenge to the party's authority. For all of its truly remarkable economic progress, the PRC remains one of the world's harshest dictatorships. The rift between China's authoritarian political system and its increasingly modern and globalized society remains deep and ominous.

Geographic Setting

China is located in the eastern part of mainland Asia, at the heart of one of the world's most strategically important regions. It is slightly smaller than the United States in land area, and is the fourth-largest country in the world, after Russia, Canada, and the United States.

The north is much like the U.S. plains states in its weather and topography. This wheat-growing area is also China's industrial heartland. Southern China has a much warmer climate. In places it is even semitropical, which allows year-round agriculture and intensive rice cultivation. The vast, sparsely populated western part of the country is mostly mountains, deserts, and high plateaus.

China is the most populous nation in the world with about 1.35 billion people. A little more than half of those live in urban areas. The PRC has nearly 160 cities with a population of a million or more. Beijing, the capital, has 20.7 million residents, while Shanghai, the economic heart of the country, has 23.5 million. Nevertheless, 650 million people still live in the countryside, which continues to play a very important role in China's economic and political development.

© Cengage Learning®

Although China and the United States are roughly equal in area, China's population of 1.35 billion is more than four times greater. Less than 15 percent of its land, however, can be used for agriculture. The precarious balance between people and the land needed to feed them has been a dilemma for centuries. It remains one of the government's major concerns.

In 1997, the former British colony of Hong Kong, one of the world's great commercial centers, became a Special Administrative Region (SAR) of the PRC. Hong Kong and China's other SAR, Macau, a former Portuguese colony with a thriving casino economy that became part of the PRC in 1999, have a great deal of autonomy from the government in Beijing in most matters other than foreign relations and defense.

About 92 percent of China's citizens are ethnically Chinese. The remaining 8 percent is made up of fifty-five ethnic minority groups. Most of these minority peoples live in the country's geopolitically sensitive border regions, including Tibet and Xinjiang, which has a large Muslim population. The often uneasy relationship between some of China's minorities and the central government in Beijing is a crucial and volatile issue in Chinese politics today.

Critical Junctures

From 221 BCE to 1912 CE, China was ruled by a series of family-based dynasties headed by an emperor. The Chinese empire went through extensive geographic expansion and other significant changes during this time. But the basic political and social organization remained remarkably consistent. One of its most distinctive aspects was a national bureaucracy chosen on the basis of merit, which developed much earlier than similar government institutions in Europe. Imperial officials were appointed by the emperor only after they had passed a series of very difficult examinations that tested their mastery of the teachings of Confucius (551–479 BCE), a philosopher who emphasized obedience to authority, respect for superiors and elders, and the responsibility of rulers to govern benevolently.

The Chinese empire was fatally weakened in the nineteenth century by an unprecedented combination of poor governance, a population explosion that led to economic stagnation and deepening poverty, internal rebellions, and external aggression by European powers, including the Opium War (1839–1842), which was fought over British demands that they be allowed to sell the narcotic in China. Many efforts were made to reform the imperial government. But these efforts were not enough to save the 2000-year-old imperial system, and in 1912, a revolution toppled the ruling dynasty and established the Republic of China.

Warlords, Nationalists, and Communists (1912–1949)

Dr. Sun Yat-sen*, who was partly educated in Hawaii, became the first president of the Republic. But he was unable to hold on to power, and China quickly fell into a lengthy period of conflict and disintegration. Rival military leaders, known as warlords, ruled large parts of the country. Sun founded the Nationalist Party, which he hoped would be able to reunify the country.

In 1921, a few intellectuals, inspired by the 1917 Russian revolution, established the Chinese Communist Party (CCP). They were looking for a more radical solution to China's problems than that offered by the Nationalist Party. They initially joined

---

*In Chinese, the family name come first.

with the Nationalists to fight the warlords. But in 1927, Chiang Kai-shek, who had become the head of the Nationalist Party after Sun's death in 1925, turned against the communists, who were nearly wiped out in a bloody crackdown. Chiang then unified the Republic of China under his personal and increasingly authoritarian rule.

The Communist Party relocated its headquarters deep within the remote countryside. This retreat created the conditions for the eventual rise to power of Mao Zedong, who led the CCP to nationwide victory two decades later. Mao had been one of the junior founders of the Communist Party. Coming from a peasant background, he had strongly urged the CCP to pay more attention to China's suffering rural masses. "In a very short time," he wrote in 1927, "several hundred million peasants will rise like a mighty storm, like a hurricane, a force so swift and violent that no power, however great, will be able to hold it back."[2] While the CCP was based in the rural areas, Mao began his climb to the top of the party leadership.

Under pressure from Chiang Kai-shek's army, in 1934 the communists were forced to embark on a year-long, 6,000-mile journey called the Long March, which took them across some of the most remote parts of China. Although only about 8,000 of the original 80,000 Long Marchers finished the trek, the communists were able to established a base in an impoverished area of northwest China in October 1935. It was there that Mao consolidated his control of the CCP. He was a brilliant political and military leader, but he also sometimes used ruthless means to gain power. He was elected party chairman in 1943, a position he held until his death in 1976.

Japan's invasion of China in 1937 had a major impact on the Chinese civil war. Chiang Kai-shek's government fled into the far southwestern part of the country, which effectively eliminated them as an active combatant against Japanese aggression. In contrast, the CCP base in the northwest was on the front line against Japan's troops. The Communists successfully mobilized the peasants to use **guerrilla warfare** to fight the invaders. This resistance to Japan gained the CCP a strong following among the Chinese people.

After Japan surrendered in 1945, the Chinese civil war quickly resumed. Communist forces won a decisive victory over the U.S.-backed Nationalists. Chiang Kai-shek and his supporters retreated to the island of Taiwan, 90 miles off the Chinese coast. On October 1, 1949, Mao Zedong declared the founding of the People's Republic of China (PRC).

Mao Zedong in Power (1949–1976)

The Communist Party came to power in China on a wave of popular support because of its reputation as social reformers and patriotic fighters. The CCP quickly turned its attention to some of the country's most glaring problems. A land reform campaign redistributed property from the rich to the poor and increased agricultural production. Highly successful drives eliminated opium addiction and prostitution from the cities. A national law greatly improved the legal status of women. The CCP often used violence to achieve its objectives and silence opponents. Nevertheless, the party gained considerable legitimacy among many parts of the population because of its successful policies during the early years of its rule.

Between 1953 and 1957, the PRC, with aid from the Soviet Union, implemented a **centrally planned economy** and took decisive steps toward **socialism**. Private property was almost completely eliminated through the takeover of industry by the government and the collectivization of agriculture. The Chinese economy grew significantly during this period. But Mao disliked the expansion of the government bureaucracy and the persistence of inequalities, especially those between the urban and rural areas.

guerrilla warfare

A military strategy based on small, highly mobile bands of soldiers (the guerrillas, from the Spanish word for war, *guerra*) who use hit-and-run tactics like ambushes to attack a better-armed enemy.

centrally planned economy

An economic system in which the state directs the economy through bureaucratic plans for the production and distribution of goods and services. The government, rather than the market, is the major influence on the economy. Also called a command economy.

socialism

A system in which the state plays a leading role in organizing the economy, owns m productive resour property, and act promotes equalit

GLOBAL CONNECTION

The Republic of China on Taiwan

After the Nationalists fled to Taiwan, communist forces would probably have taken over the island if the United States had not intervened to prevent an invasion. More than six decades later, Taiwan remains politically separate from the People's Republic of China and still formally calls itself the Republic of China.

Chiang Kai-shek and the Nationalists imposed a harsh dictatorship on Taiwan. This deepened the sharp divide between the Mainlanders who had arrived in large numbers with Chiang in 1949 and the native Taiwanese majority, whose ancestors had settled there centuries before and who spoke a distinctive Chinese dialect.

With large amounts of U.S. aid and advice, the Nationalist government promoted rural development, attracted foreign investment, and presided over impressive economic growth by producing globally competitive exports. Health and education levels were quickly raised and now are among the best in the world. Taiwan's GDP per capita ($39,600) is higher than that of Britain or France.

After Chiang died in 1975, his son, Chiang Ching-kuo, became president of the Republic of China and head of the Nationalist Party. He permitted some political opposition and gave important government and party positions, previously dominated by Mainlanders, to Taiwanese. When he died in 1988, the Taiwanese vice president, Lee Teng-hui, became president.

Under President Lee, Taiwan made great strides toward democratization. Laws used to imprison dissidents were revoked, the media was freed of all censorship, and multiparty elections were held. An opposition political party won presidential and parliamentary elections in 2000 to 2004. The Nationalists have been in power since 2008.

The most controversial political issue in Taiwan is whether the island should work toward reunification with the mainland or declare independence from China. Most people in Taiwan prefer the status quo in which the island is, for all intents and purposes (including its own strong military), independent of the PRC, but is not an internationally recognized country.

The PRC regards Taiwan as a rightfully part of China and has refused to renounce the use of force if the island moves toward independence. Nevertheless, the two have developed extensive economic relations and other connections. The Taiwan Straits—the ocean area between the island and the mainland—is still considered one of the world's most volatile areas in terms of the potential for military conflict.

MAKING CONNECTIONS Why would Taiwan be reluctant to reunify with the PRC?

---

communism

According to Marxism, the stage of development that follows socialism and in which all property is publically owned, economic production is coordinated for the common good, and a radical degree of equality has been achieved.

These concerns led Mao to launch the Great Leap Forward (1958–1960). The Great Leap was a utopian effort to speed up the country's development so rapidly that China would catch up economically with Britain and the United States in just a few years. It also aimed to propel China into an era of true communism in which there would be almost complete economic and social equality. These goals were to be achieved by mobilizing the labor power and revolutionary enthusiasm of the masses under the leadership of the CCP.

But irrational policies, wasted resources, poor management, and the suppression of any criticism combined with bad weather to produce a famine in the rural areas that claimed 30–40 million lives. An industrial depression followed the collapse of agriculture. China suffered a terrible setback in economic development.

In the early 1960s, Mao took a less active role in day-to-day decision making. Two of China's other top leaders at the time, Liu Shaoqi and Deng Xiaoping, were put in charge of reviving the economy. They completely abandoned the radical strategy of the Great Leap and used a combination of government planning and market-oriented policies to stimulate production.

This approach did help the Chinese economy. But by the mid-1960s, Mao had concluded that the policies of Liu and Deng had led to a resurgence of elitism and inequality. He thought they were threatening his communist goals by setting the country on the road to capitalism. China also broke relations with the Soviet Union, which Mao had concluded was no longer a truly socialist country.

The Great Proletarian Cultural Revolution (1966–1976) was Mao's ideological crusade designed to jolt China back toward his vision of communism. Its main goal was the political purification of the nation through struggle against alleged class enemies. Using his unmatched political clout and charisma, Mao put together a potent coalition of radical party leaders, loyal military officers, and student rebels (called Red Guards) to support him and attack anyone thought to be guilty of betraying his version of communist ideology, known as Mao Zedong Thought. The Cultural Revolution led to widespread destruction of historical monuments, the psychological and physical persecution of millions of people, and a series of disruptive power struggles within the top leadership of the CCP.

Mao died in September 1976 at age eighty-two. A month later, a group of relatively moderate leaders arrested their radical rivals, the so-called Gang of Four, led by Mao's widow, Jiang Qing. This marked the end of the Cultural Revolution.

Deng Xiaoping and the Transformation of Chinese Communism (1977–1997)

To repair the damage caused by the Cultural Revolution, China's new leaders restored to power many veteran officials who had been purged by Mao and the radicals. These included Deng Xiaoping. By 1978, Deng had clearly become the country's most powerful leader, although he never took for himself the formal positions of head of either the Communist Party or the Chinese government. Instead he appointed younger, loyal men to those positions.

Deng's policies were a profound break with the Maoist past. State control of the economy was significantly reduced, and market forces were allowed to play an increasingly important role. After decades of stagnation, the Chinese economy began to experience high levels of growth in the 1980s. Chinese artists and writers were allowed much great freedom. Better-educated officials were recruited to modernize the PRC government. Deng Xiaoping gathered global praise for his leadership of the reforms that were transforming nearly every aspect of life in China.

Then came Tiananmen.

Large-scale demonstrations began in Beijing in the early spring of 1989 and quickly spread to other cities. Most of the initial protesters were university students who were expressing their discontent about inflation, corruption, and slow pace of political reform. Over time, they became more vocal in their demands for democratization, although they never called for the overthrow of the Communist Party. At one point, more than a million people from all walks of life gathered in and around Tiananmen Square to show support for the students.

For a while the CCP leadership did little more than denounce the demonstrators as trouble-makers and issue vague warnings about dire consequences. But a small group of mostly elderly leaders, including Deng Xiaoping, who was 85 at the time, ran out of patience. The army was ordered to end the "counter-revolutionary rebellion" and restore order in Beijing. It did so with brutal violence on June 4th. The PRC government continues to insist that it did the right thing in the interests of national stability.

Following the Beijing massacre, China went through a couple of years of intense political crackdown and a slowdown in the pace of economic change. In early 1992, Deng Xiaoping took bold steps to accelerate reform of the economy. He did so partly because he hoped economic progress would enable China to avoid the collapse of the communist party–state such as had happened just the year before in the Soviet Union.

From Revolutionaries to Technocrats (1997 to the Present)

In mid-1989, Deng Xiaoping had promoted Jiang Zemin, the mayor and Communist Party leader of Shanghai, to become the head of the CCP. Although Deng remained the power behind the throne, he gradually turned over greater authority to Jiang, who

PROFILES

A Tale of Two Leaders

Chinese Communist leaders Mao Tse-tung and Deng Xiaoping in 1959.

Bettmann/CORBIS

Mao Zedong (1893–1976) and Deng Xiaoping (1904–1997) had much in common. They were both born in rural China and joined the Chinese Communist Party in their early 20s. Both participated in the CCP's Long March in 1934–1935 to escape annihilation by Chiang Kai-shek's Nationalist army. When Mao consolidated his power as the undisputed leader of the CCP in the 1940s, Deng became one of his most trusted comrades. After the founding of the PRC, Deng rose to the highest levels of party leadership. And both men transformed China in ways that mark them as two of the most important figures in all of Chinese—and perhaps world—history.

But, in some ways, Mao and Deng were very different. Most importantly, Deng was a pragmatist—someone who acts to get things done rather than dwelling on abstract ideas. Mao was an idealist who thought about the future in utopian terms and then tried to find ways to make reality fit his vision. Mao twice removed Deng from power during the Cultural Revolution because he concluded that Deng's economic pragmatism was taking China down "the capitalist road" and away from his communist ideals.

Less than a year after Mao died and his radical followers were purged in the fall of 1976, Deng made his way back to the inner circle of power. By 1978, he was clearly China's most powerful leader. Deng used his power to lead the country toward spectacular economic growth by taking the PRC in a very un-Maoist capitalist direction.

But another thing that Mao and Deng had in common was an unshakeable belief that communist party leadership of China should not be challenged. Mao initiated a number of ruthless movements to squash dissent. The brutal crackdown on the Beijing pro-democracy protests in June 1989 was Deng's response to those who questioned party rule.

Today both Mao Zedong and Deng Xiaoping are revered in China. Mao's legacy is tarnished by the tragic human cost of his utopian campaigns. But he is lauded for restoring China's sovereignty and dignity after more than a century of humiliation at the hands of foreign powers. Deng is seen as the architect of China's economic miracle. Few people associate him with the 1989 Beijing massacre since that remains a forbidden topic in the PRC.

MAKING CONNECTIONS How do you think history will judge the achievements and shortcomings of Mao Zedong and Deng Xiaoping?

also became president of the PRC in 1993. When Deng Xiaoping died in February 1997, Jiang was secure in his position as China's top leader.

Under Jiang Zemin's leadership, China continued its economic reforms and remarkable growth. The PRC became an even more integral part of the global economy. But the country also faced widening gaps between the rich and the poor, environmental degradation, and pervasive corruption. Overall, China was politically stable during the Jiang era. But the CCP still repressed any individual or group it perceived as challenging its authority.

Jiang Zemin was succeeded as head of the CCP in November 2002 and PRC president in March 2003 by Hu Jintao. The transfer of power from Jiang to Hu was remarkably predictable and orderly. Jiang had retired after two terms in office, as required by new party rules, and Hu had, for several years, been expected to succeed Jiang.

Both Jiang and Hu also represented a new kind of leader for the PRC. Mao and Deng had been involved in communist politics almost their whole adult lives. They had participated in the CCP's long struggle for power dating back to the 1920s. They were among the founders of the communist regime in 1949. In contrast, Jiang and Hu were technocrats. They had technical university training (as engineers) before working their way up the ladder of success in the party bureaucracy by a combination of professional competence and political loyalty.

Another smooth and predictable leadership transition took place when Xi Jinping (b. 1953) ascended to the top party position in November 2012 and the presidency of the PRC in March 2013. Xi is also technocrat (with a degree in chemical engineering). There is little reason to expect he will deviate significantly from the combination of economic reform and political repression that has been the CCP's formula for retaining power since the days of Deng Xiaoping.

The Four Themes and China

This cartoon captures the contradiction between economic reform and political repression that characterized China under the leadership of Deng Xiaoping and his successors.

China in a Globalized World of States

When the PRC was established in 1949, China occupied a very weak position in the international system. For more than a century, its destiny had been shaped by interventions from abroad that it could do little to control. Mao made many tragic and terrible blunders during his years in power. But one of his great achievements was to build a strong state able to affirm and defend its sovereignty. Although still a relatively poor country by many per capita measures, the sheer size of its economy makes the PRC an economic powerhouse. Its foreign trade policies have a significant effect on many other countries and on the global economy. China is a nuclear power with the world's largest conventional military force. It is an active and influential member of the world's most important international organizations, including the United Nations, where it sits as one of the five permanent members of the Security Council. China has become a major player in the world of states.

Governing the Economy

Throughout its history the PRC has experimented with a series of very different approaches to governing the economy: a Soviet-style planning system in the early 1950s, the radical egalitarianism of the Maoist model, and the market-oriented policies implemented by Deng Xiaoping and his successors. Ideological disputes over these development strategies were the main cause of the ferocious political struggles within the CCP during the Mao era. Deng began his bold reforms in the late 1970s with the hope that improved living standards would restore the legitimacy of the CCP, which had been badly tarnished by the economic failings and political chaos of much of the previous three decades. The remarkable success of China's recent leaders in governing the economy has sustained the authority of the CCP at a time when most of the world's other communist regimes have disappeared.

The Democratic Idea

Any hope that the democratic idea might take root in the early years of communist rule in China quickly vanished by the mid-1950s with the building of a one-party communist state and Mao's unrelenting campaigns against alleged enemies of his revolution. The Deng era brought much greater economic, social, and cultural freedom, but time and again the CCP has strangled the stirrings of the democratic idea, most brutally in Tiananmen Square in 1989. Deng's successors have been faithful disciples. They have vigorously championed economic reform in China. They have also made sure that the CCP retains its firm hold on political power.

The Politics of Collective Identity

Because of its long history and ancient culture, China has a very strong sense of collective national identity. Memories of past humiliations and suffering at the hands of foreigners still influence the international policies of the PRC. The CCP places great emphasis on nationalism as a means to rally the Chinese people behind the government, especially because faith in communist ideology has weakened as the country embraces capitalist economic policies. The enormous inequalities between those that have benefited from those policies and those left behind have led to the emergence socioeconomic class as a growing source of collective identity in contemporary China. China's cultural and ethnic homogeneity has also spared it the widespread communal violence that has plagued so many other countries. The exception has been in the border regions where there is a large concentration of minority peoples, including Tibet and Xinjiang.

In an act of outrage and protest, an unarmed citizen stood in front of a column of tanks leaving Tiananmen Square the day after the Chinese army had crushed the prodemocracy demonstration in 1989. This "unknown hero" disappeared into the watching crowd. Neither his identity nor his fate is known.

AP Images/Jeff Widener.

Theme and Comparisons

The People's Republic of China can be compared with other **communist party-states** with which it shares many political and ideological features. This raises several intriguing questions: Why has China's communist party–state proven more durable than that of the Soviet Union and nearly all other similar regimes? By what combination of reform and repression has the CCP held on to power? What signs are there that it is likely to hold power for the foreseeable future? What signs suggest that communist rule in China may be weakening? What kind of political system might emerge if the CCP were to lose or relinquish power?

China is also part of the developing world as measured by the average standard of living of its population, but its record of growth in the past several decades has far exceeded that of almost all other developing countries. Furthermore, the educational and health levels of the Chinese people are quite good for a country at its level of development. How has China achieved such relative success in its quest for economic development? By contrast, much of the developing world has become more democratic in recent decades. How and why has China resisted this wave of democratization? What does the experience of other developing countries say about how economic modernization might influence the prospects for democracy in China?

Where Do You Stand?

The Chinese Communist Party says that Mao's achievements far outweighed his shortcomings. What do you think?

Is a government ever justified in using massive force against unarmed demonstrators who are occupying a huge public space in the national capital, as happened in Tiananmen Square on June 4, 1989?

POLITICAL ECONOMY AND DEVELOPMENT

SECTION 2

State and Economy

When the Chinese Communist Party came to power in 1949, China's economy was suffering from more than a hundred years of rebellion, invasion, civil war, and bad government. The country's new communist rulers almost immediately seized most property from wealthy landowners, rich industrialists, and foreign companies. They then set up a centrally planned economy based on the Soviet model. The state owned or controlled most economic resources. Government planning and commands, not market forces, drove economic activity, including setting prices for almost all goods.

China's planned economy yielded impressive results in terms of increased production. But it also created huge bureaucracies and new kinds of inequalities, especially between the heavily favored industrial cities and the investment-starved rural areas. Both the Great Leap Forward (1958–1961) and the Cultural Revolution (1966–1976)

Focus Questions ▼

- What have been the major changes in China's approach to governing the economy since the Maoist era?

- What have been the major social consequences of China's rapid economic growth over the last three decades?

embodied the unique and radical Maoist approach to economic development that was intended to be less bureaucratic and more egalitarian than the Soviet model.

Under Mao, the PRC built a strong industrial base. The people of China became much healthier and better educated. But the Maoist economy was plagued by political interference, poor management, and ill-conceived projects. This led to wasted resources of truly staggering proportions. Overall, China's economic growth rates, especially in agriculture, barely kept pace with population increases. The average standard of living changed little between the mid-1950s and Mao's death in 1976.

China Goes to Market

In a 1962 speech about how to recover from the Great Leap Forward famine, Deng Xiaoping had remarked, "It doesn't matter whether a cat is white or black, as long as it catches mice."[3] He meant that the CCP should not be overly concerned about whether a particular policy was socialist or capitalist if it helped the economy. Such sentiments got Deng in trouble with Mao. They made Deng one of the principal targets of the Cultural Revolution.

Once he emerged as China's foremost leader in the aftermath of Mao's death in 1976, Deng let the cat loose. He launched what is referred to as the "Reform and Opening Up" policy to transform the Chinese economy. "Reform" meant letting market forces play a greater role, while reducing government control, whereas "Opening Up" meant dramatically increasing China's engagement with the global economy. Authority for making economic decisions passed from bureaucrats to families, factory managers, and even the owners of private businesses. Individuals were encouraged to work harder and more efficiently to make money rather than to "serve the people" as had been the slogan during the Maoist era.

In most sectors of China's economy today, the state no longer dictates what to produce and how to produce it. Almost all prices are now set according to supply and demand, as in a capitalist economy, rather than by administrative decree. Most government monopolies have given way to fierce competition between state-owned and non-state-owned firms. But there are still many thousands of **state-owned enterprises** (SOEs) with tens of millions of employees in China. Although vastly outnumbered by private business that employ many more workers and account for about 60 percent of China's Gross Domestic Product (GDP), SOEs still dominate critical sectors of the economy such as steel, petroleum, telecommunications, and transportation.

> **state-owned enterprises (SOEs)**
>
> Companies in which a majority of ownership control is held by the government.

But even SOEs must now respond to market forces. Some have become very profitable, modern enterprises. But many others are overstaffed economic dinosaurs with outdated facilities and machinery. The state-owned sector remains a severe drain on the country's banks (largely government-controlled), which are still sometimes required to bail out financially failing SOEs. These large loans are rarely, if ever, paid back. Many economists think that even more drastic SOE reform is needed. But the country's leaders have been unwilling to relinquish control of these important industries. They also fear the political and social turmoil that could boil up from a massive layoff of industrial workers.

The results of the PRC's move from a planned toward a market economy have been phenomenal (see Figure 9.2). China has been one of the fastest-growing economies in the world for more than twenty years. Gross Domestic Product (GDP) grew at an average rate of 10.3 percent per year from 1992 to 2012. During the same period, India's GDP growth averaged 6.7 percent, Brazil's was 3.1 percent, and the United States 2.6 percent. Although growth has slowed (to 7.7 percent in 2013), China weathered the global recession of 2008–2009 far better than any other major economy largely because of a huge government stimulus package.

Nevertheless, China's GDP per capita (a measure of the average standard of living) is still very low when compared to that of more developed countries. In 2013, GDP per capita in the United States was $52,800. In the PRC, it was $9,900; but in 1980, it was only $250, which again reflects how spectacular China's economic growth has been in recent decades.

Rising incomes have also led to a consumer revolution in China. In the late 1970s, people in the cities could only shop for most consumer goods at state-run stores. These carried a very limited range of often shoddy products. Today, China's urban areas are shopping paradises. There are privately owned stores of all sizes, gigantic malls, fastfood outlets, and a great variety of entertainment options. A few decades ago, hardly anyone owned a television. Now most households have a color TV. Cell phones are everywhere. In the cities, a new middle class is starting to buy houses, condominiums, and cars. China is even developing a class of "super-rich" millionaires and billionaires.

Despite these changes, economic planning has by no means disappeared. Officially, the PRC says it has a socialist market economy. While allowing a considerable degree of capitalism, national and local bureaucrats continue to exercise a great deal of control over the production and distribution of goods, resources, and services. Market reforms have gained substantial momentum that would be nearly impossible to reverse. But the CCP still ultimately determines the direction of China's economy.

Remaking the Chinese Countryside

One of the first revolutionary programs launched by the Chinese Communist Party when it came to power in 1949 was land reform that confiscated the property of landlords and redistributed it as private holdings to the poorer peasants. But in the mid- to late 1950s the state reorganized peasants into collective farms and communes in which the village, not individuals, owned the land, and local officials directed all production and labor. Individuals were paid according to how much they worked on the collective land. Most crops and other farm products had to be sold to the state at low fixed prices. Collectivized agriculture was one of the weakest links in China's command economy because it was very inefficient in the way

*These figures are based on official international currency exchange rates for the US$ and the Chinese RMB. If purchasing power parity (PPP) figures were available, the US$ amount would be about three times higher.

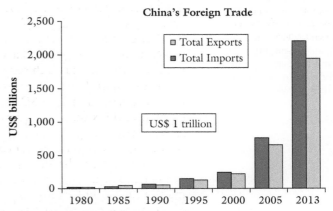

FIGURE 9.2 The Transformation of the Chinese Economy since 1980

Source: China Statistical Yearbooks; CIA World Factbook; World Bank World Development Indicators.

socialist market economy

The term used by the government of China to refer to the country's current economic system that mixes elements of both socialism and capitalism.

household responsibility system

The system put into practice in China beginning in the early 1980s in which the major decisions about agricultural production are made by individual farm families based on the profit motive rather than by a commune or the government.

it used resources, including labor, and undermined incentives for farmers to work hard to benefit themselves and their families. Per capita agricultural production and rural living standards were stagnant from 1957 to 1977.

After Mao's death in 1976, some commune leaders experimented with giving farmers more freedom to plant what they wanted, consume or sell what they produced, and engage in other economic activities, such as raising poultry, in order to increase their incomes. China's leaders not only allowed these experiments, but embraced them as national policy to be implemented throughout the country. Collective farming was abolished. It was replaced by the household responsibility system, which remains in effect today. Under this system, the village still owns the farmland. But it is contracted out by the local government to individual families, which take full charge of the production and marketing of crops. Largely because farmers are now free to earn income for themselves, agricultural productivity has sharply increased. There are still many very poor people in the Chinese countryside, but hundreds of millions have risen out of extreme poverty in the last two and a half decades because of expanded economic opportunities.

Economic life in the rural China has also been transformed by the expansion of rural industry and commerce. Rural factories and businesses range in size from a handful of employees to thousands. They employ more than 160 million people and have played a critical role in absorbing the vast pool of labor that is no longer needed in agriculture.

Society and Economy

Economic reform has made Chinese society much more diverse and open. People are vastly freer to choose jobs, travel about the country and internationally, practice their religious beliefs, join non-political associations, and engage in a wide range of other activities that were prohibited or severely restricted during the Maoist era. But economic change has also caused serious social problems.

Economic reform has created significant changes in China's basic system of social welfare. The Maoist economy provided almost all workers with what was called the iron rice bowl. As in other communist party–state economies, such as the Soviet Union, the government guaranteed employment and basic cradle-to-grave benefits to most of the urban and rural labor force. The workplace was more than just a place to work and earn a living. It also provided housing, health care, day care, and other services.

China's economic reformers believed that guarantees like these led to poor work motivation and excessive costs. They implemented policies designed to break the iron rice bowl. Income and employment are no longer guaranteed. They are now directly tied to individual effort.

An estimated 60 million workers have been laid off from state-owned enterprises since the early 1990s. Many are too old or too unskilled to find good jobs in the modernizing economy. They are now the core of a very large stratum of urban poor that has become a fixture in even China's most glittering cities. The PRC has very little unemployment insurance or social security for its displaced workers.

Economic changes have opened China's cities to a flood of rural migrants. After agriculture was decollectivized in the early 1980s, many peasants, no longer held back by the strict limits on internal population movement enforced in the Mao era, headed to the urban areas to look for jobs. This so-called floating population of about 240 million people is the biggest human migration in history. In Shanghai more than one-third of the population of 23.5 million is made up of migrants. Migrant workers are mostly employed in low-paying jobs and live in substandard housing, but fill an

iron rice bowl

A feature of China's socialist economy during the Maoist era (1949–1976) that provided guarantees of lifetime employment, income, and basic cradle-to-grave benefits to most urban and rural workers.

floating population

Migrants from the rural areas who have moved to the cities to find employment.

The futuristic skyline of Shanghai's Pudong district reflect the spectacular modernization of China's most prosperous areas in recent decades.
© Cuiphoto/Shutterstock.com

important niche in China's changing labor market, particularly in boom areas like export industries and construction.

The benefits of economic growth have reached most of China. But the market reforms and economic boom have created sharp class differences, and inequalities between people and parts of the country have risen significantly. A huge gap separates the average incomes of urban residents from those in the countryside (see Figure 9.2). The gap is also widening between the prosperous coastal regions and most inland areas. In the Maoist era, China was one of the world's most egalitarian countries; today it ranks with Brazil and South Africa as among the most unequal. Surveys show that most Chinese don't resent such inequality as long as their lives are improving and they believe their children's lives will be even better.[4] But if economic growth slows significantly and people find their rising expectations dashed, glaring socioeconomic inequalities could become a source of discontent and instability.

Some steps have been taken to improve the lot of the less well-off. In 2006, the government abolished taxes on agriculture, which had been in effect in some form in China for 2,600 years. By 2012, health insurance had been expanded to cover more than 90 percent of the population. But for most people the coverage is pretty minimal, and out-of-pocket expenses can be financially ruinous or deter the sick from seeking care.

China's economic boom and mixed state-private economy have also created enormous opportunities for corruption. Officials still control numerous resources and retain power over many economic transactions from which large profits can be made. The CCP has repeatedly launched well-publicized campaigns against official graft, with harsh punishment, even execution, for serious offenders. But corruption remains one of the biggest sources of public criticism of the government and seriously undermines the political legitimacy of the Communist Party.

The social status, legal rights, employment opportunities, and education of women in China have improved enormously since the founding of the PRC in 1949. Women have also benefited from rising living standards and economic modernization in the post-Mao era. But the trend toward a market economy has not benefited men and women equally. Although China has one of the world's highest rates of female participation in the labor force (70 percent), "[w]omen's incomes are falling relative to men's; traditional attitudes are relegating women to the home; and women's net wealth may be shrinking." Women's annual income is 67.3 percent of men's in urban areas; in the rural areas it is just 56 percent.[5]

In the early 1980s, China implemented a policy that limited couples to having just one child. The government claimed that this was necessary for the country's economic development. The population growth rate was, indeed, sharply reduced but the means used to achieve this goal were sometimes coercive, including forced abortions and sterilization. The strong preference for sons in Chinese culture also led to female infanticide and the abandonment of girl babies. In recent years, the availability of inexpensive ultrasound screenings has given rise to widespread gender specific abortions. The policy has been relaxed to allow some couples to have a second child, but the fact is that the state still claims the right to determine individual reproductive decisions.

Environmental Issues

One of the biggest downsides of China's spectacular economic growth has been the serious damage caused to the environment. Industrial expansion has been fuelled primarily by highly polluting coal. The air in China's cities is among the dirtiest in the world. The tops of ultra-modern skyscrapers are frequently obscured by dense smog. The pollution is so bad in Beijing that breathing the air is equivalent to smoking two packs of cigarettes per day. Many residents wear industrial-strength facemasks as they go about their daily business. Pollution has been linked to lower life expectancy in northern China. Private automobile use is just starting to take off and is expanding rapidly, which will greatly add to urban pollution in addition to further snarling already horrendous traffic. China has surpassed the United States as the world's largest source of carbon dioxide (CO_2) emissions, although per capita emissions remain much lower than in most developed countries. Pollution from China, much of it from export-producing industries, carries across the Pacific Ocean and contaminates air quality in the Western United States.

Soil erosion, wetland destruction, deforestation, and desertification (the loss of arable land to deserts) from unsustainable farming practices are at crisis levels. Roughly 70 percent of China's rivers and lakes are badly polluted. The government does little to regulate the dumping of garbage and toxic wastes. Nearly a quarter of the population (300 million people) does not have access to safe drinking water.

Northern China also faces a severe water shortage due to decreased rainfall, industrial expansion, and urbanization. To remedy this situation, the PRC has undertaken a multi-decade project to divert water from the Yangtze River in central China to the Yellow and two other rivers in the north. At a current estimated cost of over $60 billion, it is one of most expensive engineering projects in history. It has also raised concerns among environmentalists that the diverted water will be so polluted by factories along its route that it will be unfit for use.

The water diversion project is an example of what one scholar has called PRC's preference for an "engineering fix" to its energy needs and environmental problems.[6] So, too, is the Three Gorges dam on the Yangtze River, the world's largest and most costly ($28 billion) hydroelectric dam. The dam generates electric power equivalent to fifteen nuclear reactors and has also greatly expanding commercial shipping navigation of the river deep into China's southwest region. But the project resulted in significant ecological damage and over 1.5 million people had to be relocated.

The PRC is critical of rich countries that press it (and other developing countries) to slow down economic growth or invest in expensive pollution controls when those countries paid little heed to the environmental damage caused by their own industrial revolutions. Nevertheless, the Chinese government realizes that environmental degradation is so severe that it could threaten its modernization drive and has been paying more attention to environmental protection. China has also become a leader in the development of alternative clean energy, including wind and solar power.

China in the Global Economy

At the end of the Maoist era in 1976, the PRC was not deeply involved in the global economy. Total foreign trade was less 10 percent of GDP. Foreign direct investment (FDI) in China was minuscule. Mao's policy of "self-reliance" was intended to make sure that the PRC was not economically dependent on any foreign country. Furthermore, the stagnant economy, political instability, and heavy-handed bureaucracy were not attractive to potential investors from abroad.

In the early 1980s, as part of its "Reform and Opening Up," China embarked on a strategy of using trade to promote economic development. This followed the model of export-led growth pioneered by Japan, South Korea, and Taiwan, which takes advantage of low-wage labor to produce goods that are in demand internationally. It then uses the export earnings to modernize the economy.

The PRC is now the world leader in exports, ahead of the United States, Germany, and Japan, and is after the United States, the second largest importer of goods and services. Foreign trade accounted for 60 percent of the PRC's GDP in 2005–2012, with a relatively equal balance between imports and exports. As Table 9.2 shows, China is much more economically dependent on trade than is the United States or Japan; but, in comparison with other major economies, it is less or comparably dependent.

China is often referred to as the "factory to the world," because so many countries import large quantities of products

Table 9.2	Trade Dependency (2005–2012 Average)		
	Imports (% of GDP)	Exports (% of GDP)	Total Trade (% of GDP)
Germany	44.1	46.8	90.9
South Africa	31.3	29.6	60.9
Britain	31.4	29.2	60.6
China	27.3	32.7	60.0
Russia	21.5	30.9	52.4
India	26.5	21.8	48.3
Japan	15.1	15.5	30.6
United States	16.1	11.9	28.0
Brazil	12.2	12.9	25.1

Source: World Bank World Development Indicators.

made in the PRC. What makes these products competitive is the low cost of production, particularly wages. In 2009, according the U.S. Bureau of Labor Statistics, the average factory job in China paid $1.34 per hour compared with $32.00 per hour in the United States.

But wages are rising in China because of a labor shortage due largely to the one-child policy. It is facing increasing competition for overseas investment from Vietnam, Bangladesh, and other developing countries with lower labor costs. Long-term growth will depend on a combination of exporting more sophisticated, less labor-intensive products and focusing the production of goods and services more on the domestic market.

Where Do You Stand?

There are those who say that China's economy under Mao Zedong was better in some ways than that under Deng Xiaoping and his successors. In what ways might this be true?

Do you see the rise of China as a threat to American interests or as an opportunity for cooperation in areas of mutual interest?

THE U.S. CONNECTION

U.S.–China Relations

Shortly after the founding of the People's Republic, the United States and China fought each other in the Korean War (1950–1953). From then until the early 1970s, the two countries had very little contact because of the Cold War.

In 1972, Richard Nixon became the first U.S. president ever to visit China. Formal diplomatic relations between Washington and Beijing were established in 1979. Since then ties have deepened, despite some disruptions, such as following the Tiananmen massacre in 1989, and recurring tensions over trade, human rights, and other issues. Many believe that U.S.–China relations are the most important bilateral diplomatic relationship in the world.

China now trades with the United States more than with any other country, while China is America's second-largest trading partner (after Canada). Many in the United States think that cheap Chinese imports means lost jobs for Americans and that American firms can't compete with Chinese companies because labor costs in China are so much lower. They also say that the PRC engages in unfair trade practices, exploits sweatshop labor, and suppresses independent union activity. Some see the fact that China owns $1.2 trillion of U.S. government debt (which it bought with part of the vast reserves of U.S. dollars earned from exports) as having made the United States dangerously dependent on the PRC. Critics of Sino-American economic relations want the U.S. government

to put more restrictions on trade and financial dealings with China.

On the other side, many say that the benefits of U.S. trade with China far outweigh the negative impacts. First of all, consumers benefit greatly by the availability of a large variety of less-expensive products. In fact, although most of the things sold by companies like Walmart and Target are made in China, overall, only 2.7 percent of consumer spending in 2010 by Americans was on goods and services from China; 88.5 percent were from the United States. Furthermore, some argue that the United States should focus on developing more high-tech businesses to create jobs rather than trying to compete with China and other countries in "old-fashioned" labor-intensive industries. They also point out that many American firms have huge investments in China, which will grow—as will demand for American products—as that country becomes more prosperous. U.S. government debt is the result of American overspending, and several other countries besides the PRC own large chunks of it, including Japan and Britain. Finally, those who oppose restrictions on Sino-American economic engagement see it as one important way to promote not only the free market in China but also a more open society and democracy.

MAKING CONNECTIONS Why and how have U.S.–China relations improved since the end of the Cold War?

GOVERNANCE AND POLICY-MAKING

Organization of the State

In the early 1980s, about two dozen countries in Africa, Asia, Europe, and Latin America, with more than one-third of the world's population, were ruled by communist parties. Today, China, Cuba, Vietnam, North Korea, and Laos are the only remaining communist party–states. The political systems of these countries are characterized by the existence of an official state ideology based on Marxism-Leninism, communist party domination of all government and social institutions, and the suppression of all opposition parties and movements. Ruling communist parties claim that only they can govern in the best interests of the entire nation and therefore have the right to exercise the "leading role" throughout society.

Communist ideology is much less important in China today than it was during the Mao era when there was a great emphasis on enforcing ideological correctness. But even though the PRC has moved sharply toward a market economy in recent decades, the CCP still asserts that it is building socialism with the ultimate objective of creating an egalitarian and classless communist society. Ideology also sets the boundaries for what is permissible in politics since the party does not allow open opposition to its doctrines.

The preamble of the PRC's constitution states that the country is under "the leadership of the Communist Party of China." Article 1 defines the PRC as "a socialist state under the people's democratic dictatorship." It also declares that "disruption of the socialist system by any organization or individual is prohibited." Such provisions imply that the Chinese "people" (implicitly, supporters of socialism and the leadership of the Communist Party) enjoy democratic rights and privileges under CCP guidance. But the constitution also gives the CCP authority to exercise dictatorship over any person or organization that, it believes, opposes socialism and the party.

The Executive

The government of the People's Republic of China (the "state") is organizationally and functionally distinct from the Chinese Communist Party. Each has an executive branch, although the Communist Party exercises direct or indirect control over all government organizations and personnel. The government of the PRC acts as the administrative agency for enacting, implementing, and enforcing policies made by the party. In order to fully understand governance and policy-making in China, it is necessary to look at the structure of both the Chinese Communist Party and the government of the People's Republic of China and the relationship between the two.

CCP Organization

According to the CCP constitution (a wholly different document from the constitution of the PRC), the "highest leading bodies" of the party are the **National Party Congress** and the **Central Committee** (see Figure 9.3). But neither is as powerful as the much smaller CCP executive organizations.

National Party Congress

The symbolically important meeting, held every five years for about one week, of about 2,100 delegates representatives of the Chinese Communist Party, who endorse policies and the allocation of leadership positions that have been determined beforehand by the party's much smaller ruling bodies.

Central Committee

The top 370 or so leaders of the Chinese Communist Party. It meets annually for about two weeks and is charged with carrying on the business of the National Party Congress when it is not in session.

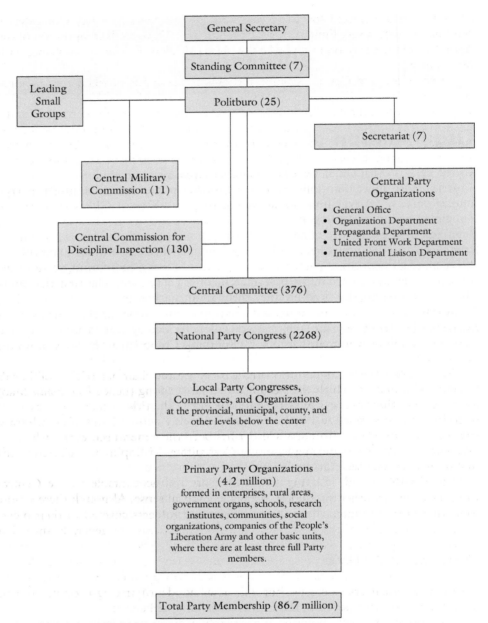

Note: Number in parentheses indicates the number of members as of 2013-14.

FIGURE 9.3 Organization of the Chinese Communist Party

The National Party Congress meets for only one week every five years, and it has more than 2, 200 delegates. This reflects the fact that the role of the Congress is more symbolic than substantive. The essential function of the National Party Congress is to approve decisions already made by the top leaders and to provide a showcase for the party's current policies. There is little debate and no seriously contested voting of any consequence.

The Central Committee (with 376 full and alternate members) consists of CCP leaders from around the country who meet annually for about a week in the late fall. Members are elected for a five-year term by the National Party Congress by secret ballot, with a very limited choice of candidates. The overall composition of the Central Committee is closely controlled by the top leaders to ensure compliance with their policies.

In principle, the Central Committee directs party affairs when the National Party Congress is not in session. But its size and short, infrequent meetings (called plenums) greatly limit its effectiveness. However, the plenums do represent significant gatherings of the party elite and can be an important forum for discussion. The announcements following the meetings are a way of telling the public of important policy changes, such as the relaxation in the one-child policy announced in November 2013 that will allow more couples to have a second child.

The most powerful political organizations in China's communist party–state are two small executive bodies at the very top of the CCP's structure: the **Politburo** (or Political Bureau), and its even more exclusive **Standing Committee**. These bodies are formally "elected" for five-year terms by the Central Committee from among its own members under carefully controlled conditions and with no choice among candidates. The slate of candidates is determined through a secretive process of negotiation and bargaining within the party elite. The first that most Chinese citizens know of the full composition of the Politburo and the Standing Committee is when they are presented on stage in rank order at the conclusion of the National Party Congress every five years. The current Politburo has twenty-five members, seven of whom also sit on the Standing Committee, the apex of power in the CCP.

Before 1982, the leading position in the party was the chairman of the Politburo's Standing Committee, which was occupied by Mao Zedong (hence *Chairman* Mao) for more than three decades until his death in 1976. The title of chairman was abolished in 1982 to symbolize a break with Mao's highly personal and often arbitrary style of rule. Since then, the party's leader has been the **general secretary**, who presides over the Politburo and the Standing Committee. Xi Jinping was elected to his first term as general secretary in 2012.

The Politburo and Standing Committee are not accountable to the Central Committee or any other institution in any meaningful sense. Although there is now somewhat more openness about the timing of and subjects covered in their meetings, the operations of the party's executive organizations are generally shrouded in secrecy. Top leaders work and often live in a huge walled compound called Zhongnanhai ("Middle and Southern Seas") on lakes in the center of Beijing adjacent to Tiananmen Square. Zhongnanhai is not only heavily guarded, as any government executive headquarters would be, but it also has no identifying signs on its exterior other than some party slogans, nor is it identified on public maps.

Two other executive organizations of the party deserve brief mention. The Secretariat manages the day-to-day work of the Politburo and Standing Committee and coordinates the party's complex and far-flung structure with considerable authority in organizational and personnel matters. The Central Commission for Discipline Inspection (CCDI) is in charge of investigating corruption within the party and other violations of party rules. Its investigations and hearings are conducted behind closed doors. If someone is found guilty, they may be demoted or even expelled from the party and, in some cases, turned over to the state judicial system for trial and, if appropriate, for punishment.

The Communist Party has an organized presence throughout Chinese society. CCP organizations in provinces, cities, and counties are headed by a party committee. There are also about 4.2 million primary party organizations, usually

Politburo

The committee made up of the top twenty-five leaders of the Chinese Communist Party.

Standing Committee

A subgroup of the Politburo, currently with seven members. The most powerful political organization in China.

general secretary

The formal title of the head of the Chinese Communist Party. From 1942 to 1982, the position was called "chairman" and was held by Mao Zedong until his death in 1976.

called branches. These are found, for example, in workplaces, government offices, schools, urban neighborhoods, rural towns, villages, and army units. Local and primary organizations extend the CCP's reach throughout Chinese society. They are also designed to ensure coordination within the vast and complex party structure and subordination to the central party authorities in Beijing.

Under Mao and Deng, power within the CCP was highly concentrated in one individual. No important policy decision was made without their consent. No Chinese leader since has had the personal authority or charisma of Mao or Deng. They have governed as a "first among equals" within a collective leadership that includes their fellow members on the Standing Committee and Politburo.

Party politics at the top has also become more institutionalized. Not only are the leaders limited to two five-year terms, they are also ineligible to be reelected if they will reach age 68 while in office. Term and age limits add considerable predictability to the leadership succession.

The route to the very top has also become more predictable. In 2007, when Xi Jinping was not only elevated to the Standing Committee, but was also given other positions, including vice president of the PRC and head of the school for training party leaders, it was clear that he had been anointed to become general secretary in 2012 and would be reelected in 2017. His predecessor, Hu Jintao, followed the same political trajectory.

In the Mao and Deng eras, few CCP leaders had an education beyond high school. Today, twenty of the twenty-five members of the Politburo (and six of the seven who sit on the Standing Committee) have a university-level degree. Two members of the Standing Committee have a BA in engineering, including Xi Jinping; others studied law, history, economics, and statistics. Almost all of China's leaders have also gained decades of experience working in party and government posts outside the capital. In fact, the only route to the top of the CCP is through the provinces. Prior to being elevated to the central leadership, Xi Jinping held key positions in four different provinces and Shanghai, where he served as both mayor and party secretary.

PRC Organization

National People's Congress (NPC)

The legislature of the People's Republic of China. It is under the control of the Chinese Communist Party and is not an independent branch of government.

State authority in China is formally vested in a system of people's congresses that begins at the top with the **National People's Congress (NPC)**, which is a completely separate organization from the National Party Congress. The NPC is China's national legislature and is discussed in more detail in Section 4.

The National People's Congress formally elects the president and vice president of China. But there is only one candidate, chosen by the top leadership of the Communist Party, for each office. The president's term is concurrent with that of the congress (five years). There is a two-term limit. As China's head of state, the president meets and negotiates with other world leaders. But the office of president is largely ceremonial and has little executive power.

The president of the PRC has always been a high-ranking CCP leader. Since the early 1990s, the general secretary of the Communist Party has served concurrently as the country's president. Thus, Xi Jinping is both General Secretary Xi and President Xi, though the source of his power clearly lies in the former position.

The premier (prime minister) of the People's Republic has authority over the government bureaucracy and policy implementation. The premier is formally appointed by the president with the approval of the National People's Congress. But in reality, the Communist Party leadership decides which of its members will serve as premier.

The premier directs the **State Council**, which is something like the cabinet in a presidential or parliamentary system. In addition to the premier, the State Council includes several vice premiers, the heads of government ministries and commissions, and a few other senior officials. Most State Council members run functionally specific departments, such as the Ministry of Foreign Affairs and the National Health and Family Planning Commission.

State Council

The highest organization in the state administration, directed by the premier. It also includes several vice premiers, the heads of government ministries and commissions, and a few other senior officials.

FIGURE 9.4 Organization of the People's Republic of China

cadre

A person who exercises a position of authority in a communist party–state; cadres may or may not be Communist Party members.

nomenklatura

A system of personnel selection under which the Communist Party maintains control over the appointment of important officials in all spheres of social, economic, and political life.

China's party–state is immense in size and in the scope of its reach throughout the country. The total number of cadres—people in positions of authority paid by the government or party—in the PRC is around 40 million. The term cadre applies to both the most powerful leaders as well as to local-level bureaucrats. Not all cadres are party members, and not all party members are cadres. The vast majority of cadres work below the national level, and a minority work directly for the government or the CCP. The remainder occupies key posts in economic enterprises, schools, and scientific, cultural, and other institutions.

The CCP uses a weblike system of organizational controls to make sure that the government complies with the party's will in policy implementation. In the first place, almost all key government officials are also party members. Furthermore, the CCP exercises control over the policy process through party organizations that parallel government agencies at all levels of the system. For example, each provincial government works under the watchful eye of a provincial party committee. In addition, the Communist Party maintains an effective presence inside every government organization through a "leading party group" that is made up of key officials who are also CCP members.

The CCP also influences the policy process by means of the "cadre list," or as it was known in the Soviet Union where the practice was developed, the *nomenklatura* system. The cadre list covers millions of important positions in the government and elsewhere (including institutions such as universities, banks, trade unions, and newspapers). Any personnel decision involving an appointment, promotion, transfer, or dismissal that affects a position on this list must be approved by a party organization department, whether or not the person involved is a party member. The *nomenklatura* system is one of the major instruments by which the CCP tries to "ensure that leading institutions throughout the country will exercise only the autonomy granted to them by the party."[7]

Other State Institutions

The Judiciary

China has a four-tiered system of "people's courts" that reaches from a Supreme People's Court down through higher (provincial-level), intermediate (city-level), and grassroots (county- and township-level) people's courts. The Supreme People's Court supervises the work of lower courts and the application of the country's laws, but it does not exercise judicial review over state policies and therefore is not a truly independent branch of government. It also does not interpret the country's constitution as it applies to laws or legislation.

At the end of the Maoist era, there were only 3,000 (poorly trained) lawyers in China; now there are more than 200,000 (compared to more than a million lawyers in the United States), with an increasingly high level of professionalism. Chinese courts can provide a real avenue of redress to the public for a wide range of nonpolitical grievances, including loss of property, consumer fraud, and even unjust detention by the police. Citizen mediation committees based in urban neighborhoods and rural villages play an important role in the judicial process by settling a majority of civil cases out of court.

China's criminal justice system is swift and harsh. Great faith is placed in the ability of an official investigation to find the facts of a case. The outcome of cases that actually do come to trial is pretty much predetermined. The conviction rate is 98–99 percent for all criminal cases. Prison terms are long and subject to only cursory appeal. A variety of offenses in addition to murder—including, in some cases, rape and especially major cases of embezzlement and other "economic crimes"—are subject to capital punishment. The number of annual executions is considered a state secret in China, but it is certainly in the thousands, and the PRC executes more people each year than the rest of the world combined.

Although the PRC constitution guarantees judicial independence, China's courts and other legal bodies remain under Communist Party control. The appointment of all judicial personnel is subject to party approval. At all levels of the system, party political and legal committees keep a close watch on the courts. Lawyers who displease officials are often harassed in various ways, their licenses to practice law might not be renewed, and they themselves are sometimes arrested.

China has become a country where there is rule *by* law, which means that the party–state uses the law to carry out its policies and enforce its rule. But it is still far from having established the rule *of* law, in which everyone and every organization, including the Communist Party, is accountable and subject to the law.

Subnational Government

China (like France and Japan) is a unitary state in which the national government exercises a high degree of control over other levels of government. It is not a federal system (like the United States and India) that gives subnational governments considerable policy-making and financial autonomy.

Under the central government, the PRC has twenty-two provinces, four very large centrally administered cities (Beijing, Shanghai, Tianjin, and Chongqing), five **autonomous regions**, which are areas of the country with large minority populations (such as Tibet).

Each level of subnational government has a people's congress that meets infrequently and plays a limited, but increasingly active, role in supervising affairs in its area. In theory, these congresses (the legislative branch) are empowered to supervise the work of the "people's governments" (the executive branch) at the various levels of the system. But in reality, subnational government executives (such as provincial governors and city mayors) are more accountable to Communist Party authority than to the people's congresses.

Despite considerable economic decentralization, the central government retains the power to intervene in local affairs when and where it wants. This power of the central authorities derives not only from their ability to set binding national priorities, but also from their control over the military and the police, the tax system, critical energy resources, and construction of major infrastructure projects.

Under the formal layers of state administration are China's 640,000 or so rural villages, which are home to a little less than half of the country's population. These villages, with an average population of 1,000, are technically self-governing and are not formally responsible to a higher level of state authority. In recent years, village leaders have been directly and competitively elected by local residents, and village representative assemblies have become more vocal. However, the most powerful organization in the village is the Communist Party committee, and the single most powerful person is the local Communist Party leader (the party secretary).

The Military, Police, and Internal Security

China's **People's Liberation Army (PLA)**, which encompasses all of the country's ground, air, and naval armed services, is, according to the PRC Ministry of Defense, "a people's army created and led by the Communist Party of China."

autonomous region

A territorial unit that is equivalent to a province and contains a large concentration of ethnic minorities. These regions, for example, Tibet, have some autonomy in the cultural sphere but in most policy matters are strictly subordinate to the central government.

People's Liberation Army (PLA)

The combined armed forces of the People's Republic of China, which includes land, sea, air, and strategic missile forces.

The PLA is the world's largest military force, with about 2.3 million active personnel (down from nearly 4 million in 1989). On a per capita basis, the PRC has 1.7 active military personnel per 1,000 of its population, compared with the U.S. ratio of 4.5 per 1,000. The PLA also has a formal reserve force of about 500,000. A people's militia of 8 million minimally trained civilians can be mobilized and armed by local governments in the event of war or other national emergency.

The key organization in charge of the Chinese armed forces is the **Central Military Commission (CMC)**. There are currently eleven members of the CMC, ten of whom are military officers. The one civilian is CCP general secretary and PRC president, Xi Jinping, who chairs the committee. The chair of the CMC is, in effect, the commander-in-chief of China's armed forces and has always been the most powerful leader of the communist party.

China's internal security apparatus consists of several different organizations. The **600,000** strong People's Armed Police (PAP) guards public officials and buildings and carries out some border patrol and counterterrorism functions. It has also been called in to quell public disturbances, including worker, peasant, and ethnic unrest. The Ministry of State Security, with a force of about 1.7 million, is responsible for combating espionage and gathering intelligence at home and abroad.

The Ministry of Public Security is the main policing organization in the PRC and is responsible for the prevention and investigation of crimes and for surveillance of Chinese citizens and foreigners in China suspected of being a threat to the state. Local public security bureaus, which carry out day-to-day police work, are under the command of the central ministry in Beijing.

The Policy-Making Process

At the height of Mao Zedong's power from the 1950s through much of the 1970s, many scholars described policy-making in China as a simple top-down "Mao-in-command" system. Since the late 1980s, terms such as "fragmented authoritarianism"[8] have been used to convey that although power is still highly concentrated in the top leadership organizations of the Chinese Communist Party, there are now many other sources of influence in the policy-making process. This model sees policy as evolving not only from commands from above, but also as a complex interplay of cooperation, conflict, and bargaining among political actors at various levels of the system. The focus on economic development has also led to the growing influence of nonparty experts, the media, and non-governmental organizations within the policy-making loop.

At the national level, flexible issue-specific task forces called "leading small groups" bring together top officials from various ministries, commissions, and committees in order to coordinate policy-making and implementation on matters that cross the jurisdiction of any single organization. Some groups, for example, the Central Leading Group on Foreign Affairs, are more or less permanent fixtures in the party–state structure, while others may be convened on an ad hoc basis to deal with short-term matters like a natural disaster or an epidemic. Since most of the members are high-ranking CCP officials, they are also a means to ensure party supervision of policy in that particular area.

China's parliament, the National People's Congress, formally passes legislation that gives policy the force of law. But it takes its cues from the Communist Party leadership and cannot be considered an independent actor in the policy-making process.

Central Military Commission (CMC)

The most important military organization in the People's Republic of China, headed by the general secretary of the Chinese Communist Party, who is the commander-in-chief of the People's Liberation Army.

Because the PRC is a unitary system, subnational levels of government have little policy-making autonomy. The central authorities pass along policy guidelines through a network of party leadership teams to be found in every locality and important government offices, and those teams closely monitor compliance with party directives. Nevertheless, the decentralization of power that has accompanied economic reform has given local governments considerable clout in policy implementation.

The policy process in China is much more institutionalized and smoother as well as less personalized and volatile than it was in the Maoist era. But it is still highly secretive, and leaders of the People's Republic are not accountable to the people of China. The unchallengeable power of the Communist Party is still the most basic fact of political life in the People's Republic of China.

Where Do You Stand?

One of the characteristics of a communist party–state is its commitment to Marxism-Leninism as the official ideology. Does the United States have an ideology?

Because of the dominant role of a single political party, China's policy-making process certainly doesn't suffer from political paralysis. Do you think that's a good thing?

socialist democracy

The term used by the Chinese Communist Party to describe the political system of the People's Republic of China. The official view is that this type of system, under the leadership of the Communist Party, provides democracy for the overwhelming majority of people and suppresses (or exercises dictatorship over) only the enemies of the people.

REPRESENTATION AND PARTICIPATION

SECTION 4

The Chinese Communist Party claims that it represents the interests of all the people of China and describes the People's Republic as a socialist democracy. In the CCP's view, this is superior to democracy in capitalist countries where wealthy individuals and corporations dominate politics and policy-making despite multiparty politics. China's *socialist* democracy is based on the unchallengeable role of the CCP as the country's only ruling party and should not be confused with the *social* democracy of Western European center-left political parties, which is rooted in a commitment to competitive politics.

The Legislature

The Chinese constitution grants the National People's Congress (NPC) the power to enact and amend the country's laws, approve and monitor the state budget, and declare and end war. The NPC is also empowered to elect (and recall) the president and vice president, the chair of the state Central Military Commission, the head of China's Supreme Court, and the procurator-general (in charge of national-level investigation and prosecution of crime). The NPC has final approval over the selection of the premier and members of the State Council. On paper, China's legislature certainly looks to be the most powerful branch of government. In fact, these powers, which are not insignificant, are exercised only as allowed by the Communist Party.

Focus Questions ▽

• What are the powers and limitations of China's National People's Congress as the legislative branch of government?

• What kinds of protests take place in China, and how does the party-state respond?

The National People's Congress is a unicameral legislature with nearly 3,000 members (called "deputies") who meet only for about two weeks every March. When the NPC is not in session, its powers are exercised by a 175-member Standing Committee (not to be confused with the CCP Standing Committee), which convenes every other month. A council of about fifteen members conducts the day-to-day business of the NPC. The chair of the NPC is always a high-ranking Communist Party leader.

NPC deputies are elected for five-year terms. Except for those from the People's Liberation Army, they are chosen from lower-level people's congresses in China's provinces, autonomous regions, major municipalities, and a few other constituencies.

Deputies are not full-time legislators, but remain in their regular jobs and home areas except for the brief time when the congress is in session. A large majority of the deputies to the NPC are members of the CCP, but many belong to one of China's eight noncommunist (and powerless) political parties (see below) or have no party affiliation. Workers and farmers make up less than 15 percent of NPC deputies; the remainder are government and party cadres, military personnel, intellectuals, professionals, celebrities, and business people.

Despite great fanfare in the press as examples of socialist democracy in action, most legislation is passed and all state leaders are elected by the NPC by overwhelming majorities and with little substantive debate. The annual sessions are largely taken up by the presentation of very long reports by the premier and other state leaders. The NPC never deals with sensitive political issues. The CCP also monitors the election process to make sure that no outright dissidents are elected as deputies.

Nevertheless, some deputies have become a bit more assertive on issues like corruption and environmental problems. Minor government legislative initiatives have occasionally been defeated or tabled. Major bills may take years to draft and be amended as a result of committee hearings, consultation with experts, and discussion among deputies. The media is not allowed to cover the legislative process in any detail or to print editorial opinions on the issues.

Political Parties and the Party System

The Chinese Communist Party

With 86.7 million members at the end of 2013 million members, the Chinese Communist Party is by far the largest political party in the world. But its membership makes up a very small minority of the population (less than 10 percent of those over eighteen, the minimum age for joining the party). This is consistent with the CCP's view that it is a "vanguard" party that admits only those who are truly dedicated to the communist cause. Joining the Communist Party is a time-consuming process that can last as long as two years and involves a lengthy application, interviews, references, a background check, and a probation period.

The social composition of CCP membership has changed profoundly since the party came to power in 1949. In the mid-1950s, peasants made up nearly 70 percent of party members. Figure 9.5 shows the composition of the CCP as of late 2012. The party now claims that rather than representing just workers and peasants, it represents the interests of the overwhelming majority of people in China and is open to all those who are committed to promoting national development and are willing to accept party leadership in achieving that goal.

The CCP welcomes members from what it calls the "new social stratum" that has emerged in the process of market reform and globalization of the Chinese economy. The new social stratum includes private business owners ("entrepreneurs")

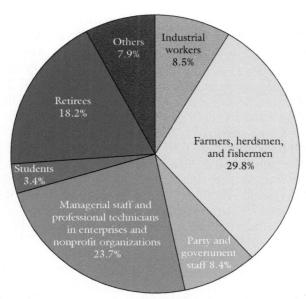

FIGURE 9.5 Occupation of CCP Members (2012)

Source: Organization Department of the Chinese
Communist Party

and managerial-level staff in private or foreign-funded companies. This is a dramatic change from the Maoist era when any hint of capitalism was crushed.

Women make up only 23.8 percent of the CCP membership as a whole and just 4.9 percent of the full members of the Central Committee elected in 2012. The Politburo has two female members. No woman has ever served on the party's most powerful organization, the Politburo Standing Committee.

Between 1.5 and 3.0 million people join the CCP each year. Even though many Chinese believe that communist ideology is irrelevant to their lives and the nation's future, being a party member remains a prerequisite for advancement in many careers, particularly in government.

China's Non-Communist "Democratic Parties"

China is rightly called a one-party system because the country's politics are so thoroughly dominated by the Chinese Communist Party. But, in fact, China has eight political parties in addition to the CCP. These are officially referred to as China's "democratic parties," which is said to be another example of socialist democracy in the PRC. Each non-communist party represents a particular group in Chinese society, such as overseas Chinese who have returned to live in the country. But these parties, all of which were established before the founding of the PRC in 1949 and accept the "guidance" of the CCP, have a total membership of only a little over half a million. They provide advice to the CCP on nonpolitical matters and generate support within their particular constituencies for CCP policies. Individual members of these parties may assume important government positions. But politically, these parties are relatively insignificant and function as little more than "a loyal non-opposition."[9]

New political parties are not allowed to form. When a group of activists who had been part of the 1989 Tiananmen protests tried to establish a China Democracy Party in 1998 to promote multiparty politics, they were arrested or forced into exile abroad, and the party was banned.

Elections

Most elections in the PRC are mechanisms to give the communist party–state greater legitimacy by allowing large numbers of citizens to participate in the political process under very controlled circumstances. But elections, especially at the local level, are becoming somewhat more democratic and more important in providing a way for citizens to express their views and hold some local officials accountable.

Most elections in China are *indirect*. In other words, the members of an already elected or established body elect those who will serve at the next-highest level in the power structure. For example, the deputies of a provincial people's congress, not all the eligible citizens of the province, elect deputies to the National People's Congress. A comparable situation would exist in the United States if members of Congress were selected by and from state legislatures rather than by popular vote (as was the case with the Senate before the Seventeenth Amendment to the Constitution was enacted in 1907).

Direct elections in which all voters in the relevant area cast ballots for candidates for a particular position are most common in China's rural villages. Elections for village head and other leaders are generally multicandidate with a secret ballot. Villagers have used elections to remove leaders they think are incompetent or corrupt. The village CCP committee closely monitors such grassroots elections. In many cases, the local Communist Party leader has been chosen to serve simultaneously as the village head in a competitive election. This is often because the Communist Party leader is a well-respected person who has the confidence and support of the villagers. Some observers believe direct elections at the village-level could be the seeds of real democracy that will spread to higher levels of the political system. Others see them as a façade to appease international critics and give the rural population a way to express discontent without challenging the country's fundamental political organization. In any case, village elections have given residents some measure of meaningful input into local governance.

Many direct and indirect elections in China now have multiple candidates and open nominations, with the winner chosen by secret ballot. A significant number of independently nominated candidates have defeated official nominees, although even independent candidates also have to be approved by the CCP. And the most powerful positions in the government, such as city mayors and provincial governors, are appointed, not elected. Recent electoral reform has certainly increased popular representation and participation in China's government. But elections in the PRC still do not give citizens a means by which they can exercise effective control over those who have the most power to affect their lives. Top Chinese communist leaders, from Mao to now, have repeatedly claimed that multiparty democracy is unsuited to China's traditions and socialist principles.

Political Culture, Citizenship, and Identity

From Communism to Consumerism

Marxism-Leninism is still important in Chinese politics, since the Communist Party proclaims that it is China's official ideology. Serious challenges to that ideology are not permitted. The CCP also tries to keep communist ideology viable and visible by efforts to influence public opinion and values through its control of the media, the arts, and education. Political study is still a required but now relatively minor part of the curriculum at all levels of the school system, and more than 80 percent of China's students between the ages of 7 and 14 belong to the Young Pioneers, an organization designed to promote good social behavior, community service, patriotism, and loyalty to the party. The Communist Youth League, which serves to foster commitment to socialist values and generate support for party policies, has about 90 million members between the ages of 14 and 28.

Alternative sources of socialization and belief are growing in importance in China. These do not often take expressly political forms, however, because of the threat of repression. In the countryside, peasants have replaced portraits of Mao and other Communist heroes with statues of folk gods and ancestor worship tablets. The influence of extended kinship groups such as clans often outweighs the formal authority of the party in the villages. In the cities, popular culture, including gigantic rock concerts, shapes youth attitudes much more profoundly than party propaganda. Consumerism ("buying things") is probably the most widely shared value in China today. Many observers have spoken of a moral vacuum in Chinese society, which is not uncommon in countries undergoing such rapid, multifaceted change.

Freedom of religion is guaranteed by the PRC constitution (as is the freedom not to believe in any religion). Organized religion, which was ferociously suppressed during the Mao era, is attracting an increasing number of adherents. Buddhist temples, Christian churches, and other places of worship operate more freely than they have in decades. The government says there are 18 million Protestants and 6 million Catholics in China. But unofficial estimates of Christians put the figure at several times that and as high as 70–100 million.

Religious life, however, is strictly controlled and limited to officially approved organizations and venues. Clergy of any religion who defy the authority of the party–state are still imprisoned. The Chinese Catholic Church is prohibited from recognizing the authority of the pope and appoints its own bishops and cardinals.

Clandestine Christian communities, called house churches, have sprung up in many areas among people who reject the government's control of religious life and are unable to worship in public. Although local officials sometimes tolerate these churches, in numerous cases house church leaders and laypeople have been arrested and the private homes where services are held have been bulldozed.

China's media is much livelier and more open than during the Maoist period when it did little other than convey party messages. There is now much greater leeway to publish more entertainment news, human-interest stories, and some nonpolitical investigative journalism in areas that are consistent with party objectives. But all media outlets are under direct or indirect party control, and the state does shut down those that provoke its political displeasure. In 2013, China was ranked 173 out of 179 countries in the Press Freedom Index compiled annually by Reporters Without Borders.

In terms of political restrictions, the arts are the area of life that has seen the greatest change in China in recent years. Books, movies, plays, and other art forms are sometimes banned, but much of the artistic censorship is now self-imposed by creators who know the limits of what is acceptable to the party–state.

The views of Chinese citizens about what makes them part of the People's Republic of China—their sense of national identity—are going through a profound and uncertain transformation. Party leaders realize that most citizens are skeptical or dismissive of communist ideology and that appeals to socialist goals and revolutionary virtues no longer inspire loyalty. The CCP has turned increasingly to patriotic themes to rally the country behind its leadership. The official media put considerable emphasis on the greatness and antiquity of Chinese culture. They send the not-so-subtle message that it is time for China to reclaim its rightful place in the world order—and that only the CCP can lead the nation in achieving this goal.

In the view of some scholars and others, such officially promoted nationalism could lead to a more aggressive foreign and military policy. The party–state has fanned nationalist sentiment among Chinese citizens to garner support for its disputes with nearby countries over claims to uninhabited islands in the strategically important Sea of Japan and the potentially oil-rich South China Sea.

Of course, it is the cultural tie of being "Chinese" that is the most powerful collective identity that connects citizen to the nation. The Chinese people are intensely proud of their ancient culture and long history. Their enthusiasm for hosting the 2008 Olympics in Beijing reflected this cultural pride. They can also be very sensitive about what they consider slights to their national dignity. Many Chinese feel that Japan has not done enough to acknowledge or apologize for the atrocities its army committed in China during World War II. This has been a strain in relations between the two countries and has sometimes led to spontaneous anti-Japanese demonstrations by Chinese students.

China's Non-Chinese Citizens

The PRC calls itself a multinational state with fifty-six officially recognized ethnic groups, one of which is the Chinese majority, called the Han people (Han being the name of one of China's earliest dynasties). The Han make up 91.5 percent of the total population. The defining elements of a minority group involve some combination of language, culture (including religion), and race that distinguish it from the Han. The fifty-five non-Han minorities number a little more than 100 million, or about 8.5 percent of the total population. These groups range in size from 16 million (the Zhuang of southwest China) to about 2,000 (the Lhoba in the far west). Most of these minorities have come under Chinese rule over many centuries through the expansion of the Chinese state rather than through migration into China.

China's minorities are highly concentrated in the five autonomous regions of Guangxi, Inner Mongolia, Ningxia, Tibet, and Xinjiang. Only in the latter two, however, do minority people outnumber Han Chinese, who are encouraged to migrate to the autonomous regions. The five autonomous regions are sparsely populated, yet they occupy about 60 percent of the total land area of the PRC. Some of these areas are resource rich. All are located on strategically important borders of the country, including those with Vietnam, India, and Russia.

The Chinese constitution grants autonomous regions the right of self-government in certain matters. But they remain firmly under the control of the central authorities. Minority peoples enjoy some latitude to develop their local economies as they see fit. The use of minority languages in the media and literature is encouraged, as is, to a certain extent, bilingual education. Minority religions can be practiced, though only through state-approved organizations.

The most extensive ethnic conflict in China has occurred in Tibet. Tibet is located in the far west of China and has been under Chinese military occupation since the early 1950s. Tibetans practice a unique form of Buddhism, and most are fiercely loyal to the Dalai Lama, a priest they believe is the incarnation of a divine being. China has claimed authority over Tibet since long before the Communist Party came to power. Tibetans have always disputed that claim and resisted Chinese rule, sometime violently, including in 1959, when the Dalai Lama fled to exile in India following the failure of a rebellion by his followers.

During the Maoist era, traditional Tibetan culture was suppressed by the Chinese authorities. Since the late 1970s, Buddhist temples and monasteries have been allowed to reopen, and Tibetans have gained a significant degree of cultural freedom; the Chinese government has also significantly increased investment in Tibet's economic development. However, China still considers talk of Tibetan political independence to be treason, and Chinese troops have crushed several anti-China demonstrations in Lhasa, the capital of Tibet.

There are 20–30 million Muslims in China. They live in many parts of the country and belong to several different ethnic minority groups. The highest concentration of Muslims is in the far west of China in the Ningxia Hui and Xinjiang Uyghur autonomous regions.

The more secular Hui (about 10.5 million) are well assimilated into Han Chinese society. But there is growing unrest among Uyghurs (about 10 million) in Xinjiang, which borders several Islamic nations, including Pakistan and Afghanistan. Tensions between Uyghurs and Han Chinese exploded in Xinjiang in mid-2010, resulting in about 150 deaths and a thousand injuries. The government forcefully restored order and then arrested more than 1,500 people (almost all Uyghurs) in connection with the riots, twelve of whom were sentenced to death.

The Chinese government also has clashed with Uyghur militants who want to create a separate Islamic state of "East Turkestan" and have sometimes used violence, including bombings and assassinations, to press their cause. In March 2014, Uyghur separatists used knives to attack people in a train station in southwest China, killing 29 and injuring more than 140 before being killed or captured by police. The government referred to this attack as "China 9/11" but also urged that the public not blame Uyghurs as a whole for the mayhem.

China's minority population is relatively small and geographically isolated. Ethnic unrest has been sporadic and easily quelled. Therefore, the PRC has not had the kind of intense identity-based conflict experienced by countries with more pervasive religious and ethnic cleavages, such as India and Nigeria. But it is possible that domestic and global forces will make ethnic identity a more visible and volatile issue in Chinese politics.

Interest Groups, Social Movements, and Protest

Truly independent interest groups and social movements are not permitted to influence the political process in the PRC in any significant way. The CCP supports official **mass organizations** as a means to provide a way for interest groups to express their views on policy matters—within strict limits.

Total membership of mass organizations in China is in the hundreds of millions. Two of the most important are the All-China Women's Federation, the only national organization representing the interests of women in general, and the All-China Federation of Trade Unions (ACFTU), to which more than 250 million Chinese workers belong. Neither constitutes an autonomous political voice for the groups they are supposed to represent. But they sometimes do act as an effective lobby in promoting the nonpolitical interests of their constituencies. For example, the Women's Federation has become a strong advocate for women on issues ranging from domestic violence to economic rights. The Trade Union Federation successfully pushed for legislation to reduce the standard workweek from six to five days. The ACFTU also

mass organizations

Organizations in a communist party–state that represent the interests of a particular social group, such as workers or women, but which are controlled by the communist party.

represents individual workers with grievances against management, although its first loyalty is to the communist party.

Since the late 1990s, there has been a huge increase in the number of non-governmental organizations (NGOs) less directly subordinate to the CCP than the official mass organizations. There is an enormous variety of national and local NGOs. These include ones that deal with the environment, health, charitable work, and legal issues. NGOs must register with the government, but they have considerable latitude to operate within their functional areas without direct party interference *if* they steer clear of politics and do not challenge official policies.

China has certainly loosened up politically since the days of Mao Zedong, and the spread of private enterprises, increasing labor and residential mobility, and new forms of informal association and communication are just some of the factors that are making it much harder for China's party–state to control its citizens as closely as in the past. But it is still very effective in monitoring dissent and preventing the formation of organizations that might challenge the CCP's authority. For example, in 2013, leaders of the New Citizens Movement, which has protested official corruption and advocated for constitutional government, were arrested on charges of illegal assembly in order to stop the movement from spreading.

Protest and the Party–State

The Tiananmen massacre of 1989 showed the limits of protest in China. The party leadership was particularly alarmed at signs that several autonomous student and worker grassroots organizations were emerging from the demonstrations. The brutal suppression of the democracy movement was meant to send a clear signal that neither open political protest nor the formation of independent interest groups would be tolerated.

Repression has not stopped all forms of citizen protest. The Falun Gong movement has carried out the biggest and most continuous demonstrations against the party–state. Falun Gong (FLG) is a spiritual movement with philosophical and religious elements drawn from Buddhism and Taoism along with traditional Chinese physical exercises (similar to *tai chi*) and meditation. It claims 70 million members in China and 30 million in more than seventy other countries. Its promise of inner tranquility and good health has proven very appealing to a wide cross section of people in China as a reaction to some of the side effects of rapid modernization.

The authorities began a crackdown on the FLG in 1999, which intensified after approximately 10,000 of its followers staged a peaceful protest in front of CCP headquarters in the center of Beijing. The authorities have destroyed FLG books and tapes, jammed websites, and arrested thousands of practitioners. Despite a few small FLG demonstrations, the crackdown seems to have been successful.

Each year, China experiences tens of thousands of so-called "mass incidents" that involve anywhere from a few dozen to more than a thousand people protesting against a wide range of grievances. These are almost always directed against local targets, not the party–state as a whole, and are often accommodated by higher-levels who see them as a way to find out about and problems before they become even more explosive.

Strikes and demonstrations by retired industrial workers protesting the non-payment of pensions or severance packages are among the most common type of mass incident in the urban areas. Employees at some foreign-owned enterprises have gone on strike against unsafe working conditions or low wages. Such actions at plants that produce most of the world's iPhones and iPads led Apple to enhance its initiative that monitors working conditions at its supplier plants in China and elsewhere.

The countryside has also seen an upsurge of protests over corruption, exorbitant taxes and extralegal fees, and environmental damage that impairs both human health and agricultural production. Illegal land seizures by greedy local officials working in cahoots with developers who want to build factories, expensive housing, or even golf courses is one of the major sources of rural mass incidents.

Urban and rural protests in China have not spread beyond the locales where they started. They have focused on the protestors' immediate material concerns, not on grand-scale issues like democracy, and most often are aimed at corrupt local officials or unresponsive employers, not the Communist Party. By responding positively to farmer and worker concerns, the party–state can win support and turn what could be regime-threatening activities into regime-sustaining ones.

The Political Impact of Technology

Internet access is exploding in China, with more than 600 million users by the end of 2013. That represents about 45 percent of the population, which is quite high for a country at China's level of economic development. By contrast, under 20 percent of people in India use the Internet.

The Chinese party–state knows that cutting-edge technology is critical to its modernization plans and wants citizens to become computer literate. But, as with so much else in China, the party–state wants to define the way and dictate the rules. Web access in China is tightly controlled by the licensing of a small number of Internet Service Providers who are responsible for who uses their systems and how. The government has invested huge sums to develop the Golden Shield Project, which operates under the auspices of the Ministry of Public Security and is charged with monitoring and censoring the Internet, including shutting out what it deems as objectionable foreign websites such as *The New York Times*. In early 2011, the authorities moved quickly to stifle social networking calls for peaceful gatherings in several Chinese cities to show support for the democracy movements in the Middle East and North Africa during the Arab Spring.

Nevertheless, the rapid spread of the Internet and social media—especially Twitter like blogs—has empowered citizens by providing a forum for communication and a flow of information that is difficult for the party–state to proactively control. There have been numerous large-scale online postings that have exposed corrupt officials, environmental problems, and child labor exploitation—and even poked fun at the heavy-handed government control of the Internet. The Internet has also been a means of mobilizing citizen action as in the aftermath of the hugely destructive and deadly earthquake that struck Sichuan province in May 2008 when relief funds were raised and blood drives organized online.

Where Do You Stand?

China claims it is a socialist democracy. Can socialism and democracy co-exist?

Do you think Tibet can be called a colony of China? Why or why not?

CHINESE POLITICS IN TRANSITION

▼ **Focus Questions**

• What are the major economic and political challenges facing the CCP?

• Why has the Chinese communist party–state been more durable than other regimes of its type?

household registration (*hukou*)

In China, the system that registers each citizen as entitled to work and to live in a specific urban or rural location.

Political Challenges and Changing Agendas

In late 2011, China passed a milestone in its history. For the first time, more people lived in cities than in the countryside. At the end of the Maoist era in the late 1970s, the rural areas accounted for over 80 percent of the population; in 2014, that was down to about 46 percent. The pace of urbanization is expected to accelerate, and by 2030, nearly three-quarters of China's population—a billion people—will live in cities, more than 200 of which will have a million or more inhabitants. The flow of farmers to the cities in search of better job opportunities—the "floating population"—has been and will continue to be the major source of the new urban population.

Rapid urbanization is a measure of China's progress in modernization, but it also presents the country's leadership with monumental challenges. Migrants mostly work in very low-paying jobs, including export industries, hotels and restaurants, and construction, that offer no security or benefits. They live in substandard housing, often hastily constructed and jam-packed dwellings called "urban villages" located on former farmland that has been incorporated into the municipality.

Perhaps their greatest vulnerability is that their presence in the cities is technically illegal. Beginning in the late 1950s, all Chinese were given either a rural or an urban **household registration** (*hukou*) that was pegged to a specific location. They were not permitted to live or work in any other area. This system prevented the kind of uncontrolled rural flight that occurred in many other developing countries and led to the establishment of vast urban slums. But, by limiting the mobility of farmers, it also became the basis of deeply entrenched inequality between city and countryside.

The authorities allowed the recent wave of migrants to move to the cities despite their rural *hukous* because their labor was crucial to economic expansion. But the migrants have no rights in the urban areas, including access to health care or education for their children, and can be evicted if the government chooses to do so.

The new leadership under Xi Jinping that took over in China in 2012–2013 has given high priority to promoting what is called "people-centered" urbanization. The government has announced that urban registration will be extended to 100 million migrants currently living in cities while another 100 million will be moved to urban areas between 2014 and 2020. The government will also invest heavily in housing, schools, hospitals, and public transportation to meet the needs of the new city dwellers. This is a hugely ambitious undertaking that will have an enormous impact the country's economic development. But China's leaders are well aware of the political implications of a project that will profoundly affect the lives of hundreds of millions of people.

China's planned urbanization is just one part of the multifaceted challenge that its leaders face in trying to sustain and effectively manage the economic growth that has not only significantly improved the lives of most of citizens, but also is the basis of public support for the ruling Communist Party. The CCP is gambling that continued solid economic performance will literally buy it legitimacy and that most citizens will care little about democracy or national politics if their material lives continue to get better. So far this gamble seems to have paid off.

But the global financial crisis of 2008 brought a significant slowdown to China's GDP annual growth rate, largely because of deceased demand for Chinese exports in developed countries. For more than two decades prior, the economy had grown at an average of better than 10 percent per year. In 2007, the Chinese economy grew at over 14 percent. In 2008, it plummeted nearly five points, and by 2012–2013, economic growth was at 7.7 percent. By post-recession world standards, that was quite enviable, but still raised the specter of seriously dashed expectations among a population that had grown accustomed to rapidly improving standards of living, especially if growth rates dips even more. That could spell political trouble for the CCP.

The government of the PRC needs to find ways to restructure the economy so that it is less dependent on export-led growth, which is very vulnerable to shifts in the global market. This will involve promoting industries that produce for the domestic economy and its huge untapped consumer market. At the same time, the Chinese government is encouraging its citizens to spend more and save less (in a way, the opposite of America's dilemma) in order to stimulate the domestic economy.

Another major economic challenge for the Chinese leadership is to deepen reform of the country's banking system, which is still almost entirely state-owned and largely immune from market forces, by allowing more room for both private and foreign investors. And, if China is to truly become a mature, modern, and globally competitive economy, it must move beyond being the "factory of the world" and become a more innovative economy that produces international-caliber, leading-edge products of its own design.

The enormous class, regional, and urban-rural inequalities that so clearly mark modernizing China so far have not become the source of major social instability. But that could change, particularly if there is further economic contraction, which would hurt the less well-off much more than the wealthy, who are increasingly sending their assets—and their children—abroad.

Corruption affects the lives of most people much more directly than political repression. Despite well-publicized campaigns and often-harsh punishments for offenders, corruption is still so blatant and widespread that it is probably the single most corrosive force eating away at the legitimacy of the Chinese Communist Party. Environmental problems may not be far behind as a source of dissatisfaction with the political status quo.

China and the Democratic Idea

The PRC has evolved in recent decades toward a system of what has been called "Market-Leninism,"[10] a combination of increasing economic openness (a market economy) and continuing political rigidity under the leadership of a Leninist ruling party that adheres to a remodeled version of communist ideology. The major political challenges now facing the CCP and the country emerge from the sharpening contradictions and tensions of this hybrid system.

As the people of China become more secure economically, better educated, and more connected to the outside world, they will also likely become more politically active. Business owners may want political clout to match their rising economic and social status. Scholars, scientists, and technology specialists may become more outspoken about the limits on intellectual freedom. The many Chinese who travel or study abroad may find the political gap between their party–state and the world's democracies to be increasingly intolerable.

What are the prospects for democratization in China? On the one hand, China's long history of bureaucratic and authoritarian rule and the hierarchical values of still-influential Confucian culture seem to be heavy counterweights to democracy. And, although some aspects of its social control have broken down, the coercive power of China's communist party–state remains formidable. The PRC's relatively low per capita standard of living, large rural population and vast areas of extreme poverty, and state-dominated media and means of communications also impose some impediments to the spread of the democratic idea. Finally, many in China are apathetic about politics or fearful of the violence and chaos that radical political change might unleash. They are quite happy with the status quo of economic growth and overall political stability of the country under the CCP.

On the other hand, the impressive success of democratization in Taiwan in the past decade, including free and fair multiparty elections from the local level up to the presidency, strongly suggests that the values, institutions, and process of democracy are not incompatible with Confucian culture. And though it is still a developing country, China has a high literacy rate, extensive industrialization and urbanization, and a burgeoning middle class—conditions widely seen by social scientists as favorable to democracy.

Despite the CCP's continuing tight hold on power, there have been a number of significant political changes in China that could be harbingers of democracy: the enhanced political and economic power of local governments; the setting of a mandatory retirement age and term limits for all officials; the rise of younger, better educated, and more worldly leaders; the increasingly important role of the National People's Congress in the policy-making process; the introduction of competitive elections in rural villages; the strengthening and partial depoliticization of the legal system; tolerance of a much wider range of artistic, cultural, and religious expression; and the important freedom (unheard of in the Mao era) for individuals to be apolitical.

Furthermore, the astounding spread of the democratic idea around the globe has created a trend that will be increasingly difficult for China's leaders to resist. The PRC has become a major player in the world of states, and its government must be more responsive to international opinion in order to continue the country's deepening integration with the international economy and growing stature as a responsible and mature global power.

One of the most important political trends in China has been the resurgence of civil society, a sphere of independent public life and citizen association, which, if allowed to thrive and expand, could provide fertile soil for future democratization. The development of civil society among workers in Poland and intellectuals in Czechoslovakia, for example, played an important role in the collapse of communism in East-Central Europe in the late 1980s by weakening the critical underpinnings of party–state control.

The Tiananmen demonstrations of 1989 reflected the stirrings of civil society in post–Mao China. But the brutal crushing of that movement showed the CCP's determination to thwart its growth before it could seriously contest the party's authority. But as economic modernization and social liberalization have deepened in the PRC, civil society has begun to stir again. Some stirrings, like the Falun Gong movement, have met with vicious repression by the party–state. But others, such as the proliferation and growing influence of non-governmental organizations that deal with *nonpolitical* matters such as the environment, have been encouraged by the authorities. The relatively new and rapidly growing phenomenon of online activism by China's netizens also suggests the emergence of a "digital civil society" that may well become a source of pressure for democratization.[11]

At some point, the leaders of the CCP will face the fundamental dilemma of whether to accommodate or, as they have done so often in the past, suppress organizations, individuals, and ideas that question the principle of party leadership. Accommodation would require the party–state to cede some of its control over society and allow more meaningful citizen representation and participation. But repression would likely derail the country's economic dynamism and could have terrible costs for China.

Youth Politics and the Generational Divide

In most developing countries, the under-30 age group is the fastest-growing segment of the population. By contrast, in China, it is the over-60-year-olds that account for the most rapidly expanding age group. This group numbered about 185 million (13.7 percent of the population) in 2010; that will grow to 284 million (21.0 percent) by 2025 and 440 million (34.6 percent) by 2050. This demographic trend is the result of a combination of factors, including longer life expectancy and, especially, the one-child policy that was introduced in the early 1980s and only modestly relaxed in 2013.

China's "graying population" presents the country with the challenge of supporting this growing cohort of senior citizens. The burden will fall particularly heavily on the shrinking younger generation, which will bear much of the responsibility for caring for elderly parents. Since both the husband and wife in a married couple are likely to be only-children, they will wind up caring for both sets of parents for what could be a decade or two. Other countries face a similar dilemma, but almost all of them (e.g., Japan) have a much higher per capita income and much more developed pension and health care systems. In other words, China's intragenerational challenge is complicated by the fact that it is "getting old before getting rich."[12]

Higher education has expanded rapidly in China over the last three decades, but still only about 20 percent of the age-relevant population is in college. Most of that population doesn't even apply since they lack the necessary high school education. For those who do want to apply, admission is extremely competitive, with just three out of five prospective students passing the required national college entrance examination. For jobs other than in the low-wage sectors of the economy, a college degree is a necessity, and, even for a substantial portion of China's 7 million college graduates each year (compared to 1.5 million in the United States), finding suitable employment has become a challenge. These unemployed or underemployed college-educated youth have become a fixture in many Chinese cities. They've come to be known as the "Ant Tribe" because they often share crowded apartments and pass the time by hanging out together. If China's economy were to slow down even more, the ranks of the Ant Tribe could grow in size and become increasingly unhappy about their situation. Unemployed educated youth have been a source of social unrest and political protest in many countries and were a major factor in launching the Arab Spring revolutions that began in 2011.

Chinese Politics in Comparative Perspective

China as a Communist Party–State

The fact that the Chinese Communists won power through an indigenous revolution with widespread popular backing and did not depend on foreign military support for their victory sets China apart from the situation of most of the now-deposed Eastern European communist parties. Despite some very serious mistakes over the six decades of its rule in China, the CCP still has a deep reservoir of historical legitimacy among large segments of the population.

The PRC has also been able to avoid the kind of economic crises that greatly weakened other communist systems, including the Soviet Union, through its successful market reforms that have dramatically improved the lives of most Chinese. CCP leaders believe that one of the biggest mistakes made by the last Soviet communist party chief, Mikhail Gorbachev, was that he went too far with political reform and not far enough with economic change, and they are convinced that their reverse formula is a key reason that they have not suffered the same fate.

But China also has much in common with other communist party–states past and present, particularly the insistence on the unchallengeable principle of party leadership in any way that the party chooses to exert that leadership. Stalinist Russia and Maoist China were classified as examples of **totalitarianism** because of the communist party's claim to exercise nearly total control of not just politics and ideology, but the economy, culture, and society as well. Under totalitarian regimes (which also included Nazi Germany), the distinction between public and private pretty much disappears, and the party–state enforces its authority through a combination of propaganda (extended to education and the media), coercion, and terror.

China is much less totalitarian than it was during the Maoist era. To promote economic development, the CCP has relaxed its grip on many areas of life. Citizens can generally pursue their private interests without interference by the party–state as long as they avoid sensitive political issues and are not seen as challenging the Communist Party's right to rule.

The PRC can now be considered a "consultative authoritarian regime" that "increasingly recognizes the need to obtain information, advice, and support from key sectors of the population, but insists on suppressing dissent ... and maintaining ultimate political power in the hands of the Party."[13] By moderating, if not totally abandoning some its Maoist totalitarian features, the Chinese Communist Party has shown remarkable adaptability that so far has allowed it to both carry out bold economic reform and sustain a dictatorial political system.

China as a Developing Country

The development of the PRC raises many issues about the role of the state in governing the economy. It also provides an interesting comparative perspective on the complex and much-debated relationship between economic and political change in the developing world.

When the Chinese Communist Party came to power in 1949, China was a desperately poor country, with an economy devastated by a century of civil strife and world war. It was also in a weak and subordinate position in the post–World War II international order. Even at the end of the Maoist era in the late 1970s, the PRC was among the poorest nations in the and little more than a regional power. Measured against these starting points, China has made remarkable progress in improving the well-being of its citizens, building a strong state, and enhancing the country's global role.

Why has China been more successful than so many other nations in meeting some of the major challenges of development? Those with political power in the developing world have often served narrow class or foreign interests more than the national interest. The result is that governments of many developing countries have become **predatory states** that prey on their people and the nation's resources to enrich the few at the expense of the many. They become defenders of a status quo

---

totalitarianism

A political system in which the state attempts to exercise total control over all aspects of public and private life, including the economy, culture, education, and social organizations, through an integrated system of ideological, economic, and political control. Totalitarian states rely on extensive coercion, including terror, as a means to exercise power.

predatory state

A state in which those with political power prey on the people and the nation's resources to enrich themselves rather than using their power to promote national development.

built on extensive inequality and poverty rather than agents of needed change. In contrast, the PRC's recent rulers have been quite successful in creating a **developmental state**, in which government power and public policy are used effectively to promote national economic growth. In this very important way, China has become a leader among developing nations.

developmental state

A nation-state in which the government carries out policies that effectively promote national economic growth.

But, in an equally important way, China is lagging behind many other countries in Africa, Asia, and Latin America. Whereas much of the developing world has been heading toward democracy, the PRC has stood firm against that wave of democratization. According to the 2012 edition of the annual Democracy Index produced by the highly respected magazine, *The Economist*, China ranked just six places from the bottom among 167 countries according to a survey that uses a variety of measures, including the fairness of elections, political participation, and civil liberties.[14]

There is a sharp and disturbing contrast between the harsh political rule of the Chinese communist party–state and its remarkable accomplishments in improving the material lives of the Chinese people. The CCP's tough stance on political reform is in large part based on its desire for self-preservation. But in keeping firm control on political life while allowing the country to open up in other important ways, Chinese Communist Party leaders also believe they are wisely following the model of development pioneered by the newly industrializing countries (NICs) of East Asia such as South Korea and Taiwan.

The lesson that the CCP draws from the NIC experience is that only a strong government can provide the political stability and social peace required for rapid economic growth. According to this view, democracy—with its open debates about national priorities, political parties contesting for power, and interest groups squabbling over how to divide the economic pie—is a recipe for chaos, particularly in a huge and still relatively poor country.

But another of the lessons from the East Asian NICs—one that most Chinese leaders have been reluctant to acknowledge—is that economic development, social modernization, and global integration also create powerful pressures for political change from below and abroad. In both South Korea and Taiwan, authoritarian governments that had presided over economic miracles in the 1960s and 1970s gave way in the 1980s and 1990s to democracy.

China is in the early to middle stages of a period of growth and modernization that are likely to lead it to NIC status within two or three decades. In terms of the extent of industrialization, per capita income, the strength of the private sector of the economy, and the size of the middle and professional classes, China's level of development is still below the level at which democracy succeeded in Taiwan and South Korea. Before concluding that China's communist rulers will soon yield to the forces of democratization, it is important to remember that "authoritarian governments in East Asia pursued market-driven economic growth for decades without relaxing their hold on political power."[15]

But economic reform in China has already created social groups at home and opened up the country to ideas from abroad that are likely to grow as sources of pressure for more and faster political change. And the experiences of many developing countries suggest that such pressures will intensify as the economy and society continue to modernize. Therefore, at some point in the not-too-distant future, the Chinese Communist Party is likely to again face the challenge of the democratic idea. How China's new generation of leaders responds to this challenge is perhaps the most important and uncertain question about Chinese politics in the early decades of the twenty-first century.

Where Do You Stand?

Do you think that the Chinese Communist Party will still be in power in 2049, one hundred years after the founding of the People's Republic?

Do you think China is ready for democracy? Would democracy be good for China?

Chapter Summary

For more than 2000 years, China was a hereditary monarchy headed by an emperor until it was overthrown by a revolution in 1912. From then until 1949 it was known as the Republic of China, but the central government was never in full control. Warlords ruled various parts of the country, a civil war broke out between the American-backed Nationalist Party government and the Chinese Communist Party, and Japan occupied almost all of eastern China during World War II. In 1949, the civil war ended with the victory of the Communist Party under Mao Zedong and the establishment of the People's Republic of China. From then until his death in 1976, Mao launched several radical campaigns that had a disastrous political and economic impact on China. Deng Xiaoping became China's most powerful leader in 1978. He implemented major reforms that helped make China the fastest-growing major economy in the world. But he also made it very clear that he would not tolerate any challenges to the authority of the Communist Party. Deng's successors have largely followed his model of economic reform and political repression.

During the Maoist era (1949–1976), the state thoroughly dominated the economy through a system of central planning in which government bureaucrats determined economic policies. Any kind of private economic activity was suppressed. This approach achieved some success in promoting industrialization and raising the educational and health standards of the Chinese people. But, overall, it left China as a very poor country with little involvement in the global economy. Under Deng Xiaoping and his successors, the state has given up much of its control of the economy and encouraged free-market forces, private ownership, international trade, and foreign investment. Living standards, modernization, and globalization have all increased dramatically. But serious problems, such as socioeconomic inequality and pollution, are a challenge for China's current leaders.

China is one of the few remaining countries in the world still ruled by a communist party. Even though the CCP has moved China in the direction of a capitalist economy, it still proclaims it is following communist ideology. The CCP insists it is the only political party that can lead the country toward economic development and maintain stability, and it prohibits any serious challenge to its authority. Power is highly concentrated in the top two dozen or so leaders of the CCP, who are chosen through secretive inner-party procedures. The government of the People's Republic of China is technically separate from the CCP, and political reform in China has brought some autonomy to government institutions, such as the national legislature and the judiciary. But, in fact, the government and policy-making operates under the close supervision of the Communist Party and almost all high-ranking government officials are also members of the Communist Party.

Representation of citizen interests and political participation in China are carried out under the watchful eye of the Chinese Communist Party. The National People's Congress, the legislature of the PRC, has become more active as the country's focus has shifted from revolutionary politics to economic development. Elections, particularly at the local level, have become more democratic. The Communist Party has also changed significantly, not just welcoming workers, peasants, and political activists into its ranks, but even recruiting members from among China's growing capitalist class of private business owners. Although they are much more open than during the Maoist era, the media, the arts, and education are still ultimately under party supervision. Communist ideology is declining as a unifying force for China's citizens, and the ability of the communist party–state to control and influence its citizens is weakening. The Internet, religion, consumerism, and popular culture are growing in influence. These all present a challenge to the CCP, which now emphasizes Chinese nationalism as a source of citizen identity. Some of the greatest political tensions in China are in parts of the country with high concentrations of non-Chinese ethnic minorities, such as in Tibet and among Muslims in Xinjiang. Protests by farmers and industrial workers with economic grievances have been on the increase, but these have not become large scale or widespread.

The legitimacy of the Chinese Communist Party to rule China rests heavily on the fact that it has presided over three decades of phenomenal economic growth that have dramatically improved the lives of most people in the country. Party leaders face major challenges in continuing to manage the economy, especially in light of the global financial of 2009. These challenges include rapid urbanization, reform of the banking system, and the transition from an export-led model of growth to one that depends more on domestic consumption and innovation. The CCP is also very likely to face increasing demands for a political voice from different sectors of society as its citizens become more prosperous, well educated, and worldly. In comparative perspective, China has proven more economically successful and politically adaptable than other communist party–states, including the Soviet Union, which collapsed in 1991. China has also been much more successful than most other developing countries in promoting economic growth, but so far resisted the wave of democratization that has spread to so many other parts of the world.

Key Terms

autonomous region
cadre
Central Committee
Central Military Commission (CMC)
centrally planned economy
communism
developmental state
floating population
general secretary
guerrilla warfare
household registration (*hukou*)
household responsibility system
iron rice bowl
mass organizations

National Party Congress
National People's Congress (NPC)
nomenklatura
People's Liberation Army (PLA)
Politburo
predatory state
socialism
socialist democracy
socialist market economy
Standing Committee
State Council
state-owned enterprises (SOEs)
totalitarianism

Suggested Readings

Davin, Delia. *Mao: A Very Short Introduction*. New York: Oxford University Press, 2013.

Fenby, Jonathan. *The Penguin History of Modern China: The Fall and Rise of a Great Power, 1850 to the Present*. New York: Penguin Global, 2013.

Gao Yuan. *Born Red: A Chronicle of the Cultural Revolution*. Stanford, CA: Stanford University Press, 1987.

Joseph, William A., ed. *Politics in China: An Introduction*, 2nd edition. New York: Oxford University Press, 2014.

Kraus, Richard Kurt. *The Cultural Revolution: A Very Short Introduction*. New York: Oxford University Press, 2012.

Lampton, David M. *Following the Leader: Ruling China, from Deng Xiaoping to Xi Jinping*. Berkeley, CA: University of California Press, 2014.

McGregor, Richard. *The Party: The Secret World of China's Communist Rulers*. New York: Harper, 2010.

Nathan, Andrew J., Larry Diamond, and Marc F. Plattner, eds. *Will China Democratize?* Baltimore, MD: The Johns Hopkins University Press, 2013.

Schell, Orville, and John Delury. *Wealth and Power: China's Long March to the Twenty-First Century*. New York: Random House, 2013.

Wasserstrom, Jeffery. *China in the 21st Century: What Everyone Needs to Know*, 2nd edition. New York: Oxford University Press, 2013.

Suggested Websites

The Central Government of the People's Republic of China
http://www.gov.cn/english/

China Brief (The Jamestown Foundation)
http://www.jamestown.org/programs/chinabrief/

China in the News
http://chinapoliticsnews.blogspot.com/

China Leadership Monitor (Hoover Institution)
**http://www.hoover.org/publications/
    china-leadership-monitor**

International Department of the Communist Party of China
http://www.idcpc.org.cn/

News of the Communist Party of China
http://english.cpc.people.com.cn/

China Digital Times (University of California at Berkeley)
http://chinadigitaltimes.net/

Endnotes

CHAPTER 1

[1]See Philippe Schmitter, "Comparative Politics," in Joel Krieger, ed., *The Oxford Companion to Comparative Politics* (New York: Oxford University Press, 2013), pp. 223–231. For a collection of articles in the field of comparative politics, see Mark Kesselman, ed., *Readings in Comparative Politics*, 2nd ed. (Boston: Wadsworth, 2010).

[2]See, for example, Gerhard Loewenberg, Peverill Squire, and D. Roderick Kiewiet, eds., *Legislatures: Comparative Perspectives on Representative Assemblies* (Ann Arbor: University of Michigan Press, 2002).

[3]See, for example, Merilee S. Griddle, *Despite the Odds: The Contentious Politics of Education Reform* (Princeton: Princeton University Press, 2004), which compares education policies in several Latin American countries; and Paul F. Steinberg and Stacy D. VanDeveer, *Comparative Environmental Politics: Theory, Practice, and Prospects* (Cambridge, MA: MIT Press, 2012).

[4]See, for example, Benedict Anderson, *Imagined Communities: Reflections on the Origins and Spread of Nationalism*, rev. ed. (London: Verso, 1991); and James DeFronzo, *Revolutions an Revolutionary Movements*, 5th ed. (Boulder, CO: Westview Press, 2014).

[5]Peter A. Hall, *Governing the Economy: The Politics of State Intervention in Britain and France* (New York: Oxford University Press, 1986); and Mark Blyth, *Great Transformations: Economic Ideas and Institutional Change in the Twentieth Century* (Cambridge: Cambridge University Press, 2002).

[6]See, for example, most of the chapters in William A. Joseph, ed., *Politics in China: An Introduction*, 2nd ed. (New York: Oxford University Press, 2014).

[7]For discussions of rational choice theory in the popular press, see "Political Scientists Debate Theory of 'Rational Choice,'" in the *New York Times*, February 26, 2000, B11; and Jonathan Cohn, "Irrational Exuberance: When Did Political Science Forget About Politics?" *New Republic*, October 25, 1999, 25–31.

[8]On democratic transitions, see for example, Samuel P. Huntington, *The Third Wave: Democratization in the Late Twentieth Century* (Norman: University of Oklahoma Press, 1993); Larry Diamond, Marc F. Plattner, and Philip J. Costopoulos, eds., *Debates on Democratization* (Baltimore: Johns Hopkins University Press, 2010); and Barbara Wejnert, *Diffusion of Democracy: The Past and Future of Global Democracy* (Cambridge: Cambridge University Press, 2014).

[9]See Joel Krieger, ed., *Globalization and State Power: A Reader* (New York: Pearson/Longman, 2006).

[10]This term is borrowed from Peter A. Hall, *Governing the Economy.*

[11]Peter A. Hall and David Soskice, eds., *Varieties of Capitalism: The Institutional Foundations of Comparative Advantage* (New York: Oxford University Press, 2001). See also David Coates, ed., *Varieties of Capitalism, Varieties of Approaches* (Basingstoke, UK: Palgrave/ Macmillan, 2005).

[12]See, for example, Chalmers Johnson, *MITI and the Japanese Miracle: The Growth of Industrial Policy* (Stanford: Stanford University Press, 1982); and Meredith Woo-Cummings, ed., *The Developmental State* (Ithaca, NY: Cornell University Press, 1999); Robert Wade, *Governing the Market: Economic Theory and the Role of Government in East Asian Industrialization* (Princeton: Princeton University Press, 2003); Dwight H. Perkins, *East Asian Development: Foundations and Strategies* (Cambridge, MA: Harvard University Press, 2013); and Linda Yueh, *China's Growth: The Making of an Economic Superpower* (New York: Oxford University Press, 2013).

[13]Adam Przeworski et al., *Democracy and Development: Political Institutions and Well-Being in the World, 1950–1990* (Cambridge: Cambridge University Press, 2000).

[14]Amartya Sen, "Democracy as a Universal Value," *Journal of Democracy* 10, no. 3 (July 1999): 3–17. This article is included in Kesselman, *Readings in Comparative Politics*. For a study that finds a positive correlation between democracy and economic growth, see Daron Acemoglu, Suresh Naidum, Pascual Restrepo, and James A. Robinson, "Democracy Does Cause Growth," Working Paper 20004. Cambridge, MA: National Bureau of Economic Research, 2014.

[15]Freedom House's annual Freedom in World Reports are available at www.freedomhouse.org

[16]Sen, "Democracy as a Universal Value," 3.

[17]Andrew Roberts, "Review Article: The Quality of Democracy," *Comparative Politics* 37, no. 3 (April 2005), 357.

[18]For contrasting views on this debate, see Samuel P. Huntington, *Political Order in Changing Societies* (New Haven: Yale University Press, 1968); and Mark Kesselman, "Order or Movement?: The Literature of Political Development as Ideology," *World Politics* 26 (1973), 139–154.

[19]Przeworski et al., *Democracy and Development*.

[20]Alfred Stepan, *Arguing Comparative Politics* (New York: Oxford University Press, 2001), 184.

CHAPTER 2

[1]Inman, Phillip, "Minority Ethnic Workers in UK Twice as Likely to Be Unemployed as Whites." *The Guardian.* Guardian News and Media, January 9, 2014. Web. May 15, 2014.

[2]UK Office of National Statistics, 2014.

[3]Richard Heffernan, Philip Cowley, and Colin Hay. Developments in British Politics Bk. 9. Basingstoke: Palgrave Macmillan, 2011.

[4]Philip Norton, *The British Polity*, 3rd ed. (New York: Longman, 1994), p. 59.

[5]Stephen Haseler, "Britain's Ancient Régime," *Parliamentary Affairs* 40, no. 4 (October 1990): 418.

[6]See Bill Jones and Philip Norton, *Politics UK*, 7th ed. (New York: Longman, 2010), pp. 475–476.

[7]Ivor Crewe, "Great Britain," in I. Crewe and D. Denver, eds., *Electoral Change in Western Democracies* (London, Croom Helm, 1985), p. 107.

[8]See Gabriel A. Almond and Sidney Verba, *The Civic Culture: Political Attitudes and Democracy in Five Nations* (Princeton, NJ: Princeton University Press, 1963); Almond and Verba, eds., *The Civic Culture Revisited* (Boston: Little, Brown, 1980); and Samuel H. Beer, *Britain Against Itself: The Political Contradictions of Collectivism* (New York: Norton, 1982), pp. 110–114.

[9]See Chris Howell, *Trade Unions and the State* (Princeton, NJ: Princeton University Press, 2005), esp. Ch. 6.

[10]Bhiku Parekh et al., *The Future of Multi-Ethnic Britain: The Parekh Report* (London: Profile Books, 2000), p. 10.

[11]Peter Riddell, *The Thatcher Decade* (Oxford: Basil Blackwell, 1989), p. 289.

[12]Tony Blair, "Doctrine of the International Community," speech to the Economic Club of Chicago, Hilton Hotel, Chicago, April 22, 1999.

CHAPTER 3

[1]Rogers Smith, *Civic Ideals: Conflicting Visions of Citizenship in U.S. History* (New Haven, CT: Yale University Press, 1997).

[2] S. Karthick Ramakrishnan, *Democracy in Immigrant America: Changing Demographics and Political Participation* (Stanford, CA: Stanford University Press, 2005), chapters 4 and 5.

[3]Louis Hartz, *The Liberal Tradition in America* (New York: Harvest/HBJ, 1955).

[4]Randall Monger, *U.S. Legal Permanent Residents: 2009* (Washington, DC: Office of Immigration Statistics, U.S. Department of Homeland Security, 2010).

[5]Jeffrey S. Passel, *The Size and Characteristics of the Unauthorized Migrant Population in the U.S.: Estimates Based on the March 2005 Current Population Survey* (Washington, DC: Pew Hispanic Center, 2006).

[6]Gary C. Bryner, *Blue Skies, Green Politics: The Clean Air Act of 1990 and Its Implementation* (Washington, DC: CQ Press, 1995).

[7]See *The Federalist Papers*, ed. Clinton Rossiter (New York: Mentor, 1961), particularly *Federalist* Nos. 10 and 51.

[8]Deborah Avant, *The Market for Force: The Consequences of Privatizing Security* (New York: Cambridge University Press, 2005).

[9]Kristi Anderson, *After Suffrage: Women in Partisan and Electoral Politics Before the New Deal* (Chicago: University of Chicago Press, 1996), chapters 2 and 3.

[10]Ruy A. Teixeira, *The Disappearing American Voter* (Washington, DC: Brookings Institution, 1992).

[11]Raymond Wolfinger and Steven Rosenstone, *Who Votes?* (New Haven, CT: Yale University Press. 1980), chapters 2 and 3.

[12]Sanford Levinson, *Constitutional Faith* (Princeton, NJ: Princeton University Press, 1988).

[13]Sidney Verba, Kay Lehman Schlozman, and Henry Brady, *Voice and Equality: Civic Voluntarism in American Politics* (Cambridge: Harvard University Press, 1995).

[14]Robert D. Putnam, *Bowling Alone: The Collapse and Revival of American Community* (New York: Simon and Schuster, 2000).

CHAPTER 5

[1]An excellent history of this event is presented in Wayne A. Cornelius, "Nation-Building, Participation, and Distribution: The Politics of Social Reform Under Cárdenas," in Gabriel A. Almond, Scott Flanagan, and Robert J. Mundt (eds.), *Crisis, Choice and Change: Historical Studies of Political Development* (Boston: Little, Brown, 1973).

[2]A classic anthropological study on the urban poor left behind by the "Mexican Miracle" is Oscar Lewis, *The Children of Sánchez: Autobiography of a Mexican Family* (New York: Random House, 1961).

[3]Joe Foweraker and Ann L. Craig (eds.), *Popular Movements and Political Change in Mexico* (Boulder, CO: Lynne Rienner, 1989).

[4]Cohn, D'Vera, Ana Gonzalez-Barrera and Danielle Cuddington, "Remittances to Latin America Recover—but Not to Mexico," (Washington, DC: Pew Research Center, November 2013), available at http://www.pewhispanic.org/files/2013/12/Remittances_11-2013_FINAL.pdf.

[5]Roger Hansen, *The Politics of Mexican Development* (Baltimore: Johns Hopkins University Press, 1971), 75.

[6]World Trade Organization, *Trade Profiles: Mexico*, http://stat.wto.org/CountryProfile/WSDBCountryPFView.aspx?Language=E&Country=MX.

[7]For a recent study arguing that many Mexican farmers have been hurt by NAFTA, see Timothy A. Wise, "Agricultural Dumping Under NAFTA: Estimating the Costs of U.S. Agricultural Policies to Mexican Producers," Mexican Rural Development Research Report No. 7 (Washington, DC: Woodrow Wilson International Center for Scholars, 2010).

[8]For a description of how Mexican presidents went about the process of selecting their successors during the period of PRI dominance, see Jorge G. Castañeda, *Perpetuating Power: How Mexican Presidents Were Chosen* (New York: New Press, 2000).

[9]Daniel Levy and Gabriel Székely, *Mexico: Paradoxes of Stability and Change* (Boulder, CO: Westview Press, 1983), p. 100.

[10]See Luis Carlos Ugalde, *The Mexican Congress: Old Player, New Power* (Washington, DC: Center for International and Strategic Studies, 2000).

[11]See Chapell H. Lawson, *Building the Fourth Estate: Democratization and the Rise of a Free Press in Mexico* (Berkeley: University of California Press, 2002).

[12]Susan Eckstein (ed.), *Power and Popular Protest: Latin American Social Movements* (Berkeley: University of California Press, 1989).

CHAPTER 6

[1]Much of this context is recounted in James S. Coleman, *Nigeria: Background to Nationalism* (Berkeley: University of California Press, 1958).

[2]Obafemi Awolowo, *Path to Nigerian Freedom* (London: Faber and Faber, 1947), pp. 47–48.

[3]Billy Dudley, *An Introduction to Nigerian Government and Politics* (Bloomington: Indiana University Press, 1982), p. 71.

[4]Robin Luckham, *The Nigerian Military: A Sociological Analysis of Authority and Revolt 1960–67* (Cambridge: Cambridge University Press, 1971).

[5]Peter Ekeh, "Colonialism and the Two Publics in Africa: A Theoretical Statement," *Comparative Studies in Society and History* 17, no. 1 (January 1975).

[6]Richard A. Joseph, *Democracy and Prebendal Politics in Nigeria: The Rise and Fall of the Second Republic* (Cambridge: Cambridge University Press), pp. 55–58.

[7]Gavin Williams and Terisa Turner, "Nigeria," in John Dunn, ed., *West African States: Failure and Promise* (Cambridge: Cambridge University Press, 1978), pp. 156–157.

[8]Michael J. Watts, *State, Oil and Agriculture in Nigeria* (Berkeley: University of California Press, 1987), p. 71.

[9]Watts, *State Oil and Agriculture in Nigeria,* p. 67.

[10]Tom Forrest, *Politics and Economic Development in Nigeria,* 2nd ed. (Boulder, CO: Westview Press, 1995), pp. 207–212.

[11]Dele Olowu, "Centralization, Self-Governance, and Development in Nigeria," in James S. Wunsch and Dele Olowu, eds., *The Failure of the Centralized State: Institutions and Self-Governance in Africa* (Boulder, CO: Westview Press, 1991), p. 211.

[12]Robert Melson and Howard Wolpe, *Nigeria: Modernization and the Politics of Communalism* (East Lansing: Michigan State University Press, 1971).

[13]Toyin Falola, Violence in Nigeria: *The Crisis of Religious Politics and Secular Ideologies* (Rochester, NY: University of Rochester Press, 1998).

[14]Pat A. Williams, "Women and the Dilemma of Politics in Nigeria," in Crawford Young and Paul Beckett, eds., *Dilemmas of Democracy in Nigeria* (Rochester, NY: University of Rochester Press, 1997), pp. 219–241.

[15]Anthony Kirk-Greene and Douglas Rimmer, *Nigeria since 1970: A Political and Economic Outline* (London: Hodder and Stoughton 1981), p. 49.

[16]Rotimi Suberu, *Federalism and Ethnic Conflict in Nigeria* (Washington, DC: U.S. Institute of Peace, 2001).

[17]Suberu, *Federalism and Ethnic Conflict in Nigeria,* pp. 119–120.

[18]Henry Bienen, *Armies and Parties in Africa* (New York: Africana Publishing, 1978), pp. 193–211.

[19]Richard Joseph, *Democracy and Prebendal Politics in Nigeria: The Rise and Fall of the Second Republic* (Cambridge: Cambridge University Press, 1987), 55–68.

[20]Samuel DeCalo, *Coups and Army Rule in Africa* (New Haven, CT: Yale University Press, 1976), p. 18.

[21]Joseph, *Democracy and Prebendal Politics in Nigeria,* pp. 52–53.

[22]Richard Sklar, *Nigerian Political Parties* (Princeton: Princeton University Press, 1963).

[23]Babafemi Badejo, "Party Formation and Party Competition," in Larry Diamond, Anthony Kirk-Greene, and Oyeleye Oyediran, eds., *Transition without End: Nigerian Politics and Civil Society under Babangida* (Boulder, CO: Lynne Rienner Publishers, 1997), p. 179.

[24]Eghosa Osaghae, *Crippled Giant: Nigeria Since Independence* (Bloomington: Indiana University Press 1999), pp. 233–239.

[25]Peter M. Lewis, Barnett Rubin, and Pearl Robinson, *Stabilizing Nigeria: Pressures, Incentives and Support for Civil Society* (New York: Council on Foreign Relations, 1998), p. 87.

[26]Donald L. Horowitz, "Making Moderation Pay: The Comparative Politics of Ethnic Conflict Management," in Joseph V. Montville, ed., *Conflict and Peacemaking in Multiethnic Societies* (New York: Lexington Books, 1991), chapter 25.

[27]Rotimi Suberu, *Public Policies and National Unity in Nigeria,* Research Report No. 19 (Ibadan: Development Policy Centre, 199), pp. 9–10.

[28]Sayre Schatz, "'Pirate Capitalism' and the Inert Economy of Nigeria," *Journal of Modern African Studies* 22, no. 1 (March 1984): 45–57.

[29]Peter Lewis, Etannibi Alemika, and Michael Bratton, *Down to Earth: Changes in Attitudes to Democracy and Markets in Nigeria,* Afrobarometer Working Paper No. 20, Michigan State University, August 2002.

[30]See Terry Lynn Karl, *The Paradox of Plenty* (Berkeley: University of California Press, 1997); and Michael Ross, "The Political Economy of the Resource Curse," *World Politics* 51 (January 1999), 297–322.

[31]Michael Bratton and Nicolas van de Walle, *Democratic Experiments in Africa* (Cambridge: Cambridge University Press, 1997).

CHAPTER 7

[1]http://pussy-riot.livejournal.com/11352.html (accessed January 1, 2014).

[2]State Statistical Service of the Russian Federation, http://www.gks.ru/bgd/free/b13_00/IssWWW.exe /Stg/dk11/8-0.htm (accessed August 13, 2014).

[3]Richard Pipes, *Russia under the Old Regime* (London: Widenfeld & Nicolson, 1974), pp. 22–24.

[4]The Economist Intelligence Unit, *Country Profile Russia* (London, 2008), pp. 49–50.

[5]Transparency International, Corruption Perceptions Index Results 2013, http://cpi.transparency.org/cpi2013 /results/#myAnchor1 (accessed May 21, 2014).

[6]Jan Burck, Franziska Marten, and Christoph Bals, *The Climate Change Performance Index: Results* (Bonn: Germanwatch, 2014), p. 6.

[7]Russian Statistical Agency, gks.ru; and the European Commission, "European Union: Trade in Goods with Russia," http://trade.ec.europa.eu/doclib/docs/2006 /september/tradoc_113440.pdf pp. 7, 10, 11 (accessed May 21, 2014).

[8]Federal State Statistics Service of the Russian Federation, http://www.gks.ru/bgd/regl/B11_58/IssWWW.exe /Stg/d2/06-09.htm (accessed May 22, 2014).

[9]*EBRD Transition Report*, 2006.

[10]See Joan DeBardeleben and Mikhail Zherebtsov, "The Transition to Managerial Patronage in Russia's Regions," in *The Politics of Sub-national Authoritarianism in Russia*, edited by Vladimir Gel'man and Cameron Ross (Aldershot: Ashgate, 2010).

[11]http://rt.com/politics/defense-draft-russia-shoigu-529 (accessed November 11, 2013).

[12]State Duma of the Russian Federation, http://www .duma.gov.ru/structure/all/. One seat was apparently vacant (accessed March 1, 2014).

[13]David Lane, *State and Politics in the USSR* (Oxford: Blackwell, 1985), pp. 184–185; and Andrea Chandler, "Has the tandem improved women's rights?," in J. L. Black and Michael Johns, *Russia After 2012* (Routledge, 2013), p. 80.

[14]*Rossiiskaia gazeta*, May 28, 2012, http://www.rg.ru /2012/05/26/partiya-site.html (accessed May 21, 2014).

[15]Stefan Oeter, "International norms and legal status of minority languages in Russia," in *Managing Ethnic Diversity in Russia*, eds. Oleh Protsyk and Benedikt Harzl (Routledge, 2013), p. 38.

[16]Reporters without Borders, Press Freedom Index, http://en.rsf.org/press-freedom-index-2013,1054.html (accessed May 21, 2014).

[17]Levada Center, "Rossiiane o SMI," February 18, 2014, http://www.levada.ru/28-02-2014/rossiyane-o-smi (accessed May 21, 2014).

[18]Committee to Protect Journalists, "56 Journalists Killed in Russia since 1992," http://cpj.org/killed/europe /russia/ (accessed March 1, 2014).

[19]Levada Center, "Internet i SMI," September 9, 2013, http://www.levada.ru/19-09-2013/internet-i-smi (accessed May 21, 2014).

[20]Sarah Oates, *Revolution Stalled: The Political Limits of the Internet in the Post-Soviet Sphere* (Oxford University Press, 2013), p. 63, Ch. 7.

[21]Dmitry Medvedev, "Rossiia Vpered" (*Go Russia*, September 10, 2009), http://www.kremlin.ru/news/5413 (accessed January 30, 2011).

[22]Levada Center, "Vybory prezidenta" March 27, 2012, and "Rossiiane o raspade SSSR," Jan. 14, 2014, http:// www.levada.ru/27-03-2012/vybory-prezidenta-kak -golosovali-sotsialnye-gruppy, http://www.levada.ru /14-01-2014/rossiyane-o-raspade-sssr (accessed May 21, 2014).

CHAPTER 8

[1]British Financial Adviser to the Foreign Office in Tehran, *Documents on British Foreign Policy, 1919–39* (London: Her Majesty's Stationery Office, 1963), First Series, XIII, 720, 735.

[2]M. Bazargan, "Letter to the Editor," *Ettela'at*, February 7, 1980.

[3]*Iran Times*, January 12, 1979.

[4]Cited in H. Amirahmadi, *Revolution and Economic Transition* (Albany: State University of New York Press, 1960), p. 201.

[5]International Labor Organization, "Employment and Income Policies for Iran" (unpublished report, Geneva, 1972), Appendix C, 6.

[6]U.S. Congress, *Economic Consequences of the Revolution in Iran*, 5.

[7]Cited in *Iran Times*, July 9, 1993.

[8]J. Amuzegar, *Iran's Economy under the Islamic Republic* (London: Taurus Press, 1994), p. 100.

[9]A. Rafsanjani, "The Islamic Consultative Assembly," *Kayhan*, May 23, 1987.

[10]S. Saffari, "The Legitimation of the Clergy's Right to Rule in the Iranian Constitution of 1979," *British Journal of Middle Eastern Studies* 20, no. 1 (1993): 64–81.

[11]Ayatollah Montazeri, *Ettela'at*, October 8, 1979.

[12]O. Fallaci, "Interview with Khomeini," *New York Times Magazine*, October 7, 1979.

CHAPTER 9

[1] Timothy Brook, *Quelling the People: The Military Suppression of the Beijing Democracy Movement* (Stanford, CA: Stanford University Press, 1999), p. 129.

[2] "Report on an Investigation of the Peasant Movement in Hunan Province," *Selected Works of Mao Zedong*, Vol. 1. (Beijing: Foreign Languages Press, 1965).

[3] "Restore Agricultural Production," *Selected Works of Deng Xiaoping (1938–1965)* (Beijing: Foreign Languages Press, 1984).

[4] Martin King Whyte, *Myth of the Social Volcano: Perceptions of Inequality and Distributive Injustice in Contemporary China* (Stanford, CA: Stanford University Press, 2010).

[5] Isabelle Attané, "Being a Woman in China Today: A Demography of Gender." *China Perspectives*, no. 4 (2012): pp. 5–15.

[6] Katherine Morton, "Environmental Policy," in William A. Joseph, ed., *Politics in China: An Introduction,*" 2nd ed. (New York: Oxford University Press 2014), p. 360.

[7] John P. Burns, *The Chinese Communist Party's Nomenklatura System: A Documentary Study of Party Control of Leadership Selection, 1979–1984* (Armonk, NY: M. E. Sharpe, 1989), pp. ix–x.

[8] See Kenneth Lieberthal and Michel Oksenberg, *Policy Making in China: Leaders, Structures, and Processes* (Princeton, NJ: Princeton University Press, 1988); and Andrew Mertha, "'Fragmented Authoritarianism 2.0': Political Pluralization in the Chinese Policy Process," *China Quarterly*, no. 200 (December 2009), pp. 995–1012.

[9] James D. Seymour, *China's Satellite Parties* (Armonk, NY: M.E. Sharpe, 1987), p. 87.

[10] Nicholas D. Kristof, "China Sees 'Market-Leninism' as Way to Future," *New York Times*, September 6, 1993.

[11] Guobin Yang, "Internet and Civil Society," in William Tay and Alvin So, eds., *Handbook of Contemporary China* (Singapore: World Scientific Press, 2011), p. 443.

[12] "China's Predicament: 'Getting Old before Getting Rich," *The Economist*, June 25, 2009.

[13] Harry Harding, *China's Second Revolution: Reform after Mao* (Washington, DC: Brookings Institution, 1987), p. 200.

[14] *The Economist* Intelligence Unit, Democracy Index 2012, http://eiu.com/democracy.

[15] Nicholas Lardy, "Is China Different? The Fate of Its Economic Reform," in Daniel Chirot, ed., *The Crisis of Leninism and the Decline of the Left* (Seattle: University of Washington Press, 1991), p. 147.

Glossary

5 percent clause This rule obliges a German political party to get at least 5 percent of the "second votes" in order for its candidates to enter the *Bundestag* (or the state parliaments). This rule depresses votes for "splinter" parties unlikely to meet this threshold. Again, the term second votes will be wholly opaque at this point.

A

accommodation An informal agreement or settlement between the government and important interest groups in response to the interest groups' concerns for policy or program benefits.

accountability A government's responsibility to its population, usually by periodic popular elections, transparent fiscal practices, and by parliament's having the power to dismiss the government by passing a motion of no confidence. In a political system character-ized by accountability, the major actions taken by government must be known and understood by the citizenry.

acephalous societies Literally "headless" societies. A number of traditional Nigerian societies, such as the Igbo in the precolonial period, lacked executive rulership as we have come to conceive of it. Instead, the villages and clans were governed by committee or consensus.

anticlericalism Opposition to the power of churches or clergy in politics. In some countries, for example, France and Mexico, this opposition has focused on the role of the Catholic Church in politics.

Articles of Confederation The first governing document of the United States, agreed to in 1777 and ratified in 1781. The Articles concentrated most powers in the states and made the national government largely dependent on voluntary contributions of the states.

Assembly of Experts Group in Iran that nominates and can remove the Leader. The assembly is elected by the general electorate, but almost all its members are clerics.

authoritarian A system of rule in which power depends not on popular legitimacy but on the coercive force of the political authorities.

authoritarian regime A system of rule in which power depends not on popular legitimacy but on the coercive force of the political authorities. Hence, there are few personal and group freedoms. It is also characterized by near absolute power in the executive branch and few, if any, legislative and judicial controls.

autocracy A government in which one or a few rulers has absolute power, thus, a dictatorship.

autonomous region A territorial unit in China that is equivalent to a province and contains a large concentration of ethnic minorities. These regions, for example, Tibet, have some autonomy in the cultural sphere but in most policy matters are strictly subordinate to the central government.

ayatollah Literally, "sign of God." A high-ranking cleric in Iran.

B

balance of payments An indicator of international flow of funds that shows the excess or deficit in total payments of all kinds between or among countries. Included in the calculation are exports and imports, grants, and international debt payments.

bazaar An urban marketplace in Iran where shops, workshops, small businesses, and export-importers are located.

bicameral A legislative body with two houses, such as the U.S. Senate and the U.S. House of Representatives. Just as the U.S. Con-stitution divides responsibilities between the branches of the federal government and between the federal government and the states, it divides legislative responsibilities between the Senate and the House.

Bill of Rights The first ten amendments to the U.S. Constitu-tion (ratified in 1791), which established limits on the actions of government. Initially, the Bill of Rights limited only the federal government. The Fourteenth Amendment and subsequent judicial rulings extended the provisions of the Bill of Rights to the states.

bureaucracy An organization structured hierarchically, in which lower-level officials are charged with administering regulations codified in rules that specify impersonal, objective guidelines for making decisions.

C

cabinet The body of officials (e.g., ministers, secretaries) who direct executive departments presided over by the chief executive (e.g., prime minister, president).

cabinet government A system of government in which most executive power is held by the cabinet, headed by a prime minister.

cadre A person who exercises a position of authority in a communist party-state; cadres may or may not be communist party members.

411

Glossary

caudillos Charismatic populist leaders, usually with a military background, who use patronage and draw upon personal loyalties to dominate a region or a nation in Latin America.

causal theories An influential approach in comparative politics that involves trying to explain why "if X happens, then Y is the result."

Central Committee The top 370 or so leaders of the Chinese Communist Party. It meets annually for about two weeks and is charged with carrying on the business of the National Party Congress when it is not in session.

Central Military Commission (CMC) The most important military organization in the People's Republic of China, headed by the general secretary of the Chinese Communist Party, who is the commander-in-chief of the People's Liberation Army.

centrally planned economy An economic system in which the state directs the economy through bureaucratic plans for the production and distribution of goods and services. The government, rather, than the market, is the major influence on the economy. Also called a command economy.

checks and balances A governmental system of divided authority in which coequal branches can restrain each other's actions. For example, the U.S. president must sign legislation passed by Congress for it to become law. If the president vetoes a bill, Congress can override that veto by a two-thirds vote of the Senate and the House of Representatives.

citizen initiative Clause in 2009 Lisbon Treaty allowing citizens to propose referendums to initiate EU legislation, provided 1 million legal signatures have been obtained in a "significant number" of different EU member states.

civil society Refers to the space occupied by voluntary associations outside the state, for example, professional associations (lawyers, doctors, teachers), trade unions, student and women's groups, religious bodies, and other voluntary association groups.

clientelism An informal aspect of policy-making in which a powerful patron (for example, a traditional local boss, government agency, or dominant party) offers resources such as land, contracts, protection, or jobs in return for the support and services (such as labor or votes) of lower-status and less powerful clients; corruption, preferential treatment, and inequality are characteristic of clientelist politics.

clientelistic networks Informal systems of asymmetrical power in which a powerful patron (e.g., the president, prime minister, or governor) offers less powerful clients resources, benefits, or career advantages in return for support, loyalty, or services.

Cold War The hostile relations that prevailed between the United States and the Soviet Union from the late 1940s until the demise of the USSR in 1991.

collective identities The groups with which people identify, including gender, class, race, region, and religion, and which are the "building blocks" for social and political action.

collectivization A process undertaken in the Soviet Union under Stalin from 1929 into the early 1930s and in China under Mao in the 1950s, by which agricultural land was removed from private ownership and organized into large state and collective farms.

Common Foreign and Security Policy (CFSP) Commitment in the Maastricht Treaty for deeper cooperation in international affairs and defense in the EU.

communism According to Marxism, the stage of development that follows socialism and in which all property is publically owned, economic production is coordinated for the common good, and a radical degree of equality has been achieved.

communist party–state A type of nation-state in which the communist party attempts to exercise a complete monopoly on political power and controls all important state institutions.

community method The EU method of making decisions in which the European Commission proposes, the Council of Ministers and European Parliament decide, and the European Court of Justice reviews European law.

comparative politics The field within political science that focuses on domestic politics and analyzes patterns of similarity and difference among countries.

comparativist A political scientist who studies the similarities and differences in the domestic politics of various countries.

consolidated democracies Democratic political systems that have been solidly and stably established for an ample period of time and in which there is relatively consistent adherence to the core democratic principles.

constitutional monarchy System of government in which the head of state ascends by heredity but is limited in powers and constrained by the provisions of a constitution.

corporatist state A state in which interest groups become an institutionalized part of the state structure.

Corruption Perceptions Index A measure developed by Transparency International that ranks countries in terms of the degree to which corruption is perceived to exist among public officials and politicians.

country A territorial unit controlled by a single state.

coup d'état A forceful, extra-constitutional action resulting in the removal of an existing government.

critical juncture An important historical moment when political actors make critical choices, which shape institutions and future outcomes.

D

Declaration of Independence The document asserting that the British colonies in what is now the United States had declared themselves independent from Great Britain. The Declaration of Independence was signed in Philadelphia on July 4, 1776.

democracy From the Greek *demos* (the people) and *kratos* (rule). A political system that featuring: selection to public offices through free and fair elections; the right of all adults to vote; political parties that are free to compete in elections; government that operates by fair and relatively open procedures; political rights and civil liberties; an independent judiciary (court system); civilian control of the military.

democratic centralism A system of political organization developed by V.I. Lenin and practiced, with modifications, by all communist party-states. Its principles include a hierarchical party structure.

democratic transition The process of a state moving from an authoritarian to a democratic political system.

dependent variable The variable symbolized by Y in the statement that "If X happens, then Y will be the result"; in other words, the dependent variable is the outcome of X (the independent variable).

developmental state A nation-state in which the government carries out policies that effectively promote national economic growth.

dictatorships A form of government in which power and political control are concentrated in one or a few rulers who have concentrated and nearly absolute power.

distributional politics The use of power, particularly by the state, to allocate some kind of valued resource among competing groups.

distributive policies Policies that allocate state resources into an area that lawmakers perceive needs to be promoted. For example, leaders today believe that students should have access to the Internet. In order to accomplish this goal, telephone users are being taxed to provide money for schools to establish connections to the Internet.

dominant party A political party that manages to maintain consistent control of a political system through formal and informal mechanisms of power, with or without strong support from the population.

dual society A society and economy that are sharply divided into a traditional, usually poorer, and a modern, usually richer, sector.

E

Economic and Monetary Union The 1991 Maastricht Treaty federalized EU monetary policy, created a European Central Bank and founded the Eurozone and its single currency, the euro.

ejido Land granted by Mexican government to an organized group of peasants.

Environmental Performance Index A measure of how close countries come to meeting specific benchmarks for national pollution control and natural resource management.

European Commission The EU executive, which has a legal monopoly on proposing EU legislation and overseeing its implementation as "guardian of the treaties."

European Council An EU institution made up of heads of state and government of EU member states that meets periodically to provide general EU strategy.

European Court of Justice EU Supreme Court that decides the legality of EU legislation and its implementation.

European Parliament The Parliament of the European Union, which meets in Strasbourg and Brussels, "co-decides" EU law with the Council of Ministers, but it cannot initiate legislation.

European single market Official title of the EU's barrier-free economic space created after 1985.

Eurozone crisis Crisis of sovereign debt within Eurozone that broke out after 2009 that led to frantic emergency efforts by Eurozone members and the European Council to bail out Greece, Ireland, and Portugal and reconfigure EMU rules.

executive The agencies of government that implement or execute policy.

Expediency Council A committee set up in Iran to resolve differences between the *Majles* (parliament) and the Guardian Council.

F

Farsi Persian word for the Persian language. Fars is a province in Central Iran.

Federal Reserve Board The U.S. central bank established by Congress in 1913 to regulate the banking industry and the money supply. Although the president appoints the chair of the board of governors (with Senate approval), the board operates largely independently.

federal system A political structure in which subnational units have significant independent powers; the powers of each level are usually specified in the federal constitution.

federalism A system of governance in which political authority is shared between the national government and regional or state governments. The powers of each level of government are usually specified in a federal constitution.

floating population Migrants from the rural areas of China who have moved temporarily to the cities to find employment.

foreign direct investment Ownership of or investment in cross-border enterprises in which the foreign investor plays a direct managerial role.

Foundation of the Oppressed A clerically controlled foundation set up after the revolution in Iran.

free market A system in which government regulation of the economy is absent or limited. Relative to other advanced democracies, the United States has traditionally had less market regulation.

Freedom in the World rating An annual evaluation by Freedom House of the state of freedom in countries around the world measured according to political rights and civil liberties.

fusion of powers A constitutional principle that merges the authority of branches of government, in contrast to the principle of separation of powers.

G

general secretary The formal title of the head of the Chinese Communist Party. From 1942 to 1982, the position was called "chairman" and was held by Mao Zedong until his death in 1976.

glasnost Gorbachev's policy of "openness," which involved an easing of controls on the media, arts, and public discussion in Russia in the 1980s.

Global Gender Gap A measure of the extent to which women in 58 countries have achieved equality with men.

globalization The intensification of worldwide interconnectedness associated with the increased speed and magnitude of cross-border flows of trade, investment and finance, and processes of migration, cultural diffusion, and communication.

gross domestic product (GDP) The total of all goods and services produced within a country that is used as a broad measure of the size of its economy.

gross national product (GNP) GDP plus income earned by the country's residents; another broad measure of the size of an economy.

Guardian Council A committee created in the Iranian constitution to oversee the *Majles* (the parliament).

guerrilla warfare A military strategy based on small, highly mobile bands of soldiers (the guerrillas, from the Spanish word for war, *guerra*) who use hit-and-run tactics like ambushes to attack a better-armed enemy.

H

hegemonic power A state that can control the pattern of alliances and terms of the international order and often shapes domestic political developments in countries throughout the world.

hegemony The capacity to dominate the world of states and control the terms of trade and the alliance patterns in the global order.

Hezbollahis Literally "partisans of God." In Iran, the term is used to describe religious vigilantes. In Lebanon, it is used to describe the Shi'i militia.

hojjat al-Islam Literally, "the proof of Islam." In Iran, it means a medium-ranking cleric.

household responsibility system The system put into practice in China beginning in the early 1980s in which the major decisions about agricultural production are made by individual farm families based on the profit motive rather than by a people's commune or the government.

household registration (hukou) In China, the system that registers each citizen as entitled to work and to live in a specific urban or rural location.

Human Development Index (HDI) A composite number used by the United Nations to measure and compare levels of achievement in health, knowledge, and standard of living.

hung parliament A situation after an election when no single party comprises a majority in the British House of Commons.

I

Imam Jum'ehs Prayer leaders in Iran's main urban mosques.

independent variable The variable symbolized by X in the statement that "If X happens, then Y will be the result"; in other words, the independent variable is a cause of Y (the dependent variable).

indigenous groups Population descended from the original inhabitants of the Americas, present prior to the Spanish Conquest.

indirect rule A term used to describe the British style of colonialism in Nigeria and India in which local traditional rulers and political structures were used to help support the colonial governing structure.

Industrial Revolution A period of rapid and destabilizing social, economic, and political changes caused by the introduction of large-scale factory production, originating in England in the middle of the eighteenth century.

insider privatization The transformation of formerly state-owned enterprises into joint-stock companies or private enterprises in which majority control is in the hands of employees and/or managers.

institutional design The institutional arrangements that define the relationships between executive, legislative, and judicial branches of government and between the national government and subnational units such as states in the United States.

interest groups Organizations that seek to represent the interests—usually economic—of their members in dealings with the government. Important examples are associations representing people with specific occupations, business interests, racial and ethnic groups, or age groups in society.

international financial institutions (IFIs) This term generally refers to the International Bank for Reconstruction and Development (the World Bank) and the International Monetary Fund (IMF), but can also include other international lending institutions.

International Monetary Fund (IMF) The "sister organization" of the World Bank, which also has more than 180 member states. It describes its mandate as "working to foster global monetary cooperation, secure financial stability, facilitate international trade, promote high employment and sustainable economic growth, and reduce poverty." It has been particularly active in helping countries that are experiencing serious financial problems. In exchange for IMF financial or technical assistance, a country must agree to a certain set of conditions that promote economic liberalization.

interventionist An interventionist state acts vigorously to shape the performance of major sectors of the economy.

iron rice bowl A feature of China's socialist economy during the Maoist era (1949–1976) that provided guarantees of lifetime employment, income, and basic cradle-to-grave benefits to most urban and rural workers.

iron triangles A term coined by students of American politics to refer to the relationships of mutual support formed by particular government agencies, members of congressional committees or subcommittees, and interest groups in various policy areas.

Islamism The use of Islam as a political ideology. Similar to political Islam and Islamic fundamentalism.

J

jihad Literally "struggle." Although often used to mean armed struggle against unbelievers, it can also mean to fight against sociopolitical corruption or a spiritual struggle for self-improvement.

judicial review The ability of a high court to nullify actions by the executive and legislative branches when it judges that they violate the constitution.

judiciary One of the primary political institutions in a country; responsible for the administration of justice and in some countries for determining the constitutionality of state decisions.

jurist's guardianship Khomeini's concept that the Iranian clergy should rule on the grounds that they are the divinely appointed guardians of both the law and the people.

Justice and Home Affairs (JHA) Engagements to make legal and regulatory changes to allow free movement of EU citizens throughout the EU.

K

Keynesianism Named after the British economist John Maynard Keynes, an approach to economic policy in which state economic policies are used to regulate the economy in an attempt to achieve stable economic growth. During a recession, state budget deficits are used to expand demand in an effort to boost both consumption and investment, and to create employment. During periods of high growth when inflation threatens, cuts in government spending and a tightening of credit are used to reduce demand.

L

laissez-faire A term taken from the French, which means, "to let do," in other words, to allow to act freely. In political economy, it refers to the pattern in which state management is limited to such matters as enforcing contracts and protecting property rights, while private market forces are free to operate with only minimal state regulation.

Leader/Supreme Leader A cleric elected to be the head of the Islamic Republic of Iran.

legislature One of the primary political institutions in a country, in which elected or appointed members are charged with responsibility for making laws and usually providing for the financial resources for the state to carry out its functions.

legitimacy A belief by powerful groups and the broad citizenry that a state exercises rightful authority.

Lisbon Treaty After a decade of efforts to redesign EU institutions in light of enlargement to Central and Eastern Europe, the treaty created new positions of the President of the European Council and High Representative for foreign and security policy and increased the powers of the European Council and European Parliament.

M

Maastricht Treaty Treaty renegotiations (ratified in 1993) that gave the EU its present name, created the EMU and the CFSP, and granted the European Parliament power to "co-decide" EU legislation.

macroeconomic policy Policy intended to shape the overall economic system by concentrating on policy targets such as inflation and growth.

Majles The Iranian parliament, from the Arabic term for "assembly."

manifest destiny The public philosophy in the nineteenth century that the United States was not only entitled but also destined to occupy territory from the Atlantic to the Pacific.

maquiladoras Factories that produce goods for export, often located along the U.S.–Mexican border.

Marbury v. Madison The 1803 U.S. Supreme Court ruling that the federal courts inherently had the authority to review the constitutionality of laws passed by Congress and signed by the president. The ruling, initially used sparingly, placed the courts centrally in the system of checks and balances.

market reform A strategy of economic transformation that involves reducing the role of the state in managing the economy and increasing the role of market forces.

maslahat Arabic term for "expediency," "prudence," or "advisability," now used in Iran to refer to reasons of state or what is best for the Islamic Republic.

mass organizations Organizations in a communist party–state that represent the interests of a particular social groups, such as workers or women but which are controlled by the communist party.

mestizo A person of mixed white, indigenous (Amerindian), and sometimes African descent.

middle-level theory Seeks to explain phenomena in a limited range of cases, in particular, a specific set of countries with particular characteristics, such as parliamentary regimes, or a particular type of political institution (such as political parties) or activity (such as protest).

mixed electoral system A system of electoral representation in which a portion of the seats are selected in winner-take-all single-member districts, and a portion are allocated according to parties within multi-member constituencies, roughly in proportion to the votes each party receives in a popular election.

mixed systems Countries whose political systems exhibit some democratic and some authoritarian elements.

monetarism An approach to economic policy that assumes a natural rate of unemployment, determined by the labor market, and rejects the instruments of government spending to run budgetary deficits for stimulating the economy and creating jobs.

N

National Party Congress The symbolically important meeting, held every five years for about one week, of about 2,100 delegates representatives of the Chinese Communist Party, who endorse policies and the allocation of leadership positions that have been determined beforehand by the party's much smaller ruling bodies.

National People's Congress (NPC) The legislature of the People's Republic of China. It is under the control of the Chinese Communist Party and is not an independent branch of government.

nation-state Distinct, politically defined territory in which the state and national identity, that is, a sense of solidarity and shared values based on being citizens of the same country coincide.

neoliberalism A term used to describe government policies aiming to promote free competition among business firms within the market, including reduced governmental regulation and social spending.

nomenklatura A system of personnel selection under which the communist party maintains control over the appointment of important officials in all spheres of social, economic, and political life.

North American Free Trade Agreement (NAFTA) A treaty among the United States, Mexico, and Canada implemented on January 1, 1994, that largely eliminates trade barriers among the three nations. NAFTA serves as a model for an eventual Free Trade Area of the Americas zone that could include most nations in the Western Hemisphere.

O

oligarchs A small group of powerful and wealthy individuals who gained ownership and control of important sectors of Russia's economy in the context of privatization of state assets in the 1990s.

Organization of Petroleum Exporting Countries (OPEC) An organization dedicated to achieving stability in the price of oil, avoiding price fluctuations, and generally furthering the interests of the member states.

P

parliamentary democracy System of government in which the chief executive is answerable to the legislature and may be dismissed by it.

parliamentary sovereignty The doctrine that grants the legislature the power to make or overturn any law and permits no veto or judicial review.

pasdaran Persian term for guards, used to refer to the army of Revolutionary Guards formed during Iran's Islamic Revolution.

patrimonial state A system of governance in which the ruler treats the state as personal property (patrimony).

People of the Book The Muslim term for recognized religious minorities, such as Christians, Jews, and Zoroastrians.

People's Liberation Army (PLA) The combined armed forces of the People's Republic of China, which includes land, sea, air, and strategic missile forces.

police powers Powers that are traditionally held by the states to regulate public safety and welfare. Police powers are the form of interaction with government that citizens most often experience. Even with the growth in federal government powers in the twentieth century, police powers remain the primary responsibility of the states and localities.

Politburo The committee made up of the top twenty-five leaders of the Chinese Communist Party.

political action committee (PAC) A narrow form of interest group that seeks to influence policy by making contributions to candidates and parties in U.S. politics.

political economy The study of the interaction between the state and the economy, that is, how the state and political processes affect the economy and how the organization of the economy and strategic choices made by the government and state actors affect political processes.

political Islam A term for the intermingling of Islam with politics and often used as a substitute for Islamic fundamentalism.

power vertical A term used by Russian president, Vladimir Putin to describe a unified and hierarchical structure of executive power ranging from the national to the local level.

prebendalism Patterns of political behavior that rest on the justification that official state offices should be utilized for the personal benefit of officeholders as well as of their support group or clients.

predatory state A state in which those with political power prey on the people and the nation's resources to enrich themselves rather than using their power to promote national development.

property taxes Taxes levied by local governments on the assessed value of property. Property taxes are the primary way in which local jurisdictions in the United States pay for the costs of primary and secondary education. Because the value of property varies dramatically from neighborhood to neighborhood, the funding available for schools—and the quality of education—also varies from place to place.

purchasing power parity (PPP) A method of calculating the value of a country's currency based on the actual cost of buying goods and services in that country rather than how many U.S. dollars the currency is worth.

Q

qualified majority voting Method in the Council of Ministers for deciding most EU legislation that weights member state voting power depending upon size and defining how many votes constitute a majority.

quangos Acronym for quasi-nongovernmental organizations, the term used in Britain for nonelected bodies that are outside traditional governmental departments or local authorities.

Qur'an The Muslim Bible.

R

rational choice theory An approach to analyzing political decision making and behavior that assumes that individual actors rationally pursue their aims in an effort to achieve the most positive net result. Rational choice is often associated with the pursuit of selfish goals, but the theory permits a wide range of motivations, including altruism.

redistributive policies Policies that take resources from one person or group in society and allocate them to a different, usually more disadvantaged, group. The United States has traditionally opposed redistributive policies to the disadvantaged.

regulations The rules that explain the implementation of laws. When the legislature passes a law, it sets broad principles for implementation: how the law is actually implemented is determined by regulations written by executive branch agencies. The regulation-writing process allows interested parties to influence the eventual shape of the law in practice.

remittances Funds sent by migrants working abroad to family members in their home countries or by urban migrants to their families in rural areas.

rentier state A country that obtains much of its revenue from the export of oil or other natural resources.

rents Economic gains that do not compensate those who produced them and do not contribute to productivity, typically associated with government earnings that do not get channeled back into either investments or policies that benefit the public good. Pursuit of economic rents (or "rent-seeking") is profit seeking that takes the form of nonproductive economic activity.

resource curse The concept that revenue derived from abundant natural resources, such as oil, often bring unforeseen ailments to countries.

S

Schengen area EU area, named after small city in Luxembourg, where freedom of transnational movement without border controls was first agreed in 1985. Schengen now includes all EU members except Romania, Bulgaria, Croatia, the United Kingdom, and Ireland. It also includes non-EU countries Norway, Iceland, and Switzerland.

separation of powers An organization of political institutions within the state in which the executive, legislature, and judiciary have autonomous powers and no one branch dominates the others. This is the common pattern in presidential systems, as opposed to parliamentary systems, in which there is a fusion of powers.

sexenio The six-year term in office of Mexican presidents.

shari'a Islamic law derived mostly from the Qur'an and the examples set by the Prophet Muhammad in the Sunnah.

siloviki Derived from the Russian word *sil*, meaning "force," Russian politicians and governmental officials drawn from the security and intelligence agencies, special forces, or the military, many of whom were recruited to important political posts under Vladimir Putin.

single-member plurality (SMP) electoral system An electoral system in which candidates run for a single seat from a specific geographic district. The winner is the person who receives the most votes, whether or not they amount to a majority. SMP systems, unlike systems of proportional representation, increase the likelihood that two national coalition parties will form.

social class A group whose members share common world views and aspirations determined largely by occupation, income, and wealth.

social movements Large-scale grassroots action that demands reforms of existing social practices and government policies.

Social Progress Index A composite measurement of social progress in countries that takes into account basic needs, their food, shelter, and security; access to health care, education, and a healthy environment; and the opportunity for people to improve their lives.

social security National systems of contributory and noncontributory benefits to provide assistance for the elderly, sick, disabled, unemployed, and others similarly in need of assistance. The specific coverage of social security, a key component of the welfare state, varies by country.

socialism A system in which the state plays a leading role in organizing the economy, owns most productive resources and property, and actively promotes equality.

socialist democracy The term used by the Chinese Communist Party to describe the political system of the People's Republic of China. The official view is that this type of system, under the leadership of the Communist Party, provides democracy for the overwhelming majority of people and suppresses (or exercises dictatorship over) only the enemies of the people.

socialist market economy The term used by the government of China to refer to the country's current economic system that mixes elements of both socialism and capitalism.

soft authoritarianism A system of political control in which a combination of formal and informal mechanisms ensure the dominance of a ruling group or dominant party, despite the existence of some forms of political competition and expressions of political opposition.

sovereign democracy A concept of democracy articulated by President Putin's political advisor, Vladimir Surkov, to communicate the idea that democracy in Russia should be adapted to Russian traditions and conditions rather than based on Western models.

special relationship Refers to relations between the United States and Britain and is meant to convey not only the largely positive, mutually beneficial nature of the relationship but also the common heritage and shared values of the two countries.

Standing Committee A subgroup of the Politburo, currently with seven members. The most powerful political organization in China.

state The most powerful political institutions in a country, including the executive, legislative, and judicial branches of government, the police, and armed forces.

state capitalism An economic system that is primarily capitalistic but in which there is some degree of government ownership of the means of production.

State Council The highest organization in the state administration, directed by the premier. It also includes several vice premiers, the heads of government ministries and commissions, and a few other senior officials.

state formation The historical development of a state, often marked by major stages, key events, or turning points (critical junctures) that influence the contemporary character of the state.

state-owned enterprises Companies in which a majority of ownership control is held by the government.

structural adjustment program (SAP) Programs established by the International Monetary Fund and the World Bank intended to alter and reform the economic structures of highly indebted developing countries as a condition for receiving international loans. SAPs often require privatization, trade liberalization, and fiscal restraint, which typically requires the dismantling of social welfare systems.

subsidiarity Principle consecrated by the 1991 Maastricht Treaty that the EU should seek decision making at the level of the lowest effective jurisdiction.

sustainable development An approach to promoting economic growth that seeks to minimize environmental degradation and depletion of natural resources.

T

technocrats Career-minded bureaucrats who administer public policy according to a technical rather than a political rationale.

theocracy A state dominated by the clergy, who rule on the grounds that they are the only interpreters of God's will and law.

Tokai Village A seaside community lying about ninety miles northeast of Tokyo that is Japan's major nuclear research center with reprocessing and enrichment facilities.

totalitarianism A political system in which the state attempts to exercise total control over all aspects of public and private life, including the economy, culture, education, and social organizations, through an integrated system of ideological, economic, and political control. Totalitarian states rely on extensive coercion, including terror, as a means to exercise power.

typology A method of classifying by using criteria that divide a group of cases into smaller cases with common characteristics.

U

unfinished state A state characterized by instabilities and uncertainties that may render it susceptible to collapse as a coherent entity.

unitary state In contrast to a federal system, a system of government in which no powers are reserved for subnational units of government.

V

vanguard party A political party that claims to operate in the "true" interests of the group or class that it purports to represent, even if this understanding doesn't correspond to the expressed interests of the group itself.

W

warrant chiefs Leaders employed by the British colonial regime in Nigeria. A system in which "chiefs" were selected by the British to oversee certain legal matters and assist the colonial enterprise in governance and law enforcement in local areas.

welfare state A set of public policies designed to provide for citizens' needs through direct or indirect provision of pensions, health care, unemployment insurance, and assistance to the poor.

Westminster model A form of democracy based on the supreme authority of Parliament and the accountability of its elected representatives; named after the Parliament building in London.

World Bank (officially the International Bank for Reconstruction and Development) The World Bank provides low-interest loans, no-interest credit, policy advice, and technical assistance to developing countries with the goal of reducing poverty. It is made up of more than 180 nations. All members have voting rights within the Bank, but these are weighted according to the size of each country's financial contribution to the organization.

World Trade Organization (WTO) A global international organization that oversees the "rules of trade" among its member states. The main functions of the WTO are to serve as a forum for its members to negotiate new agreements and resolve trade disputes. Its fundamental purpose is to lower or remove barriers to free trade.

About the Editors and Contributors

Ervand Abrahamian is Distinguished Professor of History at Baruch College and the Graduate Center of the City University of New York. He was elected Fellow of the American Academy of the Arts and Sciences. His publications include *Khomeinism: Essays on the Islamic Republic* (University of California Press, 1993), *Tortured Confessions: Prisons and Public Recantations in Modern Iran* (University of California Press, 1999), *A History of Modern Iran* (Cambridge University Press, 2008), and *The Coup: 1953, The CIA and the Roots of Modern U.S.-Iranian Relations* (The New Press, 2013).

Joan DeBardeleben is Chancellor's Professor in the Institute of European, Russian, and Eurasian Studies (EURUS) and Director of the Centre for European Studies (EU Centre of Excellence) at Carleton University in Ottawa, Canada. Her research work deals with EU–Russian relations, the EU's policy toward its eastern neighbors, and electoral politics in Russia. Her recent publications include *Economic Crisis in Europe: What It Means for the EU and Russia*, co-editor and contributor (with Crina Viju) (Palgrave Macmillan, 2013); "New EU-Russian borders after enlargement: From local to transnational linkages," in *Shifting Priorities in Russia's Foreign and Security Policy*, Roger E. Kanet and Remi Piet, eds. (Ashgate, 2013); and "The 2011–2012 Russian elections: The next chapter in Russia's post communist transition?," in J. L. Black and Michael Johns, eds., *From Putin to Medvedev to Putin – Continuity, Change or Revolution?* (Routledge, 2013).

Louis DeSipio is Professor of Political Science and Chicano/Latino Studies at the University of California, Irvine, where he directs the Center for the Study of Democracy. His research interests include Latino politics, the process of political incorporation of new and formerly excluded populations into U.S. politics, and public policies shaping immigrant incorporation such as immigration, immigrant settlement, naturalization, and voting rights. His most recent book is *U.S. Immigrant and Immigration Policies in the Twenty-First Century: Making Americans, Remaking America* (Westview Press, 2015).

Halbert Jones is a senior research fellow at St Antony's College, University of Oxford, where he directs the North American Studies Programme. His research interests include U.S.–Latin American relations, the international relations of North America, and twentieth-century Mexican political history. He is the author of *The War Has Brought Peace to Mexico: World War II and the Consolidation of the Post-Revolutionary State* (University of New Mexico Press, 2014). He wishes to acknowledge the role of Professor Merilee S. Grindle of Harvard University in the development of the chapter on Mexico in previous editions.

William A. Joseph is professor of political science and chair of the department at Wellesley College. He is also an associate in research of the John King Fairbank Center for Chinese Studies at Harvard University. His major areas of academic interest are contemporary Chinese politics and ideology, comparative revolutionary movements, and the Vietnam War. He is the editor of and a contributor to *Politics in China: An Introduction*, 2nd edition (Oxford University Press, 2014).

Mark Kesselman is Senior Editor of the *International Political Science Review* and Professor Emeritus of political science at Columbia University. His research focuses on the political economy of French and European politics. His publications include *The Ambiguous Consensus: A Study of Local Government in France* (Knopf, 1967), *The French Workers' Movement: Economic Crisis and Political Change* (HarperCollins, 1984), *The Politics of Globalization: A Reader* (Houghton Mifflin, 2012), and *The Politics of Power: The Politics of Power: A Critical Introduction to American Government* (with Alan Draper), 7th edition (W.W. Norton, 2013). His articles have appeared in the *American Political Science Review*, *World Politics*, and *Comparative Politics*.

Darren Kew is Associate Professor of Conflict Resolution and Executive Director of the Center for Peace, Democracy, and Development at the University of Massachusetts, Boston. He studies the relationship between conflict resolution methods and democratic development in Africa. Much of his work focuses on the role of civil society groups in this development. He also monitored the last three Nigerian elections and the 2007 elections in Sierra Leone. Professor Kew is author of numerous works on Nigerian politics and conflict resolution, including the book: *Democracy, Conflict Resolution, and Civil Society in Nigeria* (Syracuse University Press, 2015).

Joel Krieger is the Norma Weilenz Hess Professor of Political Science at Wellesley College. He is author of *Reagan, Thatcher, and the Politics of Decline* (Oxford University Press, 1986) and *British Politics in the Global Age* (Oxford University Press, 1999). Prof. Krieger is the Editor in Chief of the *Oxford Companion to Comparative Politics* (2013) and *The Oxford Companion to International Relations* (2014).

Peter M. Lewis is Director of African Studies and Associate Professor at the Johns Hopkins University, School of Advanced International Studies (SAIS). His work focuses on economic reform and political transition in developing countries, with particular emphasis on governance and development in Sub-Saharan Africa. He has written extensively on questions of economic adjustment, democratization, and civil society in Africa; democratic reform and political economy in Nigeria; public attitudes toward reform and democracy in West Africa; and the comparative politics of economic change in Africa and Southeast Asia. His book, *Growing Apart: Politics and Economic Change in Indonesia and Nigeria* (2007) is concerned with the institutional basis of economic development, drawing upon a comparative study.

George Ross, ad personam Chaire Jean Monnet, Université de Montréal. Author of *The European Union and Its Crises* (Palgrave-Macmillan, 2011), *Jacques Delors and European Integration* (Oxford UP 1995), co-editor of *Euros and Europeans* (Cambridge University Press 2004) and *What's Left of the Left?* (Duke University Press, 2011).

Index

A

Abacha, General Sani, 224, 228, 229, 246
Abiola, Moshood, 224
Abubakar, General Abdulsalami, 224
accommodation, **203**
accountability, **217**
acephalous societies, **220**
Action Group (AG), 221
Affordable Care Act (U.S.), 51, 81, 96, 101, 103, 112
agriculture
    in China, 373
        Mexican reforms in, 175
    in Russia and, 275
    in United States, 87, 91–92
Ahmadinejad, Mahmoud, 314, 327, 347
American Revolution, 84
Amsterdam Treaty, 159
anticlericalism, **200**
Arab Spring, 160, 163
Articles of Confederation, **85**
Assembly of Experts, **323**, 336
authoritarian regimes, 22
authoritarianism, **216**
autocracy, **227**
autonomous regions, **385**
ayatollah, **314**

B

Babangida, General Ibrahim, 224
balance of payments, **229**
Barroso, Jose, profile of, 140
bazaar, **321**
Berlin Wall, 136
Biafran War, 228
bicameral, **109**
Bill of Rights (U.S.), **86**, 114
Blair, Tony, 43–44, 48, 55, 57, 60, 66–67, 72, 76
Boko Haram, 225, 234, 249, 253, 256–257
Bolshevik revolution, 266–267
Bretton Woods, 97, 131, 134
Brezhnev, Leonid, 268
Britain, 36–79
    "Big Society," 44–45
    British Empire and, 42
    bureaucracy in, 58
    cabinet government in, 56–58
    civil service in, 58
    collective identities in, 75
    collectivist consensus in, 43
    colonial rule in Nigeria, 221
    comparative politics, 77

consensus era in, 49
Conservative-Liberal Coalition, 44
Conservative Party, 66
    as constitutional monarchy, 56
    constitutional reform in, 74
    critical historical junctures of, 40–45
    decolonization, 45
    economy in, 51–53
    election of 2010 in, 68
    elections in, 68–69
    electoral system in, 68
    environmental issues, 53
    ethnic and racial groups in, 69
    European Union (EU) and, 46, 55, 63
    executive institutions in, 56
    gender gap in, 52
    generation gap in, 75–76
    geographic setting of, 38–39
    globalization and, 54
    governance in, 55–63
    Great Recession, 48, 51
    hung parliament, 68
    immigration in, 52
    industrialization and, 42
    inequality in, 52
    Iran and, 319
    Iraq war and, 57, 61, 72
    judiciary of, 61
    Labour Party, 66
    legacies of empire and, 76
    legislature of, 64–65
    Liberal Democrats, 67
    making of the modern British state, 37–47
    military and police in, 60
    national identity and citizenship in, 70–72
    New Labour Party, 43
    other state institutions, 60–62
    parliamentary committees, 65
    parliamentary system in, 59, 64–65
    policy-making process in, 55–63
    political challenges and changing agendas in, 73–75
    political culture in, 70–72
    political economy and development in, 48–55
    political impact of technology in, 72–73
    political parties of, 66–67
    political themes in, 45, 47
    politics in action, 37–38
    politics in transition, 73–77
    prime minister in, 57
    public and semipublic institutions, 60
    reforms in behavior, 65
    representation and participation, 63–72
    royal family and, 46
    seventeenth-century settlement in, 41
    social activism in, 72

social class in, 71
social policy in, 50
Society and Economy, 51–53
society in, 51–53
"special relationship" with the U.S., 76
State and economy, 48
state organization in, 55
subnational government in, 61
surveillance and, 72
terrorist attacks in, 44, 73, 75
trends in electoral behavior, 70
unitary state, 55
voting rights in, 42
women in, 52, 69
world of states theme, 45–46
World War II, 46
Brown, Gordon, 48–50, 54, 66
Buhari, Muhammadu, 224, 228
Bukharin, Nikolai, 267
bureaucracy, **8**
    in Britain, 58
    in Iran, 339
    in Mexico, 192
    in Nigeria, 238
    in Russia, 285–286
    in United States, 103
Bush, George W., 88, 110, 178, 325–326, 344, 348, 355

C

cabinet, **8**, 56
    in Britain, 56–57
    in Mexico, 190–191
    in United States, 103
cabinet government, **56**
Calderón, Felipe, 169, 178, 179, 191–192, 200, 205, 207
Calles, Plutarco Elías, 175–176
Cameron, David, 44, 57, 61, 67, 75, 147
    profile of, 46
Cardenas, Cuauhtémoc, 201
Cárdenas, Lázaro, 176, 188
    profile of, 176
Carter, Jimmy, 233
Castro, Fidel, 122, 176
Castro, Raul, 122
caudillos, **172**
causal theories, **9**
Central Military Commission (CMC), **386**
centrally planned economy, **365**
checks and balances, **105**
Chernobyl, 279
Chiang Ching-kuo, 366
Chiang Kai-shek, 365, 366
    profile of, 368

421

China, 359–402
  agriculture in, 373–374
  CCP organization, 379–381
  Chinese Communist Party, 388
  communism in, 366
  communists, 364
  comparative politics, 399–400
  consumerism in, 390–391
  countryside life in, 373–374
  critical historical junctures of, 364–368
  Cultural Revolution, 371
  democracy and, 370, 397
  Deng Xiaoping transformation, 367
  development in, 371–377, 400
  economy in, 371, 374–375
  elections in, 390
  environmental and energy issues, 374–375
  ethnic and racial groups in, 361, 364, 392
  executive institutions in, 379
  generation gap, 399
  geographic setting of, 363
  globalization, 377–378
  governance in, 379–386
  Great Leap Forward, 366, 371
  Great Proletariate Cultural Revolution, 366–367
  Han and, 392
  household responsibility system in, 374
  internal security in, 385
  Islam in, 364, 393
  Japanese invasion of, 365
  judiciary in, 384
  legislature, 382
  Mao Zedong in power in, 365–366
  market and, 372
  military and police in, 385
  national identity and citizenship in, 390–392
  nationalists, 364
  non-Chinese citizens in, 392
  non-communist "Democratic Parties" in, 389
  NPC, 382
  organization of the state, 379
  other state institutions, 384–385
  policy-making process in, 379–386
  political challenges and changing agenda of, 396
  political culture in, 390–392
  political development of, 360–370
  political economy in, 371–377
  political impact of technology in, 395
  political parties in, 388–389
  political themes in, 369–370
  politics in action, 360–362
  politics in transition, 396–401
  PRC organization, 382–383
  press in, 391
  protest and the party-state, 394
  relations with United States, 378
  religion in, 361, 391, 394
  representation and participation in, 387–395
  from revolutionaries to technocrats, 368
  social activism in, 393–394
  society in, 374–375
  SOEs in (state-owned enterprises), 372
  Soviet Union and, 365–366
  state, 371
  State Council in, 383
  subnational government, 385
  Taiwan and, 366
  as Third World, 400
  Tianamen massacre in, 360
  trade with Brazil, 376–377
  warlords, 364
  women in, 376, 389
  world of states theme, 369–370
Chinese Communist Party (CCP), 362, 364–365, 368–369, 371, 379–381, 388
Churchill, Winston, 45
citizen initiative, **146**
civil society, **181**, 181
Civil War (U.S.), 86
clientelism, **361**
clientelistic networks, **287**
Clinton, Hillary, 306
Cold War, **2**, 60, 89, 378
collective identities, **4**
  in Britain, 75
  as comparative theme, 19–20
  in Iran, 327
  in Mexico, 180
  in Nigeria, 259
collectivization, **267**
Colosio, Luis Donaldo, 177
Common Agricultural Policy (CAP), 127, 152
Common Foreign and Security Policy (CFSP), 128, **128**, 158
Common Market, 127
Common Market of the South (MERCOSUL), 376–377
Commonwealth of Independent States (CIS), 270
communism, **366**
  in China, 366, 390–391
  in Soviet Union, 268, 282–283
Communist Party of the Russian Federation (CPRF), 296–297
Communist Party of the Soviet Union (CPSU), 268, 282, 283
communist party-state, **14**
community method, **140**
comparative data charts, 27
comparative politics, **5**
  approaches to, 5–11
  Britain and, 77
  causal theories in, 9–11
  China and, 399–400
  global challenge of, 2–4
  international relations, 5
  internet and, 6
  introducing, 1–34
  Iran, 356
  Mexico, 210
  Nigeria, 248–260
  Russia, 310
  themes for, 11–20
  in turbulent times, 4–5
  United States and, 122
comparative rankings, 34
comparativist, **7**
Confederation of Mexican Workers (CTM), 199
Congress (U.S.), 107
Conservative Party (Britain), 66
consolidated democracies, **21**
constitutional monarchy, **56**, 56
consumerism (China), 390–391
corporatist state, **180**
Corruption Perceptions Index, 6, 34
Cortés, Hernán, 174
Council of Europe, 281
country, **7**
coup d'état, 173, 320
CPSU, 294
critical historical junctures, **3**
  in Britain, 40–45
  of China, 364–368
  of Iran, 318–324
  of Mexico, 172
  of Nigeria, 219–224
  of Russia, 266–271
Cuba
  relations with United States, 122
Cuban Revolution, 176
current events, Internet source for, 6

D

Dalai Lama, 392–393
de Gaulle, Charles, 133
Declaration of Independence (U.S.), **84**
democracy, **16**
  China and, 370, 397
  as comparative theme, 16–20
  global spread of, 16
  Iran and, 326
  in Mexico, 177, 180
  multiparty, 177
  in Nigeria, 259
  socialist democracy, 387
  sovereign democracy, 300
  in United States, 89
democratic centralism, **266**
Democratic Party (U.S.), 81, 110
democratic transitions, **11**, 364
Deng Xiaoping, 366–369, 382
dependent variable, **9**
development
  in China, 371–377, 400
  in Iran, 328–334
  in Mexico, 176, 182–188
  in Nigeria, 227–234
  politics of rapid development, 176
  in Russia, 274–281
developmental state, **401**
developmentalism, **371**
dictatorships, **11**
distributional politics, **20**
distributive policies, **95**
dominant party, **296**
drug traffic
  in Mexico, 178
dual society, **331**

E

Economic and Monetary Union (EMU), 128, **128**, 129, 154
Economic Community of West African States (ECOWAS), **233**, 234
economic development
  measuring, 15
economic governance
  as comparative theme, 13–16
  Iran, 326
  Mexico, 179
  Nigeria, 258
Economist Intelligence Unit Democracy Index, 34
economy
  in Britain, 51–53
  in China, 371, 374–375

in Iran, 328, 330–332
under Islamic republic in Iran, 329
in Mexico, 185–186
in Nigeria, 228–232
in Russia, 274–278
education
in Iran, 330, 355
in Russia, 277
ejido, 175
elections
in Britain, 68–69
in China, 390
internet source for, 6
in Iran, 348
in Mexico, 202
in Nigeria, 243
in Russia, 295, 298–299
in United States, 112–113
Electoral College (U.S.), 100
environmental and energy issues
in Britain, 53
in China, 374–375
in Iran, 333
in Mexico, 184, 187
in Nigeria, 232
in Russia, 279–280, 307
in United States, 97
Environmental Performance Index (EPI),
    6, 34
ethnic and racial groups, 392
in Britain, 69
in China, 361, 364, 392
in Iran, 317, 349
in Mexico, 170–171, 208
in Nigeria, 217–218, 221, 231
in Russia, 263–273, 300
in United States, 83, 88, 90, 96,
    109–110, 113
European Central Bank (ECB), 63, 130
European Coal and Steel Community (ECSC),
    126–127, 155
European Commission, **133**
European Common Market, 132
European Convention on Human Rights
    (ECHR), 61, 281
European Council, **130**
European Court of Justice (ECJ), 55, 61, **133**,
    147–148
European Economic Community (EEC),
    127, 133
European integration, 126
    chronology of, 127
European Monetary System (EMS), 134
European Parliament, **129**
European single market, **141**
European Union (EU), 125–167, 280, 281
    agriculture, 151
    Britain and, 46, 55, 63
    competition policy, 150
    Council of Ministers, 142
    crisis and renewal 1970-1993, 134
    critical historical junctures of,
        126–128
    economic governance in, 131–134
    environmental policy, 157
    EU budget, 153
    Euro and EMU, 153–154
    Euro-Politics in Transition, 164
    European Commission, 141–142
    European Council, 143–144
    European Court of Justice (ECJ), 146–147
    European Market and, 149

European Parliament, 145–146
Eurozone crisis, 137–139
foreign and security policy, 160–163
globalization and, 135–140, 155
governance of, 140–148
Great Recession and, 137–139
institutions of, 140–148
intergovernmental Europe, 158–163
international connections, 136–137
justice and home affairs, 159–160
the making of, 126
policies of, 149–163
politics and economics in the development
    of, 131
politics in action, 126
regional development, 152–153
Russia, 304
shared policies, 155–157
social policy, 156
starting in the Cold War, 131
themes and comparisons, 129–130
United States and, 161
Eurozone crisis, 138–139, **164**
executive, **7**
executive institutions, 8
in Britain, 56
in China, 379
in Iran, 336–339
in Mexico, 190
in Nigeria, 237
in Russia, 284–287
in United States, 101–102
Expediency Council (Iran), **338**, 345
export-led growth, **369**

F

Falun Gong (FLG), 394
Farsi, **316**
Fedayin (Iran), 347
Federal Republic of Germany (FRG), 132
Federal Reserve Board (U.S.), 91, **92**
federal system, **289**
federalism, **82**, 100, 106, 113
    asymmetrical, 289–290
    in Nigeria, 235–236
    in Russia compared to United States,
        289–290
    in United States, 82
Federation of Independent Trade Unions
    (FITU), 303
floating population, 374, **374**
Ford, Gerald, 87
foreign direct investment (FDI), **54**
Foundation of the Oppressed, 338, **339**
Fox, Vicente, 177, 179, 191, 200, 205, 207
Franco, Itamar, 366
free market, **91**
Freedom in the World rating, 6
Fulani Empire, 218–219
fusion of powers, **56**

G

Gaddafi, Muammar, 61
Gang of Four, 366–367
gender gap, 6, 34
    in Britain, 52
General Agreement on Tariffs and Trade
    (GATT), 132, 136, 188

general secretary (China), **381**
generation gap
in Britain, 75–76
in China, 399
in Iran, 356
in Mexico, 209
in Nigeria, 257
in Russia, 309
genetically modified (GM) food, 53, 72
genocide, 137
geographic setting
    of Britain, 38–39
    of China, 363
    of Iran, 315–317
    of Mexico, 170
    of Nigeria, 217–218
    of Russia, 264
Germany
    Great Recession in, 138
glasnost, **270**, 270, 279, 292
globalization, 6
    Britain and, 54
    China, 377–378
    Iran and, 333
    Mexico, 188
    Nigeria, 233–234
    Russia, 280–281
    United States and, 97–98
Gorbachev, Mikhail, 270, 279, 292, 294
governance
in Britain, 55–63
in China, 379–386
in Iran, 335–344
in Mexico, 189
in Nigeria, 235–241
in Russia, 282–292
Gowan, Yakubu, 223
Great Depression, 43, 87, 120, 267
Great Leap Forward (China), 366
Great Proletariate Cultural Revolution (China),
    366–367
Great Recession (2008), 138–139, 164
    Britain, 48, 51
    Eurozone crisis and, 137–138
    Greece, 138–139
Greece, 138–139
gross domestic product (GDP), **15**
    by country, 30
gross national product (GNP), **15**
guanxi, 392
Guardian Council, **315**
guerrilla warfare, **365**

H

Han, 392
hegemonic power, **42**
hegemony, **26**
Hezbollahis, **323**
Hidalgo, Miguel, 172
HIV/AIDS
    in Nigeria, 231
    in Russia, 301
hojjat al-Islam, **323**, 336, 347
House of Commons (Britain), 57, 63–64, 68
House of Lords (Britain), 57, 63–64, 65
household registration (*hukou*) (China), **396**
household responsibility system (China), **374**
Human Development Index (HDI), 6, 34
hung parliament, 68, **68**
Hussein, Saddam, 324–325

I

Imam Jum'ehs, **338**
immigration
    European Union (EU) and, 159
    in United States, 90, 95, 99
Immigration Reform and Control Act
    (IRCA), 186
import substitution industrialization (ISI), **370**
    Mexico and, 182–183
independent variable, **9**
indigenous groups, **170**
indirect rule, **221**
Industrial Revolution, **42**
industrialization
    in Britain, 43
    in Mexico, 172, 179–180, 185
inequality
    in Britain, 52
    in China, 375
    in Iran, 327, 331
infant mortality, 33
informal economy, **371**
    in Mexico, 184
Inner Mongolia, 392
insider privatization, **275**
institutional design, **11**
Institutional Revolutionary Party (PRI), 169,
    181, 184, 188, 191, 197–201, 403
interest groups, **88**
internal security
    in China, 385
international financial institutions (IFIs), **229**
International Monetary Fund (IMF), **12**, 97,
    132, 280–281, 376
Internet, as comparative politics source, 6
interventionist, **226**
interventionist state, **370**
interventores, **362**
Iran, 313–358
    agriculture in, 320
    Assembly of Experts in, 323, 336
    as "axis of evil," 325
    bureaucracy, 339
    clerical power in, 336–337
    collective identities, 327
    comparative politics, 356
    constitution of, 319, 336
    coup d'état in, 319
    critical historical junctures of, 318–324
    democracy, 326
    development in, 328–334
    dual society in, 331
    economy in, 328, 330–332
    economy under Islamic republic, 329
    education system in, 330, 355
    elections in, 348
    environmental and energy issues, 333
    ethnic and racial groups in, 317, 349
    executive institutions in, 336–339
    Expediency Council in, 338
    Fedayin in, 347
    generation gap, 356
    geographic setting of, 315–317
    globalization, 333
    governance in, 335–344
    governing the economy, 326
    Guardian Council in, 315
    inequality in, 327, 331
    Iraq war and, 324
    Islamic Republic, 323
        Islamic Revolution in, 321–322
        Israel and, 325, 326
        Jews in, 349
        judiciary in, 340
        labor movement in, 320, 351
        legislature, 346
        Liberation Movement in, 347
        military and police in, 341
        Mojahedin in, 347
        National Front in, 347
        national identity and citizenship in,
            349
        nuclear power and, 326
        other state institutions, 340–342
        Pahlavi dynasty in, 319–320
        policy-making process in, 335–344
        political challenges and changing agenda of,
            353–355
        political culture in, 349
        political development of, 314–327
        political economy in, 328–334
        political impact of technology in, 352
        political parties in, 346–348
        political themes in, 325–327
        politics in action, 314
        politics in transition, 352–357
        public and semipublic
            institutions, 342
        Qajar rule in, 319
        relations with United States, 344
        religion in, 314, 316–317, 338, 345,
            349, 354
        representation and participation in,
            345–352
        Safavid dynasty in, 318
        September 11 terrorist attack
            and, 324
        social activism in, 350–351
        society, 330–332
        state in, 328
        state organization in, 335
        subnational government, 342
        Supreme Leader in, 336–337
        themes and comparisons, 327
        Tudeh in (Party of the Masses), 348
        unemployment in, 329
        United States and, 325
        women in, 350–351
        world of states theme, 325
Iranian Revolution, 323
Iraq war
    Britain and, 57, 61, 72
    Iran and, 324
    United States, 88–89, 104, 324
iron rice bowl, **374**
iron triangle relationships, **104**
Islam, 316
    in China, 364, 393
    in Iran, 329
    jihad and, 219
    in Nigeria, 219, 240
    political Islam, 321
    shari'a law of, 231, 240, 249, 319–320,
        340–341
Islamic Iran Participation Front, 346
Islamic Labor Party, 347
Islamic Republic (Iran), 323
Islamic Revolution (Iran), 321–322,
    326
Islamism, **327**
Israel, 325

J

Japan
    invasion of China, 365
Jews
    in Iran, 318, 349
Jiang Qing, 366–367
jihad, **219**
Jonathan, Goodluck, 216, 225, 231, 236–237,
    248
    profile of, 241
judicial review, **61**
judiciary, **8**
    in Britain, 61
    in China, 384
    in Iran, 340
    in Mexico, 194
    in Nigeria, 239
    in Russia, 288
    in United States, 105
jurist's guardianship, **322**
A Just Russia, 296–297
Justice and Home affairs (JHA), **128**,
    158–159

K

Kennedy, John F., 102
Keynes, John Maynard, 49
Keynesianism, 7, **49**
KGB (secret police of Soviet Union), 268, 290
Khamenei, Ali, 336
Khomeini, Ruhollah, 321–322, 325–326,
    336, 339
Khrushchev, Nikita, 268
Kissenger, Henry, 334
Korean War, 378
Kubitschek, Juscelino, 363
Kurds, 350
Kyoto Protocol, 97, 158, 280

L

labor movement
    in China, 393
    in Iran, 320, 351
    in Mexico, 175, 199, 205
    in Nigeria, 250
    in Russia, 303
    in United States, 110, 117
Labour Party (Britain), 66
laissez-faire, **47**
Land Use Act of 1978 (Nigeria), 232
Lázaro Cárdenas, 175
Leader/Supreme Leader (Iran), 315
legislature, **8**
    in Britain, 64–65
    in China, 382
    in Iran, 346
    in Mexico, 197
    in Nigeria, 242
    in Russia, 293
    in United States, 108–109
legitimacy, **8**
Lehman Brothers, 137
Lenin, Vladimir, 266
Liberal Democrat Party (LDP), 67
Liberal Democratic Party of Russia (LDPR),
    297
Liberation Movement (Iran), 347

life expectancy, 187
  by country, 32
Lincoln, Abraham, 102
Lisbon Treaty, **129**, 148, 159

M

Maastricht Treaty, 130, **135**, 138, 159
macroeconomic policy, **49**
Madero, Francisco I., 174, 180
Madrid, Miguel de la, 177
Magna Carta, 41
Majles, **315**
Major, John, 49, 57
manifest destiny, **82**, 82
Mao Zedong, 365–368, 372, 381–382,
  386, 394
  China and power of, 365–366
  profile of, 368
maps, 6
maquiladoras, **172**
Marbury v. Madison, **105**
market
  China, 372
market reform, **275**
Marshall Plan, 132
Marx, Karl, 20
Marxists, 266–267
maslahat, **345**
mass organizations, **393**
Mbeki, Thabo, 234
Medvedev, Dmitry, 272, 278, 282, 285–286,
  290, 292, 296
MERCOSUL, 375
mestizo, **170**
Mexican Revolution, 180
Mexico, 168–212
  agriculture and agrarian reform, 175
  bureaucracy, 192
  cabinet, 190–191
  collective identities, 180
  comparative politics, 210
  constitution of, 176, 189
  crisis and reform, 177
  critical historical junctures of, 172
  democracy, 177, 180
  development in, 182–188
  dictatorship in, 172–173
  drug traffic in, 169, 178
  economy in, 187
  elections in, 202
  emigration to U.S., 172
  environmental and energy issues, 184
  environmental issues, 187
  ethnic and racial groups in, 170–171, 208
  executive institutions in, 190
  generation gap, 209
  geographic setting of, 170
  globalization, 188
  governance in, 189
  governing the economy, 179
  import substitution industrialization (ISI)
    in, 182–183
  independence in, 172–173
  industrialization and, 172, 179–180, 185
  instability in, 172–173
  judiciary in, 194
  labor movement in, 175, 199, 204
  Lázaro Cárdenas, 175
  legislature, 197

Mexican economy today, 185–186
migration to the U.S., 185–186
military and police in, 193
NAFTA and, 185
national identity and citizenship in, 174, 202
organization of the state, 189
other parties, 202
other state institutions, 193
PAN, 178, 200
Parastatal Sector, 193
policy-making process in, 189, 195
political challenges and changing
  agenda of, 207–208
political culture in, 202
political development of, 169–181
political economy in, 182–188
political impact of technology in, 205
political parties in, 198
political themes in, 179–180
political transition and, 206–210
politics in action, 169
politics of rapid development, 176
PRD in, 201
president, 190–191
PRI, 199
relations with United States, 99
religions in, 171
representation and participation in, 196–205
Revolution of 1910, 174
social activism in, 203–204
society in, 187
Sonoran Dynasty, 174
as Spanish colony, 174
structural reforms and, 185
subnational government, 195
themes and comparisons, 181
unemployment in, 187
United States and, 169, 175, 178, 180
world of states theme, 179
middle-level theory, **10**
military and police
  in Britain, 60
  in China, 385
  in Iran, 341
  in Mexico, 193
  in Nigeria, 223, 237
  in Russia, 290–291
  in United States, 104
Mitterand, François, 136
mixed electoral system, **293**
mixed systems, **22**
moderating power, **360**
modernity vs. traditionalism
  Nigeria, 248
Mojahedin
  in Iran, 347
monarchy
  in Britain, 56
  constitutional, 56
monetarism, **49**
Mota, Josefina Vázquez, 200
Muhammad, Murtala, 223
Murdoch, Rupert, 72

N

nation-state, **9**
National Action Party (PAN), 178, 191–192,
  197–198, 200
National Congress Party (China), **379**

National Convention of Nigerian Citizens
  (NCNC), 221–222
National Front (Iran), 320, 347
National Health Service (NHS), 51
national identity and citizenship
  in Britain, 70–72
  in China, 390–392
  in Iran, 349
  in Mexico, 174, 202
  in Nigeria, 248–249
  in Russia, 300
  in United States, 114
National Party of Nigeria (NPN), 223
National People's Congress (NPC), **382**
National Regeneration Movement
  (MORENA), 201
nationalism, **363**
Nationalist Party (China), 364, 366, 368
nationalized industries, 60
NATO-Russia Summit (Lisbon, Nov. 2010),
  307
Nazi regime (Germany), 319–320
  invasion of Soviet Union, 267
neoliberalism, 7, **48**
New Deal (U.S.), 86, 89, 101–102
New Economic Policy (NEP), 266
New Labour Party (Britain), 43
Nieto, Enrique Peña, 169, 178–179, 191–192,
  205
Nigeria, 213–260
  AG in, 221
  British colonial rule in, 221
  the bureaucracy, 238
  business community, 251
  civil war in, 223
  collective identities, 259
  colonial rule and, 221
  comparative politics, 248–260
  constitutional governance, 235
  critical historical junctures of, 219–224
  democracy, 259
  development in, 227–234
  economy in, 228–232
  ECOWAS, 233
  elections in, 243
  environmental and energy issues, 232
  ethnic and racial groups in, 217–218, 221
  executive institutions in, 237
  Federalism, 235–236
  First Republic, 222
  Fourth Republic, 224, 237
  gender in, 232
  generation gap, 257
  geographic setting of, 217–218
  globalization, 233–234
  governance in, 235–241
  governing the economy, 258
  Islam in, 219, 240
  Jonathan Administration, 237
  the judiciary, 239
  labor movement in, 250
  legislature, 242
  military and, 223
  military and police in, 223, 237
  military in, 223
  modernity vs. traditionalism, 248
  national identity and citizenship in, 248–249
  NCNC, 221–222
  NPC, 221
  Obasanjo Administrations, 237
  organization of the state, 235

Nigeria (*Continued*)
  other social groups, 251
  other state institutions, 239
  PDP and other parties of the Fourth
    Republic, 246–247
  policy-making process in, 235–241
  political challenges and changing agenda of,
    253–256
  political culture in, 248–249
  political development of, 216–227
  political economy, 227–234
  political impact of technology in, 251
  political parties in, 243
  political themes in, 225–226
  politics in action, 216
  politics in transition, 253–259
  prebendalism, 239
  precolonial period, 219–220
  press in, 249–250
  relations with United States, 233
  religions in, 217, 231, 249
  representation and participation in,
    242–251
  Second Republic, 223
  semipublic institutions, 238
  shari'a law in, 249
  social activism in, 250–251
  society in, 231–232
  state structure, 228–230, 235–236
  subnational government, 240
  themes and comparisons, 227
  Third Republic, 223
  United States and, 233
  women in, 232, 242, 250
  world of states theme, 225–226, 257
  Yar' Adua Administrations, 237
Nigerian Labour Congress (NLC), 250
Ningxia, 392
Nixon, Richard, 87, 334, 378
nomenklatura system, **283**, **384**
nondepartmental public bodies (NDPBs), 60
North American Free Trade Agreement
    (NAFTA), **12**, 82, 97, 177, 179, 188
  Mexico and, 185
North Atlantic Treaty Organization (NATO),
    60, 127, 132, 162, 268, 281
Northern Ireland, 61–62
Northern People's Congress (NPC), 221
nuclear weapons
  United States, 104

O

Obama, Barack, 38, 81, 97, 102–103, 118,
    325, 326
  profile of, 103
Obasanjo Administration (Nigeria), 237
Obasanjo, Olusegun, 223–224, 230, 234–235
Obrador, Lopez, 201
oligarchs, **275**
Orange Revolution (Ukraine), 306
Organization of Petroleum Exporting
    Countries (OPEC), 134, 234, **334**

P

Pahlavi dynasty (Iran), 319–320
Palestine, 325
Papandreou, George, 138–139
parastatal sector (Mexico), 193

parliamentary committees, Britain, 65
parliamentary democracy, **55**
parliamentary sovereignty, **55**
parliamentary system
  in Britain, 59, 64–65
  European Union (EU) and, 145–146
Party of the Democratic Revolution (PRD), 178
  Mexico, 201
pasdaran, **322**
patrimonial state, **266**
People of the Book, **318**
People's Democratic Party (PDP), 224,
    246–247
People's Liberation Army (PLA), **385**
perestroika, 270
personalist politicians, **368**
Plaid Cymru (Wales), 70
police powers, **91**
policy-making process
  in Britain, 55–63
  in China, 379–386
  in Iran, 335–344
  in Mexico, 189, 195
  in Nigeria, 235–241
  in Russia, 282–292
  in United States, 99–108
Politburo, CCP, 282, **381**
political action committee (PAC), **117**
political challenges and changing agenda
  of China, 396
  of Iran, 353–355
  of Mexico, 207–208
  of Nigeria, 253–256
  of Russia, 305–308
political culture
  in China, 390–392
  in Iran, 349
  in Mexico, 202
  in Nigeria, 248–249
  in Russia, 300
political development
  of Britain, 48–55
  of China, 360–370
  of Iran, 314–327
  of Mexico, 169–181
  of Nigeria, 216–227
  of Russia, 263–273
  of United States, 81–90
political economy, **14**
  in Britain, 48–55
  in China, 371–377
  in Iran, 328–334
  in Mexico, 182–188
  in Nigeria, 227–234
  in Russia, 274–281
  in United States, 91–98
political impact of technology
  in China, 395
  in Iran, 352
  in Mexico, 205
  in Nigeria, 251
  in Russia, 303
political Islam, **321**
political parties
  in Britain, 66–67
  in China, 388–389
  in Iran, 346–348
  in Mexico, 198
  in Nigeria, 243
  in Russia, 294–297
  in United States, 110–111

political systems, classifying, 21–23
political themes
  in China, 369–370
  in Iran, 325–327
  in Mexico, 179–180
  in Nigeria, 225–226
politics in action
  China, 360–362
  Iran, 314
  Mexico, 169
  Nigeria, 216
  Russia, 263
politics in transition
  China, 396–401
  Iran, 352–357
  Mexico, 206–210
  Nigeria, 253–259
  Russia, 304–310
populism, **363**
Porfiriato era (Mexico), 172, 174, 182
Porfirio, Díaz, 172, 179
power vertical, **289**
prebendalism (Nigeria)
  in Nigeria, 239
predatory state, **400**
presidency
  Mexico, 190–191
  in United States, 101–102
press
  in China, 391
  in Nigeria, 249–250
  in Russia, 303
property taxes, **87**
protest and the party-state
  China, 394
public and semipublic institutions
  in Britain, 60
  Iran, 342
  Russia, 287
purchasing power parity (PPP), **15**
  by country, 31
Pussy Riot, 263–264, 302
Putin, Vladimir, 263, 271–272, 274, 277, 278,
    282, 284–287, 290, 292, 296, 304
  power vertical initiative of, 289
  profile of, 286

Q

Qajars
  Iran, 319
qualified majority voting, **133**
quangos, 56, **60**
Qur'an, 318, **318**

R

rankings and ratings, 6
rational choice theory, **10**
redistributive policies, **95**
Regional Development Agencies (RDAs),
    61–62
regulations, **97**
religion, 171
  in China, 361, 391, 394
  in Iran, 314–317, 336–338, 345, 349, 354
  in Mexico, 170
  in Nigeria, 217, 231, 249
  in Russia, 263, 273
  in United States, 83, 88, 114–115, 120

remittances, **185**
rentier state, **328**
rents, **228**
representation and participation
  in Britain, 63–72
  in China, 387–395
  in Iran, 345–352
  in Mexico, 196–205
  in Nigeria, 242–251
  in Russia, 292–303
  in United States, 108–117
Republican Party (U.S.), 81, 110
resource curse, **334**
Resurgence Party, 321
Revolution of 1910 (Mexico), 174, 180–182
Roosevelt, Franklin D., 87
Roosevelt, Theodore, 102
Rouhani, Hassan, 240, 314, 333
  profile of, 340
Russia, 262–311
  agriculture and, 275
  Bolshevik Revolution, 266
  bureaucracy in, 285–286
  collapse of the USSR, 270–271
  comparative politics, 310
  Council of Europe and, 281
  CPRF in, 296
  critical historical junctures of, 266–271
  destalinization, 268
  development in, 274–281
  economy in, 274–278
  education system in, 277
  elections in, 295, 298–299
  environmental and energy issues,
    279–280, 307
  ethnic and racial groups in, 263, 273, 300
  European Union (EU) and, 265, 281, 304
  executive institutions in, 284–287
  federalism in United States compared to,
    289–290
  generation gap, 309
  geographic setting of, 264
  glasnost in, 270
  globalization, 280–281
  governance in, 282–292
  international organizations and, 281
  Iran and, 319
  judiciary in, 288
  A Just Russia in, 296–297
  LDPR in, 297
  legislature, 293
  liberal democratic parties in, 297
  military and police in, 290–291
  national identity and citizenship in, 300
  North Atlantic Treaty Organization
    (NATO), 281
  other state institutions, 288–290
  perestroika in, 270
  policy-making process in, 282–292
  political challenges and changing agenda of,
    305–308
  political culture in, 300
  political development of, 263–273
  political economy, 274–281
  political impact of technology in, 303
  political parties in, 294–297
  politics in action, 263
  politics in transition, 304–310
  press in, 303
  public and semipublic institutions, 287
  relations with Ukraine, 272–273, 304

religion in, 263, 273
representation and participation in,
  292–303
Russian Federation, 270–271
social activism in, 301–302
society in, 277–278
Soviet Union and, 266
Stalin Revolution, 267–268
state, 274–277
State Duma in, 292–293, 295–297
state organization in, 282–283
subnational government, 288–289
themes and comparisons, 272–273
tsar rule and decline in, 266
Ukraine, relationship with, 265
United Russia party in, 296
women in, 301
world of states theme, 311

S

Safavid dynasty (Iran)
  Iran, 318
Salinas, Carlos, 177
same-sex marriage, 115
SB 1070 law (U.S.), 99
Schengen area, **159**
Schulz, Martin, profile of, 140
Schuman Plan, 132
Schuman, Robert, 132
Scotland, 61–62, 65, 70
Scottish National Party (SNP), 65, 70
semipublic institutions
  Nigeria, 238
separation of powers, **89**, 100
September 11 terrorist attack
  Iran and, 324
  Mexico and, 178
  Russia and, 291
  United States and, 88, 104, 119, 121
September 11th (9/11) Commission, 110
sexenio, 185, 190
Shagari, Shehu, 223–224
Shah, Reza, 319–320, 323, 328, 339
shari'a law, 231, 236, 240, 249, 319–320,
  340–341
Shariati, Ali, 332
Shi'i, 316–318, 323, 325–327, 345, 348, 350,
  354
siloviki, **287**
single-member-plurality (SMP) electoral
  system, **90**
slavery, in United States, 86
Snowdon, Edward, 11, 304, 396
social activism
  in Britain, 72
  in China, 393–394
  in Iran, 350–351
  in Mexico, 203–204
  in Nigeria, 250–251
  in Russia, 301–302
  in United States, 116
social class, **19**
  in Britain, 71
Social Democratic Party (SDP), 243, 363
social movements, **18**
  democracy and, 18
Social Progress Index (SPI), **15**
Social Security, **87**, 102
socialism, **365**
socialist democracy, **387**

socialist market economy, **374**
society
  in Britain, 51–53
  in China, 374–375
  in Iran, 330–332
  in Mexico, 187
  in Nigeria, 231–232
  in Russia, 277–278
  in United States, 93–96
soft authoritarianism, **272**
Sokoto Caliphate, 219
Sonoran Dynasty (Mexico), 174–175
Sotomayor, Sonia, 106
sovereign democracy, **300**
Soviet Union
  collapse of, 270–271
  critical historical junctures of, 266–271
  Glasnost in, 270
  Nazi invasion of, 267
  perestroika in, 270
  Stalin Revolution in, 267–268
  state organization in, 282–283
Stalin, Joseph, 267, 268
  Soviet Union revolution of, 267–268
Standing Committee (China), **381**
state, **7**
  British organization of, 55
  China organization of, 371, 379
  Iran organization of, 328, 335
  Mexico organization of, 189
  Nigeria organization of, 228–230, 235
  Russia organization of, 274–277, 282–283
  United States organization of, 99–100
state capitalism, **182**
state corporatism, **363**
State Council (China), 383
State Department, 6
State Duma (Russia), 284, 292–293, 295–297
state formation, **9**
  modern, 23
state institutions
  China, 384–385
  Iran, 340–342
  Mexico, 193
  Nigeria, 239
  Russia, 288–290
state-led economic development, **365**
  United States, 91
state-owned enterprises (SOEs), **372**
state technocrats, **370**
statistics
  Internet source for, 6
Strategic Arms Reduction Treaty, 307
structural adjustment program (SAP) **228**, 510
structural reforms
  Mexico and, 185
subnational government
  in Britain, 61
  in China, 385
  in Iran, 342
  in Mexico, 195
  in Nigeria, 240
  in Russia, 288–289
  in United States, 106
subsidiarity, **146**
Sun Yat-sen, 364
Sunni, 316–318, 323, 325–327, 345, 348,
  349–350, 354
Supreme Court (U.S.), 96, 106
Supreme Leader (Iran), 315
sustainable development, **14**

T

Taiwan, 366
Taliban regime, 325
Tea Party (U.S.), 110, 112
technocrats, **192**
terrorism
    in Britain, 44, 73, 75
Thatcher, Margaret, 37–38, 48–50, 57, 134, 136
themes and comparisons
    Iran, 327
    Mexico, 181
    Nigeria, 227
    Russia, 272–273
theocracy, 314–315, **315**
Third Republic
    Nigeria, 223
Third World
    China as, 400
Tiananmen massacre (China), 360, 370, 378, 394
Tibet, 370, 392–393
Torah, 318
total geographic area, 28
total population by country, 28
totalitarian regimes, **400**
Treaty of Lisbon, 137
Treaty on European Union (TEU), 128
Truman, Harry, 268
Tudeh (Iran), 320, 348
typology, **20**, **21**

U

Ukraine, 306
    Russia relationship with, 272–273, 304
unemployment
    in Iran, 329
    in Mexico, 187
    in United States, 96, 103
unfinished state, 217, **218**
Union of Soviet Socialist Republics (USSR), 126–127, 132, 266–268
    Bolshevik revolution and, 266–267
unitary state, 55, **56**
United Nations Economic Commission for Latin America (ECLA), 370
United Nations Framework Convention on Climate Change (UNFCCC), 158
United Russia, 296
United States, 80–123
    agriculture, 87, 91–92
    American Revolution, 84–85
    Bill of Rights, 86
    bureaucracy in, 103
    cabinet and, 103
    Civil War and Reconstruction, 86
    Civil War (U.S.), 102
    collective identities, 89, 120
    comparative politics, 122
    constitution of, 90, 100
    critical historical junctures of, 84–89
    democracy, 89
    development in, 91–98
    divided government in, 87

economy in, 91–98
elections in, 81, 112–113
environmental and energy issues, 97
equality in, 114
ethnic and racial groups in, 83, 88, 90, 96, 109–110, 113
European Union (EU) and, 161
executive institutions in, 101–102
Federal Reserve Board, 92
federalism in, 82
federalism in Russia compared to, 289–290
generation gap, 121
geographic setting of, 82
globalization, 97–98
governance in, 99–108
governing the economy, 89
immigration from Mexico, 185–186
immigration in, 90
Immigration Reform and Control Act (IRCA), 186
invasion of Afghanistan, 324
Iraq war and, 88–89, 104, 324
judiciary in, 105
legislature, 108–109
Mexican constitution compared to, 189
Mexican immigration to, 172
Mexico and, 169, 175, 178, 180
military, 104
military and police in, 104
national identity and citizenship in, 114
national security agencies, 104
New Deal Era, 86
Nigeria and, 233
other state institutions, 105–106
policy-making process in, 99–108
political challenges and changing agenda of, 118–120
political culture in, 114–115
political development of, 81–90
political economy in, 91–98
political impact of technology in, 117
political parties in, 110–111
political themes in, 89–90
politics in action, 81
politics in transition, 118–122
presidency in, 101–102
relations with China, 378
relations with Cuba, 122
relations with Iran, 344
relations with Mexico, 99
relations with Nigeria, 233
religion in, 83, 88, 114–115, 120
representation and participation in, 108–117
separation of powers, 89
September 11 terrorist attack and aftermath, 88, 104
slavery in, 86
social activism in, 116
society in, 93–96
state in, 91–92
state-led economic development, 91
state organization in, 99–100
subnational government, 106
unemployment in, 96, 103
War in Afghanistan, 104
women in, 100
women's suffrage, 116

world of states theme, 89
World War II, 87, 89
U.S. Central Intelligence Agency (CIA), 320

V

Van Rompuy, Herman, profile of, 140
vanguard party, **266**
Vargas, Getúlio, 362–363, 367
    profile of, 378
Villa, Francisco (Pancho), 175
Vision 2010, 229, 250
Voting Rights Act (VRA), 86, 113

W

Wales, 61–62
Warlords (China), 364, 366
Warlords, Nationalists, and Communists
    China, 364
warrant chiefs, **221**
Warsaw Pact, 268
Watergate, 120
welfare state, **43**
Westminster model, 47
women
    in Britain, 52
    in China, 376, 389, 393
    in Iran, 350–351
    in Nigeria, 232, 241, 250
    in Russia, 301
    in United States, 100, 113
World Bank, 6, 97, 228, 281
world of states theme, 11–13
    China, 369–370
    Iran, 325
    Mexico, 179
    Nigeria, 225–226, 257
    United States, 89
World Trade Organization (WTO), **12**, 72, 188, 280, 376–377
World War I
    Britain and, 43
World War II, 87, 126, 266

X

Xinjiang, 364, 392

Y

Yar' Adua Administrations (Nigeria), 237
Yar'Adua, Umaru Musa, 216, 224, 230, 233, 235, 237, 241, 248, 254
Yeltsin, Boris, 270–271, 275, 282–283, 288, 292
Yom Kippur war, 134

Z

Zapata, Emiliano, 175, 182
Zapatista Army of National Liberation (EZLN), 177, 181
Zedillo, Ernesto, 177, 191